# TEACH

## LIKE A

### CHAMPION

## 3.0

# TEACH
## LIKE A
## CHAMPION
## 3.0

## 63 Techniques That Put Students on the Path to College

## DOUG LEMOV

**JB** JOSSEY-BASS™
A Wiley Brand

Jossey-Bass
A Wiley Imprint
111 River St, Hoboken, NJ 07030
www.josseybass.com

Jossey-Bass books and products are available through most bookstores. To contact Jossey-Bass directly, call our Customer Care Department within the U.S. at 800-956-7739, outside the U.S. at +1 317 572 3986, or fax +1 317 572 4002.

Wiley also publishes its books in a variety of electronic formats and by print-on-demand. Some material included with standard print versions of this book may not be included in e-books or in print-on-demand. If this book refers to media such as a CD or DVD that is not included in the version you purchased, you may download this material at http://booksupport.wiley.com. For more information about Wiley products, visit www.wiley.com.

*Library of Congress Cataloging-in-Publication Data is Available:*

ISBN 9781119712619 (paperback)
ISBN 9781119712626 (ePDF)
ISBN 9781119712466 (epub)

Cover Image: PAUL MCCARTHY
Cover Design: © JJ IGNOTZ PHOTOGRAPHY
        TEACHER ON COVER: DENARIUS FRAZIER

**THIRD EDITION**

SKY10028098_080421

*For Mike and Penny Lemov,*

*my first teachers*

# Conten

**1  Five Themes: Mental Models and Purposeful Execution**

# Acknowledgments

This book would have been impossible without the team of people whose work is reflected in almost every line. My colleagues on the *Teach Like a Champion* team have made untold contributions, both direct and indirect. There are hundreds of their insights about videos or techniques in this book—and in the rest of the work we produce. But they have also contributed something that's harder to define. The moments when they offer a phrase to describe exactly what a teacher is doing or when we roll back the tape because they've seen something fascinating in a student's response are just as likely to come right after some moment in which they laugh with self-deprecating humor at something they've said, acknowledge a teammate's efforts, or defer credit to someone else. They are wise, gracious, funny, humble, discerning colleagues, this is to say, who create an environment where doing the work of studying teaching is rewarding, challenging, and even fun.

When we get teachers and school leaders together for professional development—in person or, now, virtually—our goal is always to honor people by helping them get better at such important work and to ensure that everyone—us and them—learns a lot, but also to have fun doing it—to make teaching a team sport marked by joy and camaraderie. Teachers deserve to work in that kind of environment, and I know that because I am lucky enough to appreciate it firsthand.

That team includes Emily Badillo, Jaimie Brillante, Dan Cotton, John Costello, Colleen Driggs, Dillon Fisher, Kevin Grijalva, Kim Griffith, Brittany Hargrove, Joaquin Hernandez, Tracey Koren, Jasmine Lane, Hilary Lewis, Rob Richard, Jen Rugani, Hannah Solomon, Beth Verrilli, Michelle Wagner, Darryl Williams, and Erica Woolway. I am grateful to each of them, though several played roles in the production of this volume who deserve particular mention.

The videos in this book—and all the videos we use in training and study—were edited and produced by Rob Richard and John Costello. Theirs is both technical and intellectual work—not just showing what a teacher has done on screen but then making it optimally legible to viewers by focusing in on the good stuff without distorting the reality of the classroom overall. This can mean removing the moment when the classroom phone rings or the child in the third row knocks everything off his desk or deciding that two *great* examples of a teacher using *Cold Call* is more useful than five *pretty good* examples. Every video is a sort of visual poem, and John and Rob have authored them all while also building a system to keep track of thousands of such poems. Think for a moment about what it means to keep 20 years of video organized so a team of people can say, "Remember that classroom from the school in Tennessee that we watched about four or five years ago?" and later that day we're all watching it again.

Hannah Solomon serves many roles on our team but one of them was developmental editor for this book. It might not have been "herding cats," exactly, but only because there was just one cat and "herding" implies that he is heading in the right direction—or at least making something like progress—and you are merely nudging him back on course. Hannah's work included project management—keeping me on task is hard enough; doing that and keeping track of the all the tasks, not to mention all the drafts, is an order of the highest magnitude; now imagine doing it with your most disorganized and distracted student who very earnestly tells you over and over he'll have it by Wednesday when in your heart you know otherwise. Meanwhile, Hannah also provided round after round of gracious and candid feedback on drafts, gathered and designed support materials, helped to select videos, and generally offered good advice and counsel in a hundred ways. There were dark and hopeless hours in writing this book. But then I would get my draft back and she would have taken the time to spell out exactly why she liked a phrase or a paragraph in the most supportive way and I would keep going. I am profoundly grateful for that and also for the many times she pushed me to change my thinking as we reflected on and revised the techniques.

Emily Badillo also played a critical role in the writing of this book. If the name is familiar it's because her videos appear throughout the book as well. She too was invaluable in reading and marking up drafts—and in drafting sections and sourcing support material, as well as screening and recommending videos.

As I was writing this book, my team and I were also providing training and curriculum to thousands of teachers in the United States and abroad. We had an organization to run, in other words. Every leader brings their own unique skills to such an effort. My own leadership skills include leaving emails unanswered for months, making sure meetings begin awkwardly and sometimes before everyone knows about them. Also: hiding in my office for days at a time to obsess over a paragraph while deadlines go hurtling past. Thus my partners in leading Team TLAC, Chief Academic Officer Erica Woolway and Co-Managing Director Darryl Williams, deserve a double dose of thanks and credit—for their ideas, insights, and deep understanding of teaching, as well as for their ability to gently manage around my "skills." I couldn't ask for better partners.

Writing can be a slow process, but the process of writing this book was especially challenging given that it was done during the year 2020. Amy Fandrei and Pete Gaughan at John Wiley & Sons were supportive and understanding, not to mention unflappable, throughout. I hope the result seems close to worth the headaches I caused them.

Rafe Sagalyn continues to guide and support my work as an advocate and agent, and I am grateful to have the guidance of someone so wise whose goal is to help me find my own vision for my writing and bring it to reality.

This book also reflects the insights of a broader community of teachers and educators—in the United States, in England, even around the world—who share their insights and observations with me and each other. Many days I think social media is a pox on civilization but it is also a means through which, thanks to the thousands of teachers who see it as a tool to share knowledge and insights positively and constructively, I have been able to learn an immense amount very quickly. I have tried to quote a few of the teachers whose comments have particularly struck me. I describe a few cases where, in a pickle, I asked a question of my Twitter colleagues and found myself blessed to share in their wisdom and insight. Thank you, then, to everyone who teaches and thus does the most important work in society, and doubly so to those who have shared their knowledge of that work with me.

Finally, as I have written and rewritten three volumes of this book, my own three children have grown up. Needless to say, I love them immensely and am proud of them. They are bigger now, they were littler then, and yet still there is no sacrifice I wouldn't make for them. But you knew that and I mention it here because the work that I do has always been connected to my own parenting. I wake at night and struggle with some anxiety about my children and I know other parents lie awake struggling too, often with even greater anxieties. I think often of those parents who love their children as deeply and as profoundly as I do mine but cannot rely on sending them to schools and classrooms that provide them with the fullest opportunity to learn and thrive. This book is an effort to ensure the best possible classrooms everywhere—for my own children and for every other parent's children.

I'll close with the biggest thanks I owe: to my wife, Lisa. To thank her for making this book possible is a bit unfair when there's so much more to be thankful for in a thousand ways. So, Lisa, thank you for the sunshine, which, among other things, creates the light by which I've been able to write.

# The Author

**Doug Lemov** is a managing director of Uncommon Schools and leads its Teach Like a Champion team, designing and implementing teacher training based on the study of high-performing teachers. He was formerly the managing director for Uncommon's upstate New York schools. Before that he was Vice President for Accountability at the State University of New York Charter Schools Institute and was a founder, teacher, and principal of the Academy of the Pacific Rim Charter School in Boston. He has taught English and history at the university, high school, and middle school levels. He holds a BA from Hamilton College, an MA from Indiana University, and an MBA from the Harvard Business School. Visit him at www.teachlikeachampion.com.

# About Uncommon Schools

At Uncommon Schools, our mission is to start and manage outstanding urban public schools that close the achievement gap and prepare scholars from low-income communities to graduate from college. For twenty years, through trial, error, and adjustment, we have learned countless lessons about what works in classrooms. Not surprisingly, we have found that success in the classroom is closely linked to our ability to hire, develop, and retain great teachers and leaders. That has prompted us to invest heavily in training educators and building systems that help leaders to lead, teachers to teach, and students to learn. We are passionate about finding new ways for our scholars to learn more today than they did yesterday, and to do so, we work hard to ensure that every minute matters.

We know that many educators, schools, and school systems are interested in the same things we are interested in—practical solutions for classrooms and schools that work, that can be performed at scale, and that are accessible to anyone. We are fortunate to have had the opportunity to observe and learn from outstanding educators—both within our schools and from across the United States—who help all students achieve at high levels. Watching these educators at work has allowed us to identify, codify, and film concrete and practical findings about great instruction. We have been excited to share these findings in such books as *Teach Like a Champion* (and the companion *Field Guide*), *Practice Perfect*, *Driven by Data*, *Leverage Leadership*, and *Great Habits, Great Readers*.

Since the release of the original *Teach Like a Champion*, Doug Lemov and Uncommon's Teach Like a Champion (TLAC) team have continued to study educators who are generating remarkable results across Uncommon, at partner organizations, and at schools throughout the country. Through countless hours of observation and analysis, Doug and the TLAC team have further refined and codified the tangible best practices that the most effective teachers have in common. *Teach Like a Champion 3.0* builds off the groundbreaking work of the original *Teach Like a Champion* book and shares it with teachers and leaders who are committed to changing the trajectory of students' lives.

We thank Doug and the entire TLAC team for their tireless and insightful efforts to support teachers everywhere. We hope our efforts to share what we have learned will help you, your scholars, and our collective communities.

Brett Peiser
Chief Executive Officer
Uncommon Schools

Uncommon Schools is a nonprofit network of 57 urban public charter schools that prepare more than 22,000 K–12 students in New York, New Jersey, and Massachusetts to graduate from college. A CREDO study found that for low-income students who attend Uncommon Schools, Uncommon "completely cancel[s] out the negative effect associated with being a student in poverty." Uncommon Schools was also named the winner of the national Broad Prize for Public Charter Schools for demonstrating "the most outstanding overall student performance and improvement in the nation in recent years while reducing achievement gaps for low-income students and students of color." To learn more about how Uncommon Schools is changing history, please visit us at **uncommonschools.org**.

# Preface to the 3.0 Edition: Equity, Justice, and the Science of Learning

I've called this opening section of the third edition of this book a "preface," but only because I had to call it something. I mostly skip prefaces and perhaps you do, too.

Please don't skip this one. I am going to tell you the story of this book's relationship to a rapidly changing world: How it fits within larger questions of equity and social justice. How it connects to the growing insights of cognitive science on learning.

Whether you're a TLAC veteran or new to the book, it will help you to make sense of what you read in the rest of this volume.

In the summer of 2019 I set out to revise *Teach Like a Champion* for a second time. I'd revised it once before, sharing what I'd learned from further study and tapping into the wisdom of teachers who'd adapted the original techniques. I'd watch them teach and think, *I never would have thought of that* or *How could I have not thought of that*? And so version 2.0 came about.

This time around I again wanted to tap into that wisdom, but I wanted to make a bigger change as well. I wanted to discuss research in cognitive psychology that was rapidly adding to our knowledge of how the human brain worked and how learning happened. The fact that what University of Virginia cognitive psychologist Daniel Willingham calls the "cognitive revolution" was not showing up in classroom instruction was, to me, an equity issue. Students deserved teaching informed by science. It was no longer viable to leave the connections to research implicit in my own book, or not to use the research to understand more clearly not only *what* was (and wasn't) important to do in the classroom but *why*.

Great teaching "always begins with clear vision and a sound purpose," Adeyemi Stembridge writes in *Culturally Responsive Education in the Classroom*. "The teacher who deeply understands this is often able to evoke brilliance from even the most mundane of strategies." But if a clear purpose could make mundane strategies brilliant, a lack of clarity about purpose could also cause an effective strategy to fail. To know why is to be several steps closer to consistently knowing how.

I wanted to do more of that. If you knew that, as Willingham puts it, students remember what they think about, you could be intentional about using *Everybody Writes* and *Cold Call* to help ensure that everyone thought deeply about the lesson content; if you knew that students need to feel psychological safety in order to learn, you could be intentional about using *Habits of Attention* to wrap them in a culture that ensured constant messages of support from peers.

So version 3.0 began to take shape. I replaced the chapter on lesson planning with one on lesson preparation. The two things are not the same, of course. Preparation is what you do *after* the plan is written—by you or somebody else—to get ready to teach it. Time spent in schools was convincing me of its profound importance—and the frequency with which it is overlooked. The first technique in that chapter is *Exemplar Planning*—writing out the ideal answers you want students to give to important questions you'll ask during class.[1] That might seem like a superfluous task. You might think, *I already have a good sense for what students should say*. But writing it out helps clear your working memory and this has a very important effect, I now understood.

I'll discuss working memory—essentially what you are conscious of thinking about—more in Chapter One, but when you are thinking hard about something and your working memory is full, the quality and depth of your perception is reduced. If you're driving a car while talking to your significant other on the phone, you're far more likely to misjudge the rate of approach of an oncoming vehicle and have an accident. It's not so much that your *hands* aren't free but that your working memory isn't. In critical moments, doing one thing implies not doing another. That's true for students and it's true for teachers. If you're trying to remember the answer you wanted students to give while they're answering you, you won't hear what they say as accurately as you could. But write the answer out and glance at it even briefly and it will make a profound difference. You will hear your students' thinking more clearly.

Cognitive psychology was also increasingly clear about the importance of background knowledge and long-term memory so I added new techniques based on how teachers were applying *Retrieval Practice* and *Knowledge Organizers*. Dylan Wiliam has called Cognitive Load Theory "the single most important thing for teachers to know," and you'll see its relevance throughout the book and especially in technique 21, *Take the Steps*. Eventually I decided to add Chapter One, as well, which summarizes key principles that might compose a strong mental model of classroom instruction—a mental model being itself something cognitive psychologists had identified as necessary to guide strong decision making.

That the book was changing was inevitable—not only because of the useful and sometimes brilliant adaptations I saw teachers make but also because of honest and earnest mistakes.

There were classrooms I'd visit that took my breath away and also classrooms where a teacher was "doing TLAC" and I didn't like what I saw, and that, too, was cause for reflection. How could it be that I would see two teachers using similar techniques in nearby rooms and one made me feel pride and exhilaration and the other distress?

I say that without judgment. One of many broader life lessons I've learned from great teachers can be found in technique 59, *Positive Framing*, and specifically in the section on *Assume the Best*, which involves avoiding the urge to attribute negative intention to an action unless it's unambiguously the case. When a couple of students don't follow your directions, for example, if you are assuming the best, you might say, "Guys, I must not have been clear enough about how to do this; I'd like you to work silently," or "Pause. A couple of us forgot that this was supposed to be a silent task. Let's fix that now." Assuming the best—*I must not have been clear* or *you probably forgot* versus *you don't care* or *you ignored the directions*—not only builds stronger, more positive relationships but it causes you to perceive your classroom—and the world—differently because what you practice seeing is, in the end, what you come to see. In *The Happiness Advantage*, Shawn Achor calls this the Tetris Effect. If you play the game Tetris long enough, you begin to imagine its brightly colored shapes falling everywhere. If you make a habit of naming things you are grateful for each day, you come to see a world full of things worthy of gratitude. If you practice assuming good intentions you see a world striving for goodness and this makes you happier, more optimistic, and probably a better teacher.

It's the same for students, incidentally. When we help them to make the most charitable interpretation possible of their peers—are you *sure* she meant to push you? are you *sure* he meant that as a slight?—we give them a better world. As John Haidt and Greg Lukianoff point out, having a charitable, positive, and optimistic mindset is a healthier way to go through life.[2]

All of which is a bit of a digression—at least if thinking about student well-being is ever a digression. My point is that as teachers, remembering to assume the best and say to students "My directions must not have been clear enough" rather than "Some of you weren't listening to the directions" actually causes us to interrupt our own tendency to make the fundamental attribution error[3] and instead ask: *Actually, were my directions clear enough? Perhaps not.*

When I saw classrooms where techniques I'd described were used in a way that did not feel right, I strove to ask myself: *Were* my directions clear enough? *Why* might people forget? Was the reason techniques were occasionally misapplied a result of what I'd written—or of what I had left unsaid?

The answer, of course, was sometimes *yes*. How could it not be? Teaching is difficult work done under complex and often challenging conditions. It would be impossible to get everything right—for a teacher and certainly for someone seeking to describe what teachers did or might do.

I return to this topic later, but for now I'll describe one resulting change in this version of the book: Keystone Videos. These are extended videos (most are about ten minutes long) intended to show a longer arc of a teacher's lesson where they use multiple techniques in combination. They convey a broader sense of what the culture and ethos of exceptional classrooms look like and the ways techniques combine and interact. I've added them because to show a technique with clarity sometimes requires a degree of focus that both reveals and distorts a teacher's work.

Take Christine Torres: You'll see several videos from her classroom in this book. I first saw her teaching on an impromptu visit to Springfield Prep in Springfield, Massachusetts, and the moment I stepped into her room I was blown away. Her lessons were impeccably prepared. I would use the word *scholarly* to describe the rigor of the content and the ideas her students developed. She expressed her belief in their capacity for excellence in everything she did, and while she expected effort and focus from students, love, joy, and even playfulness also shone through.

I had observed as one of her students, making a comment intended for his peers, had muttered inaudibly while facing away from them as he spoke. "*Don't talk to the wall 'cuz the wall don't ca-are,*" Christine sang in a lilting voice. The student turned and smiled cautiously, noticing his classmates' supportive gazes looking back at him. The wall might not care but his classmates were telling him with their eye contact that they did. He braced himself and offered an insight about the novel in a halting but clear voice, and you could see, afterwards, that he was happy—and just maybe a tiny bit surprised. He had done it; *he could do it*. This was a classroom that raised you up—it drew your best out of you.

Christine's classroom was, to use a phrase I will return to, a *bright mirror*. It *reflected* her students, revealing and appreciating who they already were, but it also *changed* them by bringing out things that had not been visible. It didn't just *give them an opportunity*, it influenced them intentionally to engage in positive behaviors they might not have risked, might not have even known existed, without the light of an intentionally supportive culture shining on them. *Every* environment socializes the people within it to make certain choices and exhibit certain behaviors, Cass Sunstein and Richard Thaler explain in *Nudge*. *There is no neutral case*. There are merely cases of greater or lesser intentionality. A classroom where students react with disinterest to their classmates' comments is no more "natural" than one like Christine's where they react with encouragement. One is just harder to create.

Later we sent our cameras to Christine's classroom and among the things we cut from the video was a series of tiny moments where Christine did some version of what she had done when she sang, "Don't talk to the wall 'cuz the wall don't care" and socialized her students to speak audibly and *to* one another. "Loud and proud" was how she most often put it.

It would be hard to understand how she does that—the speed, the tone, the variation in the phrases she uses—if you didn't see a series of examples in rapid succession. You need a montage—a series of moments when she took those actions spliced together tidily. But if you only saw the montage you'd only get part of the picture. You'd also need a taste of what I'd seen and felt standing in the back of Christine's classroom that first morning—a sense for how rigorous her teaching was and of the love her students felt from and for her. You'd need to see those things to understand how her use of *Format Matters* (technique 18, which includes pushing students to speak audibly) interacted with the other things she did. So we added the keystone videos, which you can read descriptions of in the introduction. They are often taken in classrooms from which you can also see shorter, more focused clips that demonstrate a specific technique; my hope is that watching the Keystone videos will give you the bigger picture.

* * * * * * *

That was where this version of the book stood when, suddenly, 2020 happened.

It goes without saying that the disruption resulting from the COVID-19 epidemic had profound effects on schools and teaching. Some of that is reflected in this book—I've included sidebars with examples of techniques used in an online setting on the assumption that remote teaching will play a role in schooling in some capacity even after schools come back to (or closer to) normal.[4]

But growing urgency in the movement for social justice and social change also exploded in 2020 in the wake of the killing of George Floyd at the hands of police in Minneapolis,[5] the most recent example of a horrifying pattern of Black and Brown citizens being killed by law enforcement. And of course it recalled the long history of systemic inequities in other institutions, including schools. This stirred me and my colleagues to more explicitly define the role we wanted to play in the fight for a more equitable and just society.

I want to say as directly as possible that *Teach Like a Champion* is and always has been a book about social justice. (The systematic inequality of the American education system has been obvious to anyone who cared to look since long before 2020.) Its premise is that students not born to privilege and opportunity—often Black and Brown—deserve schools and classrooms that don't just provide them an *opportunity* to achieve—implying that the chance is there if they choose it—though far too many go to schools that fail that test. Its premise is that the opportunity to sit in classrooms where one can cautiously pursue an interest in scholarly endeavor is not good enough. Social justice means (to me, at least, and I hope to the people who read this book) every student's right to be in classrooms that consistently ensure they can pursue their dreams of becoming scientists, engineers, and artists, the presidents of banks, organizations, and nations in classrooms that socialize scholarship and protect and create the optimal conditions for achievement. They deserve schools that encourage and push them to engage in behaviors that foster their own learning and the learning of those around them. And they deserve something that the author and literacy expert Alfred Tatum calls "disciplinary equity."

"There are dozens of disciplines taught at the university level in which it feels like there is a Black eraser," Tatum wrote recently. It's imperative that "all disciplines belong to all groups,"[6] he noted, but the feeling of erasure exists (in engineering and computer science and biochemistry, for example) because we do not sufficiently "provide the foundation in elementary, middle and high schools." Providing that foundation requires strength of academics and strength of culture—a bright mirror in every classroom that reflects students and draws them into the light.

The moment when Christine's student turned hesitantly to face to the room—unsure that he could do it—and saw not only encouragement and support in his classmates' eyes, but also a social norm reflected, one that said: *we participate with enthusiasm Ms. Torres' room; we are unabashedly intellectual,* and so found that he could do it—*that* was a moment of social justice.

When culture is *not* strong like that, when it does not foster positive and productive engagement as the norm, teachers make compromises. A lesson plan's primary attribute must then be its capacity to win students' attention with something catchy because they are not expected and socialized to pay attention. The question *How rigorous can I make this lesson?* is off the table.

This trade-off is by no means limited to certain schools. As you read this, there are tens of thousands of students across almost every strata of American society sitting in classrooms in various states of compromise, where a quiet tyranny—more or less invisible but still potent—exerts itself. TNTP's 2018 report, *The Opportunity Myth,* suggests how endemic this quiet tyranny is. Following nearly 4,000 students in five diverse school systems, TNTP found that even when they had completed the work they were given, even when they strove to give their best and set a goal of further study, students were routinely, overwhelmingly not on track to accomplish the things they aspired to. The work they did in school was not challenging or demanding enough. Even those who received high marks were not prepared. "Their lives," the authors wrote, "are slipping further away each day, unbeknownst to them and their families—not because they can't master challenging material, but because they're rarely given a real chance to try. Students spent more than 500 hours per school year on assignments that weren't appropriate for their grade and with instruction that didn't ask enough of them—the equivalent of six months of wasted class time in each core subject."

Social justice to me is classrooms that are *radically better,* classrooms that foster academic achievement and that prepare every student to accomplish their dreams. If a classroom does not operate as if the young people in it were capable of greatness, it will never be a just class-room. But operating as if young people are capable of greatness does not mean pandering. It means loving young people enough to push them, with warmth, grace, and humanity, to work harder than they may be inclined to. It means loving them enough to set limits, with humanity, constancy, and steadiness, of course. Those of us who are parents know this is true with our own children.[7]

The term *social justice,* I am aware, means different things to different people. Different teachers will in good conscience answer the call of equity in different ways,[8] but if students attend schools that do not foster in them excellence in reading, writing, science, and math, and therefore leave them unprepared to achieve excellence and leadership in their chosen field, we have not created a more socially just world, no matter how committed to action we may be. Equity starts with achievement.

Further, as one of the best school leaders I know observed,[9] if our students do not bring knowledge and analytical skills *to the discussion of social justice itself*, we risk giving rise to lethal mutations—poorly thought-through best intentions that are more harm than good. In 2021, educators in Oregon received an official document advising them that asking students to show their work on math problems was a form of "white supremacy." A friend shared an online discussion in which educators argued that homework and grading were "colonialist constructs." It's hard to tell how many people believe specious arguments that striving to reach the highest levels of achievement, accomplishment, and excellence is somehow anti-thetical to people of color or tantamount to "embracing Whiteness." It's alarming to even have to wonder. This book is written in the belief that such propositions are not just wrong but destructive and that academic achievement is the enabling engine of equity and social justice.

One of the most memorable texts I've read in the past year or so is Damon Tweedy's *Black Man in a White Coat*, a memoir of the author's experiences during his medical education and as a practicing doctor. If nothing else, the COVID crisis has proven that, as with almost every other benefit of our society, quality medical care is unevenly distributed. To anyone who had read Tweedy's book this could not have been a surprise. If we aspire to a just, equitable, and fair society it will require an abundance of doctors of every background but, doubly so, doctors from communities of color and others who are poorly served by the medical field. Social justice likewise relies in the long run on our educating a diverse array of doctors and engineers, scientists and lawyers, artists, financiers, and tech entrepreneurs.

Here is an example: during COVID, pulse oximeters, the devices used to measure oxygen levels in the blood, were three times more likely to give incorrect readings for people with Black skin than with White, *The Economist* recently reported.[10] This is because the devices were designed with more translucent, white skin in mind. Unknown numbers of patients with darker skin in distress were sent home in error due to this design bias. And of course *design bias* exists in a thousand places and will likely continue to live in those places until greater diversity is achieved among the engineers who create and manufacture medical devices. That—per Alfred Tatum's argument—means "disciplinary equity": highly trained and prepared students of color in advanced science and math courses—and in every other field.

So if social justice to you means marching in protest, I support you. Many of your students may line up behind you, too. But know also that some will want to engineer information systems instead[11] and this too is important. Some will choose to lose themselves in the color and composition of the painting they are working on. This too is important. Their right is to be prepared by our schools and our classrooms to go wherever those passions take them. That is also part of social justice: every young person made able to define and pursue their own dream. Is it necessary to point out for the majority of children of poverty, for the majority of Black and Brown children, and just possibly for the majority of children, period, this is not reliably the case?

While the role of teaching in a just and equitable society is my passion, I should note that I do not think that this is a book about educating "poor kids" or "Black and Brown kids." Kids are kids, even if schools are not always what they deserve. This is a book about teaching better, though it is true that I learned what I learned by studying teachers in the part of the education sector that is most important to me, personally.

But I am not foolish enough to think that because I have strong feelings for this aspect of social justice that I fully understand it or the experience of the communities I seek to serve, so part of writing this book involved a months-long process of learning and study of my own, often in the company of my colleagues on the Teach Like a Champion team. The range of the research I read expanded to include social theory, social justice, and culturally responsive teaching, for example. You will see some of the authors I read in that process referenced in the pages of this book: Zaretta Hammond, Lisa Delpit, Alfred Tatum, Rudine Sims-Bishop, and Adeyemi Stembridge.

My entire staff also participated in an internal review of all of our work. This was led by my co-Managing Director, Darryl Williams—it's hard to lead the process of questioning one's own thinking—but involved feedback and insights from all of my colleagues as well as partners and school leaders who use *Teach Like a Champion* in organizations and schools. We discussed at length the techniques and terms in the book to ensure that the tone felt right and descriptions would reduce the possibility of misapplication or misinterpretation. We carefully watched and rewatched videos, paying close attention to how techniques were portrayed so that teachers would apply and adapt them successfully to dignify, uplift, and honor students. There were times, to be honest, when the videos or my writing did not accurately capture what we set out to convey and this resulted in my rewriting passages of this book, renaming techniques or concepts within techniques, and retiring some videos.

I am aware that many readers of *Teach Like a Champion* may have heard critiques of some techniques—Format Matters and what was then called SLANT, for example. And it was with some surprise that, while engaging in the process of revision, I opened my copy of *Teach Like a Champion 2.0* to reread it and was surprised to find how little of what I believed about *why* and *how* I had included in some techniques. You will find those sections of the book in particular extensively revised to help frame them carefully and ensure that all readers fully grasp *why* as much as *how* so they can use them with confidence to help students thrive and succeed. I want to be clear—I think those techniques, done right, are among the most critical levers of success and social justice. You could see that in Christine's classroom as you will see it in a dozen more. But they are powerful tools, too, so it is important to get them right. Critiques that claim they are a form of tyranny or an effort to "control Black and Brown bodies," when they are not informed by deliberate distortion, miss the point: The freedoms gained from a culture that asks students to track one another, and where students' ideas are therefore deliberated, refined, and celebrated, far outweighs the supposed restrictions it imposes. That said, I, too, have been in a room where the application felt wrong. A flawed application does not indict a sound principle—but it does remind us of how important better and more responsive application is.

There were other areas of revision, too. In reading back over my original work I could occasionally see negatively framed examples and at times descriptions that seemed not to assume the best about students. Part of the reason for this was and is my deep appreciation for teachers. My desire for this book is that it will prepare teachers for the most challenging scenarios they will face—the ones that erode their faith that they can succeed and cause people to leave the profession—as much as the happy and sunny times that inspire them and make teaching the best job in the world. There are precious few books that talk about those difficult moments. And so at times I have written examples that show students at their most challenging. It is not my assumption that young people are "usually" this way. My presumption is always that it is understood that educators love young people even—well, especially—when they set limits and provide structure for them, but I can see how some examples might have read otherwise. If nothing else I have gone back through them and tried to reduce any implication that students are out to misbehave. It is also important to be honest about the job, however. Students in any classroom anywhere represent a cross section of human nature.

Any classroom anywhere is a room full of goodness and weakness, virtue and silliness, wisdom and folly. That's why the job is so hard. I'm grateful if, as a reader, you understand that the reason I sometimes give examples of challenging behavior is because it's a reality teachers deal with—too often in silence and without systematic support.

In the end, the process of self-reflection and examination has also helped me to be clear about what I believe. What I believe is that issues of social justice are inseparable from issues of teaching and that issues of teaching include the necessity of deliberately designing classroom cultures to ensure the most supportive culture for young people.

Some people are uncomfortable with this. They see engineering cultures as coercive, an exercise in the excess of power and authority. But I return to the Fundamental Attribution Error. We attribute other people's behavior to "abiding personal characteristics" and "minimize the influence of the surrounding situation." We see permanent traits—*he doesn't care*—instead of a person who might care deeply in a different context. We think insufficiently about environment—*how do I create conditions that make him want to care?*—and underestimate how people respond to cues and norms. At times those norms are practically shouting at us and yet we somehow cannot seem to hear them at all.

Yet another field of study that has been influential to me in writing this book is evolutionary biology, the net of which is that the humans who won out in the struggle for evolution won by coordinating in groups and have evolved to be exceptionally responsive to what is required for inclusion in the group—it is of the highest importance from an evolutionary point of view. We are creatures of culture first, supremely responsive to social norms, and every young person deserves to step into a classroom where social norms are as positive and constructive as possible.

Let me explain what I mean by describing a moment in the life of a student. We'll call her Asha. She is sitting in Biology class and has just had an idea. It's half developed—a notion still—but she wonders if she has thought of something that others have not. *Maybe this is something smart*. She's a bit scared to share what she's thinking. Her idea could be wrong or, just as bad, obvious already to everyone else. Maybe no one else cares much about DNA recombination and the fire it has suddenly lit in her mind. Maybe saying something earnest about DNA recombination makes you *that kid*—the one who raises her hand too often, who tries too hard, who breaks the social code. These sorts of thoughts have heretofore led her to adhere to a philosophy that counsels *Keep it to yourself; don't let anyone see your intellect; take no risks; fit in*. But somehow in this moment the desire to voice her thought overcomes her anxiety. She raises her hand and her teacher calls on her.

What happens next is critical to Asha's future. Will her classmates seem like they care about her idea? Will she read interest in their faces? Will they nod and show their appreciation? Ask a follow-up question? Jot down a phrase in their notes? Or will they be slouched in their chairs and turned away, checking their phones literally or metaphorically, their body language expressing their indifference? *Oh, did you say something?* Smirk. Will the next comment ignore her idea? Will there *even be* a next comment, or will her words drift away in a silence that tells her that no one cared enough to acknowledge or even look at her after she spoke?

These factors are Stations of the Cross in Asha's journey. They will influence the relationship she perceives between herself and school and her aspirations. She is a vibrant soul, full of ideas she does not ordinarily share and wondering quietly if maybe someone like her could become a doctor. She doesn't know anyone who's done that, but she finds herself thinking about it sometimes.

Obviously, those dreams don't all come down to this moment, but we would be foolish to dismiss its relevance. It could be the first tiny step on the path to medical school. Or it could be the last time she raises her hand all year.

Yes, it matters whether her teacher responds to her comment with encouragement—but perhaps not as much as how the social environment, the rest of Asha's peers, respond. If her teacher praises Asha's comment amidst scorn and resounding silence from her peers, the benefit will be limited. The teacher's capacity to shape norms in Asha's classroom matters at least as much as her ability to connect individually with Asha. Relationships matter, but the social norms we create probably matter more. That's a hard thing to acknowledge. It removes us from the center of the story a little bit. But it's a powerful thing to recognize as well. In many classrooms there is no model for what the social norms should communicate while Asha speaks or after she has spoken and her words hang in the air. Is it really their business whether students show an interest in what their classmates say? Or perhaps there is a model, but it is mostly words—her teacher and maybe her school do not believe that what happens in that moment is within their control. Imagine what a headache it would be to try to make that happen with hundreds of students, many of whom "just don't care"? In the end, what happens in this moment and a thousand like it will most likely be an accident: lucky or unfortunate, supportive or destructive, with immense consequences for Asha and her classmates.

Something close to optimal culture, where Asha's classmates are communicating with eye contact and body language: *we are listening; we respect your idea; it interests us; keep raising your hand*, does not occur naturally or by accident. It occurs when adults cause it to happen.

Let me close with a short parable about something I call the Band-Aid Paradox.

At the beginning of his book *Predictably Irrational*, a study of "why people misunderstand the consequences of their behaviors and for that reason repeatedly make wrong decisions," Duke behavioral economist and psychologist Dan Ariely tells a story about bandages.

Nurses often operate under the belief that that ripping bandages off quickly delivers less pain to patients than slower, more gradual removal. Fast bandage removal is proven to be the preferable form of treatment, many believe.

A burn victim during his youth, Ariely had a great many bandages removed by this method and was skeptical. His feelings must have been strong, because studying psychology years later, he tested the idea empirically and found that slower bandage removal was in fact more preferable to patients.

Ariely returned to the hospital where he had spent months in recovery and presented his findings to the nurses there but was surprised to find that even in the face of his research, nurses persisted with suboptimal treatment.

Ariely had failed to account for the psychological discomfort nurses felt as they removed bandages. Patients expressed anxiety, fear, and discomfort as nurses slowly pulled their bandages. The feeling that they might be hurting someone was bad, even if they knew rationally that they were helping, and drawing those moments out made it even worse for the nurses.

Turns out that for caregivers, the psychological aspects of administering treatment—even clearly beneficial treatment—is a significant factor in determining the care they provide. I'm going to call this the Band-Aid Paradox. Caregivers' anxiety about treatment can cause them to choose a suboptimal form of treatment and *explain it via an argument apparently grounded in patients' interest.*

A similar Band-Aid Paradox influences practices in the field of teaching. Administering "treatments" often results in a conflict between what "feels good"—or feels safe or jibes with the practitioner's self-concept or perceptions about equity. Doubly so when, like doctors whose self-concept is based on being a healer, our identity is intertwined with beliefs about right and wrong.

Teachers are constantly faced with challenging and difficult tasks and must contemplate the very real possibility that they will struggle or fail, publicly and in front of an unforgiving audience, as they endeavor to execute them. It is, we should always remain aware, easier to rationalize the preferential treatment for the caregiver than try the riskier one that will serve students in the long run. Faced with making a classroom where students are socialized to show they value one another's ideas through prosocial nonverbal actions including eye contact, the path of explaining why students should not be coerced to track their classmates in the first place beckons.

The harder the task, the greater the risk some educator somewhere will create a very smart or righteous-sounding rationale against it. That is certainly a far less risky path than the difficult and thankless work of shaping norms to ensure the rights of all children to learn in classrooms that truly prepare them to achieve their dreams.

I have written, in the margin of my version of Teach Like a Champion 2.0, a phrase that I have tried to use frequently in this book: *loving accountability*. That might not be a phrase that would naturally occur to a lot of people. Admittedly, it took several years of writing about teaching for it to come to me. But it is deeply important. It reminds us, first, that moments of accountability can and should be done with a smile to remind students that we care about them, and, second, that accountability is a form of love.

When we *Cold Call*, for example, we are drawing students—sometimes willingly, sometimes hesitantly—into the conversation and thus telling them their voice matters. We are building for them a habit of paying attention more fully, and sustaining that habit of attention. As Zaretta Hammond writes, in a phrase I will return to, "Before we can be motivated to learn what is in front of us, we must pay attention to it. The hallmark of an independent learner is his ability to direct his attention toward his own leaning." Building someone's attentiveness in class is a gift.

And if students feel a hint of anxiety, OK, that comes with growing sometimes. Knowing that learning requires you to speak up at times and knowing from experience that you are able; learning to pay attention—at first because you know your teacher is probably going to call on you to keep you honest and later because, well, it has become a habit—those are the gifts of a classroom led with love. A smile during the *Cold Call* reminds both your students and yourself—because pulling Band-Aids slowly is hard—that it's a good thing.

In the section on *Cold Call* you can see Denarius Frazier and BreOnna Tindall do this. They are smiling reassuringly and warmly at their students as they *Cold Call* and you can feel the love in those moments. They will remind you, I hope, that it is *not* a contradiction to call accountability a form of love. It's not always what students would choose at first if they were given a choice, but they often prefer it in the end when teaching informed by lovingly accountability—like Denarius's and BreOnna's and Christine's and a score of other teachers in this book—results in not only success but in engagement, when students lose themselves in the lesson and feel learning as a state of flow.[12] Then they are happier even if they never connect the happiness to the accountability that started it.

Even knowing that, though, some of them would *still* take the easier path. In such cases it is helpful to think of whom we serve in education. We serve the version of our students looking back on their schooling ten or fifteen years later, in light of its long-run effect on their lives. And we serve their parents, who are counting on us to push their children to create a future for themselves even in a world that surrounds them with distractions and messages that it's OK, cool even, not to do the things now that will create opportunity later. There is some tradition of young people not wanting to do what their parents say but coming, in the end, to say the things their parents said to them to their own children. Education is a long game and parents are counting on us to take the long view. You can hear this in the interviews in Robert Pondisicio's outstanding *How the Other Half Learns*. Among the most gut-wrenching are the parents whose own educations were unsuccessful, and who seek schools and classrooms that will prevent the same outcome from befalling their children. "I got lost in the system," one mother tells Pondiscio, "and I refuse to let that happen to my son." The sense of desperation is palpable.

Part of teaching well is teaching students to choose a path that is steep and rocky, that they will sometimes complain about. It's a long way up and perhaps others appear to be on what seems like an easier path, even if it does not lead to the summit. The steeper path involves not just harder work but *psychologically* harder work—for teacher as much as student. It involves slowly pulling off Band-Aids. It involves knowing that love is sometimes paradoxical.

If you seek justification for doing what is easy, this book will not likely please you. That said, there are many books that will. If your purpose is to find the most effective and caring way to do what needs doing to best serve students, even when it is difficult—especially when it is difficult—my goal is to provide that. If that is the book you are looking for, please turn the page.

## Notes

1. The idea began with Paul Bambrick-Santoyo and his team at Uncommon Schools.
2. See *The Coddling of the American Mind: How Good Intentions and Bad Ideas Are Setting Up a Generation for Failure* (New York: Penguin Books, 2018).
3. Fundamental Attribution Error: "The tendency to overestimate the degree to which an individual's behavior is determined by his or her abiding personal characteristics, attitudes, or beliefs and, correspondingly, to minimize the influence of the surrounding situation on that behavior" (APA Dictionary of Psychology, https://dictionary.apa.org/fundamental-attribution-error).
4. More thoughts on remote learning are included in the book my team and I wrote to support teachers during remote instruction: *Teaching in the Online Classroom*.
5. I don't mean to imply that Floyd's killing was the sole source of the outrage and anger so many felt. Obviously, the long string of killings of citizens of color in the care of institutions whose job was to protect them has been a source of ongoing consternation and frustration.
6. Tatum is the Provost and Executive Vice President for Academic Affairs at Metropolitan State University in Denver. His comments were made in a series of tweets on April 12, 2021.

7. When a small child would like to eat ice cream in lieu of dinner, all but the most indulgent parents understand that to love the child is to say no. When the child is older they will have days when they want to do what is hurtful to themselves in the long run or challenge the rules we set for their benefit: *I'm quitting the track team; I'm not writing my essay; I'm going to stay out past curfew.* Teenagers are wired to do these things; adults who love them are supposed to do what will help them thrive throughout their lives, even if it is difficult. To love them is to say, "Get your shoes; I'm driving you to practice," "Let me help you start your thesis paragraph before it gets late," or "I'll see you here at 11 sharp if you plan on using the car again." A loving adult says this even if it results in temporary resentment.

8. To some it implies that teachers should encourage students to participate actively in social protest, for example. To some it implies that issues of social justice should be a major focus of the books students read and the topics they study. To others it is more important that students prepare themselves for professional success by more traditional means such as reading Shakespeare and studying cell structure.

9. Brandi Chin of Denver School of Science and Technology. You should see her school. (Actually, you can see it, when you watch video of ace teacher BreOnna Tindall later in this book.)

10. "Design Bias Is Harmful, and in Some Cases May Be Lethal," Working in the Dark, *The Economist*, April 10, 2021.

11. I am reminded of a quote from Adeyemi Stembridge: "In any given school with any particular student, race may mean everything or nothing at all. We must make ourselves available for the discomfort inherently accompanying the topic of race and we must also be prepared to dismiss everything we know about race to allow students to show us who they are as unique individuals with agency and their own catalogue of concepts, contexts and lived experiences." A responsive educator must always see and respond to the student he or she serves. Even when they do not share the interests of their teachers it is those interests we must serve.

12. I discuss the idea of "flow" in learning in the introduction to Chapter Six, "Pacing," but *Cold Call* can be a key tool to achieving the dynamic momentum that brings it about.

# Introduction to the Third Edition: The Art of Teaching and Its Tools

Great teaching is an art. In the other arts—painting, sculpture, the writing of novels—great masters leverage a proficiency with basic tools to transform the rawest of materials (stone, paper, ink) into the most valued assets in society. This alchemy is all the more astounding because the tools often appear unremarkable to others. Who would look at a chisel, a mallet, and a file and imagine them producing Michelangelo's *David*?

Great art relies on the mastery and application of foundational skills, learned through diligent study—"craftsmanship," if you will. You learn to strike a chisel with a mallet and refine the skill with time, learning at which angle to strike the chisel and how tightly to hold it. Far more important than any theory is your proficiency with the lowly chisel. True, not everyone who learns to drive a chisel will create a *David,* but neither can anyone who *fails* to master the tool do much more than make marks on rocks.

Every artist—teachers included—is an artisan whose task is to study a set of tools and unlock the secrets of their use. The more you understand the chisel, the more it guides you to see what is possible. Rounding a contour with unexpected smoothness, the chisel causes you to realize, suddenly, that you could bring added subtlety to a facial expression, more tension to the muscles of the figure. Mastery of tools does not just *allow* creation; it *informs* it. The process is often far from glamorous; an artist's life is a tradesman's life, really, characterized by calluses and stone dust, requiring diligence and humility, but its rewards are immense. It is a worthy life's work.

Traveling abroad during my junior year in college, I saw Picasso's school notebooks on display at the Picasso Museum in Barcelona. What I remember best are the sketches filling the margins of his pages. These weren't sketchbooks, mind you. These were notebooks like those every student keeps: notes from lectures. The tiny sketches memorialized a teacher's face or Picasso's own hand grasping a pencil, with perfect perspective, line, and shading.

I had always thought Picasso's work was about abstraction, about a way of thinking that rendered the ability to draw accurately and realistically irrelevant. His sketches told another story, bearing witness to his mastery of fundamentals and constant drive to refine his skills. Even in the stray moments of his schooling, he was honing the building blocks of his technique. He was an artisan first and then an artist, as the fact that he filled, by one count, 178 sketchbooks in his life further attests.

This book is about the tools of the teaching craft and so I hope it will be useful to teachers everywhere. But it takes a special interest in the sector of the profession that is most important to me personally: public schools, particularly those that serve primarily students of poverty and who therefore walk a narrow and uncertain path to the opportunity they deserve. It should not be that to be born with fewer financial resources restricts one's opportunity, certainly not in a nation that believes in meritocracy, but the truth is what it is. The price of failure in schools serving students on the wrong side of the privilege gap is often high, the challenges significant. Teachers there often work in a crucible where our society's failures are paramount and sometimes seem nearly overwhelming. Still, every day in every such neighborhood, there are teachers who without much fanfare take the students who others say "can't"—can't read great literature, can't do algebra or calculus, can't and don't want to learn—and help, inspire, motivate, and even cajole them to become scholars who do. Impossibly, we often don't know who those teachers are, but they are everywhere—generally laboring unnoticed down the hall from one of the 50 percent of new hires in urban districts who leave teaching within their first three years. Think about that: It turns out that for those struggling new teachers, solutions to the challenges that will ultimately drive them out of the profession flourish just a few yards away. It turns out that for students, walking into the right classroom can pry the doors of opportunity back open. The problem is that we aren't serious enough about learning from the teachers who can provide these answers.

My goal was to find as many such teachers as I could and honor them by focusing on, and studying, their teaching. To write this book, I spent a lot of time standing in the back of classrooms and watching videotape of great teachers in action. I used Jim Collins's observation from *Built to Last* and *Good to Great* that what separates great from good matters more than what describes mere competence. I wanted to know not what made a teacher pretty good but what made her exceptional, able to beat the odds. Were there consistent ideas that allowed them to more reliably transform lives? Were there words and actions the rest of us could copy and adapt? Were there general trends to provide a road map, were there principles behind the excellence? Or was their excellence idiosyncratic and unmappable?

What I found was that while each great teacher is unique, as a group their teaching held elements in common. I started to see both theme and variation, so I began to make a list of the things they did and the ways in which they did them. I gave those actions names so I could remember them, and over time my list grew in both the number of topics and the level of specificity. Ideas coalesced into techniques. But I also found that great teachers came in every stripe and style: They were extroverts and introverts; planners and improvisers; quick-witted and serious. But in the aggregate, a story emerged. There *is* a toolbox for excellence even in the face of challenge, it turns out. The contents have been forged by ten thousand teachers working quietly and usually without recognition at the end of cracked-linoleum hallways. I am sure that some of my analysis of what they do is wrong. In fact, I have rewritten this book several times to try to capture more of what I am learning about what exceptional teachers do with better accuracy. One point I have tried to stress is that having a tool is not an argument for using it heedlessly. A painter has a case full of brushes and painting knives, but she does not use every one of them with each portrait or landscape.

If you're a teacher near the beginning of your study of the craft of teaching, my aim is to help you become one of those teachers who, for a long and distinguished career, unlocks the latent talent and skill waiting in students, even if previous efforts have been unsuccessful. If you commit yourself and your talents to this work, you deserve to be successful and to change lives. If you are successful, you will most likely be happy in the work, and when you are happy, in turn, you will do better work.

If you are a master teacher already, I hope a discussion of tools and their applications, the framing of a vocabulary for talking about the critical and sometimes overlooked moments of your day, will inspire you not only to refine your craft but also to love doing so and to feel the pleasure of committing (or recommitting) to the deepest possible mastery of the complex and worthy endeavor that is your life's work. I assume that in many cases this book may describe things you already know and do. That's great by me, and in that case, my goal is to help you get a little better at them, perhaps seeing useful applications and variations you haven't considered. Either way, your growth is at least as important as that of a novice teacher. Teaching is the best and most important work in our society. Those who do it deserve to experience constant growth and learning. That, after all, is what we wish for our students.

If you lead a school, I hope this book will help you in helping teachers do this challenging work as successfully as possible. In our field, the first obligation of an organization is to help its people succeed. When teachers end the day with a sense of accomplishment, when they feel they are both successful and growing more so, they stay in our schools for a long time, do outstanding work, work joyfully, and inspire others, and thus pay the organization back many times over.

The pages that follow are an effort to describe and organize the tools used by game-changing teachers, and to reflect on how and why they use them so that you can make informed decisions of your own.

My work has not been to invent the tools I describe here but to explain how others use them and what makes them effective. This has meant putting names on techniques in the interest of helping create a common vocabulary with which to analyze and discuss the classroom. The names may seem like a gimmick at first, but they are one of the most important parts. If there were no word *democracy*, it would be a thousand times harder to have and sustain a *thing* called "democracy." We would forever be bogged down in inefficiency—"You know that thing we talked about where everyone gets a say . . ."—at exactly the moment we needed to take action. Teachers and administrators must be able to talk quickly and efficiently with colleagues about a clearly defined and shared set of ideas in order to sustain their work. They need a shared vocabulary thorough enough to allow a comprehensive analysis of the wide range of often complex events that happen in a classroom. I believe that names matter and are worth using. Ideally, they will allow you to talk about your own teaching and that of your peers in efficient, specific language.

But I want to be clear. Despite the names, what appears here is neither mine, especially, nor a theory. It is a set of field notes from observations of the work of others, some of whom you will meet in this book, and many others whom you will not. I wish to thank them all for the diligence and skill that informed and inspired this work.

## SPECIFIC, CONCRETE, ACTIONABLE TECHNIQUES

When I was a young teacher, I'd go to trainings and leave with lofty words ringing in my ears. They touched on everything that had made me want to teach. "Have high expectations for your students." "Expect the most from students every day." "Teach kids, not content." I'd be inspired, ready to improve—until I got to school the next day. I'd find myself asking, "Well, how do I do that? What's the action I should take at 8:25 a.m. to demonstrate those raised expectations?"

What ultimately helped me improve my teaching was when a peer told me something very concrete like, "When you want them to follow your directions, stand still. If you're walking around passing out papers, it looks like the directions are no more important than all of the other things you're doing. Show that your directions matter. Stand still." Over time, it was this sort of concrete, specific, actionable advice, far more than reminders that I must have high expectations, that allowed me to raise expectations in my classroom.

My approach in this book reflects that experience. I have tried to describe the techniques of champion teachers in a concrete, specific, and actionable way that allows you to start using them tomorrow. I chose to call these tools "techniques" and not "strategies"—even though the teaching profession tends to use the latter term—because to me, a strategy is a generalized approach that informs decisions, whereas a technique is a thing you say or do in a particular way. If you are a sprinter, your strategy might be to get out of the blocks fast and run from the front; your technique would be to incline your body forward at about five degrees as you drive your legs up and out ahead of you. If you wanted to be a great sprinter, practicing and refining that technique would help you achieve more than refining your strategy. And because a technique is an action, the more you practiced it, the better you'd get. Mulling over your decision to run from the front a hundred times doesn't make you any better; practicing a hundred sprints with just the right body position does. This is why, I think, focusing on honing and improving specific techniques is the fastest route to success.

It's also worth noting that this set of techniques is not a "system." For me, the benefit of considering individual techniques is that they are small, discrete units of inquiry. You can choose something that interests you and study it, improving quickly and seeing the results. And you can incorporate a new technique into what you already do without having to redesign your entire approach or buying in to everything in the book. As Chip and Dan Heath point out in their book *Switch,* how people encounter useful information has a lot to do with whether they are successful in using it to change and improve their lives. Oftentimes what we conclude is resistance to change—by teachers, say—is in fact lack of clarity about what concrete thing to do next to begin the change: "OK, I get that I should be more rigorous, but how do I do that, or start to do that in a concrete, manageable way?" Giving people tools to try might seem less efficient than giving them an overarching system that encompasses everything they do, but trying to do everything at once is a recipe for lack of action. Having a manageable focused idea to work on can help make change and improvement safe and easy to pursue, with the result that the technique becomes part of your life. We often achieve more change over the long run via small changes in the short run.

Another key observation from *Switch* is that we tend to assume that the size of a solution must match the size of the problem. You were observed; there were criticisms; it seems you have to make wholesale changes to everything you do. Or do you? Perhaps just connecting with a few students who appear disinterested via *Cold Call,* or preparing differently so you can listen better during your classes, would make a huge difference and cause other things to fall into place. Little changes can often make a big difference.

## THE ART OF USING THE TECHNIQUES

Many of the techniques you will read about in this book may at first seem mundane and unremarkable. They are not always especially innovative. They are not always intellectually startling. They sometimes fail to march in step with educational theory. But used well and responsively they yield an outcome that more than compensates for their occasionally humble appearance. They are worth your time and effort sometimes *because* they are so mundane and easy to overlook. *Simple* and *useful* can be beautiful words. But I want to emphasize that the art is in the discretionary application of the techniques. I've tried to help artisans be artists, not because I think the work of teaching can be mechanized or made formulaic. There is a right and wrong time and place for all of the tools. Effective application will always fall to the unique style and vision of great teachers. That, in a word, is artistry. Great teaching is no less great because the teacher systematically mastered specific skills than is *David* a lesser reflection of Michelangelo's genius because Michelangelo mastered the grammar of the chisel before he created the statue. I believe that given the tools here, teachers will make insightful, independent decisions about how and when to use the techniques of the craft as they go about becoming masters of the art of teaching.

## DEFINING WHAT WORKS

If you've read previous versions of this book you know that my process of finding teachers to study began with test scores. I looked for individuals and schools that, controlling for poverty, were positive outliers. These were teachers (and sometimes whole schools) who worked with students in neighborhoods where often only a fraction of students graduate from high school, never mind go on to college, or where typically only 10 or 20 percent of students might pass a given state test (an incomplete but still important measure of progress) in a typical year. And yet working in that same landscape, the teachers I was studying helped their students achieve at a dramatically higher rate than anyone would have predicted: they might have double the number of students passing . . . or *four times* the number of students passing. Sometimes every single kid passed. Sometimes they had more kids score "advanced" than teachers in surrounding schools had kids score "proficient." Their results often closed the gap between kids born to poverty and kids born to privilege.

Test scores of course are an imperfect measure. They tell us a lot but not nearly everything and are often best used to generate and test hypotheses: You watch a series of teachers with unusually strong results and start to see trends and commonalities. So whenever possible, I tried to use as much additional data as I could get, and to look for signals that were durable over time—sustained results as opposed to one-time blips. When a school was successful for a long time, I also considered the principal's guidance and input in sourcing teachers. Although there are data to suggest that the average principal is only so-so at identifying the best teachers, very good principals are, of course, different from the average. One could argue that the reason they are successful is their ability to understand whose teaching is especially effective. And over time I came to rely on my team—by now they've spent hundreds and hundreds of hours studying and discussing classroom video—to spot moments that would be useful for teachers to study—moments that were replicable, and adaptable, and likely to help teachers help students thrive.

## THE KEYSTONES

As I mentioned in the Preface, one major change in this third edition of the book is the inclusion of longer Keystone videos that show how a selection of truly exceptional teachers use and combine techniques over a sustained arc of their lesson. Sharing these videos shows how the pieces fit together and helps balance the inevitable distortion of seeing only a single technique in sharp focus. Here's a list of the Keystone videos and some of the things I appreciate about the craft of the teachers they profile. I hope you will watch them multiple times. If you're the head of a school or train teachers, I think they're ideal for repeated viewing and study.

*Julia Addeo* (North Star Academy HS, Newark, NJ): Julia's outstanding Checking for Understanding (Chapter Three) is enabled by *Exemplar Planning* (technique 1). Her review of the *Do Now* (technique 20) relies on a balance of *Means of Participation* (technique 36) that includes *Cold Call* (technique 34) and *Show Call* (technique 13). There's not a minute of wasted time.

*Akilah Bond*, then of Leadership Prep Carnasie Elementary School, is reading a Cam Jansen story with her second graders. Her Wait Time is exemplary. She uses *All Hands* (technique 29), asking students to put their hands down so their classmates don't feel rushed, and she ensures productive *Wait Time* (technique 33) by prompting thinking skills. She consistently holds out for "all the way right" answers (*Right Is Right*, technique 16). When Anthony answers you can see both how he uses *Habits of Discussion* (technique 44) to show he's been listening and how supportive his classmates' *Habits of Attention* (technique 48) are in making him feel confident as he strives to explain his own thinking. And when Michael crushes it, his triumph is in part brought about by clear Procedures and Routines (Chapter Ten)—students know not to call out while he is thinking.

*Jessica Bracey:* Reading with her fifth-grade students at North Star Academy Clinton Hill Middle School, Jessica executes gold standard *FASE Reading* (technique 24), with her students, showing pleasure and skill in bringing the book to life. She *Fronts the Writing* (technique 40), asking them to respond in writing before they discuss the book. Her exemplary Procedures and Routines (Chapter Ten) mean they transfer all their thinking to the page and her *Silent Solo* (technique 39) means they're thinking deeply and industriously in complete sentences the whole way. No wonder they're so eager to share out! When they do, you can see a combination of *Habits of Attention* (technique 48) ensuring that they listen well and *Habits of Discussion* (technique 44) building the listening skills that make for a real discussion.

*Na'Jee Carter:* I write about Na'Jee's *Cold Calling* (technique 34) in the clip extensively in Chapter Seven but note also his outstanding *Habits of Discussion* (technique 44): his students listen as well as they speak. His impeccable Procedures and Routines (Chapter Ten) not only help keep his reading group on task and make sure transitions are efficient but they ensure that the students not in his reading group are happily and productively engaged the whole time. His *Accountable Independent Reading* (technique 23) is super productive because he is so clear on the annotation task and this allows him to observe clearly how his readers are doing, but before he sends everyone off to read he *Replaces Self-Report* (technique 6), asking students a series of questions to assess their understanding of the task instead of merely asking them if they understand.

*Denarius Frazier* (Uncommon Collegiate Charter High School): I discuss a section of this video extensively in Chapter Three, Check for Understanding. Denarius models almost every technique in the chapter, starting with Active Observation and ending with *Show Call* in manner that is fundamental to understanding the reality of how productive and enduring relationships are built in the classroom. But notice also how he moves to the corner and uses *Radar and Be Seen Looking* (technique 53) and a *Least Invasive Intervention* (technique 55) to ensure that everyone is attentive. And notice how his *Emotional Constancy* (technique 62) assists him in building a *Culture of Error* (technique 12) that makes students willing participants in the task of learning from their mistakes.

*Arielle Hoo* (North Star Vailsburg Middle School) asks her students to write at a key moment in the lesson about how they'll know a solution is correct. Notice the word "conjectures"—it's a great example of a formative prompt that not only makes it safe to be wrong but socializes students to think of writing as something you do to discover new insights, not just explain them. This is a key aspect of *Everybody Writes* (technique 38). Notice the *Silent Solo* (technique 39): Everyone is writing right away. Notice how the exemplary discussion she has, full of keen insights and technical vocabulary, starts with her, like Denarius, moving to "Pastore's Perch" and using *Radar and Be Seen Looking* (technique 53) to ensure that everyone is with her. Sidney kicks off the discussion (so well!) and the eye contact and pro-social body language she receives (technique 48, *Habits of Attention*) remind her—and everyone else—that *what you are saying is important.* Next Sadie speaks, hesitating while using the technical term *coincidental* to describe two lines. Possibly it's the first time he's used this term. Notice how he persists and takes the risk of doing so. The Habits of Attention help but so do a larger nexus of Procedures and Routines (Chapter Ten): No one shouts out the answer or waves their own hand in the air or says anything distracting while he struggles for the right word. The sequence ends with students revising their original conjectures in writing, an example of the revision you can read about in both *Front the Writing* and *Regular Revision* (techniques 40 and 42).

*Sadie McCleary* (Western Guilford High School): Sadie's Pacing (Chapter Six) and *Means of Participation* (technique 36) are brilliant—perhaps the latter leading to the former—and I discuss them both at length later in the book, not to mention her *Board = Paper* (technique 22), *Turn and Talk* (technique 43), and *Call and Response* (technique 35). She's successful at all of these because her *What to Do* directions (technique 52) make it just so clear to students how to participate and be successful. Sadie's easy, warm, gracious style expresses loving accountability.

*Narlene Pacheco:* Working with her kindergartners at the Immaculate Conception School in the Bronx, Narlene is crystal clear on how to participate successfully through a combination of economy of language (see technique 58, *Strong Voice*) and *What to Do* (technique 52) directions, which she combines with immense warmth. She's also great at carefully observing for errors (*Active Observation*, technique 9) while building a *Culture of Error* (technique 12), correcting mistakes without a hint of judgment or negativity.

*BreOnna Tindall:* Watching this class at Denver School of Science and Technology first led me to coin the term "bright mirror"—the idea that BreOnna is changing students while also letting them reveal themselves. She is both bringing out something that is new and giving students the chance to show what is already there. She begins with an impeccable *Turn and Talk* (technique 43), but notice how her system allows her to vary shoulder partners (next to you) and desk partners (across from you). All of this is built into habit and shows how impeccable Procedures and Routines (Chapter Ten) lead to a warm, trusting, and supportive environment. The warmth of her *Cold Call* (technique 34) shows just how inclusive this technique really is.

*Christine Torres:* You've already read a bit about Christine's teaching at Springfield Prep in Springfield, Massachusetts, in the Preface—the magic with which she brings *Format Matters* (technique 18), *Habits of Attention* (technique 48), and *Habits of Discussion* (technique 44) to life. Chapter Two starts with a discussion of her preparation. To make the keystone I had to cut from two sections of her lesson—the vocabulary review and the discussion—because

I've rarely seen a class where students participated with such effort and openness and her playful personal style combined with constant loving accountability makes this class sing.

*Nicole Warren:* This lesson with her third graders at Leadership Prep Ocean Hill Elementary Academy positively crackles to life from the outset. There's a quick chant that everyone is all-in on (Procedures and Routines, Chapter Ten, will help you do this). Then it's right into a *Turn and Talk* (technique 43). She *Cold Calls* coming out of it (technique 34) before transitioning to independent practice. It's also *Retrieval Practice* (technique 7). The movement from each activity to the next is a model of the sort of flow that a well-paced lesson can build (Chapter Six). Notice in particular how well she *Brightens the Lines* (technique 28) with lightning transitions like "Tell your partner" and "Go to work!" as well as economy of language (part of technique 58, *Strong Voice*). The tiny *Call and Response* (technique 35) of "Happy Birthday" leaves Crystal smiling. There's also top-of-the-line *Active Observation* (technique 9) and *Standardizing the Format* (technique 8) that allow her to know how students are doing and to build the positive and warm relationships you will undoubtedly notice.

*Gabby Woolf:* Reading *Dr Jekyll and Mr Hyde* with her year 10 English class at King Solomon Academy in London, Gabby models *FASE Reading* (technique 24) beautifully as her students make meaning audible. Next there's a bit of *Cold Call* (technique 34) as she *Replaces Self-Report* (technique 6) with targeted questions to review the passage. She makes sure to reinforce that discussion starts with being heard by stressing audible format from *Format Matters* (technique 18). Her *Circulate* (technique 25) is outstanding and her *What to Do* directions (technique 52) keep everyone on task: "Text in front of you, please." There's a great *Stretch It* (technique 17) in there too when she asks, "What are we imagining when we read the word 'clubbed'?" "Neanderthal," replies an astute student. It's a good answer and Gabby honors it by following up with more questions: "Why?" and when he explains, "So that links to the character of Hyde how?" The message is: The reward for right answers is harder questions, though his answer—he notes that Hyde has devolved—is a sort of reward too.

*Sarah Wright:* Reading *Esperanza Rising* with her fifth-grade boys at Chattanooga Prep in Chattanooga, Tennessee, Sarah proves that the best way to have students take pleasure in learning is to have clear procedures (Chapter Ten, Procedures and Routines) so things work right and students know how to do things. Her students write first before bursting into a *Turn and Talk* (technique 43). Her circulation here allows her to overhear some great answers and she honors one student by *Cold Calling* him. Notice also how when Akheem reads his sentence, everyone in class is looking at him and showing with their body language that his words matter (technique 48, *Habits of Attention*). Notice how the *Turn and Talk* snaps to life because she has such a clear in-cue for it, because students have practiced it, and because they know every classmate is going to join in enthusiastically along with them.

Notice how the *Turn and Talk* ends quickly when needed because she also has a clear, practiced procedure for calling the class back to order. Notice how she has a system that she uses to let students celebrate one another's work and how, as eager as they are to answer, the boys don't shout out their answers; this lets Sarah *Cold Call* and give Akheem just the right chance at just the right time. The joy is palpable, and the clear procedures, the structure, the systems, and routines are not its antithesis but part of its source.

## BEYOND THE BOOK

### How to Access the Videos

Access the videos in the text (as well the videos for all of your *Teach Like a Champion* books) at my.teachlikeachampion.com. Follow the instructions on the website to create an account or to add new books to an existing account.

Companion files to accompany this book can be found at www.wiley.com/go/teachlikeachampion3e and at teachlikeachampion.com/3.0/welcome.

# Five Themes: Mental Models and Purposeful Execution

For carpenters, attaching two pieces of wood at right angles has for centuries been a complex challenge, especially if they have not wanted any nails or screws to show—or if such hardware was not available. Over time, though, woodworkers gradually surmounted this challenge through a technique called *mortise and tenon*. Refined over centuries, the method involves narrowing a section of one piece of wood (a tenon) and wedging it into a gap cut in another (a mortise) and ensures that joints can be made snug and sturdy, even at 90 degrees, without hardware.

Within the mortise and tenon technique, however, a wide range of adaptations are required to overcome different challenges. For a dining room table, the joint must be trim, elegant, and all-but-invisible. The joints for the beams of a barn must be massively strong but designed for quick assembly while they are held aloft. For a ramp, the joint may need to be removable. Thus there are stub mortises, through mortises, and wedged mortises; tusked tenons, pegged tenons, and biscuit tenons.

For carpenters, terminology memorializes the insights of a thousand fellow craftsmen, just as it empowers an individual facing a challenge to more clearly consider the solutions available and engage other carpenters in discussing them with precision.

It's the same, of course, for teachers—or at least this book is an effort to make it that way. Want to engage more students more intentionally in the work of thinking? Try a *Cold Call*—that is, calling on students regardless of whether they've volunteered—and doing so with warmth and genuine interest in their answers—"inclusively," as I like to describe it. Even so, a wide range of adaptations are possible with the *Cold Call*. Asking the question before stating the name of the student you are calling on can cause other students to answer the question in anticipation of possibly being called on themselves. Breaking apart a large question into smaller ones can involve more students in answering. *Cold Calling* a second student to respond to the first answer can help socialize pupils to listen carefully to one another. We can call those things *timing the name*, *unbundling*, and *follow-on*.[1] To name the details of a technique and its adaptations leaves a trail of bread crumbs that you can use to refine its use.

But technique and the ability to describe it are not enough. We execute, many of us, nearly a thousand lessons a year—some we've designed ourselves and some in which we bring someone else's blueprint to fruition. We do this with thirty seventh graders on a Tuesday morning. And then again with thirty different seventh graders that afternoon, at which point the second group will surely remind us that we never teach the same lesson twice. Expertise—making the plan come out right for each class—means solving for a steady stream of variables and contexts. Your lesson plan assumed that students would understand *juxtaposition*, but they don't. You thought students would eagerly offer myriad thoughts about the chapter, but the first class weighed in tepidly and only one student raised her hand in the second.

And so a teacher, even one ready with a box of tools she has mastered, makes decisions not only about which tool to use, but how. A dearth of hands? You could *Cold Call*, but you could also *Turn and Talk*, or use a quick low-stakes writing prompt—a *Stop and Jot*. Your tone could be whimsical: "Usually I can't keep you guys from a conversation about *The Giver*. Has something terrible happened to the Kardashians and I'm the last to know?"[2] You could go philosophical: "Yes, it's a hard question. Who will be brave enough to answer it?" You could be blunt: "I need to see more hands." You could say nothing.

In a typical lesson you decide, often quickly. Then you decide, decide, and decide again. You are a batter facing a hundred pitches in a row—a comparison I will return to in a moment, but first it's worth asking: What do you need to decide quickly, reliably, and well, while thinking about other things and often under a bit of pressure in the form of, say, twenty-nine restless students, twenty-five minutes' worth of work left to get done, and a ticking clock to remind you that you have fifteen minutes left in the class period?

Cognitive science would tell that having a strong mental model is critical. In this case that means having a clear conception of what the elements of a successful lesson should look like. This too, benefits from intentional language to frame the principles reliably.

## MENTAL MODELS

One evening a few years ago I watched a soccer match with a coach named Iain Munro who had played professionally for nearly twenty years in the UK and then coached for twenty more. At one point during the match he was having a bite to eat, and I was in the middle of asking him a question. Suddenly he looked up and interjected: "The right back is out of position."

"Sorry?" I said, wondering which team's right back, and whether he was talking about the game unfolding in the stadium far below or something more abstract and metaphorical.

"He's come too far towards the center and cannot see his man," Iain said. He gestured with his sandwich to point this out to me. As he did so an opposition player noticed the same thing. He drove a pass to a teammate on the dead run in the right back's blind spot. Moments later it was 1–0.

We'd been watching the game for half an hour in a relaxed way when suddenly, one player among twenty-two was out of position for a few seconds, and Iain had seen it instantly, from eighty yards away, while chatting and eating a sandwich. A sort of alarm had gone off. You could see it in his body language: He knew it meant trouble.

How had he done that? The key was his knowledge of what things were *supposed* to look like. "The back four have a proper shape," he said. "Together they should look a bit like a saucer. The saucer should tilt a bit in response to where the ball is," he said, gesturing with his hands.

What Iain was describing was a *mental model*, a framework that people use to understand complex environments. His mind was continually comparing what was in front of him to this mental model and it helped him to notice quickly things that were important or out of place.

Teachers too have mental models. You briefly turn your back on your class but can distinguish without looking the normal and natural chatter of students busily on-task from talking that "sounds wrong." You might not be able to explain how it's wrong, but hearing it, you know distraction is afoot. You have a mental model of classroom noise.

Research tells us that mental models are critical to effective decision making in almost every field of expertise but especially in fields where people are asked to make a great many decisions quickly while they are focused on multiple things.

In his research on teacher expertise, David Berliner[3] showed video of classrooms to novice and expert teachers. Novices struggled to make sense of what they saw. "They often reported contradictory observations and appeared confused about what they were observing," Berliner writes. Like Iain, however, experts often appeared to be observing passively until something looked out of place. This triggered a reaction. "When anomalies occurred," experts responded "effortlessly and fluidly," in part because they were quickly able to discern what was an anomaly. They didn't overreact to what was normal, but they noticed potential problems quickly. They could distinguish students who were quieter than normal because they were thinking deeply from students who were quiet because they were bored. They were able to quickly separate signal from noise, in part because they were comparing what they saw to a mental model.

So where the rest of this book discusses specific techniques, this chapter describes core principles that can help teachers build a stronger mental model and thus choose among techniques and make better decisions while teaching, with "better" defined, most of all, as resulting in more learning and development among students. Deciding begins with accurate perception—a mental model aids in perception—but while perception derives from experience it develops more rapidly when it is informed by understanding of key principles.

This is something I did not include in earlier iterations of the book but have added to this edition to put even greater emphasis on understanding the purpose of the techniques. "Brilliant teaching always begins with clear vision and a sound purpose," Adeyemi Stembridge writes in *Culturally Responsive Education in the Classroom*. "The teacher who deeply understands this is . . . able to evoke brilliance from even the most mundane of strategies" (p. 154). Put another way, "Everything works somewhere and nothing works everywhere," as Dylan Wiliam writes. Impeccable technique at exactly the wrong time or for the wrong reason is a dead-end street.

After a school visit not long ago, my colleague Darryl Williams reflected on an example. We'd seen a teacher engage her students beautifully—every hand eagerly in the air for most of her lesson. The energy was palpable and, as a reader of *Teach Like a Champion* might point out, the participation ratio was high. There were lots of opportunities to *Turn and Talk*. But Darryl had felt as though something was off. The questions themselves were insubstantial and the answers were vague. The teacher had not thought through what the most important questions were and what good answers would sound like in advance. "If people try to use techniques to compensate for a lack of clarity about their content, the lesson won't work," Darryl said.

Compare that to Sadie McCleary's teaching in the video *Sadie McCleary: Keystone*. She too uses *Turn and Talks* to boost the ratio in her classroom. Hands are in the air and students engage dynamically. But her intentionality about what technique she's choosing and why is remarkable. Sadie described her thinking this way:

> If it's a meatier question, I always have students write or *Turn and Talk* first to increase participation, then circulate while they're talking and choose a kid or two to *Cold Call*.
>
> If it's something that is easier, I might ask out loud but gather data in the moment by *Cold Calling* specific students—I often choose kids who I think of as bellwethers—indicative of how kids often think about things. If it's something really simple that I want all students to quickly remind themselves of, I might use *Call and Response* and we'll all say it aloud.

Sadie thinks carefully about technique, but her understanding of the principles of how learning happens frames her decisions—her goal is to keep students thinking constantly and actively building long-term memory. Sailing along, there are knots to tie and sheets to trim, but a teacher also has to keep an eye on the compass.

You might argue that the chapter titles of this book are already a set of design principles for a model of the effective classroom—that one should "check for understanding" and have high academic and behavioral expectations, for example, or that the "ratio" of student work should be high and include a balance of writing, discussion, and questioning. In many ways they are, but they are *teaching* principles and even those principles need to be supported by principles of *learning* that can help to explain why certain methods work as well as how and when to use them.

First, though, let me make a brief digression on the topic of perception. Perception is crucial for educators to understand because it shapes decision making. We can only make decisions about what we see. For a teacher to recognize that Julissa is slowly growing despondent over the math, she must first perceive Julissa's body language and facial expression. Many people assume that this is far simpler than it actually is, that if we look at Julissa we will see her, but seeing is in fact far from automatic. The first, often overlooked step in making better decisions is seeing better.

"We are aware of only a small portion of our visual world at any moment," Christopher Chabris and Daniel Simons write in *The Invisible Gorilla*, their study of a topic teachers will know a little something about: inattentional blindness. That's the technical term for every person on earth's ability to look directly at something important and simply not see it: a car entering the intersection, a student tentatively raising her hand or, frankly, an eraser flying across the room. It happens all the time to people who work in complex perceptive environments. We want to think perception is objective and automatic. We don't really believe that we fail to perceive. That's the tricky part. Chabris and Simons write that it is "flatly incompatible with how we understand our own minds."

So what do you do when perception is fallible but really matters—when it's critical to note the student who is quietly edging toward frustration, for example, or when you've been working area problems for ten minutes and Daphne has not picked up her pencil yet? "There is one proven way to eliminate inattentional blindness—make the unexpected object or event less unexpected," the authors conclude. In other words, the best way to see well is to know what should occur. Your mental model guides what you look for. The more we understand, the more we see. And when we don't understand what we're seeing this too influences our looking. A recent study found that skilled radiologists were more accurate in making correct diagnoses from X-rays than novices (that is, they were more likely to perceive them correctly), but the errors of less skilled radiologists were not randomly distributed.[4] They feared "missing something" and this anxiety caused them to consistently overdiagnose conditions that did not exist. Even worrying that you don't understand what you're seeing shapes how you see it.

With that in mind, it's worth spending some time discussing five guiding principles, which I hope will provide a helpful mental model of how learning works and increase your ability to perceive accurately in the classroom and to apply the techniques in this book in a way that gets the most out of students. They are:

1. Understanding human cognitive structure means building long-term memory and managing working memory.
2. Habits accelerate learning.
3. What students attend to is what they will learn about.
4. Motivation is social.
5. Teaching well is relationship building.

## PRINCIPLE 1: UNDERSTANDING HUMAN COGNITIVE STRUCTURE MEANS BUILDING LONG-TERM MEMORY AND MANAGING WORKING MEMORY

Here is a simple model of the structure of human cognition as provided by Daniel Willingham in his outstanding book *Why Don't Students Like School?*

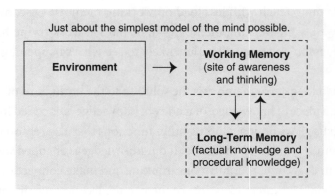

Among the things it points out is the fact that working memory is the means through which we consciously interact with the world. Any thinking we're aware of doing, such as critical thinking, occurs here.

The power of working memory is prodigious. It has allowed humankind to discover penicillin, create the musical *Hamilton*, and conceptualize String Theory. But beyond its immense power the most dominant characteristic of working memory is its tiny capacity. We struggle to hold more than one or perhaps two ideas there at a time. Here's a way to test the limits of your own working memory. Reread the first two sentences of this paragraph. Then close the book and try to copy out the sentences verbatim on a piece of paper. You will likely struggle to remember even those two simple sentences. That's you coming up against the limits of your working memory. You just can't hold much information there at any given time. A version of this problem—cognition being constrained by the limits on working memory—occurs over and over for learners. If we try to keep too much information in working memory, we will fail to remember it.

If we persist in overloading working memory we force ourselves to choose among the things we are trying to work on. For example, if you are driving and also trying to use working memory for another task—having a conversation on the phone with your partner about things to pick up at the store, for example—you are suddenly several times more likely to have an accident if you make a left turn across traffic. This has nothing to do with whether your phone use is "hands free." The problem is not free hands but free working memory. A heavy load on working memory degrades your perception and you are less able to judge the approach of other vehicles. You perceive less from the environment when your working memory is taxed and more when it is free. This by itself has profound implications for teaching, one of which I'll discuss in Chapter Two—the idea that effective preparation is designed to allow you to teach with less load on working memory. Or conversely that if you haven't prepared well, your working memory will be hard at work trying to remember what comes next in the lesson and you will be less likely to see what's happening in the classroom accurately.

A well-developed long-term memory is the solution to the limitations of working memory. If a skill, a concept, a piece of knowledge, or a body of knowledge is encoded in long-term memory, your brain can use it without degrading other functions that also rely on working memory. And long-term memory is almost unlimited. If our knowledge is encoded well and we are able to retrieve it, we can draw on it to inform our thinking and make connections. The scourge of the new-age educator, facts, mere facts, lots of them, encoded carefully in long-term memory and easily recalled through practice, are in fact the foundation of higher forms of cognition. You begin to think consciously about something in working memory—a scene in a novel you are reading, say—and suddenly the connections from your long-term memory start to pour in. It's like another book you read; it's an example of a sociological theory; what you are reading is not historically accurate. These forms of critical thinking are relying on knowledge encoded in long-term memory. As Willingham writes, "Data from the last 30 years lead to a conclusion that is not scientifically challengeable: Thinking well requires knowing facts. . . . The very processes that teachers care about most—critical thinking processes like reasoning and problem solving—are intimately intertwined with factual knowledge that is in long-term memory."[5] "Much of the time when we see someone apparently engaged in logical thinking, he or she is actually engaged in memory retrieval," Willingham continues.

This notion should inform every teacher's mental model. First, critical thinking and problem solving are not the opposite of factual knowledge. They rely on it. This is important to note because a great many educators are scornful of facts. Why teach them, the argument goes, when you can Google anything? We should teach critical thinking instead. The answer to that rhetorical question as Willingham tells us is that you *can't* teach critical thinking without facts. Problem solving is "domain specific"; for the most part you can have deep thoughts only about things you know something about.

In a recent workshop with school leaders I tried to add a bit to Willingham's diagram to capture a bit more about what it tells us. I came up with something like this:

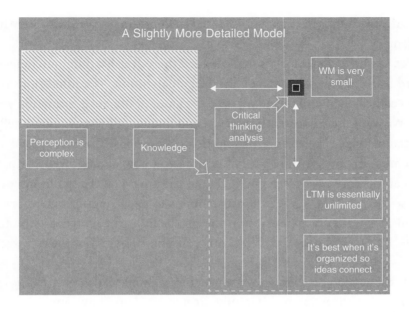

In my version I've tried to make working memory very small to remind you that its capacity is limited. But long-term memory is large. The dotted line suggests that as far as cognitive scientists know, it is all but unlimited. Not only does having more knowledge in long-term memory not make it harder to add something new there, it may make it easier. The more you know, the more connections you can perceive to new knowledge; this makes it easier to remember more of that new knowledge and gives you more connections to help you recall it. An expression among cognitive scientists is "things that wire together fire together." If we think about them at the same time, recalling them will also happen in concert and, in an ideal case, remembering something from long-term memory will enhance recall of related concepts and ideas. The antidote to the argument that memory is merely isolated facts is, in part, to organize our memories so that knowledge is connected to other facts, insights, and observations. This is how initially isolated facts become something broader that we call knowledge. Remembering something requires successful storage *and* successful retrieval, however, and the speed and ease with which you can find it is *the* critical factor in your ability to use it so again organized memories with lots of connections among lots of information are also more likely to have more ways to recall the knowledge they contain successfully.

I also added the idea to my model that perception is complex because one of the things that working memory does most effectively—help us to perceive the outside world—is much more complex and fallible than we think. Broadly, if working memory is overloaded—students will both perceive and remember less. The solution is to have knowledge encoded in long-term memory. Once information is stored there it can be used with very little load of working memory.

Of course, if working memory is underloaded there are also poor outcomes—boredom and reduced learning, for starters, but also lack of attention. The mind finds other things to do. So it's critical to attend to and manage the amount of new information young brains work with. We want them constantly engaged and interested but not overloaded with more than they can manage. The science behind this is known as "Cognitive Load Theory." It's among the most important things for educators to know about. Sweller, Kirschner, and Clark, who are its foremost researchers, define learning as a change in long-term memory and observe that "The aim of all instruction is to alter long-term memory. If nothing has changed in long-term memory, nothing has been learned."[6] That's why forgetting is so important to think about. You'll find this concept in several of the new techniques in this book.

A last critical note on managing working memory: Sweller's *guidance fading effect* argues that experts and novices learn differently. Problem-solving environments where learners are tasked with inferring solutions rather than being provided with guided instruction work well for experts because they perceive these environments accurately and can quickly connect what they see to their vast background knowledge. For novice learners this does not occur. They are likely to perceive incorrectly or attend to low-value phenomena or use up their scarce working memory searching for the right information. With little knowledge on the topic in their long-term memory, they make far fewer connections. For novices, carefully guided instruction is far more effective. However, too few educators are aware of this distinction. They tend to presume what works for experts is therefore best for everybody. If it's how elite mathematicians learn, well then, let's give it to everyone. But in fact the guidance fading effect tells us that this is a mistake. "Students should initially be given lots of explicit guidance to reduce their working memory load, which assists in transferring knowledge to LTM," Sweller writes. "Once students are more knowledgeable, that guidance is unnecessary and interferes with further development of expertise and should be faded out and replaced by problem solving." Students in a K–12 setting are usually novices, although this definition is fluid. You can be an expert on *Macbeth* but a novice as soon as you start reading *Hamlet*. Or vice versa. Technique 21, *Take the Steps*, in particular discusses several issues raised by the interactions of working and long-term memory— "the curse of expertise" and the necessity of parsing out new information in steps with practice interspersed to address the capacity issues of working memory—but it will play a role throughout the book. You'll want to use retrieval practice frequently to install knowledge in long-term memory and use *Cold Call* to ensure that everyone is getting the practice, for example. You'll want to ask students to write before discussions to reduce the strain on working memory of having to remember what they wanted to say, leaving them free to listen to one another's comments, for example.

A final point about the importance of long-term memory comes from a glimpse at what's known as the forgetting curve, which demonstrates the rate at which the typical person forgets things they've learned.

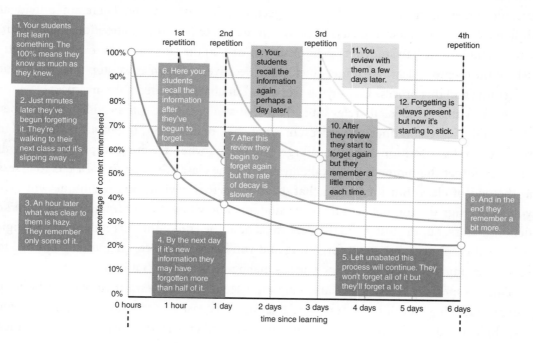

The original forgetting curve was derived in the 1880s by the German psychologist Hermann Ebbinghaus and plotted the actual rate at which he was able to remember a series of nonsense syllables after learning them. Though your students aren't learning nonsense syllables, the rate at which they forget what they have learned after they learned it is captured here, and the principle is broadly accepted by cognitive psychologists. The forgetting curve tells us that:

- As soon as you learn something, you begin forgetting it almost immediately.

- The rate of forgetting is often shockingly high; a few hours after learning something, people routinely remember only a small fraction of it.

- Each time you practice recalling what you know, the rate and amount of forgetting is reduced somewhat.

- Retrieving something back into working memory slows the rate of forgetting, but how and when the retrieval happens is important. (I discuss the details of retrieval more in technique 7, *Retrieval Practice*.)

That's immensely useful information, but forgetting curves can't tell us everything. They cannot tell you exactly what the rate of retention will be for your students generally or for a specific student at time A or time B for a specific topic you've taught. There are individual differences and factors in the learning environment, like how much attention students are paying and how new to students the information was, so the curve in most cases is theoretical but the theme is clear: We forget quickly and decisively as soon as we stop thinking about something and this process is always at work. Left unabated its effects are massive.

One way this is especially relevant is that what students appear to be able to remember at the end of a lesson does not represent what they really know, because the knowledge is not yet in long-term memory and forgetting begins when teaching stops. Students will begin to forget the moment they walk away from the class. Yes, use *Exit Tickets* to assess at the end of class. But know also that, barring further review, this technique will give you a false signal.[7] You will assume your students know how to add fractions with unlike denominators, but the test given the next week or at the end of the year will measure original learning minus subsequent forgetting and you likely won't see what you had hoped to see. Managing forgetting is as important as managing learning (but isn't as visible).

This is especially relevant because only knowledge in long-term memory can be used without reducing working memory available for other tasks or eroding perception. If you ask a higher-order question, such as "Can you find another way to solve this problem?" then the answer is likely to be *no* if working memory is required in service of the calculations. If you want higher-order thinking or greater perception from students, help them to free their working memory at the moment you want them engaging with those tasks by making the skills they're using in the moment more fluid. This is why reading fluency and automaticity with math facts are critical—they are necessary because we don't want students thinking about these things at crucial moments, and fluency is the only way around the problem of working memory. You cannot perceive the author's tone if your working memory must be engaged to parse the syntax of the passage you are reading. When the foundational skills are not fully automatic it is very difficult to have profound or insightful thoughts during reading; bright and eager children can thus fail to have much to say about a passage they have read because their working memory was spent figuring out the words. Background knowledge is similar. You cannot make a leap to connect the prime minister's attitude to his predecessor a century before unless that knowledge is in your long-term memory. "Looking it up on Google" actually requires your working memory.[8]

So what's the ideal number of interactions required with content if we want to encode it in long-term memory? Research suggests three or four but with many caveats and a lot of unknowns. In *The Hidden Lives of Learners*, Graham Nuthall, for example, finds that whether students have had three interactions with material determines with 80 percent accuracy whether they will have learned it. That is, when he and his colleagues sorted through the things that were taught during a given class and determined whether students had encountered it and attended to it—either through the teacher's instruction or through some other interaction (with peers say)—they could predict with 80 percent accuracy whether students had learned the material. So predictive was this method that Nuthall hypothesizes it is at least possible that "other factors (such as the use of open-ended questions, feedback, advance organizers, relevant examples and analogies and the interest level of the material) . . . may not be relevant to student learning except to the extent that they enhance the likelihood that students will encounter [and attend to] relevant content."[9]

But of course even if Nuthall's research were conclusive, the complexity and familiarity of content, never mind the quality of the presentation of the material and the attentiveness of students could alter this number. Further, the idea that if you don't hear it all three times you won't learn it becomes especially important in light of research on the constancy of low-level distractions in many classrooms. So would the degree of fluency the content required. "Remembering it" can mean different things. With some knowledge it's fine if I need a few seconds to pull it out of long-term memory. There's no rush. But some things I need in the blink of an eye and therefore, we can presume, require more iterations to ensure ease and speed of recall.

So how should this principle inform teaching decisions? You'll want to keep working memory free for students, so roll out new content in manageable chunks and be sure to constantly embed short sequences of practice and retrieval. *Cold Call* is a great tool for making everyone do the work of retrieval, even those whom you don't call on. You can also use *Everybody Writes* and other forms of writing to cause student thinking to be more durably encoded in memory. Remember that thinking hard about things encodes them in memory. A good adage to remember is that students remember what they think about, so get the ratio high and build habits of attention and focus. Constantly have an eye to building knowledge (knowledge organizers can be helpful) and reinforce reading fluency with *FASE Reading*.

But also don't forget your own working memory. Chapter Two will help you use lesson preparation to free it for perceiving what's happening with students while you teach.

When gathering data on student mastery, remember that the data can quickly overload your working memory so track it via *Active Observation*.

## Online Lessons

Managing the limitations of working memory is one of the core challenges of teaching in any setting. Online, its challenges are magnified since we are always competing against potential distractions and because attention is fractured online. So while one of the silver linings of online instruction was how easy it was to gather data by, say, asking students to respond in the chat, the challenge was at times that this yielded *too much* data. The "velocity of data" was often too much for working memory: thirty student responses scrolling upwards across the screen is more than teachers or students can process—and the result was at times everyone chatting and no one able to read or attend to the comments with adequate attentiveness. The video *Harley and Clayton: Slowing the Data* shows Rachel Harley and Hasan Clayton, two teachers at Nashville Classical Charter School, providing an elegant solution. They ask students to chat their responses only to them, not to "everyone," then curate a few exceptional answers from the chat stream and post them where the class can read and reflect on them with more deliberate focus. There's really no reason teachers couldn't curate a set of interesting examples from students and present them to guide and inform discussion in a similar manner in brick–and-mortar classrooms as well.

## PRINCIPLE 2: HABITS ACCELERATE LEARNING

One corollary of the fact that working memory is both powerful and limited is the realization that every task you can manage to do with a minimal load on working memory allows you to use the remaining capacity for something more important. Fluent reading is perhaps the most important example of this. When students can read with fluency, their working memory is freed to think deeply about the text and their comprehension and ability to analyze increases.

This also explains why forming habits is so critical to learning. Making common, everyday activities familiar enough that we can do them without having to think about them makes it easier for us to do them—and therefore more likely that we will—and means we can free our minds up to think more deeply while doing them.

Your alarm goes off in the predawn darkness and your hand slaps the snooze button. You are in a half-waking state but soon standing at the sink, toothpaste on your brush; now the shower is running. Likely you are operating based on habit as your brain sleepily struggles to engage the new day. You do what you do because that's what you do. Your actions would happen more slowly and require more willpower and working memory (or might not happen at all) if they were not a habit. A familiar routine allows you to save your willpower for something else. Interestingly, research suggests that willpower is indeed finite in this way. Most of us can use it up. The term "ego depletion"[10] describes this effect.

But something more happens as a result of habits. Likely some of the freest and widest ranging thoughts you will have today will occur while you are doing things you do out of habit: brushing your teeth; standing in the shower; perhaps driving to work. Your mind can do these things at very little cost to working memory; suddenly it is free to roam. Before you know it, you are thinking about where to put the couch so the living room makes sense or what the best question is to unlock last night's reading for your students.

Think about that in classroom terms. When you ask your students to write in response to something you've been reading or discussing, the more the process is established as a habit—"get out your Reader Response Journal and begin writing"—the more working memory is left over to think about the novel. You can see that play out in a sequence from Jessica Bracey's fifth-grade classroom in Newark, New Jersey, in the video *Jessica Bracey: Keystone*. Jessica says: "Tent your books. Question 87 in your Reader Response Journals. You have evidence in the text. Go!" Less than three seconds later, every pencil in the room is moving and, more importantly, every student is thinking deeply about the book. Compare that to Ms. Bracey's counterpart down the hall, Ms. Yecarb. Her classroom is the opposite of Ms. Bracey's. She thinks students get bored doing things the same way every day, so she often improvises new ways to make familiar tasks interesting. "Take a few minutes to write down your thoughts about why Maddie does what she does," Ms. Yecarb says. "Write this down in sentences?" one student asks. "Yes," says Ms. Yecarb. "On what?" another student asks. "Anything will do; scrap paper or your notes. Use a big purple crayon if you have one! Just try to think deeply," Ms. Yecarb responds. "Is this OK?" asks one, holding up her notebook. "I can't find a piece of paper," says another student. "Hey!" says a third. Her deskmate has been looking for a pencil in his backpack and has unsettled her desk.

It's not just that time has been wasted, though it clearly has. It's that continuity has been lost and focus squandered. By the time her students begin writing they will remember less about the text. Ideas that were beginning to develop a few seconds before have been driven out of working memory by the demands of getting pencil and paper. Their insights will be scattered on the wind. And as they write, some part of them will be thinking about mundane aspects of task completion—Am I writing enough? Are other people writing more?—because responding in writing is not yet a habit. Ironically, in an effort to make it "interesting," Ms. Yecarb focuses more attention on the task of writing and less on the book itself.

In Jessica's class, however, the ideas are flowing right away because there is both habit and procedure. There's a journal in everyone's folder; the folder is on everyone's desk, and pencils are in the trays. They have done this, her narrative reveals, eighty-seven times already, and so it is the equivalent to them of brushing their teeth. They can do it not just quickly but with their minds on bigger things—the book, in this case. Jessica's students are likely to think more deeply and creatively specifically because she's made the logistics of responding in writing a habit. You can see the benefits of this in the rest of the video. What you do out of habit takes less willpower—so every student is writing the whole time. What you do out of habit allows your working memory to be on things of substance—so students have engaged Jessica's questions in thoughtful and reflective ways. No surprise then that when she prompts them, every child's hand goes up eagerly. She has built a setting in which it is easy for their minds to engage and they have responded.

Habits, Charles Duhigg tells us in *The Power of Habit*, are the brain's way of saving energy, or allocating its energy to other more pressing things and they are just as important for teachers as they are for students. According to a study by social psychologist Wendy Wood and colleagues at Duke University, up to 45 percent of our daily behaviors are automatic.[11] These make it easier to operate—thinking is hard work and the brain is always trying to conserve energy and focus for when it really needs it. You can't plan your lesson if you're thinking about brushing your teeth. But there are also habits you develop to help you think more deeply about what you're doing, like your process for lesson preparation. "I always prepare my lessons the same way," Sarah Wright told me. The morning of the beautiful lesson in her Keystone video, in which she is so compellingly responsive to her students and seems to make every decision right, she "did the lesson as if I was a student, thinking it through from their perspective and writing out the answers I hoped I'd get." Teachers like Sarah use a familiar and productive habit to prepare. That it's a routine means that she isn't thinking about how to get ready, but rather about what a good student answer looks like.

It's the same for students. We want to optimize their use of their thinking by filling their school days with two kinds of habits: (1) having a way of doing relatively unimportant things quickly and easily and (2) having a way of doing important things well and in a way that channels the greatest amount of attention, awareness and reflection on the content. It's obvious that we want consistent habits for the trivial stuff, in other words, but it's less obvious that we want consistent habits for the most important tasks. True, there are useful habits like how to come into a classroom and how to pass out materials. But academic habits—how to hold a discussion and how to write in response to text—are even more critical. What we do frequently benefits most from being done consistently, so building habits around paying attention well (*Habits of Attention*) and listening and building community during discussions (*Habits of Discussion*) pay massive dividends, as do consistent routines for different ways of participating (*Turn and Talk, Silent Solo*), not to mention expectations like putting hands up to answer (there's nothing worse than interrupting a student who makes a good comment to ask the student who shouted out—again—to desist from shouting out) and down when others are talking (see technique 29, *All Hands*).

So build your classroom around procedures that become habits. Education writer Tom Bennett describes the shared habits that become a routine in a good classroom as being like a "superpower." Habits, he writes, become part of students: "They behave the way they need to behave, without thinking. And that means . . . time and head space to think about the things you want them to think about—the learning. Routines are the foundation of good behaviour. They take time to communicate and imbed. But nothing is worth your time more." Tom's right, of course. And what he says of positive behavior is even more true of thinking behaviors and academic habits. Ironically this often makes students happy because they take comfort—and sometimes pride—in knowing how to do things quickly and well. But either way, you will be transferring the focus of their working memory from how to do a task to the significance of the question. So a classroom infused with strong habits is usually a happy and scholarly place too.

There's a third, more subtle aspect of habit building that's worth thinking about, and a story from my visit to London's Michaela Community School, which serves students from some of the poorest sections of London, will help to explain why. At Michaela—which was recently the top-scoring school in England on at least one math exam—students at the school stand up at lunch each day and give thanks. I saw this myself on a visit in 2016.

After eating, the pupils were offered the chance to stand and express gratitude in front of half the school. Their hands shot into the air. All of them. Everyone wanted to be chosen to say thanks.

Students thanked their classmates for helping them study. They thanked their teachers for expecting a lot and helping them. One student thanked the lunchroom staff for cooking for them (incidentally, cafeteria food in the UK is far superior to that in the United States and much more likely to involve on-site cooking). And still the hands shot up into the air.

A student thanked his mother for everything she did to provide for him. He was perhaps thirteen years old and shared his appreciation in front of perhaps a hundred other teenaged boys, speaking haltingly but honestly about how grateful he was for how hard she worked and the sacrifices she made. You don't see that every day. The gratitude seemed to be endless and came pouring out of them until the teacher in charge said it was time to go back to class.

I found myself wondering about it for a while afterwards. Here were kids from some of the poorest sections of the city, kids who might have faced difficulty at home and on their way to school. Many had left (or even lived still) in places racked by violence and difficulty. But at Michaela, their days were punctuated not by someone reminding them that they had suffered or been neglected by society, but by the assumption that they would want to show their gratitude to the world around them.

What did this mean? Well, first of all, it gave rise to a culture of thoughtfulness. Everywhere I looked students did things for one another. In one class a student noticed another without a pencil and gave her one without being asked. In the hallway a student dropped some books and suddenly three or four students were squatting to pick them up. When students left a classroom they said, "Thank you" to their teacher.

Maybe thanking makes behavior worthy of gratitude more likely to occur. Students know their goodness is seen and valued, not just by their teachers but their peers. It spreads. Maybe at first it's due to the plausibility of appreciation but after a while it just takes on a life of its own. People are kind and considerate because, at Michaela, it's what they do—it's their habit.

But the gratitude, I think, is as much about the giver as the recipient. Maybe that's the most important point. To show gratitude causes you to look for and then to see the goodness around you, and therefore to perceive a world full of goodness all around you. Which makes you happy. And just maybe optimistic—to think the world is the kind of place that will embrace you when you give your best. The habit of showing gratitude caused students to see more things to be grateful for, to have a more positive view of the world. They saw it as a place where people were likely to smile at them, help them, support them. Building a habit of seeing it made it appear everywhere. In the *Happiness Advantage*, Shawn Achor describes this as the Tetris Effect. You play enough Tetris and you see its characteristic shapes everywhere. Similarly, you see enough hard work behaviors from your peers, enough generosity and kindness, enough academic success, and it changes your view of the world. And this, too, is something we can use in the classroom, recognizing that where we direct our students' attention can be a self-fulfilling prophecy. Narrating the good, the hard work, and the productivity around them helps them to see it when it is present and to learn more from observing it.

## PRINCIPLE 3: WHAT STUDENTS ATTEND TO IS WHAT THEY WILL LEARN ABOUT

Graham Nuthall's *The Hidden Loves of Learners* is a fascinating book in part because of its description of tiny and otherwise mundane moments in the lives of ordinary students.[12] As I noted before, one of his main premises is that students learn ideas and content that they come into contact with three different times—especially if each interaction is comprehensive and if the interactions present the information in slightly different ways. But, he notes, this only applies if students are paying attention, and Nuthall describes a series of experiences that will be familiar to all of us. A group of students are learning about Antarctica, for example, and are supposed to have learned that Antarctica is one of the driest places on earth. Some have and some haven't. Nuthall notices that a student named Teine is whispering to a peer and passing notes while a video is describing the desert nature of Antarctica. Teine fails to learn the content. Another student, Tui, often decides that he already knows the content being taught and so fails to listen carefully. He's not passing notes but he's not attending, and he, too, fails to learn.

This reveals an obvious but important fact about education: In any learning environment some people develop quickly and some people develop more slowly. One major factor in the rates at which individuals learn is their ability to concentrate for a significant period of time. Half-focused or fleetingly focused learners master things more slowly and with more difficulty. This is often apparent to us when we work with students with diagnosed attention issues, but of course the ability to sustain focus is spread unevenly across all students (and adults); its strength is a hidden driver of progress.

As I discuss at greater length in technique 48, *Habits of Attention*, "selective attention" is the term for the ability to focus on the task at hand and ignore distraction. It is the ability to select what you pay attention to—to lock out distractions and lock in on the signal—and has "reverberating effects" on success in language, literacy, and mathematics, note cognitive scientists Courtney Stevens and Daphne Bavelier. They add that there are potentially "large benefits to incorporating attention-training activities into the school context."[13]

Not surprisingly, it turns out that building strong habits for focusing and maintaining attention—a key aspect of how educators help support students with attention deficits—is useful for all students. Still, attention may vary from moment to moment even for the same person. Learners may concentrate deeply in one setting and be scattered in another, and this variability reminds us that learning environments shape habits of attention. Attending to attention—building habits of sustaining focus—is one of the most important things that teachers can do. If there's a mental model of a productive classroom it surely includes students able to lose themselves in a task and work at it steadily for a significant period of time, which means a setting where concentration can reliably be maintained and tasks and activities where the ability to focus is carefully cultivated.

This has always been true—and has always been a challenge, perhaps—but probably never more so than today, when the capacity of technology to affect and erode attention is exponentially greater than ever before. Yes, educators in the 1960s argued that television eroded students' attention and focus, but young people at the time did not walk around with a television in their pocket. Television was not the medium through which all of young people's social interactions were funneled. Young people did not surreptitiously—or openly—check their TVs every few minutes during class. They were not habituated to need to check their televisions every few seconds. A young person—and an adult—today owns very few garments that do not have a pocket for a smartphone. The assumption—written in the language of fabric—is that our phones are and must always be within reach. Quietly, gradually, the dosage and accessibility of technology has increased to the point where it has affected not only the level of attentiveness but the overall capacity for attentiveness of most people in profound ways. While a teacher's approach to attentiveness has always been a critical if unspoken part of a productive classroom, it is rapidly becoming more urgent. We aren't just struggling to help students learn to concentrate on what's important, we are struggling against a massive and pervasive technology that acts on our students—and ourselves—to erode that critical capacity in almost every minute of the day. Schools and teachers now must constantly design their choices and decisions with this challenge in mind if they hope to succeed. This is by far the single biggest change to emerge in education since the previous version of this book was published.

In his book *Deep Work,* Cal Newport examines the phenomenon of attention in the workplace, studying the conditions necessary to produce world-class knowledge work. Success in such a setting requires that you "hone your ability to master hard things," he notes. A computer scientist by training, he uses writing code as an example. To be able to write complex, technical code is an outstanding thing to be good at, especially today, because knowledge work has never been more highly valued in society. Code moves freely and at light speed around the globe; if you write it well your audience of potential users is almost limitless. But this state of affairs—you in your happy place, writing code and sipping a latte while the world clamors for more and more of it—has a downside. Everyone else's code also moves freely and at light speed around the globe. Any line of it written anywhere in the world immediately competes with yours. All knowledge work is increasingly like this, Newport writes, and to succeed you not only must be able to concentrate to produce something uniquely intelligent, but "you must be able to do it quickly, again and again," with "it" being the ability to achieve mastery of new and difficult things. The key to mastering complex material with speed and flair, Newport writes, is the ability to sustain states of unbroken attention and deep concentration. Those who can focus best for longest separate themselves from the crowd.

However, Newport also observes that it has never been harder to build these focused mindsets because our daily lives (which include our work and learning environments) socialize distraction, lack of concentration, and states of constant half-attention. They erode rather than build the sorts of locked-in mental focus that ultimately drive so much of success. Concentration, he concludes, has never been better rewarded and never harder to achieve.[14]

A useful term in understanding why is "attention residue."[15] When you switch from one task to another, your mind remains partially focused on the previous task. You pause during a project to check your email and when you've returned to the project your mind is still partially on your email even if you don't realize it. You're now less likely to do your best work. This is especially corrosive, Newport points out, to learning new and difficult things, but researchers have found that people in most working environments operate in constant states of low-level distraction. It's common for students, too. The average undergraduate student, presumably more mature than K–12 students and an example of academic success and interest, still switches windows every nineteen seconds when working on his or her laptop, for example.

But beyond attention residue is a larger issue: Our brains are neuroplastic, which means they rewire according to how we use them. And the way we, and especially young people, use them increasingly involves constantly switching tasks. Every two and a half minutes is average for an adult; it is surely more for young people. The result is not just that we are often more distracted than we ideally would be, but that we are increasingly less able to sustain focus. Our brains increasingly expect distractions to "pop up," and become agitated and distracted by the deferral of this gratification. As productivity expert Maura Thomas put it in a recent article,[16] "Our productivity suffers not just because we are distracted by outside interruptions, but also because our own brains . . . become a source of distraction in and of themselves."

"Skimming is the new normal" writes Maryanne Wolf in *Reader Come Home*, one of the most profound and important books on learning in recent years. She describes how constant exposure to technology not only distracts us in the moment but rewires our brains to be less attentive, less capable of attention, and less able to sustain reflective states required in particular for deep and meaningful reading. Perhaps you notice this in yourself: Suddenly in the last few years you've found your eye rapidly skimming down the page while you read, inching ahead to look for . . . something. This is your brain, having been wired for distraction by a digital environment in which your average sustained attention to any task is under two minutes, looking for something new and flashing. In other words, this is you not only failing to pay attention, but losing the capacity to do so. You notice it because you once lived a low-tech life and feel the absence of the focus you used to have. Your students did not and do not. For most this is the only reality they have ever known.

This raises several questions for teachers. Do the environments they build in their classrooms socialize sustained attention or fractured and skittish attention? What can they do to help their students if they observe them, singularly or as a whole, to require stronger attention skills?

Recently I ran into a principal I know and I asked him about his students and how they are changing. "Attention spans are shorter and shorter," he noted. "Especially because most students don't read outside of school anymore, unless they have parents who make them. But we're doing our best to adapt our instruction." It was a short conversation and I never found out whether he meant *We are adapting instruction to respond to the reduced attention of students by giving young people learning tasks that require less sustained focus* or *We are adapting our instruction to try to intentionally socialize concentration and improve student attention spans by engaging in sustained periods of a working on a single task*. Were they acceding to the change or fighting back, in other words? This is a critical question. The latter can—and just possibly must—be accomplished. If you look at the videos referenced in this book, I believe you will see plenty of joy and energy and fast-paced learning, but you will reliably see in almost every high-achieving classroom students who can sustain focus on a single task, often quietly, deliberately, and independently. This is in part because their teachers have prioritized it and have built it up over time until it was a habit.

You will also see in the videos environments where constant disruptions to work, to thinking, and to reflection are rare. This is because teachers know that students deserve as much.

Even if the ability to focus varies widely among students and they walk through our doors with different levels of it, we can still seek to develop the ability to focus and pay attention as much as possible. Accomplishing this has always been one of the most important outcomes of schooling—even if this fact is not always recognized or acknowledged. Schools are increasingly one of the last places that can aspire to insulate young people from constant distraction, digital overstimulation, and task switching. There is a place for digital devices in learning, certainly, but there is just as much a place for sustained time without them. Providing steady doses of screen- and distraction-free time characterized by sustained meditative reflection—pencil, paper, book—is the greatest gift we can give to young people.

In 1890 (when high-tech meant newfangled innovations like the tabulating machine), the psychologist William James noted in *The Principles of Psychology* something else about attention: that what we pay attention to shapes our cognition more broadly. "My experience is what I agree to attend to," he wrote, anticipating a vast array of twenty-first-century research that suggests how profoundly what we pay attention to shapes us. Attention, in other words, is not just a sort of "muscle that allows us to keep looking" as my colleague Hannah Solomon put it in a conversation on this topic, but also "the lens through which we students look," and this is also critical to consider.

So how might attending to attention play out in the classroom? Here are some initial thoughts. You will surely find more.

You'll want to build strong habits for focused sustained writing through *Silent Solo* and then extend the amount of time that students can engage in writing over time. You'll want to use *FASE Reading* to train students to focus on what they are reading without interruption for a period of time and to help them experience the pleasure of focus—"flow" as some people call it, the moment when you lose yourself in a task and the rest of the world—including its phones and screens—fades away. You'll want to help students learn to concentrate during teaching and discussions via *Habits of Attention* and *Habits of Discussion*. You'll want to put *Turn and Talk* on rails. And you'll want to think about how to bring the concept of "flow" to your own instruction via the tools in the "Pacing" chapter. Another key question is the cultural and behavioral environment in your classroom. Can you sustain times for thinking free from interruption? If students shout out answers as soon as you ask, you cannot enforce wait time as a key tool that allows students to reflect and focus on questions. If this is the case, start with *Means of Participation*.

As the preceding paragraph reminds me, this book may in the end be first and foremost about building and sustaining attention.

Finally, there is technology to consider. Too many classrooms presume that doing a task with technology or on a screen adds value. Educators think that it is inherently good to wire the classroom. Technology gives us immense power but comes with profound downsides, as well. When you don't use technology, when you prevent it, in fact, is at least as important as when you do use it. School is one of the last places where we agree to mutually not introduce constant distractions. Pencil-to-paper writing, taking notes by hand, reading in hard copy books—there is ample research to support each of these activities as far more beneficial than the same task done on a screen.

## PRINCIPLE 4: MOTIVATION IS SOCIAL

The research that is powerful in understanding learning is not limited to cognitive psychology. Some of the most important insights come from a surprising source: evolutionary biology, or the history of how we came to be as we are. The most important word

s "we." While humans evolved to develop individual characteristics that were
our survival—large brains, opposable thumbs, the ability to stand, and so
lutionary success was primarily a group endeavor—the result of a profound
rd coordinated group behavior.

ut over other groups, members of groups that survived had to prove themselves strong and able as individuals but also at least as capable in their ability to form loyal and cohesive groups. "The outcome of between-group competition is determined largely by the details of social behavior within each group in turn," writes the biologist Edward O. Wilson in *The Social Conquest of Earth*. It was important to be strong individually—there was competition within groups too—but a strong individual not embraced by a group was doomed. What primarily determined which humans would thrive and survive were traits such as "the tightness of the group, and the quality of communication and division of labor among its members. Such traits are heritable," Wilson concludes, and so who we are is a "consequence of individual selection and group selection."

Thanks to this dual-level selection—what evolutionary biologists call parallel processes of group and individual competition—our characteristics are complex, fascinating, and sometimes contradictory, not least because we are usually not aware of what we seek. After all, the point is that we evolve to do what has helped us survive without being aware of it.

The term "prosocial" describes animals that engage in individual behavior that benefits the larger group. Few animals will do this. The term "eusocial" goes a step further and describes species that coordinate and sacrifice to an even greater extent. And it is far rarer. Wilson suggests that we are among only two eusocial mammals.[17] Lions and wolves will coordinate to hunt, but they will not sacrifice their lives for the good of the group; they will not raise each other's young or take care of the aged. Only humans do that, though for what it's worth humans also compete with fellow group members for food or mates or status.

Since ancient times, intense awareness of what was happening within the group was required to survive—to ensure one's connections and to watch out for potential betrayal, for instance. "The strategies of the game were written as a complicated mix of closely calibrated altruism, cooperation, competition, domination, reciprocity, defection and deceit," Wilson writes. "The human brain became simultaneously highly intelligent and intensely social. . . thus was born the human condition, selfish at one time, selfless at another, the two impulses often conflicted."

The brain is a "social organ" is how Zaretta Hammond puts it in *Culturally Responsive Teaching and the Brain*, but the degree to which this is true is striking. One example is the physiology of our eyes. We are the only primate with sclera—what we call the whites of the eyes. All other primates have dark eyes surrounding the pupils. Why? The answer, many evolutionary biologists think, is that tracking what fellow group members are looking at and thinking about is urgently important. We need to know what the group thinks, where we stand in its hierarchies and alliances, and how each action was received. The information critical to our survival is revealed in furtive glances and fleeting expressions of admiration, dismissiveness, and/or respect. Our eyes have evolved to better reveal the crucial details of approval, acceptance and scorn.

And our deep sociality also shows up in the ways we make decisions. "Social norms" are what we call the unwritten social rules of any group. "The highly social nature of human behavior means that the actions of colleagues and the broader culture of the school will have a persistent effect on how things pan out in your classroom. This is why building motivation is best done collectively," writes Peps Mccrea. "Norms are so powerful they override more formal school policies or rules . . . However their largely invisible and unconscious nature makes them easy to underestimate if not totally ignore." That there will be norms is "inevitable"; the key is to recognize this and shape them intentionally and positively.[18]

To modify motivation we must change what our students see and what they perceive as normal, acceptable values.

To be clear, some norm or other will emerge in every classroom. "There is no such thing as a neutral design," Richard Thaler and Cass Sunstein tell us in *Nudge*. *The environment will shape the behavior of the individuals within it.* We choose the norms or they choose us. And if we want more productive norms, we have to find ways to make them appear universal and more visible.

How does this affect classroom decisions? It reminds us that classrooms are first and foremost cultures that shape the actions and beliefs of the people within them. We have to establish positive prosocial norms that value student work and encourage our pupils to do what will help them succeed and thrive.

Is a culture where students look at the speaker and so reinforce that they care what the speaker is saying "natural"? Of course not. There is no natural case. A good classroom nudges students to scholarly identity through *Habits of Attention* and *Habits of Discussion* (not to mention great lessons, rigorous curriculum, and an insistence on honoring students' time). It ensures that students see their peers eagerly reading and writing as this a great way to get any individual student to want to—or at first, be willing to—read or write. It explains why *Brightening the Lines* is so powerful in causing students to join in activities. And of course why procedures and routines are so powerful—they start by norm setting. "The biggest mistake" teachers make, Tom Bennett writes in *Running the Room*, is "to wait for behavior to occur and then react to it." The best teachers prevent counterproductive behavior in the first place.

A final note. The strength of a norm's influence "depends on how much we feel a part of and identify with those exhibiting the norms" writes Mccrea. We are motivated by belonging. The last principle I will discuss in this chapter is relationships, which obviously are profoundly important. But it is worth remembering, too, that a student's sense of belonging to a culture is different from his or her relationship with the teacher. By joining with peers in actions and feeling honored, supported, and respected by them, students will do many of the things that some educators presume they will only do if a teacher inspires them. Again relationships matter—but the peer-to-peer cultures we build through the norms students perceive are at least as important.

## PRINCIPLE 5: TEACHING WELL IS RELATIONSHIP BUILDING

A common belief among teachers is that they must build relationships with students before they can make progress teaching them. "Students won't care what you say," an oft-repeated aphorism goes, "until they know that you care." The presumption is that students can't learn from someone who doesn't care about them and the result is often teachers seeking to connect with students and show their caring *so they can teach them*. That statement is informed by good intentions, but still mistaken in important ways. Should students know and feel that we care about them? Absolutely. Do relationships matter? Yes, of course—often immensely. But the assertion that no teaching can happen until a relationship exists is inaccurate,[19] in part because teaching well is the most effective way to show a student that you care and to establish a relationship with them in the first place.

Recognizing that relationships matter is the easy part, in other words. The difficult questions are: what kinds of relationships—and relationship-building actions—are most helpful? Is the aphorism about students knowing you care a rationale for any and all relationship-building actions? Some students might be quite happy if you were to show up at their dance recital or stop them to chat about their home life in the hallway. Others might find this strange and even invasive. This should remind us that we can understand that relationships are important and still take steps to develop them that are counterproductive.

So, while still affirming the deep importance of relationships, here are some important observations about how to seek them most productively.

First, we are teachers to our students. We seek a specific kind of relationship that is unique to our role. Those relationships "are based on trust," ResearchEd founder Tom Bennett wrote recently. "Trust is best built in safe calm ordered environments where adults can be relied upon to be dependable. Trust is built on predictability of action and character," Bennett noted.[20] Being reliable, humane, and consistent is the center of relationships. But learners also must feel that the *environment* in which they learn communicates these things. When a student talks about her relationship with Ms. Smith she in some ways means Ms. Smith's classroom. She will not come to trust Ms. Smith if Ms. Smith allows her to be subtly mocked by peers when she speaks, or if Ms. Smith is unable or uninterested in making sure the time spent in her classroom feels valuable and productive. Trust for a teacher is in part an affirmation of their competence and diligence in building the right environment.

Second, successful teaching is at least as much the cause as the result of effective relationships. At a minimum the process is iterative. You demonstrate your respect for and belief in students by putting their time to good use. You show that you are worthy of their respect by creating a productive learning environment. As you do this you are warm, encouraging, and welcoming. You now have begun a relationship. It may form the foundation for a greater connection with some students; with others it will be sufficient. Chatting after class about your favorite shows with students is nice but not required and can distract you from the job at hand, teaching well, which is the primary tool by which teachers build relationships with students. "A relationship is a tool that helps students understand how to connect to the content," Adeyemi Stembridge writes in *Culturally Responsive Education in the Classroom*. It's supposed to be about them and what will help them learn and thrive, in other words, and that's a key reminder because teachers' needs are also met by relationships. We can at times fall prey to wanting too much to be needed or, worse, wanting to assume that our students lack something that only we can provide.

A skeptical reader once observed about previous editions of this book: "You don't have a chapter about relationships, You must not think relationships are important." *But to me the whole book is about building relationships.* A teacher who observes her students carefully, who notices and responds effectively when they struggle, and helps them see that they can be successful, is building relationships in a way that is not achieved by a teacher who gets frustrated and tells students to "figure it out." Or even one who warmly and lovingly greets them every day but fritters away time in activities they know don't result in learning. A teacher who pushes students to work hard, to write an essay they are truly proud of, a teacher who does not have to shout at students for work to get done, a teacher who, by teaching well, builds a student's interest in and then love for a subject, builds relationships.

I recently came across a list for teachers on a popular website: "Ten Ways to Build Relationships with Students." It included some good advice ("Apologize when you mess up") but also some more questionable guidance: "Do crazy things," "Talk to them about non-school-related subjects," and "Share inspirational stories from your life." It's worth considering whether those actions can be distractions from more important things.

Talking to students about unrelated subjects is fine—some may appreciate it—but not nearly as important as talking to them about school-related subjects. Sharing inspirational stories might be fine, but proceed with caution. My own children have heard mine many, many times now and it's possible they don't find them to be quite the touchstones I do. One teacher I had in school could reliably be counted on for a twenty-minute digression if you got him going on his stories. I'm not sure how many relationships were built but his interest in telling them would reliably result in the test being pushed back by at least a day. As for doing "crazy things," it risks as much harm as good. You're a teacher, not a performer. It makes more sense to spend your time preparing to teach really well, with warmth, humanity, attentiveness, and encouragement. The real question is whether you can inspire young people by awakening their curiosity and opening the doors of knowledge to them.

The relationship we want is at least in part a triangle, with the teacher connecting to the student about content and with the goal of inspiring them to build a relationship to the things they learn. The following illustrates how Adeyemi Stembridge expresses that.

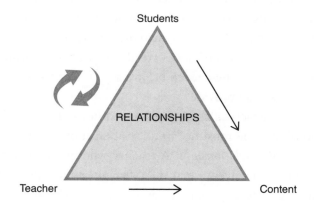

"I'm just not sure you can say you can build relationships with students unless you teach them well," my colleague Darryl Williams said after we watched a video in our offices one day. (I'm going to show you that video in a moment.) I went home that night and thought long and hard about that statement because at first it appeared to be false. Of course you can have good relationships with students if you don't teach well. Darryl's statement was the opposite of the oft-repeated quotation. He was suggesting that students won't know you care until they know you can teach them well.

But over time I came to see Darryl's observation operating in many of the videos in this book. In the one that prompted his comment *Denarius Frazier: Remainder*, Denarius circulates among students in his class giving them feedback on their math. "Killing it," he says to one student to reaffirm her progress. "Much better," he says to another. Consider that tiny phrase for a moment. Much better than what? Much better than the last time you attempted problems like this. What this says is: *I see you as you work. Your progress is important to me.* And in the case of a teacher as good as Denarius, *I'm going to help you to succeed.*

Denarius speaks to *everyone* as he works the room and he speaks to them *about their academic work.* Over and over, the message is *I know you; I will help you.* There could be flashier videos about connecting with students, but there probably aren't many more substantive videos about building relationships.[21]

Denarius's students love and respect him because of how he *teaches* them. This is how he builds core relationships. Fittingly, I have taken this video of Denarius from the chapter on Checking for Understanding. What that tells you is that to know and care deeply about your students' progress is relationship building and that each aspect of the core job of teaching which a teacher executes with skill, humanity and warmth forms the foundation of relationships.

Part of the argument here is about where to focus our energy. It is easy to assume that if relationships are beneficial, then the more extensive the relationship, the better. But it's not that simple. Some of us may play the role of mentor to some students in our lives—if we do, the benefit is at least half ours—but students do not need to see you as a confidant. Some students may appreciate that you care in a manner that involves chatting with them in the hallway or encouraging them to come to you with details about their personal lives and even sharing their difficulties. But plenty of them have no interest in or need for that. They are waiting for you to teach them with care and humanity. Believing that relationships start with our playing some meaningful role in students' lives other than being their teacher can distract us from the fact that classroom relationships begin with our competence as teachers.

On the first day you should smile, welcome students, and put their time to good use. As you do so, make a point of beginning to learn names. Or perhaps you've already begun this process before students arrive and can surprise them by knowing their names and how to pronounce them. Tiny moments of humanity sprinkled in—You're Damani's sister, right? How's he doing? Say hello for me!—can be powerful, but as much or more of relationship building is being prepared for class, demonstrating the capacity to help students succeed, even if they have struggled in the past, and doing that with enough skill that you can smile and encourage students. Students will be looking to see that you take their learning seriously, that you can do your job. It's hard to smile and encourage students when some are ignoring your directions or distracting you and their peers, for example. Not being able to run the room is one of the fastest ways to lose the respect of students. They may still be friendly with you, knowing your lessons are simplistic or you are easily manipulated by mischievous classmates, but those relationships are not ones that lead to learning and growth for young people.

As you teach, endeavor to show that you like your students as much as you can in simple, subtle ways. Smile, for example. As teacher and writer Jo Facer puts it, "Everything is easier when students think you like them." But students knowing that you care about them does not mean that you are friends. Part of caring about young people will almost assuredly include setting limits or pushing them to work harder than they otherwise might. You should be as warm as you can and also expect to be strict when needed. Again, if you can build an environment where students are on task, work hard, and treat you and all of their peers with respect and appreciation, it's much easier to be positive, warm, and encouraging.

Let me try to frame this distinction with vocabulary. There are *supplementary relationships*—connections with certain students about their lives outside the classroom—and *core relationships*—positive, mutually respectful relationships in the classroom that help to ensure students' learning and growth with warmth and humanity. I am not dismissing supplementary relationships. Many teachers have played profound roles in students' lives; they can be valuable to young people and gratifying to teachers. I hope you will experience a few in your life. But it is a trap to presume that supplementary relationships are a requirement of success, when it is core relationships that do the work. Seeking the former too ardently can detract from the latter.

So what is a core relationship like? It is one in which students feel, as my colleague Dan Cotton frames it, *safe, successful,* and *known.* That is, their teacher sees them as an individual, has the competence to ensure that they will learn, and provides an environment where they need not worry.

*Safe* is perhaps easy to overlook when we think about relationships. It means students must not only feel like they won't be bullied or mocked but that they will be respected and appreciated. Students must be able to take intellectual risks without fearing chastisement or judgment—from you or from their peers. Their relationship is heavily influenced by their sense of belonging within the class. If you smile after a student answers and show appreciation for her thinking but allow her, within the space under your authority, to be snickered at or the subject of eye-rolling, or if the moments when she reveals her intellect are met with disinterest and silence from the class, your relationship will not likely flourish. If it does it will be a Pyrrhic victory. Successful relationships require teachers to make use of the authority vested in them to build a culture that ensures students feel safe and supported *by the community.* It is not just your own actions you must shape to create the conditions under which students grow and thrive. Students see this clearly. You can tell Melissa you loved her comment after class all you want. If she knows that during class she will be an object of strange curiosity every time she makes a similar comment, she will be less likely to feel the trust in you that relationships require.

*Successful,* as I have tried to explain throughout this chapter, derives from your over-all effectiveness at the core tasks of teaching. When you do those tasks well, students see themselves progressing and succeeding, and this causes them to feel trust and appreciation. A corollary: Helping students to feel successful and to see convincing evidence of their own progress also helps to build relationships.

But what about the idea of students feeling *known*? Let's say you have a student. Let's call her Elicia. She'd like to know that you see her as unique, different from Candace to her left and Edward to her right. Begin by knowing her name and how she likes to say it (EE-lee-cee-ah rather than Uh-lee-sha). Use her name whenever you can: Every time you use a student's name you remind her that you know her. Perhaps you've got a couple of simple downtime questions you ask for when she and other students are first to arrive to class: *Morning, Elicia. Everything go OK on the homework for you?* Perhaps occasionally you even *Cold Call* Elicia to show that you are thinking about her experience in class. "Elicia, you feel confident at these problems?" "Elicia, were you convinced by Kennedy's argument?"

In doing these things you have begun to establish that Elicia is an individual to you—one whose opinion you care about. I had a colleague once, a math teacher, who loved to learn little details about each student and drop them into playful word problems: If Elicia loved Beyoncé he would write, "Elicia wants to build a platform for the Beyoncé statue she has created in art class. Its dimensions are . . ." Great, if that's you, but you don't need a bag of tricks like that. It's more important to know Elicia as a learner, to walk by her desk and say, "Don't rush, Elicia. Your last paper was good because you took your time." Your statement shows that you remember her last paper. That you know what she is capable of. That you know and care about her progress. That you see her as an individual, in other words. This most of all is what young people crave and deserve.

A final note. Teachers who work with students who grow up in poverty should be especially careful to avoid a potential assumption that growing up with limited financial resources implies growing up impoverished in other ways—without strong social networks or parents who can support you, for example. I wish to go on record stating that of the 100 best parents and guardians I have met in my life, 99 of them have been parents who were raising their children with limited financial means, sometimes in real financial difficulty, and who provided their children with exemplary love, support, guidance, and wisdom nonetheless. Many students have people they can confide in and share their lives with, in other words. Please do not presume that they need an advocate more than they need someone to teach them chemistry. What young people need most reliably is an opportunity to learn and grow under the guidance of someone who cares about their progress in doing so. This is nonnegotiable. Do some students lack relationships in their lives and yearn for an adult who can be a confidant or a mentor? Sure, some do. These students come from every socioeconomic stratum. A few times we may meaningfully provide supplementary support for a student whose social network does not provide everything they need, but it is also easy to convince ourselves that a relationship that makes *us* feel important and needed is the one that most students need and this may not be the case.

So how might getting relationships right play out in the classroom? Here are some initial thoughts. You will surely find more.

The first step to relationship building, I have intimated, may be the opposite of what you expect: making your classroom an orderly place where the procedures for doing everyday things are familiar and happen as if by routine. When students also have a very clear mental model of the behaviors required in a productive classroom, it will be easier for them to do those things with at most small reminders. Further, *safe, successful, and known* starts with safe—that is, with a learning environment where students can struggle and will never be mocked or laughed at. Young people should be able to rely on adults to provide such a setting for them to learn in, and to provide it is a form of caring. Better for you to provide an orderly classroom where students encourage one another than to fail to do so and spend your time as the lone voice encouraging students. Further, an orderly classroom will allow you to listen to and attend to what students say and to focus on understanding each of them as a learner. Denarius's classroom is a relational place, first and foremost, because it is orderly.

Lesson planning and preparation are also critical to relationships—and again, perhaps unexpectedly so. A well-planned and well-executed lesson tells students that they matter and their learning is at the forefront. And an engaging and energetic lesson draws students in. Watch a few moments of Sadie McCleary's chemistry class at Guildford East HS in Guildford, North Carolina. Students are happy *because* they are busily engaged in meaningful work throughout; because when they walk in the room the chemistry lesson starts right away and has them thinking deeply and actively from the first minute. This is arguably more gratifying than walking into a classroom where a teacher spends the first five minutes asking everyone how they're doing.

In his book *The Happiness Advantage*, Shawn Achor reminds us that there are several parts to the concept of happiness. Accomplishment (seeing your own progress) and engagement (losing yourself in something) are critical components of happiness—as powerful as pleasure in causing happiness, even if far less often acknowledged. Further, when you know your lesson well and aren't thinking of what question to ask on the spur of the moment, you can be more responsive and observant; your working memory can be employed in perceiving how students are reacting to the work and how effective their answers are. Quite simply, you are more present.

Relationships are often based on the mastery of a dozen tiny skills from across the chapters in this book. A small element of the technique *Positive Framing* called Assume the Best is a game changer, for example. As with all of *Positive Framing* it will help you to give students the constructive feedback they deserve in a way that reminds them that you care about them and believe in them. Furthermore, it asks you to construct plausible reasons for low-level unproductivity. "Sorry, my directions weren't clear; this is a silent writing activity," is a big improvement on "It needs to be silent in here." It exudes calm and poise and shows students that when they don't follow direction your first instinct is to think: *Well, there must be some reason for that*, and it also causes you to consider and then verbalize some of these reasons, some of which will often turn out to be right. Sometimes it will just be lack of focus by the class; but sometimes you will *not* have been clear. When you make a habit of seeing the best in your students you are more likely to notice it when it is present. *What to Do* is another example. Nothing corrodes relationships like not being sure what you're supposed to be doing—times ten if it happens over and over and nobody gets much done, and times ten again if students get "spoken to" for not following a direction that's not clear to them.

## Notes

1. If you're new to Teach Like a Champion and don't follow all the wherefores and whys here, don't worry. You can get full explanations of all the terms and variations in *Cold Calling* (technique 34) in Chapter Seven.
2. I am just showing you how to be hilarious in an ironic, talking-to-teenagers kind of way with this comment about the Kardashians. I actually have no idea who the Kardashians are—I only know they're famous. Also, if you're wondering about taking advice on humor from me, my teenaged kids tell me I'm truly hilarious ("OMG, Dad, you're so hilarious" [insert withering stare]).
3. https://eric.ed.gov/?id=ED298122
4. http://web.stanford.edu/~gentzkow/research/radiology.pdf.
5. https://www.aft.org/sites/default/files/periodicals/WILLINGHAM%282%29.pdf.

6. Paul A. Kirschner, John Sweller, and Richard E. Clark, "Why Minimal Guidance During Instruction Does Not Work: An Analysis of the Failure of Constructivist, Discovery, Problem-Based, Experiential, and Inquiry-Based Teaching," *Educational Psychologist* 41, no. 2 (2006): 75–86. http://mrbartonmaths.com/resourcesnew/8.%20Research/Explicit%20Instruction/Why%20minimal%20guidance%20instruction%20does%20not%20work.pdf.

7. This is the difference between "performance" and "learning."

8. And of course you can only look up what you already know is relevant and connected.

9. Graham Nuthall, *Hidden Lives of Learners* (NZCER Press, 2007), p. 69.

10. Baumeister et al. proposed this concept in a 1998 paper in the *Journal of Personality and Social Psychology*, "Ego Depletion: Is the Active Self a Limited Resource?" They found, for example, that "people who forced themselves to eat radishes instead of tempting chocolates subsequently quit faster on unsolvable puzzles than people who had not had to exert self-control," and that "an initial task requiring high self-regulation made people more . . . prone to favor [a] passive-response option." Some further research has challenged their findings.

11. David T. Neal, Wendy Wood, and Jeffrey M. Quinn, "Habits—A Repeat Performance," *Current Directions in Social Science* (August 1, 2006), https://dornsife.usc.edu/assets/sites/545/docs/Wendy_Wood_Research_Articles/Habits/Neal.Wood.Quinn.2006_Habits_a_repeat_performance.pdf.

12. Nuthall's research involved taping and studying a sample of students during each lesson. He was often uninterested in what the teacher did and very interested in what students did and how it affected their learning. Many of his most interesting observations come from moments when we hear the children, whom he has mic'd, talking to themselves after an interaction with a teacher, for example.

13. www.researchgate.net/publication/225304965_The_role_of_selective_attention_on_academic_foundations_A_cognitive_neuroscience_perspective.

14. Ironically for a computer scientist, he has managed to achieve this himself by dramatically restricting the presence of technology, with its strong tendency to fracture and distract his concentration, as the title of another of his books, *Digital Minimalism*, suggests. (I recommend both it and *Deep Work*.)

15. The phrase was coined by Sophie Leroy at the University of Minnesota, based on her research on workplace productivity.

16. https://hbr.org/2018/03/to-control-your-life-control-what-you-pay-attention-to.

17. The other is—yup, you guessed it—the naked mole rat. They, too, will sacrifice unto the last full measure of devotion for one another. But God bless the little fellas, I don't

mind being outshone by them one bit—they're miraculous and quirky in a dozen ways. Also—honestly—they're funny looking and don't smell great. Let them have eusociality to brag about, I say.

18. Peps Mccrea, *Motivated Teaching: Harnessing the Science of Motivation to Boost Attention and Effort in the Classroom*, p. 74.

19. Everyone learns from people without having strong relationships. You have and will again have to learn many times in settings where the teacher did not know you from Adam—a large lecture in your university days or a Khan Academy video are examples. Obviously, as teachers we want to build relationships that help students thrive but it's important to be clear that everyone can and will have to learn in situations where a relationship doesn't exist at different times throughout their lives.

20. Tom's remarks were made in a series of tweets on March 5, 2021.

21. You've probably seen videos on the Internet of teachers who give each child their own distinctive greeting at the door. Arrival is a celebration of personalized handshakes and fist bumps. I find them lovely too. If you want to be that teacher, wonderful, but recognize that thousands of teachers build enduring relationships with students without those moves and, furthermore, the results are only likely to be substantive and enduring if you also teach well, your students feel safe, and you let them know that you see them for who they are.

# Chapter 2

# Lesson Preparation

If you're familiar with the 2.0 version of *Teach Like a Champion*, you may notice that some of the most significant changes in this latest edition come in this chapter. While much of what I wrote about in the second edition focused on how to *plan* an effective lesson, this chapter endeavors to shine a light on the methods my team and I have observed teachers use as they *prepare* to teach their lessons, instead. Essentially, I've replaced one chapter with another based on the importance implied by the change of a single word: from "plan" to "prepare." What's the difference, you might ask, and why the change?

First, preparation is universal. Not everyone writes their own lesson plan every day. Many teachers use a plan written by a colleague or a curriculum provider. Some reuse a plan they wrote previously. But everyone prepares (or, I argue, *should* prepare) their lesson before they teach it. If a lesson plan is a sequence of activities you intend to use, lesson preparation is a set of decisions about *how* you will teach them. Those decisions can determine the lesson's success at least as much as the sequence of activities, but because planning and preparation are readily confused, it's easy to overlook the latter and think once the plan's done, you're ready to roll.

Say you teach the same lesson twice a day: third period and fifth period. Your third-period class is verbal and eager—sometimes so eager that you have to cut off the chatter and digressions to keep them on track. Fifth period is more introverted. Pretty cerebral, actually, but they need some prodding to speak up. You use the same lesson *plan* for both classes, but you *prepare* it differently.

"The techniques that work to support engagement with one group of learners may need to be applied differently from one classroom to the next," notes Adeyemi Stembridge. "The design of highly engaging learning experiences requires a keen sense of context because human beings are a highly social species and interpersonal and cultural contexts matter."[1]

Perhaps on Tuesday, that means a bit more writing to get third period to slow down and reflect and a few more *Turn and Talks* to draw the fifth period classroom out. Perhaps a student in fifth period used a beautiful phrase to describe a passage from the novel and you want to remember to go back and ask her about it at a critical point in the lesson. Despite using the same lesson plan for both lessons, an effective process for lesson preparation has caused you to plan for crucial differences in how you'll teach each class.

The first step in preparation is to know the content of your lesson well. You can't teach at your best if you're not sure what comes next and have to read ahead when you should be listening, explaining, or observing. Managing working memory is important for teachers, not just students. I'll come back to this idea at the end of this section because there's more to it than first appears. But beyond the necessity of developing familiarity with *what* you're teaching, developing habits that can help you adapt your lesson successfully to the setting and react effectively to events as you teach is critical to a teacher's short- and long-term success. Such habits might seem like they would add to your workload, but done well they will reduce it, helping you succeed while maintaining balance and sustainability in your teaching life.

The reasons lesson preparation matters relate to cognitive science and the importance of perception, which is one of the most important skills of a teacher. "Experienced teachers develop a high level of sensitivity to students' level of interest, their involvement and their motivation," Graham Nuthall writes in *The Hidden Lives of Learners*. They "can tell from the atmosphere of the classroom, from the look in the students' eyes, from the questions and answers, from the way they engage in activities, how much the students' minds are engaged. Effective teachers . . . use these signs to tell whether they need to change what they are doing, to speed up or slow down, to introduce more or less challenge." Some caution may be warranted—even when we think we know students are engaged (or not) it's good to remember that we can be wrong and that reviewing written student work is a critical check on our assumptions—but for the most part we succeed when and if we perceive what is happening in our classrooms accurately and we make key instructional decisions accordingly. If you do not see the relevant cues, you cannot decide reliably. You will zig when students need you to zag.

But of course it's not quite true that "experienced" teachers do this. Those who have learned most productively from their experiences do, but you could have a twenty-year veteran who still fails to read a room or a first-year teacher whose read on the class is stellar. In fact, the real question is how every teacher can accelerate and improve their process of learning to "read the signs," as Nuthall puts it. Adeyemi Stembridge argues that responsiveness, too, starts with perception. "We want to sharpen our perception and capacities for leveraging strategies in ways that are most beneficial to students in need of specific support," he writes.[2] A key part of teaching responsively is reading the reactions and needs of our students as we teach. An important question, then, is how we can "see" better and more fully as we teach.

It might sound like something intangible, but perception responds to preparation. To perceive well, you need to prepare for what you'll be looking for and, ideally, free as much working memory as possible to be available, unencumbered, for observation. Inattentional blindness, I noted in Chapter One, is the name for the phenomenon whereby people frequently fail to see what is plainly before their eyes—never mind what is hidden or concealed. We are all at constant risk of failing to notice important details, especially when they occur in a complex visual field, and the classroom is almost always that.

We have to accept this and prepare with it in mind if we want to perceive more accurately, as Chabris and Simons remind us when they write: "There is one proven way to eliminate inattentional blindness: make the unexpected object or event less unexpected." If you think through potential errors in student thinking before you teach, you'll be more likely to notice them—or any mistakes. You learn to see in part by preparing to see. If you're clear in advance about what you want to see in the end product of student work, you'll look more precisely and notice more whether students are actually doing it.

But we also know that perception is affected by the load on our working memory. Pick up your cell phone and call your spouse or partner and you become less alert to what's happening on the road around you. Try to think about what's the best answer to a question while you're listening to your students and you become less alert to what's happening around you. You'll have less cognitive bandwidth to use for perception. You are likely to miss signals. But if you think through—and write down—details of an ideal student answer to key questions—what we will call in this chapter an "exemplar"—you can process what students say and write with less load on working memory.

Your ability to foster student engagement is another aspect of teaching that responds to preparation. If you have thought through how you're going to ask students to participate during the *Do Now*, say, and who you're going to call on to answer it, you make it more likely that you will follow through on those actions and the result will be students who feel accountable to participate and who benefit from a classroom where everyone—not just the eager hand-raisers or call-out-the-answer types—gets a fair chance to speak. Do that and your lesson is likely to crackle with engagement and energy. If you don't, you're likely to find yourself reminding students that you're seeing the same two or three hands on every question. Making a statement like that to your class should be a reminder to yourself to prepare better.

So lesson preparation is the process of going back through the lesson plan and thinking what it will look like not just in *a* classroom but in your fifth-period classroom tomorrow. When and how do you want to be more intentional about drawing out some of the quiet kids? Which questions should students answer in writing so you can see what they're thinking? It will be different for third period, where you'll have to watch the clock so you don't glance up and realize that a "five-minute discussion" is now entering its twenty-fifth minute. You'll need *time stamps*—if you're going to get to the demonstration of plate tectonics, you'll have to keep the *Do Now* to seven minutes, no matter how eager the waving hands. The vocabulary review gets three minutes and a stopwatch on the smartboard to make certain you don't miss the second half of the lesson.

With all this in mind, let's step into Christine Torres's fifth-grade classroom at Springfield Prep in Springfield, Massachusetts, to understand a bit more about the connection between preparation and teaching. In the video *Christine Torres: Keystone*, you will probably notice almost immediately how dynamic her lesson is—every student locked-in to learning in the most positive way and each second used for a productive activity that causes students to think. They work hard and seem to love it. Goodness, you're thinking, if my class looked like that, I could do this job forever. We had the same response. In fact we shot this video of Christine because we'd visited her school—without our cameras, alas—a few weeks earlier and had been immediately transfixed by the joyful, energetic, thoughtful lesson Christine was teaching. We could barely drag ourselves out of her classroom, and then only because they promised we could videotape her as soon as possible. That's the back story on where this video comes from. But one other detail is relevant from that first visit to Springfield Prep. Christine shared a copy of her packet—the place where she prepares her lesson, a copy of which is available on the website www.wiley.com/go/teachlikeachampion3. This is the tool she used to get ready to teach a different lesson from the one you just watched, but one which reveals the process she uses for every lesson—which is interesting in and of itself. She is consistent in how she *prepares* and so her lessons are consistent in quality, engagement, and energy. Remarkably so, which is sort of the point. The first step in making your classroom look more like Christine's is to copy—or at least study and adapt—her approach to preparation.

You can see that Christine has spent time in "exemplar planning": Before the lesson she took the time to write out the answer to each question as she hoped a top student would. This helps to focus her in discussions—to draw out the right points and hear the gaps. And she can glance at these notes as she teaches if she needs a quick reminder, so her working memory can stay relatively free.

Christine has also written out additional reminders to herself—the number of minutes she wants an activity to take, "back-pocket questions (BPQ)" she could use to support confused students, and, crucially, notes on how students will answer. After all, she could ask the same question of two classes but ask one to respond in writing via a *Stop and Jot* and the other to go straight to a *Turn and Talk*. These processes she goes through of marking up and preparing her lesson are different from the lesson plan—these are her handwritten, game-time adaptations to the prepared sequence of activities. Both tasks are necessary. The researching and careful crafting of lesson plans like this one take time and could not be done sustainably the night before (we know; she's using lessons as part of a pilot of the Reading Reconsidered Curriculum our team wrote) but preparation adapts that carefully crafted plan to ensure success with *this* group of students, *today*, with up-to-the minute knowledge of what the best moves will be, given the detail of how students are progressing and even what happened in class the day before. Even the best plan will not succeed without effective preparation and even great preparation of a poor plan will fall short. You need both.

And you can see the results in the video. Christine appears to be making the perfect decision to maximize the level of participation by all students over and over throughout her lesson. Christine's teaching is magical, but like every great magician there's some sleight of hand involved. Her decisions are outstanding, but she only appears to be making them on the spur of the moment. She's planned out many of them, or has narrowed the choices she'd consider, in advance. If you look at her version of the student packet, where she's done her preparation, you can see that there are both decisions ("Turn and Talk here") and options ("If time. Show Call exemplar."). Some people worry that too much preparation will make it harder to express themselves and connect with students, but the opposite is true here. Christine is prepared and so she is able to be fully responsive. Students feel seen and known by their teacher and as though they have her full attention. Her warmth and humor are magnified by virtue of her being calm, relaxed, and ready—and perhaps from the students' pride in their work and willingness to engage successfully with the tasks presented. Her careful planning sets a pattern in the first few minutes of class: She's clear with students about the task, they respond positively, and she can relax and express all her humor and brilliance as a teacher. They lather, rinse, and repeat all class long. It all starts with what's on her "Preparation Page."

James Clear's *Atomic Habits* lends insight into another way to understand why the time Christine invests in preparation results in such a powerful outcome in her classroom.

Clear cites a British study where three groups of people were asked to try to begin exercising. The control group received no special treatment. The second group received motivational materials. The third group received motivational material *and* was asked to complete the following sentence: "I will take 20 minutes of vigorous exercise on [DATE] in [TIME] at [PLACE]." The rates of people from the three groups who actually exercised were 35 percent, 38 percent, and 91 percent. The follow-through rates when people committed to a particular action for time and place nearly tripled over those who wanted to do those things but weren't specific in planning time and place. In Clear's words, "People who make a specific plan for when and where they will perform a new habit are more likely to follow-through. Too many people try to change habits [or apply teaching techniques] without these basic details figured out."

Christine's notes reveal that she has done something similar to what Clear advises. Every time she jots "Cold Call here" or "Turn and Talk here," Christine has made a specific plan for where and when she will take a particular action and thus has tripled the chances that she'll actually do these things. More specific preparation makes it more likely that we'll do the things we hope to do in teaching. It is a follow-through multiplier that helps us become the teachers we want to be.

Christine's lesson preparation habits are impressive but there isn't one universal method for Lesson Preparation. Situations are different and people are different. When your intuition and curriculum have been sharpened by years of instruction, you may be able to prepare simply—perhaps scripting the exemplar to a single critical question and then entering the classroom confidently. . . at least on a routine day with a lesson you've taught before. But it may take some time before you get there. Perhaps you're a teaching a new class this year. You'd probably want to increase your preparation level at the outset even if over the course of the year you began to simplify or adapt the process you used at the outset. But it's important to make it a habit. Naming the core preparation practices, making sure they're productive and useful, and committing to when you'll complete them is critical. Just as the preparation itself increases the chances you will take the actions you plan on when you teach, so too your chances of preparation will multiply if you commit to consistent time, place, and methods.

This is likely to result in stronger student achievement  and a more positive and engaging experience for your students, not to mention more enjoyment of teaching for you. I will return to this idea later but as Adeyemi Stembridge puts it, reflecting on his own lesson preparation habits in *Culturally Responsive Teaching in the Classroom*, "I always start my planning with time to think carefully about what I want my students to understand and feel." What students feel is critical to their sense of belonging is made up of many things. Part of it is the connection to the content and the teacher; part of it is being caught up in the flow of a lesson that moves briskly with what Mihaly Csikszentmihalyi calls "flow" and therefore moves them to another world—in Christine's case to Denmark in 1943—and fires their imaginations. The journey begins when one is made to feel included in something dynamic and engaging. An artfully crafted and executed lesson does that.

Before we define specific techniques for lesson preparation, let me return to the most basic question about preparation: How well do you know the content covered in your lesson? This might seem like a pointless question. No teacher except one thrown suddenly into emergency duty outside her subject would answer: "Oh, not very well, really." But there is a huge range of what teachers mean when they say they know their content and it's worth asking if knowing more about the context and the facts really matters.

Research tells us that higher-order thinking relies on facts and is only possible when people are possessed of a strong body of knowledge about a given topic. Here's a demonstration of that.

Imagine that you woke up tomorrow morning and the sky was green rather than blue. In the box below, jot two possible explanations of what, from a scientific perspective, could conceivably have caused that to happen:

Well, how'd you do? Were you creative? Brilliantly analytical? Did you suggest that something would have to affect the particles in the Earth's atmosphere, causing them to absorb blue light more than it currently does, but only slightly so as to leave green, with the next shortest waves, as the most visible? Did you suggest that perhaps an increase in water droplets in the air might reflect the yellows and oranges of sunrise and combine with the natural blue of the sky, perhaps against a backdrop of clouds, to make it appear green?

Or were you unable to answer? Did you guess something implausible, maybe about the reflection of the ocean (a common misconception) and then give up on the project? Is your thinking box blank? If that's the case, then you've just been reminded of the point made in Chapter One: Higher-order thinking is context-specific and knowledge-dependent. If you don't have knowledge about what causes the sky to be blue (or any other color) this exercise in creative and analytical thinking is lost on you. You can think deeply only about things you know something about—the more you know, the more deeply and creatively.

From a student learning perspective this means that we must consider our pupils' level of background knowledge in advance if we want real rigor during lessons. Preparing a lesson by noting that you will ask "probing questions" is insufficient unless you have ensured that students have knowledge to draw on as you probe and ask them "Why?" I'm actually pretty shaky on my knowledge of the atmosphere so you could have asked me a thousand probing questions about the color of the sky and not elicit much more than resentment. At some point in your asking me ". . . but might it have something to do with particles in the air?" I would get angry and frustrated. *I've already told you that I don't know. You can keep asking me "why" if you want but I still won't know, so perhaps you should stop asking.*

Compare that response to how Christine's students act in her lesson: the eager hands, the vibrant burst of ideas when she offers a *Turn and Talk*. Her students engage because she has leveled the playing field for them. You can see the places where her lesson plan infuses knowledge deliberately to prepare them to think deeply—the articles about rationing, the fairy tales of Hans Christian Andersen, and the description of what a trousseau is, but Christine has also prepared to feed knowledge where necessary and made thinking about gaps in knowledge part of getting ready to teach. Notice, for example:

- The sentences she's underlined in the article about rationing because they contain key background knowledge that will allow students to better analyze the book and her note to add these to the slide.

- Her notes on ensuring that students understand that "past perfect" implies that something *was* but no longer *is*, so they can think more deeply about the unspoken fact that Annemarie's sister is deceased.

*But knowledge also matters for teachers.* That's the sleeper. It is also true that we can think more deeply and creatively about our lessons if we know more about them, if we have reviewed key knowledge beforehand so that it is encoded in long-term memory. Imagine trying to teach the preceding green sky lesson based only on having read the answer and brief explanation I've provided. You certainly wouldn't teach it well or flexibly. More likely you'd teach it in a way that forestalled the likelihood of getting questions from students you couldn't answer. Your unsteady knowledge would constrain your teaching moves. You'd be reluctant to ask probing "why" questions if your answer to every student conjecture was, "Hmmm. Interesting. Maybe we can look it up later and find out." You'd do much better to have thought through a few likely responses and ensure you were clear on why they did or did not make sense. And though that's obviously true for a lesson on the visible light spectrum, it's just as true for topics like archetypes and fairy tales, as my colleague Hannah Solomon pointed out. Without first having made sure to reflect deeply on them, your lesson might still fail. But you'd be more likely to overlook the importance of reading up on fairy tales and the like because of their familiarity. Notice, however, this screenshot from Christine's lesson. She's annotated the plan with notes of preparation that show she's been thinking about fairy tales and why they are particularly relevant to a story about life during wartime. Not only does her lesson plan provide background knowledge but her preparation shows that she's reviewed and reflected and applied what she knows to be ready to teach it.

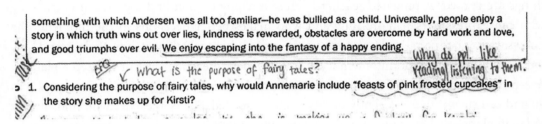

So perhaps it's worth asking: What habits do you have as a teacher to ensure that you are always investing in your knowledge? In this chapter we'll discuss a few, but I'll also observe that several successful schools I know use the phrase "intellectual preparation" to describe a key step in lesson preparation and they build this into professional development. Teachers get together before they teach a book or unit to talk through its important questions and share and prioritize key background knowledge that will allow them to teach it. I love the idea of such a meeting. The message is: *How much you know about what you're teaching is a key part of how you prepare.*

## TECHNIQUE 1: EXEMPLAR PLANNING

Teachers and school leaders tend to have an overwhelming response to clips of Sarah Wright's teaching. The video *Sarah Wright: Tio Luis*, shot in her fifth-grade classroom at Chattanooga Prep in Chattanooga, Tennessee, shows why. The joy and purposefulness of Sarah's classroom are striking. Her students, all boys in this case, grin from ear to ear as they dive into a *Turn and Talk* in which they imagine they are the villainous character, Tio Luis, from Pam Muñoz Ryan's *Esperanza Rising*. They write eager, detailed responses. The boys delight in using—sometimes imperfectly but always enthusiastically—rich new vocabulary words and in celebrating a peer's exemplary response. All the while they are locked-in to the novel. Perhaps as you watch you hear a faint echo of Christine Torres's lesson, which we discussed in the introduction to this chapter. And in fact the echo you might hear is not a coincidence. The similarities include the way students are universally engaged in quality learning activities without a second of downtime; the way they seem to think studying this book is just about the greatest thing in the world. And there's one more parallel that's not quite as clear from watching the video but that is at least as profound as any of the other likenesses: Sarah and Christine achieve similar outcomes because they prepare similarly.[3]

What you see in their classrooms is a product of decisions made hours before the lesson began as much as it is a product of those made in the moment, though of course the two things are related. A prepared teacher is often a happy teacher and a poised teacher—one who can express herself more fully and who makes better decisions in the moment. She knows where she's going and isn't anxious or worried about what's next, how to do it, and how long it will take; her working memory is free to listen to each answer or to keep a planned five-minute discussion to five minutes in real time because she knows where she wants it to go and can steer it there as gently or decisively as needed. She is a teacher who finds it easy to laugh alongside her students and celebrate their work like Sarah does. You can't be fully present unless you're prepared.

Like Christine's preparation, Sarah's is a product of habit and experience. Sarah initially prepared her lesson much like Christine did: planning her key instructional moves—her *Means of Participation*—and the mistakes she thought she might see, but her final step came that morning. "I had 45 minutes," she told me, referring to a busy morning on the day she taught this lesson. So she went through and reviewed her exemplars.

Exemplars, you'll recall, are correct answers that you write out to your own questions. They are the answers you hope a student will give to your question. It would be easy to overlook this step or underestimate its value in planning. It seems perhaps both obvious and redundant. You might argue that you have the answer "in your head" and don't need to write it out. But this simple action might be the single most important step in preparing to teach.

To see why, let's take a look at a tiny moment from two lessons where you can see exemplars being used. First, there's the clip *Denarius Frazier: Remainder*. Check what he does at 1:12 in this lesson on dividing polynomials—you'll see the whole lesson in Chapter Three, "Check for Understanding." Explaining to a student why her work is incorrect, he quickly glances at his *exemplar*, which he's carrying with him. It helps him to diagnose what she's done wrong more quickly and accurately. "Your remainder is off because this value right here is incorrect," he says. He is able to spot the incorrect value quickly and easily because he has the ideal answer ready to compare it to. He doesn't have to strain to keep all of the information in his working memory. About a second is enough to remind him.

Julia Addeo does something similar in the clip *Julia Addeo: Keystone*, which I'll also discuss more fully in the "Check for Understanding" chapter. The first thirty-seven seconds show her comparing students' work to her exemplar and quickly and easily spotting their mistakes by comparing their work to the exemplar. She's able to move fast and get to multiple students. But she's also able to free more of her working memory to think about why they are making these mistakes and what she can do about it. You can see her do this. She steps back from her observations to think about how she wants to address the misconceptions she's seeing and, in so doing, glances again at her exemplar. "What should be happening to make this process go right?" she appears to be asking herself. The exemplar helps her to see that clearly.

In *The Checklist Manifesto*, the science writer Atul Gawande describes situations in which trained professionals use a similar tool—checklists—to assess the final outcome of a process. "Under conditions of complexity," he writes, checklists "are required for success." Good checklists "provide reminders of . . . the most critical and important steps. They allow for precision and efficiency. The user can make sure the final result is thorough and preserve working memory in assessing it at the same time." A lot like an exemplar, in other words, with the difference being that an exemplar can be narrative and each element need not be satisfied in a particular order. Both tools are valuable because they discipline the process of looking and free working memory. Interestingly, Gawande argues that checklists are most valuable in two situations. First, they are useful when performing especially complex and sophisticated work. Surgeons use them, for example—though they resisted them for years. So do engineers who build massive skyscrapers. In each of these examples, "the volume and complexity of what we know has exceeded our individual ability to deliver its benefits correctly, safely, or reliably." A tool to focus observations is more important for experts because they know much more than they can keep in working memory while observing! Certainly this is true for teachers, who balance a complex daily instructional plan filled with challenging content and the individual learning needs of up to thirty twelve-year-olds, for example.

The second situation when checklists are especially valuable is when you want reliable results across a large organization with a lot of autonomy—a school, for example. If everyone agrees on what *right* looks like, it can reduce variability in execution while preserving autonomy. Want to start having "intellectual preparation" meetings at your school? Writing and comparing exemplars to various key questions might be the ideal activity. When we ask students, "How is Jonas changing in this chapter?" discussing the nuances of what could or should be in your exemplar is a perfect way to discuss interpretations and insights about the text.

There's a bit of humility necessary to unlock the power of exemplar planning. It seems like such a mundane task at first, but the more you know, ironically, the more you need to organize what you're looking for. I assure you, Denarius knows his division of polynomials and Julia knows her binomials. Christine knows *Number the Stars*. Sarah knows how Tio Luis feels upon discovering Abuelita's disappearance. But they write the ideal answer out anyway and this helps them to organize and reinforce in their own minds what they want to see and hear when their students respond.

So perhaps it's not surprising that Sarah chose, with her limited preparation time on her busy morning the day of her Esperanza lesson, to review and revise her exemplars. She went back over them and made small adaptations and additions. This helped to refresh the sequence of lesson activities in her mind, caused her to review the contents of the book so it was sharper in her memory, and ensured that she had an ideal answer to refer to as she listened to her students. It also caused her to think, with the lesson that day, of who she might call on when or how she might ask students to participate (topics I cover in the technique *Delivery Moves* further on). You can add other elements to your lesson preparation—this chapter will describe several that are immensely valuable, but when you have "one of those days," and forty-five minutes is all you get, exemplar planning is the one task to fall back on.

Sarah is an English teacher, of course, so her process of writing out exemplars reflects that. She often focuses on key words or phrases she wants her students to use or a section she wants them to refer to in the text. Were Sarah a chemistry or math teacher, her process might include showing her work, then setting up each problem in the same format expected of students for easy reference during class. But no matter the subject the key is that the *exemplar planning must be written down*. This forces you to put your thinking into words as students must. It allows you, as Sarah did, to revise and amend as other thoughts come to you, and it makes your thinking portable, which as I noted earlier can allow you to share and discuss it with colleagues during professional development. And most of all it means you can take it with you when you teach, as we've seen Julia and Christine doing. And you can see that Sarah has hers in hand as well. She puts it down briefly to celebrate Akheem's answer but when the clapping and celebrating is done, she picks it right back up again.

Why, you might wonder, has Sarah's exemplar plan become her right hand (and Denarius's and Julia's and Christine's, as well) as she teaches? Thinking back to our discussion of the limited capacity of working memory can help to explain it. By familiarizing herself deeply with the target answer to every question, Sarah can be thinking not "What's the answer?" when she hears or reads student work but rather "Where and how are they confused?" She is able to respond quickly and nimbly and to be fully present while teaching because far more of her working memory is allocated to perception than a comparable teacher who is also using working memory to remember things. She is calm enough to remember to smile, confident enough in her plan to celebrate greatness, to laugh at silliness, and to encourage risk-taking.

Having the exemplar in hand speeds her progress around the room and helps her get to everybody.

A final point to reiterate about exemplar planning: It makes for excellent professional development in two ways. First, there are arguably few better conversations among teachers in a department than "What constitutes an outstanding answer to the following (important) question?" To discuss those things for six or eight questions would be a crucial and powerful form of intellectual preparation. It's hard to imagine a better department meeting. We review the book, but we also hear ideas that we may not have considered. A teacher saying *Oh, I'm definitely adding that to my exemplar* is a teacher expanding their knowledge of the content they teach. My colleague Paul Bambrick-Santoyo calls this process "sparring with the exemplar": You script your best answer and then sit down with colleagues and compare yours to theirs. Teachers leave intellectually prepared, with a deep understanding of the book and quite possibly differing perspectives on it. And of course it's the ideal kind of professional development because it happens before teachers teach their lessons. It makes them better *now* rather than in some far-off sunny day next year when they teach the book again. Of course if your department doesn't offer this kind of professional development you can do it virtually, finding colleagues elsewhere with whom to spar.

For this reason the English curriculum we've developed comes with exemplar student answers in the teaching material, but our recommendation is always that teachers not read them until they have written their own. You learn more when you've thought it through in advance. That said, we also script exemplars because it helps our lesson designers to refine their questions. If they struggle to answer or don't like their answer, well, they know the question has to change—a fact we mention because for those teachers who do write their own lesson exemplar planning is an even more powerful step.

## TECHNIQUE 2: PLAN FOR ERROR

In Chapter One I discussed Christopher Chabris and Daniel Simons' observations about inattentional blindness, our frequent tendency simply not to see what is right before our eyes. The one proven way to eliminate it, they write, is to "make the unexpected object or event less unexpected."[4] A critical step in preparing to teach is recognizing that in a complex visual environment, what we have prepared ourselves to look for is what we are likely to notice. This means that anticipating specific mistakes we think we're likely to see from students can be as valuable as exemplar planning. One of the most productive questions you can ask yourself is: *What will they get wrong*? Or perhaps *What will they misunderstand*?

Asking and answering such questions has profound effects.

First, if you have thought through the question (or task or problem) from the students' point of view and thought about what they may misunderstand, you are more likely to spot those misunderstandings when they occur. This will not only help prevent inattentional blindness—that is, students make mistakes, but you don't notice it—but it will also help you to take more productive action in at least two ways if you do observe misunderstandings.

Thinking through likely student errors in advance helps you to avoid "burying the data." Let's say you're teaching the subtly crafted scene in *The Giver* where the narrator, Jonas, sees color for the first time but, because he doesn't understand what color is, remains confused. The scene is written to merely suggest what's happened to Jonas. It describes the flashes of red he sees from an uncomprehending point of view. It ends unresolved. Students often remain confused as well.

A teacher would want to anticipate that students might not understand this scene or its importance. But merely noticing that students get this wrong is not enough. Teachers frequently "bury the data"—that is, they recognize that students are making an error or are struggling with a misunderstanding but they fail to address it, perhaps hoping that it will resolve itself. Perhaps sometimes it will, but more often the misunderstanding compounds. Students read several chapters without realizing that they should be very attentive to the changes in Jonas's vision.

Why do we sometimes ignore the data in this way, recognizing a misunderstanding but not doing anything about it? Honestly, there are lots of reasons. Acting on the data means tearing up your lesson plan in front of thirty seventh-graders and planning an alternative on the spur of the moment. If it works, you return to your original plan but with the timings all a mess. If it fails, well, then you're really stuck. But if you've anticipated the likely errors you're going to see you can also plan what you'd do about them. And planning that response—building some if/then contingency into your lesson (if X happens, then I will do Y) makes you more likely to take action. You've removed the disincentive of improvising live in front of thirty students.

So by planning for error you're more likely to see the error if it happens and you're more likely to act on it. To do the things teachers do successfully in the Check for Understanding chapter, that is, teachers must prepare for mistakes.

A second way planning for error helps you take more productive action is that it helps you to treat your observations like data—another topic discussed more fully in the chapter on Check for Understanding. Watch again the moment 44 seconds into the clip *Denarius Frazier, Remainder* when Denarius makes a tiny hash mark on his clipboard in response to a student's struggle to find the remainder. Denarius does not take the time to write down "remainders" or "struggling to use remainder theorem." Why? He is able to make a hash mark because he has already written that phrase down before the lesson. On his clipboard Denarius has a list of possible errors. Now he can merely begin quantifying them when and if he sees them. There are six hash marks next to "struggling to use remainder theorem." Denarius might have planned three potential errors his students could make. His planning allows him to see quickly which ones they're actually making and how often. Planning for errors in advance makes it much easier to turn observations into data during a lesson.

Anticipating errors in the passage from *The Giver* in which Jonas sees color reveals something else about planning for error: There are decisions to be made. Yes, the scene intimates subtly that Jonas can see color. I might want my students to focus on that. But I might decide that it's more important for them to see how disorienting what's happening is to Jonas. Something is wrong, mysterious, unexplained for the first time in his life. He repeatedly attempts to "test" his vision. He breaks the rules to take the apple home and examine it. There are two aspects of the passage that might easily be missed. It might be that students don't need to fully understand that Jonas sees color as long as they recognize how troubling and confusing whatever was happening to Jonas is.

The question of how much to emphasize each of two things students might not understand in a difficult passage might seem arcane to all but English teachers or fellow *The Giver* enthusiasts, but there is a larger point about process that's relevant to all teachers here: I realized that those were two different potential misreadings and two approaches to teaching the passage *because I was trying to think about the errors students might make*. The process of planning for error caused me to better understand the book through a student's eyes. The more I do this, the better I get at understanding the types and causes of student misunderstandings, and the better I get at designing my teaching with that in mind the first time around. It almost doesn't matter if you guess correctly about the mistakes students will make. By predicting them and then noticing whether they occur, you'll get better at seeing your lessons through a student's eyes.

But planning for error is not just identifying the mistakes that might occur. It's planning what you'd do about it too. In my example from *The Giver*, I might go back to the line: "Then [the apple] was in his hand, and he looked at it carefully, but it was the same apple. Unchanged. The same size and shape: a perfect sphere. The same nondescript shade, about the same shade as his own tunic."

I might first draw students' attention to the words "nondescript shade." Why those words for the apple's color? What did it imply? Were apples usually noted for being nondescript in color? Why were they throwing an apple, by the way? Why not a ball? Could there be something symbolic there?

Or, depending on the group, or how much time I had, I might say, "This passage implies that Jonas is seeing color for the first time, but he doesn't know what it is because he's never seen it. Let's go back and reread this scene and I want you to tell me how Lowry communicates both the fact that he could see color but also his confusion."

Now I've developed two possible responses. I can read the room and my students and make a decision about which way to go. But in the moment I decide I won't be starting from scratch and choosing a lesson path I have considered only on the spur of the moment.

To review what we've discussed so far, planning for error means predicting errors and planning how you will respond, intentionally thinking through (and writing down) what students will misunderstand about key questions in the lesson and then planning potential corrective actions should those misunderstandings occur.

This is potentially a time-consuming process, so I think it's important to be realistic about it. Should you do it for every question you ask? I would argue not. The goal is to build a manageable and sustainable habit. Again how much depends on teacher and context: New or experienced teacher? New or familiar content? Challenging topic? As a starting point I might recommend doing it for the most important question or two in every lesson.

Throughout this book I talk about the critical nature of perception. Teaching is a decision-making endeavor and to make the right decisions we have to approach the work in a way that maximizes our ability to see and understand what we are seeing. Planning for error increases the likelihood that we will see misunderstandings and be able to make sound decisions about what steps to use to adjust our lesson plan. And, frankly, the likelihood that we will be brave enough to act on them under duress.

But there's another aspect of perception at work here, too. Teachers are experts in their domain and this means they perceive differently from their students, who are novices. A study by Chi, Glaser, and Feltovich revealed how novices and experts perceive differently. Studying novices and experts solving physics problems, they noted that "whereas novices categorize problems by the surface structure of the problem," experts saw "deep structure" to categorize and solve them.[5] Novices might observe that two problems involved moving objects and try to solve them similarly, Carl Hendrick and Paul Kirschner note in discussing the study, but experts would quickly see that one was an acceleration problem and the other a constant velocity problem. "What you know determines what you see," Hendrick and Kirschner conclude, and this represents a double challenge. First, novices don't know as much and so don't perceive things as well as experts and, second, experts are not often aware of this or at least cannot easily unsee what they notice as a result of their expertise. It takes practice to see what people who know less about a topic will not understand. The discipline of planning for error and testing those predictions is the process of investing in your ability to see beyond this expert–novice divide and into the cognitive lives of your students.

There's one final benefit to planning for error. If you practice anticipating what students will struggle with during your planning, you are also internalizing the assumption that *there will be misunderstanding and mistakes*. There is a presumption now of their inevitability, which means you are far less likely to get frustrated with students when mistakes emerge. You're less likely to blame learning gaps on students or see their struggles as signs of some flaw. When errors are inevitable and the challenge is predicting and reacting to them teaching becomes a problem-solving challenge more than a question of assigning blame, and this will help to preserve students' trust in you.

## TECHNIQUE 3: DELIVERY MOVES

There is a constellation of things a typical teacher does to adapt a lesson and bring it to life for a certain group of students on a certain day. The adaptations are made in response to a variety of factors: the differences between third and fifth period (each class having its own slightly unique personality and group dynamic) or the mood on a Wednesday in October versus the last day before spring break, or how yesterday's lesson went. These actions prepare teachers to deliver a lesson uniquely and responsively to each class.

The first is Means of Participation (MOP) planning. MOP, as I discuss in technique 36, is choosing not just what question you will ask but also how you will ask students to answer that question—and then clearly communicating that expectation back to them. The lesson plan tells you the question, but how it's asked and answered—via *Turn and Talk* and/or a *Cold Call*; with *Wait Time*, or via *Everybody Writes*—is just as important. The best question in the world can still not "work" from a learning perspective if everyone doesn't answer it with their full effort and reflection. So lesson preparation should involve drafting a plan for how you will engage students in your questions with intentional decisions—a few *Cold Calls* at the outset to engage everyone. A few *Stop and Jots* to push for deeper thinking in the middle, and to give them the chance to write and rehearse their ideas. Some *Turn and Talks* to keep the energy rolling. Of course because you've planned these things doesn't mean you can't change them. It just means you start with a game plan, and, as we learned earlier from James Clear, then you're more likely to do the things you want to do instructionally.

**Plan for Who:** The next question after you've decided *how* students will participate is often: *who*. One of the reasons to not always take hands or let students call out is "voice equity." The ideas of quiet students—the ones who think more deliberately, the ones who worry about how they might come across if they volunteer to speak—matter, too. So if you are *Cold Calling* or taking hands, thinking about whom you want to call on is often critical. A *Cold Call* might be a perfect tool to use at a given moment to get a little "voice equity" and ensure that everyone feels central to the discussion. But whom will you call on? Just *Cold Calling* would not solve the problem if, in the moment, you called on one of your students who always had their hand up anyway. Your decisions about the right *Means of Participation*—in this case *Cold Call*—will be much stronger if you have also thought through who would most benefit from being invited into the conversation or who might add the most to it.

When you plan whom to call on, you might think about individual students—it may be James you want to check in on or draw out—or certain characteristics of students—if a student who I think is often a reliable bellwether has got it wrong, lots of people probably do, say. Sometimes, I might steer questions to Jabari, because he struggled on perimeter questions on the quiz but has been making great progress. I'll let him answer during class, so he feels the progress. Or my goal could be to make sure everyone speaks and is included and feels the "voice equity." I might make a note to "call on Tyson or Mary" because they are quieter, or to "call on quieter kids," because I don't know who will be quiet that day. In other words, my goals can be individual or categorical. Making a note to call on someone with an "almost there" answer is one of my favorite examples of a categorical preparation note. Seeing the note—"Show Call an almost there"—in the margin, I would then circulate around the room, glancing over students' shoulders as they worked and choosing a strong answer that was lacking a key detail (i.e. "almost there"), and starting the discussion there. "Naveen has some really provocative insights and I think we can also help her make her good work even better. Let's have a look. . . ."

When reviewing the lesson online, you can see that Christine has done this at the bottom of page 3 and again at the bottom of page 6. She's got a list of kids whom she might want to call on for this. You can see some cross-outs. The list is changing. She's got a list for her co-teacher Kait Smith, too, who's leading a pull-out group.

**Time Stamps:** How do good lessons go bad? Slowly, then all at once. Everything is going fine if a little slower then you anticipated and then you look up and realize that you are having the discussion you hoped you'd have but twenty-five minutes later in the lesson than you'd planned. Suddenly you are in trouble. There'll be no independent practice, no written reflection, no time to review for the quiz. This is why using Time Stamps is important. They push you to intentional allocation decisions about your dearest resource.

How much time on the *Stop and Jot* before the discussion, how much time on the discussion, and how much time on the written reflection afterwards. This helps you to see more quickly when you're getting behind. Time is finite so these are important trade-offs and the right decisions might change. It might be different for third period (honestly, they could use some time to slow down and think about other people's opinions) versus fifth period (they could learn to verbalize a bit more). It might be different on Wednesday than on Tuesday. It might be different Wednesday *because* of Tuesday, so if you planned on Monday you might want to go back through and update your time allocations as close to when you teach as possible.

Christine has done this on page 6 of her lesson. Next to the annotation box where students take notes on the reading, she's allocated five minutes. Next to question five she's allocated three minutes. When she says: *two minutes on the clock to write your answers,* that's because she's planned it: two minutes to write and one to hear an answer out loud. Then we move on. She gives seven minutes to the question about the fairy tales. There are going to be eager hands wanting to read their answers to question 5. The temptation will be to hear more and more of them. But Time Stamping lets Christine see that it's a trade-off between that and getting to the rest of the lesson, and she chooses the latter. She is prioritizing: The question about fairy tales is more important than some other things: more critical to understanding the book; more central to the writing they'll be doing. It's hard to prioritize when we want kids to learn everything, but even imperfect compromises made with foresight are better than the accidental prioritization of, "Whoops, we're out of time." After all, what comes last is often there because it helps us make sense of what we've done. It's likely to be important. Maybe that's why at one point Christine's notes remind herself: "Do Not need to capture all examples!" and: "Can skip: pacing." If she gets in trouble, that's the first question to go. One very small detail you might consider: including the actual time of day as opposed to running time of your lesson. It's easier to see when you are over time at 10:35 a.m. than "at twenty-two minutes."

**Back-Pocket Questions:** Back-pocket questions are the ones you'll fall back on when students struggle with the initial question in your lesson. They're hard to think of in the moment and trying to do so slows you down. Plus you may not think of exactly the right follow-up question in the moment and there's a greater chance than normal that the question won't be perfect, so may confuse the student you're hoping to help. So sketching out a few potential back-pocket questions in the calm before you teach and writing them down where you can find them easily is a great practice. You can see examples of this in Christine's packet. You can see how she's planned to respond in case students struggle to make sense of the sentence "We enjoy escaping into the fantasy of a happy ending." She'll ask, "Why do people like reading and listening to them?" to help students realize fairy tales are a form of pleasure that's not supposed to be realistic—they're supposed to be escapist.

~~Anderson was all too familiar. He was bullied as a child. Universally, people enjoy a~~ ins out over lies, kindness is rewarded, obstacles are overcome by hard work and love, ~~ov~~er evil. We enjoy escaping into the fantasy of a happy ending. *why do ppl. like reading/ listening to them?*

· *What is the purpose of fairy tales?*

rpose of fairy tales, why would Annemarie include "feasts of pink frosted cupcakes" in ~~is up for Kirsti?~~

**Segues:** Part of what makes well-prepared lessons effective is that the teacher connects upcoming content to the previous task or to what's coming. Take this example from Laura Baxter's fourth-grade class in Nashville, Tennessee, in their study of *Esperanza Rising*. The class has just wrapped up the vocabulary portion of the lesson, and Laura shares that her favorite of the new words they've studied is *irritable*. "Oh, wait till you see how irritable Esperanza is on this train ride," she says, intrigue in her voice, and after a few crisp *What to Do* instructions—"Packet in the corner [of your desk], text in front of you. Ready to read on page 72," she's reading and the chapter is underway. Her segue has students looking eagerly forward to see how irritable, in fact, Esperanza will be. Preparing a segue means looking ahead to connect content and helping students to see how the parts of a lesson fit together via a very transitional phrase. The segue becomes a through-line for students, to make the lesson feel more like a whole, and the things they do more connected.

"I almost always start our reading with a question that connects the prior day's reading to this day's," ace literature teacher Sarah Wright told me. That form of a segue "is like a hook," she noted. "You've got the hands going up . . . and then . . . every student is on the edge of his seat because you've made the connection to what they care about. The more you can make those connections, the more you are connecting the brain neurons and helping students remember and build on all of their knowledge as they are going through the text."

By writing segue statements, you shape how students will experience the overall lesson by telling them—and yourself—the story of how the discrete pieces come together in one unified, objective-driven whole.

## Rigor Checklist

A few years ago I watched a day's worth of lessons at schools in a major East Coast city school district. They had been working with a program that was using *Teach Like a Champion* to train new teachers and wanted feedback on how the teachers were doing. One classroom stayed with me more than the others. The teacher had done a lovely job of establishing productive procedures and routines and positive culture. Her students sat eagerly at their desks, ready to learn, listening expectantly. She had worked hard and done well to set the stage for an outstanding lesson. But there were crucial things missing. The lesson involved simplistic tasks—underlining a sentence in an article that was too easy. Students circled answers to multiple-choice questions but didn't do any writing. They sat at their desks, waiting for some worthy and inspiring task to begin, the brightness ebbing slowly away from their faces. This was what school was, they were learning.

The journalist Ellis Cose writes of sitting in his second- or third-grade classroom this way: "It came to me as I was sitting at my desk trying to keep myself interested as the teacher led the class, one listless word at a time, through the book I had read the first day of school, a book (and not a particularly interesting one) she would end up taking the entire semester to slow walk us through."[6] Alfred Tatum summarizes Cose's realization this way, noting that it applies to far more students than one: "The longer he went to school the more he was convinced that real learning would not take place."[7] In this way what Tatum calls "anti-intellectualism" develops in American classrooms. Students are bored when challenge, rigor, and a feeling of momentum are lacking. Teachers read this boredom as a signal that students cannot or will not do more advanced work. They do more mundane work instead. A sort of death spiral ensues. The moments that have most frustrated my own children in school have been the moments when they have realized that lessons marked by tasks devoid of rigor were also what tomorrow and the next day would look like.[8]

Elsewhere in the school were a few classrooms led by a few masters and a shockingly large number of disorderly and chaotic classrooms where no learning happened because teachers lacked the tidy systems and carefully built expectations that the teacher I was observing had constructed. And yet here, in this promising teacher's room, an opportunity was lost. The teacher had lost sight of what a worthy lesson should look like—what its component parts should be. Perhaps her mental model was incomplete; perhaps she was just focused on other things.

At about this time I was reading about the power of checklists, "quick and simple tools aimed to buttress the skills of professionals," as Atul Gawande puts it. A checklist is, in a sense, a reminder that ensures key aspects of the final product don't get left out. I found myself imagining a rigor checklist. A gut check teachers could use—even or perhaps especially when they were focused on other things like installing strong procedures—that would let them assess: Was this lesson worthy? Were the core things in place? Every lesson wouldn't need every piece, but over time if a teacher had to say, no, we didn't write today, no, we didn't read any challenging grade-level-or-above text, they would know they needed to make some changes.

The goal wouldn't be comprehensiveness. It would be a gut check. A quick and efficient tool to help teachers make sure they weren't consistently missing something.

Here's what I put together:

- Students write frequently and describe or reflect on at least one important idea in complete sentences (Grade 1 and above).

- Teacher consistently asks students to improve, develop, and revise initial answers both verbally or in writing.

- Teacher introduces new and advanced vocabulary and students use these words frequently to engage and discuss the content of the lesson.

- Students read challenging text (grade level or above) and text-dependent questions are used to ensure they are able to establish meaning. The discussion is not limited to the establishing of meaning but the step is not overlooked.

- Teacher achieves voice equity; almost everyone participates by speaking; everyone participates by listening. Teacher uses *Cold Call*, follow-ons, and formative writing among other tools to achieve this.

- Students use retrieval practice to encode key knowledge in long-term memory.

It's imperfect. Other people would name different things. In fact you can make your own if you don't like mine. But to me this would be a great tool to give teachers—especially when they were training on other important aspects of building an effective classroom that might distract them from the big picture—so that when they finished preparing a lesson they could ask themselves, *In the long run, am I on the right path?*

## TECHNIQUE 4: DOUBLE PLAN

Here's something possibly obvious about Christine Torres's lesson preparation—so obvious that it might be easy to overlook even though it's one of the most important things she does.

She's working from a copy of the student packet—the document they are working from throughout the lesson. It's what she holds in her hand as she teaches; it's where she makes her preparation notes. Her starting point, in other words, is a document that outlines what students will be doing at each stage of the lesson. Just the fact that there is such a document is profound. Yes, there's a lesson plan also that Christine can consult if she needs it. It contains more detail about what she will do and how. But more central to the preparation of the lesson is the document that describes what *students* will be doing each step of the way.

A lesson plan describes a series of activities you will lead or topics you will discuss, but what the teacher is talking about or doing is not the same as what students are doing. *Double Planning* describes in detail what *students* will be doing each step of the way. A lesson plan might say that a teacher should lead a discussion about a line in the text. A double-planned lesson would describe what students should be doing during the discussion: jotting down notes about insights their peers make that they find useful, for example. A packet goes a step further and gives them an actual place to do so. A lesson plan might say, "The teacher should read the passage with students." *Double Planning* clarifies this: What should the students be doing? Is listening sufficient? They'll be a lot more successful if you tell them what to listen for (examples of irony) and if you plan for them to be jotting notes while you read. You might even think about where they should jot those notes. Their actions while you're teaching are key drivers of how much students learn, this is to say, so it should be part of the planning process.

For teachers like Christine that often means not just planning for students to answer a given question in writing, say, but providing a specific place that communicates to students, in its design or in the directions, whether they are casually brainstorming—in which case the packet might include bullets or a box with no lines—or writing multisentence paragraphs—in which case she would surely want not only lines (and enough of them to communicate her expectations for length) but perhaps a space for outlining as well. A packet like Christine's does this. It translates her plan into a document students can work from directly to ensure efficiency and simplicity. There's space to take notes and a reminder of what to take notes about.

Do you have to have a packet, then? No. Would high school students preparing for college be better served by the experience of note-taking sometimes, often, or perhaps always? Yes. But the lesson should still be double planned, perhaps via a sort of T-chart in which the teacher's actions are described on the left side and what students should be doing on the right.

Still, don't sleep on the packet. Its value is high—a fact that's mildly ironic because some educators dismiss materials copied and given to students as "worksheets" and presume that implies banality and superficiality. A reminder then: The means by which instructional materials are reproduced and disseminated has no correlation to their quality.

Designing a lesson packet in fact is one of the most effective tools for *Double Planning*. Here are five ways well-designed packets can improve your teaching and increase students' learning.

## Goal 1: Everything in One Place

A well-designed packet provides students with all (or many) of the lesson materials in one place, where they are easily accessible, and thus minimizes the need to distribute additional materials, take out new documents, and move back and forth between them. Students can read and write about a text seamlessly in one place. Christine's packet, for example, includes the nonfiction articles she'll read to illuminate the chapter from the novel as well as definitions of the vocabulary she'll teach, the *Exit Ticket*, and various places to take notes. It's all in one place and that streamlines her lesson.

## Goal 2: Synergy with Pacing

The packet allows Christine to be able to manage the student experience easily and effectively: she can jump ahead and skip an activity to save a little time but still have students complete it for homework; she can have students go back and reread a passage or check the Do Now at almost no transaction cost. It reduces the time required to change tasks and activities to a minimum. She can skip passing out the vocabulary sheets or collecting notes. Although it may seem trivial, saving minutes this way each day helps her add back days of lost instructional time to each school year.

As I discuss in the chapter on pacing, one way to draw attention to mileposts (see Chapter Six, "Pacing,")—reference points inserted along the route of a journey to make the distance covered more visible to travelers—is evident in Christine's packet. Each question or activity stands out as something new and discrete as opposed to a muddled mass of undifferentiated responses to the novel. Students can see clearly that they are moving dynamically from activity to activity.

One effective tool I've seen in some packets—particularly London's Michaela Community School—is line numbering. If you're spending a significant chunk of time discussing a passage, it's often worth copying it into your packet with line numbers added to ensure more continuity, quality, and efficiency in discussion. The following image shows the first paragraphs of Linda Sue Park's novel *A Single Shard* with line numbers added. Reading this, Carlise can easily draw the class's attention to Tree-ear's use of the phrase "later today" in line 9 rather than everyone using up their working memory searching for the spot "in the middle of the third paragraph" she's referring to. Afterwards, the teacher might draw students quickly and easily back to a different spot: "What does the narrator's reference to 'the well-fed of the village' in line 3 tell us?"

---

1    "Eh, Tree-ear! Have you hungered well today?" Crane-man
2    called out as Tree-ear drew near the bridge.

3    The well-fed of the village greeted each other politely by
4    saying, "Have you eaten well today?" Tree-ear and his friend
5    turned the greeting inside out for their own little joke.

6    Tree-ear squeezed the bulging pouch that he wore at his waist.
7    He had meant to hold back the good news, but the excitement
8    spilled out of him. "Crane-man! A good thing that you greeted
9    me so just now, for later today we will have to use the proper
10  words!" He held the bag high. Tree-ear was delighted when
11  Crane-man's eyes widened in surprise. He knew that Crane-man
12  would guess at once–only one thing could give a bag that kind
13  of smooth fullness. Not carrot-tops or chicken bones,
14  which protruded in odd lumps. No, the bag was filled with rice.

15  Crane-man raised his walking crutch in a salute. "Come, my
16  young friend! Tell me how you came by such a fortune–a tale
17  worth hearing, no doubt!"

---

## Goal 3: A Clear Road Map

When you have a million things on your mind, it's easy to overlook an activity, forget a question, or neglect a topic that you intended to cover. Because *Double Plan* packets provide teachers with such a clear road map about what they and students should do at every step, teachers are less likely to let activities slip through the cracks or to shortchange important content.

On a similar note, when you script your questions into your packets, it also holds you accountable to ask them in the same form that you planned. This prevents you from unintentionally diluting the rigor of your planned questions or leading students astray with tangential prompts (for more information, see Chapter Nine). The same holds true for *What to Do* directions: The more clearly you script those into your packets, the easier it will be to ensure that students do what you planned, in the manner you intended.

## Goal 4: Standardize the Format

Well-designed packets *Standardize the Format* (see technique 8). Everyone in Christine's class answers question number 6 in the same place and she can circulate quickly and easily and get a strong sense of what they are writing about because she's always looking in the same place. It makes it easier to move quickly and to compare students' written work with her exemplars, which she's written in the same place into her own packet. What they're doing is mirrored on her page. The demands on working memory are reduced and her capacity to observe accurately is increased.

Formatting the workspace for students helps in other ways too. Whether you include eight blank lines or two after a writing prompt implicitly communicates to students how extensive their answer should be; a "notes" box during a *Turn and Talk* reminds them that they should (or could) take notes on what they discuss.

## Goal 5: Embedded Adaptability

Another detail of Christine's packet worth noticing: a partial answer to the ageless question of what's out there for the strivers who are done first on the *Do Now* or some other question and want to know what's next. Will their teacher have something ready? What if she doesn't see them? Will they have to sit and wait for the class to catch up? What about the kid she doesn't realize is a striver, but who wants to show her he can be? On Christine's *Do Now* there's a challenge question embedded at the end, waiting for the strivers. Strive on.

This is a reminder that better planning does not imply a loss of flexibility—the opposite, in fact. Troy Prep math teacher Bryan Belanger regularly includes more questions in his packets than his students will do in a lesson so that he can jump ahead to harder problems or double back for more review, depending on student progress. Brooklyn teacher Taryn Pritchard divides her independent practice into sections by level of challenge: "mild," "medium," and "spicy." That way she and her students can adapt by adding more "mild" or "spicy" work to their diets, as a group or as individuals; thus, students can speed ahead or double back on their own. Other teachers embed "Challenge" or "Deep Thinking" questions in their packets. Individual students can try them on their own or if things are going well the teacher can use them as a class activity.

## TECHNIQUE 5: KNOWLEDGE ORGANIZERS

Few schools have had as profound an impact on the education sector as London's Michaela Community School. Founded at a moment when schools were often encouraged to eschew facts and knowledge in favor of transferable "thinking skills," tiny

Michaela dissented, and set about to build a school with a true knowledge curriculum. At first, they were a lonely dissenting voice, but they were unapologetic and unwavering, and several years later their results, combined with a larger researched-based return to the recognition of the crucial role knowledge plays in thinking, have caused the world to sit up and take notice.

One of the key tools in Michaela's work was developed by then–English teacher Joe Kirby. The idea was a *Knowledge Organizer*, a one-page document that outlines the most important knowledge students need to understand to engage a unit of study. It presents that information in a format designed to make it easy to encode in memory. The idea was straightforward: Students shouldn't have to guess what it is important to remember. Make it clear to them what's most important to know; put it in one place so it's easy for them to study. Over time the idea has caught on. In thousands of schools, each unit begins with a one-page summary of critical background knowledge that allows students to think more deeply about the unit and that forms the framework of their knowledge about the topic after the unit is completed.

The version I recommend may place slightly more emphasis than Joe's on knowledge that students should know at the beginning of the unit to fill in knowledge gaps that might prevent them from understanding the unit, but either way it's both a short-term strategy—it makes students learn from and enjoy the unit more—and a long-term strategy—it systematically gives students a wide-ranging knowledge of critical facts. Either way you frame it, given how much we now know about the profound importance of background knowledge in higher-order thinking, the idea is powerful.

As Joe envisioned them, *Knowledge Organizers* should be one-page documents (or, occasionally, one page with two sides, if it's heavy with things like maps). The organization—the categories—are often nearly as important as the knowledge. Categories like key terms, important figures, and a timeline of important events communicate what sorts of things are important to know when exploring a topic.

If you set out to design a *Knowledge Organizer* for *Number the Stars*, the book Christine is reading, for example, you might include a timeline of key events in World War II. You might also want to include key historical figures and terms: It's hard to make sense of the book if you don't know what an occupation is or what the Star of David symbolizes. When you do, the scenes where Annemarie's little sister speaks boldly and dismissively to a Nazi soldier or where Annemarie grips her friend's Star of David necklace suddenly make sense. *Now* students can analyze them. If they don't understand those things—and it's a big assumption that all students do—it's going to be hard to read the book well.

Reflect back on the earlier exercise in which I asked you to speculate on why the sky might appear green. Imagine how much more substantively you'd have been able to engage in that activity if you knew a body of rules and principles describing the physics of visible light and why colors appear as they do. Your reflections probably would have been much more rigorous.

To demonstrate the various ways a *Knowledge Organizer* might work, here are two fairly different ones that my team developed for two books in our Reading Reconsidered Curriculum. The first is for *Brown Girl Dreaming*, Jacqueline Woodson's verse memoir of her girlhood in South Carolina and New York during the Civil Rights era.

*Brown Girl Dreaming* **Knowledge Organizer**

| Poetic and Literary Terms | | |
|---|---|---|
| *Poems are written in verse. Unlike **prose**, the ordinary language used in speaking or writing, **verse** has a rhythmic structure and often rhymes.* | | |
| Term | Definition | Example |
| Free Verse | Nonrhyming lines that do not follow a formal poetic structure | |
| Poetic License | The understanding that a poet might change or "break" rules of grammar that govern other forms of writing | *february 12, 1963* |
| Rhythm | A pattern of sound set by the syllables in lines of poetry | |
| Refrain | A phrase or line repeated within a poem | *Hold fast to dreams* |
| Stanza | A series of lines arranged together to create divisions in a poem | |
| Enjambment | The running-over of a sentence or phrase from one poetic line to the next, without end punctuation | |
| End-Stopped | A poetic line ending with punctuation to show the completion of a phrase | *Uhmm, my mother says.* |
| Anaphora | The repetition of a word or phrase at the beginning of lines or stanzas | *Maybe the car [. . .]* |
| | | *Maybe right before [. . .]* |
| Caesura | A pause within a line of poetry, usually marked by punctuation | *can grow up free. Can grow up* |
| Haiku | A Japanese poetic form; three unrhymed lines of 5, 7, and 5 syllables | *Even the silence has a story to tell you. Just listen. Listen.* |
| Language of Memory and Storytelling | | |
| **Memoir** | A collection of memories written about important moments and events in person's life | |
| **Subjectivity** | The way a person's memory or judgment is shaped by their opinions or experiences | |
| **Reliability** | The degree to which a person's narration or memory is trustworthy or accurate | |

| Words to Describe Family and Heritage | |
|---|---|
| **Ancestry** | The line of people in a family's past |
| **Genealogy** | An account of a person or family's descent from past generations |
| **Heredity** | The passing of personal characteristics from one family's generation to another; we say that a trait that is passed (e.g., brown eyes) is **inherited** or **hereditary** |

| Timeline of the Text | | |
|---|---|---|
| In Jaqueline Woodson's Family | Year | In the United States |
| Woodson's great-great-grandfather is born free in Ohio | 1832 | Slavery is still legal and practiced throughout the southern United States |
| | 1865 | The **13th Amendment** to the U.S. Constitution abolishes slavery, but **segregation** and racism continue to restrict the rights of Black Americans |
| | 1916 | The **Great Migration**, a mass movement of Black Americans out of the American South, begins |
| | 1954 | In *Brown v Board of Education*, the Supreme Court outlaws segregation in public schools |
| | 1955 | **Rosa Parks** is arrested, beginning the **Montgomery bus boycott** |
| | 1960 | **Greensboro lunch counter sit-ins** begin sit-in protest movement to desegregate public spaces; **Ruby Bridges** desegregates her elementary school |
| Jaqueline Woodson is born in Columbus, Ohio | 1963 | The **March on Washington** is one of the biggest events of the **Civil Rights Movement** |
| Woodson and her family move in with their grandparents in Greenville, SC | Mid-1960s | |
| Sterling High School in Greenville, SC, burns down | 1967 | |
| Woodson and her siblings move to New York City with their mother | Late 1960s | The **Black Panther Party** is founded to advocate for Black American rights |
| | 1968 | **Martin Luther King, Jr.** is assassinated |
| Woodson writes *Butterflies*, her first book of poems | Early 1970s | |

Reading and making sense of several hundred pages of verse as rich as Woodson's will require some technical terminology so the organizer starts with terms like *refrain*, *stanza*, and *poetic license*. Now students will be armed with a range of terms to discuss Woodson's craft. And they can communicate their ideas to each other because everyone in the room will know the term when a peer uses it. Just as important is historical context, and in this case a two-sided timeline helps students both understand important events in the Civil Rights movement and also understand when they happened relative to events in the Woodson narrative.

Compare by contrast the *Knowledge Organizer* for Pam Muñoz Ryan's novel *Esperanza Rising*. It includes two timelines. There's one to help students understand Mexico, where the first half of the novel takes place and where the civil unrest post-revolution sets the plot in motion. There's a second one outlining the history of California, where the second half of the novel takes place, and describing key social events of the era: the Great Depression; the Okie Migration; the Dust Bowl. This demonstrates the double power of a *Knowledge Organizer*. Students will understand the book more—and enjoy it more and bring more insight to it—by knowing these things as they read it, and they will end the unit with knowledge of those events that they will carry forward. Both novels are now truly historical fiction as opposed to stories set in past times that the students reading can scarcely understand.

| History of Mexico <1930 | |
|---|---|
| The first part of the book takes place in Mexico, mostly in Aguascalientes, a region in the central part of the country. | |
| 1521 | Spain conquers the Aztecs and establishes the Spanish Empire in Mexico. They control and discriminate against native people ("Indians"). |
| 1821 | War of independence: Spain defeated and Mexico founded. It is larger than today and includes the present-day U.S. Southwest. |
| 1846 | Mexican-American War begins when the United States annexes Texas. |
| 1848 | Mexico loses Mexican-American War and gives up Texas, California, New Mexico, and Arizona. Sixty years of rule by dictators follows. |
| 1910 | Mexican Revolution begins; **Campesinos** (poor farm workers) promised rights if they win. They do and the last dictator is forced out. |
| 1917 | Adoption of the Mexican Constitution, but there is continued conflict. |
| 1930 | Period of relative stability begins. |

| History of California | |
|---|---|
| The second part of the book takes place in California's San Joaquin Valley, the primary food-growing region in the United States. | |
| 1846 | The United States takes over California as a result of the Mexican-American War. |
| 1848 | Gold is discovered. Thousands migrate to seek their fortune as part of the **Gold Rush**. |
| 1850 | California is admitted to the Union as the 31st state. Population < 350,000 |
| 1890 | Mass irrigation to and farming of the **Central Valley** and **San Joaquin Valley** begins. |
| 1910 | California becomes the leading food- and oil-producing state in the United States. |
| 1920 | **Population explosion:** population of California reaches 3.5M (10x the population in 1850). |
| 1933 | **Okies** (migrants from Oklahoma and other states) begin arriving—as many as 7,000 per month. |
| Terms for the Labor Movement | |
| **Migrant Workers** | Farmers who move from place to place to harvest different crops in different seasons |
| **Strike** | When workers refuse to work and try to prevent others from working to get better conditions or pay |
| **Picket** | The act of standing outside a business and protesting, usually while carrying signs and sometimes preventing people from entering |
| **Wages** | Hourly pay given to workers such as farmers |
| **Conditions** | The setting in which workers work: can be safe/unsafe; clean/dirty |
| **Union** | An organized group of workers who take action together |
| The Migration Crisis | |
| A westward migration of farmers from the Great Plains happened just before Esperanza arrives in California. | |
| **Great Depression** | The stock market crashes in 1929, wiping out much of people's savings and devastating the economy. The unemployment rate reaches 25%. |
| **Dust Bowl** | Overfarming on the Great Plains leads to massive dust storms that ruin farms. Tens of thousands of farmers and their families are forced off their land. |
| **The Golden State** | Farmers head west with their possessions to seek jobs in California—"the Golden State"—which seems like paradise. |
| **Okie Migration** | Desperate, poor, farmers arrive in masses—up to 7,000 a month. There are not enough jobs and they are often turned away at the border. They are disparagingly called "Okies." |
| **Labor Unrest** | Farm workers form unions and strike in response to poor treatment by farm owners. |

| Key Quotes |
|---|
| *Between them ran a deep river. Esperanza stood on one side and Miguel stood on the other and the river could never be crossed. (p. 18)* |
| *"I hear that in the United States, you do not need una palanca [a lever]." (p. 75)* |
| *"I am poor but I am rich. I have my children, I have a garden with roses, and I have my faith and the memories of those who have gone before me. What more is there?" (p. 76)* |
| *"Full bellies and Spanish blood go hand in hand." (p. 79)* |

| Key Literary Terms | | |
|---|---|---|
| Term | Definition | *Esperanza Rising* Example |
| Juxtaposition | Placing two (or more) images or ideas close together to emphasize the contrast between them | Esperanza's clothing vs. the campesinos', the hands of a wealthy woman from Mexico and a poor campesina |
| Personification | The attribution of human characteristics or emotions to inanimate or nonliving things | "This whole valley breathes and lives" |
| Motif | An idea, symbol, or image that occurs multiple times throughout a text | The river that divides Esperanza and Miguel |
| Symbol | When an object, person, or idea in a text has an additional meaning beyond its literal one | Papa's roses, Abuelita's crocheted blanket |
| Foreshadowing | A hint that suggests what events might happen in the future | Esperanza pricks her finger on a thorn |

One takeaway from these examples might be about theme and variation. These *Knowledge Organizers* for two middle-grade novels with mid-twentieth-century settings are both similar and different. There are consistent principles but no formula.

You're probably wondering about adapting *Knowledge Organizers* to other grades and subjects. To help, here's a reflection by chemistry teacher Sadie McCleary on designing and using *Knowledge Organizers* and an example of one of her *Knowledge Organizers*. After that I'll share some examples of *Knowledge Organizers* for much younger students.

# Sadie McCleary's Reflections on Knowledge Organizers

I almost always include vocabulary terms in my *Knowledge Organizers*. These are the foundational terms students should know in order to increase the rigor of the questioning possible by the teacher and increase the quality of student responses. Note that these are not the only terms/concepts students will learn this unit! They will continue to build on these and complicate their ideas. These are simply a starting place.

Studying is a skill! Remember to teach students to study with *Knowledge Organizers*. This needs to be modeled and students need to practice—even simple vocabulary drills.

- Take two minutes several times in the first unit to show students how to fold their KO to hide the definitions and self-quiz. Follow this up with several minutes of students doing their own silent self-quizzing and an oral drill or recall quiz.

- Partner quizzing: Provide opportunities for students to quiz one another for one to three minutes in class. Explicitly name for students that this should be replicated at home with a family member or friend. Model partner quizzing for students, and set clear times for when partners should switch who is quizzing whom. If time allows, follow up partner quizzing with an oral drill or recall quiz. You can grade these sometimes but you don't need to. Research on frequent low-stakes assessment shows how effective this is without grades.

I often ask students to annotate diagrams, definitions, or other information in their *Knowledge Organizers* during lessons. This adds to their understanding of the core concepts and makes the organizer into a living document. It also draws their attention. If we're getting out our organizers to add a note, it must be something very important.

You can build the organizer into the fabric of your class. Reference it frequently. If a student is stuck, ask them to check their organizer first, often before they raise their hand in class. You can make it part of their desk setup: at the beginning of class every students should have out homework, notebook, *Knowledge Organizer*, and pencil.

# An Example of One of Sadie's Knowledge Organizers

Knowledge Organizer #4
Unit I – Matter: Properties of Gases & Calculations        NAME: _____,        PD: ___

## Vocabulary:

|  |  |
|---|---|
| Heat | Form of energy that flows between two samples of matter due to the difference in temperature. Heat flows from a sample with higher average kinetic energy to a sample with lower avg. kinetic energy. |
| Temperature | The measurement of average kinetic energy of a sample. Units used: K, °C (converted between using equation C below). |
| Kinetic Energy | The energy an object possesses due to its motion. Calculated using equation B shown below. |
| Pressure | Force exerted by the substance per unit area on another substance. The pressure of a gas is the force that the gas exerts on the walls of its container. Units used: atm, kPa, mmHg |
| Volume | Amount of space occupied by a three-dimensional (3-D) object. Units used: mL, L (liquid), $cm^3$ (solid) |
| Velocity | Speed of an object (primarily particles in this case). Units frequently used are m/s or cm/s. |
| Mass | Measure of the amount of matter in an object. Units used: g, kg |
| Particle Diagram | Visual representation of the particles of a substance, where the particles are shown as dots. Allows us to represent samples in different phases. |

## Equations:

**Equation A. Combined Gas Law:**

$$\frac{P_1 V_1}{T_1} = \frac{P_2 V_2}{T_2}$$

- $P_1$ = initial pressure
- $V_1$ = initial volume
- $T_1$ = initial temp
- $P_2$ = final pressure
- $V_2$ = final volume
- $T_2$ = final temp

**Equation B. Kinetic Energy:**

$$KE = \frac{1}{2} mv^2$$

- $KE$ = kinetic energy
- $m$ = mass
- $v$ = velocity

**Equation C. Temp Conversions:**

$$°C + 273 = K$$

- °C = Celsius
- K = Kelvin

## Content

- The relationship between pressure and volume at constant temperature is

- The relationship between temperature and pressure at constant volume is

- The relationship between temperature and volume at constant pressure is

## Relevant Diagrams/Calculations

**Calculation Ex 1: T conversions**

**Calculation Example 3: Combined Gas Law**

### Diagram Set 1. P. V. T. Graphs

**Diagram 1a:** $P$ vs. $V$ with constant $T$

**Diagram 1b:** $V$ vs. $T$ with constant $P$

**Diagram 1c:** $P$ vs. $T$ with constant $V$

**Calculation Example 2: Combined Gas Law**

# Primary-Level Knowledge Organizers

## Year One Science: Seasons and the Weather

### "Foul Weather"

| | |
|---|---|
| Flood | So much rain that rivers overflow their banks. |
| Hurricane | Huge swirling storm with heavy rains and dangerous winds. Comes off the water. Take cover! |
| Blizzard | A big snow storm. Often windy and hard to see. |
| Tornado | A small but dangerous swirling cloud. Formed on land mostly. Take cover! |

### Measuring Weather

| | |
|---|---|
| Data | A collection of facts, often numbers, that can tell us important things |
| Rain Gauge | A tool for measuring how much rain has fallen |
| Weather Vane | A tool that measures the direction and speed of wind |
| Thermometer | A tool that measures how warm or cold it is |

### Types of Clouds

Cirrus Cloud — Thin and delicate, high in the sky, "wispy" like feathers

Cumulus Cloud — Puffy or fluffy, like cotton balls, sometimes piled up high.

Stratus Cloud — "Blanket clouds," low, thick without a shape.

### The Seasons

| | |
|---|---|
| Spring | After Winter. Plants begin growing. Temperatures warm. Animals come out of hibernation. |
| Summer | After Spring. The warmest season. Days are longest and the sun rises early and sets late. |
| Autumn | After Summer. Temperatures cool and days get shorter. Leaves fall. Crops are harvested. |
| Winter | After Autumn. The coldest season. Short days. Trees are often bare. Some animals hibernate. |

### Ghana and the Ashanti

| | |
|---|---|
| Ghana | A country in West Africa with grasslands and rich forests. |
| Ashanti | A group of people who have lived in Ghana for over 400 years. Storytelling and art are important in their culture. |

| Folktales and Mythology | |
|---|---|
| oral tradition | • the practice of a culture or group of telling stories out loud instead of writing them down |
| folktale | • a story passed down from one generation to another as part of an oral tradition<br>• helps us understand something about the people who tell it |
| myth | • a traditional story meant to explain something about the world<br>• usually have magical or impossible elements |
| moral | • a lesson a story teaches about what is right or wrong |

Note that *Knowledge Organizers* need not be as complex as the examples included here. Just because it shouldn't be more than one page doesn't mean it has to take up the whole page. A *Knowledge Organizer* could be perfectly good if it consisted of a single box with key literary terms or people to know, say, as a starting point, and if starting with less helps make it easy for you to get started and try them out, all the better.

How *Knowledge Organizers* are used is just as important as how they are designed. They are intended to be used frequently for retrieval practice and self-quizzing, if not every day, then a least several times a week. Constant quizzing and review encodes the content in long-term memory. At Michaela, when I visited, homework every night was simply to review and quiz yourself on the *Knowledge Organizers* from each of your classes. It was so simple and direct. The homework was always the same, so it was easy to do. Parents quizzed children while they cooked dinner. (They often focused on just one portion of the organizer rather than trying to learn the whole thing at once.) That's why one thing you'll notice about these *Knowledge Organizers* is that they are designed with limited verbiage so that students can learn the answers by heart, and with two columns to facilitate easy self-quizzing by covering up one side.

*Knowledge Organizers* are sometimes confused with study guides, which are documents that summarize a unit of study after it is completed—often to aid in preparation for a test. That's not what a *Knowledge Organizer* does. It goes out at the beginning of a unit to ensure all students have the knowledge that will help them engage in each lesson fully.

*Knowledge Organizers* appear in the lesson preparation chapter because designing them is useful for the teacher as well. Thinking through what students will need to know to be successful in your unit has the benefit of causing you to think deeply about what they need to know and often do a bit of research. In writing a *Knowledge Organizer* you'll come to know ten times more than what you put into the organizer. In other words, it's a habit that builds your own content knowledge, and knowledge matters for teachers, too.

## Notes

1. *Culturally Responsive Education in the Classroom*, p. 70.
2. Ibid., p. 66.
3. Another is that they are using the Reading Reconsidered Curriculum, which gives me the opportunity to observe that having a lesson plan allows them to spend more time preparing to teach (and perhaps adapting content) than sourcing content and writing a detailed plan. When a teacher's time is limited, preparation is often a better use of it than planning.
4. *The Invisible Gorilla*, p. 17.
5. Micheline T. H. Chi, Paul J. Feltovich, and Robert Glaser, "Categorization and Representation Physics Problems by Experts and Novices," *Cognitive Science: A Multidisciplinary Journal* (April 1981). The implication of the article for teachers is discussed in Carl Hendrick and Paul Kirschner's excellent *How Learning Happens: Seminal Works in Educational Psychology and What They Mean in Practice*.
6. Ellis Cose, *The Envy of the World: On Being a Black Man in America* (2002), p. 69.
7. Tatum discusses Cose in *Teaching Reading to Black Adolescent Males* (2005), p. 13.
8. For what it's worth, this was most likely to happen in their foreign language classes, marking a dramatic contrast with schools in other countries where the study of other languages was treated as a serious endeavor, the equivalent of math, science, English, and history. It most certainly isn't that in most U.S. schools I've been to.

# Chapter 3

# Check for Understanding

The great basketball coach John Wooden—a former English teacher before he won ten NCAA championships in twelve years at UCLA—defined teaching as knowing the difference between "I taught it" and "they learned it." Part of what's so profound about this perfect expression of the core challenge of teaching—in any setting—is its calm presumption that errors will emerge. It is not whether, but when. Every teacher seeks to present material clearly and memorably so that their students grasp meaning and importance. You want the initial presentation to be as good as it can be, but mopping up afterwards is inevitable. No matter how well you explain or demonstrate the material, gaps in understanding will emerge. It's what you do next, how you respond to errors, that matters most. Will you see misunderstandings? Will you ignore them? Can you fix them? Will you blame students and express your frustration? There will be a gap between what you taught and what they understood. Regardless of why it will be your job to fix it.

With that in mind I can safely say that one of the most useful teaching videos you're likely to see is *Denarius Frazier: Remainder*. It's a thing of quiet beauty and I'll discuss it extensively in this chapter. But for now here's a brief overview and some highlights.

The video starts with students hard at work on a pair of problems. Denarius wants to use the independent work to gauge how his students are doing, so he begins to go from student to student to observe their work. Quickly he assesses where each student is and provides useful and supporting feedback. "[You're] killing it," he tells one young man. "Keep going," he tells a young woman. "Make sure you have the remainder and the quotient."

"What's going on here?" he asks the next young woman, and spots the fact that her digits are not lined up. A few seats later he tells one young woman quickly, "Oh, much better, thank you," affirming both her progress and his own awareness of the progress of her learning.

As he works, Denarius is able to assess not only the progress of individuals but also of the class. The class is dividing polynomials and the most frequent issue is lack of clarity about how to find the remainder. He pauses, presents an example to the class, guides them through an analysis of where it was effective and where it went wrong, and sends them back to their quiet, productive practice.

Every student feels seen and supported. It is evident that their teacher can and will help them succeed. It's a case study in how effective teaching builds relationships. Because Denarius is alert to gaps in understanding as they emerge, he is able to help each student, calmly and steadily, and create an environment of trust and respect. The trust, as I argued in Chapter One, is not a precondition to Denarius teaching them, but in many ways an outcome. At the very least the two develop in synergy. You teach me well and I will come to have faith in you.

This chapter is about the gap between teaching and learning: about how to see it, how to respond to it, and how to make students comfortable with the struggle it implies. It's going to be technical stuff. What should you look at and look for? How can you respond to mistakes? How can you get students to reveal misunderstandings to you willingly? But don't be fooled. The consequences of a teacher mastering such technical details are not arcane. As Denarius shows, they create the conditions under which students thrive.

## TECHNIQUE 6: REPLACE SELF-REPORT

One of the most common methods teachers use to find out whether their students understand what they've been teaching is to ask them directly, "Do you understand?" This seems logical enough, but it turns out to be a relatively ineffective (if easily improved upon) way to assess student understanding.

Let's say a science teacher has just finished explaining cellular structure to her sixth graders. "OK," she says, "those are the basics of cellular structure. Does everyone understand?" Or perhaps she's a bit more specific: "Is everyone clear on the differences between plant and animal cells?"

She'd likely get what seems like confirmation: mutters and nods from a smattering of students. Perhaps a "yeah" or "uh-huh," though perhaps she won't hear anything. Either way, she's likely to take it as evidence that students are with her—call it *apparent assent*—and say something like: "Good. Let's push on to the role of chloroplasts."

But questions that ask students to evaluate their own understanding of something they've just learned tend to yield false confirmation—especially when they are framed as a yes/no question. The primary reason for this is that the questions rely on self-report, which is notoriously inaccurate. People, especially novices, often don't know what they don't know about a topic, and even if they do they are often unlikely to acknowledge it when asked.

If, for example, you ask a group of students, "Are you clear on the causes of the American Revolution?" and everyone says yes, it is because they are clear on *the causes they are aware of knowing about at the moment.* If they missed some, if their conception contains misinformation, they won't know it without some way of checking themselves against a fuller description of the concepts they should know and which, to you, are implicit in the question. Ironically, someone with deep understanding of the causes of the Revolution is more likely to answer in the negative: "I still don't totally understand why the Intolerable Acts unified dissent rather than isolating colonial radicals . . ."

Ask me, a novice, "Are you clear on the differences between plant and animal cells?" and really you are asking me, "Are you aware of some differences between plant and animal cells?" or "Are you aware that there are differences between plant and animal cells?" "Yes," I will tell you, as I think of those things I do know which come readily to mind. *They are shaped differently and plant cells have a cell wall that's relatively inflexible,* I think. *Got it.* As I tell you this, though, I remain unaware that the nucleus is positioned differently within the cell, and I have no idea what lysosomes are. My honest answer is yes, but I don't know what I don't know. Sadly then, the less your students know about a topic, the more likely their *apparent assent* is to be inaccurate.

However, even this example presumes that I am trying very hard to share everything I know about plant and animal cells with you, my teacher. Just as often there are social and psychological barriers that prevent students from revealing their confusion. Let's say that I am aware that I didn't understand the difference between plant and animal cells. Saying "Actually, I don't know" means stopping the room—causing the teacher to go back and re-explain, when the presumption is clearly that she and my classmates do not want to. It means appearing to be, possibly, the only person in the room who didn't get it. Or the only person in the room who doesn't get that you're not supposed to say you don't get it. All this for the uncertainty that the re-explanation will really help. It's easier just to tell myself I'll figure it out on my own. Such factors prevent most people, not just students, from speaking up when they are confused. When was the last time you stopped the room during a meeting to say, "Wait, I don't get it"? If a colleague did this, what are the odds that you felt (or expressed) appreciation rather than exasperation? Students may occasionally say, "No, I don't get it," but not reliably so. There are too many implicit social pressures pushing them to keep their confusion to themselves.

A final factor that makes "Everybody get it?" questions ineffective is the format of the questions. They offer two bad choices. In most cases students' understanding is somewhere in the middle; whether they get "it" is actually a series of questions in which the answer is yes to some and no to others. The answer to a yes/no "Do you get it?" question requires the conflation of a lot of data points; it causes students to choose one oversimplification or the other.

The good news is that when we ask questions like "Everybody get it?" we are recognizing that we are at a point when it would be beneficial to check for understanding. If we notice when we ask these sorts of questions, we can replace them with some more productive alternatives, what I call "targeted questions," specific, objective questions focused on the content in question and asked in an open-ended format.

Imagine for a moment that our sixth-grade science teacher notices herself saying "Everybody get it?" during her introduction to plant and animal cell differences and tries to replace that question with something better. She might then say:

"OK, let's just check a few of the key ideas. If I was looking at a photograph of some cells and they were rounded and spaced randomly, would I be looking at plant or animal cells? Jasmine?"

"Good, and if I were looking at plant cells, what would cause them to have a more rectangular pattern? Louis?"

"Great. So which types of cells have a membrane, Kelsey, plant cells, animal cells, or both?"

"Good. Finally, Shawn, what are lysosomes and which kinds of cells would I find them in?"

First, you'll notice that our science teacher's questions are now objective. They don't ask whether students *think* they know, they ask them to *demonstrate* if they do, so the accuracy of the data is now far better.

Second, these are not yes/no questions. This makes it harder to guess the right answer or to get it right with only the most basic understanding.

One common solution to the problem of apparent assent is worth being wary of. Many teachers try to replace the yes/no question with a signal from students: *Thumbs up if you understand the differences between plant and animal cell structure, thumbs down if you don't, thumbs sideways if you're not sure.* This may seem like an improvement—you're likely to get more responses from students—but the problems of self-report remain—you're still relying on students' perception of whether they know something and the fact is, even if they're totally honest, many are probably still wrong on that account. Putting your thumb up or down may make the self-report more engaging and thus remove some of the awkward silence but in terms of giving you better data on your students' understanding, it's mostly an illusion. Targeted questions are far better.

Targeted questions work best when you plan them in advance, by the way. It's hard to think of the four questions that will quickly reveal where your students stand on the spur of the moment. And if you're trying to think of the next question you won't be able to listen to the answers very well. Or to think about your tone of voice. That's important because if you asked targeted questions in an environment where, say, you smiled warmly to show that getting it wrong would not make you frustrated, then you would make the opportunity to check for understanding more productive. Smiling when you ask your targeted question or perhaps when students struggle to answer reminds your class that you want honesty and that knowing about misconceptions early makes them easier to fix. This is a topic I will discuss further in technique 12, *Culture of Error*.

There's one other thing that will help you ensure that your students succeed: *Cold Calling* (see technique 34). This technique allows you to gather data from a sample of students from around the room. If you rely instead only on students who volunteer to answer, you will gather erroneous data. Students who volunteer to answer mostly do so when they think they know. Students who don't think they know are less likely to raise their hands. Unless you find a way to call on those pupils, you will always overestimate the proportion of your class that understands a concept.

*Cold Calling* also helps in another way. It helps you to move quickly through your questions. That might seem counterintuitive; wouldn't a teacher want to assess as thoroughly as possible? But one reason why teachers so routinely recognize the need to check for understanding but fail to act on it—or act on it in a cursory way—is time pressure. There's never enough time, as you know if you're a teacher, and taking five minutes to circle back to double-check that everyone understands is stressful when you have ground to cover. If it takes forever and disrupts your pacing, or causes you to drop the last activity of your lesson plan, *of course* you won't do it. But if you could double-check in thirty seconds then you might really do it, so one of the keys to replacing self-report with targeted questions is to do it quickly—ideally in less than a minute. If (and only if) you can do it fast will you be likely to do it often. So even if it yields imperfect data, seek to gather what you can through the best questions you can design in a minute or less. You can use the remaining time to review if necessary.

Asking targeted questions can be just as valuable for assessing understanding of *tasks students are about to do* as it is for assessing understanding of *content you've just taught*. If you're sending students off for eight minutes of independent or partner work, it's really good to ask them a few targeted questions about the task so that you don't find out half-way through that they weren't really clear on how to write up their discussion notes or even that they had to write them. Generally speaking, the longer the task you are sending students off to do, the more important it is to assess their clarity on the task beforehand via targeted questions.

Recently I observed a lesson where a teacher wanted her students to read a text, note phrases and phrasings that were intentionally repetitive, and track shifts in who the implicit audience was. They were supposed to work solo for five minutes and then discuss with a partner.

Before she sent students off to do this task, she asked them targeted questions to review. It took her about twenty seconds and she used *Cold Call* to ensure that she wasn't just calling on the kids who thought they knew:

*Teacher:* Nelson, tell me the two things I want you to look for while you're reading this.
*Nelson:* Repetition and shifts in audience.
*Teacher:* Good, and Tina, what should you do when you see examples of repetition?
*Tina:* Box them in the text.
*Teacher:* Yup. Nice. And Gary, is this partner work or independent work?
*Gary:* First by ourselves, then, after five minutes, work with a partner.
*Teacher:* Perfect. Off you go.

It would be so easy to have some portion of the class set off earnestly but do the wrong task! Ten minutes spent on a task for thirty students is *five hours of learning time* allocated with a single set of directions! Replacing "Everyone understand what we're doing?" with targeted questions is a smart investment.

It's crucial to remember that the goal of targeted questions isn't to be comprehensive but to create a small data sample where previously no data existed. It's often better to be quick and bring data to multiple places in your lesson than to be comprehensive and exhaustive, but assess infrequently.

You might be wondering if this means you're doing something wrong if you still occasionally ask students, "Got it?" or "Everybody clear on that?" Don't worry. There's no reason to be absolutist; you will almost assuredly say those phrases sometimes (I know I do); it's almost impossible to root out familiar rhetorical habits and if you did, the self-consciousness it requires might be a distraction. It's just important to recognize *how often* we use self-report and how much of an illusion it creates. When you use such phrases you are telling yourself: *I have reached a natural transition point where I should check in with students and find out how they are doing.* Hopefully in the aggregate that consciousness can be curative.

The video *Gabby Woolf: Dr Jekyll and Mr Hyde* shows an interesting adaptation of *Replace Self-Report.* If you're not familiar with it, Robert Louis Stevenson's novella is a challenging read. For example, the passage Gabby was reading with her Year 10 class at London's King Solomon Academy begins: "Nearly a year later, in the month of October, 18—, London was startled by a crime of singular ferocity and rendered all the more notable by the high position of the victim. The details were few and startling."

Gabby and her students read the passage aloud—you can hear them doing a lovely job reading it via FASE Reading in the clip *Gabby Woolf: Keystone*—and because of its complexity, Gabby paused after reading and told the class she wanted to "check that you understand." She then projected a series of short targeted questions on the board and gave students a minute or so to review the answers in pairs. The questions were straightforward and designed to yield short answers that revealed student understanding (or the lack of it) quickly:

"What month did the murder take place in?"

"Why was London particularly startled by the victim?"

"Who saw the murder?"

"Where did she see the murder from?

"Who is the murderer?"

Gabby wanted to ensure that despite archaic syntax such as "singular ferocity" and "rendered all the more notable" they had grasped the critical details of what had taken place.

You can see her reviewing these answers with her students in the video. Notice her warm tone and brisk pace. Her constant encouragement—"OK, good"—and the way her *Cold Call* keeps the pace moving allows her to sample a cross-section of students. She also slows the pace of her speech a bit to imply a slightly more reflective tone when she transitions: "Good, so we get the picture of what's happened. Now go back to this question: How does Stevenson sensationalize the murder?"

Had Gabby asked this question without first checking for understanding, students might have engaged in the analysis confused about basic facts. But her questions, planned in advance for precision and speed, allow her to ensure that they are ready for a deeper discussion. The pair review prior to her questions also has the effect of allowing students to encode the answers more strongly in memory. And her tone is warm and her pace brisk, so she accomplishes the whole thing in about a minute.

## TECHNIQUE 7: RETRIEVAL PRACTICE

Forgetting is a constant problem in almost any setting that involves learning—so familiar and pervasive that we almost overlook it. Hours after demonstrating their understanding of juxtaposition in *Romeo and Juliet* or how to find the area of an irregular polygon, students may remember only a fraction of that knowledge. In a few days, they may have forgotten the majority of it. This simple if frequently overlooked fact is one of the most important considerations in teaching: Once students have initially learned something, they quickly begin to forget it.

You have probably seen this play out in your own classroom. On Tuesday you are confident in your students' skill and knowledge. They're solid on the what, why, and how. But when you assess them a week and a half later, it's as if Tuesday's lesson never happened. Then, Rodrigo completed five complex area problems with ease; now you glance over his shoulder and see that he has gotten even simple problems wrong.

There is a silver lining, however, to this persistent challenge. The process of forgetting contains the seeds of its own solution. If you ask students to recall what they learned yesterday about the area of polygons or juxtaposition in *Romeo and Juliet* they will strain to remember but if successful, that struggle will more deeply encode the material in their long-term memories. They will remember a little more and forget a little less quickly.

*Retrieval Practice*, or the process of causing students to recall information they've learned after a strategic delay, is a practical solution to the problem of forgetting. If you graphed the process of retrieval practice it might look something like this, with each repetition along the top axis an iteration of retrieval practice and the percentages on the $y$-axis representing how much of a given body of content students remember.

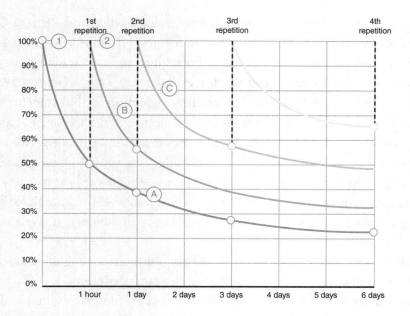

This illustration is an example of what's called a forgetting curve.[1] It represents the nature of forgetting as educational psychologists understand it. At point 1, the end of your lesson, students have acquired a certain amount of knowledge and skills. But as soon as the bell rings, the forgetting begins. And forgetting is a relentless enemy. Even a few minutes later some of the details will have gotten hazy. By the next day students will have forgotten even more—possibly more than half of what they learned. If steps aren't taken to arrest this process, they may lose most of what they know. On the curve, the process of unchecked forgetting is represented by line A.

Point 2, however, represents what happens when you come back to the content and review it. Perhaps this happens the next day. When you do so, students' knowledge is recalled into working memory. Having done so, their knowledge of it returns roughly to the level it was at by the end of the original lesson.

Of course, after this review, forgetting begins again. What students know again starts to slip away. The second downward sloping line (B) captures this. But the rate of forgetting is slower now and the line starts to flatten sooner—which suggests that more remains in long-term memory. If you review again, knowledge is refreshed and forgetting again resumes immediately after—represented by line C—but again the rate is slower yet and the floor (total amount of knowledge retained) is higher still.

As the cognitive psychologists Paul Kirschner, John Sweller, and Richard Clark write: "The aim of all instruction is to alter long-term memory. If nothing has changed in long-term memory, nothing has been learned."[2] If we spent an hour studying the systems of the human body only to have students forget it—a day later, a week later, a month later—then the lesson might have been interesting and engaging, but students would have learned precious little. Even the deepest and most profound discussions remain at risk of evaporating as if into ether. As Harry Fletcher Wood puts it, "Student performance while being taught is a poor indicator of lasting learning." We should by all means check for understanding at the end of a lesson. But just because students appear to know something at the end of that hour does not mean they will know it in a week, a month, or a year. If we want lasting learning, we have to get things into long-term memory, and retrieval practice is the best way to do that.

Since the concept of *Retrieval Practice* is discussed throughout cognitive psychology in a wide variety of contexts, the following is a useful "teacher's definition."

*Retrieval Practice* occurs when learners recall and apply multiple examples of previously learned knowledge or skills after a period of forgetting. This definition suggests two key things. First: intentionality. You might say, "Oh, asking kids about concepts we previously learned? I do that all the time," but what we're talking about here is more than just occasional episodic review—"Remember how we talked about juxtaposition when we read *Romeo and Juliet*?" It's the strategic use of retrieval, systematically and regularly. This might even mean *Retrieval Practice* becomes a discrete part of your lessons—a chunk of time you design with the explicit purpose of causing students to recall important things in strategic ways, probably using tools like *Cold Call* and *Call and Response* to ensure that every student recalls the requisite information. Retrieval in these settings need not be simplistic or rote. A bit of challenge is beneficial, so changing formats or asking students to apply concepts in new ways is likely to help.

Second, the definition suggests strategic delay. Notice on the Forgetting Curve that the delay between rounds of retrieval increases slightly each time. Gradually increasing the intervals between rounds of retrieval aids memory because the best time to remember something is when you have begun to forget it, and the rate of our forgetting is constantly changing. And if nothing else, a glance at the Forgetting Curve should confirm that it is almost impossible to master a concept in a durable and enduring way in a single lesson.[3]

You might be tempted to think of *Retrieval Practice* as a recipe for mere rote memorization, but this is not the case. Retrieval is an opportunity for what Brown, Roediger, and McDaniel call "elaboration": connecting an idea to other ideas, reflecting on it, and expanding it as you review it. Elaboration aids in retrieval, in fact.[4] When a concept is connected to other related ideas and when students can describe it in different ways, it becomes more powerful. So you might, in reviewing juxtaposition, deliberately ask for elaboration. "Asha, what's juxtaposition? Darius, what's an example from *Romeo and Juliet*? Katie, what's another? Roberto, what's another example of two characters who are juxtaposed from something else we've read? Good, and Kyra, in your own words, why might an author use juxtaposition?" The elaboration, causing students to explain and put into new words, to make connections, increases their knowledge of the concept and the likelihood that they will remember it when they need it.

The first half of the video *Christine Torres: Keystone* is a great example of other ways that *Retrieval Practice* can work. Christine is reviewing vocabulary words with students. Notice the richness of the questions Christine asks. *Retrieval Practice* questions don't have to be simple recall. Christine asks her students to apply the vocabulary words they're learning in different ways and new settings. That's important, because words work differently in different settings. To truly understand a word, you'd want students to constantly encounter it in all its nuanced shades of meaning. Christine asks students to know the definition, but also to apply the word in challenging and interesting ways. It's both simple and more elaborated retrieval. Christine makes sure that every student wrestles with almost every question. She uses *Turn and Talk* (see technique 43). For retrieval practice, we can't just take hands from volunteers or let a few highly verbal kids call out answers. We need to cause everyone to remember and apply the concept.

Interestingly, the period of delay between initial learning and retrieval is short in Christine's classroom. Forgetting, she knows, starts right away. With challenging and potentially confusing concepts, especially, it's not too soon to begin retrieving right away. So even though students learned what the words meant just a few minutes ago, Christine is already trying to get them into long-term memory. And Christine will be sure to follow up the next day and/or a few days later—and again a few days after that—with more fun and engaging questions to retrieve and apply their knowledge of their vocabulary words. She also frequently includes previously mastered vocabulary words when she's retrieving new words. In this way they will have both depth and richness of understanding and long-term memory of the words.

It's not just that *more* of the original material remains in long-term memory that matters with *Retrieval Practice*. It's that the knowledge that is there is *easier for students to recall*. After three rounds of review, the neural pathways back to those discussions about juxtaposition in *Romeo and Juliet*, for example, are well worn. When students come upon an example of juxtaposition in some other text they are reading, the examples from Shakespeare will snap readily to mind. They will form connections. Easier retrieval leads to more than just knowing facts, in other words. Having various models of juxtaposition that come easily and naturally to mind becomes a schema—a connected body of knowledge that becomes familiar enough that people can use it quickly and easily to process information at minimal load to working memory as they interact with the world around them. Knowledge in that form—encoded in long-term memory and easily accessed—helps students perceive and understand more. This is one key reason why educational psychologists like Daniel Willingham remind us that knowledge easily accessed in long-term memory is the key to higher-order thinking.[5] The best way to maximize the capacity of working memory for higher-order thinking, as I discussed in Chapter One, is to give it access to lots of ideas in long-term memory that it can draw upon.[6]

You can see some unexpected benefits of retrieval practice in the video *Lauren Moyle: Cranium*. Lauren here is asking her first-grade students to retrieve into active memory key details about the body. The brain is an *essential* organ that controls our decision making. It is encased in a bone called the *cranium*. The heart is a *pump* that distributes blood to the body like an engine. You can see them recalling the pieces of this content in different ways: What's it called, Why is it called that, What does it do? Every child is engaged with the task.

Interestingly this video is about ten years old and only recently did I come to understand it! We used to show it at workshops, inspired by Lauren's dynamic teaching—the questioning that fostered eager hands supported by the use of *Cold Call* and with *No Opt Out*, to ensure accountability and engagement. We were focused on *how* Lauren taught and didn't spend much time thinking about the value of *what* she was doing. In fact, ironically, when what she was teaching came up in discussions at workshops, I often found myself apologizing for it. Participants would occasionally note that she was *just recalling facts*, the phrase implying there wasn't much substantive teaching going on. Eventually we stopped showing the video altogether.

Now I can see much more clearly that *what* Lauren is doing is at least as valuable as *how* she's doing it. Future discussions in her class will be richer and based on firm knowledge because of what she does here. The other unexpected thing the video shows is how much students tend to like *Retrieval Practice*. Lauren's students are eager, happy, and confident. Teachers sometimes presume that facts are boring for students and so focusing on retrieval practice will make their classes dull, but the opposite is often the case. Students who know their material are proud to know it and eager to use it. And as they begin they see examples of what they know in more and more places, their confidence grows, often transferring to more complicated tasks in which they are asked to put those facts to use.

I'll close the discussion of *Retrieval Practice* by sharing a video, *Retrieval Practice Montage*, of several teachers employing the concept in different ways. Art Worrell's AP U.S. History students stand to answer his retrieval questions. It's a regular and intentional part of the day and the importance of *Retrieval Practice* is transparent to students. This helps them to understand how important it is for them to use in their own studying! Art again undercuts the idea that *Retrieval Practice* questions have to be simple. He asks Tarik what the compromise of 1877 was, but also why it was important. He then asks Kamari to expand on Tarik's answer. As Kamari's answer shows, it's broad knowledge, not just narrow facts, that they're recalling.

Annette Riffle uses *Retrieval Practice* in her middle school math classroom to make ideal use of what might otherwise be down time—one student is at the board modeling a problem and, rather than allowing everyone else to sit passively, she peppers them with key questions about coordinate geometry.

Barry Smith's use of *Retrieval Practice* in his French class shows two things: first, a variety of ways to engage—*Cold Call, Call and Response*, hands raised—and also that the content goes in two directions. Barry asks his students to go both from French to English and English to French. Teachers of other content areas might think about naming a concept and asking students to describe it and then flipping the process: describing a concept and asking students to name it, asking, for example, "What is hyperbole?"; "What is it called when authors intentionally exaggerate to make a point?"; and perhaps even "If I say I've got a million things to do today, what literary device am I using?" All of these strengthen the neural pathway.

Finally, Alonte Johnson reminds us in his literature classroom that we can ask students to retrieve a full range of content types: plot, character, background knowledge, and even themes.

## TECHNIQUE 8: STANDARDIZE THE FORMAT

Though asking questions of students is a great tool to check for understanding, gathering data through observation is arguably even more effective when you can use it. One major benefit of relying on observation to assess student understanding is that it allows you to respond quickly to more complex ideas in more formats than you can assess through questioning alone. Another benefit is that you can "parallel-process"—you can be checking for understanding while students are working. For example, you can quickly observe the quality of your students' thesis paragraphs as they are writing them.

But the greatest advantage of gathering data through observation is its efficiency. Done well it allows you to gather data quickly and about everyone. This is important because gathering data in the midst of instruction is almost always subject to significant time constraints. Say you assign independent work to students for five minutes. By the time you've given students a chance to get started, have answered their questions, and checked to make sure everyone has gotten underway, you might have three minutes to assess thirty students—six seconds per student on average. Many teachers might successfully assess ten students in that amount of time but if you can gather information twice as fast with half as many distractions, you suddenly become able to assess and respond to students in situations where you weren't previously able to. Suddenly six minutes is enough. In some cases two or three minutes can be profoundly useful. If you maximize the efficiency of data gathering, you also increase the times and places when you can use it without redesigning your lessons. You become able to assess what happens during parts of your lesson that might otherwise go unmonitored.

So while efficiency might seem at first like one of the least compelling words in teaching, it turns out to be critical to many of the most important things that differentiate great lessons from others.

*Standardize the Format* focuses on streamlining data-gathering and making your observation more efficient and accurate. It means designing materials and space so that you're looking predictably—in the same, consistent place every time—for the data you need. You might ask for work to be shown in the margin of a specific page of your students' books, for example, or for students to circle their final answer to a problem set. Or, at the beginning of class, you might give students a "packet" (see technique 4, *Double Plan*) in which to do key aspects of their work that day, and include clearly visible, preset places to write or take notes.

The following details from lesson packets in the Reading Reconsidered Curriculum my team and I developed offer some examples of ways carefully designed materials can organize the space where students work to make observation and assessment easier.

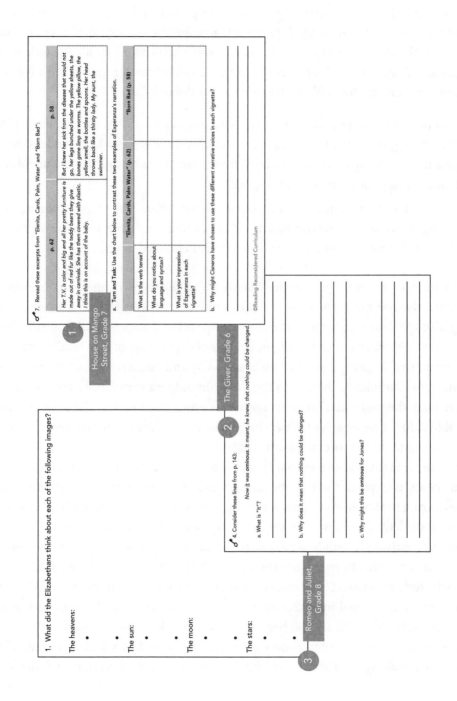

**House on Mango Street, Grade 7**

7. Reread these excerpts from "Elenita, Cards, Palm, Water" and "Born Bad":

| p. 62 | p. 58 |
|---|---|
| Her T.V. is color and big and all her pretty furniture is made out of red fur like the teddy bears they give away in carnivals. She has them covered with plastic. I think this is on account of the baby. | But I knew her sick from the disease that would not go, her legs bunched under the yellow sheets, the bones gone limp as worms. The yellow pillow, the yellow smell, the bottles and spoons. Her head thrown back like a thirsty lady. My aunt, the swimmer. |

a. Turn and Task: Use the chart below to contrast these two examples of Esperanza's narration.

| | "Elenita, Cards, Palm Water" (p. 62) | "Born Bad" (p. 58) |
|---|---|---|
| What is the verb tense? | | |
| What do you notice about language and syntax? | | |
| What is your impression of Esperanza in each vignette? | | |

b. Why might Cisneros have chosen to use these two different narrative voices in each vignette?

©Reading Reconsidered Curriculum

**The Giver, Grade 6**

4. Consider these lines from p. 143:

Now it was ominous. It meant, he knew, that nothing could be changed.

a. What is "it"?

b. Why does it mean that nothing could be changed?

c. Why might this be ominous for Jonas?

**Romeo and Juliet, Grade 8**

1. What did the Elizabethans think about each of the following images?

The heavens:
•
•

The sun:
•

The moon:
•

The stars:
•
•

Some notes about the examples:

- In example 1, the use of a chart helps students keep track of their progress and make sure to answer all parts of a complicated question (three questions about two different excerpts). It also lets the teacher do this as well and to see at a glance how far along students are and to quickly differentiate which part of the task students are struggling with (presumably because they are leaving it blank, writing less, or doing it last).

- In example 2, dividing the task into parts a, b, and c again allows the teacher to Check for Understanding on individual components and quickly assess where students are in the process from a pacing point of view, but here the use of lines reinforces the use of complete sentences versus informal notes in responding.

- In example 3, the scaffolded structure separates the different elements students should be reflecting on without being too structured or leading (or asking for more writing than is needed). It also models for students how to take organized notes.

In addition to enabling you to find answers (or key steps in the work process) more quickly, *Standardize the Format* allows you to disrupt students less. You won't spend time flipping through their work or asking them to help you find answers and this will allow them to concentrate. Most important, though, instead of expending energy (and using your own working memory) locating answers, you can identify and assess trends among your students' work and spot examples to share with the class. Simplifying search tasks reduces extraneous cognitive load; the more consistent the appearance and placement of the data, the more you will be able to focus on what it's telling you. You perceive more accurately, remember more of what you see, and think more productively about it.

There are some surprising relational benefits to all this "efficiency" and "productivity" and you can see an example of them in the video *Nicole Warren: Keystone*. As she circulates and observes during the last few minutes of the clip you may notice the beautiful connections she makes with students. There are sincere encouragements and acknowledgments. These little moments of relationship building are surely something most of us seek, so it's important to observe that they stem in part from the ease with which she can find what she is looking for in each student's work. The easiness leaves her relaxed and confident. With her working memory only lightly taxed by search costs, her mind is free to think about each student in turn as she works the room, and all her warmth and graciousness can show.

There are other ways you can continue to prioritize your focus on the content of student work by *Standardizing the Format* even further. In addition to directing students to answer in the same space, you can also ask them to lift up the key pieces of the answer that you are looking for as you circulate. "Box the equation you used to calculate the sum," or "Underline the appositive you added to your thesis." These additional directions not only make it easier for you to focus on the most important aspect of student work when time is of the essence, but also heighten student awareness of the most important variable to include in their work. Boxing the remainder or circling the active verbs in their topic sentence helps students to focus and prioritize.

My team and I recently tried to use *Standardize the Format* ourselves at a workshop on CFU. The topic was "Reject Self-Report" and the activity was a series of case studies: six transcripts from classroom situations where a teacher had initially relied on student self-report to assess mastery. Teachers in the workshop were asked to rewrite cases, scripting their questions to better gather data about student mastery in lieu of self-report. Workshop participants were asked to complete several of the scenarios over the course of a few minutes. At the bottom was an additional section where people were asked to identify and rewrite a case from their own experience. The page we provided looked like Figure 3.1.

| Self-Report Statements | Rewritten to Reject Self-Report |
|---|---|
| **Example 1:**<br><br>**Teacher:** A "regular polygon" is a two-dimensional shape with sides that are all equal and angles that are all equal. Got it?<br><br>**Student:** Yes. | |
| **Example 2:**<br><br>**Teacher:** To *glare* and to *gaze* are similar because they both mean that you are looking at someone or something—usually for a long time. They're different because when you glare, you're looking at someone angrily, and when you gaze, you're looking with great interest or wonder. *Glare* has a negative charge, whereas *gaze* has a positive charge. Get it?<br><br>**Students:** Yes. | |

Figure 3.1  *Reject Self-Report* Mini Case Studies

As my team and I circulated, we were able to ascertain the following quickly and easily:

*How quickly people were working and how many scenarios they had completed.* This allowed us to make a simple but fundamental decision: How much time should we allocate for the activity? Did people need more time?

*Which scenarios people chose to work on. It was clear at a glance which of the scenarios they'd chosen to rewrite.* Each was in its own box of about a quarter page. I could glance over twenty shoulders and know which topics people had found interesting and would want to discuss during the post-activity discussion. It also helped us write scenarios for future workshops. If very few people chose example 5, for example, we could replace it.

*What good ideas and common misunderstandings we could talk about during the debrief.* It was easy for me to look for more evidence of something specific; for example, if I saw something intriguing in one participant's answer to example 3 and wanted to know if it was typical, it was ten times easier for me to track other people's responses to that example.

It was also easy to scan to the final question and differentiate those answers. That is, I wanted to look differently at the scenario of their own experience to get a quick sense of the sorts of settings they were finding applicable. This was easy to do because the answer I wanted to analyze more closely was located in the same place on every participant's paper. I could find it and tell it apart in an instant.

People worked for three or four minutes, and the room had about 120 people in it. But at the end of that time, I had a pretty good sense of what the strengths and gaps in understanding were, and it was mostly thanks to an apparently mundane design decision. Merely using *Standardize the Format* in a very simple way greatly leveraged my ability to understand what was happening in the room.

## TECHNIQUE 9: ACTIVE OBSERVATION (ACTIVEOBS)

Here is a simple observation about teaching: What we are looking at as our students are working is a stream of data. But this is in fact two statements at once. The first—that it is data we are looking at—tells us that it contains the seeds of insight if we think analytically and purposefully about it. The second—that it is a stream—tells us that the information may come at us fast and furious; there will often be too much to make sense of all at once, or even to remember. Happily, making a few small changes to what you do when, and before, you observe student work can help you make more sense of the data stream.

The first change is to track what you see in writing. You can see Denarius Frazier doing this in the clip *Denarius Frazier: Remainder*, which you watched at the beginning of the chapter. He is carrying a clipboard, and as he moves around the room he makes slight notations—about a consistent kind of error he's seeing or about students who can provide strong examples, or who will need extra support. Just this simple move is a game-changer.

If we think we're going to circulate around the room making "mental notes" about thirty students' work on two problems with four steps each, while perhaps taking a few questions and offering occasional encouragement, and still be able to remember at the end of it what the most common error was and which students struggled where, we are kidding ourselves. Working memory is small; even the slightest distractions cause us to forget what we're trying to remember and in an environment as complex as a classroom working memory is quickly overwhelmed. In such a setting there's really no such thing as taking mental notes.

Denarius, however, is able to give individualized feedback to each student, note their progress, and at the same time discern the common error, or the most germane topic for intervention. "Much better," he says to one student as he circulates. Think about that. He remembers how she did on a similar problem earlier in the day or perhaps the day before and tells her he can see the difference in her work. He's able to do this because in tracking the data on student performance he engages more actively with it, and therefore remembers it. And with his observations written down, he can review his notes after one lesson or before the next. When you put your observations on paper you create a permanent record, increase the amount you remember, and free your working memory to perceive more. The result is that Denarius remembers how his student did yesterday and can affirm her progress today. Could there be a stronger statement of the fact that he believes her progress is important?

More than just writing things down, *Active Observation* means deciding intentionally what to look for and maintaining discipline in looking for what you have prioritized. We know from cognitive psychology that observation is subjective and unreliable; we won't notice what's most important unless we prepare to focus on it and are looking for it.

We're also inclined to think that looking for more things is better than attending to fewer things, but that's often not the case in the classroom.

In one of my first teaching jobs a mentor advised me to circulate around the room when my students were doing independent work. That was good advice. Walking around and looking over this or that student's shoulder encouraged students to do their best work, in part because my actions suggested that I cared about what they were writing and was interested in their ideas, and, frankly, that I would know how hard they were working. But there was a lot more I could have done to get the most out of that "walking around."

For one thing, while I believed I was very observant, I probably was not. Usually I would be looking passively, waiting to be struck by spontaneous observations about what students were doing. This can sometimes be useful, but it meant that I was prone to inattentional blindness—not seeing what was plainly before me—for example, that students were not successfully able to do the task I'd assigned. What I noticed was often a random event. What I gave students feedback on was also likely to be accidental. If on any given day there were ten really important things you could say about students' writing, I might notice something about number seven on the list. Or number nine. The cost was that I wasn't talking about topics one, two, and three consistently—and sometimes not at all.

And honestly, without a real purpose for what I was looking for, I sometimes allowed myself to become more passive. I really wasn't looking that carefully. I'd mimic the actions of a carefully observing teacher, nodding approvingly and squinting as if in keen interest, but my mind would wander.

I would often be looking mostly for whether my students appeared to be working hard. Their topic sentences were poor and yet I'd walk right past because their pencils were scribbling away. Effort is generally a good thing but it doesn't guarantee learning. "Never mistake activity for achievement," the coach and teacher John Wooden advised. Just because students are working hard at a task does not mean they are learning from it. Understanding whether students are making real progress requires more careful observation. Were they using strong active verbs as they scribbled away? Were they able to cite evidence both directly and indirectly?

Compare my well-intentioned but mostly subpar observation to the deliberateness we see in the clip *Julia Addeo: Binomials*. Like Denarius, she's carrying a page of notes as she works the room. She explained what was on it.

"My 'key' mirrors exactly what students should have on their paper, including the question, the work that they should be showing, and the correct answer, boxed," Julia told me.

"I leave some room on the side to make checks and notes as I monitor the classroom. I keep a tally of how students did or the initials of names that I know I want to *Show Call* or *Cold Call*."

As she observes, she quickly notes that students are doing fine with problem number 1. She won't need more than a quick review afterwards to reinforce technical vocabulary. But her observations reveal that there's something going on in problem 2. You can see her marking up her notes with details on the errors students are making. Then you can see her literally step back, review the data, and make a decision about how to proceed—as that decisive nod of her head about thirty-seven seconds in reveals.

Tracking the data in writing has freed her working memory. Rather than merely trying to remember what she's seen, it can now focus on analyzing what students are doing. Her use of *Active Observation* allows her later to *Cold Call* students who she knows will contribute strong explanations when she's reviewing the problem. These students often do an exemplary job of explaining concepts to their peers. This is not a lucky accident. She has used the knowledge gained from her *Active Observation* to choose participants intentionally and even strategically.

In *Front the Writing* (technique 40) and *Disciplined Discussions* (technique 46) I call this idea "Hunting, Not Fishing." You *hunt* for productive answers that will move the conversation in a productive direction as you circulate. Then later you draw on them while teaching so you don't have to *fish*—call on students more or less randomly, hoping they will have useful responses. This allows you to let students do more of the cognitive work, and build a culture where the strength of students' thinking is more visible to their peers and where being *Cold Called* is as often as not a sign of the quality of their work. "Hunting" for answers in this way and remembering whom to call on eight or twelve minutes later demands more of working memory than almost any teacher has available in a busy classroom. It requires *Active Observation*.

But *Active Observation* is not just taking notes. It's deciding what you should see and then looking carefully for whether you see it. It's thinking about what mistakes might occur and being ready to respond. Crucially, Julia's ability to observe and assess what's happening begins with the exemplar she's planned (technique 1, *Exemplar Planning*) and that she carries with her as she goes. To observe effectively in real time, you must think through what you'll look for in student work beforehand.

Let's focus in on how Denarius uses his exemplar in the clip *Denarius Frazier: Remainder*, which we began discussing earlier. You'll notice that he's making tiny, quick notations as he circulates, for example, in the following image.

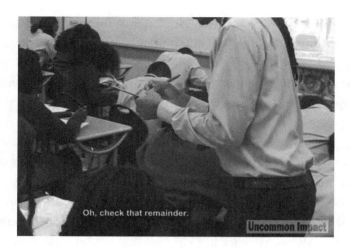

Oh, check that remainder.

Uncommon Impact

Students are dividing polynomials and a student has struggled to find the remainder. But Denarius doesn't write "David: can't find remainder" or something like that. We know this because his notation is a tick mark, done in a fraction of a second, which thus allows him to keep circulating quickly with his working memory free. That might seem like a mundane observation but it tells us something profound: Denarius has made a list of likely errors and he's marking up this list each time he sees one. Not only can he now move quickly as he makes his rounds but as a trend in the data emerges he will see it in the data instantly. In fact in this clip Denarius recognizes that eight or nine students are struggling with the remainder and is able to target his reteach to exactly this issue—the one most relevant to the greatest number of students. He doesn't even need a step-back moment to analyze the data as we see Julia Addeo use; he simply glances at what is essentially a histogram of mistakes that he's generated as he walks. By the time he's halfway around the room much of his working memory is focused on how he'll reteach the example. And he is able to draw an excellent example from a student for a *Show Call* because, like Julia, this is something he's made note of.

Discussing this video afterwards, Denarius noted that his seating plan is also critical to his success. The two front corners of the room are the places he always starts his observational rounds. He sets his seating plan so the first four students he observes in each of those corners present what is often a statistical sample of the room—a mix that includes at least one student who often struggles, one student who's often typical of the group, and one who is often a high performer.

"After looking at four kids' work I often have a decent hypothesis for how the room overall is doing. I'm testing that hypothesis already as I work the first column, and by the second column I'm deciding what to do about it."

"A lot of people think I'm tracking who got it right and who got it wrong but I track the nature of the errors I see. When I finish my observations, knowing what they misunderstand rather than what number of kids got it right is much more useful. And that, too, helps me develop my plan to reteach as I work."

As I'm sure you're recognizing, the design of the tool you use to track and analyze data in real time is critical. The following illustration shows some examples.

In this example the teacher has to focus on who's demonstrated proficiency, student by student. It's probably a pretty straightforward skill—punctuating a complete sentence—which is why she can give it a yes/no check. This approach wouldn't work for everything teachers assess, but the emphasis on ensuring that she checks in on every student's progress is powerful. She has also left space for narrative notes if she needs them, which allows the tool to gather both quantitative and narrative data about the work.

Story Problem: Yedidah is making friendship bracelets for her birthday party. At the store, beads are sold in packs of thirty-five. She decides to buy six packs. When she gets home, her mother suggests using twenty beads on each of her friends' bracelets. How many complete bracelets can Yedidah make for her friends?

| Point of Error | Number of Students Making Error |
|---|---|
| **Error 1:** Scholars incorrectly multiply 6 × 35 | |
| **Error 2:** Scholars incorrectly use the total of 210 beads in the final step of the problem | |
| **Error 3:** Scholars create a bracelet with less than 20 beads | |

In this example the teacher is more focused on error trends rather than individual student progress. During class she'll make a hash mark each time she sees a mistake, regardless of who made it, so she can sum things up quickly at the end of her circulation and determine what she needs to review. Again, there's room here for narrative detail. Denarius's tracker likely looks similar to the one we see above.

This exemplar also offers insight into how teachers plan when they will gather key data. Notice the difference here between Error 2 and Error 3. Clearly these are two pieces of the same math problem, but the teacher has divided the errors into two separate rounds of observation. Julia Addeo told us something similar when we spoke to her. "I'll always include the laps that I make. So on lap number one I'm just coming around to look at your multiplication. Or I'm just coming around to just see how you isolated the variable. I'll include that for most essential questions on either a *Do Now* or a problem set." In other words, she's not looking for everything at once but imagines a series of observational rounds, each focused on a slightly different aspect of the task.

"I check every student multiple times during math block," fourth-grade teacher Nicole Warren told me (you can see her *Active Observation* in the video *Nicole Warren: Keystone*). "I first observe for procedural norms, including marking up the problem and labeling work. Then I circulate for conceptual understanding and record which students are on track, which students have basic mathematical errors, and which students might have a deeper conceptual misunderstanding. This helps to make the plan for the discussion and also helps build accountability around student work."

"When students know you'll be circulating to them every couple of minutes," Nicole Willey said, "they work quickly and efficiently. They love being rewarded by a smiley face on their paper or a high-five. [The joy students feel in Nicole's small notes and appreciations as she observes is extremely evident in the video.] There's also a lot of celebration around success and growth. At the end of the (class) each day, I announce which students achieved 100 percent, as well as which students improved. Students are highly invested in this moment of public recognition. We also have group goals that if, as a class, we get 100 percent on each of the questions the class gets a special prize. These incentives, while external, build a sense of community and showcase that working hard leads to long-term success."

Often teachers make their observational focus transparent to students. "I'm coming around to look at your hypotheses," they might say. At that time they'd try to give feedback only on that topic before adding additional rounds; for example, "This time I'm coming around to see whether you have described clear experimental and control groups." This influences student actions even before they've given any feedback. Students see their teacher approaching and think about their hypothesis because they know she will be looking for it. Perhaps they focus on it more in the first place. Teachers influence students to focus on key tasks when they tell them that they are looking for them.

You can see evidence of these actions in Rafael Good's tracking sheet from his math class. He's worked the problem himself so he can use his own model to see gaps in student thinking more quickly, made notes on delivery moves ("*Show Call* exemplary work!"), and notes the time allocated for the work ("4 mins") so he doesn't lose track. He's written out the initial phrase he wants to say when he sends students off to work ("Make sure to show multiplication steps") and finally his Lap 1 focus ("L1"). He's written out the exact phrase he wants to use before he starts observing—"Checking for your multiplication steps to be written out."

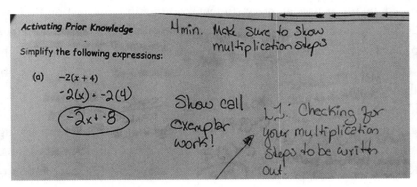

Focusing on limited and specific priority elements when you give feedback makes it easier to give immediate feedback to every student and, perhaps unexpectedly, this is often helpful in building relationships. The most important and genuine tool for relationship building is something you might call relational teaching—using the way you teach the content to build trust. Trust comes when your teaching demonstrates your skill as a teacher and your interest in and ability to help students learn. Giving effective and precise feedback communicates to each student:

Your success is important to me. I am aware of your progress in this endeavor.

I will help you succeed.

I believe you will succeed.

That is more important in the long run to building trust with students than whether you chat with them in the hallways or ask them about what shows they like to watch. And it ensures that the relationships we build are about learning and the topics we study.

In *Culturally Responsive Education in the Classroom*, Adeyemi Stembridge writes, "Depth of learning requires that students enter into a meaningful relationship with the content itself. . . . This is most often profoundly facilitated through modeling of a relationship with content by teachers." Relationships are valuable because they are "the channel through which investment in school is personalized."

The quality of feedback enabled by *ActiveObs*, effective, focused, informed by an understanding of each student's learning, brings the interconnection between student, teacher, and content to life. Consider the dynamic between students and teachers in the video *Active Observation Montage*. The three clips are a case study in relationship building. In the first classroom, we see Nicole Warren giving feedback on a math problem. "Super smart," she says, "going and checking every answer choice while you have extra time. . . . Really nice." The smile on the student's face lights up the screen. Though Denarius Frazier's style is a bit more muted, he too pauses at every student, commenting not just on their work in the moment. "Killing it," he says, as he delivers a fist bump and a smile. His "much better" shows that he knows where his students struggle and therefore is able to celebrate growth. Tamesha McGuire's first-graders get the same mix of affirmation—"Nice work, my love!"—and meaningful, targeted feedback.

I should note that people sometimes confuse *Active Observation* with "aggressive monitoring," which is a term Paul Bambrick-Santoyo has coined to describe giving feedback to every student using a monitoring key over a series of specific rounds or laps. Much of the guidance I've provided here reflects Paul's insights and the implementation of teachers trained by him, so I hope it's clear that I see immense value in that approach. Teachers should use it! But it's also important to recognize the value in balancing it with a broader array of data-gathering approaches. Using *Active Observation* therefore includes also using alternative approaches to giving every student immediate feedback as you observe because alternative observational tools can create balance and emphasize different aspects of the learning process. The following chart provides three options for *Active Observation*:

| Option 1 | Option 2 | Option 3 |
|---|---|---|
| Sometimes called "Aggressive Monitoring." Teacher tracks progress of and gives immediate feedback to each individual student. | Teacher gives feedback to the group after tracking and completing observations (and does not provide individual feedback during observing). | Teacher gives feedback (and makes observations) focused on specific individuals (and not the whole group). |

Though Option 1 is often excellent, one limitation—and therefore one reason to occasionally balance it with other approaches—is that the need to get to every student can lead to rushed feedback or a tone that feels hurried or transactional—it feels like the teacher's goal is to get around the room.[7] This can crowd out time for questions, for example. There may be times when you ask students to hold their questions—the data could be more important—but there will also be times when it's valuable to respond and linger. Sometimes it's valuable to give feedback right away but sometimes it's appropriate to let students struggle for a bit and not receive immediate feedback on their progress.

It's worth considering that Option 1 could be adapted. You could, for example, still try to observe and gather data from every student's work but *not* try to give live feedback as you circulate, giving feedback only to the group at the end of your lap. This would allow you to make independent work feel more autonomous for students. Careful observation accompanied by silence can be powerful, especially if your feedback to the group makes it clear you were observing carefully. Perhaps you want students to struggle a bit or not know right away whether they are on the right track. Not attempting to give feedback as you circulate could also allow you more time and working memory to observe trends and issues in student work. On the other hand, you might risk allowing individual errors to persist and/or students not feeling the same level of support and/or accountability, so it is important for you to choose intentionally, based both on the objective for the day and the moment in the lesson, as well as what you see as you observe.

You can see a strong example of the quieter approach to *ActiveObs* in the clip *BreOnna Tindall: ActiveObs* cut from her seventh-grade ELA classroom. As the clip opens, students are reading and annotating a short nonfiction text about the concept of "blind justice."

This is part of their larger reading of the *Narrative of the Life of Frederick Douglass*. BreOnna, clipboard in hand, is circulating and reading over students' shoulders, occasionally nodding appreciatively as she comes across ideas that will be useful in the discussion. "I'm treasure hunting," is how BreOnna described it. "I'm looking for the pieces of the conversation that I'm going to highlight so we can come to those key understandings in the lesson."

Her route around the classroom seems planned but not rushed, and she doesn't pause to read every student paper. Most students do not get feedback. Her goal is to inform the coming conversation. So she's still taking notes and she still occasionally asks clarifying questions ("What's this underline mean here?"), but mostly they are intended to ensure that *she* understands what students are thinking, rather than to give them guidance. She's noting ideas rather than addressing misconceptions. When she writes on her clipboard, she's not tracking every student's accuracy, but rather taking notes on the trends she's seeing and highlighting students she might choose to call on later in discussion. In the subsequent discussion, you can see the results of BreOnna's *ActiveObs*. It's a great example of "hunting, not fishing." BreOnna calls on Adriel, whose answer she knows is a good starting point, then Renee, who she knows has used the word "exonerates."

"I try not to go for the kid who has the all-the-way right answer first," BreOnna said. "I try to find people who have pieces of the right answer. As opposed to saying 'build' arbitrarily, I try to find people who have pieces of the right answer so they can really understand how a discussion works—what does it really mean to build?"

BreOnna's observation allows her to honor student voice but still curate the conversation for focus and quality, and, she noted, it allows her to ensure that students hear a high-quality response without having to provide it herself. "I don't always want to be the person stamping the right answer—that's boring! Also, that takes away the kids' belief that they know," BreOnna said. "I try to find other kids in the classroom to unearth the key point."

## *ActiveObs* in the Early Grades

You can see another example of a quieter form of *ActiveObs* in the video *Narlene Pacheco: ActiveObs*. She's done a great job of *Standardizing the Format* in her kindergarten classroom at Immaculate Conception School in the Bronx. Everyone's workspace is set up the same—clean and tidy. It's easy for her to see what she's looking for at a glance. She circulates around the room carefully but doesn't give feedback to every student. Instead, she's looking for overall trends, and she shares a reminder about that (make sure you're going from left to right) to the whole class. She's already adapting her teaching to the data. Perhaps because what she's looking for—and the range of possible errors—is smaller, she's not using a clipboard. But she uses a hint of *Affirmative Checking*—"Hands on your head when you are ready." Students can signal when they are ready to be checked. This lets her know where to look first. She spots Clara struggling and uses *Break It Down* (technique 37) beautifully for her, prompting her to find the error for herself. This is successful in part because Ms. Pacheco shows such patience and emotional constancy. But it's also worth noting that she has lots of time to spend with Clara, in part because she's not trying to give feedback to every student. On the second round of observation—for the word "yet"—you can see that she's deliberately checking back on Clara to see how she does. Clara's got it, now. She smiles and Ms. Pacheco is sure to reinforce her success.

---

To return to Adeyemi Stembridge's observations about the nature of relationships, the responsibility of being a teacher lies in building students' relationships with learning and content. Their relationships with us are the means to achieve that goal. The strongest and most productive teacher relationships are built by establishing a triangle in which we connect to students and (help to) connect them to content.

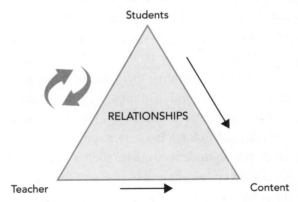

We are conduits, in other words. If students do not develop a valuable relationship to the things they study in school, their relationship with their teacher will not have accomplished its full purpose. This challenges us to resist the desire to be the center of the story; the goal is not to be loved and remembered forever but for students to take away a belief in their own capacity, to value the process of learning, and just possibly love or at least appreciate deeply the ideas of science, math, music, or literature. *ActiveObs* is a primary tool teachers can use to help relationships serve this purpose.

## TECHNIQUE 10: SHOW ME

Another useful tool in making effective and efficient observations of student work involves flipping the dynamic in which a teacher works to gather data about a group of students whose role in this process is largely passive. Instead, in *Show Me*, students actively present the teacher with visual evidence of their understanding. This gives teachers a way to quickly assess an entire class's understanding, more or less at a glance, and has the added benefit of often being enjoyable to students.

*Show Me* could mean students presenting answers on mini-whiteboards, as you'll see in the video *Dani Quinn: Show Me* (which we'll study more in a moment) or holding up a number of fingers, each representing the answer to a multiple-choice problem on cue, as Brian Belanger/Denarius Frazier do in the video *Belanger/Frazier: Show Me Montage*. They've cut out the need to circulate around the room to gather data but still are able to get a strong sense for where everyone in the class stands.

Here are the basic criteria for a good *Show Me*. It should ask students to (1) *present objective data,* (2) usually *in unison*, and (3) *in a format that the teacher can assess at a glance.* It's worth taking a moment to go a bit deeper into each of these criteria.

*Present objective data:* When Denarius and Brian ask students to respond by showing on their fingers which answer they chose, they are presenting their actual answer, not their (subjective) opinion about their own understanding. Self-report, as we discussed earlier, is notoriously unreliable. So versions of *Show Me* that take subjective self-report data and make it visible (e.g. "Tell me if you understand: Thumbs up, thumbs down, thumbs sideways") don't help much. You want to see their actual answer. "Hold up one finger if you chose answer A, two if you chose answer B," and so forth is a better approach.

*In unison:* In most cases asking students to share their answers visually works best when it happens in unison, for efficiency reasons and to preserve the integrity of the data. Imagine you're a student. You chose answer B, but for whatever reasons don't share your answer right away when the teacher asks the class to hold up their answer. Glancing around the room, you see eighteen classmates showing they chose answer C. If you reveal that you answered B, you will likely be the only one. Will you change your answer? Studies have repeatedly shown that people are deeply swayed by the answers of their peers. In a classic study by Solomon Asch, for example, experimental subjects were placed in a group of "participants," who were in fact confederates of the experimenters. The group was asked to compare the lengths of a series of lines that were clearly of different lengths. Without confederates present, subjects reported the length of the lines incorrectly less than 1 percent of the time, but in a setting where confederates consistently reported believing the lines were the same length, most people made efforts to conform, giving an answer they knew to be wrong at least some of the time. A third of participants changed any given answer on average and 75 percent of participants changed an answer at least once over twelve trials. Conclusion: Most people will change their answers to something they don't believe is right in order to conform. If everyone presents their data point simultaneously and on cue, it prevents students from changing their answer based on their peers' responses. Ensuring that answers are given in unison also maximizes pacing and flow. *Show Me* can often feel energetic and game-like to students, and their crisp and coordinated participation facilitates the sense of momentum it creates.

*In a format that the teacher can assess at a glance.* The data in *Show Me* are actively presented by students in visual form—held up so you can see and scan them quickly from where you're standing; limited circulation required. The clearer you are about what the presentation of the data should look like, the better. You'll want to decide and explain to students whether they should hold their fingers up in the air (so you can see them easily) or in front of their chests (so they are less visible to peers), for example. If they're writing on a whiteboard, are the answers boxed? How high must the whiteboards be held? This is important because the less of your working memory you have to use in searching, the more you can spend analyzing the data.

There are two common versions of *Show Me*: the first is *hand signals,* and the second is *slates*.

## Hand Signals

Although there are a variety of ways to employ hand signals, the key to the approach is that on a specific cue, students hold up digits in unison to represent their answer.

In *Belanger/Frazier: Show Me Montage*, Bryan Belanger uses hand signals to gauge student mastery of a multiple-choice question about rates of change. Within seconds of the morning greeting, Bryan prompts students with the cue "rock, paper, scissors . . . one, two!" On "two," students pound their desks three times in unison before they raise their hands to reveal their response (one finger for answer choice A, two for B, and so on). Bryan has made the act of showing him their answers so familiar that this routine goes like clockwork.

Once students' hands are up, Bryan scans the room, narrating what he's looking for ("making sure they're nice and high") as well as what he sees ("I see lots of twos, a couple of fours"). This reinforces the procedural expectations and reminds students that he's *observing carefully.*

He then asks students to be ready to defend their answer. In doing so, he acknowledges that multiple responses have been given but, crucially, he has withheld the answer (see technique 12, *Culture of Error*) and not yet told them which one is correct.

Instead of revealing the answer himself, Bryan calls on Blaize (who correctly selected B) to explain his answer and reasoning. He affirms Blaize's answer but also calls on Elizabeth (who incorrectly chose D) to reiterate it. Bryan then asks students to "check or change" their work for that problem, saying, "Give yourself a check if you picked answer choice B. If you did not, circle that, and fix it now." By insisting that students *Own and Track* (technique 14), he ensures that they *all* internalize the answer and the reasoning behind it.

While the multiple-choice format of Bryan's question lends itself well to *Show Me*, it's also possible to use hand signals to gather data on questions that were not originally designed as multiple choice, as Denarius Frazier shows in the same video. Denarius has written out on chart paper two solutions for a problem that students have been working on independently. He asks students to evaluate the two solutions and then says, "Let's take a poll. We'll reveal on one. One finger if you agree with solution A, two for B. Where are we, in three, two, and one?" Notice how careful he is to ensure that answers are revealed in unison. Thus he is able to instantly read the room and see that students are divided between the two solutions. He sends them into a *Turn and Talk* (technique 43) to discuss their thinking. Afterwards, Denarius takes another poll to see if their thinking has shifted as a result. He scans the room to assess the new data, and begins the discussion with a student who chose B. Other students share their thinking, and then Denarius shifts focus and asks someone who chose A to explain. Note that he is withholding the answer and managing his tell (see *Culture of Error*)—students still don't know which is the right answer. Finally, after a student comfortably and confidently changes her answer, Denarius confirms that A was correct. His use of *Show Me* has allowed him to efficiently poll the room multiple times, note trends in data, and determine which students he should call on when.

In the video *Lisa Wing: Boom, Boom, Pow*, you can see Lisa using hand signals with her seventh graders. She's asked them to evaluate three anonymous thesis paragraphs written by class members. She reinforces the fun and engaging procedure (*boom, boom, pow*) and gets really crisp, timely follow-through. She then follows up with questioning, asking students to discuss their opinions. It's a nice example and suggests how you could even ask students to use hand signals to respond to a question for which answers were a matter of opinion. By the way, it's also a great clip because there's so much "reality of the classroom" baked in. Not only do we get to see Lisa's gracious response when she calls on a student who's lost his voice, but there's a story playing out between the two girls in the front row at the beginning of the clip. One girl is proudly telling her friend that one of the paragraphs chosen as an example is hers! It's a lovely scene that reminds us how meaningful it is for students to see their work valued, but it should also remind us how easy it is for students to influence the answers other students give if the procedure for hand signals isn't crisp. The student could just as easily be "helping" her classmate by telling her, "Pick #2."

## Slates

Slates is another form of *Show Me* in which students complete their work at their desk and then, on a signal, hold it up to show their teacher. Often teachers use small erasable whiteboards to do this, as Dani Quinn's students do in the video *Dani Quinn: Show Me*, shot at London's Michaela Community School. Notice Dani's consistent upbeat cue for students to show their work ("Hold up!") and the way she makes reviewing the boards easier by going row by row and asking students whose work she's reviewed to put their boards down. She offers individual feedback to students as she scans, building a *Culture of Error* by keeping her tone similar whether students got it wrong—"Sam, what's five times five?"—or right—"Bianca, very good." The impressive number of names she's able to use lets many students feel seen and acknowledged, and we see her reinforce the procedure when she asks for "Boards down" and a faster response.[8] Finally, Dani does an excellent job of not just gathering data but adapting instruction to that data: "A few mistakes. We'll do one more . . ."

Slates needn't be done only with whiteboards—you might have students hold up their work in other ways: sketch a line on graph paper; write a sentence defining *verisimilitude*, perhaps "double spaced" so you can read it a bit easier from afar; add a margin note on page 26. Although scanning the responses might not be quite as simple in those cases, the approach can still be revealing (and effective in supporting accountability).

## TECHNIQUE 11: AFFIRMATIVE CHECKING

A final tool that can help you use observation to check for understanding, *Affirmative Checking*, involves the strategic use of checkpoints where students must get confirmation that their work is correct or on target, and that they are ready to move on to the next stage—a new paragraph, a second draft, a harder set of problems, the last step in a lab. In many cases students determine their own timing for doing so, which can create opportunities for self-assessment.

You can see Hilary Lewis using the technique in her first-grade classroom in the video *Hilary Lewis: Green Post-It*. This clip appeared in previous versions of the book and is one of our longest-serving clips at workshops; we continue to use it because Hilary does such a beautiful job of gauging student mastery before independent work. She's warm, attentive, and exudes high expectations. She asks students sitting on the carpet to complete a math problem on a green sticky note, which she calls a "ticket." Students must show that ticket to her as proof that they're ready to start independent practice (IP) at their desks. She stokes their interest in a perfect first-grade way by comparing this to the experience of "going into a movie." By requiring students to "earn" the opportunity, she turns IP into a kind of reward.

When the first student comes to have her work checked, it looks for a moment like a race is on to get in line first. Students start to scramble to show Ms. Lewis their work, but Hilary checks that trend in a loving voice: "Scholars, the only way you can come up here is if I ask you to come."

One by one, students complete the problem and await Hilary's signoff. She calls them up, first individually and then row by row. For correct work, she responds, "Go get started" in a warm, quiet way. Not unexpectedly a few students have done the problem incorrectly—or perhaps hastily—to which Hilary responds: "Please go back and check your work." Her reaction is emotionally constant. When one student shows her work for the wrong problem, Hilary uses the same warm, supportive tone: "OK. You did your own problem, which is great. I need you to do *that* problem" [as she points to the board].

Having everyone complete a gatekeeper problem before they move on to the full problem set lets Hilary correct small misunderstandings and reinforce working carefully and it helps students see that they are "ready" for a larger task, when they work carefully and attentively.

You can see a useful adaptation of this idea with older students in the clip *Jessica Madio: Silent Hand When You Have It*. Flipping the idea of an *Exit Ticket,* which her seventh-graders at St. Athanasius School in New York City are familiar with, Jessica uses an entrance pass prior to a section of independent practice. Getting it right shows you're ready to work on your own successfully.[9]

Jessica has *Standardized the Format* so answers are easy for her to find and assess quickly, and she tells students to raise "a silent hand when you have it. I'll come around and I'll check it." Instead of checking students based on seating plan, Jessica has given students agency over when their work will be checked. They are familiar with this routine and jump into the problem on cue. As each student finishes and raises a hand, Jessica simply says, "Thank you," and checks off the problem if it's correct. Students then transition immediately to independent practice problems without additional directions. Of course Jessica is also using *Active Observation* and taking notes on which students struggle and why. She uses this data to call a handful of students to work at the back table with her. These students have all made a similar mistake, and so they get additional support while others work independently. When they appear to be able to solve on their own, she sends them back to practice independently. Jessica offers a great reminder that classroom differentiation starts with data gathering.

One of the nice things about *Affirmative Checking* is the avenues to self-assessment it can create. *Affirmative Checking* offers students an opportunity to gauge their own work and decide when they are ready for the teacher to evaluate what they've done. This empowers students to assess their own work first—*Am I done? Do I feel ready for the next step?*—before asking for a response from the teacher. Because students elect the moment they'd like feedback, *Affirmative Checking* gives us additional data on student thinking about their own work that we might not see when we're reading over students' shoulders ("Oh, I see—you thought this was finished, but let's think about . . ."). Like *Stretch It* (technique 17), it can contribute to a culture in which correct answers are rewarded with future challenge—for example, "Great, now you're ready to move onto some advanced problems." That sense of accomplishment from seeing themselves pass through checkpoints successfully also help students develop confidence. Their progress is made more legible to them.

One of the keys to using *Affirmative Checking* effectively, however, is minimizing or eliminating the time students spend waiting for evaluation. The time students spend with a hand in the air, waiting for a teacher to come around (or even less productively, arms folded, pencil down, chatting with a neighbor) is a waste of precious instructional time and a risk that students will lose both their momentum and train of thought. The following tips for designing effective *Affirmative Checking* will help you balance student independence with efficiency.

Consider whether the content of your lesson is conducive to staged checking. The checkpoint(s) should ideally pass quickly—recall how efficient Hilary is when she reads each sticky note. If student work requires lengthy analysis or detailed feedback, it may not be feasible to ask everyone to wait for the next step while you read and respond.

Have a rubric or an answer sheet ready even if the work appears pretty straightforward. *This will free working memory and speed your ability to process.*

Consider how long each student might need to complete the task. Work would ideally be challenging or complex enough that students would tend to finish at different times, spreading out the checking required of the teacher so there was less waiting. *Affirmative Checking* might work well in writing classes, for example, where students typically complete drafts at very different paces, staggering the checkpoints from the teacher's perspective; however, it would be important to keep the check focused. You won't be able to read each student's first draft but you could ask students to circle five dynamic verbs or two indirect quotations or their thesis paragraph.

It can be helpful to add optional work. If you gave students three problems in one stage of a problem set but made the third a bonus question (or extra credit, perhaps), you could start checking students who had completed one or two. If students finished simultaneously and had to wait, they could go on to the third problem while you checked others' work. This might sound contradictory—isn't the point here to check before you go on? The difference is that the third problem would be at the same level of difficulty as the first two, so it would create an extra buffer of (productive) time in which you could complete your checking.

You may also consider making the signal for "I'm ready" the sort of cue that students can give while continuing to work. Keeping his or her hand in the air for three minutes makes it all but impossible for the student to go on to another problem. But an index card that's green on one side and yellow on the other, for example, can be flipped to show "I'm ready to be checked" while continuing to work on the bonus problem.

Another way to increase efficiency is by combining *Affirmative Checking* with *Show Me*, having students hold up their work for you to sign off on. You can see this in the video *Jon Bogard: Go to IP*, in which Jon uses whiteboards to dispatch some students to independent practice and to require more guided practice of others.

## Student-Driven Affirmative Checking

Another approach to *Affirmative Checking* is to allow your students to own more of the process of checking for accuracy and then present the data to you. Students could self-check on a key you provide and report their results. Or they could be responsible for checking one another's work in partners and then report the results to you, which would reduce the number of checks you needed to make. This works best when it relies on objective rather than subjective assessments.

One important fact to consider if you have students participate in *Affirmative Checking* is that there are two key purposes to the technique. One is to make sure that students are successful before going on to more complex work; the other is for you to gather data on how your students are doing. Distributing the checking accomplishes the first with more efficiency, but risks reducing your access to the data: If students self-check, will you know how they did? I'm sure you will find a way to balance these goals—either by using student-centered checking sometimes and checking yourself other times, or by engineering ways to track the data during student-centered checking (or both). For example, if students self-checked against a rubric, they could check a box to show how they did so that you could track it later. It's just important to be aware of the challenge and the possible trade-off as you're out there adapting and designing new and better solutions.

# TECHNIQUE 12: CULTURE OF ERROR

In a recent article about his development as a musician, the pianist Jeremy Denk observed a hidden challenge of teaching and learning: "While the teacher is trying to . . . discover what is working, the student is in some ways trying to elude discovery, disguising weaknesses in order to seem better than she is."[10]

His observation is a reminder: If the goal of *Checking for Understanding* is to bridge the gap between *I taught it* and *they learned it,* that goal is far easier to accomplish if students *want* us to find the gap, if they are willing to share information about errors and misunderstandings—and far harder if they seek to prevent us from discovering them.

Left to their natural inclinations, learners will often lean toward the latter. Out of pride or anxiety, sometimes out of appreciation for us as teachers—they don't want us to feel like we haven't served them well—students will often seek to "elude discovery" unless we build cultures that socialize them to think differently about mistakes. A classroom that has such a culture has what I call a *Culture of Error*.

Those teachers who are most able to diagnose and address errors quickly make *Check for Understanding* (CFU) a shared endeavor between themselves and their students. From the moment students arrive, they work to shape their perception of what it means to make a mistake, pushing them to think of "wrong" as a first, positive, and often critical step toward getting it "right," socializing them to acknowledge and share mistakes without defensiveness, with interest or fascination even, or possibly relief—help is on the way!

The term "psychological safety" is often used to describe a setting in which participants are risk-tolerant. Certainly psychological safety is a critical part of a classroom with a *Culture of Error*, but I would argue that the latter term goes farther: it includes both psychological safety—feelings of mutual trust and respect and comfort in taking intellectual risks—and appreciation, perhaps even enjoyment, for the insight that studying mistakes can reveal. In a classroom with a *Culture of Error*, students feel safe if they make a mistake, there is a notable lack of defensiveness, and they find the study of what went wrong interesting and valuable.

You can see this happening in the video *Denarius Frazier: Remainder*. Gathering data through *Active Observation* (technique 9), he spots a consistent error. As students seek to divide polynomials they struggle to find the remainder. Fagan is one of many students who have made the mistake. Denarius takes her paper and projects it to the class so they can study it. His treatment of this moment is critical. There is immense value in studying mistakes like this if teachers can make it feel psychologically safe. Unfortunately, it doesn't take a lot of imagination to picture the moment going wrong—badly wrong. The student could feel hurt, offended, or chastened. Her classmates could snicker. Perhaps you are imagining the phone call that evening: *Let me see if I have this right, Mr. Frazier. You projected my daughter's mistakes on the overhead for everyone to see?*

But in Denarius's hands, the moment proceeds beautifully and, more importantly, as if it were the most normal thing in the world to acknowledge a mistake and study it. How does he do it?

First, notice his tone. Denarius is emotionally constant. He is calm and steady. There's no suggestion of blame. He sounds no different whether he is talking about success or struggle. Next, he uses group-oriented language to make it clear that the issue they'll study is common among the class. "On a few of *our* papers, I'm noticing that *we're* getting an incorrect remainder . . ." he says. The mistake is ours; it's relevant to and reflective of the group, not just the individual. There's no feeling that Fagan has been singled out.

Another important characteristic of classrooms like Denarius's has to do with how error itself is dealt with. It is best captured in a phrase math teacher Bob Zimmerli uses in the video *Culture of Error Montage*: "I'm so glad I saw that mistake," he tells his students. "It's going to help me to help you." His phrase suggests that the error is a good thing. He calls the class to attention to show it is a worthy and serious topic, but he simultaneously normalizes the error through tone and word choice.

This is different from—the opposite of in many ways—pretending it is not really an error. Notice that Bob explicitly identifies the mistake as a mistake. His goal is to make it feel normal and natural, not to minimize the degree to which students felt they had erred. I mention this because sometimes teachers struggle with this distinction. In workshops we occasionally ask teachers to write phrases that they could use to express to students the idea that it is normal and useful to be wrong. They sometimes suggest responses like "Well, that's one way you could do it," or "Let's talk about some other ways," or "OK, maybe. Good thinking!"

These phrases blur the line between correct and incorrect or avoid telling students they are wrong. There are, of course, times when it's useful to say, "Well, there's no right answer, but let's consider other options." But that is a very different moment from the one in which a teacher should say something like "I can see why you'd think that but you're wrong, and the reasons why are really interesting," or "A lot of people make that mistake because it seems so logical, but let's take look at why it's wrong."

You can see another example of this in the *Culture of Error Montage*. Mathew Gray, like Denarius, is sharing a mistake—this one made by a student named Elias (a *Show Call*, technique 13). He notes this right away: "Elias has made a mistake," but he notes that this is not a surprise because he made the question difficult and that others have made the mistake as well. Then crucially he adds, "It's a mistake that I made when I first read the poem." He is the teacher and he, too, has struggled to understand. What could more fully contradict the idea that being an expert somehow means that one does not make mistakes? The idea is not to forestall defensiveness by making students believe they are correct, in other words, but to forestall defensiveness by helping students to see that the experience of making a mistake is normal and valuable.

Here are some other phrases that do that:

- "I'm glad I saw that mistake. It teaches us something we have to fix before we've mastered this."

- "I like that your first instinct was to use geometry, but in this situation, we have to solve algebraically."

- "Yes, the writing here makes it very challenging to follow who is saying what. But that phrase is spoken by Mary and not by John. Let's take a look at how we know that."

- "What I am asking you to do is difficult. Even working scientists struggle with it. But I know we'll get it, so let's take a look at what went wrong here. . . ."

It's worth noting that the statements are different. The first flips student expectation; the teacher is glad to have seen the mistake. The second gives credit to the student's understanding of the mathematical principles—but makes it clear that she's come up with the right answer for a different setting. The third and fourth acknowledge that the task is not the sort of thing you try just once and get right. They normalize struggle.

As this *Culture of Error* is created, students become more likely to *want* to expose their mistakes. This shift from defensiveness or denial to openness is critical. As a teacher you can now spend less time and energy hunting for mistakes and more time learning from them. Similarly, if the goal is for students to learn to self-correct—to find and address errors on their own—becoming comfortable acknowledging mistakes is a critical step forward.

## Building a Culture of Error

A teacher alone cannot establish a culture in which it is safe to struggle and fail. If snickers greet a classmate who gets an answer wrong, for example, or if impatient hands wave in the air while another student is trying to answer, very little that a teacher does will result in students feeling safe exposing their mistakes to the group.

Shaping how students respond to one another's struggles is, therefore, a must. It is a process that starts with teaching students the right way to handle common situations.

That is, explain how you expect them to act when someone struggles *before it happens*, share the rationale, practice the expected behaviors in hypothetical situations, and if (when) a breach occurs, reset the culture firmly, but with understanding. You might say something like, "Just a minute. I want to be very clear that we always support each other and help one another in this classroom. And we never, ever undertake actions that tear down another person. It's difficult but I will expect that of all of you. Among other things, we know that person could just as well be us."

When you think about making it safe to struggle, it's important to consider that the goal is not just eliminating potentially negative behaviors among students. Even better would be fostering a culture where students actively support one another as they struggle through the learning process. Collegiate Academies in New Orleans does a great job of encouraging this culture. When someone is struggling to answer a question, peers (or teachers) "send magic," making a subtle hand gesture that means, "I'm supporting you." After an answer, if peers wish to show appreciation (they often do), they show it with snapping fingers, thus creating a system for positive student-to-student feedback for quality work.[11] This positive culture is one of the most remarkable and powerful things about a remarkable group of schools.

And of course having strong *Habits of Attention* (technique 48) is critical to ensure that signals of belonging are strong and the importance of each student's ideas is regularly reinforced.

That said, building a classroom culture that respects, normalizes, and values error is complex work, so I've named and described some of the key culture building moves in greater detail so they're easier to use intentionally in your classroom.

## Expect Error

After a mistake occurs, strive to show that you are glad to know about it. We want the overall message to be that errors are a normal part of learning—a positive part, often—and are most useful when they are out in the open.

Consider how Roxbury Prep math teacher Jason Armstrong communicated the normalcy of error even before he started reviewing answers to a problem recently. "I suspect there's going to be some disagreement here, so I might hear a couple different people's answers," he said, before taking *four* different answers from the class. His words implied that the normal state of affairs is to see different answers among smart people doing challenging work. This also serves to teach that math is not just a matter of deciding between a right answer and a wrong one but, sometimes, a matter of deciding among a wide array of plausible answers. If the questions are hard, Jason's teaching intimated, of course people will disagree.

## Withhold the Answer

In the video *Culture of Error Montage* you can see Jason introduce a second problem from the same lesson. His choice of language was again striking:

> OK, now for the four answers we have here, A, B, C, and D, I don't want to start by asking which one you think is right, because I want to focus on the explanations that we have. So let me hear what people think of D. I don't care if you think it's right or wrong; I just want to hear what people think. Eddie, what did you say about it?

You've probably noticed that Jason's language emphasizes the importance of mathematical thinking (as opposed to just getting it right). That's valuable. In situations when many teachers say things like, "I want to focus on the explanation. How you think about this is as important as whether you got it right," what Jason does is different because *students don't know whether or not they are discussing a right answer.* He has asked them not to discuss how they got the answer *they* gave—and therefore think is right—but an answer that he chose.

We often begin reviewing a problem by revealing the right answer and then, suspense alleviated, talking about it. However, as soon as students know the right answer, the nature of their engagement tends to change. They shift to thinking about whether they got it right and how well they did. No matter how much they love the math for the math's sake (or history or science or literature for its sake), part of them is thinking "Yes! I got it," or "Darn, I knew that," or "Darn, why do I keep messing up?" If Jason had said, "The answer here is B, but I want to look at D," some students would almost assuredly have thought, "Cool, I knew that," *and then stopped listening as closely because in their minds they had gotten it right and didn't need to listen.*

One of the simplest and easiest things you can do to begin building a *Culture of Error* is to delay revealing whether an answer is right or wrong until after you've discussed it, and perhaps an alternative.

You can see Katie Bellucci do this in the video *Katie Bellucci: Different Answers*. She begins by asking students to use hand signals (see technique 10, *Show Me*) to reveal their answers to a multiple-choice question. "We have some different answers out here," she says, "I see some twos, threes, and fours. B, C, and D." Her tone is cheery, indicating that disagreement—and therefore wrong answers—is not a bad thing. It only proves the discussion will be interesting. But notice what she does next. As she begins reworking the problem with the help of her students, she does not tell them which of those answer choices was correct.

By *withholding the answer* until after she's discussed the question fully, Katie retains a bit of suspense, keeps students productively engaged, and avoids the distraction of "Did I get it right?" for a few seconds. This can be very productive, not just as an intellectual exercise, but as a cultural one, in causing students to spend less energy evaluating their work and more energy thinking about the underlying ideas ("I hadn't thought of doing it that way. I wonder if she'll get the answer I got").

Her lovely move to normalize and celebrate error—"Put your hand up if you changed your answer. Yes, be proud! You figured it out," is a perfect way to express the core of the idea in *Culture of Error—the fun is in the process*. She celebrates struggle in the most compelling way, but that moment is really only possible if everyone is invested in "figuring it out" with her throughout the process, and it all starts with her decision to withhold the answer.

## Manage the Tell

In poker circles, players have to watch their "tell"—the unintentional signals they give that reveal the status of their hand to savvy opponents. A good player can figure out that an opponent's habit of rubbing his eyes or rechecking his cards is a nervous tic revealing a poor hand. Having a tell puts you at such a disadvantage that some elite players wear sunglasses and hooded sweatshirts to ensure they don't reveal too much.

As teachers, we also have tells—unintentional cues that reveal our hand, such as whether an answer was right or wrong or whether we valued what a student said. A tell causes us to communicate more than we realize. It compromises our ability to withhold the answer. And it can often result in our unwittingly communicating disdain for errors.

One of my tells as a teacher was the word "Interesting," offered in a benign but slightly patronizing tone of voice and usually with a "Hmmm" in front of it and a single, long blink of both eyes. I would use it, without realizing it, in my English classes when a student offered an interpretation I thought was flimsy. I know this was my tell because one day after a student comment, I said, "Hmmm. Interesting." At that point, a student named Danielle said quite clearly from the back of the classroom, "Uh oh. Try again!" She knew what "interesting" meant: "Well, that was disappointing." Like most teachers, I was saying a lot more than I thought I was. My message really was, "You probably should have kept that thought to yourself," and the student who'd spoken and all my students knew that. So much for making it safe to be wrong.

Compare that to Emily Badillo's response to student errors in the video *Emily Badillo: Culture of Error*. Her facial expression does not change whether students are right or wrong. She's the same steady, emotionally constant self. It helps that she withholds the answer. There's no giveaway at all.

We all have tells—several, probably—and because they are unintentional, we may send them over and over, communicating a message to students that undercuts what we might intend to say. One of my most capable colleagues describes a different tell. When students gave an answer in her class, she would write it on the board if it were correct, but wouldn't bother to write it if it were wrong. Sometimes she would call on a student and turn to the board, marker poised as if to write, only to turn back to the class upon hearing the answer, and recap the marker: *Click*. Message received.

Students figure out our tells surprisingly quickly, so it's important to seek them out in our own teaching and manage them. Of course, we'll never be perfect. Of course, it's fine to say, "Interesting" or even to explicitly say, "I think we can do better" or "No, I'm sorry, that's not correct." You just want to be aware of and intentional about what you communicate and when. Think for a moment about what might be the most common teacher tell: "Does anyone have a *different* answer?" (When was the last time you said *that* when someone got it right?) In using this phrase without intentionality, you would first communicate that the answer was wrong and therefore risk discouraging students from thinking as deeply about it as they would if they didn't know. Second, you would imply to the student who answered, "If that's all you've got, please don't speak again."

It's worth noting that the most persistent tells are usually in response to wrong answers, but we can also have tells for right answers—a big, bright face or perhaps the inflection on the word "why" in a statement like, "And can you tell us *why* you think Wilbur is afraid?" Clearly, it's not a negative to show appreciation and enthusiasm for a great answer. But it *is* worth considering whether that enthusiasm sometimes gives away too much, too soon or, if it's used too often, what its absence communicates. Ideally, we are all alert to our tells and manage them—replacing them as often as possible with a consistent and balanced expression of appreciation that's not quite approval.

## Praise Risk-Taking

The final aspect of creating a *Culture of Error* is to praise students for taking risks and facing down the challenge of a difficult subject. It's especially useful to encourage students to take risks when they're not sure. A statement such as, "This is a tough question. If you're struggling with it, that's a good sign. Now, who'll be bold and start us off?" reminds students that being a scholar means offering your thoughts when you're not sure, and sometimes *because* you're not sure. You can reinforce that positively by saying, for example, "I love the fact that this is a hard question and so many of you have your hands in the air," or you can shorthand that by simply referring to your students' "brave hands" when you see them raised (for example, "Who wants to take a shot at our challenge question? Beautiful. Love those brave hands . . . Diallo, what do you think?"). If discussing a particularly difficult passage in a book, you could try acknowledging the difficulty by saying something like, "This is a question that people have debated for decades, but you're really attacking this." You can see Denarius Frazier do this in the *Culture of Error* montage. "Ohhh, I like this bravery," he says, looking out at a handful of students willing to try to answer a difficult question. In a *Culture of Error*, students should feel good about stepping out on a limb, whether they're right or wrong.

## Putting It All Together: Jasmine Howard, Nicole Warren, and the Back (or Front) Table

The video *Jasmine Howard: College Bound* provides a beautiful example of *Standardize the Format*, *Active Observation*, *Show Me*, and *Culture of Error* in a single clip, shot in her eighth-grade math class at Freedom Prep in Memphis, Tennessee. She's chosen one problem within a larger problem set as a sort of gatekeeper. It's a sort of mid-class *Exit Ticket*. Jasmine circulates and observes. She's using a version of *Active Observation* that's more focused on preparing to give group feedback than on giving individual feedback to every student. Based on these observations, she reviews the problem with the whole class and, as she does so, uses *Show Me* to check that students arrived at answer A. She then sends students to independent practice but walks around and signals subtly to four students to meet her at the back table. There, Jasmine teaches a targeted mini-lesson for the students who needed more help, observing and supporting them as they work. Here you can see her *Standardizing the Format* as she asks students to circle the rate of change to ensure that they both calculated it correctly and know what it is. She does this with impeccable *Culture of Error*—steady, supportive, nonjudgmental. You can see how much the students feel this as they get up from their desks to come to the back table. The first student she taps starts to gather his things and move right away. He's not embarrassed and he's not trying to hide. He trusts in Jasmine to help him and you can see why when you watch her reteach. Jasmine has caught a simple misunderstanding early, before it snowballed, and adeptly has given them just the support they need to understand the concept. It's one of the most impressive takes on differentiation through *Check for Understanding* I've had the pleasure of watching.

Not only that, but Jasmine's forming a group for reteaching in "real-time" *Checking for Understanding* reminded me of another clip of Nicole Warren doing something similar. You can see this in the clip *Nicole Warren: Front Table* in her third-grade classroom at Leadership Prep Ocean Hill. Nicole calls students up to the front table for extra practice after the previous day's *Exit Ticket* revealed that they continued to struggle with story problems.

In part, she told me, she wanted to pull them up front to watch them solve the problem "so I could stop them in the moment, if necessary, and be sure they were using the strategy we had discussed the day before. Since we already spent time debriefing this problem, I wanted to be sure they were practicing correctly to solidify the skill."

In other words, Nicole observes all students carefully, but she also structured her classroom so she can occasionally observe students she's worried about even more carefully. Everyone gets real-time feedback; but this allows her to give a double dose to those who need it most. And you'll notice that they get a ton of feedback—positive in tone but rigorous—and they get the implicit feedback of knowing—when they are sent back to their seats—that they've mastered, at least for the moment, the skill that Nicole had targeted.

One of the most important things Nicole does to make her front table system work is to think about how to leverage her *Culture of Error*—there has to be no judgment, no stigma, no snickering about working at the front table. Nicole's messaging sets that up.

"Pulling a small group has never had a stigma. I think it has to do with how we frame it. We tell students, 'This is a moment to get extra practice one-on-one or in a small group with your teacher.' We never make this time feel negative in any way and students leave feeling successful, after getting the problem correct. We use stickers, high-fives, and smiles to commend them for showing effort through a tricky problem. In addition, the students who come up to the table are always different, based on the [most current] data. Sometimes it is students who are on the higher end, too. This helps to normalize the idea that everyone struggles and that this struggle is a part of the process that leads to mastery."

By the way, a couple of other favorite *Teach Like a Champion* moments from this Nicole Willey clip: Nicole uses *Brighten the Lines* (technique 28), when she uses the prompt "Go!" after her directions to help ensure that students jump right into their work. She also uses *What to Do* (technique 52) beautifully to make sure one of her front-table scholars is listening to her feedback. The student looks like he wants to start going before he really hears what she's saying, so she says, "Look at me" (twice!), in a warm, supportive tone backed by a smile.

Like Jasmine, Nicole has designed her classroom around the idea of *Checking for Understanding*.

# TECHNIQUE 13: SHOW CALL

Let's return to what is perhaps the crucial moment in the clip from Denarius Frazier's math class that we've been examining in the course of this chapter, *Denarius Frazier: Remainder*. Circulating and observing actively, Denarius recognizes that there's something his students have misunderstood about finding the remainder when dividing polynomials. He has recognized an error in real time but this is only half of the equation in *Checking for Understanding*. The second half, deciding how to address it, is a much more challenging question than it appears. Teachers bury the data—recognize student misunderstandings and fail to take action on them—all the time. In many cases this is because of the difficulty of changing one's lesson plan on the spur of the moment in front of thirty students. Or a failure to address the error may be due to the pressure of time. But Denarius hardly bats an eye. He chooses the work of a student, Fagan, who made a characteristic error, walks to the front of the room and projects it to the class. Seconds later the class is engaging with interest and openness in a study of the mistake, why it happened, and what it could teach them.

What's the quickest and most productive way to respond to an error in the midst of teaching, in other words? Often it's to study the error itself.

If you can pull that off, you have a simple, reliable tool to use in response to student errors. If students struggle to understand the first time, you may not have to plan a backup lesson or a new way of teaching the material if you can instead make a useful version of the error instantly visible and then build a culture that supports open study of the thinking that led to a mistake.

That's a powerful idea. If we can find and study our mistakes with openness and fascination, if we can discuss them in substantive conversations, then we have a replicable way to react to error when we see it and we are teaching a process we'd wish our students to copy for much of their lives: Find the mistake. Study it without defensiveness. Relish it as a learning opportunity.

The technique Denarius uses to accomplish this is *Show Call*, choosing a student's work and sharing it, visually, with the class so they are not just talking about it but studying it in a durable sustained way. An essential component of making this sustained study possible is the fact that the mistake is visible to all students. If Denarius had not projected Fagan's work to the class, the class would have learned far less from it.

This opportunity for learning is too important for Denarius to accept anything but the most productive example. Using *Show Call* effectively implies being able to choose deliberately whose work to project. *A Show Call is therefore not just projecting work but selecting the example regardless of who's volunteered to share. Show Call is a visual Cold Call.* To learn optimally from an example, students must see it well, and they need to be looking at just the right case study.

You will also probably notice that Fagan, the accomplished young woman whose work he's chosen, is not bothered when Denarius takes her paper. She doesn't look surprised, as you might expect her to have been. It's a familiar procedure, in other words, one that happens, if not daily, then regularly, and one that began with Denarius explaining to the class what he would do and why before he did it the first time. Then they practiced it—tried the idea out under controlled circumstances where success was more assured. For example, the first few times he used *Show Call*, Denarius probably focused on making *Show-Called* students feel honored by and comfortable with the process. Over time his *Show Calls* became more rigorous. Now he doesn't need to explain why he is taking Fagan's or any student's paper, and students all have learned to engage in error analysis respectfully and productively.

Further, the culture Denarius has built—and which we can see him reinforcing in this clip—communicates the importance of studying mistakes and reinforces a strong sense of psychological safety for students as they do so. Ironically, students in classes like Denarius's often come to love *Show Call*. If they don't love it, they certainly see the value of it. In observing how Denarius approaches the technique we can learn a lot about why. It's also worth noticing that *Show Call*, used frequently, reinforces accountability for written work. On tomorrow's problem set, students will be strongly incented—perhaps even motivated—to do their best work. This will result in better and better examples to share with the class.

Notice Denarius's actions when he begins his *Show Call* and how much importance he assigns to the task of shared error analysis. He deliberately ensures full attention—notice his formal body language (technique 58, *Strong Voice*) and his use of a brief positive group correction, "Waiting on one" (see technique 55, *Least Invasive Intervention*), before commencing. He is communicating the heightened importance of the upcoming task.

As soon as he begins the process of studying a student mistake, he deliberately reinforces a few essential cultural messages. "As I walked around, on a few of our papers I'm noticing that we're getting an incorrect remainder," he says. Immediately it's a "we" issue. He's going to show one example of what is a classwide challenge. Message: It's our work we're studying, not just that of a single *Show-Called* student. "We have check mechanisms in place that we can use to check this," he says, again stressing the class's group ownership of the problem and the solution.

Now to Fagan's work. "Snaps first to Fagan for using long division," Denarius says. "You didn't have to use long division. You don't have to use synthetic. There's even another approach that I saw on Quinetta's paper. . . ." In introducing Fagan's work, the teacher first establishes that there is plenty of successful work in the classroom, even if they are going to improve something about it. Fagan's first instinct may have been to think, *Oh, I got it wrong*, but in fact she *didn't* get it all wrong. She got a *small piece* of it wrong and a lot of it right. She's doing fine, and he's helping her to see that.

Notice also Denarius's emotional constancy and how he treats the error as being completely normal. As I discuss in technique 12, *Culture of Error*, Denarius establishes that mistakes are interesting, valuable even, and definitely not something a teacher gets frustrated at learners about. This is not a culture where people are afraid to discuss a mistake. Why would they be afraid when mistakes have been established as a necessary and helpful part of the learning process and the examination of them is a completely routine part of class?

Students do most of the analysis throughout this *Show Call*, even when he guides them to recognize that they should use the remainder theorem. Denarius doesn't solve the problem; all he really does is tell them how to perceive that their answer does not make sense. Once he's guided them to that realization, they know how to solve it.

*Show Call* is a simple and powerful concept but one that can feel risky to try for some teachers. If you've never done it, you can imagine how you or your students would feel if it didn't work.

In light of that I will describe a typical progression—what *Show Call* might look like at different stages in a classroom so the pathway to a lesson like Denarius's becomes clear. The technique involves shared culture and routines that must be intentionally built. A *Show Call* is unlikely to look like Denarius's the first time a teacher and her students try it.

An early *Show Call* could, however, look a bit like Paul Powell's in the video *Paul Powell: Show Call*.

The student whose paper Paul takes is Kahlila. Here's a still shot of him doing that. Paul's pretty nonchalant in his body language—casual (see technique 58, *Strong Voice*), but Kahlila is not. It's likely she feels a bit anxious; even if Paul has explained what a *Show Call* is and why he does it, she's nervous. *My paper? Oh no!*

That's why Paul's framing when he presents student work is so important. "The theme of the day is showing your work," Paul says. "So I'm going to show off Kahlila's work." Suddenly everything has changed. My team and I refer to this moment in the *Show Call* as "the reveal": the moment when you show the student work and frame how the class should think about it. You'll notice again and again how important the reveal is in building culture. Kahilia now knows that Paul's sharing her work is a good thing. He's showing it off.

"Look at that," Paul continues, pointing out details of her now-projected work. "*Boom.* Formula. Plugged it in. Very neat. *Boom.*" If, a moment before, Kahlila's primary emotion was anxiety, it's now pride.

The culture Paul is building isn't simplistic, though. He's also sowing the seeds of self-study and improvement—a good-to-great culture. As he highlights the many things to love about Kahlila's work, he normalizes the process of making it better. "There's one little thing we're going to fix here in a second," he says, making sure that the first few times he asks students to share their mistakes feel especially safe and nonthreatening.

A few moments later, Paul returns to the idea of improvement. "What is the one little thing she can fix?" he asks, and here is Kahlila's reaction:

There are lots of hands up, but Kahlila's is the straightest. Her body language is unmistakable. "Call on me now, Mr. Powell! I can make it even better!" She's proud, in other words, and eager to show how much else she knows.

What we see here is not just a single *Show Call* that helps students to better see how to solve a problem and how to avoid a common mistake, but a procedure—and the culture to support it—that makes students feel lovingly accountable for their written work and unafraid of having it presented to the class. Paul's example is a road map for the first few times you use the technique; emphasize positivity and make students feel honored by and comfortable with the process.

Over time the goal is to build a culture in which, as we saw in Denarius's class, students understand implicitly that one of the ways they honor a classmate's work is by helping them to see both its success and also how to improve.

You can see this progression of Show Call culture clearly in the video *Ijeoma Duru: Almost-There Work*. Ijeoma is sharing the work of a student named Deborah and starts by asking students to give Deborah some "snaps and shine." This ideally makes Deborah feel supported; it also, perhaps even more importantly, reminds the class: this is a classmate's work. We'll study it and improve it, but don't forget to be appreciative in your tone and comments as we discuss.

Like Denarius and Paul, Ijeoma uses her "reveal" to shape the culture that surrounds the *Show Call*: "Deborah has some 'almost there' work but I want us to work together and use her annotations to fix it," she says. She then asks students to focus on the second half of Deborah's work and "snap if you see something you agree with." This is a clever move. Every one of Deborah's classmates just affirmed that, like Fagan, she got plenty right in her answer. Even if there's something to improve on, there's a lot to the good and it's obvious to everyone. Ijeoma next asks a few students to describe what they agree with. This isn't just about building Deborah up; it also reinforces their understanding. It's a form of *Retrieval Practice* (technique 7), encoding knowledge more deeply in long-term memory via recall and, here especially, elaboration. "Beautifully explained," Ijeoma says to Jules, whom we can't see, after he has put the ideas he sees on the graph into new words. He's done well, but it was hard work. You could hear the labor in his voice. Memory is the residue of effort. He's worked hard to elaborate precisely, and this will help him remember and encode, and Ijeoma shows her appreciation for his work.

But there's another crucial benefit to *Show Call* that we see evidence of in Ijeoma's class. Deborah has annotated the diagram to show that there are corresponding angles in it—she's written the phrase across the side—but not *where* they are. She knows they're there —she just isn't sure how to find them. This underscores the critical and underrated role of perception in learning.

"She says that there must be corresponding angles somewhere," Ijeoma says, referring to Deborah's annotation, "and I agree," but then she asks: "Where should I place a star for the other angle that corresponds to that 25?" She calls on Michaela and as Michaela narrates her thought process, something very important is happening. *Everyone is looking at what Michaela is describing as she describes it*. If you want a group of people to problem solve, they need to all be looking at the same version of a problem. With the work projected, Ijeoma can guide students' eyes through their study of it. She is teaching them mathematical concepts *and how to perceive on their own when they apply*. While this is an example from a math class, perception is equally important, if not more critical, in studying a section of text, either from a writing or a close reading perspective. The discussion can be radically improved when a student states vaguely that she likes the "details" or the "writing style" in a peer's passage. "Great," you can suddenly say, "let's take a look at some of the details that stand out to you," or "Great, let's read it together and annotate some of the lines that help her create such a distinctive tone."

Learning starts, most often, with perception, something so basic we often overlook it. Most of our brain is a system for visual perception—much of it unconscious. We look where we look out of habit, and if we learn to look in the right places, we're far more likely to be successful. Decisions almost always start with our eyes. In that sense, students are a bit like athletes. Those who see at a glance where to pass or how to block an opponent make their decisions first and foremost because they are looking for the right things and in the right places. Their eyes go to the parts of a problem where the relevant signal will appear. This is a key piece of their expertise. The more expert the decision maker, the more likely this precise looking is to happen. Or perhaps it's the other way around. The more likely a decision maker is to look at the right things, the more expert they are likely to be.[12] Projecting a problem allows us to engage student's perception in the problem-solving process. In a moment, I'll show you another example of this.

*Show Call* works because there is learning power in looking: we build students' perception ability. The content that we look at together remains fixed in students' attention and engages the portions of their brains—the majority of the brain—that rely on and process visual information.

Watch how powerfully Julia Addeo leverages the idea of guided or shared perception in the video *Julia Addeo: Expand,* in which she *Show Calls* Monet's work and where Monet, interestingly, has made two different efforts to solve a problem. Julia doesn't tell students which one is correct. The goal is for students to discern which solution is correct and why—or for them to be able to look and perceive what mathematical tool will work. Notice how focused on perception Julia's questions are: "What did Monet do on the left?" The first student Julia calls on does not correctly perceive the strategy Monet is using and Julia's response is powerful. "What did she do in this first line here?" She still hasn't told them the answer; she's just helping them know where to see it.

*Show Call* can also work by asking students to use comparative judgment—it can place two examples close together and ask students to discern the differences. When the next student describes Monet's first step correctly, Julia labels it. Now that they can see the math, she wants to associate a name with it. "Let's write that in our notes: expand," Julia says. Now they can see what it looks like and associate it with its technical name. Then another perception question: "Once she [Monet] expanded, what did she do then?" And then for the other side, Julia again asks a perception-based question, "What did she do?" To perceive is to understand. Now that they understand the steps Monet took in each case, students have to decide which solution was more useful. Julia goes to a *Turn and Talk* (technique 43) and then uses *Show Me* (technique 10).

In the video *Rousseau Mieze: Source Line*, you can observe Rousseau *Show Calling* two examples of student work and asking the class to discern why one of them is stronger than the other. Once again this demonstrates how *Show Call* can be especially powerful when it asks students to compare examples because it leverages the power of a cognitive principle called "the law of comparative judgment"—simply put, this is the idea that people are better at making comparisons between pieces of work than at making absolute judgments about quality. Humans are likely to learn more by comparing one piece of work to another, rather than to an abstract standard.[13] Want students to see the subtle differences between good and great writing? Show them two different examples and suddenly the conversation will accelerate— and the subtler the differences, the more advanced and more nuanced a conversation they will yield. In other words, if you want to do really rigorous study of student writing, compare a very good example to a great one. Or show the class two similar approaches and study how the small differences allow them to achieve different ends. "I want to talk about which one is strongest," Rousseau tells the class in his reveal. Then notice how he reads the two student answers aloud, one immediately after the other, to make subtle differences as apparent to students as possible.

The video *Rose Bernunzio: Good Catch* also shows the benefit of using *Show Call* to compare two students' work, and it's worth comparing some of the similarities and differences between Rose's approach and Rousseau's. Both begin with a question that emphasizes perception—essentially, what's the difference—and both intentionally try to boost their ratio in this critical moment, getting every student to discuss via a *Turn and Talk*. They want everyone doing this cognitive work. But whereas Rousseau asks students to "snap it up" for two classmates whom he identifies, Rose deliberately keeps the identities of her students anonymous. Balancing anonymity and credit is a variable you can consider in the "reveal."

There are also variables in the "take," the name we use for another key culture-setting part of the *Show Call*, the moment when you take a student's paper. Do you explain why? Do you merely take it and presume it's understood? Do you ask? In this case, Rose subtly asks the student whose paper she takes. It's more of a courtesy than anything else. Rose also diffuses the pressure a bit by saying, "Lots of people are making this mistake." Ironically, the "take" is often smoother if it's simpler. Rousseau, like Denarius and Paul, uses an "unnarrated take." He does not ask permission. It's important to note that he can do this because, in his classroom, *Show Calling* is an established procedure that students understand clearly. And because a *Culture of Error* is intact, an unnarrated take won't work without those things in place. Another important difference between the clips is what happens afterwards. Rousseau asks students to revise their answers. Rose asks students to apply the same method to parts B and C of the problem. Two slightly different applications of an idea we also saw in Ijeoma's *Show Call*, which ended with the phrase "Make sure you have this written on your paper." The message in all three cases is: *We just spent a lot of time learning something important; make sure you have it down.* This foreshadows technique 14, *Own and Track*.

*Show Call* can also help students to see and understand their mistakes by showing the solution rather than the error. You can see Sarah Wright do the first of those in the video *Sarah Wright: Show Call Discussion*. In her study of the novel *Esperanza Rising*, her reveal explains the purpose of her *Show Call*: "We are going to *Show Call* some students' work, have them explain their work a little bit, and then you'll be able to add to your paper." She's *Show Called* some of the strongest pieces of work in the room; she wants the rest of the class to take notes on the gaps between their own work and these examples. Multiple times she returns to Trey's paper to point out what's excellent about it. She uses Trey's observations, perhaps the strongest in the class, to start a conversation in which students expand and elaborate on his ideas. What they ultimately write down is Trey's answer plus the class's further reflections on the best-written ideas that emerged.

A final note: *Show Call* appeared in TLAC 2.0 as part of a section on Building Ratio. And, indeed, it does boost the amount of cognitive work that students do, but it's most powerful, I have been arguing, as a tool to respond to error as a group, and so I have moved it to an earlier spot in the text. That said, as Sarah intimates here, it is also an excellent tool for revising and expanding ideas and so I will return to it in Chapter 8, "Building Ratio Through Writing."

## During the *Show Call*: Two Key Moments

There are two especially important moments to manage during a *Show Call*: the *take*—the moment when you take a student's paper off his or her desk with the intent to project it—and the *reveal*—the moment when you show the work to the class. What you say and how you frame what you are doing are especially important at these points of inflection.

### The Take

The goal is to make the *take* feel familiar to a student. We want to remind them that *Show Call* is an everyday event and that almost everyone's work will be projected at some point. And we want *Show Call* to feel safe. Nothing bad or humiliating will happen. In many ways those things go together. A seamless "take" where the teacher calmly selects a students' paper from their desk and says very little—perhaps offers a nod of thanks or a brief smile, or whispers

"Can I borrow this?" mostly as a courtesy—communicates best the calm normalcy of *Show Call*. It suggests routine.

That said, "If the culture is built right" is a statement not to take lightly. Strong positive cultures constantly need reinforcement and reinvigoration, so mixing in a bit of positive framing is also sometimes helpful. Arielle Hoo offers a great example of that in the video *Arielle Hoo: Strong Work*. "I'm coming around to look for strong work to *Show Call*," she says matter-of-factly, reminding students that *Show Call* is an honor. Suddenly, Ms. Hoo lingering at your desk is a sign that all is well. Then you'll notice when she takes Tyler's paper she looks at it admiringly but says nothing:

An alternative might be a quiet explanation to a student to remind them of the purpose: "Your work is really interesting. I'd love to share it with the class." You might do more such framing early on in your use of *take*, transitioning later to more unnarrated takes. But less is often more. There are definitely times to say, "Oh, this is great. I can't wait to share it," but if you have to say it every time you wish to "take" a paper, it becomes nearly meaningless.

In some cases (it's early in the year and you're building culture; or a student may be self-conscious about the mistake they've made) a bit more of an "ask" is appropriate with the take, but often a simple statement of purpose preceding the question is helpful: "I'd love to share this with the class, OK?" is even better than "Can I share this with the class?" A smile or some positive words of affirmation, "You're doing fine; I'd love to share your work," always helps. It can also help to crouch down and put yourself on an eye level with the student.

It's up to you whether you want to give students the right to say no when you ask, but for most teachers, it's more of a courtesy than a real option. That said, if a student were to object, you might respond with, "Well, let's see how it goes. I really think it will be worthwhile," or "OK, how about if I keep you anonymous?" or "Why don't I start, and if you get uncomfortable you can signal me to stop."

## The Reveal

The way you "reveal" written work to the class frames the way students interpret it and sets the tone for the rest of the *Show Call*. One factor to consider is whether you want to name the student whose work you show. Naming a student can help you make *Show Call* feel like a reward, but anonymity can be effective as well, especially if it makes you and your students more comfortable being constructively and positively critical in the revision stage.

Another important part of the reveal is whether and how the work is read. You could have students read it silently, but often you or a student may want to read part of it aloud. Reading written work with expression, careful attention, and appreciation is one of the best and most sincere ways to show how much you value and appreciate it. It also unlocks much of the meaning and expression in the words.

A last factor in the reveal is whether you want to tell students what they should look for ("Let's look to see if Martina has used active, dynamic verbs. What do you think?") or use a nondirective reveal ("Here's what Martina wrote. What do you think?") A directive reveal can help you be more efficient and focused, ensuring a tight, productive discussion on what's *most important*. Giving students more latitude via a nondirective reveal can allow students to simulate the revision process more closely and to identify issues they consider relevant. Noting what students observe unprompted can also be a useful source of data.

Arielle Hoo's clip is a model of subtlety. The *reveal*, "Let's take a look at Tyler's work. Tyler, please explain what you did to check," is a model of *Culture of Error*. She's calm and steady but withholds the answer. Only after Tyler's description of his own work does it turn out that he's checked his work in a way that a few students have forgotten to do. Then there's further study by the class of all the reminders of strong mathematical habits that his solution provides.

# Low-Tech *Show Call*

No document camera in your classroom? So be it. While you're in the process of petitioning district higher-ups to provide the single most useful and affordable piece of technology to enhance teaching available, here are four ways to do a low-tech *Show Call* in the meantime:

1. *Show Call* a piece of writing from yesterday's class or last night's homework by collecting it and making a transparency for use with the 1980s version of the document camera: the overhead projector. There's probably one sitting in a closet somewhere.

2. If there's no overhead projector, you can always simply copy the student work (last night's homework or yesterday's in-class writing) and ask students to edit at their desks.

3. Ask students to work on "slates"—mini whiteboards students can write on at their desks. Select one and show it to the class as your *Show Call*.

4. Transcribe a crucial sentence from one student's work on the board and "live edit" it with the class. My colleague Paul Bambrick-Santoyo recommends using flip chart paper for this purpose. Then the notes that capture the class's analysis can live on in your classroom as a permanent record of your collective thinking.

## TECHNIQUE 14: OWN AND TRACK

One morning a few years ago I stopped in on Bryan Belanger's math class. Bryan had given his students this problem to solve:

Which of the following functions would be parallel to the line $y = 3x$? *Select all that apply.*

| | | | | | |
|---|---|---|---|---|---|
| A | $y = -3x - 5$ | B | $y = 3x - 5$ | C | $y = -3x$ |
| D | $y = -3x + 5$ | E | $y = 3x + 5$ | F | $y = 3x + 0$ |

He *Cold Called* students to name the correct answers, and most students understood the problem very quickly and eliminated A, C, and D, though one or two chose A as the correct answer, so Bryan quickly reviewed: "What must every answer need to have to be correct?" he asked.

"A slope of 3," a student replied, so Bryan annotated the problem, writing "m = 3" above the prompt and asked his students to do the same. He didn't want to just correct the understanding, he wanted them to have a record of it.

Then Bryan challenged his students. "Actually," he said, "one of the three other answers is also not correct. Can anyone tell me which one and why?"

He took hands here, and one of his students observed that "F had the same slope but also the same y-intercept."

"Yes," Bryan said. "That's subtle but important. It's the same line and a line can't technically be parallel to itself."

Then again Bryan locked down the teaching point through mark-up.

He asked students to be sure to cross out answer F in their packets and to write in the margin "same line" so they remembered not only that F wasn't correct but why. Then he had them add a note so that above parallel they wrote: "Same slope but different y-intercept."

Thus in the end students had in front of them a perfect record of what they'd learned. It looked something like this:

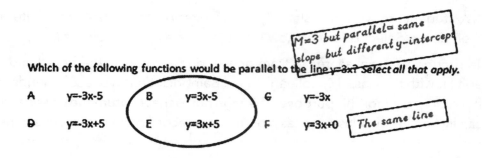

Bryan's actions were intended to increase the value of the time he spent studying common errors by making sure that students took careful note of what they learned. They knew not only which were the right answers, but which one had fooled many of them and why. And they had the rule as they now understood it handy for easy review. That's the idea behind *Own and Track*. If you're going to invest time studying mistakes, make sure students get the most out of it by "owning" the learning and tracking it.

Studying mistakes can be powerful but it's not without risks. It can lead to confusion on the part of students. They could walk away unsure of which part of the discussion was correct, with the muddled and confused memory that there were lots of ways to be wrong, but, hmmm, which was right? In fact, there's research to suggest that discussing wrong answers can result in students, especially the weakest students, failing to differentiate correct answers from incorrect ideas and merely remembering even better the errors you describe. One study found that "incorrect examples supported students' negative knowledge more than correct examples." Error analysis benefited only students who had a strong working knowledge of how to arrive at the answer already, and students needed an "advanced" level of understanding before they were ready to benefit from analyzing errors. For other students, it actually made things worse! Now *that* is a note of caution!

An additional way in which error analysis can go awry would be that you invest a ton of time studying mistakes and students just don't attend to it very intently. The cognitive scientists Kirshner, Sweller, and Clark point out that any lesson that does not result in a change in long-term memory has not resulted in learning. A terrific discussion is important to building understanding but hasn't achieved learning yet. Students have to remember it. Thus, the more time you invest in studying error, the more important it is to end with students having a written record of key insights, terms, and annotation. They need a record of what they've learned both to refer back to later and to build their memory as they go by, causing them to engage with the intention of remembering. These kinds of activities are part of the final CFU technique, *Own and Track*.

We will distill this *Own and Track* process down to three possible steps that teachers can encourage students to follow:

1. Lock in the "right" answer in writing.
   Make sure at the end of your error analysis that students know what the right answer was.

2. Get "meta" (metacognitive) about wrong answers.
   Have students take notes on why wrong answers were wrong. That's often where you spend most of your teaching time. It's immensely valuable because it's a window into students' confusion. But as we know, forgetting happens fast. They should track the learnings so they can review them later and be more likely to remember them.

3. Get "meta" about the right answers, too.
   It's also useful to have students make notes on why correct answers were correct.

Below you can see an example of all three from science teacher Vicki Hernandez's class. Her class was discussing photosynthesis.[14] As you can see, the right answer is clearly marked. And in the box the student has explained to herself why that answer is right. She's also explained why each wrong answer is wrong. This is a student with deep understanding of the question and a record of it for future reference.

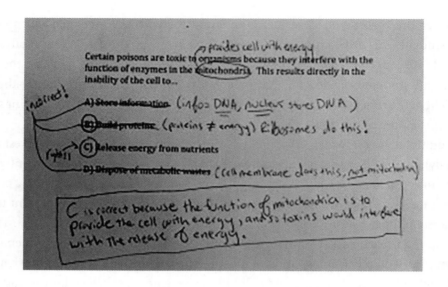

In the video *Vicki Hernandez: Let's Make a Note,* Vicki starts with appreciation for the student whose work she has *Show Called,* praising him for correcting his own answer. She also has the work clearly displayed on her document camera, so the students can see Vicki make notes on the correct answer. She's seen that the common error was a confusion around grass, so she asks them to lock in what they learned about what confused them. "Grass," she says (and writes), "is a producer because it is a plant and goes through photosynthesis."

*Own and Track* is a critical time for *Circulation* and *Active Observation,* as you provide time for students to explain the right answer, appropriately denote the wrong answer, and label their errors. You'll see that in Vicki's clear scan at the end of her clip—she knows the bit of information about grass is critically important for her students, and so she takes the time to make sure everyone has jotted it down.

Another way to help students engage with the content as they correct their answer is to have them reflect on the steps that they did (or did not) take, as Paul Powell did at the end of the video *Paul Powell: Show Call.* Paul and his students have established the correct answer for a multiple-choice question. "Are you showing your work even on a multiple-choice question?" he asks. "Pick your pencil up and give yourself a check for each one of these steps." By building in this written reflection for students, Paul not only ensures they walk away with a clear understanding of what is right (and what is wrong); he also guarantees that their papers reflect the process they took to arrive at the accurate answer; a valuable engagement task turns into a record of lasting value. Some things you could say to help students *Own and Track* include:

"Give yourself a check for every one of these steps that you got correct. If you're missing one, make a note to yourself."

"Circle answer B and write a margin note that explains that it uses the wrong operation."

"Draw a line through the [insert grammar mistake] and rewrite it correctly in the space in the margin."

"Make your paper look like mine."

"Reread your response. Add at least one piece of evidence from our discussion to better support your answer."

"I'm coming around to check that you've defined *fortuitous* in the margin and that your definition includes the word *lucky*."

You can see the benefit of this written record of learning in action in the video *Jon Bogard: Back to Your Notes*. After a robust conversation trying to determine the nature of a classmate's error, a student, India, has the chance, as Jon puts it, to "arbitrate." To determine who is wrong and who is right, she refers back to her notes—with great glee, I might add—to prove that her conclusion is correct. (Don't miss the snaps of support from her classmates, which validate India's scholarly engagement and the high-five from the student in front of her after she drops her evidence on the class.) Here we see the long-term benefit of a clear *Own and Track* system. India is able to engage in this analysis independently because she has referred back to notes that she took the previous day. Then we see the system in action: Jon says to his students, "Fifteen seconds, back to your notes, update what you had before in light of what India just said." He capitalizes on the moment of her insight by asking every student to record it, both increasing the chances that they will remember it and creating a record of it that they will be able to refer back to.

## Lessons from Online

Some of our greatest lessons from remote and online instruction have to do with *Checking for Understanding*. The video *Sadie McCleary: Get You There*, for example, is an exceptional example of how to create a *Culture of Error* online. The first thing you'll notice is that the video is a montage of tiny moments from one of Sadie's chemistry lessons at Western Guilford High School in Greensboro, North Carolina. *Culture of Error* is built up through the aggregation of tiny moments from throughout your lessons. It's a seasoning you are frequently shaking on the meal. But if AP Chemistry is challenging in the classroom, it's exponentially harder when learned on your laptop. Sadie normalizes the struggle constantly and gracefully. She asks Sierra to explain the impact of solution B on reaction rate from a slide she's projecting. "I'm going to be honest, Ms. McCleary," Sierra replies. "I'm so confused."

"That's OK," Sadie replies, but then continues, "I'm going to ask you a couple of questions to get you there—because I know you can get there." Her tone is steady and without judgment. She expresses her belief in Sierra. And then they get to work. So much of what students are responding to when they develop a sense of trust in a teacher, my colleague Dan Cotton observes, is the teacher's competence. Sadie is calm and confident when she finds that the material is difficult for Sierra and she reminds Sierra that it's a struggle, not a crisis—they'll get to work and solve the problem.

Later in the lesson Sadie is more proactive. "Finding the units for K is always the hardest skill of this unit and if it feels tricky that's OK . . . we'll continue to practice it." She's reminding students beforehand that parts of chemistry are difficult—for everyone—and that they don't need to respond to difficulty with panic or frustration but with steady diligence and the willingness to practice.

Later again in the lesson Sadie asks Kendall to explain how to get the exponent in an equation. Kendall's answer is wrong, but Sadie's first words are telling: "I'm glad you said that. That's not why. That's not where we get our exponents, but Kendall has lifted up something that is a common mistake. The coefficients do not matter . . . you have to use your concentration data, and we're going to keep practicing that." Earlier I noted that one key to building a *Culture of Error* was to diffuse defensiveness and anxiety about mistakes while still making it clear that mistakes were mistakes. Sadie does that beautifully here. It's a useful answer, she notes—she's glad Kendall offered it—*because* it's wrong. Sadie's management of her tell is impeccable: She's warm and supportive and unflappable. Her first words are of appreciation and then she gets down to explaining the useful lesson of Kendall's answer.

# Notes

1. The first Forgetting Curve was drawn by Hermann Ebbinghaus in 1885, tracing the rate at which he remembered (or failed to remember) nonsense syllables. The findings have been replicated in principle but how quickly forgetting happens in any specific case depends on who is trying to remember what and under what conditions. Still the principle endures across settings: forgetting starts right away and is always at work. Repetition matters.

2. Paul A. Kirschner, John Sweller, and Richard E. Clark, "Why Minimal Guidance During Instruction Does Not Work: An Analysis of the Failure of Constructivist, Discovery, Problem-Based, Experiential, and Inquiry-Based Teaching," *Educational Psychologist* 41, no. 2 (2006): 75–86, doi: 10.1207/s15326985ep4102_1.

3. You might be wondering *How many times do I have to review a concept to get it into long-term memory?* There's no clear answer—a lot depends on who is learning what, when—but in his long-term study of student learning, *The Hidden Lives of Learners*, Graham Nuthall found that he and his colleagues could predict with 80–85 percent accuracy whether a student in a given class would learn something they did not previously know, based on whether they had encountered the full concept three different times during class. Given that students are sometimes not paying full attention or do not get the whole concept and that facility and speed of access continue to increase and improve one's ability to perceive and connect, there may be an argument for more than three repetitions for many concepts, even if Nuthall is correct.

4. Brown, Roediger, and McDaniel elaborate on elaboration in *Make It Stick*: "Elaboration is the process of giving new material meaning by expressing it in your own words and connecting it with what you already know. The more you can explain about the way your new learning relates to your prior knowledge, the stronger your grasp of the new learning will be and the more connections you create that will help you remember it later" (p. 5).

5. Factual knowledge enhances cognitive processes like problem solving and reasoning. The richer the knowledge base, the more smoothly and effectively these cognitive processes—the very ones that teachers target—operate. https://www.aft.org/periodical/american-educator/spring-2006/how-knowledge-helps.

6. "What you know determines what you see," write Karl Hendrick and Paul Kirschner; it is the knowledge you have deeply encoded in long-term memory and can access simply and easily in the blink of an eye that allows you to see more—literally and figuratively.

7. For this reason I don't personally use the term "aggressive monitoring" as it can unintentionally reinforce this transactional feel in application. "Active Observation" is a bit more neutral to me but if you prefer "aggressive monitoring" that's fine. It's a common term and there's an argument for using *lingua franca*.

8. She also does a nice job of double-checking on Juliana by asking her to rework the original problem while others start in on a new problem. This is a demonstration of the effort Dani has put into building a *Culture of Error* that results in students feeling psychological safety. See technique 12 for more on how teachers like Dani do this.

9. The idea that both Hilary and Jessica use a ticket metaphor for their *Affirmative Checking* is coincidental and actually fairly atypical.

10. *New Yorker*, April 8, 2013, https://www.newyorker.com/magazine/2013/04/08/every-good-boy-does-fine.

11. You can see examples of this in two clips from Jon Bogard's classroom from this chapter. Note the snaps of support "India" gets in the video *Jon Bogard: Back to Your Notes* from the technique *Own and Track* and in the support various students get in the clip *Jon Bogard: Go to IP*.

12. If you're interested, I discuss the science of this extensively in my book *The Coach's Guide to Teaching*. This video of one of the world's best soccer players, Cristiano Ronaldo, wearing eye-tracking glasses is a fascinating study in how important looking is to problem solving.

13. As I note in Chapter Five, Dylan Wiliam has applied this idea to the idea of self-assessment. Giving students work samples to compare to their own is far more effective than using a rubric. https://teachlikeachampion.com/blog/dylan-wiliam-advises-forget-rubric-use-work-samples-instead/.

14. We transcribed the student's notes because they were only partially legible to others.

# Chapter 4

# Academic Ethos

## TECHNIQUE 15: NO OPT OUT

Consider this moment from a recent lesson in Denarius Frazier's tenth-grade geometry class (video: *Denarius Frazier: Quadrilateral*). His students are about to attempt to prove that a given shape is not a square, but first Denarius pauses and asks the class, "Before we get into that, what is the definition of a square?" It's important that every student start with sound knowledge of the basics.

He calls on Aaron, who responds: "All four angles and all four sides are equal." It's a solid answer, one that might suffice in another class, but Denarius says, "Hmm . . . that's about 80 percent of the way there. It can be a little more specific." It's a bit of a *Right Is Right* moment (technique 16)—Denarius is holding out for *all-the-way right* rather than *mostly right*, even while acknowledging the value of Aaron's answer.

Next Denarius calls on Anastasia, who has raised her hand. She adds precision: "A quadrilateral with four 90-degree angles and four congruent sides." At this point, with the fully correct answer having been shared, many teachers might simply move on and return to the proof. But Denarius has something else on his mind, and he instead returns to Aaron: "Back to you, Aaron. What was the difference?"

Aaron says, "I didn't add the quadrilateral."

"The quadrilateral and . . .?" asks Denarius.

"And the degrees of the angle," Aaron finishes.

"Yes, so it's, 90-degree angles and all four sides are congruent." Denarius confirms before moving on to the proof: "How can we prove that this is not a square?"

Denarius's standard of correctness is high and that helps make his classroom a rigorous place. And his preparation is impeccable. But the heart of the interaction is something else subtle but powerful called *No Opt Out*, which is the name for the moment when he returns to Aaron, whose initial answer was not correct.

When a student does not answer correctly, teachers often call on another student or provide the correct answer themselves. But the class hearing the right answer is different from the original student understanding it and being accountable, with caring and humanity, for expressing that understanding.

When Denarius returns to him, Aaron explains the difference between his own answer and Anastasia's. The "return" closes the loop and ensures understanding.

There are a variety of ways to return productively in a *No Opt Out*. For example, Denarius could have asked Anastasia not to answer herself but to provide a cue (a focused and productive hint) to Aaron and then returned to him for the answer. Or he could have asked Anastasia for the correct answer but, in returning to Aaron, had him begin by repeating Anastasia's answer in an effort to encode it in long-term memory. Or he could have shared a gold standard definition of a square himself and then returned to Aaron to ask for the gap between the original answer and the model. He could have asked Aaron to both repeat Anastasia's answer and explain the gap between his own and hers. If it had been a problem such as *What's the measure of the angle here?*, he could have given Aaron another example to try and succeed on, upon returning to him. I'll discuss these variations later, but the core idea is that when a sequence beginning with a student unable or (as we will discuss) unwilling to answer ends with a return in which the student answers successfully the result is progress toward mastery—and a culture that promotes learning.

For now, though, it's most important to focus on Denarius's tone. He's emotionally constant, signaling steady support with his voice and body language: *In this class, we get things wrong and then get them right and we keep moving. That's normal. You're doing fine.* A teacher executing a *No Opt Out* should avoid indicating frustration at the original response but also, in most cases, go easy on the "awesome awesomeness"—that is, in praising a student's small success so highly that the teacher seems either disingenuous or surprised by the student's success (*OMG, you got it right!*).

In this example, Denarius chooses his words wisely in other ways as well. "About 80 percent of the way there," he says, which both diffuses any anxiety for Aaron—after all, he's mostly right—and also cues him to attend carefully to Anastasia's response because there's a fair chance that Denarius is coming back to him to close the loop. In some cases—for example, earlier in the year before students have come to understand that Denarius commenting on the almost-ness of the answer is a signal that he is probably going to coming back to with a question—Denarius might be more explicit: "Not quite. Listen to the next answer and I'll come back to you."

It's worth noting that teachers often promise students they "will come back" to a student when they struggle publicly but, barring their use of *No Opt Out*, often forget to do so. I suspect this is because (a) our working memory is always taxed when we are teaching, so the longer the amount of elapsed time, the harder it is to remember that a student got it wrong or what she got wrong, or (b) we intend to go back but can't exactly imagine what that would look like, so mostly we are announcing our intent. *I am concerned that you struggled and know I should address it. I should not leave this as is.* If we don't have a technique for putting that intent into practice, we're likely to insert a bookmark that we never return to.

One of the benefits of *No Opt Out* is that it gives you a model—or a series of models—for how to go back to a student and *quickly* so you don't lose sight of the moment. This is not to say that you should use the tool reflexively—not every erroneous response needs to trigger a *No Opt Out*. A thousand good things exist in balance and compete for time and focus in a classroom. There's plenty of discretion to be had in when, how often, and what type, but the idea is powerful—returning to a student who hasn't gotten an answer correct and allowing, encouraging, sometimes prompting them to answer again ensures that students rehearse success rather being left dangling when they don't succeed. Done well it often goes a step further, affording a student who's struggled an opportunity to "get it right" in front of peers. It can also be an effective response to learned helplessness—the awkward moments when a student simply won't try. But we will come to all of that.

For now, let's watch a second example from one of Denarius's classes. In *Denarius Frazier: Cosine*, ninth-grade students are solving algebraic equations during guided practice. "Two cosine theta equals the square root of 2," Denarius says, explaining the next step to students.

"Wrap this problem up . . . Shayna," Denarius says. He's going back and forth between modeling steps himself and allowing students to solve parts of the problem, using what Barak Rosenshine would define as guided student practice and others might call the "we" stage in an overall lesson arc of I do/we do/you do. The class's pace is quick and efficient—the *Cold Calls* are predictable—and Shayna hasn't raised her hand but she also doesn't seem the least bit surprised to be called on. And the tone is supportive.

"Divide [by] two on both sides," Shayna advises.

"And we're left with what?" Denarius asks. Shayna responds and Denarius sends the class into a *Turn and Talk* (see technique 43) to solve the problem in pairs ("Turn and talk to your partner; I want an answer for theta in thirty seconds").

Out of the *Turn and Talk*, Denarius *Cold Calls* Deandrea and she's ready with the answer: "Forty-five degrees." Other students snap to show they agree.

But Denarius wants to test for reliability, to make sure students understand the process Deandrea used to solve. "What do we have to do to get that forty-five degrees? Michael?" It's a *Cold Call*—crucial in checking for understanding, as Denarius is doing here. And it's a good thing he asked because, despite snapping along in support of his classmate, Michael is a bit unclear. "Um . . . reverse?" he says, before trying again, "Oh, I'm sorry . . . secant?"

Michael is confused and, rather than waiting for further guesses, Denarius steps in. "We're coming back to you," he says, warmly and without judgment, before calling on Kayla, who begins: "We have to do the inverse of cosine . . ." Moments later Denarius returns to Michael: "Why do we have to do the inverse of cosine, Michael?" Whereupon Michael explains the importance of solving algebraically.

Denarius's tone is supportive throughout, but he also signals normalcy. Of course some students were momentarily confused. Of course Michael got it right in the end. "Go ahead and flip to your *Exit Ticket*. You have three minutes," he says.

Before his "return" to Michael, Denarius uses that phrase, "We'll come back to you" here. The powerful thing is that with a clear procedure or recipe to follow that outlines his reaction—a technique he'd made familiar almost to the point of automaticity—he actually does return to Michael and helps him progress in his understanding.

## Theme and Variation

*No Opt Out*, as I mentioned, comes in various forms and it's worth comparing the two examples from Denarius's classroom to begin considering both themes and variations.

In both cases, going back to the student who was initially incorrect (or partially correct) provides them the opportunity to improve or clarify their original answer. It also gives another student in the room the opportunity to provide an "assist." Allowing students to help their peers in a positive and public way builds community and culture—or, more precisely, if you've established an intentional culture where teamwork thrives, and students support one another, then *No Opt Out* enhances that culture richly and lets students help their peers via their academic accomplishment.

In both cases, tone matters: Denarius is consistent, clear, and steady. *Culture of Error* (technique 12) thrives: Mistakes are useful learning tools. When confusion emerges, the class works through it. There's no blaming of the learner but also not a profusion of "awesome awesomeness." In most cases a sprinkle of subdued positivity suffices ("Well done, Aaron" or "Now you've got it, Michael"). There will be occasions when celebration is warranted; it will sing more if it is reserved mostly for those moments.[1]

A subtle difference between these two clips also highlights the flexibility in the technique. Michael is confused; Aaron's response was strong and very close to gold standard, so Denarius "previews" for Michael—that is, he lets him know explicitly that he'll be coming back to him. This makes the process transparent and reminds Michael to listen carefully to Kayla's response.

The setting is also worth noting in the two clips. The first happens during a brief interval of retrieval practice. The second comes at the end of guided practice and right before students solve on their own. Both of these moments of transition are critical from a Check for Understanding perspective when you would especially want to ensure student knowledge. You can't always use *No Opt Out* but Denarius has chosen his timing strategically.

The second example also might have offered Denarius the alternative of using a cue if he'd wanted to. That is, instead of asking Kayla for the answer he could have first previewed—"OK, Michael, let's get you some help. I'm going to come back to you"—and then asked, "Without giving Michael the answer, who can tell him one word that will help him here?" Let's say that here Kayla raises her hand and replies, "Inverse. He has to use the inverse of something." He can see now in Michael's face that this has been enough and returns to him: "Ready now, Michael?"

"Yes. We need to take the inverse of cosine and then . . ."

We've come across three terms that are helpful in using to the technique so far. The *return* is the part of the *No Opt Out* when you go back to a student who initially struggled to answer fully. A *preview* is when you tell that student explicitly that you are coming back to them to encourage them to listen carefully to peers, as in: "OK, listen carefully and I'll come back to you." You don't have to use a preview, but it can be helpful in establishing familiarity with and transparency in the process for students. Just make sure to remember to return to a student when you've said you will! Finally there's the *cue*. That's the idea that you can sometimes ask additional students you call on to provide key information that the initial student can use to answer after the return rather than the complete answer. This allows the initial student to do more of the work (and show that he or she can do more of the work). Note that, as I discuss below, a cue is different from a hint because the teacher guides the student to give especially useful information.

## On Cues, Hints, and Questions

If I ask James to identify the subject of the sentence "My mother wasn't happy" and he can't answer, I might say: "Can anyone give James a hint to help him find the subject?" and a helpful student might offer, "It starts with the letter *m*." This would help James guess the answer, but it wouldn't teach him anything that would help him in future situations.

I use the word *cue* in place of hint then to refer to a prompt that offers additional information that is useful in building understanding.

Five types of cues are particularly useful in a *No Opt Out*. Here are some examples and the answers they might yield. You'll likely find even better ways to cue students in your own subject and grade.

1.  The place where the answer can be found
    "Who can tell Julia where she could find the answer?" [It's in the diagram at the top of page 3.]

2.  The next step in the process that's required at the moment
    "Who can tell Justine what the next thing she should do is?" [Justine, try to distribute first.]

3.  Another name for a difficult term
    "Who can tell Kevin what *distribute* means?" [Kevin, when you distribute you multiply the outside term by each term inside the parentheses.]

4.  An identification of the mistake
    "Who can explain what Roberto might have done wrong here?" [He might have dropped a negative sign when he distributed.]

5.  A word that might be useful
    "Who can tell Michael a word that might be useful to him in solving?" [Michael, the word *distribute* is really important here.]

An alternative to cuing is to allow students to ask questions as part of a *No Opt Out*. I got this idea from Michael Towne, one of the winners of the 2014 Fishman Prize, a national award given to top teachers in the country. "If I ask them, 'What's the speed of the magnetic flux here?'" Michael told me, "I want them to be able to say, 'I'm actually not that clear on what you mean by magnetic flux.'" To Michael that's a sign of maturity, so he explains to students that they always have this option and encourages them to use it. But the sequence still ends with a *No Opt Out*: "OK, now that we've clarified what magnetic flux is, what's its speed here?"

You can see a really engaging example of cuing in the video *Derek Pollak: Fifth Root*, shot at North Star Academy High School in Newark, New Jersey. Notice Derek's warm and encouraging demeanor as both he and then a peer provide cues to a student solving a problem during retrieval practice.

---

I mentioned previously that there were variations to the *No Opt Out* technique. I'm going to map them out a bit more now.

## Options for What Happens Before the Return

*Go to another student and ask for the answer. Return.*

"Not quite. Who can tell us the definition of juxtaposition?"

*Go to another student and ask for a cue. Return.*

"Not quite. Who can give Kayla an example of juxtaposition? And then, Kayla, I'll ask you to tell us the definition."

*Give a cue yourself. Return.*

"Not quite. Kayla, what if I told you that juxtaposition always involved two characters, images, or things. That help?"

If it didn't help, you might go to another student for the answer—"OK, who can give us a definition of juxtaposition?"—and then return yet again to Kayla after: "Great, now, Kayla, you tell me." The last step might seem unnecessary, but it does several key things. It ensures that Kayla listens to the answer. By causing her to repeat it, it helps her to encode it in long-term memory, and it reduces the chances that Kayla might use "I don't know" on purpose to avoid having to answer. I'll return to this idea later.

*Give a gold standard answer. Return with "Try to tell me that back."*

"Not quite. I'll give you what I think is the ideal definition of juxtaposition, then you try to tell me back. Juxtaposition is when an author places two unlike objects or characters in close proximity within the text to emphasize their contrast. See if you can tell me back?"

This is the least common form of *No Opt Out* (I'll discuss at least one application later), but if you do use it be sure to follow it with a *Stretch It* (technique 17) to give the student the chance to show that they can do more than repeat. As in, "Good. Now that you've got the definition, can you think of an example from the play?" Or, "Good, now that you've got the definition, who is Callie being juxtaposed with in the novel?" Or, to use a different example:

"Jasmine, an inverse is what I multiply a number by to get a product of 1. What's an inverse?

"What you multiply a number by to get the product 1."

"Good, so what would I multiply one-half by to get 1?"

"Two."

"Good, and what's the inverse of one-half?"

"Two."

"Yeah, and what's the inverse of two?"

"One-half."

"Beautiful. Now you've got it."

## Options for What You Ask a Student to Do After the Return

The point of *No Opt Out* is to cause the original student to give the correct answer and successfully solve the problem or encode the information. After that you can add other steps that increase the value of the interaction.

*Explain why the answer is the answer.*

Ask the original student to explain or analyze the answer in some way. Denarius uses this in the second example. "Why do we have to take the inverse of cosine, Michael?"

*Explain the difference between original and final answers.*

Denarius uses this in the first example: "Back to you, Aaron. What's the difference?" Aaron has to note what he left out.

*Apply the idea or complete a similar example.*

"Good, now that you've got the definition, Kayla, who was the author juxtaposing Martina to in the opening scene?"

Or perhaps:

"What's eight times six? Justin?"

"Fifty-six."

"Hmm. Listen carefully to Danielle because the eights are tricky. Danielle, what's eight times six?"

"Forty-eight."

"What's eight times six, Justin?"

"Forty-eight."

"Good. What about eight times seven?"

"Um . . . fifty-six."

"And eight times eight?"

"Sixty-four."

"Good. And eight times six once more?"

"Forty-eight."

"Well done."

## Some Combination of the Above

Once a student gives you a correct answer, you may want let them use it or apply it in a variety of ways. Balancing the needs of time is always a challenge. There's only so much time you can spend doing *No Opt Out*, so you won't be able to do it with every wrong answer. But often it's surprising and unexpected to a student to have a teacher cause them to succeed on a question when they first appeared to struggle, so occasional opportunities to let a student shine a bit after the return can be powerful.

## Aidan Thomas Sticks with It

You can see another example of *No Opt Out* in the video *Aidan Thomas: Y Intercept*. The clip starts with Aidan calling on Jahiem to plot a point on the graph of a line. He's asking for the *y*-intercept, in other words the point (0, X). It looks as if Aidan thinks this question will yield a quick and easy right answer, but Jahiem answers that it's the origin. "No," Aidan chimes in. "That's the trick. Not anymore." His language is masterful here in normalizing the error and making Jahiem feel supported. Jahiem learns that what he thought was the answer (the same answer to a recent problem) was in fact "a trick." This suggests that a common and natural mistake has been made.

He refers the question to Shawn, who answers that the *y* value is −1 and Aidan quickly makes his return: "Yeah, why is it −1, Jahiem?" The return shows faith in Jahiem. By asking him to explain Shawn's answer, he's arguably giving him the harder question. My reading of it is that Aidan thinks he'll get it right and have a chance to shine.

Unexpectedly, Jahiem struggles a bit, but with a bit of prompting, fixes his mistake. Aidan's response—"Nice self-correction," he says, in a steady constant tone—is another bit of culture building. It reinforces the idea that making a mistake and catching it is normal and natural and lets Aidan give Jahiem credit for doing something well: spotting and fixing a mistake. Note that he doesn't overdo the positive reinforcement.

But the data also tells him Jahiem is confused, so eight minutes later, he *Cold Calls* to ask a question that again causes Jahiem to find the *y*-intercept. "What's the point on this graph that we know . . . [pause for everyone to think] . . . Jahiem?"

Again we see Aidan's mastery of creating an environment characterized by a supportive tone but that also ensures that Jahiem is caused to get lots and lots of practice at something he hasn't yet mastered. "You're just using the wrong language," he says when Jahiem struggles. There's no judgment or frustration in his tone. If anything, he's reminding Jahiem that he's closer than he thinks, but he avoids the temptation to gloss over his mistake (e.g. "You meant to say 'y-intercept,' right?") and instead causes Jahiem to use the correct term.

Still Jahiem guesses wrong. Aidan goes to Tavon for the answer (0,2), and then returns again with a *Cold Call*, informed by the previous question Jahiem could not answer. It's still part of the *No Opt Out* in my mind—"That's called the what, Jahiem?" Jahiem's a little flummoxed, but once DJ gives Aidan the correct answer, he circles back to Jahiem and another student, CD, to make sure they lock in the term and, incidentally, hear themselves getting it right.

Throughout this sequence of events Aidan's tone remains warm and supportive. His positivity and equanimity show students that this *No Opt Out* is an expression of caring from an adult who seeks to ensure that they solidify their knowledge and help them succeed.

---

One thing you've probably noticed about the classrooms in which we've studied *No Opt Out* is the larger culture. Denarius has clearly established a climate of trust with his students. In both cases his students give full effort on the initial question and on the return. In Aidan Thomas's and Derek Pollak's classrooms, they persist even on multiple returns.

What if that's not the case? What if individual students or a roomful of students are not yet willing to struggle forward like that? What if they do not yet fully trust the process and are reluctant or resistant? What if they start not at a very good answer, as Aaron does, but at "I have no idea"? How to help them then?

Worse, what if they start at "I have no idea and am not sure I wish to try"? Or even "I have no idea, so leave me alone"?

The reality of teaching is that we are often tasked with addressing reluctance, resistance, learned helplessness, or even outright refusal on the part of students. Some students may give up in the face of what seems to us like a minor challenge. You ask and the answer is very quickly "I don't know." Others may not be willing to even try in the first place. You ask and the answer is "I don't know," and whether they realize it or not, if the *I don't knows* continue, they create an easy out for themselves because in many cases teachers don't know how to respond to "I don't know"—times 100 if it's delivered with a bit of sharpness, as if to say *I already told you I don't know*. When teachers don't know how to respond to that, the result is often that they leave the student alone for the rest of the class.

Or the rest of the week.

Or the rest of the year.

It's a case of the Band-Aid Paradox. We're asked to do what's difficult and sometimes scary. It's easier to make "the deal" with students, which is basically, *I will expect nothing challenging or effortful from you if you agree not to disrupt my class or behave negatively.* You can sit in the corner and I will call on someone else. We all know that there are classrooms where this happens. Students may not see the long-term consequences of this terrible bargain, but teachers should be able to. I hope it is obvious to say that adults who care about young people cannot leave students alone like that and allow them to opt out of learning. That's not love and that's not respect.

Let me be clear—I recognize the complexity of such situations. They reflect Adeyemi Stembridge's observation that "Learning depends on trust that the ground will not give way beneath us, trust that effort is worthwhile." Fixing a context where some students seek to opt out of learning requires a broad range of remedies. We always have to be building trust, for example—in the processes, in ourselves as teachers, or in the endeavor of school—and seeking to ensure that students who don't yet feel that trust come to do so. We need to build cultures that make students feel safe, successful, and known. Much of this book is about that struggle. It's why robust positive cultures that seek not just to limit negative behavior but build positive pro-learning behaviors like *Habits of Attention* (technique 48) are so profoundly important. People's actions are shaped, more than any other single thing, by the norms of others around them. When students are asked a question in class, whether they see their peers' encouraging faces supporting them, or the backs of uninterested heads goes a long way toward determining whether they take the risk of revealing what they know and what they don't. Similarly, we have to build cultures of error (Chapter Two), seek to motivate and inspire, and establish the caring and expectations of *Warm/Strict* (technique 61).

But even as we do these things, even if we have accomplished them for the majority of students in our classes, the moment will come when a student will not be able to answer or won't want to answer and will choose to opt out. The student will say *I don't know* in one of the ways described above, or will say nothing at all, or will say nothing at all with their words but a great deal with their eyes, and no matter how much you understand the imperative of trust and relationships, in that moment you will still be standing there in need of a solution that can bring the situation toward a positive resolution, set basic expectations around effort, and reinforce both caring and accountability. Just telling students you care and want the best for them every so often is not likely to be sufficient to shift established behaviors and mindsets. You will require some option other than "the deal."

Using a *No Opt Out* in this situation gives you a viable and productive response. In order to help students make the change from reluctance or refusal to effort, teachers must first reduce or eliminate the pathway to the "easy out," forestall the opportunity for students to not engage a question when they don't know or don't want to try. It reduces the chances that a student might use "I don't know" on purpose to avoid having to answer because you have required effort of them (even if merely repeating an answer) and so have reduced the incentive. Then teachers must make a base level of effort a habit. That teachers should do this with understanding, humanity, and emotional constancy and that students should do it in a safe environment characterized by mutual respect and decency among students goes without saying.

*No Opt Out* can also help you to understand the student more. If you're not sure whether a student is trying, then simplifying the task, even to the point of asking for a mere restating of an answer, helps to reveal whether you are dealing with a confused student or an unwilling participant. A confused student can always make an effort to repeat. Once they've done that, you can start building them up, via little successes, *Stretch Its*, and positive reinforcement. The path forward involves showing them that they can succeed—at first perhaps at small tasks and because you have insisted. Their success will grow from there.

In fact it's worth noting that while the culture you see in Denarius's classroom clearly supports his use of *No Opt Out* it is also in part a result of his use of the technique as well. His students eagerly engage because Denarius has insisted along the way, with care and humanity, that they do so. He has forestalled the easy out and his students, encouraged to take the riskier path, have mostly come to appreciate that and to trust him. In the end most students know the teacher who makes "the deal" is not the one who cares most about them.[2]

And while the progress a student makes in answering correctly via *No Opt Out* may seem trivial, research on motivation tells us that succeeding makes students want to try more. This is true even of small successes. So when students are stuck and they don't know, letting them see themselves answering correctly not only helps in the short run but in the long run.

And if your *No Opt Out* reduces the task to something very simple and a student persists in refusing to try, then you know clearly that you will have a time for limit setting, a different conversation, perhaps in private, along the lines of: "Charlie, you don't have to get the answers right in my class, but you will be expected to try. You're too capable not to." There are, sadly, students for whom we will have to make it harder not to try than to try. I hope that most of your use of *No Opt Out* is not in such settings. I too wish that such cases were not the reality of our world, but they are and it's our responsibility to be prepared.

## Adding Rigor to *No Opt Out*

Over time my team and I have found that *No Opt Out* often works best when it is most rigorous—the more it rehearses success and lets a student have something to be genuinely proud of at the end of the sequence, the better. This turns setback to triumph and I've often noticed that many of the most able teachers with *No Opt Out* follow up right away to add a challenge or an extra practice, much as you'll read about in *Stretch It* (technique 17).

Consider this very basic interaction:

*Teacher:* What's three times five? Carson.

*Carson:* Eight!

*Teacher:* It's not eight. Who can tell Carson what operation he used?

*Jalani:* He used addition instead of multiplication.

*Teacher:* That's right. So, Carson, what's three times five?

*Carson:* Three times five is fifteen.

*Teacher:* Yes, good. And what's five times three?

*Carson:* It's fifteen, also.

*Teacher:* Good. And four times five?

*Carson:* Twenty.

*Teacher:* Oh, you've got it now! I can't stump you.

This teacher not only gives Carson extra practice at a skill he struggled with but also engineers the experience so the sequence ends with Carson showing that his success was no fluke. He answers several questions correctly; his teacher can't "stump" him. Consider how this sort of interaction turns the tables after a "wrong" answer. Or consider how some small tweaks of this interaction could make it not only positive but more rigorous:

*Teacher:* What's three times five? Carson.

*Carson:* Eight!

*Teacher:* It's not eight. Who can tell Carson what operation he used?

*Jalani:* He used addition.

*Teacher:* That's right. So, Carson, what's three times five?

*Carson:* Three times five is fifteen.

*Teacher:* Yes, good. And if I wasn't sure, what operation could I use to check that?

*Carson:* You could use division.

*Teacher:* Good. Tell us how.

*Carson:*  Well, you'd divide fifteen by five and get three, and you'd know your multiplication was right.

*Teacher:*  Thank you, Carson.

In this case, the teacher has focused on asking not another version of the same question, but a different, related question. In both cases, she is using her follow-up to shape Carson's experience of success, as well as to push his skills.

The following case studies show ways you might use a "stretch" after a successful *No Opt Out* to build rigor and culture.

---

## Case Study 1

*Ms. Klein:*  What's the definition of *vengeance*? Carla.

*Carla:*  Um . . .

*Ms. Klein:*  Shakani? *Vengeance*?

*Shakani:*  Vengeance is violent revenge, getting back at someone who got you.

*Ms. Klein:*  Thanks, Shakani. So what's vengeance, Carla?

*Carla:*  Violent revenge.

*Ms. Klein:*  So who seeks vengeance in *Romeo and Juliet,* Carla?

*Carla:*  Tybalt, when he says, "This must be a Montague. Fetch me my sword."

*Ms. Klein:*  Tybalt is doing what when he says that?

*Carla:*  Looking for vengeance.

*Ms. Klein:*  And would you agree that examples of people seeking vengeance are rare indeed in the play?

*Carla:*  No. Pretty much everyone is seeking vengeance.

*Ms. Klein:*  Nice, Carla. It does seem like just about everybody had vengeance on the brain.

---

## Case Study 2

*Mr. Vaca:* What's the multiplicative inverse of negative three, Jason?

*Jason:* Three.

*Mr. Vaca:* But if I multiply negative three times three I get negative nine. Who can tell Jason what the multiplicative inverse of negative three is? Carlos?

*Carlos:* The multiplicative inverse of negative three is negative one-third.

*Mr. Vaca:* What is it, Jason?

*Jason:* Negative one-third.

*Mr. Vaca:* Good. Why, Jason?

*Jason:* Because negative three times negative one-third equals one.

*Mr. Vaca:* Good. So now tell me the multiplicative inverse of negative one-fifth.

*Jason:* It's negative five.

*Mr. Vaca:* And four?

*Jason:* One-fourth.

*Mr. Vaca:* *(Smiling)* Well, now you're just showing off.

## TECHNIQUE 16: RIGHT IS RIGHT

In almost every lesson, there comes a moment when a student's answer is similar to what you hoped you'd get (or, even better, to the exemplar you wrote when preparing your lesson), but something is still missing. The gist is there, or a kernel of the insight, but it's also not a response that fully answers the question or completely captures the key idea. It's not a mistake, it's just not all the way complete.

What happens next? How do we validate a student's contribution while continuing to push for deeper and more precise thinking?

If we struggle in this moment, it may be in part because of our best intentions. We want to encourage students or we want to keep the class engaged or we need to make sure we get to the *Exit Ticket* before the bell rings, so we say "right" or "good" or "yes" to that almost-there response. However, there are real risks to calling "right" that which is not truly and completely right. Students look to their teachers as arbiters of quality. They rely on us to communicate with honesty and objectivity, using our expertise to evaluate whether responses have answered a question fully and well, so that they may better understand their own progress in learning. If we are not fully honest when we say, "Yes, you have done work of merit," we not only misinform them but sow seeds that eventually erode that essential trust.

*Right Is Right* is about how to respond in the way that's most beneficial to students when an answer is almost right—pretty good, but not 100 percent.

Although it seems obvious that we should set a high standard, we often drop our standards unintentionally. Consider a common teacher habit that I refer to as "rounding up." Rounding up involves a teacher responding to a partially or nearly correct answer by affirming it and in so doing, adding critical detail (perhaps the most insightful or challenging detail) to make the answer fully correct. Imagine, for example, a student who's asked at the beginning of *Romeo and Juliet* how the Capulets and Montagues get along. "They don't like each other," the student might say, in an answer that most teachers would, I hope, consider to be not fully correct—the gist, perhaps, but none of the detail and specificity that indicate a quality understanding. "Right," the teacher might reply. "They don't like each other, and they have been feuding for generations."

Did you catch the rounding up? The student hadn't included "and they have been feuding for generations." That was the teacher's work, though she gave the student credit for it.

Sometimes a teacher will be even more explicit in giving a student credit for the rounding up, as in "Right, what Kiley said was that they don't like each other and have been feuding. Good work, Kiley." Either way, the teacher has set a low standard for depth and accuracy. The student who answered may think, "Good, I did it," when in fact she didn't. Moreover the teacher has crowded out Kiley's own thinking by doing cognitive work that she could—and should—do herself. She has eliminated the opportunity for Kiley to recognize the gap between what she said and what would have constituted a top-quality answer.

Over time, persistent rounding up may cause students to internalize a low standard—they may believe they're prepared and ready to succeed when, in fact, they're not. The story of the American high school, TNTP's *Opportunity Myth* tells us, is an overwhelming number of students believing they've done everything right and still not being prepared to succeed in college. Resisting this kind of subtle erosion of expectations is part of our responsibility to students.

Another, possibly more likely outcome of persistent rounding up is an erosion of trust in and respect for the teacher. Students are highly attuned to moments of inauthenticity in the classroom. Rather than feeling the boost of confidence her teacher might have hoped for, Kiley might be thinking, "That's not what I said . . . Was she actually listening to me?" Perhaps she thinks it's funny and she laughs. Or perhaps she thinks *I didn't say any of that*, and she starts to suspect that her teacher will accept the bare minimum from her. As Adam Smith points out in *Theory of Moral Sentiments*, "It is only the most . . . superficial of mankind who can be much delighted with that praise that they themselves know to be . . . unmerited."

Is "in the ballpark" good enough for Kiley? For all students? Rather than giving students the chance to persevere through a challenge or marshal additional cognitive resources, the teacher takes over and, in so doing, may actually (and paradoxically) signal a *lack* of confidence in Kiley's abilities. As Peps Mccrea writes in his study of the science of motivation, "Success is not about making things easier for pupils. It is about helping them to do something they couldn't do before." Perversely, rounding up devalues students' voices and insights, denying them that chance. False attributions of quality "only serve to undermine motivation and erode trust."

Fortunately, a few specific actions can make it easier to consistently help students arrive at academically rigorous answers. Of course, in talking about right answers, I also acknowledge that there are questions for which there is no right answer. Every teacher asks questions that are open to interpretation or require nuance, but even in such cases, there remains a standard for what constitutes a complete, high-quality response. That standard too requires our daily attention and self-discipline.

## Holding Out for All-the-Way Right

The most basic form of *Right Is Right*, holding out for all-the-way right, means using phrases that cause students to elaborate on and add to their initial thinking and so come to recognize what fully correct looks like—the opposite of rounding up. A teacher might use one of the following phrases in response to Kiley's answer about *Romeo and Juliet*:

"True. They don't like each other. But can you observe a bit more about their relationship?"

"Good start, Kiley. Can you develop your answer?"

"Can you elaborate on what you mean by 'don't like each other,' Kiley?"

"Thanks for starting us off, Kiley. Can you talk about the word Shakespeare uses to describe their relationship [that is, *feud*]?"

"OK. Kiley said the Capulets and Montagues don't like each other. Can we put some more precise language to the task here?"

"Thanks, Kiley. When you say they don't like each other, is that how they'd describe it?"

"Thanks for kicking off our discussion, Kiley. Can you point us to some language in the Prologue that can help us get more specific?"

In holding out for all-the-way right, you set the expectation that ideas matter, that you care about the difference between the facile and the scholarly, *and that you believe your students are capable of the latter*. This faith in your students' ability sends a message that will guide students long after they've left your classroom. They will have been pushed and know they can do it if they push themselves.

There are two excellent examples of holding out for all-the-way right answers in the video *Akilah Bond: Keystone*. As students strive to figure out why Cam is helping Eric in the Cam Jansen story they are reading, Cheyenne gives a strong answer that includes one of two possible reasons. At about 2:00 in the video Akilah says (with students chiming in): "Nice work, Cheyenne," and praises her for having talked about both characters. She's reinforced her effort. But then she adds, "There is something else we know about both characters that makes me think there's another reason Cam is helping Eric." There's positive reinforcement for Cheyenne and also clarity about the fact that they've not yet arrived at a fully correct answer and Kimayah weighs in to add the critical detail.

Later Akilah asks Sonoa to explain why Eric asks Cam a question. Sonoa's response is good, but afterwards, Akilah notes, "We're missing something from Sonoa's response. What are we missing?" she asks, and by not accepting an almost-right answer or not crowding out student thinking by rounding up herself, she allows Michael to do the work (and, as you'll notice, be the hero).

A word about tone. Holding out for high standards does not imply being harsh or punitive—in fact, the opposite is true. As you read the responses to replace rounding up above, I hope you imagined a teacher smiling gently, nodding to encourage her students, and/or speaking in a supportive tone. "Personal warmth combined with active demand-ingness," Zaretta Hammond writes in *Culturally Responsive Teaching and the Brain*, "earns the teacher the right to push for excellence and stretch the student beyond his comfort zone." Students must feel that you believe in their ability to produce ideas of depth and quality, and when this is the case it yields a happy irony: Using *Right Is Right* demonstrates that you value the student as much as the answer. The goal isn't simply to get the right answer spoken aloud (by *someone*), but to help each student push their answer to the level of precision and accuracy you believe them capable of, and in so doing to believe them-selves capable of excellence.

You can see that dynamic—personal warmth and high expectations for the quality and correctness of answers combining to express an ardent belief in what a student is capable of—in the video *Emily Badillo: Traitor*, which shows Emily's fourth-grade classroom at Excellence Girls Charter School in Brooklyn. After a student, Chassity, offers a convoluted (if earnest) response to her initial question, Emily explains with patience and emotional constancy what the question was asking and offers Chassity a moment to get her thoughts together. Chassity, perhaps feeling Emily's belief in her, does not give up and her hand is soon back in the air.

Emily does not forget her. "Back to you, Chas," she says lovingly, but again Chassity struggles. There's lots of thinking there, but not yet a right answer. "Eyes here," Emily instructs the class, drawing attention away from Chassity for a moment to ease any tension she might feel. She then explains what the question is asking for, making the presumption that if Chassity is unclear, others in the room are likely to be as well. She wants a description of the change from one opinion to another among the soldiers. This time she gets an excellent answer from a classmate, but Emily still wants *Chassity* to get it right. And she wants Chassity to believe she can get it right. So she goes back to her. Chassity again struggles to focus on the question, so Emily steps in, again with warmth and care, to help her focus on the question as she begins framing her response with a sentence starter.

At this point Chassity's answer is dramatically improved. That's the good news. But it's still not right. And Emily thinks Chassity can get all the way there. So where most teachers would pull the ripcord and says "Great work, Chassity," or round up and say, "What Chassity means is. . . ," Emily tells her, "You are so close. Add in your . . . keyword about the soldier's perspective. At first, what?" and now, at last, Chassity nails it. And when her classmates celebrate with her, she knows her accomplishment is real and that she has done something of merit. When Emily says Chassity's work is good, Chassity knows it's good. Recall what we've learned from Peps Mccrea: "Success . . . is about helping [students] do what they could not do before." When that happens, he observes, their motivation increases.

It's important to note that it can take quite a bit of time, as we see in this clip, to help a student get from "not quite" to "nailed it." In this case, Emily knew it was worth investing the whole class's time (as opposed to privately intervening with Chassity at another time) because Chassity's thinking was going to form the thesis of the essay every student was about to draft. They all benefited, culturally and academically, from Emily's investment in their peer.

## The Power of Scripting "Right"

Many factors account for why we sometimes don't hold out for all-the-way right answers. There's a time investment in pushing students to find the rest of the answer instead of simply providing it yourself, and we're always under pressure for time. "OK," we think, "I have ten minutes left, and I just might make it through everything I planned," and then we get an answer that's almost what we wanted. It's easy to jump at the quick fix. Another reason is that we want to be encouraging. It is the first time you can recall ever seeing Linda raise her hand. Her answer isn't perfect, but you want to be positive, make her feel successful, and encourage her to raise her hand again. So you avoid any implication of "not good enough."

It turns out that preparation is one of the keys to keeping standards high. If we haven't clearly defined what a high-quality answer will include beforehand, it's hard to hold out.

If you're not sure of exactly what a great answer should contain, you won't be able to hold students to an exacting standard. Therefore, *Exemplar Planning* (technique 1) can help you do some of the "Is that good enough?" and "Is that all-the-way right?" thinking in advance. Of course this doesn't mean you can't override your initial model answer when you're surprised by an unexpected insight from a student; it just means you've started with a more concrete sense of the end goal, particularly for the most critical questions.

## Keeping "Almost There" Phrases in Your Back Pocket

A final reason why we sometimes accept answers that are less than fully correct is that we are not neutral observers of our own lessons. At the end of the day, we evaluate ourselves as teachers based in large part on how much we think our students learned. It's not just our students we're assessing but also ourselves, and we have a vested interest in telling ourselves that our students were successful. In a sense, if we give students credit for a correct answer, we give ourselves credit too. The phrase "I know what she was trying to say," which is sometimes heard among teachers, acknowledges the problem; the unsaid second part of the sentence is, "but she didn't actually say it." A lifetime of caring about students, of wanting to believe in them, and wanting to believe we've served them well puts us at risk of giving full credit for partial answers and pits us against some of our strongest impulses as educators.

Getting the most out of *Right Is Right* often means crafting two-part phrases that capture how we feel about our students' effort on one hand and how correct their answer was on the other. This makes it easier to be honest about both—that you *like what they've done so far* and that they're *closing in on the right answer*, that you *think they know more than they said* but that *there's still some work to be done* or that you want them to *push themselves to be even more precise with their words*.

Take, for example, a scene from Lauren Harris Vance's class some years ago at Roxbury Prep Charter School in Boston. Lauren asked a student for the slope of a line. The actual slope was negative four-fifths, but the student gave the slope as four-fifths. Where another teacher might have said, "Right, except you need a negative sign," Lauren said, "Hmm. I like *most* of that"—expressing in five short words both "You did some good work" and "You're still not all the way there, but I know you can close that gap." The positivity, honesty, and simplicity of Lauren's response provides a road map for *Right Is Right* responses. To be effective with *Right Is Right,* reply to "almost right" answers in a way that is appreciative and often upbeat about what's been accomplished.

It's worthwhile to come up with a few commonly used phrases of your own—planned ways of saying just what you want in common situations. Keep them at the ready—in your back pocket, so to speak. Once you've come up with two or three phrases, use them to simply and consistently enforce *Right Is Right* and make rigorous answers a habit for your students. Your phrases should:

- Show appreciation for good work that's been done.

- Be clear and honest about the fact that more work is needed.

- Be fast enough in the delivery to allow you and the student to quickly get back to the thinking.

- Be simple and familiar enough that you can use them with near-automaticity.

Finally, it's important—and often difficult—to remember that *Right Is Right* is a technique you use when an answer is mostly right rather than when it's just plain wrong. When you encounter a fully wrong answer, you'll want to use more of the techniques described in *No Opt Out*. Affirming a fully wrong answer as partially correct may only lead to additional confusion (and potentially consume more class time).

## Beyond Holding Out: More Versions of *Right Is Right*

Imagine a typical student in your classroom. You've called on her to explain Shakespeare's use of light and dark imagery in *Romeo and Juliet*, and she gamely gives it her best shot. While she's done the reading, you can tell as she begins her response that she's not exactly sure where she's going (and might be hoping to find her way onto more solid ground as she shares). Eager to please, this student may inadvertently reach into a bag of tricks many well-intentioned students before her have discovered. They include:

**The Kitchen Sink:** Sometimes students who are confused or unsure will simply start talking and say everything they can think of about the topic. The right answer might be in there somewhere, but so is a lot of other stuff and it's not at all clear that they know which is wheat and which is chaff. We should recognize that such "kitchen sink" answers require us to ask students to narrow in on the most important ideas. "Let me pause you for a second because you've said a lot there. Which part of what you said best answers the question?"

**Bait and Switch:** Students may at times choose to answer the question they *wished* they'd been asked instead of the one they *were* asked. This could be because they misunderstood what you were specifically asking or because they understood one aspect of the text or question better than another and want to keep the discussion in "safe" territory. Thus students often need reminders to answer the actual question. "Yes, she's an inspiring hero.

But just to bring us back a bit, the question was about how we'd characterize her relationship to her sister."

**Heartfelt Topic:** Students may feel more comfortable sharing personal opinions, anecdotes, and affective responses because these opinions and observations are low-risk ways to engage with challenging material (and are unlikely to feel like "wrong" answers). And it's easy as a teacher to want to reinforce and respond to stories that start "something this made me think of that happened to me once was . . ." Sometimes the best response is to say, "Love that you're making connections, but for now let's stay focused on the question at hand. . . ."

**Vague Vagaries:** Students who are hazy on the details might respond in vague language, relying on pronouns or abstractions instead of names and concrete details. Rather than assuming we know (and the class knows) what they mean, we can push for precision, ensuring that we're all on the same page while helping students practice specificity in their language. We might say, "When you say "she gave it to her," just tell us who 'she' is and who is the 'her' that she gave it to."

To see *Right Is Right* in action, look at the video of Jennie Saliba's Year Five (fourth-grade) class at Great Yarmouth Academy in Great Yarmouth, England, where students are reading a nonfiction text on factory workers' lives in Dickensian England. "What made life in the workhouse so tough, Alf?" she asks. Alf, eager to demonstrate his comprehension but perhaps not as focused on the precision of his answer as he might be, offers: "What made life in the workhouse so tough was the jobs, and that many people had . . . they were too young, too old, too ill to work, and also many people had to work." Though his answer isn't wrong, it's imprecise and unclear. He has included several ideas, commingled, and Jennie can't be sure if he knows clearly. "You gave me three or four answers there in one," she responds with emotional constancy. "Just give me your first answer again, please." Given the chance to revise his answer, Alf shows a more precise understanding of the text. "What made life so tough in the workhouses was that . . . some jobs were very physically demanding," Jennie seizes this moment not only to appreciate Alf's answer, but to show him (and the rest of the class) how his increased precision improved the quality of his response. "In your first [answer] you gave me four bits of quite vague information. In that one, you perfected it with . . . the words you chose." Jennie has both given Alf a chance to shine and moved the class toward a more specific understanding of the text—and how to respond with clarity.

There are other reasons why students sometimes answer a question other than the one you asked. For example, they sometimes conflate different types of information about a topic. For example, you ask for a definition ("Who can tell me what a compound word is?"), and a student replies with an example ("Eyeball is a compound word!"); or you ask for the description of a concept ("When we refer to the area of a figure, what are we talking about? Who can tell me what area is?"), and a student replies with a formula to solve for it ("Length times width"). In the thick of the action, it's easy to miss that these are right answers to the wrong question. And as you begin to listen for them, you'll find that these kinds of exchanges are far more common than you might expect. If you ask students for a definition and get an example, try saying, "Kim, great example, but we need a definition." After all, knowing the difference between an example and a definition matters and students need authentic opportunities to practice responding accurately to each type of question.

When student responses are vague, you can respond with a slightly different approach—asking for technical vocabulary or precise language. A student might indeed answer your question, but answer it like a horoscope—in such generalities that the answer could apply to any person or situation. Whereas *good* teachers get students to develop effective right answers using terms they are already comfortable with ("Volume is the amount of space something takes up"), *great* teachers get them to use precise technical vocabulary they're developing comfort with ("Volume refers to the cubic units of space an object occupies"). This response expands student vocabularies and builds comfort with the knowledge students will need throughout the unit (and even when they are in college). These teachers ask for specificity and follow up to reinforce.

To help you remember the scenarios in which we're most at risk of failing to set a high bar for right answers, here are four common scenarios and names to help recall them:

1. *Hold out for all-the-way right:* When we resist "rounding up" and saying that a student is right when he or she is only partially so.

2. *Answer my question:* When we push students to be disciplined about answering the question they were asked.

3. *Specific vocabulary:* When we ask students to lock down the details in precise words and technical terminology.

4. *Leaner language:* When we ask students to improve an answer by using *fewer* words . . . and sometimes clearer syntax.

## TECHNIQUE 17: STRETCH IT

In the classrooms with the highest academic expectations, right answers aren't the end of the learning process; instead, they open the door to further challenge. "The reward for right answers will be harder questions," is how music teacher John Burmeister describes it to his students, and over time *Stretch It*, the simple habit of responding this way—perhaps not every time but often enough—builds a powerful culture of self-confidence and curiosity.

What does this look like in practice? Let me start by showing you two classrooms where this happens. The first, the video *Arielle Hoo: How Did You Know?*, is a middle school math class. Even before Arielle starts questioning her students, you can sense the heightened level of expectations that have become part of Arielle's classroom culture. Her student, Sarah, explains how she knew a proposed solution to a system of equations would be false: "I knew by looking at the graph, because the two lines are parallel so they would never intersect, which shows there is no solution." Without being asked, Sarah uses technical vocabulary, and offers a full explanation for her response in a cogent and precise sentence.

Arielle is probably fairly happy with Sarah's response. Proud of her even. But instead of saying simply, "Great work Sarah," she responds: "How did you prove that algebraically? What method did you use?"

Arielle's response to Sarah's answer shows both cause—how does one get a classroom where students answer like Sarah—and effect—what do you do to push the learning even further when you start to get answers like this.

"I used elimination," Sarah says. "After I eliminated the $x$ and the $y$ I saw that it ended up with $0 = 2$, but that's not true, so that's a false statement."

"Awesome," says Arielle before moving on to a question about a pair of coincidental lines.

Jaheem volunteers to answer this one and again we hear complete thoughts with technical vocabulary rather than simple one-word answers.

"The way you can figure out how many solutions [the system of equations] has is by looking at the graph, and you'll find that it has infinite solutions," Jaheem says.

Which is true. And which causes Arielle to ask, "How do you know?" She wants to challenge Jaheem but also make sure the right answer is not a lucky guess. She wants to understand how he approached the problem and ensure he (and other students) can repeat the process on other problems.

Moments later, noting a tiny slip-up Arielle asks, "By two?" This allows him to catch his own error. "You'd multiply it by four and you would get the same equation," he clarifies.

"Talk about the result," Arielle continues, subtly giving him the opportunity to connect what he's said to other pieces of knowledge and thus build schema (connected bodies of knowledge).

Jaheem keeps going: "The result will be $0 = 0$, which is infinite solutions."

"Great," says Arielle, "because it's what kind of statement?"

"A true statement."

"Nice job. Send Jaheem some love," she says to the class. His classmates make a gesture of support to "shine" on him while she says with a bright smile, "I loved your explanation." This puts a bow on the interaction but even without the praise, I suspect Jaheem knows he's done well and feels a growing, well-earned confidence. He's connected the ideas he's begun learning into something cohesive. It's a great example of what a cognitive scientist would call elaboration, which takes place during retrieval practice. Arielle prompts Jaheem to review his understanding of an idea, connecting pieces and straining slightly to describe it in a new context and with new words. This elaboration will build Jaheem's knowledge and long-term memory, along with his confidence.

You can see a similar process in the video *Michael Towne: Red Dye*, from Michael's Physics classroom. Gathered around two beakers of water, one heated and one at room temperature, Michael places drops of dye in each and gives students a brief opportunity to discuss observations with a partner. The basic observation he knows they'll make is that the dye spreads more quickly in the warmer water. "It's way faster," you can hear one student observe. But Michael's focus is not just on a simple observation but rather a deeper understanding of what students are seeing—as becomes clear when his questioning begins.

"What do you notice happening here? Go ahead," he says, *Cold Calling* one student.

"The dye disperses faster in the hotter water than it did in the cooler," the student responds. As in Arielle's classroom, you can almost hear him anticipating Michael's expectations: he's careful to use technical vocabulary (disperses) and to be precise in noting that he is comparing the "'faster" movement of the dye in the warmer bath than in the cooler water. A correct observation made in a scientific manner. But this correct answer has opened the door to a new challenge and Michael decides to *Stretch It.*

"OK, so what?" he responds.

The student pauses briefly, suddenly realizing he will now have to explain what's happening at a more substantive level. He's unsure at first but as he starts to articulate what's happening at a molecular level, he starts to gain confidence.

"The hotter the molecules get, the faster they move around in the beaker so if you put . . ."

Michael steps in briefly here:

"Which molecules?" he asks.

"The water molecules," his student answers, but the challenge continues:

"Can you see any molecules?" Michael asks.

"No, but the dye movement shows how they're moving around," the student pushes on.

Now Michael turns unprompted to another student—the *Cold Call* reminding everyone of the importance of listening to peers—and asks, "What's he talking about, Melanie?" subtly giving the first student credit for knowing something scientific after holding up under a challenging bout of inquiry.

You can see Melanie composing herself before she answers. It's going to be a challenge to put all of this into scientific terms but after steadying herself, she goes for it.

"He's talking about that, when you put another liquid substance in the water, that's . . . the atoms are moving faster, so in this case when it's hotter, the atoms are moving faster than the ones that are in the cold water." Again we see the idea of elaboration at play here, retrieving an idea from long-term into working memory but also connecting it and expanding upon it. It's long-term knowledge formation.

"Tell me more," Michael says turning to yet another student. The *Cold Call* here seems part of the fun. The message to students is *We're being pushed to the limits.* Treated like working scientists; everybody's in the game of imagining ourselves in that setting.

"Atomic theory says that everything's made up of matter and the atoms in it," the next student answers as the video closes—a small scene from a classroom marked by constant questions. No answer taken for granted. Always searching for why. Being in this classroom is like being a real scientist, in other words, and it just may be the kind of place that makes young people decide to pursue further studies in science.

When you give students ways to apply their knowledge in new settings, think on their feet, and tackle harder questions, they usually like it, at times quite a lot. This kind of questioning keeps them engaged and sends the message that we, their teachers, believe deeply their intellectual capability. *Stretch It* shows young people what they can do. You can almost see that in Melanie's response. She wonders for a moment, braces herself —she's beyond her comfort zone—but then she carries on and finds that she is up to the task. To find you can, over and over in the face of challenge, is to come to believe in yourself.

It's not just that students learn more in classrooms like Michael's and Arielle's; it's that, if you asked them, these would be those classrooms where they felt important as learners, valued and respected as students, most capable as thinkers. They're the places where young people rise to the challenge and start to think: *Yeah, I'm a math kid*, or *Yeah, science is my thing.* Many times, by challenging students, we tell them more about what we think they are capable of than when we say, "I think you are smart. I think you are capable of science." Kids want proof, and in these classes, they get it, seeing themselves succeeding in the face of real challenges.

What Arielle and Michael show us is that by treating correct answers as a step in the learning process, *Stretch It* can help students build long-term memory, expand and connect pieces of knowledge into cohesive schema, and build curiosity and confidence. The greater challenge brings about a cultural change.

*Stretch It* involves:

- Making a habit of asking follow-up questions in response to successful answers

- Asking a diversity of types of follow-up questions

- Building a culture around those interactions that causes students to embrace, and even welcome, the notion that learning is never done

## Other Advantages of *Stretch It*

*Stretch It* can often also help you learn more about student thinking and ensure the reliability of correct answers. In Jaheem's case, for example, I read Arielle to be deliberately making sure he understood the initial answer he gave and why it was true, challenging him to accurately explain his correct response rather than accepting it at face value and moving to another student. This allows you to avoid false positives—moments when luck, coincidence, or partial mastery can lead you to believe that students have achieved a more complete understanding than they really have.

Further, in classes in which there isn't necessarily one "correct" answer—analyzing complex literature, for example, or formulating a hypothesis—*Stretch It* questions give students the opportunity to pursue their singular train of thought, supported by their teacher's authentic curiosity about their insights. *Stretch It* is an opportunity to demonstrate your interest in students' thinking (rather than simply accepting a student's response that aligns with your objective or exemplar) and thus create an academic culture in your class that values students' perspectives and thoughtful engagement with the content.

*Stretch It* can also help you solve one of the thorniest classroom challenges: differentiating instruction for students of different skill levels. Asking frequent, targeted, rigorous questions of students as they demonstrate mastery is a powerful and much simpler tool for differentiating than breaking students into different instructional groups. By tailoring questions to individual students, you can meet them where they are and push them in a way that's directly responsive to what they've shown they can already do.

### Varying Your Questions

In the next section, I describe six different categories of *Stretch It* questions. My purpose in doing so is to help teachers provide a rich and diverse range of ways to extend student thinking. Although there's value in categories, it's also important not to get too hung up on them. The categories are merely tools to help you think about how to bring variety to the important task of challenging students in the moment of success.

## Ask How or Why

The best test of whether students' answers are reliable—of whether they can get questions right consistently on a given topic—is whether they can explain how they arrived at the answer. Asking a student "why" can push them to explore their own thinking and go beyond a "simply" accurate answer into new depths of insight or nuance. In his sixth-grade English classroom at Brooke East Boston, Rue Ratray stretched a student in this way during a discussion of a pivotal moment in *The Giver*:

*Teacher:* What can we infer about how Jonas's father feels about what he did?
*Student:* He didn't give much thought into what he did to the baby and he acted fine with it.
*Teacher:* Why?
*Student:* He was talking to the baby like he talked to Gabriel.
*Teacher:* Why?
*Student:* On the last sentence, it says, "a shrimp" and he's acting like this always happens, and he's talking to the baby in a baby voice.

## Ask for Another Way to Answer

Often there are multiple ways to answer a question. When students solve it one way, it's a great opportunity to make sure they can use all available methods. Arielle Hoo is essentially using this approach in her math class when she asks students to "solve algebraically" what they have understood from looking at a graph of the system of equations, and you can tell from Jaheem's and other students' responses that they almost expect, having initially solved graphically, to be asked to solve via another method as a follow-up.

Alternatively, imagine a teacher is reviewing a short, written paragraph by a student about a scene in *A Raisin in the Sun* as she circulates around the classroom. The student has written:

> Responding to Asagai, Beneatha says, "You didn't tell us what Alaiyo means . . . for all I know, you might be calling me Little Idiot or something." This reveals her skepticism.

Her teacher might respond. "Nice choice of supporting evidence, now see if you quote Beneatha indirectly rather than directly."
The student might then revise:

> Beneatha reveals her skepticism by asking Asagai what Alaiyo means and suggesting, perhaps with a hint of cynicism, that it might mean "Little Idiot."

The teacher, circulating around the class a few minutes later, might follow up with a further *Stretch It*: "Nice change. How do you think it changed the argument to quote the play indirectly rather than directly?"

## Ask for a Better Word

Students often begin framing concepts in the simplest possible language. Offering them opportunities to use more specific words, as well as new words with which they are gaining familiarity, reinforces the crucial literacy goal of developing vocabulary. Pushing for the inclusion of vocabulary can also develop students' confidence in their thinking and support mastery of new words.

I mentioned regarding the video of Michael Towne's class that the first student to answer seemed to me to be anticipating Michael's follow-up question and deliberately using the most technical vocabulary he could. You could imagine a day previously where a student might have said, "The dye spreads faster in the warm water." To which Michael might have said "Can you use a scientific term?" or "a term from our Knowledge Organizer," or perhaps, "a more precise term for that idea."

"The dye disperses."

"Yes, thank you."

Similarly you could imagine the day when a student said in Arielle's class: "The lines cross once." And she said, "What's the technical term for that?" allowing the student to retrieve the term "intersect." Students make a habit of using advanced vocabulary because teachers push them to. Once that becomes a habit they do it even when not promoted. They *self-stretch*.

This can also happen in nontechnical cases.

"How did Kika respond when she received the trophy?" a teacher might ask her students.

A student responding, "She smiled" would be correct, but the teacher might stretch her by asking: "Can you capture more of the feeling of her response in your word choice?" Or "Can you use one of our vocabulary words?"

Hopefully she'd then get a more powerful word, like "She beamed."

If she got a response like "She smiled strongly" or "She had a broad smile on her face" the teacher might stretch again. "Yes, much better. Glory for you if you can capture 'a broad smile' in a single precise word. Can you?"

## Ask for Evidence

By asking students to describe evidence that supports their conclusion, you emphasize the process of building and supporting sound arguments. In the larger world and in college, where right answers are not so clear and the cohesiveness of an argument is what matters, this will prove invaluable practice. You also avoid reinforcing weaker subjective interpretations, a task that is often challenging for teachers. You don't have to label an argument as inadequate; instead ask for the proof and give the student an opportunity to reflect, refining her response and potentially revising herself.

You might ask students for evidence to support a student's assertion that Beneatha is struggling to express her identity in *A Raisin in the Sun*. Or for evidence of times when she seems more and less confident in what she believes. Or you might say, "Yes, I think that's true. But many people remark on the way she subtly changes in the course of the play. Can you find me some evidence to support or refute that reading?" Or perhaps, "Yes, I think that's true, but can you find me an example of how that struggle becomes more intense when her mother is present?"

## Ask Students to Integrate a Related Skill or Additional Knowledge

In the real world, questions rarely isolate a skill precisely. To prepare students for that, try responding to mastery of one skill by asking students to integrate the skill with others recently mastered.

*Teacher:* Who can use the word *stride* in a sentence?
*Student:* "I stride down the street."
*Teacher:* Can you add some detail to show more about what *stride* means?
*Student:* "I stride down the street to buy some candy at the store."
*Teacher:* Can you add an adjective to modify *street*?
*Student:* "I stride down the wide street to buy some candy at the store."
*Teacher:* Good. Now, can you add a compound subject to your sentence?
*Student:* "My brother and I stride down the wide street to buy some candy at the store."
*Teacher:* And can you put that in the past tense?
*Student:* "My brother and I strode down the wide street to buy some candy at the store."

For students to encode concepts in their long-term memory, they need to consolidate knowledge from multiple sources. *Stretch It* questions can help students practice this consolidation.

*Teacher:* What might Bradbury be alluding to in this image?
*Student:* Maybe a bomb that went off, destroying the whole town.
*Teacher:* What do we know was happening in America at the time Bradbury was writing?

*Student:* The United States ended World War II by dropping nuclear bombs on Hiroshima and Nagasaki.

*Teacher:* So what might Bradbury be alluding to specifically?

*Student:* This image might be an allusion to nuclear destruction, like what happened in Japan in 1945.

## Ask Students to Apply the Same Skill in a New Setting

Once students have mastered a skill, consider asking them to apply it in a new or more challenging setting.

*Teacher:* Which letters make up the digraph in the word "stop"?

*Student:* "ST."

*Teacher:* Excellent. What word in this sentence contains a digraph? "Last, he jumped."

*Student:* "Last."

*Teacher:* And what is the digraph?

*Student:* "ST."

## Prompting

For the most part, the six types of *Stretch It* I've presented are directive: They guide students to think further *in a specific way* about something they've shown mastery of. Questions like "Can you give me a better word?" or "Can you tell me why?" and "How would the answer be different if the exponent was a zero?" shape the way students think about their original answer, and that's part of their strength. There are times, however, when it's also valuable to be nondirective. Prompting is a form of *Stretch It* that is nondirective, and the teacher's intervention is kept to an absolute minimum. Saying "Tell me more" or "Can you develop that?" doesn't tell a student how to think, merely to think further. Nondirective prompts allow students to decide what they think is most important to talk about and help students develop intellectual independence.

Prompting is often beneficial because it minimizes the disruption to a student's thinking. "Say more" comes faster and with less disruption to a student's train of thought than does a specific question about the author's purpose. It's easier for a student to immediately pick it up and develop it, so student thought remains center stage. As the buzzing of our electronic devices constantly proves, even a few seconds' distraction is enough to break the spell of deep thinking. The absolute simplicity of prompting is critical, and many of the ways we see champion teachers prompting are about minimizing interruption and shifting the ratio toward student thinking. Prompting is also helpful for those moments when you just need to know more about what a student is thinking in order to know how to respond. A simple "tell us more" opens up the floor for them to expand on their idea without influencing the content, and gives you valuable data about what the student is able to understand independently and in what areas he or she may need additional support.

The most common type of prompting is the verbal variety, whereby a teacher vocally indicates that a student should continue developing a particular idea. Some typical examples include:

"Say more."

"Keep going."

"Develop."

As teachers make prompting a habit, they can begin to remove the verbal portion of the prompt and replace it with a nonverbal prompt, which yields the ultimate in minimal transaction cost. It's also the least directive type of *Stretch It*. Effective nonverbal prompts include:

- Making a rolling gesture with your hands, like the "traveling" signal in basketball
- A head nod and/or sounds of encouragement ("*Mmm hmm*")
- Raised eyebrows or other distinctive facial gestures

One caveat to offer on nondirective prompts is that while they clearly offer students more autonomy, and that can certainly be a very good thing, people often assume that increased autonomy always leads to increased rigor. It's not necessarily true that prompting a student with "Say more" is more rigorous than asking, "How is Langston Hughes's vision of internalized anger different from that of another author we've read this semester?" In fact, the opposite is often true. The specificity of a good teacher's question is just as likely, if not more so, to result in rigorous thinking as a student's merely adding whatever was on her mind. (It may be helpful to state the obvious here that, of course, teachers will likely be more ready to respond with this kind of directive prompting if they've planned out the target response they are looking for, as discussed in technique 1, *Exemplar Planning*.) Answers that are left open to chance are, well, open to chance, which can mean high-or low-quality answers, answers that are relevant and useful for classmates to reflect on, and answers that are meandering or derail the class's progress toward an understanding.

Given the trade-offs between directive and nondirective forms of *Stretch It*, the best approach is probably to seek balance, in two ways: by using both directive and nondirective prompts or by combining the aspects of both approaches in semi-directive prompts. To do that, a teacher might use the "Say more" prompt, for example, but direct it to a specific part of the answer that she thought was most worthy of follow-up.

Let's say I ask my students how Jonas is feeling during a section of *The Giver* where he is experiencing both horrible and pleasurable feelings for the first time. A student replies, "Jonas is confused and feeling scared. He never felt any of this before, and he feels isolated." One solution would be to say, "Tell me more about his confusion" or "Tell me more about why he feels isolated." Now I'm giving my student significant autonomy, but still helping her see where the most productive part of her observation might be. This would be a semidirective prompt.

\*\*\*

As you're probably starting to recognize, you could put a variety of *Stretch Its* on a spectrum to reflect their degree of directness. Figure 4.1 arranges three different levels of prompting according to the degree of direction they offer.

It's important to see these possibilities as a spectrum, not a hierarchy. Sometimes the power of *Stretch It* lies in your capacity to shape the answer and steer students to the most important ideas and concepts. In other situations, the most important factor is a low transaction cost or a student's decision about what's worthy of further comment. There's a place for both directive and nondirective forms of *Stretch It,* and I suggest using all types. That said, where to strike the balance is a necessary question.

Part of finding that balance lies in recognizing the synergy between directive and nondirective versions of the technique. Asking lots of rigorous directive *Stretch It* questions is likely, over time, to teach students how to think more productively about developing their own answers. Then, when you stretch those students with less directive follow-ups, they're likely to do so, out of habit, in rigorous ways. This suggests that it may be worthwhile to invest time at the outset in directive questions, working in more nondirective prompts over time.

The type of question you're asking and the type of discussion you hope to have will also impact the balance of directive and nondirective versions of *Stretch It* you use in your classes.

| Prompt— Nondirective | Prompt—Partially directive | Prompt—Directive |
|---|---|---|
| "And?" | "Tell me more about the first part specifically." | "What evidence tells you that?" |

Figure 4.1 *Stretch It* Prompts: Degree of Directedness

When you are eager for an array of answers—when exploring affective responses to a text, for example, or engaging in literary analysis that encompasses a range of plausible thinking—nondirective *Stretch It* prompts can yield a fascinating array of student thinking, perhaps even unearthing meaty insights you hadn't predicted. On the other hand, if there is a specific outcome you have planned for, the balance probably shifts in favor of more directive prompts. In short, you'll want to match the decision you make about the balance you strike among *Stretch It* prompts to your objective. If you want students to understand how isolated Jonas feels, be more directive. If you want students to reflect on how Lowry's language reflects his isolation (or identify moments in which they empathize with Jonas's feelings of isolation), be less directive.

## *Stretch It* Loves Objectives

Let's assume you asked a student to add three and five. After she correctly gave you an answer of eight, you decided to *Stretch It* a bit and reward correct work with harder questions. Here are a number of ways you might stretch her:

"Good. What's 13 + 5?"

"Good. What's 30 + 50?"

"Good. What's 8 – 5?"

"Good. What's 5 + 3?"

"Good. What's 4 + 5?"

"Good. Can you write me a story problem?"

"Good. Can you show me how you know?"

These are all fine follow-ups to the original problem, but which one do you choose? With so many options for stretching even a very simple question, how do you keep your stretching from becoming scattershot and haphazard? How do you keep your lessons from stretching all over the map?

Your being aware of a variety of types of questions can help you push yourself to be broad and diverse in the ways you challenge your students; at the same time, some strategic focus can help you ensure that your use of *Stretch It* accomplishes important, *objective-aligned goals* in your classroom.

Regardless of the type of question, it's always useful to remember lesson objectives. Although it's good to do some "lateral" stretching (that is, into new areas), and it's good to do some reinforcement stretching (that is, to keep skills students have mastered alive by circling back to them for occasional practice), reserve *most* of your *Stretch Its* for questions that align most closely to your objectives for that day or your current unit. This will help you keep the technique focused and productive.

## TECHNIQUE 18: FORMAT MATTERS

There is no one right way to speak a language, especially one as polyglot and complex as English. This is manifested in the fact that nearly every speaker of English is in fact a speaker of "Englishes," using different versions of the language depending on the setting: at work versus with friends or family, for example. Let me state directly, then: there is beauty and value in everyone's voice and in all our different ways of speaking.

Yet at the same time *teachers have a special responsibility no one else in society has.* We are tasked with developing students' mastery of a *particular* English.

It is the version of English in which almost every article, scientific study, legal brief, or memo is written. It is used before the court of appeals, in presentations to the board, among physicians during rounds.

Call it Standard English if you like. Some people don't like that name, but we have to call it something and the fact is that there is a vernacular your students must master if they are to be prepared to participate fully and equitably in civic and economic life.

It may anger you to know that someone might prejudge your students' ideas because they were not communicated in Standard English; perhaps you'd rather argue against accepting a standard form,[3] but as teachers we must put those feelings aside. Or feel both things: love for our students and their forms of expression *and also* embrace the responsibility of ensuring that they are prepared to speak the language of the professions with fluency. School is the institution that provides students with the opportunity to master those language forms. If it does not, then full access to opportunity will accrue only to those whom privilege or happenstance prefers.[4]

"Pretending that gatekeeping points don't exist is to ensure that many students will not pass through them," Lisa Delpit writes. "To imply to children or adults that it doesn't matter how you talk or how you write is to ensure their ultimate failure."[5]

Delpit calls language a "game," with rules students must learn to play by. I might opt to call it a convention,[6] one that we inherit and that changes more slowly than society,[7] but whatever you call it, we have a responsibility to prepare students to master it. As the teacher and writer Jasmine Lane observes, "School is a place of preparation, a place where you learn the codes of the mainstream not necessarily because the mainstream is better . . . but because if you want to make significant changes to any systems, you have to be able to first get in by the gatekeepers' standards."[8]

Some people worry that this will cause students to feel like they or their own forms of language are somehow inferior, but why assume that? Would you presume as much about yourself? If you moved to England (or if you are English, if you moved to the United States), you would start speaking differently in certain public settings; do you imagine that you would lose your sense of identity and self-worth? I suspect you would remain very much you despite adapting your language habits in some settings. Our students are strong; why think them less capable than ourselves of making language choices without a loss of identity? If you are worried that some might feel their own language implicitly undervalued, it is certainly something you can address as a teacher. Writing about her own experience in school, Lane observes that she never felt learning to use language differently was a rejection of who she was, "I just needed someone to explicitly teach me the importance of both [ways of using language]."

Our job, in other words, is to teach students—with sensitivity, nuance, and judgment—to master Standard English. For some, our classrooms may be their only chance to learn it. And the best way to do this is to build verbal and written habits. *When we are in the classroom* we shift to a mode of discourse that ensures consistent and sustained exposure to the standard form so that all students will be able to use it naturally and effortlessly.[9]

I'll begin by describing the *what* of *Format Matters*, but I'll also discuss the *how*—an issue that is equally important.

There are four specific actions I think teachers can take within *Format Matters*:

1. *Grammatical format* involves asking students to phrase (or rephrase) their answers in Standard English.

2. *Complete sentence format* involves asking students to expand answers into full phrases or complete sentences to ensure they get extensive oral practice at sentence and complex syntax formation.

3. *Audible format* involves reminding students to speak audibly. The value of students' ideas is undercut if no one can hear them.

4. Finally I propose an idea called *Collegiate format*. Informed by Basil Bernstein's research on elaborated code, the idea is to prepare students for some of the particular demands of college and university by pushing for comfort not just with "Standard English" but the form of language, more formal and distinctive still, frequently encountered in an academic setting.

## Grammatical Format

When students make grammatical errors (that is, variations from Standard) in class, they are often unconscious of them. Our goal should be to help them to hear when this happens and know how to correct the errors.[10] They will be able to assess them themselves. And we want them to build habits so that when they are in the classroom Standard English comes to them naturally. An understanding of working memory tells us that if students have to consciously translate while they are speaking, the effort required to do so will interfere with other uses for working memory. We want our students to not have to use up scarce working memory thinking about how to say something so that it can instead be focused on thinking and perceiving.

If habit is the goal, then it is not enough just to tell a student that they have made an error; it's better to ask them to fix it. In this way their learning isn't much different from what we might experience learning sports or music. Coaches and music teachers will quickly recognize that offering a critique—telling a young person that they need to face the basket or that a note needs to be played more quietly—will not be nearly as effective as giving them a chance to correct and build fluent memory of the desired outcome: "Try that again and let me see you square up to the basket before you shoot" or "Let me hear you play that again but play that last note gently." It's the doing that builds the habit.

Building a habit also implies a fair amount of frequency and consistency in correcting, and that can be a challenge. Must you correct every single time you hear nonstandard usage? Of course not. There's a delicate balance to be struck. It may be worth skipping a correction in the middle of an especially profound thought, or at least delaying the correction until the thought is compete. Better to wait until after a student says, "We was discussing the ironic nature of a law that says it protects people by taking away their rights," to say, "Interesting, can you start, 'We were . . .'" than to interrupt the thought and risk its never being completed. It's hard to keep two things in working memory at once. There's always the risk that thinking about the correction can drive the sentence you sought to improve out of working memory. And certainly there are times when you'll want to be careful not to suggest that your first thought on hearing a student's heartfelt thought was: "Oh, subject-verb agreement."

Correcting a few times early in class—before you get to the deepest thinking and when you can remind students early of the expectations—is often especially effective.

You'll also want to explain to students what you're going to do and why in advance so they understand it. That means a brief rollout speech, perhaps something like this: "I'll often help you identify how to say it in the language that college and the workplace will expect of you. How you speak in your lives outside the classroom is beautiful to me, but my job is to help you learn a specific version of the language so you are ready for the world. So I'll often tell you how to say things in Standard English. When I do, do your best to fix it but know that I'm never judging you. I speak differently outside these four walls too."

As this rollout suggests, it's important that corrections be kept judgment-free—our goal is to prepare students for the world while reinforcing their faith in themselves and their ability. In *Culturally Responsive Teaching and the Brain*, Zaretta Hammond reminds us to make sure that language correction is "instructive feedback" that helps learners focus on making "specific adjustments." It should always be "timely" and "delivered in a low-stress environment" rather than evaluative.

So the goal is to find simple techniques to identify and correct errors with minimum distraction. Two simple methods are especially helpful:

1. *Identify the error.* When a student makes a grammatical error, merely repeat the error in a gently interrogative tone. You can watch Darryl Williams do this in the video *Darryl Williams: Has to Be.* "It gots to be?" Darryl asks when a student uses that phrase. He then allows the student to self-correct—he's previously explained that they should plan to correct if he points out an error.

2. *Begin the correction.* When a student makes a grammatical error, begin to rephrase the answer, then allow the student to complete it. In the second example in the video, Darryl begins, "It has . . ." leaving the student to provide the full correct answer. This version is useful if you try identifying the error and your student fails to self-correct.

Remember to exercise discretion. *There will be times to let the sentence be completed and not step in right away.* If you're doing work where students are expressing especially strong opinions or thoughts, you'll probably want to let them finish their thought before correcting. And there will of course be times not to step in at all.

In *Motivated Teaching*, Peps Mccrea points out the risk that good ideas can become lethal adaptations if teachers aren't careful about how they use them. Often this is true of the most important tools we have, and *Format Matters* is no exception. The most important part of the technique is tone. Students have to know that we care about them, value their ideas, and still have a responsibility to shape their communication habits. Be humane and gracious but also not apologetic. Notice that Darryl doesn't make a fuss about his decision to correct. Sometimes being matter-of-fact draws less attention to a correction and suggests its normalcy.

## Complete Sentence Format

A *notion*, a professor of mine once argued, is a fragment of an idea, an impression, belief, or opinion not yet fully formed in your mind. Only when you put it into words does it finally become an idea. Before it has been encapsulated in language, it is not fully formed.

You know you feel something, but you don't yet know what it is until it becomes a string of words. "Language," as the poet W. H. Auden put it, "is the mother, not the handmaiden of thought."

Our facility with the process of wrestling ideas into words and syntax helps (or limits) their creation. One definition of a sentence is "a complete thought," which reminds us that sentence creation is therefore complete-thought formation and surely one of a handful of the most critical skills for any student.

Given that, it's a gift to students to give them lots of practice building complete sentences—in spoken as well as written discourse, upon reflection, and on the spur of the moment. A student's truncated answer—in a single word or a fragment of a phrase—in other words, can often be an opportunity to practice using and developing fluency with the syntactic forms that will shape their thoughts for the rest of their lives.

You can start by simply asking for a complete sentence, either *after* a truncated answer, as in:

*Teacher:*  James, what's the setting of the novel?
*James:*  Oakland, California.
*Teacher:*  Yes, good . . . and in a sentence?
*James:*  The setting of the novel is Oakland, California, in 1968.

Or before the answer is given:

*Teacher:*  Who can tell me in a complete sentence what the setting of the story is?

Notice in the first example that the teacher has *praised the thinking* ("Yes, good") before asking for a revision. This is an easy way to keep the tone positive and underscore that practicing sentence formation is not a judgment on the answer. A smile helps make this point too.

You'll notice, too, in the example that James adds a bit more information (he includes the year 1968). Of course that won't always happen. But often when you ask for a slightly more elaborated answer or a more formal form of expression students sense the expectation and willingly add more details.

Alternatively, you could challenge James by suggesting an interesting way to start the sentence, ideally one that uses challenging syntax:

*Teacher:*  James, what's the setting of the story?
*James:*  Oakland, California.
*Teacher:*  Good. Can you tell me again starting, "The novel is set . . ."
*James:*  The novel is set in Oakland, California, in 1968.

Again the teacher here has praised the thinking before asking for a revision, but the revision has also caused James to use "set" as a verb. This involves taking a noun and turning it into a verb—a challenging task—and applying usage that is less common verbally than in writing. Both are likely to help expand students' syntactic control.

You can see this play out in the video *Jasmine Howard: Unique Output*. Jasmine asks a student to define a function. "It has an output and it's unique," the student replies. Her answer is largely correct. At least it is if you make some assumptions about what her pronouns refer to, so Jasmine pushes her to clarify:

"'It has its own output and it's unique,'" she repeats. "What's the 'it'?"

"The input," her student replies, and Jasmine now asks for a complete sentence with an encouraging tone and demeanor that affirms the answer: "Go ahead and say that in a complete sentence." In other words, she's asking her student to embed the second answer in the original answer and express them as a complete thought.

"Every input in a function has a unique output," her student says. She's not just demonstrated understanding, she's practiced creating an elegant and concise expression of a complex idea in the midst of discussion and she's further specified her point in adding the word "every" of her own accord.

In another interaction she asks a student, "Is this a linear function?"

"Yes," the student replies.

"Why?"

"Because it forms a straight line."

"All right. Say it in a complete sentence and do not use 'it,'" Jasmine replies. This requires the support of a classmate who ultimately arrives at: "The equation represents a linear function because the points are in a straight line on a graph."

I hope it's not necessary to add that an argument in favor of frequent practice at sentence formation is not an argument for reflexively asking for answers in complete sentences. As always, judgment applies. Too much of a good thing can make it a bad thing. But please don't overlook the influence of oracy—the ability to express oneself clearly, fluently, and grammatically in speech. Elegant and concise expressions of a complex idea offered in the midst of discussions, along the lines of what Jasmine's student creates, make a student stand out in a class and feel the confidence to express her ideas.

Further, as I discuss elsewhere, it is important to recognize that the data is sadly clear: students read less and less, and the trend is going in the wrong direction. Reading is in a death struggle against the smartphone and it is losing. Given that written text uses a much wider range of not just vocabulary but also syntax than spoken language, one of the many ways this is relevant is that students are less frequently exposed to those forms of language. Allowing for more intentional use of elaborated and elevated syntax in your classroom can help to bridge at least some of the resulting gap.

## Audible Format

Take a moment to watch the brief segment of discussion about Lois Lowry's novel *Number the Stars* in the second half of the video *Christine Torres: Keystone*. Then watch the clip *Christine Torres: Loud and Proud*, which shows the influence of Christine asking students to speak audibly. In this clip you can see her reinforcement of the expectation during the discussion as well as during a series of moments earlier in the lesson. These results are striking. Students express themselves with confidence as if their ideas were valuable, and their classmates hear them clearly and all the nuances of what they say. The rich discussion you hear comes about in part because of this. Students hear arguments clearly and expressed as if they matter and respond accordingly. Combined with *Habits of Attention* (technique 48) and *Habits of Discussion* (technique 44), this sews the fabric of a culture where people listen to each other, value ideas, and thus speak honestly and openly with confidence.

None of this would happen if, when called upon, Christine's students mumbled or muttered so that other people in the room could not hear them.

There's not much point in discussing ideas with people who can't hear them, in other words; a classroom where marginally audible statements are common suggests that the ideas expressed in those statements don't matter very much. And it's hard to make listening well an expectation unless speakers are audible. If it matters enough to say in class, it matters that everyone can hear it.

Perhaps the most effective way to reinforce the expectation of audibility is with a quick, crisp reminder that creates the minimum distraction from the business of class. Christine uses the phrase *loud and proud*. She's consistent and her implementation shows clearly her respect for students. You can hear this in the additional reinforcement Christine occasionally gives. She is warm, supportive, and occasionally playful, but always insistent on excellence:

To Mark: "Go for it. Loud and proud. Boom it."

To Jasmine: "Louder, you got this, girl."

To Didi: "Loud, girl!"

To Jovon: "Louder and prouder, 'cuz you got this."

Again to Jovon: "Pause. Jovon. You got this. Match my voice . . ."

There are other phrases you might use. Just make sure that what you choose is quick and consistent (always preferable to distracting or disruptive), and heed Zaretta Hammond's advice that corrections of this sort should be "instructive and actionable rather than evaluative." You can see this over and over in Christine's class. The explicit or implicit message is: your words matter; share them with us so we can hear. "Voice" or "with voice, please" is a good simple and noninvasive option. It might work better, depending on your setting and style—"loud and proud" probably wouldn't work well in a high school classroom, for example.

You can observe a further example for audible format in the video *Gabby Woolf: Keystone*. As Gabby reviews a challenging section of *Dr Jekyll and Mr Hyde* to ensure that all students understood the key events, Imran answers the question and Gabby reminds the class, "Good. Can we keep voice loud, please." She's reinforced this not when Imran's answer was inaudible but as it slipped toward quiet. Catching it early is better, when a reminder will do rather than a correction. Moments later, Ahmed answers and Gabby reminds students again, "Keep your voices loud, please." Her tone is clear but without pique. Notice that she addresses her comments to the whole class as well, ensuring the universality of the reminder and diffusing any criticism Ahmed or Imran might feel. This too is easier to do when you are reminding students *before* voices have actually become inaudible. Once they have you'll have to ask the speaker to repeat and draw far more attention to him.

Reinforcing audible format is best when introduced by a rollout in which you explain to students what you'll do and why. You might consider language like "What you have to say is important, so everyone should be able to hear it." Students may feel uncomfortable at first, so the reinforcement of the purpose behind the expectation is essential in helping them embrace the challenge and contribute audibly to the learning community. So is a bit of warmth as you begin reinforcing the expectation so students understand that it comes from your faith and caring for them. This is evident in Gabby's teaching and in Christine's, where the upbeat tone is as noteworthy as her persistence.

## Collegiate Format

Watch the interaction between Beth Verrilli and her student Ashanti in the video *Beth Verrilli: Hither*. Students are reading a scene from Shakespeare where Lady Macbeth seeks to inspire her husband to ruthless ambition. (Note the beautiful oral reading by Jennifer.)

"What's she going to do when he gets home?" Beth asks, to which Ashanti replies: "She's gonna talk all this evil stuff in his ear." Which is true and shows a strong understanding of Shakespeare's play, and frankly of Lady Macbeth.

But how would that response play in a college class just a semester or two on in a student's journey? It might work fine. Her classmates and her professor might love the easy casual wisdom of *she's gonna talk all this evil stuff in his ear*. They might even try to use a bit of it themselves in their own answers; it's fun to capture the essence of Shakespeare so casually, as if it were easy. But Ashanti will also need to write a paper using more academic language She'll have to be able to sit in the professor's office chatting about Lady Macbeth's "insidious influence on her husband's worldview." It's fine to use informal discourse if you know you can shift it up a level or two when you need to.

College and university are settings where words matter and elevated formal discourse is at times expected. No one tells you that explicitly. In fact they will sometimes pretend otherwise but this is only hiding the keys—keeping the secret to themselves. Your ability to shift into such forms of discourse, to frame ideas in precise words or elevated or new words—or frankly sometimes the ability to frame tired and rehashed ideas in new words—is part of the unspoken code of success. These are the forms of language that mark one's expertise in and mastery of a profession—whether anyone tells you that or not.

So consider the value in what happens next. "In AP language, she's gonna talk all this evil stuff in his ear . . ." Beth says, directing the question back to Ashanti.

"She's going to try to impose her negative beliefs onto Macbeth," Ashanti explains.

Ashanti's first answer was in many ways just as good. In some settings it might have been better. Notice that Beth is clearly expressing appreciation of Ashanti's original answer. She's merely helping her ensure that she's also ready to prove her bona fides by taking it up a level if she needs to. Her request for elevated discourse suggests the quality she sees in Ashanti's thinking.

Collegiate Format, in other words, refers to moments when teachers cause students to practice elevating their discourse and allows them to express their belonging and readiness to contribute in even the most advanced contexts.

# TECHNIQUE 19: WITHOUT APOLOGY

The belief that students can't do an assignment or that content will be too difficult or uninteresting to students can slip unintended into our classrooms . . . and mindsets. *Without Apology* offers reminders of some ways that can happen and some language that can be useful in preventing it.

## Apologies for Content

When I returned to campus at Hamilton College after studying abroad my junior year, every other class in my major was full except *British Romantic Poets* with Patricia O'Neill. There could not have been a topic less compelling. I imagined a semester of highbrow recitations on the nature of love, but I needed the credit for my major, and so I walked reluctantly and, if I am honest, a little sullenly into the single best class I took in college.

Adeyemi Stembridge points out that a passionate teacher can be the link between student and content, that the teacher's purpose is to model and foster a relationship with the content. So it was that Professor O'Neill somehow convinced me that it was urgent to stay up late reading William Wordsworth and permanently changed the way I think and read. There were classes I took that I knew I would love, but Professor O'Neill managed to inspire me with content that, with my comprehensive nineteen-year-old wisdom, I was sure was irrelevant to me. I suspect most people have had a similar experience, finding that the subject that seemed least interesting came to life in the hands of a gifted teacher.

There is no such thing as boring content, in other words, only content that is waiting for you to bring it to life, to find a way in. In the hands of a great teacher, the material students need to master is exciting, interesting, and inspiring, even if we sometimes doubt that we can make it so. If nothing else, there is always the pleasure of rising to a challenge.

I often hear this argument about book choice: let students choose what they like and they will love reading. That's often fine for independent reading but only by reading the same book can all of us discuss and understand our different perspectives on a given story. Someone is not going to get their choice. Perhaps no one will. And just maybe that's a good thing. It is folly to imagine that an eleven-year-old or a fourteen-year-old knows enough about the options available to know fully what they like. The whole point is to expand young people's horizons, not accept them, and reinscribe them in permanent marker. The more you prove to a fourteen-year-old that his or her knowledge of the world is as yet imperfect, the better. The same child thinks they do not like a certain cuisine because they have not tasted it cooked by an expert. The gift, in fact, is in part learning that what you love may surprise you.

Nor does merely shifting to content that we think will speak to students make a culturally responsive classroom. The foundations of teaching must make the classroom a warm, vibrant, inclusive place that tells students their learning is important. Meaningful teaching helps students feel a sense of belonging in the classroom and connection to the content. As Zaretta Hammond writes, it is "simplistic to think that students who feel marginalized, academically abandoned or invisible in the classroom would reengage simply because we mention tribal kings of Africa or Aztec empires of Mexico."

## Assuming Something Will Be Boring Is a Big Assumption

We often presume that students will find something boring. Think for a moment about accounting, for example. The epitome of boring, right? And yet there are thousands of accountants who love their job and find it fascinating; who read books about accounting for pleasure. They follow fascinating accountants on social media. Perhaps we assume accounting is boring because we don't know much about it. Perhaps we fail to account for variability in tastes. Someone loves every food that you despise and vice versa. Saying something like, "Guys, I know this is kind of dull. Let's just try to get through it" or even "You may not find this all that interesting" as a way of getting students through a topic is apologizing—it's assuming it will be boring to others—and perhaps a bit defensive: If I tell you I don't like it, then if you don't like it, you'll know it's not my fault. You won't think it's me that's boring.

A belief that content is boring is a self-fulfilling prophecy. No one lights a lesson on fire when they've just announced it's no fun. And yet there are teachers who make great and exciting and inspiring lessons out of every topic that some other teacher considers a grind. Our job is to find a way to make what we teach engaging and never to assume that students can't appreciate what's not instantly familiar or does not egregiously pander to them.

## "They'll Like It" Can Be Superficial

Just as our reasons for assuming students won't like something can be superficial, so can our reasons for assuming they will. Rudine Sims-Bishop observes that lesson content provides "views of worlds that may be real or imagined, familiar or strange." She uses the analogy of mirrors and windows. In a mirror I see myself reflected. In a window I see a different world brought to life. All students deserve and respond to both. For example, as Sims-Bishop points out, "children from dominant social groups . . . too have suffered from the lack of availability about books about others. They need books that will help them understand the multicultural nature of this world." And it's also true that students of color are just as likely to be moved and inspired by Shakespeare's words as any other students. "All texts belong to all students," writes Alfred Tatum. Shakespeare—like Morrison, like Marquez, like Neruda, like Hurston, like Murakami—belongs to everyone.

But there is perhaps a tendency to presume that the mirror will be more engaging than the window, to assume that students will only want to see themselves in content, just as many may be inspired by books or lessons about people of different backgrounds from their own. For some, interest and identity align to the terms by which we see them ("I am Latina"). To others it is less visible ("I am a scientist"). A just school is a school in which every child gains the fullest opportunity to pursue their dreams. We have to stay open to the wide variety of their dreams. Some students will find inspiration in Malcolm X and some in Gregor Mendel. We—and, honestly, they—will never know which is going to be which. When it comes to windows and mirrors, every student should have both.

### Blaming the Context

A teacher who assigns the responsibility for the appearance of content in her class to some outside entity—the administration, state officials, or some abstract "they"—starts with two strikes: she is undercutting the content's validity to students and eroding her own enthusiasm for teaching it. The blaming might sound like this: "This material is on the test, so we'll have to learn it" or "They say we have to read this, so . . ." The negativity here is a self-fulfilling prophecy and also a bit lacking in perspective: if it's "on the test," it's also probably part of the school's curriculum or perhaps your state standards. You're never going to agree completely with anyone's judgment on what gets included in the curriculum and standards, but it's just possible that the (also smart) people who put it there had a good rationale for putting it there. Reflecting on that rationale can be a good place to start: "We're going to study this because it's an important building block for things you do throughout your life as a student."

### Loving Challenge

Carol Dweck's important work on growth mindset has been widely discussed and applied—sometimes well and sometimes poorly. At its core it reminds us that the fact that something is challenging is a good thing. A willingness to embrace challenge may well cause us to learn more. It certainly prepares us for life's difficulties. So a tiny shift from "I'm sorry, this is going to be hard" to "This is going to be really challenging (and that's a good thing)" can help. Here are some phrases that can help turn apology into opportunity:

- "This topic is great because it's really challenging!"
- "Lots of people don't understand this until they get to college, but you'll know it now. Cool."
- "This gets more and more exciting as you come to understand it better."
- "A lot of people are afraid of this stuff, so after you've mastered it, you'll know more than most adults."
- "There's a great story behind this!"

## Apologies for Students

At the first school I helped found, students learned Mandarin Chinese as their foreign language. None were Chinese and many were English Language learners. They were a polyglot of every background culture and color. Knowing how difficult Mandarin is—the tens of thousands of *Hanzi*, the four tones that cause words to take on new meanings, the simplified and complex alphabets—many outsiders, a few staff members, and even many parents, responded, "How in the world are they going to learn Chinese?" The principal at the time calmly responded that if they'd been born in China, they'd learn Chinese. And so we started. And so they learned. Often with great pride and success. The first step was to believe.

"As educators we have to recognize that we help maintain the achievement gap when we don't teach advanced cognitive skills to students," writes Zaretta Hammond. We stand at risk of serving students poorly when we "underestimate what disadvantaged students are intellectually capable of [and] postpone more challenging and interesting work until we think they have mastered the basics."

Sticking with kids, telling them you're sticking with them, and constantly delivering the message "I know you can" raises a student's self-perception. Here are some phrases that can help frame challenge when you present it to students:

- "This is one of the things you're going to take real pride in knowing."
- "When you're in college, you can show off how much you know about . . ."
- "Don't be rattled by this. There are a few new words, but once you know them, you'll have this down."
- "This is tricky. But I haven't seen much you couldn't do if you put your minds to it."
- "I know you can do this. So I'm going to stick with you on this question."
- "It's OK to be confused the first time through this, but we're going to get it, so let's take another try."

## Notes

1. Tone and praise are also age-related variables. This means that if you teach kindergarten, make a fuss over every tiny moment. If you teach tenth grade, go a bit easy.
2. This is one of a hundred reasons why behavioral culture matters. It is not enough to eliminate negative behaviors. We have to install and instill learning-positive behaviors among students so the classroom culture supports changes in behavior that benefit young people. Please remember this moment when you read Chapters Ten through Twelve.
3. I've seen several critiques of the idea of reinforcing standard grammar and syntax in school. Several found my argument oppressive or offensive. For what it's worth, they were all written in impeccable Standard English.

4. Consider for a moment recent articles about the increasing importance of college essays in an era of growing SAT optionality. Ask yourself whether you would consider it an advantage or a disadvantage for your own child's college essay to be written without mastery of Standard English.

5. *Other People's Children* (New Press, 1995), pp. 39–40.

6. It's also possible that it is an inevitability—are there languages in the world where there is not a standard form that must be learned, where "rules," often passed down and therefore feeling archaic to some, do not need to be followed? If there are, they are rarely written languages. Rules, after all, are the purpose of grammar.

7. Often for legitimate reasons. One benefit of the slowing influence on linguistic change via standardized grammar is that it sustains our access to older texts and ideas. Spelling was far less standardized before the publication of Johnson's first dictionary in 1755. Reading texts written before that where spelling is unpredictable is extremely challenging.

8. https://citizen.education/2019/08/09/schools-dont-need-to-teach-our-students-to-act-white-but-they-should-prepare-them-for-mainstream-america/.

9. Am I just talking about adjustments in discourse for certain Black and Brown kids? I am not. To varying degrees, learning to use the standard form is an issue across the majority of young people in society. Part of standardization is not about cultural but about generational differences. Young people speak like young people and their parents want schools to ensure that they can speak in a way that is more like how the adults talk. Any student's language habits, in other words, are informed by a combination of influences and factors and it may be a false judgment to assume that a teenager's way of speaking is a representation of his or her culture. For all you know it makes their parents crazy. Most of us went through a process as teenagers of learning to speak in a way that was accessible to the broadest swath of society.

10. This then is something they can choose not to do if they wish; we are empowering choice.

# Chapter 5

# Lesson Structures

## TECHNIQUE 20: DO NOW

The way we start class sends a strong message to students about the culture, purpose, and expectations of the community they are entering, so teachers should be intentional about it. We want students to engage in productive and high-quality work that interests and challenges them right away, and over time we want to make a habit of this, so they expect to be actively and meaningfully engaged any time they enter our classrooms. We want them to know we are prepared and value their learning. They will not be passive; there will be very little downtime.

So consistently starting quickly and with a quality task is important. A predictable familiar activity that students know how to do lets them get started actively and with confidence.

The first step in a great lesson, then, is a *Do Now*—a short pencil-to-paper activity that is waiting for students as they enter the classroom and that they can and should start without any directions from you.

The secret is the "without directions from you" part. A procedure that does not require guidance from you beyond posting the task beforehand benefits you as well as your students, especially when you are teaching a full schedule. It gives you the chance to take a final glance at your lesson preparation document, make sure the classroom is arranged how you want it, connect with an individual student or two, or pass back some papers—perhaps even somewhere in there you manage a sip of coffee. All this happens, efficiently and smoothly, while students are busily and productively engaged. At the same time, it's a moment for students to mentally transition to your classroom. Regardless of what happened in the hallway or at the close of a prior class or at lunch, beginning with a few quiet, focused minutes can help students be ready to succeed.

An effective *Do Now* should meet three critical criteria to ensure that it's focused, efficient, and effective:

1. The *Do Now* should be in the same place every day so it becomes habit for all your students. You can write it on the board, post it on a piece of chart paper in advance, or put it on a sheet of paper you leave in a stack by the door. Wherever you put it, keep it consistent.

2. Students should be able to complete the *Do Now* without any direction from you, without any discussion with their classmates, and in most cases without any materials beyond what they always bring to class. So if the *Do Now* is to write a sentence interpreting a primary source document that is a nineteenth-century *Punch* cartoon, that cartoon should be copied into the *Do Now* materials or posted somewhere easily visible. Some teachers misunderstand the purpose of the *Do Now* and start by explaining to their students what to do and how to do it (for example, "OK, class, the *Do Now* is on the board. You'll notice that it asks you to do X and then Y. Please get started."). This defeats the purpose of a self-managed routine to start class. If you have to give directions, it's not independent enough.

3. The activity should take about five minutes to complete and should require putting a pencil to paper. That is, there should be a written product from it. This not only makes it more rigorous and more engaging but also enables you to better gather data through *Active Observation* and reinforce students who've done good work.

In the great majority of cases, the *Do Now* is silent work. I can imagine an occasional exception for peer-to-peer quizzing with a Knowledge Organizer or some other form of retrieval practice, but only occasionally and for a class with a well-established routine.

With regard to the content of the *Do Now*, I favor three options. The activity can (1) preview the day's lesson (you are reading *The Jacket,* and the *Do Now* asks students to write three sentences about what they'd do if they thought someone stole their little brother's favorite jacket); (2) review a recent lesson (you recently introduced three new vocabulary terms and want students to review the definitions so they don't forget them); or (3) build background knowledge that will be necessary for the upcoming lesson (you are reading *Number the Stars* and want students to read a short nonfiction excerpt about rationing during World War II). Though all options can be powerful, I want to take a moment to highlight the particular benefits of using the *Do Now* as an opportunity for regular, low-stakes review.

In *Small Teaching*, James Lang notes that "a brief (and ungraded) multiple-choice quiz at the beginning and end of class and one additional quiz before the exam raised the grades of all students by a full letter grade." These brief low-stakes "quizzes" (you can choose if you grade them or have students grade against a key) actually lowered students' anxiety on end-of-unit assessments, because they reported feeling more prepared. Of course, as I discuss in *Retrieval Practice* (technique 7), this is because, as Lang puts it, "Every time we extract a piece of information or an experience from our memory, we are strengthening neural pathways that lead from our long-term memory into our working memory, where we can use our memories to think and take action." By using *Do Now* as a way for students to quickly review critical information from prior lessons, you are setting them up not only for increased engagement in the upcoming lesson, but also ensuring that they are able to retrieve that information at relevant moments later on.

Just as important as the content of your *Do Now* is how you review it with students. The most common downfall I observe is a teacher losing track of time while reviewing answers. Fifteen minutes into a *Do Now* the "opening" has replaced the lesson that was originally planned—or at least has crowded out all of the independent practice and pushed all the timings to the breaking point. Set a timer so you complete your review in about the same amount of time you give students to work on it: three to five minutes. This may require the art of selective neglect. If you give your students eight problems to complete, you may not be able to review all of them. You'll have to choose the two or three that are most important. This makes the period when students are working critical from a Check for Understanding perspective—you'll want to observe carefully to make sure you know which questions most require review, as well as which students can provide answers that are correct or contain useful errors. You'll only have a few minutes to decide this so be ready to draw on the ideas in *Active Observation* (technique 9).

You can see a great example of Sarah Wright debriefing a *Do Now* in the video *Sarah Wright: But Esperanza*. Here's a copy of her *Do Now* from a lesson on Pam Muñoz-Ryan's novel *Esperanza Rising,*

## Do Now

1. Develop this sentence: Miguel warned to prove to Esperanza that "things would get better."

   - Miguel wanted to prove to Esperanza that "things would get better," **but** _____

     _____

     _____

   - Miguel wanted to prove to Esperanza that "things would get better," **because** _____

     _____

     _____

   - Miguel wanted to prove to Esperanza that "things would get better," **so** _____

     _____

     _____

2. Imagine Tio Luis discovers that Abuelita has disappeared. Write down what he might say to himself as he burns with **unrelenting** anger. **Challenge:** use two of our vocabulary words!

   _____

   _____

   _____

Notice Sarah's *Show Call* of exemplary answers, which socializes students to work their hardest at written work. She also makes explicit reference to her purpose in designing the *Do Now* as she has: She wants students to review key events from the previous day's reading and reflect on important characters' motivations to give context to the final scenes of the book. She uses rich and engaging Because, But, So questions—a method I discuss in *Art of the Sentence* (technique 41) that comes from Judith Hochman and Natalie Wexler's book *The Writing Revolution*—to build the complexity of students' thinking. You can see how engaging students found it in the enthusiasm and rigor of their comments in the discussion. But notice how briskly Sarah moves through the review. Her goal is an attentive and enthusiastic discussion but not a long one. It's so easy to assume that the discussion deserves more time given all the enthusiasm, but by keeping her discussion tidy Sarah transfers energy to the next task.

Since the *Do Now* is a consistent procedure we want students to follow every day, it's important to reinforce process and expectations. In the video *Christine Torres: Silently to Seats* you can see Christine Torres do this, appreciatively and quietly naming students as they meet expectations in completing this *Do Now*. Here's what her students are working on, by the way. It's designed to build background knowledge for the passage from the novel *Number the Stars* that students will study in class that day (in which the protagonist journeys through the woods).

Christine reminds us, as Tom Bennett observes in *Running the Room*, that the best time to reinforce expectations is when students are doing things well. "One of the most underused strategies is to reinforce norms when they are happening," he writes. Especially when they're going well. "Calm, quiet, and settled" is the ideal emotional state for receiving guidance on how to do things.

## Do Now

### Reading Symbolically: The Woods

The forest is a mysterious place; in legends and fairy tales, the woods are usually full of mysterious creatures, symbols of all the dangers which young people must face if they are to become adults. "Hansel and Gretel," "Snow White," "Little Red Riding Hood" —in these and many more tales, the forest is a place away from civilization, a place of testing, an unexplored land full of the unknown.

The forest is often the home of the outlaws or a place where typical rules no longer apply. Since its trees obscure the light of the sun, it's often a place of literal and figurative darkness and mystery. Entering the forest can be seen as a metaphor for entering the unknown. Sometimes it is also a place of opportunity and transformation—the hero enters the forest and discovers something about him- or herself.

*(continued)*

(continued)

1. Consider the final line of this text: "Sometimes it is also a place of opportunity and transformation—the hero enters the forest and discovers something about him- or herself."

   a. What does the pronoun "it" refer to? _____

   b. What might Annemarie have discovered about herself during her journey through the forest?

   _____

   _____

   _____

2. Why might Lowry have chosen to have Annemarie journey through a forest, instead of, say, through a town or a field? Underline any words or phrases in the text above that support your thinking.

   _____

   _____

   _____

Finally, some of the masters of the *Do Now*, in my opinion, are effective because of the speed with which they transition from completing the *Do Now* to reviewing it. They might count down the end of the *Do Now* with something like, "OK, pencils down when you hear the beep, and we'll talk about some of these questions." Or when the timer starts to beep, they might immediately start in with a *Cold Call* (technique 34) or a *Show Call* (technique 13), not wasting a second of time. This creates a strong sense of momentum from the outset. The sensation of "flow," which, as I discuss in Chapter Six, is a state of mind in which people lose themselves in a fast-paced and engaging activity, is among the most pleasurable experiences you can create in the classroom. The pace of a good *Do Now* can get a lesson flowing right from the outset.

## Online Lessons: The Remote *Do Now*

The start of a lesson is especially important online. When students are far from us and the classroom it's often doubly important to remind them of familiar routines and habits—providing comfort and continuity in a topsy-turvy world.

We loved watching Joshua Humphrey do this with his students at KIPP St. Louis High School in the video *Joshua Humphrey: Pause It Right Now.* Joshua starts his online lesson—it's asynchronous, meaning students will watch the recorded lesson later—with a *Do Now* and the phrase "just like we always do," reminding his students of the familiar moments and habits of their in-class life. Of course he's made some adaptations too: in an asynchronous lesson he can't just leave his *Do Now* passively on the screen and assume students will complete it, so class begins with a short greeting before the *Do Now*, for example. And he has to be direct and clear about pausing the video to complete the task. But Joshua's review of his *Do Now* afterwards is instructive to both remote and in-person instruction. His tone is perfect—his emotional constancy in describing errors makes it safe to struggle. His pacing during the explanation of the answers is crisp but not rushed, and most of all he uses colored highlights to guide students' eyes through the review of right and wrong answers to help them focus on and attend to the most important things. Students learn about what they attend to. The difficulties of online learning caused us to see the value of guiding students' eyes to focus on key details, but this lesson is surely applicable everywhere.

Another *Do Now* that we learned from online was Hasan Clayton's at Nashville Classical Charter School. Hasan's lesson in the video *Hasan Clayton: Two Noses* is synchronous—his students are with him live—so he greets them warmly but quicky and then asks them to complete their *Do Now* task "in the chat." They can send their answers to him and he can instantly review. And of course this way he'll know who's completed the task when. Notice that the substantive part of his *Do Now* in an online setting is reduced to just one question: "In one artful sentence, summarize the nature versus nurture debate. Include a word that shows contrast...." You can read more about Hasan's decision to have his students respond in "one artful sentence" in technique 41, *Art of the Sentence*. Hasan has students chat their answers just to him so he can choose a few thought-provoking or exemplary answers and share them with the class (a sort of an online *Show Call*) to prompt a rich discussion and honor students who've done quality work. Notice also, though, that Hasan adds a second, more playful question to his *Do Now* (Would you rather have one eye or two noses?). The purpose is in the playfulness. Hasan is using the question to build community and connection among students when they are isolated and separated by circumstance. He's careful to spend only a little time on this but he and his colleagues did it regularly when teaching online to build positive culture, and you can imagine how the occasional playful *Do Now* question could be a bonus, even in a brick-and-mortar classroom.

## TECHNIQUE 21: TAKE THE STEPS[1]

Strong content knowledge is essential to excellence in teaching but it also has a downside. Expertise carries with it what some cognitive scientists call it the "curse of knowledge:"[2] It's hard for experts to understand why things are hard for novices. What's obvious to us is not obvious to students.

Consider: You flash a slide showing cell structures and organelles like the following illustration on the screen and begin explaining it to your class:

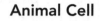

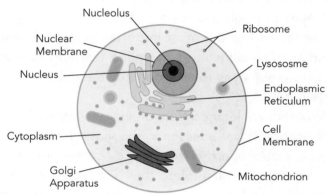

As you talk you hold in your mind a thousand implicit understandings: That the cellular organisms are enlarged relative to the size of the cell in the image to make them more visible. That the colors are for the purpose of demonstration, and aren't realistic. That actual cells are three-dimensional. That animal cells feature huge variety in their shapes, and few if any animal cells are actually *this* shape. That the images of the organelles are supposed to represent cross-sections. That the mitochondria aren't in fact all the same size. That the organelles are always moving and changing. And on and on.

At best, your students might vaguely understand a few of these things. More likely they'd know none of them. But you wouldn't think to mention them in your explanation of the diagram because what they don't understand is hidden from you. For all intents and purposes, you and your students are looking at different diagrams.[3] What's obvious to an expert is hidden to a novice, even in terms of perception.

In fact I generated my list of what an expert understands about a cell diagram with the help of dozens of colleagues on Twitter.[4] *What was obvious to a biology teacher and not to students*? I asked. Most people contributed one or two of these ideas. Nobody saw all of them, and there were more suggestions than I could keep track of.

Combine this with the Dunning-Kruger Effect, the tendency of unskilled individuals to overestimate how much they know, and you have "an unwitting conspiracy," writes Greg Ashman. "The teacher thinks their students understand and the students think they understand, and they don't understand."

There's no reliable "cure" for the curse of knowledge. Perceiving subtle hints of confusion in your students' countenances can suggest that maybe you've overlooked something, so prepare your lessons well and keep your working memory free to observe students. Experience also helps: You develop intuitions about students and their misunderstandings from years of hearing them say wonderful things like, "That can't be the mitochondria—it's not orange!" during a lab. But it will always plague us. Still, there are two things you *can* do in terms of teaching methods that make you *more likely* to instill successful understandings in students' minds and to avoid massive misunderstandings or simple failures of learning.

The first is to break up new material into steps and teach and practice them sequentially. The second is the use of annotated models or work samples instead of rubrics to help students develop an understanding of the parts of a complex task.

Perhaps consciousness, too, is curative. Teachers should always be on the lookout for any points they may have overlooked, which may be obvious to them but a source of confusion to students. You have listed the hard vocabulary words in the chapter and taught them, but there are some simpler words that confuse your students. You understand that two events happened a hundred years apart but your students lack your chronology and think they happened at roughly the same time. What exactly the points of confusion will turn out to be remains a mystery. That they exist is a very good bet.

## THE GUIDANCE FADING EFFECT

Novices learn differently from experts. This is one of the most important findings of educational psychologists and, as far as I can tell, one of the least recognized by educational theorists. The tendency of novices to benefit from more direct guidance and experts to get more from problem-solving situations, cognitive psychologist John Sweller calls *the guidance fading effect*. "Students should initially be given lots of explicit guidance to reduce their working memory load, which assists in transferring knowledge to long-term memory," he writes. "Once students are more knowledgeable, that guidance is unnecessary and . . . should be faded out and replaced by problem-solving." This is both useful and unusual guidance. (Unusual because Sweller does not propose one inherently better methodology for every situation. He seems to have heeded Dylan Wiliam's admonition "Everything works somewhere and nothing works everywhere.")

Open-ended problem-solving activities play an important role. So does direct instruction. The answer to the question of which to use is: It depends. But what it depends on most, Sweller tells us, is the degree of knowledge about the topic among students, and here it is important to recognize that outside of a university setting students are most often novices and, further, that people go back and forth between novice and more knowledgeable states frequently, even within a subject. On Friday, at the end of a well-taught and organized unit, your students may be fairly knowledgeable; then they start a new unit on Monday and move back to square one again. This would imply different teaching techniques for each day.

Consider an experience one of my own children had building a model rocket in Science class. One day my daughter announced with no small degree of excitement that they were going to be building and flying rockets in class later that week. "Great," I said, "Are you studying air resistance? Or aerodynamics?" That sounded super-geeky, so I rephrased: "You know, the sort of things that might make a rocket fly better."

"I'm not really sure," she said, "We haven't yet. I think it's the introduction to a new unit."

A few days later I asked her how the rocketry lesson went. "*Great*," she said. They had made the rockets out of paper and gone out to the back fields to fly them. "Our team won!" she told me breathlessly—meaning that her group's rocket had stayed aloft the longest. "Double-cool," I said, "What made your rocket work so well?" I asked.

"I'm not really sure," she said. "I think maybe our wings. They looked different from other people's."

"Oh," I said. What had she and her teammates tried to do with them? How were they different?

Silence.

If their wings had been better, in other words, it had been a lucky guess, which was fun and memorable but not all that instructive. They hadn't been testing an idea—"Hey, since we know X, let's see if . . ." It wasn't an application of knowledge, in other words.

I should be clear: I liked the rocket activity. It was fun and inspiring and typical of why my daughter loves science. But it would have taught her more to do it after she was no longer a rank novice. A few lessons on the principles of air resistance followed by some small experiments with different wing shapes would have helped. Or, to capitalize on the rockets as a "hook,"[5] you might fire them twice—once to make some conjectures at the beginning, and then again after students know enough to cement their knowledge and ask: "What do you notice now that you didn't know when we first fired the rockets?"

If students have knowledge they can use it to describe, explain, and perceive why some rockets fly better than others:

*We had larger wings with more surface area* or

*Maybe it was the size of the nose cone that created less air resistance.*

The value of hands-on learning, in other words, correlates to how much students know when they engage in it. To use hands-on activities before you've shared knowledge overlooks the differences between how experts and novices learn.

Watch the video *Michael Towne: Red Dye* from *Stretch It* (technique 17) again and notice how, as Michael drops dye into water of two different temperatures, his students apply knowledge that he has taught them. They are able to see what's happening because they have the prior knowledge to do so.

"Present new material in small steps with student practice after each step," advises Barak Rosenshine in *Principles of Instruction*, his guide to teacher effectiveness. This takes time but is worth it. It makes the implicit explicit for students and uses practice to consolidate understanding before working memory is overloaded. This, cognitive psychologists suggest, is the way students learn best when they are not experts. "Teaching in small steps requires time, and the more effective teachers [in studies] spent more time presenting new material and guiding student practice than did the less effective teachers," Rosenshine notes. "In a study of mathematics instruction, for instance, the most effective mathematics teachers spent about twenty-three minutes of a forty-minute period in lecture, demonstration, questioning, and working examples." In contrast, less effective teachers spent only eleven minutes methodically explaining and practicing new material, Rosenshine notes.

Working memory is quickly overloaded by too much new material at once. Solution: Break down what you're doing into steps. Take the steps one by one. Let students practice each one. As they practice, ask questions of two different types: conceptual (what are we doing?) and procedural questions (how do we do it?), going back and forth between the two when possible.

The video *Rachel Boothman: We Are Solving* provides an excellent model of Rosenshine's idea of methodically explaining and practicing new material as well as the idea of going back and forth between procedural and conceptual questions.

"When we are solving it means we are finding the value of the letter. So we want $x$ on its own and we have solved the equation," Rachel begins, reminding her class of a key definition. Then she asks a procedural question to start: "What's my first step here?"

Brandon answers and Rachel asks a conceptual question: "What is the mathematical name for what Brandon has just done?"

Moments later she's back to procedural questions, *Cold Calling* Ella and then Arian to ask, "What do I do next?"

"OK, this time we are simplifying," she says as she moves on to a new problem. Now she starts conceptually: "Who can tell me another word for simplifying?" She gets a correct answer, finding like terms, so asks Karis, "So here where are our like terms?

Karis has left off the negative sign and Rachel asks, "Can anyone improve on Karis's answer?" But of course there are multiple sets of like terms so she asks Azaria for another set. After these conceptual questions—What are like terms? How can I spot them?—she goes back to procedural questions, asking Hannah to add $-3x$ and $5x$ and Ellis whether she can simplify any further. When he answers correctly, she asks a conceptual question: "What do I mean when I say index? What's the index here?"

Later, after students have mastered concepts, a less methodical approach might well work, but remember this caution: Our own memories of our experiences as learners sometimes work against us. We remember moments that were unforgettable to us later in our studies. They were unstructured. We were granted the opportunity to explore. Suddenly: an epiphany. Perhaps you still remember walking out of some building on campus after a class in your major with your mind exploding. Surely if you re-created this activity for your students it would be equally profound. Surely it would add rigor to your class. The challenge is that you were an expert when you explored your way to this insight. You were perceiving far more meaning in each interaction than a novice would. Your students will eventually get to a place where they, too, will derive profound benefit from the open-ended exercise. But until they know more, they are likely to get less out of the experience than you did, and adding it to your lesson won't necessarily make your class equally profound and memorable to your students.

## WORK SAMPLES VERSUS RUBRICS

The message so far: Introduce new content in discrete steps, interleaved with practice and reflection to allow students to manage the load on working memory and gradually begin encoding ideas in long-term memory. But what about content that can't be easily broken into sequential steps? Writing an essay or painting a watercolor, say. They are still tasks that involve mastery of separate elements, but they cannot be easily broken into steps.

One solution is to share an annotated exemplar marked up by the teacher for students to study. In *Embedding Formative Assessment*, Dylan Wiliam and Siobhan Leahy suggest replacing the commonly used rubrics with "work samples" as tools to explain how to complete tasks successfully. This is interesting in part because rubrics, carefully crafted but relatively abstract descriptions of the characteristics of high-quality work, are full of things that are obvious to experts and hidden to novices. They "rarely have the same meaning for students that they do for teachers," Wiliam and Leahy note. For example, a common rubric might note that a proficient essay "uses words and phrases, telling details, and sensory language to convey a vivid picture of the experiences, events, settings, and/or characters." But what does it mean to use telling details and sensory language if you are a novice, and how do you determine their quality? An "inadequate" essay, according to the rubric, "merely tells experiences, events, settings, and/or characters." So the difference is that a better essay uses sensory language and is vivid. Do students know what vivid language looks like? Do they know if their language is sensory? What would it mean in their minds to write in sensory language? Would it make the essay better if the author suddenly dropped in details about things he or she smelled and tasted? It might just as likely sound absurd.

Instead, Wiliam and Leahy suggest looking at high-quality examples that include explanations of *how key elements were created.* Such a work might point out several passages that included vivid language or sensory detail. With a series of concrete examples, a novice now might really understand what it looks like and see how to embed it in a larger work. How are sensory details effectively included so they are not just greater in quantity but better in quality?[6] Essentially, you are building a mental model for students so they can imagine and understand the component parts of the end product.

The idea that the starting point for an assignment could be public work sampling—rather than abstract rubrics—is compelling. The key is to make the work samples concrete—to guide students through three or four examples of key elements, and then allow them to practice them discretely.[7] This might result in several shorter exercises—studies—where students seek to master various parts, or solve smaller problems before composing a larger work. This is in fact how many of the great masters worked. Their canvases are the product of study after study in which solutions to the painting's component problems are modeled. Figure out the light and shadow on the house in the foreground first. Then sketch the figures in the field and explore how you'll use shading. Several times, perhaps. Then put them together.

An exceptional example of this was provided to me by Nina Troiano, then an Art teacher at Troy Prep Middle School in Troy, New York. I was always stunned by the quality of student work in the hallways at the school and observed several of Nina's lessons. Typically she would build skills and knowledge progressively through a series of exercises leading up to a final piece. Here's her process for breaking down the process of painting formation as she described one project to me.

"It's a pretty academic first day," she said. "We started by reading about the artist in the *Do Now*—maybe two paragraphs with questions to answer. We discussed her approach and then we looked at one of her drawings.

"We talked about why she did what she did and we were pulling out elements we'd use in our projects through guided discussion," Nina said.

"I was trying to allow the kids to give their own spin on what I think was a really eerie approach to landscape.[8] We talked about how the house was isolated, and that there were no people. But also that there were strange elements like a ladder up to a window that made you realize there might have been activity at one point. It made you realize there were no people but there should be. We talked about how the houses and trees were stylized and the houses were drawn in two-point perspective, but a distorted imperfect version of that."

Here Nina was essentially annotating an exemplar, telling her students: Here is a model of a possible finished work. Here are some of the key elements that make it powerful. Here are words to describe those things.

Next Nina's kids practiced, a lot, before they tried to produce a final drawing. "The first day, we all draw together. We start with a house. We go step by step and break the house apart into shapes and angles and lines and what each line is doing. For example, to make the house look as if it's receding in space, the front edge would be longer and then gradually narrows toward the back. So I draw it and we copy it together. After they've done that, it starts to make sense. Then I give them half-complete houses that they have to complete. It becomes more independent. Toward the end they draw a full house. Then we start adding horizon lines and landscape details." By the end of the first day Nina's students have done multiple sketches and drawings of the houses that they may put in their final project.

On day two they practiced the elements of landscape, especially the trees, in the same way. And on subsequent days they got more practice. "On day two for the *Do Now* we start with what we did previously. I had a half-drawn house for them to complete. On day three I gave them a house and they had to add the landscape with stylized trees," Nina said.

After a few days of practicing sketching the elements, students did a final draft. "I tell them it's like a test. They have to show that they understand the points that we've hit. There are composition requirements: one house; at least four stylized trees, all of the tress with cast shadows, all of them pointing in the correct direction, aligned with the sun; a mysterious element that suggests missing people. Then they could think about color. They draw a first draft with crayons and colored pencils. They use that to guide their final copy. But before that, we do demos with oil pastels. How to get a vibrant color. How to blend."

You can see in the story how Nina builds up knowledge piece by piece, helping students to not only understand how to successfully create a larger complex work but also develop skills and knowledge they can apply in future paintings and drawings. In part, this is about managing student's working memory. By allowing them to apply all of their conscious thought in a sustained way to a smaller task she helps them make each element special and the overall result memorable. Certainly the resulting works were full of creativity and self-expression, but there's also such immense respect for the knowledge of craft implicit in being able to create and express. Did students enjoy it? Overwhelmingly. There was such a sense of competence and confidence. They knew how to create. And of course the degree to which one can bring one's creative vision to reality is a result of the knowledge and skill she has built.

Perhaps my perception is wrong, but I don't often see an approach like this used in art classrooms. Students are most often assigned a painting and they have a go at it all at once.

In her outstanding book *Making Good Progress*, Daisy Christodoulou makes a fascinating point. If teachers don't break down complex tasks into component parts, the alternative is to practice summative tasks as whole exercises. Sort of like doing whole landscape paintings over and over, except that in academic subjects the tasks often become very focused on tested outcomes. That is, teachers do over and over tasks that replicate what students will be assessed on in the end. "Assessment for learning [what teachers in the UK might call data-driven instruction] became excessively focused on exam tasks not just because of the pressures of accountability," Christodoulou writes, "but because the dominant theory of how we acquire skill suggested it was the best thing to do." We blame teaching to the test on the tests when part of the problem is our own conception of teaching. Lessons, she says, should look very different from the final skill they are hoping to instill. The goal is to make what's intuitive to experts legible to novices so they can master it.

## TECHNIQUE 22: BOARD = PAPER

I have a colleague who can still tell me what we said about each classroom we observed during a series of school visits we made more than a decade ago. I know this because once, several years after the visit, she did exactly that, flipping back through a trusty old spiral note-book until she found the date and heading, thumbing down through a tidy transcription of the salient points about each teacher we'd watched until she found the one we were discussing. "Yes," she confirmed, "we loved her upbeat, positive tone even then."

I have another colleague who can flip back through her notes and remind everyone what we decided at a meeting or what we thought of a video we watched eighteenth months ago.

Unlike these colleagues, my own notes are more or less useless to me after I have taken them. I never learned (or, more precisely, never built a habit of using) an intentional system of note-taking. Perhaps teachers in my schools assumed my peers and I knew how to take notes, perhaps they thought it was up to us to figure out, but in school my notes then were a mess of hasty scrawls with little organizational structure. This pattern persists to this day, and I find this weakness to be an enduring drain on my productivity.

Taking notes is a critical but easily overlooked skill that allows students to organize and review material over the long run: across a unit, a semester, or a lifetime. And in the short run—that is, during class when they are actively taking notes—the process can cause students to focus and prioritize their attention.

To state the obvious, note-taking is progressive: a habit that builds over time from a simple model in the primary years to something more complex when students are older. At the elementary level, students should know that "written on the board" means it's important and should be written down by them as well. At the middle school level, they should systematically record the important ideas from the class and differentiate them from less salient points. At the high school level they should leave class with a record of the proceedings that will allow them to study the ideas in depth and with clarity even weeks later.

Perhaps some students do. But too many, likely, will produce haphazard scrawls scattered across the page like I did because the process of learning to make notes is so easily overlooked. Others will not know that *if it's on the board it matters*. Taking good notes requires and therefore builds attentiveness, and too-brief notes not only will be largely useless later on but also may reflect a fractured state of attention during the lesson. At the other end of the spectrum, some students will try to write everything down and have little attention left to reflect on the ideas from class. They may have little sense for what information was actually important when they return to review. Left uncorrected, each of these untaught note-takers will carry a hidden disadvantage to every classroom they inhabit.

With that in mind, it's worth watching the video *Sadie McCleary: Board Equals Paper*, a series of moments from Sadie McCleary's Chemistry lesson at Western Guilford High School in Greensboro, North Carolina, in which she guides her students through the process of creating a written record of the day's learning. As the clip opens, Sadie instructs her students to get a page set up for note-taking. She is clearly modeling and practicing a *method* of note-taking as much as she's seeking to help them master the details of the day's lesson: "You are writing at the top 'Unit 2: Matter,'" she says. "Today's lesson is lesson 14: *Combined Gas Law*." The system—with references to units and sequences of lessons—is implicit in the set-up.

After guiding the students through several practice problems, Sadie says, "We're going to write that into our notebook." Notice the 'we' language here and throughout—the clip reminds students: *What I am doing at the board, you are doing at your desk—all of us are doing this together.* You can also see Sadie reach for her own version of a notebook and place it under the LCD projector. She's completing a "worked example": a high-quality model completed live in front of students in which she comments on the process as she completes it. She models and describes at the same time. It's not trivial that she keeps her own version of a student notebook. At the end she'll have a record of what they have in their notebooks, which Sadie reflects comes in handy to help with absences, lost notebooks, and students in need of study tips. And having a consistent place to take notes is part of the system. She's modeling that, too.

Sadie's pace is stately. "So we'll write $P_1V_1$ over $T_1$," she says, and then leaves a few seconds for students to get that down. "It used to drive me crazy when a teacher said *write this down* but then was already talking about something else when I was trying to do just that," recalled my colleague John Costello as we screened this video at our offices. "But she goes slowly. There's time to do what she asks." In part that's because she is making actual notes live rather than, say, projecting a version she created in advance. This causes her to be doubly attentive to pace—she understands the time that students need for tasks because she's doing them herself. That said, only teachers with strong established class cultures can write while still scanning for follow-through and behavior, so while it's ideal to write along with students, having prewritten notes that you narrate is acceptable if your culture is still developing. It will give you less to manage in your own working memory and let you observe more accurately. Just be sure to go slowly. And work toward the sort of live modeling Sadie uses.

Watching this video as a team, we also noted how important planning was. Having a clear sense of what students should write (and possibly even having written out an exemplar version of their notes beforehand to guide you) will help make the notes organized and thoughtful. If you're figuring out how to structure the notes or what to write in real time, the result is likely to be confusion.[9] In a later interview Sadie noted how important it is for her to think through in advance exactly what she wants in her notebook. Turns out she keeps two! One she fills out in advance, so she knows what to write. The second she completes along with her students so she can model and describe the process to them in real time.

Throughout the video, you'll also notice how carefully Sadie scans to make sure students feel accountable to follow-through. She is sending the message "I care about you getting this down and I'm watching to make sure you do." As we discuss in *Radar and Be Seen Looking* (technique 53) this makes it so much more likely that the students will, in fact, make sure to get every note down. You can see Sadie looking several times and even carefully adjusting the projector at one point to make sure students can see perfectly. The message is *This has to be just right so you can all get it down perfectly.*

Sadie models a two-part process in which students include both "content" and "commentary" in their notes. She shows them how to write down elements of the lesson and how to mark them up with their own thoughts and reminders. At one point you can see Sadie model for her students how and where to include marginalia and commentary, such as labeling one part of the equation "initial" and adding side notes about how to use the formula: "It must be the same gas" and "No added or removed particles."

Here's a side note about the video, based on a conversation that came up in our team's screening of the video: *How can we prepare students to take notes on laptops in college?* One of the most important parts of this video to me is that Sadie is modeling handwritten notes. Recent data[10] has made it pretty clear that handwriting your notes leads to greater recall than typing your notes. You remember more, think more deeply, and are less likely to be distracted by other things that pop up when your laptop is open. The more students work by hand, the better, so I think my response is to prepare students not to take notes on laptops, if possible. I'd be transparent about this, and remind them of the benefits of handwriting their notes—presently and when they get to college and in a university setting.[11]

Seeing Sadie's work with her high school Chemistry students is powerful, but as I noted before *Board = Paper* involves "progressive habits that build up from the primary to the university years." What skills and habits should a classroom reinforce when students are younger?

Begin with the idea that students should know to track what the teacher is writing on the board. When a teacher writes it on the board, it means *This is important.*[12] Students should know to write it down.

The best way to start students on the path to autonomous note-taking is to make your overhead a mirror image of the graphic organizer you give to students to take notes on. As you fill in a blank, they fill in a corresponding blank. You fill out the projected worksheet on the board and say, "Make your paper look like mine." Even as students earn more autonomy, having your overhead match the format in which they are taking notes allows you to model what note-taking—one of the most important skills for any student—should look like.

Gradually, students should develop note-taking independence, filling out longer and longer passages of their graphic organizers on their own, before you ultimately ask them to take notes on a separate sheet of paper as Sadie does. But know that it may take time before students are ready to take full responsibility for such a critical piece of the process and that along the way they'll need lots of feedback. At her previous school, Sadie notes, when students got to the point where they were simply taking their own notes without guidance, she used to collect class notes to give them feedback and/or to share exemplars to compare their own notes to.

## TECHNIQUE 23: ACCOUNTABLE INDEPENDENT READING

Independent reading is critical to student success in every subject. It is a base operating system that supports nearly every academic endeavor. Even a problem-set in math assesses, in some part, students' ability to independently read a short passage about drawing colored beans randomly out of a bag or the details of how many lawns Tyson mowed when.

As they progress toward adulthood, advanced study, and professional careers, students must be able to read complex texts specific to each discipline independently, even when those texts are challenging. To be a lawyer, a scientist, or an engineer is to be prepared for texts not necessarily designed to engage the reader or yield their meaning easily. If students cannot sit down and successfully make thorough sense of such texts on their own, their horizons will be constrained.

Maryanne Wolf points out in *Reader Come Home* that independent reading is also critical to building the capacity to sustain attention and concentration.[13] Learning to read deeply and well "rewires the brain," she says, creating "sophisticated neural circuits" capable of reflection, concentration, and empathy. A fractured half-attentive society shouting at one another, in other words, is one outcome of a culture that does not read much.

And young people increasingly do not read. A 2020 study by the Literacy Trust in England found the lowest rates of student independent reading so far recorded.[14] When students do read, they typically read in states of distraction: on the couch with a smart phone buzzing away on their stomach, say.[15] To read and half-attend or vaguely understand is an increasingly normal cognitive state. Being distracted trips no internal alarms.

Providing periods of sustained, focused independent reading, especially with challenging texts, is among the most valuable things teachers can do in school, in every subject, and at every grade level. For many students, school is increasingly the only place this activity is likely to happen—there are few other places safe from the reach of technological distraction.[16]

However, many teachers don't ask students to read in class because students don't do it productively or they—or their administrators—don't think of it as a form of teaching.

**Accountable Independent Reading** (AIR) is a set of tools to ensure that independent reading during class is successful and productive. It has three tenets. First, assign reading in smaller durations at first in order to make adaptive decisions based on how well students read an initial sample (or samples). Second, assess intentionally, ideally through observable tasks, to make decisions about how effectively or how much of a given text students can read on their own. Third, embed the reading within the arc of the instruction so it is not a separate activity but rather one where ideas apply and connect to the rest of the lesson.

Much of the rationale for this approach comes from the recognition that students' ability to read independently is not static—it depends on the text they are reading and varies given their own background knowledge and experience with different forms of syntax.[17]

Further, the goal is for students to read attentively and with understanding when they read as much as it is to increase the amount of their reading. The habit we want to build is of focused attentive reading.

You can see an example of this in the video *Nicholas Hermann: Forces*. Nick has added an article to his lesson plan for his fifth-grade Science students to read. Great idea. Scientific texts read differently from other writing. It's great practice for students to read within the discipline. The article describes the forces that affect the flight of a baseball. Nicholas is very clear that they're going to start with just four paragraphs. He wants to make sure they can spot the two forces (gravity and air resistance) acting on the ball. He's prepped the text in advance, so the segment is easy for students to see "You're going to stop right next to that number three." His annotation task—put a box around the two forces acting on the baseball—allows him to clearly see if students are able to comprehend this kind of scientific writing.

Why that can be difficult is deftly revealed by the second round of AIR he assigns: *read the next section and place a star next to the line that explains how a scientific law is different from a government law.* "Law" is an apparently simple word that means something different in a scientific context, just the kind of barrier to understanding that the "curse of knowledge" might cause a teacher to overlook. But with two careful tests like this Nicholas will know: Can I give my students longer reading assignments? Can they learn reliably from this kind of reading? If they can, he can pause during a typical lesson and, rather than saying, "Let me explain to you how electricity works," he can say, "Let me give you a short article that will explain how electricity works," and let reading passages be one of his core teaching tools. If not, they will need more practice.

You can see a slightly more complex example in the video *Kirby Jarrell: A Doubtful Freedom*. Students in her seventh-grade class are reading *The Narrative of the Life of Frederick Douglass*. It's a challenging text, to say the least—published in 1845, Douglass's syntax is challenging to modern ears. His writing is rich in complex imagery and often employs a formal rhetorical style rarely seen today. But it is also a critical text for students to read. There is no other way to understand the book save to hear Douglass's voice directly. The text is both complex and necessary.

As the clip opens, Kirby's class has just read aloud. "It was so obvious from the way you read that aloud that you really understood it," she says. This small moment shows us that Kirby is already using students' fluency and expression in oral reading as data to inform choices about how ready students are to read this passage independently.[18]

Kirby asks students to read on their own to the end of the section for about two minutes and to make notes about the "lists" Douglass makes—these are critical to understanding the passage. In assigning a visible annotation task, Kirby sets out to assess students' status as independent readers—not just generally, but of *this* portion of *this* book. Because she's given them a specific annotation task, Kirby is able to use *Active Observation* (technique 9) to note trends in comprehension, and as the timer winds down she is optimistic, "Awesome job. You don't need a partner," she says, deciding to skip a planned *Turn and Talk* (technique 43). Instead she launches into a whole-group discussion. "What is he listing, and why?" she asks.

The subsequent discussion is meant to stamp the understanding students should have gleaned independently from the text, but the text is tricky, and it quickly emerges that not everyone understood as fully as Kirby thought. One student explains that Douglass is listing the challenges he faced while escaping, and Kirby calls on another student to clarify that the lists are hypothetical—none of the challenges listed had actually happened yet. This passage, critically, involves Douglass imagining the risks of escape.

But Kirby is alert to the indications of struggle and asks students to jot a note at the bottom of the page capturing the idea that Douglass is *imagining* in this section. They're doing well in the face of real challenge, but she'll have to be careful about how much she gives them to read on their own. Being able to fly solo with such a challenging book is still a work in progress.

As the clip closes, she says, "I just want to emphasize, it's been [only a few] weeks [since they started the novel] and just think about how well you're understanding this book . . . what was that like for you? . . . I think a lot of us are really able to figure out Douglass's tough language." This might seem like a contradictory thing to say after students have struggled with a key point, but both things are true.

They have made incredible progress. They are often able to read successfully from an immensely challenging text. But tricky passages will emerge. A book's "level of difficulty" is an average. Within it there are sections students can breeze through and sections of special difficulty. To say that students can read a book independently is always a generalization. There are several elements Kirby uses to ensure this segment of independent reading is productive.

First there is the gradual release in the length of the independent reading: starting small and increasing the amount of text as your confidence in students' comprehension grows. If Kirby's students had read the bulk of a chapter instead of starting as they did with just a paragraph or two, it would have been much harder for Kirby to lock in on their understanding of this passage and to use it as a test of their readiness to read similar passages solo. In the long run we want to build students' stamina for independent reading tasks, but it may take time before we know that students are up to the task of reading extended passages with accuracy.

Kirby's clear and specific annotation task—"What is he listing, and why?"—is key. Giving students a focal point allows you to monitor comprehension while they work. For younger students, this might sound like what you hear Dan Cosgrove say in the video *Dan Cosgrove: Earthworm*: "Meet me at the top of page 56 and jot one word to show how the earthworm is feeling." In a history class, you might prompt, "Underline at least two details about the conditions faced by Revolutionary War soldiers." Having a clear task also benefits students, guiding them to concentrate on the most important parts of the text by giving them something concrete to pay attention to while reading.

One important caveat on annotation tasks: It's easy to make the annotation task too complex or too vague. What we want is a task that clearly reveals whether students understood, not just the gist, but the specific language of the passage. The task should therefore be specific to understanding a particular section of text rather than the application of a universal skill. "In this paragraph, underline the three ways memory can be manipulated or changed" is better than "In this paragraph underline three examples of figurative language." A student can complete the second task and not understand what they've read. The goal in designing annotation tasks is to give yourself data on whether students understood with precision what the author is trying to say so you know how much they can read on their own.

One benefit of short and medium doses of AIR is that they allow you to integrate reading into the arc of your lesson and send the message that independent reading is one of the ways we engage content together during class and not just something we do after class and on our own. To have everyone read a passage independently and then discuss it or write about it makes reading a part of the learning process. As Nicholas Hermann's video shows, this is especially valuable outside of reading classes. Learning to read the discourse of the sciences independently and seeing reading as intrinsic to the process of learning about science is a necessity for any STEM career, for example.

A last thought on AIR. Does it always look like this? Must you always methodically assess students' readiness and release them only to what you know they can do successfully? No. The accountability is something you often use to understand and support your students' ability to read complex texts. There are times when independent reading can take other forms—students should choose and read books on their own, of course; sometimes they should struggle with a challenging text and reflect on what they initially missed or didn't fully comprehend. But AIR reminds us of how important it is to constantly assess students as independent readers so we understand the experience they are having when they read.

And AIR can help students understand the reading process better too. Like Kirby, you may opt to be transparent about your decision-making process (for example, "My sense is that we're still figuring Steinbeck out. We're going to keep reading independently in small chunks until we're a bit more familiar with his style and voice," or "This description of photosynthesis includes a lot of technical vocabulary, so you're just going to read the first two paragraphs on your own.") It also allows for celebration of success, as we can see in Kirby's clip: "That was a challenge, and you did it." This language of celebration is a way to embrace challenge and show that success brings additional autonomy: "We're really starting to get Steinbeck. I'm going to challenge you to do more on your own," or "You did a great job summarizing the section on photosynthesis—let's see how you do in this next chapter, which goes a little deeper."

## TECHNIQUE 24: FASE READING

*FASE Reading*, or, as it was formerly known, *Control the Game*, is a system for student read-alouds that maximizes the value and viability of this crucial activity, allowing you to build students' fluency in and enjoyment of reading. It has always been in the top tier of techniques in the book in terms of importance, but society is undergoing rapid and dramatic changes, the most significant of which involve the omnipresence of technology, and these have elevated even further the importance—I might even say urgency—of an intentional approach to reading in the classroom that includes the use of *FASE Reading*. This is, in my mind, one of the handful of most important techniques in the book.

What does FASE mean? It's an acronym, and even though I'm not crazy about acronyms, the previous name was obscure,[19] and this technique needed a new name that communicated something important about the technique. The previous name communicated important things about the technique mostly to me and me alone.

The new name, FASE, is intended to remind teachers about four things they should try to reinforce when students read aloud. It also sounds a bit like "phase" and this can be a reminder that it often happens in a cycle of a few minutes that yields to other activities and then is used again later. A phase—like *FASE Reading*—is often temporary but recurring.

**F is for fluency.** Fluency is hugely important for readers at all levels. We want to use *FASE Reading* as an opportunity to build it. This is because, as Student Achievement Partners note in a recent white paper, "Research shows dysfluency causes as much as 40% of the variance in students who pass [state] tests versus those who fail. This is true for every testing grade."[20] You don't have to like tests to get the point: Comprehension and understanding require fluency. You must read not just individual words but strings of words at the speed of sight[21]—with automaticity that is, so that your full working memory is free to think about the text. One of the least contemplated, obvious things about reading is that it has to happen fast—"at the speed of sight," as Mark Seidenberg puts it—for it to work. We have to be able to make sense of it as soon as we perceive it. If you're asking a student about the author's craft or what exactly the experiment says about the role of ATP and they can't process the words and syntax at the speed of sight, you're likely to be disappointed. When you have to slow down to read, when the task of reading and making basic sense of the words requires conscious thinking, your working memory is allocated to figuring out the words, what they mean, and how they fit together, not to comprehending. Perhaps this is why the students who got fluency instruction—both those in regular classrooms and those who were struggling readers—"simply read better" than those who did not get regular work on fluency, writes Timothy Shanahan, who is among the nation's foremost researchers on reading. "For many students oral reading fluency practice continues to help in the consolidation of decoding skills [and] . . . helps to support prosody development which is more directly implicated in reading comprehension."[22]

Reading aloud is critical to building fluency. It is the only reliable way to assess it and it provides students with the opportunity to practice the meaning making we express when we read aloud. To read something aloud is to interpret it and make arguments about it: In what tone should it be read? Which word gets emphasized? Think for a moment of how critical it is to know what the implicit voice of a text sounds like, not just for novels but for scientific research and historiography; now think of how often your students have heard those things read aloud. With FASE reading there's constant modeling of how a text should sound but the model comes from fellow students. I will return to this when we discuss the social aspects of reading.

Reading aloud is the best way to practice fluency and it's beneficial for *all learners*, but once they have finished the elementary grades students no longer get opportunities to read aloud and build fluency. This gap is ten times more important now when—and this will be another motif of this book—reading as we know it is locked in a death struggle with the cell phone, a battle it is losing badly. It's not just that students read less and less—the data are devastating—it's that they read less and less well. They are more distracted; in states of constant half-attention,[23] their eyes flitting down the page looking for the next new thing. So it's not just that we build fluency and reading skills that translate into silent reading as well, it's that it is one of the few ways we can cause students to read for sustained, undistracted periods of time.

**A is for accountability.** "The only way we can ever 100% know that a child is actually reading is if they are reading aloud," Jo Facer writes in *Simplicity Rules*. And it's the only way we can know *how* they are reading. Your class reading aloud is not just fluency practice, it's not just an exercise in creating community (which I'll come to in a moment), it's a constant data stream on the reading level of your students on the key texts of your classroom. Nothing could be more data driven.

Making sure students are reading is a big deal—bigger now than five or ten years ago. Yes, I can hear some teachers saying, we should socialize students to read at home as much as we can. But note also that relying on reading happening at home is in part regressive—the strong readers are likely to get more of it—and we increasingly can't be sure that many students read steadily outside of school. We are all addicts to a device engineered to absorb our full attention. Our students are in its thrall the minute they leave school.[24] "Any and all systems I have ever come up with [to ensure independent reading at home] have been gamed by students . . . If you want to ensure pupils are reading, your only bet is to make them do it with you, as a whole class. That's why things like whole class reading of a suitable novel . . . for 20 to 30 minutes a day are so beneficial. If children have read that much for that long, they will have a massive advantage over their peers," Facer writes.

**S is for social.** This is the hidden gift of *FASE Reading*. Shared experiences, especially ones with emotional weight or where significant ideas emerge, draw people into communities and give them a sense of belonging. This is what you are doing when you read together—building community and belonging and, not coincidentally, this is in part the role stories and texts have played in our society for longer than there have been schools. Stories and experiences were shared not just among groups but *in groups* as a way to draw people together. It is fitting that this aspect of reading may be our best bet now to elevate its stature above the lonelier forms of communication available through screens.

In *Culturally Responsive Teaching and the Brain,* Zaretta Hammond makes a compelling case for the importance of community in the classroom. We are the most individualist society on earth, she notes. Finding ways to balance ardent individualism with a communal approach is part of culturally responsive teaching—a key way to make the classroom more accessible to students from less individualistic cultures, she argues. At the same time it pushes us to see the benefits of greater emphasis on community and belonging conferred upon some other cultures that value it more highly.

The way we read sometimes reflects that ardent individualism, especially in moments where everyone chooses their own book and reads it on their own. There's a common argument that students will only love reading if it involves individual choice and while some choice is nice,[25] everyone always choosing their own thing means giving up what is collective—the shared text we can all talk about because we've all read it and shared the experience of reading it together. One of the benefits of a collective task like reading together is that it builds belonging, the strongest incentive for humans there is. Ironically, reading and experiencing together often yields more enjoyment than does a setting where everyone gets choice. The moment when your class laughs or gasps aloud in the midst of a shared reading, a bond is made. The experience of reading together is as powerful to the brain as events experienced together and thus the shared connection it creates can help forge a lasting and valuable sense of community and belonging. If we want the experience of reading to be powerful and unique—social, shared, and pleasurable, more powerful than the smartphone—the key is to read communally and to emphasize that by reading aloud together.

**E is for expressive.** To read aloud well is to make meaning audible, to breathe life into a text. It's powerful when a teacher does this and it's even more meaningful when students do. It is a statement—peer to peer—that the text is worth bringing to life. To hear your peers take pride in their reading skills and show they value reading creates the sort of positive social norm that is most likely to shift reading behaviors. When students read aloud expressively, and when, as they do in the best classrooms, they implicitly compete to show who can read most expressively—they are not only bringing what you are reading to life, they are making the case for the book. Gabby Woolf does an exemplary job of this in the video *Gabby Woolf: Keystone*. Her class is reading *Dr Jekyll and Mr Hyde*, Robert Louis Stevenson's 1886 novella, which is full of archaic and unfamiliar syntax. To successfully bring it to life is to show that you understand the book. So as she begins, first modeling herself before she calls on students to *FASE Read*, she challenges students to bring out their maximum degree of expressiveness. "In the spirit of being sensationalist, we want to read it as . . . Stevenson would want his readers to imagine it." She encourages her pupils to volunteer "with your highly expressive reading" and notes, "I know several of you who would make a very good job of that." And indeed the subsequent reading by her students is rich in expression and meaning made audible.

## The Challenges of Reading Aloud

There is joy and pleasure in reading aloud but there are also challenges, and these are also worth addressing because in many ways the purpose of *FASE Reading* is to address those challenges[26]—it's a classic case of technique making strategy viable. If you have the technique that allows you to overcome a few challenges, the benefits of a powerful strategy become feasible.

So what are the challenges? The reasons can be grouped in two primary buckets: leverage concerns and self-esteem concerns.

## Leverage Concerns

Some educators react to suggestions that they include more oral reading in class with a question along these lines: "Why would you allow a single student to read aloud during class time? What are the other kids doing?" The implication is, I guess: nothing. Having a lone student reading aloud to an otherwise passive classroom can indeed be a poor use of time. And of course it's possible that the reader's peers could be checked out and gazing out the window. But in a well-designed lesson, they would be reading, too, and this is both valuable and relatively easy to accomplish.

I use the term "leverage" to refer to how much reading the rest of the class is doing when one student is reading aloud. If twenty-seven students are staring into space or listening passively, the leverage is low. But if one student is reading actively and twenty-seven students are listening carefully and reading along with her, as actively engaged in the text as if they were reading independently, then the leverage is much higher. It's also worth reflecting on the ease with which a group of people can discuss a text meaningfully when they have just experienced it together. There are no reminders: *remember the scene where this or that happened*? The memory of the scene is vivid in students' minds when you say, "Let's pause here and discuss." So a second answer to the question "What are the other students doing?" is: They are preparing to discuss. Concerns about the passivity of nonreaders are legitimate, but they're fairly easily managed by specific teacher actions, which I'll discuss in a moment.

I've also heard concerns raised that both listening and reading along at the same time will overload students' working memory—that listening will prevent reading along—or vice versa. I'm not sure there's a clear answer to that, though there's a fair amount of recent research showing that the visual and auditory channels are additive in terms of working memory.[27] Still, we can't rule out this concern. That said, reading is an immensely complex task that we use to serve a wide range of outcomes in the classroom. Among other things, we want students to learn decoding and fluency and vocabulary through reading. We want them to acquire knowledge through reading and be able to acquire knowledge through further reading of complex texts in particular. We want them to persist in reading, make a habit of it, and value it all their lives. It's unrealistic to think that any single approach is going to optimize that many diverse outcomes. Reading remains to me the first among equals—the most important among all the valuable things we teach in school—and my guidance would be to have students read a lot in class, to have them read in ways that make a text feel valuable—buy-in, a colleague of mine says, is an outcome, not a precondition for any activity—and use a variety of ways of reading so that you get the benefit of multiple approaches.

In designing our Reading Reconsidered Curriculum, my team included three forms of reading in each lesson: *Teacher Read Aloud*, *FASE Reading*, and *Accountable Independent Reading* (see technique 23). The exact balance we suggest depends on the teacher, the class, and the text. But we suggest healthy doses of all three. (That's not advice I'd limit to the ELA classroom.) The video *Eric Snider: The Wind* is a great example of a teacher using all three ways of reading in synergy: Eric reads aloud, allows his students to read for a stretch—they crush it with the complex text, by the way—and then sends them off to (accountable) independent reading. If there's a weakness to any of those forms of reading, he balances them by using the others and still reaps the unique benefits of each approach.

## Self-Esteem Concerns

Some educators have also suggested that students should not be asked to read aloud in class because they might struggle—this might shame or embarrass them, and possibly cause them to dislike reading. Essentially, the argument is that if students are weak readers, we should withhold from them one of the best tools for improving reading skills because it might cause them discomfort. Learning to be comfortable struggling is, in my mind, a much more manageable and temporary challenge than being a weak reader. Teachers, and the cultures they build, are fully capable of making it safe to struggle and take risks. It's yet another reason why building a vibrant, positive culture—not just avoiding a negative culture—is so critical in the classroom.

And fortunately everyone's reading is imperfect! So one critical step is to make this simple fact more evident. Balancing teacher read-alouds with student read-alouds is a great way to do this. If you read aloud you will surely make your share of stumbles and bobbles. I know I do. Not trying to hide them but instead making them seem normal is powerful. You could say "Whoops, let me start that sentence over," or "Whoops, that's 'flawed,' not 'flamed.'" Or you could say very little and just carry on as if it were the most normal thing in the world and let the data settle in on the class over time: Even the teacher stumbles. Having lots of students read also affords lots of opportunities for lots of students to stumble a bit, go back, reread, figure out a word—all of it public and in full view, even among the best readers. This normalizes an obvious aspect of reading that is otherwise hidden to students. The key is not to make weaker students feel like they should not stumble but to help them see that everyone does.

But of course some readers struggle more than others and it is precisely those students who struggle most who also benefit most from the practice. Planning, preparation, and culture building can address the challenges of this. Later I'll share with you a moment in Jessica Bracey's classroom where she demonstrates some excellent solutions. But first, this advice from Jo Facer: She writes that, initially, it is best to "select short, simple sentences before you teach your lesson, and underline or highlight these on your own copy. That way you will know the 'safe sentences' to get your struggling readers to succeed with." Over time this will allow them to meet with success and build their confidence, she notes.

One observation implicit in this comment is the idea that people change—not only their skills but also their perceptions. You cannot control whether a student is nervous at first. But you can control environmental variables sufficiently to change that feeling in time.

There are of course other ways to manage the experience so that students gradually get better at reading by reading aloud. I'll return to those in a moment. But for now I want to also point out that denying all students the opportunity to read aloud because some students might at first be nervous is wrong. All students deserve the right to connect with reading as a positive experience and teachers must ensure that all students develop mastery of the skill.

## How to Lead *FASE Reading*

How then do you unlock the benefits of student oral reading and mitigate its downsides? How do you ensure leverage and attentiveness and prepare for strugglers? When you lead *FASE Reading*, you ask students to read aloud, one by one, in an unpredictable pattern, usually for short durations, at least at first. By "asking" I mean most often assigning readers—*Cold Calling*. We want volunteers but we want universality and accountability, as well. Everyone has to read—and hopefully come to love reading. "The weakest readers need the *most* practice at reading, but are also the ones who tend to volunteer *least* to read aloud, as well as the ones who opt not to read privately after school hours. To serve our weakest readers, it simply must be the expectation that every child can be asked to read aloud at any time," Jo Facer writes. Here are some details on those elements.

### Keep Durations Unpredictable

If you designate a student to read in class and say, "Read the next paragraph for me, Vivian," everyone in the class knows no one else will be asked to read until Vivian finishes the paragraph. *Stating the duration for which a student will read causes other students to follow along a little less.* Instead, when you ask a student to read, don't specify how long you want her to read for. Saying, "Start reading for me please, Vivian" or "Pick up, please, Vivian" makes other students more likely to read along, since they don't know when a new reader will be asked to pick up.

In addition, keeping durations unpredictable allows you to address a struggling reader in a safe and noninvasive manner. If Vivian struggles with the paragraph you've assigned her, it means either a long, slow slog to the end, possibly exhausting for Vivian and reducing leverage with other students, or it's you suddenly cutting her short of what you promised: "OK, I'm going to stop you there, Vivian. Jelani, would you please read some?," which carries an implicit judgment. If you don't specify the length of the read initially, however, you can adapt in the interest of both the student who's reading and the rest of the class. Vivian can read two sentences really well and then stop before she struggles too much, making the experience positive, then you can move to a dynamic reader who will push the story along for the rest of the class. Or, if Vivian is doing well, you can let her keep going. All of this happens invisibly when you avoid telling students how long they'll read.

### Keep Durations Short

Reading short segments can often allow students to invest energy in expressive reading and sustain the energy required for fluent, even dramatic reading. It's better to read really well for three or four sentences and stop than to read well for two and drone through six more. Moving quickly among primary readers can yield higher-quality oral reading and make the lesson more engaging. The momentum of quick, unpredictable, and relatively frequent changes of reader makes reading feel quick and energetic rather than tedious and slow.

Knowing that segments tend to be short and may end at any time also reinforces for secondary readers that they will likely soon get a chance themselves to read, and this keeps them from tuning out.

As students develop as readers, your definition of "short" will, of course, change. Maybe the average read is two or three sentences at first, but as students get better as readers and become more able to attend carefully, as they come to love reading and lose themselves more in the text, you will naturally extend the average length of a read. Sometimes you and the class will lose yourselves in a passage, and Vivian will just keep going. The key idea is that using shorter reads can bring engagement and energy to student oral reading—perhaps at the beginning of a passage, perhaps if things slow down, perhaps all the time. When and how often is up to you.

Finally, keeping durations short enables you to take better advantage of a crucial form of data: every time you switch readers, you gather data about your leverage. When you say, "Pick up please, Charles," and Charles jumps in with the next sentence without missing a beat, you know that Charles was reading alongside the previous reader on his own. If not, you know otherwise. Ideally, you want this sort of seamless transition every time you switch readers, and frequent switching allows you to gather and manage transitions more often and more broadly. The more data you have, the more information and tools you will have to help you ensure leverage.

### Keep the Identity of the Next Reader Unpredictable

If you move quickly from one primary reader to another, students focus more closely on following along. This is doubly true if they don't know who the next reader will be. A teacher who announces that she'll go around the room in a predictable fashion gives away this part of her leverage. Students can tune out until their turn is near. Retaining your ability to choose the next reader also allows you to match students to passages more effectively. If you want to use Jo Facer's idea of preselecting sentences that developing readers can be more successful with, you'll need to be able to *Cold Call* readers and you'll need to select randomly.

Unpredictability makes for both better leverage and better reading, so when you call on students to read, it's great to call on some students who volunteer—the moment when they wave their hands in the air, desperate for their chance to read is a huge win for any teacher— just make sure not to call *exclusively* on volunteers. A significant proportion, most often a majority, of readers should include those who haven't raised their hands. This will maximize leverage and normalize full and universal participation. The message should be that reading is a pleasure and that a good teacher doesn't let just a few students hog all the fun.

### Reduce Transaction Costs

A *transaction cost* is the amount of resources it takes to execute an exchange, be it economic, verbal, or otherwise. When it comes to transitioning between readers, small differences in transaction costs can have a large effect, so it's critical to reduce them. A transition from one reader to the next that takes much more than a second steals reading time and risks interrupting the continuity of what students are reading, thus affecting how well students follow and comprehend the text.

Make it your goal to transition from one primary reader to another quickly and with a minimum of words—ideally, in a consistent way. "Susan, pick up," is a much more efficient transition than, "Thank you, Stephen. Nicely read. Susan will you begin reading, please?" The first transaction is more than three times as fast as the second, maximizing the amount of time students spend reading. A couple seconds of difference may seem trivial, but if you transition fifty times per class, those seconds very quickly translate into minutes and hours of lost reading time over the course of the year. Just as important, reducing your transaction cost when switching readers causes less interruption to the text, allowing students to concentrate and keep the narrative thread vibrant, alive, and unbroken. If you make a habit of minimizing transaction cost, you can more easily switch at almost any natural pause in the text, giving you even more control over when to choose a new primary reader. Can you occasionally drop in a "lovely" or a "thank you"? Of course. Though perhaps even better would be to express it with body language or a quiet and appreciative comment while a student was still reading.

Let me show you how those things look in two classrooms: Jill Murray's and Maggie Johnson's.

We'll start with Jill, whose video *Jill Murray: Quartering Act* my team loves because it is from a Social Studies class. *FASE Reading* should happen everywhere. Some aspects of reading are likely domain specific in a way we rarely consider: A nonfiction text about a historical event sounds different from a novel. A scientific text has its own unique conventions and rhythms. Students in Jill's class are developing an ear not just for reading but for historical text.

And of course we love it because of how the students react when she announces *FASE Reading* (she calls it by its then-common name "Control the Game"). The kids cheer! I promise we did not pay them to do that! But it suggests the powerful sense of joy and belonging fostered by shared reading. *FASE Reading* is a pleasure, they are telling us.

Jill starts by modeling. She's saying (implicitly): *Here is what a historical text sounds like read aloud.* And just as powerfully: *Here is how I'll expect you to sound when you read aloud.* She's norm setting. Notice how she doesn't race. Commonly students will try to show their skill by reading fast. She wants them to show their skill through expression—by making meaning audible—not speed. You can hear, too, that the text is challenging! But Jill's students persist with relish. They see one another openly embracing challenge—no one's reading is perfect, but everyone is OK with that. And of course as they work toward fluency at this level of complexity, Jill is gathering critical data. She is also teaching them to sustain focus and effort when the going gets hard. All those things—the persistence, the expression—will translate into their independent reading, as well.

Now let's look at Maggie's class: In the video *Maggie Johnson: Grew Serious*, her eighth graders are reading *To Kill a Mockingbird*. It's a challenging text but look how they rise to the occasion. Maggie goes first. Her reading is a model of expressive reading. Arshe is next. He begins reading ably but Maggie encourages a bit more expression: "You can give me a little bit more than that," she says. Call it gentle encouragement, permission to be expressive.

This is important. Reading is social and we want a memorable experience with the text and for students to create as much meaning as possible through their reading. We want students to see one another doing that.

Notice the faint smile on Arshe's face as he rereads. He reads beautifully. Suddenly the story does come to life a little more. Maggie laughs and gently puts a hand on his shoulder to show her appreciation.

Arshe keeps reading. It's a complex text (Lexile 870) but with encouragement he's not only thriving, he's bringing a little more expression to his reading. Another appreciative chuckle from Maggie and then it's Brianna's turn. She's perhaps a bit more halting. Again Maggie is gathering data here on how well everyone can read the text. She asks Brianna to reread a sentence to ensure correct decoding, but she does so easily and with an appreciative laugh like the one she had for Arshe's reading. Brianna gets the point: you're doing fine; keep reading. And she does. Suddenly she's cantering along and crushing it on some very challenging syntax.

Maggie steps in next. She's able to read a bit faster. There are probably kids in the room who want to move the story along. Her bridging helps keep the momentum and their attention. Notice that she's chosen an especially critical passage to read herself and notice how slow and thoughtful her model is. Then she passes the reading to Mel and then to Ronnie, who responds to her request to use expressive reading to depict an irritated Atticus.

This is the only time she's taken a volunteer—the rest of the time she's selected the reader. But here she wants real energy, top-of-the-line expressiveness, and Ronnie does a beautiful job.

It's worth noting that you are seeing effect as much as cause here. Maggie's students read this difficult text so well and with such pleasure and appreciation because they *FASE Read* so often and because the norm of expressive reading is so well established! In Maggie's classroom, expressive, joyful reading is what you do. It's also worth noting that this is an eighth-grade classroom. Sadly, few students this age get the pleasure and benefit of the kind of reading Maggie's class is doing—perhaps because teachers mistakenly think it's not beneficial for older students and perhaps because some teachers think they won't like it or won't do it. I hope the pleasure Maggie's students take in their reading gives teachers license and encouragement to read aloud with older students!

Now that you've got the idea, here are a few more key elements of the technique.

Use Bridging to Maintain Continuity

Using *FASE Reading* combines two types of reading—student oral reading and teacher oral reading. As the teacher, you are naturally the best reader in the room. In reading aloud, you model the sorts of expressive reading you want from students—joyful, scholarly, what have you. You may choose to step in yourself and read especially important or tricky passages—your reading of them can bring the nuance of the text to life and help expedite comprehension. You can also use segments to resuscitate momentum after a particularly slow or struggling reader by stepping in for a few sentences, keeping the thread of the narrative alive and engaging for other students.

In bridging, a teacher takes a turn in the *FASE Reading* rotation, reading a short segment of text—a bridge—between student readers. In a typical sequence of bridging, a teacher might ask Trayvon to read for a few sentences, then Martina and then Hilary, and then read for a stretch herself. She might have planned in advance a part she thought she should read, or she might read to model expressive reading and bring the story to life a bit. She might read because Hilary really struggled, and the teacher didn't want the slow pace to cause other readers to disengage. She might step in more or less frequently.

Sometimes teachers will start the reading themselves to set the tone, occasionally even doing so transparently: "I'll start reading, then I'll ask some of you to pick up. Be ready!" Obviously, teacher reading needn't always bridge. When you do so is obviously discretionary, and part of the art of reading well. Harder texts often demand more bridging—to create more opportunities to model, and to balance the necessarily high rate of slower student readers.

### Spot-Check, a.k.a. Oral Cloze

I learned Oral Cloze from watching Roberto de Leòn teach reading to third-grade boys at Excellence Charter School for Boys in Bedford-Stuyvesant. In one example, Roberto kicked off his reading of *Phantom of the Opera* by leaving a word out at the end of his first sentence: "Carlotta had the . . . ," he read, signaling to students with his shift in tone of voice that they should fill in the blank. On the day in question, only a handful of his boys chimed in "leading role" exactly on cue. So Rob started over: "Ooh, some boys weren't quite with us. Let's try that again. 'Carlotta had the . . . ,'" and all his boys chimed in with "leading role," demonstrating that they were now following along. This quick device, which Roberto uses throughout his lessons, allows him to assess leverage quickly and simply.

### Use a Placeholder

As you move between reading and questioning students about what they read, it can be helpful to use quick, consistent prompts to ensure that students recognize the transition and react quickly. I call this prompt a *placeholder,* because it ensures that students retain their place in the text and enables a quick and immediate transition back to reading after discussion. "Hold your place. Track me," announces Patrick Pastore, modeling for his sixth graders how to point to the spot where they left off reading *Esperanza Rising,* close their books partway, and engage his eyes to show they are ready to discuss. After a brief discussion of why Esperanza and Miguel react differently to a train ride, he instructs, "Pick up reading, please, Melanie." In less than two seconds, she and her classmates are back into the book at almost no transaction cost.

Similarly, Roberto de Leòn might intone, "Finger in your book; close your book," as he prepares his students to discuss *Phantom of the Opera*—and also prepares them to end that discussion and return to the book efficiently.

In the video *Jessica Bracey: Circle of Gold*, you can see Jessica, then at North Star Academy in Newark, New Jersey, executing a lesson with an effective segment of *FASE Reading* embedded in it.

You'll notice how engaged Jessica's students are as she keeps durations short and unpredictable, moving the reading around the room to involve lots of students. You'll also notice that even though she calls on a number of students to read, every single one picks up on cue—solid evidence that they're all reading along with her. But then again the best evidence of all comes after about a minute and a half. Jessica mixes in an opportunity for volunteers. "Please continue for me . . ." she begins, and hands shoot into the air. Students love reading when it comes to life this way; their hands show how much they feel a sense of belonging. They want to be a part of the experience.

Please continue for me.

You'll also notice a wide range of reading skills. There are outstanding readers who model expressive, engaged reading, and there are also some who struggle. Even so, those who struggle aren't afraid to read, even when it's tricky for them. There's a constantly supportive culture.

And Jessica reacts to the stream of data that students reading aloud provide her to help them. She asks them to embed meaning into their expression or to reread words they didn't get the first time. Finally, you'll notice that the girl who reads first in the video also reads again later. Not only is it the ultimate in unpredictable reader selection—just because you've read once doesn't mean the game is over in Jessica's class—but this is a girl who's still developing her fluency skills. She gets double practice! And she's happy to read.

This is no small thing. These students are fifth graders. The various stages in their development as readers are passing quickly. Compare lots and lots of joyful practice for a developing reader to the alternative: the encroaching feeling for such a reader that reading is a source of embarrassment, something she will never be good at, something he wants to avoid. This can be, and is, a self-fulfilling prophecy for thousands of students.

A final note. Earlier I noted that one of the things I liked about the name *FASE Reading* is that a phase is a stage in a series of events. *FASE Reading* ideally is combined with and embedded in other classroom activities, such as five minutes of *FASE Reading* to bring the text to life and then a bout of writing about a text that seems vivid. Or ten minutes of silent reading with the text voice and setting brought to life. Or a discussion of the book we all just read. Imagine how much richer the discussion of *To Kill a Mockingbird* will be in Maggie's class after her students have heard the story come to life through Maggie's and Arshe's and Ronnie's readings. There's a lot more depth to respond to. Imagine also how much more likely they will be to pick up the book and read it that night for homework when it made them laugh together as a group that afternoon in school.

## TECHNIQUE 25: CIRCULATE

Where you stand as you work is a critical aspect of your teaching. It shapes the information you gather about students and helps determine the types of interactions you can use to guide and support them.

Can you stand naturally at a student's shoulder as she solves a problem correctly for the first time, quietly encouraging her and preserving her privacy: "Yes, that's it," or "Much better," or "Now you've got it!"?

Can you subtly move to a spot near another student as you explain the homework, and therefore provide just enough gentle accountability to keep him on task and writing down the assignment?

Only, perhaps, if you can work the room simply and easily—if you can get anywhere in your room at any time without navigating a pile of backpacks or asking for the pushing in of chairs. In fact, if you have to ask for permission to get to any spot in the classroom or if it seems unnatural for you to stand anywhere, it's not really your room and, more importantly, you may not be able to shape it optimally to support student learning.

*Circulate* describes rules and habits for a teacher's strategic and intentional movement around the room during all parts of a lesson.

## Step 1: Break the Plane

The "plane" of your classroom is the imaginary line that runs the length of the room, parallel to and about five feet in front of the board, usually about where the first student desks start.

Some teachers are slow or perhaps hesitant to "break the plane"—to move past this imaginary barrier and out among the desks and rows. They might spend the entire lesson moving back and forth from one front corner to the other. Or just leaning on their desk in front of the board. But breaking the plane adds energy to your teaching and allows you to observe what students are doing. You can linger beside a student's desk and subtly raise your eyebrows as you ask an intriguing question or place a warm and gentle hand on his shoulder as you progress around the room.

It's important to break the plane early—within the first few minutes of the lesson, if possible. (One benefit of technique 20, *Do Now*, is that it creates a natural opportunity to circulate and observe what students are doing right away at the outset of class.) You want it to be clear to students that it is normal for you to go anywhere in the classroom at any time, and the longer you wait to break the plane, the less natural and normal it seems for you to come wandering by at any moment.

Being able to naturally and easily get near students increases the range of tools you have in interacting with them. Technique 9, *Active Observation*, for example, is dedicated to the critical role that systematic data-gathering via circulation plays in checking for understanding. The tools it discusses require breaking the plane as a matter of course.

So, too, do a series of more mundane interactions. You can be far more private with Alfred, for example. All class long it seems like he's been fussing with something on the floor, leaning under his desk and moving his chair back and forth in order to . . . well, you're not really sure. But he hasn't got anything in his notes or completed any problems. And now he's distracting the students around him. If you're only positioned at the front of the room, you're limited to a question that is likely to distract (and possibly yield a more distracting answer), such as "Alfred, what are you doing?" or "Alfred, please sit correctly in your chair."

But wandering over to investigate as you call on a student on the other side of the room, you notice that someone has spilled something sticky on the floor beneath Alfred's desk. It's getting on his shoes and he's struggling to stay focused. "Alfred, honey, move to this desk," you can now say in a low voice. Or perhaps you can bring Alfred a few pieces of paper towel a moment later as the class discussion continues and say, "Try this, sweetheart. Wipe it up and then I'll be back to make sure you've started problem number 1." Or perhaps there is no sticky something on the floor, and Alfred just needs a reminder to stay on task. Now that you're near him you can do it with a whisper. He'll appreciate that. And just maybe he will be more likely to get going.

A *whisper* solution, a *hand-you-what-you-need-while-I'm-still-teaching* solution, a *stand by you to help you complete the task or understand what the problem is* solution. These are only possible if you can get anywhere in the classroom and get there naturally, without attracting undue attention from the rest of the class: Look! She's moving toward Alfred! Your approach to Alfred is much better if he appears to be on your natural path of circulation around the room—your route. In other words, your interaction with Alfred can't be the first time in the class period you've broken the plane.

Breaking the plane, in other words, allows you to gather information constantly—even when you don't know you need to gather information; if you circulate more you will see more of what's happening in the classroom, especially from your students' perspective— and to use privacy and proximity to solve problems and communicate with individual students.

But it only works as a norm, a teacher habit. If you move out into the classroom to establish proximity only when you need to (for example, to address a behavioral situation), it will heighten attention to your actions, making it almost impossible to interact with the subtlety and finesse you sometimes need.

## Full Access Required

Once you break the plane, you must have full access to the entire room. You must be able to simply and naturally stand next to any student in your room at any time, without interrupting your teaching, listening, or observing. When you do this, you can create a climate of loving accountability.

Loving accountability means, for example, that when students are writing short responses they can predict that at some point you will glance encouragingly over their shoulder—but also that you will see whether they are doing their best work. Loving accountability means students not taking out their smartphones, in part because you have asked but in part because there is a plausible chance they'd look up from a secretive glance at their messages to find you standing there.

If moving between any two points requires the shuffling and dragging aside of backpacks or the moving of multiple chairs, you have already ceded ownership of the room. If you have to say "excuse me" to get around chairs and backpacks and desks to reach the back corner, you are asking for student permission—or interrupting their work—to stand in that space. This means there will be places safely insulated from loving accountability.

Ensure your full access in the room by keeping passageways wide and clear. Find a place for backpacks that does not impede your movement, for example, and consider seating your students in pairs rather than long arcs or rows so that you can stand directly next to anyone at any time.

## Engage When You *Circulate*

It's good to be proximate and present everywhere in the room, but it's better if you work the room a bit. If you're actively teaching, make frequent verbal and nonverbal interventions (a smile; a hand subtly on a shoulder; "Check your spelling" to a student as you gaze at her notes). If students are completing independent work, glance thoughtfully at what they're doing.

In those cases it can be useful to try to mix and match these types of interactions as you *Circulate*:

*Simple walk-by.* You walk by a student's desk slowly enough to show that you are monitoring what she's doing but without engaging more extensively.

*Tap/nonverbal.* You have a brief, unspoken interaction, perhaps just adjusting a student's paper by a fraction of an inch to show you are observing his work, say, or perhaps using a quick nonverbal—a thumbs-up for good progress, a traveling gesture for "C'mon, keep going."

*Basic read/review.* You stop and make a point of reading or reviewing what a student is working on while it is on their desk. You might comment on what a student has written, but you don't necessarily have to. Reading a student's work, alone, is a powerful message.

*Pick-up read.* You stop and pick up a student's paper and read what she is working on, intimating an even greater level of interest in or scrutiny of her work. They will be watching you now so your facial expression is critical. Generally, I think, benign interest is best. *I am reading this because I care about your ideas.* Manage your tell (see technique 12, *Culture of Error*) and don't give too much away until you decide to give feedback. If you can't think of anything to say, try: "Keep going."

These last two options are especially important. Reading, assessing, and responding to student work in "real time" are indispensable to checking for understanding, showing your interest in students' work, and setting a tone of accountability—all functions that are critical to your ability to provide academic support and rigor ("Try that one again, Charles"; "Just right, Jamel"; "You haven't shown me the third step").

# Dot Round

Recently, a colleague from the Netherlands, Carla van Doornen, shared an idea for giving feedback while circulating that I thought was fascinating: a "dot round."

The idea is simple: you assign students independent work, and as they are working, you *Circulate* to observe. If their work contains an error, you put a dot on their paper. It is very subtle, and it's not a permanent "wrong" mark—just a reminder that there's something that needs checking. The best part is that that's *all* you do. No verbal commentary. No directions to "check again." The idea is that the dot reminds students, subtly, to find their own mistake and, in time, encourages self-reflection and self-correction. You could then even ask students to discuss—Who got a dot and found their mistakes?

Later Rue Ratray, then of Edward Brooke Charter School in East Boston, took the idea of Dot Round and moved it a step further. Instead of using one general dot to indicate a wrong answer, Rue used three colors—green, yellow, and red—to indicate different degrees of accuracy. After *Circulating* for ten minutes or so and marking thesis statements, he would then ask several "green" students to read their work followed by several "yellow" students. This allowed students to discern subtle differences between work that was complete and work that was "almost there." For the students receiving red dots especially (who now knew they weren't on the right track), it was helpful for them to hear models of successful answers. This adaptation "made a huge difference in their writing right away," Rue reported, perhaps because it draws on Dylan Wiliam's observation about the benefits of models compared to rubrics and other abstract descriptors (see technique 21, *Take the Steps*) and the "Law of Comparative Judgment" to more accurately and quickly differentiate key aspects of work quality.[28]

## Move Systematically

As you move around the room, your goal is to be systematic—to cover all parts of the room and be aware of what's happening everywhere, and to show that your movements and any interactions when you *Circulate* are universal. You are likely to engage anyone at any time by checking his work, nodding at him, or sharing a smile.

In the video *Denarius Frazier: Remainder*, which figures prominently in Chapter 3, you may recall how systematically Denarius moved around the room to give every student feedback and even designed his room so that his typical route of observation revealed more data.

Recently my team and I noticed how some top teachers tended to "walk the circuit" when approaching students they needed to correct. Let's say in this case it's Alphonse, who's off task and distracting the student next to him. If you march too directly toward Alphonse, you intimate that you are anxious and tense. This is counterproductive in the long term. Moving too directly can also cause other students to watch your interaction with Alphonse. Taking a bit of a circuitous route to Alphonse can make your interaction more private and just might buy you a few seconds to choose your words carefully before you arrive.

Systematic is not the same as predictable, though. It's often beneficial to avoid using the same pattern every time (left to right; clockwise around the room). Vary your pattern, skip interacting with some students, and invest heavily in time spent with others unpredictably as you *Circulate*.

## Position for Perception

As you *Circulate,* your goal should be to remain facing as much of the class as possible. That way, you can see what's going on around you at a glance and with minimal transaction cost. You can lift your eyes quickly from a student's paper and then return to reading in a fraction of a second. Turning your back, by contrast, creates a blind spot and may even invite opportunistic behavior.

A bit like the Earth itself, it helps to turn on two axes at the same time: revolving (moving around the room) and rotating (turning to face the "center of gravity").

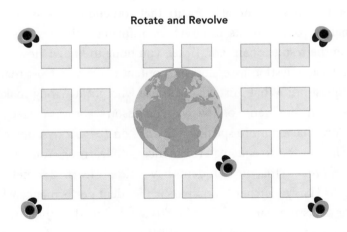

**Rotate and Revolve**

This may require you to consider what side of students you stand on as you *Circulate,* or to reorient yourself as you take a student's paper off his desk and read. Second, a bit of mystery can help. It's often beneficial to stand where you can see students but they cannot see exactly what you are doing, standing just over a student's shoulder as you peruse his work, for example, or standing at the back of the classroom as a class discusses a topic.

In addition to Denarius Frazier's exemplary circulation in *Denarius Frazier: Remainder*, several of the Keystone videos in the book are excellent examples of circulation at its best. I particularly recommend watching *Christine Torres: Keystone*; *Gabby Woolf: Keystone*; *Narlene Pacheco: Keystone*; and *Nicole Warren: Keystone*. Notice how they move easily around the class as they teach naturally. Even when classroom space is tight you'll notice teachers moving around to teach from most areas of the room, going front to back, and interacting with students as they do so.

## TECHNIQUE 26: EXIT TICKET

As the bell rings at the end of class and students gather their things, we often have an intuitive sense of how our lesson went, but without objective data, it can be hard to know for sure how student understanding has changed as the result of the hour spent together. In order for our students to make maximum progress, we need better information. In order to get a reliable snapshot of student thinking, I recommend ending your lesson with a short sequence of questions that reveals the extent to which students have mastered the central content of the day (as well as, perhaps even more important, who is still struggling and with what). When you collect this from students before they leave, and review the data, it's called an *Exit Ticket*. Use of *Exit Tickets* can establish a productive habit of student review (and retrieval practice) at the end of a lesson and also ensure that you end each session with information you can use to analyze your students' progress and inform coming lessons.

After reviewing the results of an *Exit Ticket,* you hope to know: How many of your students answered a basic question assessing the content correctly? How many could answer a more nuanced question? What mistake did those who got it wrong make? You can even reflect on whether your "gut" sense of how well the lesson went was correct, and why.

One caveat before sharing more specific guidance on *Exit Tickets*: one of the most common pitfalls of *Exit Tickets* is to equate performance with learning. You'll recall from the discussion of *Retrieval Practice* that once students have initially learned something, they quickly begin to forget it. As Harry Fletcher Wood puts it, "Student performance while being taught is a poor indicator of lasting learning." *Exit Tickets* are designed to give you more immediate data on misconceptions students may be struggling with *as they are in the process of learning*, not to measure how well students have committed previously learned knowledge or skills to long-term memory. They provide you with an opportunity to intervene as close as possible to the point of misunderstanding, so students can spend their valuable time and cognitive space remembering correctly. But once you start to see mastery on *Exit Tickets* you have understanding, not learning. For that you'll need to make sure to return to concepts over time.

## Characteristics of Effective *Exit Tickets*

Here are some general characteristics of effective *Exit Tickets*:

*They're quick:* Two or three questions is a good rule of thumb. It's not a unit quiz. You want to get a good idea of how your kids did on the core part of your objective and, given how busy you are, be able to review the data in a few minutes.

*They're designed to yield data.* Think about asking each question (or part of a question) to focus on one specific part of the lesson rather than asking several questions that summarize the whole lesson. That way, if students get it wrong, you'll know which part was the problem. Also remember to vary formats—one multiple choice and one open response, say. You need to know that students can answer both ways.

*They make great* Do Nows. After you have looked at the data, let your students do the same. When students struggle, start the next day's lesson by redoing questions or studying wrong answers from the *Exit Ticket*.

*They're predictable.* An effective *Exit Ticket* doesn't introduce new concepts or skills. It should reflect the work students did in the lesson. Honestly it's fine if a question in the *Exit Ticket* repeats or restates a key question from the lesson itself.

## Variation: The Stamp

*Exit Tickets* are designed to be quick and data friendly. Occasionally, though, you may wish to substitute another form of daily assessment in their stead. These are called *stamps*. The name was coined by Paul Bambrick-Santoyo, who uses it to refer to a student-initiated summary of key learning points. Sometimes a teacher will ask a student to "stamp the learning" during class . . . that is to recap the important points of a discussion, say. But a stamp can also be a written activity—an open-ended *Exit Ticket* if you will. A stamp is slightly longer than *Exit Tickets* and almost always open-ended. It asks a student to summarize their takeaways. In building our Reading Reconsidered Curriculum we found we used an *Exit Ticket* on the great majority of days, but occasionally we would use a stamp instead. They took twice as long but they asked students to complete a broader, more comprehensive reflection. The data isn't quite as crisp and there's more to grade. But it gives you the opportunity to assess more advanced and rigorous thinking.

For comparison, here are three examples of *Exit Tickets* we wrote in our curriculum units and one typical "stamp."

**Example 1: *Romeo and Juliet***

## Exit Ticket

1. Which of the following lines hint at the dark and **tragic** mood underlying Act 1, scene 4? Circle all that apply:

    a. "I have a soul of lead / So stakes me to the ground . . ."

    b. "I am too sore enpierced with his shaft . . ."

    c. "Borrow Cupid's wings / And soar with them above a common bound."

    d. "My mind misgives / Some consequence yet hanging in the stars."

2. Select one of the circled lines, and in 2–3 sentences, explain how it develops a **tragic** mood:

    _____

    _____

    _____

**Example 2: *The Giver***

## Exit Ticket

1. Name at least two rules that exist in the community, and list at least two things about the community that are still **ambiguous**.

| Rules | Ambiguities |
|-------|-------------|
|       |             |

2. In one carefully crafted sentence, describe the degree to which members of the community seem *apprehensive* or *obedient*. You can choose one or both words to use in your response.

    _____

    _____

    _____

**Example 3: *Roll of Thunder, Hear My Cry***

## Exit Ticket

1. Complete each of the following sentences:

   - The Logan family owns land **because** _____
   _____
   _____

   - The Logan family owns land, **but** _____
   _____
   _____

   - **Since** the Logan family owns land _____
   _____
   _____

## STAMP: *LORD OF THE FLIES*

**Stamp:** This lesson is titled: "That's how you can feel in the forest." Who says this and what does he mean by it? Explain why that might be, using one or two details from today's reading.

_____
_____
_____
_____
_____
_____
_____
_____
_____
_____

### *Exit Ticket* Advice from Teachers

Because *Exit Ticket* is one of the most commonly used and deeply trusted techniques in the book, I recently asked some teachers for their advice, and the results were pretty amazing. The insights came from the United States and the United Kingdom; they came from district school teachers, charter school teachers, and private school teachers. They came from teachers whose lessons I'd watched and admired, and teachers I'd never met. Here are a few gems.

### Review Data Efficiently

One of the key themes was reviewing the data. Teachers advised looking at the data quickly and using a standard, low-transaction-cost way of processing to make it easy to take action. Leanne Riordan of Baltimore suggests looking at the *Exit Tickets* as soon as you can, right after the lesson if possible, and sorting them into three piles—Yes, Some, and No—based on the responses. After looking for reasons that students missed a concept entirely or grasped it partially, make quick notes right on the *Exit Ticket*. You can then use these piles to differentiate small groups the next day or to create a *Do Now* for the whole class if needed.

As an added tip, keep the No pile on the top as a reminder to check in with those students more frequently the next day. Alternately, tracking the number of students who get a certain score and adding notes to sum up misconceptions can help you stay accountable for grading nightly and give you a glimpse of how the lesson went.

Hand in hand with reviewing results quickly is creating a format that makes it super easy to do. For example, Janice Smith, from Durham, North Carolina, uses sticky notes, having students write their name on the front and their answer on the back. On the way out of the classroom, students stick the notes to the door, allowing Janice to quickly flip through them between classes and easily enter data in a spreadsheet later in the day. Regardless of whether you use handouts or even just have students write their answers on something as simple as a sticky note, ensuring consistent placement (a variety of *Standardize the Format*) makes reviewing answers far more efficient.

### Have a Clear Purpose

Another common theme surrounds the purpose of *Exit Tickets*. One teacher in the United Kingdom talked about the importance of having a "clear sense of why you are using *Exit Tickets*." If *Exit Tickets* show poor understanding across the class, then reteach; if *Exit Tickets* show just a few students to be struggling, then that small group may need a separate intervention; if the class kind of gets it, but is a bit unsure, then focus on areas of uncertainty for homework or during regular ten-minute slots for a few weeks; if *Exit Tickets* reveal the class to be very secure about a certain topic, then schedule a refresher in a week or two, but don't give this topic too much time, as there will be better things to use it for. In short, responding to *Exit Tickets* is often about being entrepreneurial with time.

Alexa Miller, a fourth-grade teacher in New York, addressed that theme as well, saying that she leaves *Exit Tickets* in student mailboxes to be corrected the next morning. This works well for elementary teachers, because students can fix mistakes during breakfast while the teacher *Circulates* to assist and recheck. This extra step in the screening process for remediation helps keep groups small.

There was a great piece of planning advice from a champion teacher whose lessons I'd watched multiple times. Heather Snodgrass of Nashville advised: "[I] write the *Exit Ticket* first, before planning out any other parts of the lesson. This helps me focus in on the key points that are essential to conveying the most important content, and occasionally helps me refine the objective so I'm honing in on a manageable and appropriately rigorous skill." She added, "I also like having a consistent routine for students who frequently finish their *Exit Tickets* very quickly. One I've used for math is having students write their own problems about the skill we've learned that day. Students also like this if they get an opportunity to solve each other's problems."

## Notes

1. TLAC purists will notice the change in name of this technique from *Name the Steps* to *Take the Steps*. The core idea is breaking complex tasks up into discrete steps and teaching and practicing them. I've de-emphasized the naming part. The naming can be useful but it can also lead to an excessive focus on a resulting acronym—that is, you fall in love with your acronym and then don't retire it when students are ready.

2. Birch and Bloom coined this term in a 2007 paper "The curse of knowledge in reasoning about false beliefs." I am partial to Greg Ashman's treatment of it in *The Power of Explicit Teaching and Direct Instruction*.

3. In a study of how physicists studied complex problems, Chi, Glaser, and Feltovich found that experts see deep principles when novices see superficial features.

4. On January 30, 2021. Thank you to the lovely and insightful people who shared their thoughts. It's reassuring to know there remain corners of sanity, goodness, and community on social media.

5. I used this term in *TLAC 1.0* to refer to engaging exercises to win students' interest at the outset of a lesson or unit.

6. The addition of excess and extraneous details, notes the ghost of Hemingway, does not make an essay better.

7. *Show Call* (technique 13) is an ideal tool for this.

8. "Mysterious Houses" by Victoria Taylor-Gore.

9. There's a fair amount of research emerging about how to present material in notes so that it's most effective for students and maximizes their working memory. Diagrams are included, for example, but only carefully made with short explanatory notes and very limited extraneous information. If this topic is of interest to you, Oliver Caviglioli's *Dual Coding* is an excellent starting point.

10. Pam A. Mueller and Daniel Oppenheimer conducted three separate studies to compare longhand note takers to those who took notes on laptops ("The Pen Is Mightier Than the Keyboard: Advantages of Longhand Over Laptop Note Taking," *Psychological Science* 25, no. 6 [2014]). "In three studies," the authors wrote, "we found that students who took notes on laptops performed worse on conceptual questions than students who took notes longhand. We show that whereas taking more notes can be beneficial, laptop note takers' tendency to transcribe lectures verbatim rather than processing information and reframing it in their own words is detrimental to learning." In a 2014 discussion of Mueller and Oppenheimer's research in *Scientific American*, Cindi May notes, "Because longhand notes contain students' own words and handwriting, they may serve as more effective memory cues by recreating the context (e.g. thought processes, emotions, conclusions) as well as content (e.g. individual facts) from the original learning session." Some researchers suggest that typewritten notes offer other advantages (e.g. they may be preferable because they can be more easily edited). This may be true, but it is also true that having a laptop out during class causes students to multitask and distract themselves. Daisy Christodoulou's *Teachers vs Tech?* summarizes much of the research in this area. She cites Carter, Greenberg, and Walker's 2016 study in which students who did not bring devices to a course did better than those who did and Glass and Kang's 2018 study in which students were randomly split into two lecture groups, one with devices and one without, with the result being that students without devices did better. One possible reason might be the benefits of longhand note taking. Another might be the reduction of attentional focus caused by the presence of a screened device.

11. I took my own advice here. When my son left for college, I gave him two pieces of academic advice: (1) Never miss class, and (2) put your laptop away during class and handwrite your notes, then retype the notes afterward to review.

12. Which is important for teachers to be consistent about as they write on the board!

13. Her book should be required reading for every teacher. You can read my review of it here: https://www.educationnext.org/forgetting-how-to-read-review-reader-come-home-maryanne-wolf/.

14. Rates of reading dropped especially steeply over the years when students typically get a smartphone, from 76 percent at age 8 to 40 percent at age 14. https://files.eric.ed.gov/fulltext/ED607777.pdf.

15. Perhaps as a result the 2005 ACT revealed that "only about half of our nation's ACT-tested students are ready for college-level reading."

16. It is important to be aware that the smartphone is designed to fracture attention and addict its users and it is very successful at doing so. How far is yours from you right now? When did you last check it? Now that I have mentioned it, are you itching to have a quick peek?

17. *The Grapes of Wrath* provides a fortuitous example—it alternates between chapters written in straightforward prose and chapters written in a variety of experimental styles that merge prose and poetry. Can students read the novel independently? It depends on which chapter you assign.

18. It's also worth noting that beginning with shared reading can act as an effective transition into independent reading—it's much easier to continue reading something you've started together, rather than to jump in cold.

19. Control the Game—which you are welcome to keep using if you prefer—originally came from the game of soccer. Certain central midfielders have the job of controlling the game, not by hogging the ball themselves but by being a brief and often nearly invisible pivot point: the ball comes to them and they pass it somewhere else. They coordinate the attack and set the rhythm, determining when others get opportunities and setting them up to succeed. Such players rarely score the goals. Their job is to organize and arrange the team, to get the ball to others so they can score. This process—ball comes in briefly, they pass it on to someone new, ball comes back, and they quickly move it on again in a different direction—reminded me of what a teacher does when steering reading opportunities around the room. Truly, it was an obscure and quirky reference at best. But there were a lot of techniques to name and you can't get them all right. At least it wasn't an acronym.

20. Student Achievement Partners' report is only one of many that emphasize the critical role of fluency in comprehension at all grade levels as there is extensive research on this point. Their "Short Guide to Placing Text at the Center of Learning" can be found at their website: https://achievethecore.org/content/upload/A%20Short%20Guide%20to%20Placing%20Text%20at%20the%20Center%20of%20Learning.pdf#:~:text=Rationale%3A%20Research%20shows%20dysfluency%20causes,tests%20versus%20those%20who%20fail.&text=Students%20who%20were%20previously%20

fluent%20can%20become%20dysfluent%20when%20text%20complexity%20increases.

21. This is a deliberate allusion to Mark Seidenberg's outstanding book *Language at the Speed of Sight*. It should be required reading in every graduate and undergraduate education program.

22. https://shanahanonliteracy.com/blog/wake-up-reading-wars-combatants-fluency-instruction-is-part-of-the-science-of-reading.

23. Maryanne Wolf's book *Reader, Come Home* is an outstanding study of the ways constant exposure to technology is changing the portions of the brain that we use when we read. These portions of the brain are neuroplastic—they change in response to what they are asked to do. I strongly recommend the book. I also wrote a book review of it that makes the broader case that I don't have time for here as to why Wolf's book is so deeply important. https://www.educationnext.org/forgetting-how-to-read-review-reader-come-home-maryanne-wolf/.

24. And, sadly, even within the walls of many schools.

25. Especially for independent reading.

26. In some cases the challenges of student oral reading have come to dominate the conversation, to the point that teachers are routinely advised to "never ask students to read aloud." It's often dismissively referred to by the pejorative phrase "popcorn reading," but creating a simplistic straw man is not grounds for dismissing a crucial classroom practice. There are surely challenges to student oral reading, but they are also easily managed and overcome by a capable classroom teacher.

27. See Oliver Caviglioli, *Dual Coding*.

28. I discuss the Law of Comparative Judgments in technique 13, *Show Call*. As I noted there, it was derived in the 1920s by psychologist Louis Thurstone and demonstrates that people make better judgments about quality and learn more from analysis when asked to compare two examples of something than they do when trying to judge the quality of one example of something.

# Chapter 6

# Pacing

I recently observed Sadie McCleary's Chemistry lesson at West Guilford High School in Greensboro, North Carolina. (You can see footage of Sadie's lesson in the video *Sadie McCleary: Keystone*.) Her topic was particle motion, pressure, and the compound gas law and the lesson was bursting with focused, productive energy. Five, ten, fifteen, twenty minutes raced by as Sadie engaged the whole room in rigorous, thoughtful work that in another classroom might have felt like a slog.

As a timer went off signifying the end of the *Do Now*, students finished writing and Sadie began a quick review, via *Cold Call*, reminding students that they should know relationships between volume, pressure, and temperature by heart. Students who were called on were ready right on cue and those not called on checked and corrected their answers. Her language was clear and precise: "You should have gotten 120 liters. Give me a thumbs-up if you've got that. Great."

She transitioned seamlessly into a *Turn and Talk*, asking students to explain what happened to the pressure of a gas as temperature increased in a fixed container. After ending the *Turn and Talk* warmly and crisply ("Pause where you are") she *Cold Called* Sterling, whose response was clear, concise, and accurate. "Beautiful," said Sadie. "That was excellently said."

Next, she gave students a new problem to consider: How would temperature and volume change when pressure increased in an elastic container? "Tell your partner. Go!" she said.

Students immediately began discussing in pairs, and Sadie listened in on a conversation at the front table.

As the energy of discussion showed its first signs of ebbing, she paused the class and *Cold Called* one student then another to explain the answer. After a succinct and well-stated response (complete with "shine" for both students from their peers), Sadie moved on to a new question. Students shared once again with their partners.

Students then quickly took out their notebooks for notes on a new topic: the Combined Gas Law.

The rest of the lesson was of a piece. Students constantly engaged in rigorous thinking in a variety of formats: taking notes, chatting with a partner, answering questions from Sadie as she checked for understanding. The activities changed with some frequency but tasks were always clear, and always clearly distinguishable from the task before. There was energy and momentum: change and novelty in how students engaged, but consistent focus on the lesson topic.

The psychologist Mihaly Csikszentmihalyi coined the term "flow" to refer to a mental state in which a person performing an activity is so immersed in it that they begin to lose their sense of time. We've all had that happen: You look up and suddenly class (or practice or rehearsal) is almost over. You'd thought it had just begun! Flow states happen most often when people are highly absorbed in a task that involves a significant degree of ongoing mental stimulation. Discussions of the theory of flow often note the happiness it brings participants. To lose yourself in the work of some task is not just productive, it's gratifying.

This offers a reminder that people mostly want to be positively and productively engaged, and that students are often frustrated when they enter a classroom and realize it will not be that way. Csikszentmihalyi's chosen name for this state, flow, underscores that it is connected somehow to a perception of motion, of steady forward momentum, and this is something you could feel keenly that day in Sadie's classroom.

Teachers frequently use the term *pacing* to describe the aspects of Sadie's lesson that gave it forward motion, but the underlying idea is difficult to pin down. It has something to do with momentum, but pacing can't just be a synonym for how fast you go through content. While Sadie moved quickly from one question to the next, the class never felt rushed; in fact, while it seemed like things were always changing, Sadie stayed focused on just one or two topics.

There's something ironic there. The work of teaching and learning can feel fast when you're moving slowly—and it can feel slow when you're moving fast. Sometimes you're working on problem after problem, for example, determining the slope of a line or deep-reading just a few paragraphs of *To Kill a Mockingbird*, but there's energy crackling in the air.

Sometimes you're discussing three chapters on the American Revolution, but the minutes tick slowly away, and students stare blankly. We sometimes assume that a plodding lesson results from our overall choice of methodology: "You shouldn't lead the review; you should let them review!" But the desperate slowing of the classroom clock can just as likely happen in a less traditional setting. Who hasn't found themselves fanning barely smoldering interest during a "student-led discussion" they had assumed would excite students?

So pacing is different from the speed at which you cover content and it's not necessarily about methodology. It's more like your students' perception of progress as you teach, that is, *the illusion of speed*. A teacher with strong pacing creates a perception of rapid progress when they *want* students to feel as though they are "moving." And they balance that with times when they'd prefer a pace that feels slower and more reflective.

The architecture of the human brain is full of paradoxes, many of them created by tens of thousands of years of evolutionary refinement for an environment not quite like the one we currently live in. We know that attention and staying on task yield long-term learning, for example. "The big rewards," cognitively speaking, accrue from "sustained, focused effort," notes McGill University cognitive psychologist Daniel J. Levitin. And yet our brains are also wired for "novelty bias," and are "easily hijacked by something new."[1] "Humans will work just as hard to obtain a novel experience as we will to get a meal or a mate,"[2] Levitin writes. Gratifying the "novelty-seeking portion of the brain" induces a "feeling of pleasure."[3] We are drawn to distraction because it was often critical to survival, Maryanne Wolf points out in *Reader, Come Home*. In the long arc of pre-history, attending to a new stimulus right away meant you were ready when something burst out of the thicket, teeth bared. We evolved accordingly. Novelty bias is the term for the special attention we give to what is new.

And novelty bias, many readers will know, is the design principle behind the smartphone's hold over all of us, but Sadie's teaching harnesses it in a beneficial and balanced way. Her students are always focused on the content, but her ability to achieve the right rate of novelty at the same time draws students in and engages them. She creates strategic novelty; new and ever-changing ways of engaging that keep the focus on the same material all the way through the lesson. When you peer behind the curtain, the first ten minutes are just a series of pressure, temperature, and volume problems, but shifting the format of the way students interact with the problems at just the right rate—from *Turn and Talk* to *Cold Call* to (later) note-taking—maximizes engagement and attention. Perhaps the optimal balance of these things is the source of "flow."

The keys to pacing, then, often lie in mastering both students' perception of time and the tension between attention and novelty. Sadie's switches between activities (from writing to *Turn and Talk*, say) were invariably crisp, so students never lost focus. A long and highly narrated transition might disrupt the ideas they were holding in working memory, but careful attention to the transitions ensures that important ideas are sustained in working memory even when activities change. Clear, bright lines between activities contribute in other ways, too. Because the end of one activity and the beginning of the next are so distinct, it makes novelty, the introduction of a new activity, easier to see. And what's more, students can sense their own progress as they move from one task to another. This, too, is motivating. Here's an analogy: driving your car at 60 miles per hour on the interstate does not feel fast. Your experience is one of continued sameness—a smudge of trees or houses in the distance and the consistency of an unbroken stretch of guardrail. But drive at that rate on a narrow road or in a settled neighborhood and you suddenly feel like you are racing along. The smudge of houses in the distance becomes, in fact, one house and then another and then another. When you distinguish them each whipping past, they become like mileposts that indicate to you that something has come and gone. They create an illusion that multiplies your perception of your own progress. A teacher like Sadie often does something similar: the more she creates mileposts, the more her students realize a new task has come and gone, and she uses this to enhance the influence of novelty bias.

In this chapter, I'll discuss ways to capture and manage the kind of momentum you can see in Sadie's class. Because you sometimes need to stick with an activity for a longer period of time, I'll also describe some tools to frame activities (slow or fast) so that you can be more effective at helping students get lost in rigorous work (and lose track of the passage of time), regardless of how long you actually spend on an activity.

The tools of pacing can be broken into two groups. The first involves varying the *types* of activities your students engage in during a lesson, the goal being to cause dynamic changes in student thinking and participation by engaging them in different ways. The second set of skills involves managing activities and the *transitions* between them to ensure clear, decisive, and noticeable shifts—the illusion of speed. Many of these tools deal in perception—managing the illusion of speed, maximizing mileposts by making beginnings and endings visible so that students are more aware of the changes around them.

A final note: Generally, speed is exciting and change is interesting, but as with most good things it's best in moderation and balance, so it's useful also to think of the limits of speed. My colleague Chi Tschang once mentioned that too much passivity wasn't the only way students could get distracted. "If there are two (or three) highly active kinesthetic activities in a row, the class's energy level can shoot off the charts, and kids can lose focus." Too much speed can be as problematic as not enough. The goal is balance. And the good news is that the tools of pacing can often make what you choose to do feel dynamic and engaging, even when at its core, it's reflective, deliberate, methodical, and even slow.

# TECHNIQUE 27: CHANGE THE PACE

One of the keys to Sadie's success is her decision-making about switching activities. Students keep thinking about the same idea, but they engage it in different ways. I call this idea **Change the Pace**. It helps to achieve the proper balance of "fast" and "slow," flow and focus, momentum and attention.

## Changing Activity Types

At the risk of oversimplifying a complex topic, Let me suggest six types of activities we can ask students to participate in. Each requires students to think and engage in a different way. They are:

1. Assimilating knowledge directly from sources, such as direct teacher instruction or reading a text

2. Participating in guided practice

3. Executing skills without teacher support, as in independent practice

4. Discussing ideas with classmates

5. Reflecting independently on an idea—thinking quietly and deeply, often in writing

6. Reviewing previously mastered material to encode it in long-term memory (i.e. *Retrieval Practice*)

All six activity types are important, and students should engage in all of them frequently so they get a well-rounded mental workout.

A couple of caveats in thinking about these activity types:

All six types of activity are important for students to engage in regularly, but choosing among them requires consideration of more than just what feels right in a given moment. How and when you use one type of activity affects how well others will work. Knowledge assimilation, for example is probably the most important activity type, if not in its own right then because of its importance in making the others function well. The cognitive science on this is clear: the other activities, which we often think of, sometimes accurately, sometimes not, as more analytical and "higher order," are more productive when students have strong background knowledge to support them. Pause now, for example, and reflect for two and a half minutes on the decisions of Napoleon and Lee to attack at Waterloo and Gettysburg respectively. Were they wise? Did the decisions reflect the dominance of personality over tactics?

That's a higher-order thinking activity if you know a lot about the requisite topics, but if you don't know enough about military history, there's not much higher order in your thinking. In fact, there's not much thinking. Let me quote Daniel Willingham again here: "Thinking well requires knowing facts, and that's true not simply because you need something to think about. The very processes that teachers care about most—critical thinking processes such as reasoning and problem-solving—are intimately intertwined with factual knowledge that is in long-term memory (not just found in the environment)."

And here's the National Research Council on the topic: "Over a century of research on transfer has yielded little evidence that teaching can develop general cognitive competencies that are transferable to any new discipline, problem or context."[4] Cognition is not a transferable skill and is always context specific and knowledge dependent. Guided practice, discussion, and reflection are all ways to help students think deeply and in higher-order ways, but only if they are preceded by a strong investment in knowledge, directly taught.

In his research Barak Rosenshine provides an excellent description of this. "In a study of mathematics instruction, . . . less effective teachers gave much shorter presentations and explanations and then . . . told students to solve problems. The less successful teachers were then observed going from student to student and having to explain the material again."[5]

Second, as I will discuss in a moment, switching among activity types is often necessary to effective instruction. Your lesson would probably be less successful if you chose one activity type for the *whole lesson* and more successful if you used two or three and asked yourself, for example: when is discussion ideal and for how long and what different activity after it will create the greatest synergy? You can sense that in Sadie's class—her lesson seamlessly incorporates Direct Instruction (via students' note-taking), discussion with *Turn and Talk* partners, and guided practice.

There's no formula, of course. You won't use the same approach every time. Each lesson will require something different; each teacher's style and approach will shape the progression. The goal is to create a feeling of flow, but in fact there are *feelings* of flow—some faster, some slower, some louder, some quieter.

With that in mind, here's a bit more about those six activity types.

Activity 1: Direct Instruction/Knowledge Assimilation
When students are presented with new information while they listen, read, or take notes, they are engaged in Direct Instruction/Knowledge Assimilation (KA). This could involve a class reading a text (silently or aloud, by teacher or students) or a teacher lecturing, modeling a problem, or sharing a presentation (with or without occasional questioning of students).

The idea of Direct Instruction might at first feel antithetical to pacing, but that is only if you imagine it in caricature—like the teacher in *Ferris Bueller's Day Off* droning on to a room of half-asleep students. When Direct Instruction is implemented well, it not only has important effects on student understanding, but can be energetic and contribute positively to pacing. And the key to implementing it well? As Barak Rosenshine points out, Direct Instruction, like all methods, must respond to the limitations on working memory. "Presenting too much material at once may confuse students because their working memory may be unable to process it. . . . More effective teachers do not overwhelm their students by presenting too much material at once. Rather these teachers present only small amounts of new material at any time, and then assist the students as they practice this material."[6]

This may sound at first like it contradicts Rosenshine's observation about the importance of investing heavily in background knowledge first, before engaging students in more interactive forms of processing, but that's not the case. You could imagine how Sadie McCleary might accomplish both. She might spend a few minutes explaining a new concept with students taking notes. Then they might pause: "Discuss how this might apply to X with your partner. Go." Then perhaps a bit of *Cold Call* to make sure students understood. Then she might spend a few minutes explaining a bit more about the concept. Then a different activity to engage and give working memory time to process. "Take a minute to summarize what we've done so far in writing. Go." Then she might ask a few students who've written insightful things to share. They might then discuss briefly. Then to the board again. Slides on. Taking notes as she explains a bit more about the concept. Switching from explicit teaching or other forms of knowledge assimilation to short reflective activities and back is the key to both engaging the strengths of working memory and overcoming its limitations. Doing that requires strong pacing skills in terms of activity design and in terms of your ability to make shifts efficient and energizing and your instructional choices strike the balance between novelty and focus.

The first portion of Christine Torres's lesson where she is introducing new vocabulary words is a perfect example of this, especially because teaching new vocabulary words is, for many teachers, such a notoriously low-energy activity: "Here are our new words, please copy down the definitions." Many teachers respond to this challenge by making the activity independent: "Go look up these words." This can result in poorer understanding of the words and can take more time. But look at Christine's approach (you can watch this segment of her lesson a little over two minutes into the video in *Christine Torres: Keystone*). Her steps are:

Identify the word and ask students to repeat it.

Provide a definition.

Ask students to read a situation involving the word (in this case "caustic." (What might a judge in *American Idol* have said if they made a caustic remark?)

Ask students to *Turn and Talk* about the example.

Briefly *Cold Call* to hear a few answers.

Show a picture: "How does this image demonstrate the word 'caustic'?" *Turn and Talk* again.

*Cold Call* to hear answers.

The knowledge is disseminated via Direct Instruction and is followed by a different activity type (usually discussion in pairs) but the cycles are very short so the energy is impressively high and Christine's students learn new knowledge in a joyful flow-like setting.

### Activity 2: Guided Practice/Guided Questioning

When students engage in activities that involve more extensive back-and-forth with the teacher, practicing the use or application of knowledge, they are engaged in guided practice/ guided questioning. Rosenshine emphasizes the importance of this stage for working examples and releasing autonomy gradually to students. Guided practice might involve executing the steps in solving a problem, with the teacher asking questions to remind students what step to take next, or it might involve explication of a text passage with the teacher consistently providing new and more targeted questions to unlock understanding. It is usually used before students have independent mastery. Some examples:

After asking her students what would happen to the pressure in a fixed container if temperature increased, Sadie asks, "OK, why would the pressure increase?"

A student says: "Because there are more collisions."

"But why are there more collisions?" Sadie asks.

"Because the particles are moving faster."

"OK, what if the container was flexible? Then what?"

A class solves a problem involving systems of equations together, with the teacher asking various students to explain the steps, identify the next step or solve the calculations required in a given step.

During a close reading burst, a teacher asks his students to annotate each reference to the sun in the opening pages of *Grapes of Wrath*. Through a series of questions (some written, some oral), the class unpacks the way Steinbeck reveals the devastating impact of the sun on the land and its people.

To maximize the benefits of novelty bias with guided practice, a teacher would typically unbundle questions, that is, break questions down into smaller pieces so that she could ask them more quickly of a greater number of students, thus maximizing the perception of mile-posts. *Cold Calling* participants for each step might also create more of a sense of momentum and flow. On the other hand, a risk of moving more rapidly is that some students could struggle to keep up with or process what they'd seen, so capping a bit of guided practice off with a slower opportunity for note-taking or reflection might be beneficial, as in, "OK, take 90 seconds to make sure you've got each step down in your notes and then make a note to yourself about your takeaways for solving this kind of problem." Independent practice—"OK, now try one on your own; you have three minutes and then we'll check in"—is also a good way to let students absorb what they've learned during guided practice.

Activity 3: Independent Practice

When students complete work that they know how to do on their own, they are engaged in independent practice (IP). IP is usually done without significant support from the teacher; it's often done silently. But just because work is silent and independent does not make it IP. For example, silent reading is often knowledge assimilation, and reflecting on or brainstorming solutions to questions students don't know how to solve is reflection and idea generation, the next topic in this section. By way of distinguishing, IP implies autonomous execution of a skill or application of a knowledge base that students are in the final stages of mastering. Some examples:

- Students apply what they've learned about "showing, not telling" by writing three sentences about the experience of a character named Jonas as he rides a roller coaster (without ever saying he rode a roller coaster).
- Students independently solve a set of problems involving systems of equations.
- Students write a summary of the important ways daily life in eighteenth-century America was different from today.

Independent practice is often assigned in large chunks and at the end of the lesson in the "you have till the end of class to get started on this" variety. That's not wrong, but it can also be allocated in smaller pieces, mid-lesson. Imagine Christine Torres adding a bit of it at the end of her vocabulary lesson: "Take three minutes to write a series of sentences, each one using one of these three new vocabulary words correctly." Or Sadie McCleary in the middle of notes: "Tonight you'll have a set of problems to do for homework, but see if you can set this problem up on your own now. You don't have to solve it, just set it up correctly. One minute. Go."

Shifting into IP is also a great way to slow things down while you are maintaining flow. That is, the tension between attention and novelty is captured in the idea of shifting (change) into independent practice (highly focused).

## Activity 4: Reflection and Idea Generation

Reflection often looks like IP, but it serves a different purpose. In IP, students execute work they know how to do on their own. In reflection, students are given time to think in a more open-ended fashion about things they are in the midst of learning or do not yet understand. Reflection is often silent, and frequently involves writing. When the task involves brainstorming potential solutions, it is idea generation. Some examples:

- A teacher asks students to reflect in writing on how differences in daily life in the eighteenth century might have caused people to understand the role of family differently from how we do today.

- A teacher asks students to reflect on an author's stylistic choices and why she might have used a repeated image.

- A teacher asks students to make notes to themselves on the keys to solving a difficult type of problem after solving a few as a group.

Reflection activities are independent, so they function much like IP, but they tend to feel a bit slower as they are open-ended and more formative. Thus they can bring a sense of slowness back to a lesson even in small pieces. They are also important to include because students who, outside of school, are constantly stimulated by their smartphones, increasingly spend less and less time reflecting and letting their minds wander. There may be some value in causing that to happen in school.

## Activity 5: Discussion

Activities in which students develop ideas and answers by talking directly to one another, in small groups or as a class are called Discussion. This might involve a *Turn and Talk* (as we saw in Sadie's class) or using *Habits of Discussion* (see technique 44), which are to make a larger discussion productive and efficient. In some cases, you might insert batches of discussion during guided practice or questioning to ensure that students *Batch Process* (technique 45)—that is, make a certain number of comments without mediation from you. We call this "playing volleyball, not tennis." Some examples:

- A teacher asks students to share their opinions about the ethics of genetically modifying food and organisms. She takes three or four student comments in a row and then returns to her presentation on the topic.

- A teacher asks students to participate in a ten-minute whole-class discussion of the impact of corruption on American politics in the 1890s.

- A teacher asks students to *Turn and Talk* (technique 43) with a partner to identify where a peer made a mistake in adding two fractions with unlike denominators.

While whole-class discussions are great, they tend to have a higher transaction cost—it takes time to set them up and to give multiple people a chance to talk. Balancing larger discussions with pair discussions can allow you to include it more frequently and in shorter intervals, especially because a *Turn and Talk* can so easily be made into a routine that students begin quickly and easily, thus preserving ideas in working memory. You can see both Sadie and Christine doing this throughout their lessons.

### Activity 6: Review/Retrieval Practice

Retrieval Practice is reviewing previously mastered content to ensure its encoding in long-term memory and to facilitate its easy retrieval. Including review is not only beneficial from a learning perspective. John Sweller reminds teachers that "the major function of instruction is to allow learners to accumulate critical information in long-term memory." Sadie is doing this at the beginning of her lesson, as students solve problems they learned how to do earlier in the week.

Because it is so important to learning and so easily overlooked—and sometimes dismissed by educators who haven't read the research—*Retrieval Practice* is its own technique. But since the discussion here is about shifting among and between activities to create a dynamic flow in your lesson, it's worth noting here how helpful inserting short batches of retrieval practice in the midst of other activities can be from a pacing perspective. It's often fast and energetic; it can be done in short doses; it often makes students feel successful.

Let's take a closer look at how the different activity types can come together in a lesson—in this case, one taught by Jessica Bracey, of North Star Academy Vailsburg Middle School (see the video *Jessica Bracey: Keystone*). Consider the activities Jessica shifts between: As class begins, Jessica asks her students to summarize what happened in the previous chapter of the novel they are reading. As her students comment, she steps in to ask for clarification or steer the next question to a given student: "Yes, Angel's bracelet was stolen. What else is going on?" This is guided questioning. Jessica's students spend about two minutes engaging in it and she "unbundles" her questions, spreading the work of summarizing across multiple students. Then she shifts into *FASE Reading*, continuing the story from the prior day, before asking students to pause and respond to a question in their reading response journals. After students write independently, she leads a whole-class discussion in which students respond to one another's thinking.

We often try to keep class interesting by doing "new" things with students, but what makes Jessica's class interesting is doing *familiar* activities. By shifting between activities that students know how to do well, Jessica creates a feeling of flow. Students are constantly engaged but often in new ways. They shift from reading to writing in their reading response journals in a matter of seconds, because they've done it so many times. Stopping to explain a new activity they hadn't done before—for example, "We're going to do a new kind of writing today; let me explain how it works . . ."—would result in a lot of downtime while she explained all the details and while her students internalized the process, using valuable working memory capacity to follow a new set of directions. Even though it might seem as though a new activity would be more interesting, it would be as likely to have the opposite effect. (You can read more about the power of academic systems and routines in Chapter Ten.)

After a minute or two of discussion, Jessica's students go back to reading. In fact, Jessica repeats the same cycle again: students read, write in their reflection journals, and discuss throughout the class, with the cycles getting longer and the questions getting harder over time.

At a recent workshop, teachers shared that the shorter recurring cycle of read-write-discuss was different from what they tended to do in their classes. They did the same three activities, but in long, "nonrecurring" chunks. For example, in a typical class, they might read for fifteen to twenty minutes, write for five to ten minutes, and discuss for another ten to fifteen minutes, before tackling an *Exit Ticket* and wrapping up. As Jessica demonstrates, you can bring energy and engagement to your class merely by breaking those chunks into shorter cycles of the same activities.

## TECHNIQUE 28: BRIGHTEN THE LINES

Nicole Warren's pacing in the video *Nicole Warren: Keystone* is masterful. Class starts with incredible energy that draws students in and makes them active and engaged: a song; a *Turn and Talk*; a discussion of student reflections from the *Turn and Talk*; and a longer stretch of focused independent work, with students locked-in and focused partly because of the energy of the preceding activities. Part of what makes Nicole's lesson work is her careful design of the flow from activity to activity, in other words, but also watch her release her students into the *Turn and Talk* just under a minute into the video or the independent practice just shy of four minutes in. There's a clear and engaging task. Then a tiny delay for suspense. Then, suddenly, a crisp and quick signal to start, with students leaping into action. Part of what makes the pacing so powerful is the quality of the transitions that begin each activity.

When you take steps to make the beginnings and endings of activities visible and crisp, you *Brighten the Lines*. By calling attention to changes in activities, you ensure that your students can perceive mileposts clearly, and make it easier for them to notice and be attracted to new activity. You're essentially harnessing their novelty bias in a productive way.

## Step 1: The Go Start

The first way to *Brighten Lines* is with a *go start*—shifting from one activity to another on a cue. Starting everyone at the same time with a statement such as, "Okay, scholars. You have three minutes to write a response to this question. Ready? Go!" has several advantages.

First, making the beginning of an activity "pop" makes the activity itself feel a bit like a special event. By using the phrase "go," you build excitement and anticipation—much like a footrace—causing students to start together, as a team. Not only does this implicitly frame the forthcoming activity positively, but it also causes everyone in the class to start exactly on cue. That half-second delay causes students to work more industriously once they are "allowed" to. Plus, students see all of their peers snap to it—normalizing the idea of making productive use of time.

The cue doesn't have to be "go," of course. There are dozens of options you could use (e.g. "off you go"; "give it a go"; "begin," etc.), but as Peps Mccrea explains in *Motivated Teaching*, the cue is an essential part of the routine. He describes the ideal cue as "distinct," meaning it won't be misinterpreted, "multimodal," combining language or speech with action or position, and "punchy." With cues that fit these criteria, Mccrea argues, we make the norms more visible and thus more widespread across the class. If it's unclear whether everyone else has actually started something, there's a potential incentive to take your time so as to avoid being the outlier (the first to start). If everyone begins on cue, there are no grounds for strategically managing the optimum starting point. Everyone else just started. Better catch up!

Previously, I mentioned that you can use pacing tools to make "slower" work more reflective and engaging; some simple adaptations to the *go start* can help. You might, for example, encourage deeper, more reflective thinking by prompting students with a slower, quieter cadence, "Ah, a fascinating question: Just who *is* the hero of this book? You have three minutes to reflect in writing. [Pause] Who is the hero, and how do you know?" Now perhaps you've dropped your voice to a whisper and you say in a slower cadence: "*Begin. . . .*" This approach still socializes efficient use of time by getting students started right away and as a group, but your slower and quieter delivery of the start cue can communicate something about the tone of reflection you expect. Even using the cue "Begin" as compared to the cue

"Go!" suggests less a race and more of a journey. This way, you get the benefits of everyone starting on cue and making good use of time, but also clear and efficient communication of the idea, "I want you to think deeply here; I am looking for thoughtfulness as much as productivity."

In Christine Torres's class, we see her cue a *go start* in several different ways. During the vocabulary rollout section of her lesson, her cues to *Turn and Talk* are high energy and crisp—"Fifteen seconds with your teammate, go!" Students jump into conversation without a moment to lose. Her goal in this section of the lesson is high engagement and participation ratio; she wants to boost the energy of the room and make this section of the lesson feel fast. For a slightly more challenging question, she gives a little more time and slows the pace of her delivery "How does this image demonstrate the word 'caustic'? Look carefully at the image. Thirty seconds with your teammate to discuss. How does the image demonstrate the word 'caustic'? Ready, go." Later in the lesson, as she guides students through a rigorous discussion of Annemarie's bravery, her cues are even slower and reflect the thoughtful focus she hopes students bring to a writing task: "With a teammate . . . answer questions 2A and 2B. Three minutes, if you're not done, that's OK . . . Three minutes, go." In all three instances, students have a clear cue to begin working (as well as a precise time limit, which we'll talk more about in a moment), but the subtle variations in her tone and the speed with which she gives the directions reflect the type of energy she hopes students will bring to the task.

To see the range of ways in which teachers use clear in cues to *Brighten the Lines* (while signaling the type of work they expect students to engage in), check out the video *Montage: Brighten Lines* of teachers launching their students into independent work. First: Hasan Clayton. "Four minutes, silent solo. Let's see what you remember. Eyes in," he says. His calm, steady tone and presence indicate that this is a moment for thoughtful reflection. Even the pace with which he begins to move around the classroom signals that this activity is meant to be completed with sustained, quiet focus. In contrast, Tamesha McGuire's warm, crisp directions to her kindergarten class—"Ready . . . set . . . go to work!" (complete with a bright smile)—infuse the independent work with energy and excitement. As students begin working, her cheerful narration maintains the energy of the launch. Jamila Hammett's cue to her small group of third graders is more muted—a student reads the question and she says simply, "Go ahead, take one minute." She remains silent as students' pencils begin to move to give students space to begin grappling with the challenging *Art of the Sentence* prompt. In each example, the teacher influences the pace and energy of the room through the tone and language of their in-cues; at the same time, all three cues are clear and specific enough to *Brighten the Lines* between activities and ensure that all students are prepared to begin at the same time.

## Clean Finish

Being able to end an activity reliably on cue is also a critical skill for several reasons—the most obvious being time management. How many meetings have you been in where the person running it was unable to say, "Okay, we're done with that; now we're moving on to this," as it became increasingly obvious that the meeting would run over time or that other topics would be truncated? Time use in the classroom can be done a similar disservice when a teacher can't reliably end one activity to begin the next.

There's more value in making activities end crisply and clearly—a skill I call the *clean finish*—than just time management. Ending on cue establishes a clear and discernible transition point from one activity to the next and can actually help students maintain the continuity of their thinking across tasks. Students are better able to carry what is in their working memory from one activity to the next if the transition is efficient and our language is clear. Consider the example in the previous paragraph. You've said to your students, "You have three minutes to reflect in writing: Who is the hero, and how do you know?" If you're going to transition from writing to whole-class discussion or a *Turn and Talk*, you want to minimize disruption in the shift between activities so students can remember the insights they just developed. You want the writing to end on cue, in a single moment, so that you can immediately start looking forward to your next step without anyone losing their train of thought. If your transition from writing to discussion is fast—a few seconds at most—then the ideas that students had before the transition are more likely to cross over to the second activity.

As the three allocated minutes of writing come to a close, you might provide a preliminary reminder that you'll be wrapping up soon: something like "I'll need pencils down in twenty seconds. Try to finish that last thought." When you get to the end of the allocated time, ideally there'd be a signal. The timer would go off and you'd say, "I hear the timer, and that means pencils down and eyes up, please." The icing on the cake is that crisp, visible transitions also affect pacing. The milepost is bright and clear, and students can see it passing. Better still, when the milepost is clear, you can also connect the pieces of the lesson together through use of segues, language that highlights the most important threads of the lesson that tie multiple activities together. (For more on segues, see Chapter Five, Lesson Structures.)

A final note to observe here: The same tools used to speed up pacing, lightly adapted, can slow things down as well. For example, you might say to your class, quietly and with a slow and reflective tempo: "In thirty seconds, your journal writing session will come to an end. At the beep, please close your journals and give me your eyes." Then you might let the timer beep for a few seconds or leave a silent pause of a few seconds and add, "Good. Now we're ready to discuss." It's still a clean finish with bright lines, but it establishes a slower pace and quieter tone. In fact, you could argue that *Brighten the Lines* is *most* useful for this kind of slower, more thoughtful task, where stepping in to be more directive is also more disruptive to the quiet, reflective mood of the room. Crisp transitions are often most useful at exactly the time you would least expect them to be, and where their use is least intuitive.

## TECHNIQUE 29: ALL HANDS

Raising your hand is an act that deserves some reflection, even if at first it seems straightforward.

For example, every time students raise their hands they mark the passage of an event worthy of action. They say, both to themselves and others, "There was a question there, and I want to answer it." The question is distinguished from the previous one. It has novelty. Now it is a milepost. The intent to answer also distinguishes the moment. It's a decision that the lesson is worth it: the rewards of speaking outweigh the risks, There is a shift in student's self-perception: I wasn't just sitting here passively; I was having ideas. I want to share them. The act of hand-raising can draw students further into a lesson and change them from the outside in.

Hand-raising is also contagious. When students see their peers eagerly volunteering, a norm is established that the classroom is a safe, engaging place that others want to be a part of, and the incentive to participate spreads around the room. "The norms we hold arise predominantly from our observation of others," says Peps Mccrea. And making a decision to engage with the content publicly affirms that a student thinks being a part of the group and its activity is worthwhile. It is a referendum on the worthiness of the class or the lesson.

For teachers, the sight of a host of volunteers means not having to try to drag participants into the conversation. Few things make time move more slowly, even in a staff meeting, than a question hanging in the air as we all avoid each other's eyes. The seconds lengthen as everyone shifts uncomfortably in their seats.

Much of what we think about a classroom when we observe it is in fact a reading of the semiotics of hand-raising: Are students eager to speak? Are hands sparse and reluctant? Do students speak without raising their hands at all?

*All Hands* helps you manage aspects of student hand-raising to maximize the benefits of its influence on pacing and engagement and shape students' perception of what's happening in the classroom.

### Hands Down

It may sound counterintuitive (particularly in a technique called *All Hands*), but the act of putting your hand down is also important: It says that one question has been answered and a new one is coming. It inserts a milepost and causes students to perceive separate events. An undifferentiated stretch of time in which the class was "talking about the government" becomes a question about the Executive Branch followed by a question about the Judicial Branch followed by one about the Legislative Branch. Mileposts are speeding past. Pacing is sped up.

Alternatively, we've all had the student whose hand remains permanently raised throughout a series of questions and answers, waving in the air for minutes at a time. If you call on him you are unlikely to get a response to the most recent comment or the topic currently under discussion. You're likely to get a response to a question that caused your student to raise his hand ten minutes ago. You're more likely to be calling on someone who wants to speak but not necessarily to respond or answer or connect to the ideas of others.

Lowering your hand also communicates respect for your peers because it's difficult to listen and have your hand up at the same time. A classroom where hands are up while someone is speaking is a classroom where people are saying, essentially, "What you're saying won't change what I want to say." It's very hard to listen carefully to someone else's idea when your raised hand is a cue to try to keep your own previous idea in your working memory. Putting hands down when someone else is speaking communicates respect and interest in someone else's idea. In order to ensure that students' enthusiasm to participate isn't dampened every time they lower their hands, it's helpful to share the rationale for students and have a clear cue for when hands should be raised or lowered, even something as simple as "hands down" or a nonverbal gesture to remind students to be fully attentive to the comments of their class teammate. (For more on the effect that this peer-to-peer listening can have on the speaker, check out technique 44, *Habits of Discussion*.)

You can see an example of how this works in Christine Torres's vocabulary lesson. "The word 'implore' means what?" Christine asks, and almost every hand is in the air as she pauses briefly before identifying Jovon as the student who will answer. As she does this every hand goes down, as if to say *Jovon, we are listening. It's your turn.* Seconds later Christine says, "Read the situation for me loud and proud . . ." and again almost every hand goes up before she calls on Juju, whereupon, again, everyone's hand goes down. This reminds students: now is the time to listen to what Juju says, not to be thinking of what you would have said. Seconds later Christine asks, "What did the girl do in this situation? Use the definition." Again every hand goes up. Now it's Etani's turn and the process of putting hands down—again, this happens on cue because Christine has taught it—reminds students of the rest of the routine implicit in someone else getting called on. Putting one's hand down to listen cues the next step in listening behavior: giving Etani eye contact. James Clear describes this as "habit stacking," where one habit leads to another and a series of positive actions can reliably result if they are connected consistently to a relatively simple first action.

Beyond the effect of each individual interaction, in Christine's use of *All Hands* you can clearly see the mileposts flying past. The illusion of speed has been created. A traditionally slow activity—vocabulary—has been brought to life.

## Press Pause on Digressions

Sometimes we lightheartedly refer to managing a group of people as herding cats. In any group of people, some will occasionally just wander off in their own direction, physically or intellectually—even when it's beneficial or appropriate to stick together. When you've got ground to cover as a teacher, you can't always let everyone just head off on a tangent. A good cowboy has to know how to bring the wanderers back into the fold quickly and smoothly. A good teacher, too. It's part of the job.

Similarly, even when they are eager to share, students' comments can inadvertently derail the pacing or focus of a lesson by being digressive or just plain off-topic. Don't get me wrong. I love long and insightful student comments—when they come at the right time. However, a long and tangentially related comment that involves references to several obscure and only semi-relevant shows and movies at the wrong time is a rally-killer. (It can be that even with best intentions and offered at the "right time") There you are, finally having gotten a quality discussion about *The Giver* going with lots of kids weighing in. There are only five minutes left in class but there's so much good thinking going on and just maybe the epiphany about what "release" means is about to happen, when one young wanderer begins a long-winded and meandering discussion of some of his personal highlights of the novel. He's lost his train of thought now, so he's throwing words at the problem—trying to use quantity to make up for a loss of clarity. In that moment it feels a bit like grounding into a double play, except maybe it's multiple double plays (I say this lovingly). Suddenly the optimism that you're going to pull it out and get to the epiphany evaporates into thin air.

In this situation you need a way to press pause on the digression, to help him cut his comment off even though he hasn't offered to end it. If you can do so warmly and skillfully, without making your student feel embarrassed, it's good for the class discussion (and therefore for learning) and *good for him*. To let him go on and on is a disservice. "Helpful" is providing a gentle nudge to help young people understand how to read their audience and setting.

Ending a digression quickly and politely just takes a little technique. I call it pressing pause because the word "pause" is so helpful, especially when followed by a statement pointing out what's useful about what's already been shared. "Pause there, Daniel. You've given us so much to talk about already. Let's let some other folks respond." *Boom*. The rally is back on! The positivity is important. Some other variations might include: "Ooh. Pause there.

You mentioned the memories he's started to receive and how emotional they are. Who else thought about that?" or even "Ooh. Pause. Interesting. Yes, the memories are so emotional; who can tell us why that matters?" You also might be able to redirect students to the most productive part of their answer: "Pause. That phrase, 'more emotion than he's ever felt.' Let's focus on that for a minute." This is a way of gently cutting him off before he can get too far afield, while still extracting value from his answer and, you hope, helping him see what was valuable in it for next time.

If you are able to convey your appreciation for a student's participation while maintaining focus on the question at hand, you'll be more likely to step in and press pause when it's necessary for the sake of the learning community. Although some unexpected student comments are worth their weight in gold, some are not, and it's the job of the teacher to maintain the lesson's pacing through how time is allocated in the classroom.

A final note: I am a big fan of the word "pause," specifically, in this application, as opposed to the words "stop" or "freeze" or something else. Pause implies that the stop is temporary and has a gentleness. "Stop" tends to make it feel like you've done something wrong—"pause" implies you will start up again at some point, that you will continue to share your thinking. Which, happily, is true.

## Online Lessons: Online Needs Flow

Pacing draws on the principle of flow, the idea that people take pleasure in being swept up in an engaging and dynamic activity. This is a critical driver of excellence in the classroom. Online, it's necessary to stave off disaster. Students who are bored or feel no connection to the lesson can't walk out of a classroom. If they disengage you can see it—in the empty page before them or the lack of follow-through on task. Sometimes they'll make you see their disengagement via behavior. Not online. There, unengaged students will simply slip away. They'll turn off their camera if you'll let them and then goodness only knows what they're doing. Or they'll toggle off to another screen or engage themselves on their phone or some other device. They'll be playing *Minecraft* or be on TikTok and you'll never know they're gone.

So teaching in an online setting puts a premium on pacing—the momentum of a lesson has to draw students in right from the outset and sustain their focus. In the video *Arrianna Chopp: Means of Participation*, you can see Arrianna Chopp of Libertas Prep in Los Angeles bring pacing to her online lesson from the word go. Within seconds of starting class there's a task that everyone completes (answering in the chat). This is supported by Arrianna "narrating the chat," that is, letting students know she sees and appreciates when they participate but also building a sense of momentum to make participation visible to other students. It's like a wave of forward momentum that she quickly translates into a mini discussion where three students in a row give their opinion. It's fast and engaging and inclusive of everyone. There's not time to get lost in the far corners of the Internet. Just possibly this sense of dynamism—especially at the start of the lesson—is something we can borrow online.

## TECHNIQUE 30: WORK THE CLOCK

We measure things because they matter. Time is the greatest resource you as a classroom teacher manage, so measuring that time intentionally, strategically, and often visibly is critical in shaping your students' experience in the classroom. This skill is called *Work the Clock*.

### Show the Clock

First, *show the clock*: make time visible to students. Showing how you allocate time—indicating how much you allow for certain activities and that you track its passage during a lesson—will help students understand that you value its wise and careful allocation, and will ultimately teach them to be attentive to it as well.

Showing the clock also has the added benefit of helping you discipline yourself. What teacher hasn't planned five minutes for an activity, for example, but unintentionally spent fifteen on it? What teacher hasn't told her students, "You have ten minutes to work on this," only to lose track of time and give students twice—or half—that? The result can often be a lesson that ends incompletely; you don't get to the end of the story or the experiment, or you end with only guided practice rather than independent practice.

When you send students off to try a problem for a few minutes, make your best guess as to how long it should take and say, "OK, try one of these on your own. I'll give you three minutes." Then start your stopwatch or, better, start an overhead stopwatch—perhaps an LCD clock you can project on the overhead or on the wall. If students can see the clock, they can self-manage—learning, for example, to pace their time for a short-answer response.

Some might protest that they don't want to be locked into a specific time allocation for an activity when they don't really know how long it will take, but it's important to remember that you're not actually locked in by giving an initial time allocation. If the time you allocated wasn't enough, you can always extend it ("OK, we've been working hard, and it looks like another two minutes might help") or shorten it ("Wow, your answers are too interesting and too good to wait the full three minutes, so we'll check in at two minutes!").

Showing the clock gives rise to a time-sensitive culture. I would love to tell you that classrooms should be timeless places where we take as long as we need and follow every digression, but we all know that's not the reality of our daily periods of forty-two, fifty-five, or seventy-five minutes. And the fact is that you are more likely to be able to occasionally meander timelessly if you manage the rest of your time very well.

*Showing* time also allows you to *talk about* time less often. Projecting a clock as it counts down the minutes or seconds on an activity requires no additional narration once your students have learned to attend to it (and once they know that you're going to abide by it). You just say, "Okay, let's go," start the clock, and let it run, perhaps offering an occasional reminder ("You'll hear the beep in just under a minute," for example). Then say, "Okay, let's see how we did," when the timer has finally wound down.

Several years of applying the tools of master teachers has led my Uncommon Schools Teach Like a Champion team to use this at our workshops. During independent work (or breaks!) we often project an Internet stopwatch so that participants know where they stand on time. Generally we find that they much prefer self-management to being constantly managed by us—particularly at lunch breaks.

You can encourage students to embrace time management and develop time management skills by setting up opportunities for them to complete multiple tasks during a block of independent time. "I'm putting twenty minutes on the clock. In that time, you need to edit your paragraph and complete your self-assessment."

## Use Specific, Odd Increments

Whether you are showing the clock or are the only one who can see it, it's valuable to *use specific times and odd increments* when you discuss time allocations with your class. Consider this mundane case study. If I was leading a professional development session for teachers and said, "Okay, let's take a short break and pick up again in ten minutes," I would probably not have people return ready to work in ten minutes. The time allocation I used—ten minutes— sounds like an estimate. Round numbers often contain an implicit "about" in them, as in "Let's pick up again in about ten minutes." Ironically, I'd get people back and ready to work much more quickly if I gave them a longer time increment for their break, *as long as it was specific*. In a race between "Okay, let's take a short break and pick up again in ten minutes" and "Okay, let's take a short break and pick up again in twelve minutes," I am betting on the second group every time.

In your classroom, be specific about exactly how long students have for an activity, and vary your allocations. Four minutes of group work is usually better than five minutes of group work (and three minutes is better than "two minutes," which also sounds like an estimate), but better than both is an initial round of solo writing for two and a half minutes and then a group discussion for three minutes. The variation in allocations for different activities or different iterations of the same activity communicates your intentionality about time. You care about and are precise about time, and this makes others respect it as well. Having established such a track record, you're actually likely to get a pretty good response from folks if you do occasionally use "two minutes" and the like.

In the video *Emily Badillo: Go Right to Work*, which shows a recent fourth-grade lesson on *Number the Stars*, Emily Badillo launches a writing task with four minutes (not five!) of work time. After explaining that she'll be looking for example sentences to share with the class, Emily cues the group to begin by restating the time: "You've got four minutes. Go right to work." She immediately sets a four-minute timer on the red stopwatch attached to the front board so that all students can keep an eye on their time as they're working. As she circulates, Emily keeps one eye on the clock so she can provide verbal time stamps for students as they go. "You've been working for one minute," she says. "Looks like almost everyone is done with the first sentence. Keep up that speed." This narration helps students check their own pace and mark the passage of time—How much have I accomplished in this first minute? Am I on track with the rest of the class?—but is warmly and positively delivered, emphasizing success and encouraging those who might not be finished yet. After another two minutes of work time, Emily addresses the room again—"You have one minute and thirty-six seconds left. Get as far as you can." The precision here helps students see that she'll be taking the end of work time seriously (it's not an approximation or an estimate) but her encouragement to "get as far as you can" lessens the pressure, reassuring students that while the group will be stopping soon, each person's job is simply to make as much progress as possible in the time allotted. Finally, she tells students, "You have twenty-five seconds left, wrap up the sentence that you are on," preparing students for the end cue and ensuring they aren't caught off guard by the timer. When the timer goes off, Emily says simply, "Stop where you are, put your pencils down," pauses the timer, and begins to *Cold Call* students to share their work.

We see teachers using *Work the Clock* phrases at a few key moments of an activity—at the outset or in the launch in order to set expectations, periodically throughout work time to set benchmarks for progress or encourage stamina, at in the final thirty seconds or so, to cue students to wrap up their thinking and prepare for the transition. Here are a few phrases that might come in handy:

"You have the next two minutes to respond to Question 2. If you finish early, try Question 3 as a challenge."

"You've been working for two minutes and thirty seconds. Looks like most of us are working on the third problem."

"We have about three minutes left; you should be moving on from your reading into answering the first reflection question."

"Wrap up your conversation with your partner in the next ten seconds."

"You'll hear the timer in another forty seconds; finish the sentence you're working on."

## Using Countdowns Effectively

A *countdown* is a statement of a desire to get something done within an explicit time frame—one that's shorter than it might otherwise be. On the basis of observations, I encourage the judicious use of countdowns in most classrooms, especially when they follow some important dos and don'ts:

### Dos

Do use countdowns for simple tasks, wrap-ups, or transitions. Be aware that you will disrupt a certain percentage of work in the room. For this reason, try to transition, over time, to less narrated countdowns, advising students to be "ready for the [timer] beeps in ten seconds" or merely counting selected digits (for example, "Ten, nine [pause for a few seconds], five, four [pause], two, and one.")

Do use the lowest countdown possible. Be cautious about giving students too much time to do a simple task. Putting pencils down shouldn't take ten seconds, so don't use a countdown from ten. Try three. The idea behind a countdown is to give students just enough time to do something well. Don't rush students by setting an unreasonable goal, but do be constantly encouraging students to manage their time efficiently during transitions and other mundane tasks and to be attentive to efficiency in academic tasks.

Do narrate follow-through *during* a countdown. If I narrate during countdown, for example, "I'll need your eyes up here in five, four, Nick is ready to go, two, Sarah's ready," I am describing students who exceeded expectations. In other words, call students' attention to exemplars *during a time when they can all still meet your expectations for them.*

### Don'ts

Don't stretch a countdown—that is, don't slow it down to match student behavior. If you do, it shows that you will adjust the countdown to the alacrity (or lack of it) students demonstrate, rather than the reverse. This defeats the whole purpose. It's much better to end on time and respond with feedback: "Looks like we didn't quite make it. Next time, we have to be faster so we can get back to the novel."

Don't narrate follow-through *after* a countdown has finished. In doing so, you are describing a student who has merely done what you asked, and you risk making it sound as though you are pleading for follow-through ("Won't you please try to be like the kids who've done what I asked?"). This can undercut expectations as effectively as it can reinforce them.

Don't overnarrate students who have met your expectations. A few quick acknowledgments of those who are ready is great. Too many, and it sounds as though you're worried students won't follow through on what you've asked them to do.

## TECHNIQUE 31: EVERY MINUTE MATTERS

Respect students' time by spending every minute intentionally.

I observed one of my favorite moments in teaching—simple, humble, and powerful—early in my *Teach Like a Champion* study process when I saw Annette Riffle of North Star Academy in Newark working with her fifth-grade math students. The moment started with an utterly typical scene. Students had solved a problem on the coordinate plane independently at their desks. They'd had to plot certain points to show the outlines of a hypothetical stadium. Annette ended the independent work with a crisp, pace-accentuating clean finish—a series of claps that she gives and that students echo to bring them to attention. Then she said, "Someone come give us a stadium," handing the marker to a girl named Kadheisha, who excitedly approached the front of the room to model her work on the overhead.

Ten thousand teachers have, from time immemorial, called a million students up to the board to "show their work," and not much usually happens while one student puts said work up on the board. Twenty-nine students sit and wait for thirty seconds or a minute while the student in question completes the work they will soon review. Perhaps in some classes, three or four students put problems up on the board at once. But the rest of the group does precious little, even if told to "pay attention to what they're writing." Twenty-nine students wasting thirty seconds are the same as one student wasting almost fifteen minutes, except that, in addition, precious amounts of momentum are also squandered reenergizing students who've lost the task.

What came next in Annette's class, though, was quietly brilliant.

While Kadheisha did her work at the board, Annette did a quick review of key terms and ideas with the rest of her students. "What quadrant are we in? Fatimah? And what do we call that line along the bottom? Sean? And which direction does the *x*-axis run, Shatavia?"

The result was not only a productive use of time and the reinforcement of key facts during what would otherwise be downtime, but also an exercise that increased the likelihood that students would use key vocabulary words to analyze and describe Kadheisha's work.

Time, I was reminded in watching Annette's class, is water in the desert. It is a teacher's most precious resource—it is to be husbanded, guarded, and conserved. Every minute of it matters and the way we use it shows students where our priorities lie. We must work to maximize the precious moments of class we share with students to ensure we're using our time as intentionally as possible. This is not to say we must avoid all downtime or breaks—after all, these can be opportunities to have meaningful interactions with students—but rather to emphasize that we must be deliberate and thoughtful in our choice about how to spend even the smallest increment of time. Mastering *Every Minute Matters* means deciding how to spend time intentionally, even in the moments between activities or other everyday pockets of time that are easy to miss.

## *Every Minute Matters* . . . **Even in the Hallway**

One of the very first videos we shot in what became the *Teach Like a Champion* project, long before there was such a name, is a short video of History teacher Jamey Verilli managing his minutes one afternoon at North Star Academy. Waiting for the rest of the class to arrive with some of his students in the hallway just outside his classroom, he begins quizzing students on their vocabulary:

"What does it mean to be 'bound' to do something?"

"Can you use it in a sentence, John?"

"Who would have been bound to the land in a Middle Ages town?"

"What are you bound to be doing right now?"

Class has not even started yet. Not in the classroom, not during class time, but Jamey recognized a learning opportunity. Meanwhile, his students are excited, smiling, happy to be engaged, and showing off their knowledge.

Purposeless time can kill momentum. One reason that Jamey's students are so invested and engaged is the message he is sending. He's showing he believes that their time is important, not to be wasted, and that they and what they are learning is of great significance. A teacher like Jamey creates a sense of meaning and productivity that pervades the room.

The first step in *Every Minute Matters* is a psychological one: recalibrating your expectations so that you think not, "Well, it's just thirty seconds" but rather, "Good gosh, thirty seconds—how can we use that well?" There's a quiet confidence implicit in such a shift. The well-it's-just-thirty-seconds teacher tacitly assumes that he could not do much with thirty seconds, so why bother? The second teacher knows, believes in, and embraces how much he might accomplish even in a very short period of time. After all, almost everything we've ever learned, we learned in the end, in a minute. There was an extra minute of reflection, practice, explanation, or discussion that pushed us over the top and perfected our skill or knowledge. There's no reason to believe that the profundity of the learning has to correlate to the glamour, predictability, and formality of the setting. The critical moment can just as easily come at 2:59 p.m. on Friday afternoon as the buses start to fill the circle in front of school as it can in the middle of your lesson on Wednesday morning.

Once you've embraced that notion, you'll start seeing pockets of time everywhere, where once, it seems, none had existed. A bit of occasional advance planning will help you make the most of it. Keeping at the ready—in your "back pocket"—some activities and groups of thematic questions aligned to what you're teaching can make the difference.

## Back-Pocket Questions

If you work in a school, you are alert to the constant potential for the unexpected. Schools are complex organizations where the perfect flow of scheduled events is sometimes disrupted. So it's useful to be ready for the unexpected by having a portfolio of quick and useful back-pocket questions ready to go. These activities are also much easier to incorporate impromptu when students recognize them as something familiar that they know. You might opt to give a name to the activities you do most often so students know what to expect. For example, "Let's do a little vocab bingo" saves the time you'd need to explain a new procedure or activity. They can live in a real pocket (on a set of note cards) or a metaphorical one. Plan the questions both periodically (every three weeks or so) and in advance, so that they are aligned to key objectives for your current unit. I also know teachers who keep a mental list of good topics for Q&A among mastered skills, enabling them to strategically spiral in practice and ensure retention of mastered content. You can always review key vocabulary, just as you can always ask students to put historical events in chronological order or put events from a novel in sequence.

Without any props at all, you can always ask "math chains"—sequential math problems such as "Three times six. Now doubled. Take that number's square root. Subtract seventeen and take the absolute value. Add 104. Your answer is?" My colleague Paul Powell did this daily when he started a school—Troy Prep in Troy, New York—in a building whose layout had students regularly waiting for others to clear tiny landings and passageways before they could move between classes. There on the landings and stairs, with Paul calling problems to students a dozen stairs above or a dozen below, his students mastered hours of math—ultimately resulting in some of the highest math scores in New York State.

## Notes

1. https://www.theguardian.com/science/2015/jan/18/modern-world-bad-for-brain-daniel-j-levitin-organized-mind-information-overload.
2. Daniel J. Levitin, *The Organized Mind: Thinking Straight in the Age of Information Overload*. Quoted in Maryanne Wolf, *Reader, Come Home*.
3. https://www.theguardian.com/science/2015/jan/18/modern-world-bad-for-brain-daniel-j-levitin-organized-mind-information-overload.
4. https://sites.nationalacademies.org/cs/groups/dbassesite/documents/webpage/dbasse_070621.pdf.
5. https://www.aft.org/sites/default/files/periodicals/Rosenshine.pdf.
6. Ibid.

# Chapter 7

# Building Ratio Through Questioning

*Here's how you should think about memory: it's the residue of thought, meaning that the more you think about something, the more likely it is that you'll remember it later.*

—Daniel Willingham[1]

The term "ratio" refers to the proportion of cognitive work done by students during a lesson. This is an important thing for teachers to reflect on. Students remember what they think about, Daniel Willingham tells us. So a major goal of our teaching is to cause students—all of them, ideally—to do quite a lot of thinking about the most important content of the lesson. But of course there's a bit more to it than that. "Desirable difficulty" is what cognitive psychologists call the idea that thinking harder about something encodes it more deeply in memory and therefore makes it easier to remember—and probably encodes more things of substance in the first place, as well.

We could represent the concept of ratio graphically like this:

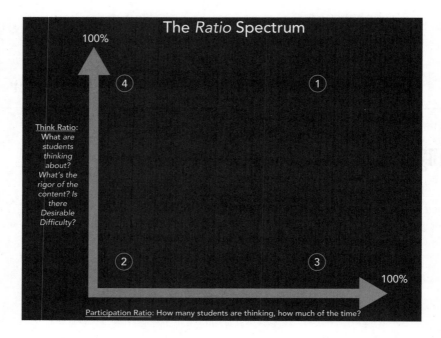

Understanding this diagram requires defining two terms for describing student thinking during the lesson. The first is Participation Ratio (PR). I've put this on the *x* axis. It asks the question of who participates and how often. If I ask a question and everyone in my classroom answers in their heads or picks up their pencil and starts writing out thoughts, my Participation Ratio is high. Everyone in the class is answering my question. If it's a discussion and everyone is listening carefully to the speaker my Participation Ratio is high. Potentially it's higher still if I occasionally divide my whole group discussion up into pair discussions (*Turn and Talks*); suddenly more people are participating. My PR is high.

If I was measuring my Participation Ratio, though, I'd have to measure it over the course of the whole lesson. A minute or two of full participation isn't nearly as good as everyone engaged and participating all class long.

One easy way to get a high Participation Ratio might be to do a lot of *Call and Response*. Students love it—at least younger ones—and I can see that everyone is answering my questions. *If I add six and six what do I get . . . class?!*

The problem of course is that while adding six and six is helpful to a degree, there's not much "desirable difficulty." My questioning isn't going to be rigorous enough to ensure deep understanding of the math. To do that I've got to ask harder questions about harder things.

Students have to strain a little. The rigor of student thinking I could call Think Ratio (TR) and put it on my $y$ axis.[2]

I could boost my Think Ratio even more if my students thought deeply about substantive questions *in a variety of ways.* Writing, for example, is especially rigorous. Writing and then listening to how others thought about the same question might be even more challenging, with unexpected ideas suggested by others to wrestle with and reconcile with my own thoughts. At least that would happen if I were a good listener. If I had to rewrite my initial idea based on what I'd heard in the discussion and then explain my changes to a partner, my thinking could have even greater depth and variety.

If that happened and it happened steadily throughout class, I might plot my class overall at point 1 on the Ratio Spectrum above. My Think Ratio would be high throughout and so would my Participation Ratio.

This would be better than my *Call and Response* lesson with math facts, which would land around point 3: high Participation Ratio but low Think Ratio.

If I instead dusted off my deepest questions about the nature of math and had a profound discussion about it with the two or three most engaged students in class, I might check in at point 4, high Think Ratio, low Participation Ratio.

Sadly it would be easier than I might think to get down to point 2: low PR, low TR. I could get there via a banal lesson plan yielding boring questions and bored students. But just as likely I could get there with a promising lesson and lack of attention to teaching technique. For example, if I allowed students to call out answers to questions, and the two or three most verbal students in my class proceeded to call out the first answer they could think of to each question, I would very quickly get to point 2. Even my two or three answerers weren't thinking very hard and everyone else would have long since realized they weren't answering and would be elsewhere, mentally. In that case I could be asking the most brilliant questions in the world. Two or three people answering them with half thought-out ideas is enough to render my perfect questions irrelevant.

The following three chapters are about increasing student understanding and knowledge—not to mention motivation and engagement—by taking three paths to point 1.

In Chapter Seven we'll address how questioning skills can increase PR and TR. For example, if I can use *Means of Participation* to signal to my three highly verbal students that I'd like them to raise their hands unless otherwise indicated, I can suddenly slow things down and cause them to think more deeply about my questions. "Perhaps your first answer is not the best . . ." I say, and they stop to reconsider. Over time I teach them to think slowly and deeply. If I then begin *Cold Calling*, I can cause more students to share answers (even those who don't at first volunteer readily) and even more students than that to answer in their heads in preparation of the fact that they might just get called on. Suddenly we are moving up and to the right on the graph.

In Chapter Eight, we'll address how writing can boost the ratio. If I pose my question and ask everyone to write out some initial thoughts, I suddenly have thirty students answering a question I might previously have had just one or two students answer. I have multiplied my PR but also my TR. Students have to choose precise coordinated syntax and verbiage to write out an idea, especially if, again, I can get them to work more slowly and deliberately at times. Or to rewrite for precision, even. Writing is inherently harder than talking. Again we are suddenly sailing upward and rightward.

In Chapter Nine we'll address discussion and how it can help boost ratio. There's a bit of a golden ticket in this chapter, a hidden gem that not everyone recognizes the value of. It's the realization that the ratio during a discussion—and indeed the quality of the discussion more broadly—is shaped at least as much, or even more, by the degree and quality of listening as it is by the degree and quality of talking. We live in a world where sometimes we're all talking (or shouting), and no one is listening (unless shouting back counts). Our classrooms are better if they are the antidote to such a world. So perhaps a better title for Chapter Nine is Ratio Through Discussion and Listening.

Before we get to these topics, there's one additional factor to consider: the knowledge prerequisite. To quote Daniel Willingham once more:

> Data from the last thirty years lead to a conclusion that is not scientifically challengeable. Thinking well requires knowing facts, and that's true not simply because you need something to think about. The very processes that teachers care about most—critical thinking processes such as reasoning and problem-solving—are intimately intertwined with factual knowledge that is in long-term memory (not just found in the environment).

The tools in the ratio toolbox are wonderful, but they work only if they are employed in knowledge-rich (and knowledge-enriched) settings. That is: where students know a lot about the topics you ask them to think about because you've taught them. If you want a high Think Ratio you must have facts. Yes, "mere facts." (I'm pausing here while a pall descends over some of my readership.) Students must have facts to use, apply, consider, connect, and reflect on. Of course, the facts are even better if they're connected in a deep and organized body of knowledge, the fancy name for which is *schema*.[3] In a knowledge-rich environment, though, even "disconnected facts," that straw man of futurist educators the world over, don't stay disconnected for long.[4] Soon enough, students will see connections among the things they know and their facts will no longer be disconnected—doubly so if we place them in situations that make it more likely for them to connect the pieces of knowledge they hold.

I share this because the power of knowledge is one of the most misunderstood things in education. You've heard those self-same futurists and their acolytes in TED Talks and out on social media telling us that facts are irrelevant because you can look anything up on Google, but this is not, in fact, true. To use knowledge in critical thinking it has to be in your long-term memory. What we call insight or even creativity is often actually a bit of knowledge from long-term memory popping up in the moment we learn about something else and announcing a previously not-obvious connection.[5] But even beyond that, the "just Google it" theory doesn't work because you're unlikely to know there's a connection between something you don't know about and what you're reading or learning about, so you're unlikely to think to look it up.[6] And even if you did, you'd have to hold it in your short-term memory once you looked it up, and this would leave you less working memory for creative leaps.

Bloom's Taxonomy, at least when presented as a pyramid, is a typical point of confusion. Educators often presume that knowledge and facts being at the bottom of the pyramid means they're the least important part. Many followers of Bloom on the other hand insist that he understood the profound importance of knowledge and meant to imply that the whole thing *rested on a foundation of knowledge* because it was so important. That's relieving to hear but doesn't change the fact that many (most?) educators don't think about it that way. If you've got a pyramid, every teacher glances at it and wants to guide his or her students to the top: *We're all in synthesis, all the time in this classroom.* Sadly, cognitive science tells us that this is wrong. It's actually the lowly facts that work like fuel and get the whole cognitive motor humming.

## Building Ratio Through Questioning

Teachers love to ask questions. Rightly. Questions can cause students to think deeply about content, and what students think about is what they are likely to learn and remember.[7] And of course questions can spark discussion and peer-to-peer learning.

But *can* and *do* are different things. We have all been inspired by profound questions but we have all also seen, and many of us (myself included) have taught lessons where questions, once asked, hang unanswered in the air. Or generate a smattering of half-hearted and obligatory responses: the same few students (or student) calling out the first thought off the top of their heads.

Just because we ask questions doesn't mean students answer them, in other words—or think much about them. So it's worth using a few tools to refine questioning and ensure that it supports strong Participation and Think Ratios. As a starting point, let's differentiate two different reactions that students may have to questions, both of which can be valuable in the classroom.

First, there is thinking. Ideally everyone in a given class would think rigorously about every question you ask and attempt to answer it *in their minds*. This is a different activity from answering the question and sharing their thinking *aloud*. Answering and thinking are separate variables.

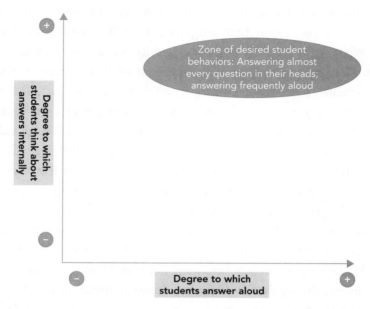

That might seem like an arcane point to make, but to be the teachers our students deserve, we need to reliably cause both to occur. Imagine you're the teacher and I am your student. When you ask a question, I think deeply about my response and also share slivers of my insights with the group. All my classmates do the same. That's the ideal, but it doesn't come about easily. I might barely think about a question and reflexively answer off the top of my head. I'd be answering, but you would have failed to elicit much thinking. Or I could think deeply but never share those private thoughts, leaving you and all my classmates to guess to what degree I was engaged in and learning about the class content. Then you'd have *thinking* but not *answering*. And of course, I could neither think about nor answer the question. I could sit and engage in flights of my own fancy while class went on around me.

In fact, the degree of thinking I do and the degree of my intent to answer are correlated; *norms of answering shape norms of thinking*. I am less likely to think fully about your questions if I know I am unlikely to share my thinking with others. On the other hand, if answering fully and well is the social norm in the classroom—that is, most of my classmates answer frequently and with full effort, so I think that's the natural thing to do—I am more likely to persist in doing the hard work of thinking because I want to be able to answer too.

Perhaps a few students will persist in the most rigorous inquiry when left to their own accord and self-discipline but most (myself included![8]) require the possibility of having to share their answer to sustain and encourage their best thinking. So unless we manage the process of who answers, when and how, we are far less likely to cause the greatest amount of thinking to occur among the widest range of students.

I am aware that I have not said anything about the content of questions yet and that may concern some readers. Needless to say, the quality of your question matters deeply. Among other benefits, a good question creates a strong incentive (or disincentive) to answer. It is also true, though, that if questions engage only a narrow group of students or only engage them half-heartedly, *the quality of the question doesn't matter much*. You can ask the most profound question in the world; if only one or two students think about it deeply with the expectation that they might answer, it's all for naught. If we want to improve questioning, it's necessary to first address the culture and context in which questions are asked.

Thus the techniques in this chapter include *Wait Time* (how to build "thinking habits" in the moments after a question is asked and before answers are given) and *Cold Call* (which among other things ensures that all students feel that they might be called on to answer and therefore engage fully in thinking about questions). I'll also discuss *Call and Response*, which can help build norms of engaged participation, and *Means of Participation*, which is a reflection on the overlooked step of communicating to students how you will ask them to answer questions. Finally, I will discuss *Break It Down*, the process of using additional questions to help students when they are stuck.

### Basic Guidance for Question Writing

Of course how you craft your questions matters, so before going deeper into these techniques for building ratio through questioning, I'm going to share notes on writing better questions that focus on two things: preparation and purpose.

1.  *Preparation:* It is difficult to think of a great question in the midst of teaching. You need your working memory elsewhere. Either your question or something else will likely suffer if you try to think of the perfect way to unlock the irony of Jane Austen's prose in the moment your students are reading it. Whenever possible, plan and write your questions out in advance—either the exact ones you will ask or key questions you *might* ask. Even a first draft helps. If you change it in the midst of the lesson that's a good thing: that a second draft improves on a first draft does not mitigate the value of the earlier draft.

2.  *Purpose:* The purpose is not to ask questions; the purpose is to use questions to elicit different types of thinking. A question is a means to an end, so if your goal is to use questioning in a lesson, it's necessary to take the next step: use it for what?

If the end purpose is to use thinking to elicit different types of thinking, it's worth noting that we often fall into unconscious habits—consistently asking the same types of questions—and thus elicit the same types of thinking, perhaps overlooking opportunities for different types of questions that elicit different types of thinking. Categorizing questions by the type of thinking they seek to foster is an imperfect endeavor at best, but it can help to push us outside our familiar habits and ways. With that in mind, here are five purposes for questions:

1. Discovery: Some questions are intended to cause students to *discover* or derive a new idea. I could ask you questions designed to make you realize that an author is talking about something that the *reader* knows but the *main character* doesn't. When you explain that this is happening, I tell you it's called "dramatic irony."

2. Application: Just as rigorous—sometimes more so—is to start with the idea and ask students to apply or explain its *application*. I tell you that "dramatic irony" is when the reader knows something the main character doesn't and then ask, "Why is the author using dramatic irony here?" or "How is it different from the last time she used it?"

3. Check for understanding: There are also *check for understanding* questions, which are retrospective: "Why did we say the author was using dramatic irony? Where was the dramatic irony in yesterday's reading?"

4. Retrieval practice: We use *Retrieval Practice* questions to encode ideas in students' long-term memory. such as "Please define dramatic irony for me, Charles."

5. Perception-based questions: *Perception-based* questions ask students to describe what they notice. These are crucial but underrated. Perception is the first step in understanding, and when describing what they see, students must prioritize what they think is most important. When you ask, "What do you notice about Emma's language in this passage, Charles?" He may tell you a lot of things but also reveal that he has missed a phrase of crucial irony. Or perhaps he has seen it. Until he can observe the key phenomena for himself he is not fully autonomous.

## Using Perception-Based Questions: What Differences Do You See?

Sensitivity Analysis is a close reading tool my colleagues and I describe in Reading Reconsidered Curriculum in which the teacher presents a sentence from a text to students and asks them to compare it to a similar version they've created with one or two small changes.

The idea is for students to analyze the impact of word choice or syntax by comparing subtly different examples. The key is in the subtlety of the differences.

Research in comparative judgment suggests this is an especially effective way to unlock understanding of nuance and complexity. Students perceive a slight difference in tone or mood and so develop an ear for language.

In testing out lesson plans for the Reading Reconsidered Curriculum we developed, I volunteered to teach a lesson on the novel *Esperanza Rising* that included a sensitivity analysis question, and I struggled badly.

The sentence in question described the protagonist's experience in a dust storm. The original was:

> "Thousands of acres of tilled soil were becoming food for *la tormenta* and the sky was turning into a brown swirling fog."

The alternative was:

> "Thousands of acres of tilled soil were blown into the air and the sky was turning into a brown swirling fog."

Students jumped in gamely. The idea was to help students see the impact of personification—that it made the storm seem alive, like a monster perhaps, but students' responses were vague. "The original was more descriptive," one student opined. "It made you feel things more," said another. They struggled to look carefully at the differences in word choice and I struggled to help them. We were fumbling around as if in a dust storm ourselves.

Afterwards, Colleen Driggs, who'd been observing, advised: "Focus on perception first. Ask them to start by observing the differences they see between the two sentences. *Then* ask them to analyze."

This was simple but brilliant. My first question should have simply been: "What differences do you see between the two sentences?" This would have caused students to describe (and see) the changes *first* and *then* think about their impacts. I needed to start by making sure they saw the difference and then ask why it mattered. Understanding almost always starts with perception . . . for me, as well as my students.

Colleen caused me to see the opportunity in shifting to perception-based questions. I'd been asking application and discovery questions. By helping me to see how a perception question was different, she allowed me to then think about how to use it. In part that's why I suggest occasionally asking yourself, "What kind of question did I use there? What was its purpose? Might I have used a different type of question?"

# TECHNIQUE 32: PHRASING FUNDAMENTALS

How we ask a question can help ensure that it is worth trying to answer from the perspective of the listener; the question's structure can have a significant influence on the degree of thinking and answering it inspires. Understanding a few "phrasing fundamentals" can help make sure your questions engage your students as you'd hope they would.

## The Obvious Trap

One reason students don't answer or think about questions is because they don't seem worth answering, often because they are either rhetorical—the teacher doesn't really expect an answer—or, worse, so obvious that they *seem* rhetorical. You might call this *the obvious trap*. Questions with obvious answers are killers of intellectual culture because they pretend to ask a question when there's really no question. *Why are you asking me that?* students think. If you're often asked meaningless questions, you become skeptical of the questioner. Students become reluctant to answer under those circumstances. When everyone clearly knows the answer, the person who gives that answer aloud appears to be a fool: oblivious and overeager. Sometimes we seek to start a discussion with an "easy" question, for example, but because the answer seems so obvious, participants are reluctant to answer, perhaps thinking they've missed something or that it was actually a trick question. The effect is the opposite of the intent. We kill the culture from the outset. In the long run, too. Over time, asking questions with obvious answers undercuts the credibility of your questioning more broadly.

Yes/no questions and questions with just two possible answers are especially vulnerable to *the obvious trap*. And, obvious or not, they often reduce the quality of the learning environment because one-word answers are the natural response.

Consider a science teacher who asks, during a lab, "Should we add our solution now or wait till it cools?"

I haven't provided enough context to indicate whether the solution should be added now but I'd wager the answer is pretty likely that we should wait. Would you stop a lesson to ask, "Should we add the solution now or wait till it cools?" if the answer was that you should add the solution now? Unlikely. You'd just say, "Now we add our solution." Or would you ask "What should we do now?" The answer is obvious and students are likely to perceive the question as rhetorical or think, *Why are you asking us?*

One reason this may happen is because a teacher is trying to ask a question when she really just wants to explain something: "It's important to remember that we should wait for the solution to cool." Or even: "It's important to remember that we should wait for the solution to cool. Why?" It's OK to tell people things directly. Appearing to ask a question when you want to tell students something wastes time and builds a culture where questions don't feel engaging and authentic. It's hard to build intellectual engagement from that kind of experience.

The questions "Should I add the solution now?" and "Should I add the solution now or wait till it cools?" are also uninspiring because they are binary. There are two possible answers in each case. "Yes" or "no" in the first question and "now" or "later" in the second. "What should I do now?" would be more interesting. "What should I look for now?"—a perception-based question for which the answer might be "the temperature"—would be better. Or "What's happening now?" which, assuming you can't see anything happening at the moment, might have more of a retrospective focus and allow you to check for understanding of previously taught content. These questions are all more interesting because there are more than two possible answers. Simply making the question nonbinary helps.

Binary questions are also problematic because they are especially prone to "tipping," which occurs when the questioner adds voice inflection on a word or phrase to suggest the answer. A bit of emphasis on "now" or perhaps on the "let it cool"—"Should we add the solution *now?* Or *let it cool*?"—makes answering doubly redundant. Your questions could be about bocce, something I know exactly nothing about, and given a binary question with a bit of voice inflection to tip me off, I'm getting ten out of ten correct answers.

## Avoid Bait and Switch

Another way questions can go wrong is because you ask a question, give students time to think about it, and then call on them to answer a different question, or a question you rephrase in a way that changes its meaning. "How is Jonas changing in this chapter? Turn and talk with your partner for ninety seconds," you say. But after the *Turn and Talk* you say, "Great. Where and how do we see Jonas's anxiety showing up?" The eager student who put her hand up thinking she'd be asked the original question is caught out. She showed her enthusiasm and now may quite publicly struggle to answer. It's bait and switch and it makes it less likely that she'll keep raising her hand as confidently or as often.

Most of the time, bait and switch happens because we haven't prepared. If you think up your question in the moment, you will have to keep it in your working memory while you listen to student responses, manage the classroom, think about the content, and so on. Under these conditions it's easy to forget your own question—or to remember only the general idea. It's one more reason to plan (and write down) your key questions in advance.[9] If you do use questions that are thought up in the moment, write them on the board when you can. The visual will help students remain disciplined to answer what you asked, and it will also help you to remember the original question.

# TECHNIQUE 33: WAIT TIME

After asking a question of his class, the typical teacher waits about a second before taking an answer. The challenges and limitations posed by such a habit are significant. The answers the teacher can expect to get after less than a second's reflection are unlikely to be the richest, the most reflective, or the most developed his students can generate. And taking answers after just a second has the effect of systematically encouraging students to raise their hands with the first answer they think of, rather than the best answer. If students wait any longer, someone else will have answered. What's more, taking immediate answers makes it more likely that the teacher will waste time. He will likely have to respond to a poorer answer before he gets a good one. A bit of waiting can often save you time in the end, as it ensures that you start with higher-quality initial answers.

*Wait Time* is the practice of inserting a short amount of waiting—often just a fraction of a second—before taking an answer. Under ideal circumstances, what happens during *Wait Time* is thinking, so it's a powerful tool for increasing Think Ratio.

The benefits of waiting a few seconds between question and answer include:

- Allowing more hands to go up
- Enabling a wider range of scholars to raise their hands
- Supporting better, more rigorous answers
- Prompting more cognitive work during the "wait"
- Increasing use of evidence in answers

You can see a great example of *Wait Time* in the video *Maggie Johnson: Focus on Why* from an eighth-grade English class at Troy Prep Middle School. The class is discussing *To Kill a Mockingbird,* and the clip begins as Maggie follows up on some writing she's asked her students to do. "As I walked around, [I noticed] many of you were able to tell me what the difference in opinion is between Aunt Alexandra and Atticus on Calpurnia," Maggie says. "The question is, why?"

After about a second (the amount of time a typical teacher waits), there's just one hand in the air. So Maggie waits. After three seconds or so, perhaps eight more students have raised their hands. Just a second or two of additional reflection time, and a spate of students enthusiastically offer to participate, having realized they have some insight on the matter.

Her smile and the playful way she raises her eyebrows diffuses any awkwardness. In another few seconds a few more hands go up, these a bit more tentative. This is especially interesting: the last group of students who've raised their hands seem as though they weren't at first sure they wanted to risk it, but have decided to after all. In many ways, these are exactly the kids you want raising their hands, and it's exciting to see the courage that a few seconds will evoke.

In the end, Maggie gives, by my count, eight seconds of *Wait Time* before she calls on Jaya to answer. As a result, she has better choices: a dozen kids who've thought through an answer. If the first student's answer needs developing she has lots of students she can call on. And they're likely to have more thoughtful answers than what she'd have likely gotten from the student whose hand went up as soon as Maggie stopped talking.

For her next question, Maggie gives almost thirteen seconds of *Wait Time*. Again, you can see students starting to raise their hands, slowly, thoughtfully. Note the girl in the front row towards the right who starts to raise her hand, puts it down, and then slowly raises it again. She's wrestling, apparently, with whether to try to join in or not. Perhaps she's wondering whether she should risk it. Perhaps she's wondering whether her answer is solid enough yet. But the extra time allows her to overcome her doubts or refine her answer. She opts in. At the same time, several students are using the time to scan the book for useful insights, a fact made evident by Maggie's narration.

A similar process plays out again in the seven seconds of *Wait Time* that Maggie offers in response to her third question: "What does Atticus say about mockingbirds again?" What's striking here are the high levels of participation, enthusiasm, and reflection among Maggie's students. They love the book, are invested in it, and so are thinking deeply. Or is it the other way around? Do they love and feel investment in the book because she's caused them to reflect deeply on it?

Implementing *Wait Time* can be challenging. It is hard to discipline yourself to allow time to pass after a question, and it takes a bit of practice. Making a habit of silently counting to three in your head or narrating your intention to wait (for example, "I'll give you a few seconds . . . OK, let's see what you have to say") can help.

Even so, there's no guarantee that students will use *Wait Time* to think. To confound the issue, it's hard to assess what students do with the time you give. It may not necessarily be apparent to students how they should respond to your waiting. What this tells us is that there are steps necessary to teach, remind, and acculturate your students to use *Wait Time* effectively and ensure it is as productive as it can be.

## Step 1: Narrate Hands

As I discussed earlier, students are more likely to think productively about a question if they expect to answer it. The degree to which students think during *Wait Time* is in part a function of their expectations about what's going to happen next. If students expect to use the ideas they generate, they are likely to put *Wait Time* to good use. *Cold Calling*, the technique I will come to next, is one way to address this—it makes it possible that anyone might be called on and so socializes readiness and engagement during time allotted for thinking. But being *Cold Called* is far from a surety and even better and more reliable, is students' own expectations of their likely actions. A student who thinks, "I seek to raise my hand" is a student who does the thinking. If students believe that what one does after time spent thinking is to offer to share ideas, if they expect to raise their hands, they have internalized a belief that causes them to engage in active thinking. The correlation is imperfect, of course, but if the expectation—I will probably raise my hand—becomes the norm, optimal thinking is likely to as well.

Sadly though, there are a great many classrooms where hands in the air are infrequent or limited to a few students, and where nonparticipation is a matter of course, sometimes a norm. In such classrooms, *Wait Time* will be less effective and the ratio will be lower. If the productivity of the *Wait Time* is influenced by the likelihood of a hand being raised afterwards, one productive move, especially early in the year, is to encourage, foster, and socialize hand-raising by *narrating hands*.

Let's say you ask, "What was the purpose of the first Continental Congress?" Maybe one or two students raise their hands. Others sit passively. Most students, probably, are engaged in a subtle and silent calculus: *Is the teacher really expecting us all to raise our hands?* Your first goal is to build a norm, the expectation that most of the class probably will. You can do this by "elevating its visibility," Peps McCrea points out, by increasing an action's "profusion" (the portion of students who do it) and its "prominence"—how much people notice the behavior and believe that you value it. "One hand," you say out loud. "Two hands. Now three." You are building momentum. Perhaps a fence-sitter, a student who had something they might offer but who was warily reading the classroom norm, now raises her hand. "Four hands," you say, smiling, relaxed, not rushed. You want hands but especially hands of students who have taken their time. "Five," you say. "Thank you, Kesha. Thanks, Lance. Nice. Now I'm starting to see those hands."

Your message is: I notice and I care when you raise your hand and, increasingly, many of your classmates are doing it.

In the video *Josefina Maino: I Need More Hands,* you can see Josefina narrating the hand-raising in her math classroom at Astoreca School in Santiago, Chile. "What does it mean that an inequality has a 'set of solutions'?" she asks. Here's the scene, after she's allowed perhaps four or five seconds of wait time:

It's typical of classrooms everywhere. Four hands are raised: enough for her to be able to find someone to call on. Over the course of the lesson, four or five hands means it won't be as awkward as when it's just two kids. She can teach under these conditions. Many teachers do.

But it's worth asking: How many of those students sitting with their hands down are thinking? How many are answering the question? Could Josefina build a culture in which they were expected to engage and thus thought more actively about things, like what we mean by a set of solutions to an inequality?

Yes, she could, as we soon see. She starts merely counting hands, making it clear that she's values breadth of participation. Just the act of counting hands out loud encourages more volunteering. She gets easily to twelve. She asks for sixteen volunteers as a minimum. Thirteen, fourteen, and fifteen go a little slower. Alonzo's is the sixteenth hand. Josefina thanks him. And calls on him. He was hesitant and she wants, now, to make him feel successful, to cause him to persist in this new behavior of hand-raising that he's embraced.

She walks towards him, repeating the question to make sure he remembers it, but also making the connection feel more personal. It's a bit of *Warm/Strict* (technique 61), too—she reminds him nonverbally to answer in a complete sentence (*Format Matters*, technique 18)—and that's the gesture she's making.

When Alonso rises to the occasion, the handshake from Josefina and the snaps of support from the class are beautiful—and encourage everyone in class to be hand-raisers as well.

There are lots of wrinkles you could add to the approach here to emphasize and value different things. For example, if you're trying to socialize risk-taking and encourage students to be comfortable raising their hands for hard questions or when they're not sure they're right, you might say, "Now I'm starting to see those *brave* hands." Or you might say, "I especially love it when students raise their hand when they *aren't* sure. That shows me fearlessness." You might signal to students that you aren't expecting a polished, final response: "This is a really tricky one. I'm curious about your initial reactions. Get us started and we'll work through it together."

Or you could slow your cadence and be double-calm. "Two hands. Three hands. Take your time but push yourself to share."

Or instead of counting you could just verbalize appreciation. "Thanks, Jeremy, for raising your hand. Thanks, Jasmine. Thanks, Carlos. Gonna give other folks a few more seconds."

If you're still not getting enough hands, keep at it. Norms and expectations won't change all at once. But you can also be ready with a few backstops, like saying "Hmmm. A lot of us seem unsure. Twenty seconds to discuss with your partner. Go." You might even tell your students to put their hands down. "I want you all to take fifteen seconds and go back to the text and find the answer. I want to see everyone rereading, and I'll tell you when you can raise your hands." After fifteen or twenty seconds, you might say, "OK, now, hands!"

Or perhaps, "Hmmm. Surprised to see so few hands. Mark, tell us as much as you *think* you know." That's a *Cold Call*, as you probably know, but a pretty supportive one. And if Mark doesn't have his hand raised but some students do, it communicates that all students in the room are part of the conversation, whether or not they've raised their hands. Reluctant students might as well get in on the game. You'd be using a bit of loving accountability to support the gentle encouragement. Together they are likely to make a difference.

The video *Aidan Thomas: Wait Time Montage* shows a compendium of Aidan's narrating hands techniques. You can see how his energy is always positive and how he varies his approach but is constantly at it throughout this class period. He's building a culture of hand-raising.

## Step 2: Prompt Thinking Skills

Once you've normalized and reinforced the expectation of hand-raising, another productive action to get the most out of *Wait Time* is to *prompt thinking skills*. This is a step by which you teach students how to make *Wait Time* useful by providing guidance about *how* to use their three or five or twelve seconds to be most productive. For example:

"I'm seeing people thinking deeply and jotting down thoughts. I'll give everyone a few more seconds to do that."

"I'm seeing people going back to the chapter to see if they can find the scene. That seems like a great idea."

"I'm hoping someone will be able to connect this scene to another play, ideally *Macbeth*."

"I'm going to give everyone lots of time because this question is tricky. Your first answer may not be the best."

It's an assumption that students know they can and should do things like this in the brief periods of time you provide for thinking, in other words. In each of these cases, the teacher is explaining things that, as expert learners, we know are productive actions. They can be pragmatic—to jot down ideas, check your notes, or glance back through the text—or more abstract: to think about broader connections or to double-check your first thought. Knowing how to use such actions starts with being aware of them.

About a minute into the video *Akilah Bond: Keystone*, Akilah asks, "How did Cam help Eric find the note?" She reminds a few students to put their hands down to ensure that they use their *Wait Time* and then, pointing to the notes of the class' earlier discussion, notes, "Imani's looking at what we know about the characters. Nice move." The purpose of the notes is to reinforce students' memory of key moments in the story. Just the kind of thing that's obvious to adults but not to second graders, perhaps, so Akilah is reinforcing that it's the ideal thing to review to help their thinking. Between that and reminding them to put their hands down and take their time, she's teaching them how to use *Wait Time* when they get it.

## Step 3: Make *Wait Time* Transparent

When you intend to give students more than a handful of seconds of *Wait Time,* it's helpful to make that fact explicit to them so that they can manage their actions accordingly, especially as they get better and better at using *Wait Time* to build ideas. Doubly so, if you are giving them longer stretches of *Wait Time.*

Let's say I'm a student in your class and you ask a rigorous question, something like, "What political forces pulled the border states toward the Confederacy, and how did Lincoln respond to them?" You give the class some *Wait Time,* and I start to reflect. After about five seconds, I've come up with a few nascent ideas—I'm ready to be called on—and I begin to wind down my thinking.

But let's say you were hoping for something a little more robust—you were hoping I'd be ready to cite a few specific incidents and describe how they connect, and you'd decided to give the class twenty or thirty seconds of *Wait Time* to make sure we thought deeply. I'd be more likely to meet your expectations if you made your intentions transparent by saying something like, "This is a hard question. It requires you to reflect on multiple factors. I'll give you thirty seconds or so."

Now I can gauge my thinking accordingly. I would start off understanding that this was no throwaway moment and would persist in reflecting because you'd told me about how much *Wait Time* to expect. If not, you might give me thirty seconds to think only to have me not use it, simply because I didn't know you were going to give it to me.

## Step 4: Give Real Think Time

The fourth step is simple: stop talking. This is critical because the first steps require you to narrate things and interrupt student thinking. This must be balanced with *real think time*, which, because it requires inaction, can be hard to remember to provide. Counting silently to yourself can help you build the necessary habit of self-discipline. You might also walk around your room as you wait, with the goal of waiting until you reach a specific spot on the other side of the room before you call on someone. Or you might use the clock to your advantage, saying, "I'll call on someone in ten seconds," and forcing yourself to wait until the second hand releases you. After the socializing of hand-raising and the praising, remember that this is the most important part: there has to be some time when no one is talking, when students are thinking. By your silence, you are intimating that this is as important as anything they will do all day.

# TECHNIQUE 34: COLD CALL

*Cold Call*, the practice of calling on students regardless of whether they have raised their hand, is a profoundly important technique that can elicit a chain of surprising and positive effects in the classroom. There are few techniques that can transform a learning environment for the better as quickly. That said, because it is such a powerful technique, it's important that it be used correctly. Fortunately, getting a few simple things right makes *Cold Call* highly likely to help you build an inclusive, rigorous, and, frankly, happy classroom.

I'm going to start by sharing two videos that I think help demonstrate with clarity how to make *Cold Call* effective. The first is of Denarius Frazier in his tenth-grade geometry class. The second is of Na'Jee Carter in his second-grade reading group. Because I love these videos and think they have so much to teach us I'm first going to narrate each of them chronologically; then I'll go back and explain the key principles of effective *Cold Calling*.

Let's start with *Denarius Frazier: Parts of a Circle*. It's the beginning of class and Denarius has planned some *Retrieval Practice* to encode key concepts in long-term memory before pushing on to new content. "Take a second to look at this diagram," he says, "And get ready for some questions. . . ." As he does this, a warm and welcoming smile lights up his face. Though he hasn't asked a single question yet, several important things have already happened.

First, Denarius has indicated to his students that he is preparing to *Cold Call* (he uses the technique frequently, especially at the beginning of class, and his statement "I'm going to ask you some questions" cues them to expect it here).

With the *Cold Call* coming, all students know they might be responsible for answering, so their attention and focus increase. This is so universally important it's easy to overlook: We can only learn what we attend to. Students are far more likely to think attentively about each question and answer it in their head because they may be asked to answer out loud. Denarius's questions are likely to elicit maximum thinking for all students and verbal answers from some of them.

Denarius's smile is also important. It says *I care about you* or *I want you to be successful* or *This is a good thing.* There's a loving accountability for students to stay focused on the math. This is what adults who care about young people do.

Denarius's first question is, "Give me an example of a radius . . . [pause] . . . Ricardo," and everyone in the room glances at the diagram and searches for an example of a radius during that pause.

If he had said, "Who can give me an example of a radius?" and taken hands, some students would have known they would be answering because they planned to raise their hands. Some, though, would not find a radius because they hadn't planned to raise their hands or weren't yet sure if they wanted to participate. The ratio would be low.

If he had said, "Ricardo, give me an example of a radius," and used the *Cold Call*, then other students might or might not have taken the time to think through the answer to this particular question about the radius since they knew the Cold Call was directed to Ricardo. But the way Denarius frames the question causes every student to do the work during the pause between the question and the identification of the person who will answer. The recipe here is: Question. Pause. Name. The timing means every student in Denarius's class is searching the diagram for an example of a radius in preparation for the possible *Cold Call*. The ratio has been multiplied, if not by thirty, at least manyfold.

A small thing: Denarius gives his students six or seven seconds of *Wait Time* here to observe and think abut the diagram before he even asks the first question. In fact there's *Wait Time* throughout. This reminds us of something else important. *Cold Call* is never a "gotcha." Denarius is not trying to catch students daydreaming or embarrass them into paying attention; the intention behind the technique is to set them up to succeed. Giving them the time to get oriented and to think through their answers helps with that. Effective teachers make students feel safe and successful even as they cause them to be more accountable and attentive.

There's further wisdom in the video as well: the universality of Denarius's *Cold Calls*, for example. It's clear he's not picking on Ricardo—or anyone else—because so many people get *Cold Called* throughout the lesson. It's not the strugglers or the kids in the back row or any identifiable group. It's just how we do it here. *Cold Call* comes to everyone because Mr. Frazier cares that everyone is thinking, engaged, and participating. By spreading his *Cold Calls* around the room, Denarius indicates that he's attentive to the progress of every single student.

Denarius also emphasizes the universality and positivity of the technique by smiling as he quizzes students. Here he is asking Shamari to identify a chord:

There's another critical moment when Denarius calls on Shamari and she answers incorrectly, mistaking a diameter for a chord. Teachers worry about what to do if a student freezes or gets an answer wrong when they've been *Cold Called* (in fact, it's one key reason why some are reluctant to try the technique, an important consideration for trainers and school leaders to be aware of), but Denarius provides a simple and effective solution. He responds with a *Turn and Talk* to let everyone discuss the question. Implicit in this decision is the idea that if Shamari didn't know, others probably didn't as well. (You could also make this assumption explicit by saying it out loud: "Hmm. Tough question. I bet lots of us are struggling with it. Let's review.") Coming out of the *Turn and Talk*, there's another *Cold Call* to make sure students engaged fully.

Now let's step into Na'Jee's classroom to watch the video *Na'Jee Carter: Cold Call Montage*. His reading group is discussing internal and external conflict in stories. After a quick *Call and Response* where students answer that there are two types of conflict, Na'Jee *Cold Calls* Marcel to identify them. "Marcel, talk to me . . ." he says. Na'Jee's language choice here is striking. He hopes Marcel will know but he's given himself a bit of wiggle room. What is the wrong answer to the question "Talk to me"? Na'Jee can turn almost any answer from Marcel into a positive starting point for the discussion. He can make Marcel and the group feel successful right from the outset, and increase their motivation and sense of progress. They will be more engaged and more willing to take academic risks throughout. We see this cycle of early success in motivating participants even with adults at our workshops, where people sometimes are reluctant to risk raising their hand in front of 100-plus people. Typically if we start the day by *Cold Calling* them in a way that ensures their success, they begin raising their hands of their own volition. Through *Cold Call*, they have successfully entered the conversation and have grown comfortable speaking in front of 100 colleagues. *Cold Call* has allowed them to take the risk and prove something to themselves; motivation, confidence, and hand-raising all increase.

With that in mind, the phrasing of Na'Jee's second question borders on brilliant: "Tell me about the internal conflict, Yedidiah . . ." Again, the openness of the question allows Yedidiah many ways to contribute to the conversation. He is capable of contributing, even if doesn't know every last piece of the answer. Na'Jee makes it safe to start without having to be perfect.

Na'Jee's third *Cold Call* is a bit trickier. He's increasing the challenge a bit now but when Yedidiah gets it, Na'Jee's appreciation is simple and quick but lovely: "You got it, dude."

There are two more *Cold Calls* immediately after: "Can you tell me about that conflict, Marcel?" and "And what kind of conflict was that, Mark?" and then Na'Jee's most interesting question stem yet: "Yedidiah, I want you to start to speak about what sort of conflict you already see evidence for. . . ."

The framing suggests, in asking Yedidiah to *start to speak,* that of course he won't be able to cover everything. He's asked merely to get the class started. If there are follow-ons to expand Yedidiah's thinking, well, we expected that from the start and Yedidiah will experience his contribution to the conversation not as incomplete, but rather as exactly what was helpful to the class at that moment. In other words, he will feel successful.

As with Denarius's class, you can readily see warmth and positivity in Na'Jee's *Cold Call.* He, too, is smiling while he *Cold Calls.* In the following photo he is listening to Marcel's answer to his first *Cold Call,* relaxed and smiling. His smile says to his student: *This Cold Call lets me hear your voice. It's a good thing.*

The first type of conflict is the internal conflict.

Notice also in the next photo, Na'Jee's body language after he has *Cold Called* Yedidiah and is listening to his answer. His body language—eyes on Yedidiah, facial expression of genuine interest, tilted head as if he's considering each fascinating phrase—is a different form of positivity. Na'Jee looks like a college student listening to a peer in a seminar. His body language says: *What you are saying is interesting and important. I am listening. I value it.* This is as important to positivity as a smile—possibly more so. He is building and reinforcing scholarly identity.

There are five key principles implicit in effective *Cold Call*, all of which Denarius and Na'Jee have modeled already. They are: positivity, predictability, universality, intentionality, and connectedness.

# Principle 1: Keep *Cold Call* Positive

Both Denarius and Na'Jee endeavor to make a *Cold Call* feel positive and natural. Their smiles are the biggest indicator of this and they remind students to relax, that their teacher wants them to do well. You can also verbalize this idea so it's even more obvious. "We're going to do *Retrieval Practice* with *Cold Call* to help us remember these ideas. I'm excited to see how we do." Or you could say what Brittney Moore says to her third graders as she's observing student work and preparing to *Cold Call* in the video *Brittney Moore: So Hard to Choose*. "It's going to be so hard to choose one person to share out," she says, her voice upbeat with excitement. The implication is clear: You choose someone to *Cold Call* because you love their work and the class will benefit from hearing their thinking. Under those conditions, there's scarcely a child who wouldn't want to be *Cold Called*. After all, it's an honor. Or check out the video *Summer Payne: Individual Turns*, which I've retrieved from the archives of *TLAC 1.0* (those super-cute kindergarteners are probably in college by now!) so you could enjoy her singing "individual tu-urns, listen for your na-ame" and be reminded that the positivity of this or any technique is almost always within your control. I mean, your *Cold Call* is your turn. Who doesn't want their turn?

Listening behaviors are also important to establish the positivity of *Cold Call*—think here of Na'Jee's tilted head listening to Yedidiah. They make the interaction feel like a conversation, not a quiz show, with the positivity deriving from the feeling that the teacher values students' ideas. A bit of head nodding or other gesturing that communicates something like, *what you are saying now is very interesting*, is always helpful, as is movement. Somehow a teacher who is walking slowly as she listens communicates a kind of professorial interest.

Of course the greatest source of positive emotions for students during *Cold Call* is their own success, and it's a powerful motivator. *Cold Call* requires that students engage in an activity that may be challenging, unpredictable, and maybe even cause a bit of healthy tension. And then they succeed. That feeling of success can be powerful, even more so because they've succeeded at something that is hard. This doesn't mean all *Cold Call* questions should be easy—the challenge has to be real. But all the more reason that teachers should plan their *Cold Call* sequences to *begin* with a question that sets students up to succeed as a preamble to greater challenge. Then students, as we saw in Na'Jee's video, can ride the cycle of success-motivating-success for the duration of the lesson.

One additional aspect of *Cold Call* that leads to positivity can occasionally elude teachers when they aren't prepared: both the question and the ideal answer should be clear. Every teacher has had the experience of asking a student a question that, in retrospect, was confusing or unclear. It's doubly important to avoid this kind of question when *Cold Calling*, when it is essential that students are maximally set up for success. Many teachers address this challenge by planning their exact questions and answers word for word as part of their lesson-planning process.

One final bit of guidance in making sure *Cold Call* is a positive experience is to do a bit of culture building around how to respond when students have been *Cold Called* and aren't sure of the answer. Consider the power of explaining to students in advance what to do if (1) they don't know the answer ("Say, 'I'm not sure' and then add 'but' and then give me your best guess," or "Restate the question and tell me why or how you're confused"); or (2) their classmate can't answer ("Be supportive. Smile warmly and keep your eyes on them. Don't raise your hand until they're done trying, and remember that all of us will be there at some point.")

## Principle 2: Make *Cold Call* Predictable

In some ways *Cold Call* works backwards: it's designed to influence what precedes it, to cause everyone to think harder by creating an expectation that anyone might end up being asked to answer just afterwards. This means that the more likely it is that students see a *Cold Call* coming, the more focused, active, and attentive they will be during the thinking that precedes it. Thus *Cold Calling* should be predictable. Using it regularly is one of the best ways to do that. If *Cold Call* is an everyday thing, students will make a habit of increased attentiveness and get better and better at responding.

It's also important to think about the converse: If your *Cold Calls* surprise students, they may learn a lesson ("Darn, I should have been ready!"), but one too late to help them. They may also feel ambushed, caught off guard, and therefore more likely to be thinking about the past (*Why did she do that?*) than about the future (*I'm going to be ready!*). A *Cold Call* should never feel like a "gotcha" to students, and to use it that way—to try to embarrass Marcus a little bit by asking, "What did I just say, Marcus?" because you don't think he was paying attention—is to take a powerful and positive learning tool and cause it to undergo a counterproductive mutation that undermines trust between teacher and students.

You can see evidence of predictability in Denarius and Na'Jee's classrooms—mostly in the fact that students seem so unsurprised by their *Cold Calling*. They react naturally and . . . well, honestly, they hardly react at all. *Cold Call* is a familiar occurrence to them. In fact there's a bit of an equation implicit in that: the *more* it happens, the *more naturally* it unfolds and the more comfortable students become. If the response by students is so-so at first, keep at it. Make sure you've got the positivity, make sure your questions are good, and then persist. Over time it will become part of the fabric of your classroom and the biggest benefits will accrue when it does that.

Another way you can make *Cold Call* predictable is to make it transparent—to tell students it's coming. For example: "Take a few minutes to work on this then I'll *Cold Call* a few of you to hear your thoughts." Suddenly the incentive to do one's best work is even stronger. "*Turn and Talk* with your neighbor, and I'll *Cold Call* a couple of groups to share after your conversations." You can also signal that students can expect it during class by *Cold Calling* right at the beginning. Not only does this let students know it's coming and keep them engaged all lesson long, but to the degree that you find it awkward to start *Cold Calling* the first few times you do it, it's actually easier to do it right away. You can plan it and then there's no awkward feeling to overcome when it suddenly starts.

Another essential step in making *Cold Call* predictable to your students is a rollout speech. Na'Jee's and Denarius's can't be seen in these videos because they happened on the first day or two of school. A rollout is the ultimate in predictability—you make the what, the why, and the how totally transparent to students before using the technique so they see it coming and know how to react. You might say something like:

> In this class I'm going to *Cold Call* you. That means I may ask for you to answer a question or share your opinion, whether or not you've raised your hand. This allows me to balance who participates and to hear from everyone. And sometimes I want to know what you and you alone are thinking. I'll try to remember to smile when I *Cold Call*, which is my way of reminding you that I always want you to do well. So if I call on you, do your best, even if you feel a little nervous. If you're stuck, tell us what you're confused about, and we'll help you out. That's what your classmates and I are here for. But, honestly, I think you're going to surprise yourself. Let's try a bit now. . .

BreOnna Tindall of Denver School of Science and Technology, whose teaching figures throughout this book, shared some great details of her rollout. "I tell them the difference between the different types of calls—I'll look for volunteers, I love hands, we'll do some warm calling. I might put a star on your page if I'm going to call on you. And there's also *Cold Call*, which is another opportunity for me to vary the voices in the room because sometimes I know that you know the material, maybe you're just shy, maybe you need a push, maybe you don't know that you know. We talk about that [when I roll out *Cold Call*] and they feel excited for the most part."

The last thing that can help make *Cold Call* feel natural and predictable in your classroom is practice—your own. An awkward and hesitant lead-in to the *Cold Calling* by the teacher makes students awkward and hesitant. Denarius and Na'Jee's *Cold Calling* seems natural, seamless, and conversational in part because they've done it a lot, but rehearsing a few times before class can help when you're just starting out. It's especially helpful to practice the first *Cold Call* or two—that's the one where you're most likely to pause or hesitate or suddenly change course. And since your working memory will likely be under intense pressure the first time you try it, practice smiling warmly when you rehearse—this will make it more likely that it comes off positively the first few times you try.

## Principle 3: *Cold Call* Should Feel Universal

Teachers who use *Cold Call* take pains to make it clear that *Cold Calls* are universal. They come, without fail, to everyone and are not an effort to single out students for lack of attentiveness, in response to specific behaviors, or according to some other hidden calculus. You can see this clearly in Denarius's class. He *Cold Calls* seven students—enough to make it clear that anyone might be called, not just particular individuals or groups of students. This is typical. He tends to *Cold Call* in batches so that it doesn't appear as though one person is "in the teacher's sights." And he's careful to *Cold Call* all types of students—not just those whose attention might be questioned, say, or who are obviously high or low on the achievement scale. Finally, there's nothing in his affect—squinting, for example—to make it seem as though he's looking for someone or some behavior to latch on to. The seven students he *Cold Calls* are evenly spread out around the room. These aspects seem trivial but they are visual reminders that *Cold Call* is about expectations—"This is how we do it here"—and Denarius underscores this by asking *Cold Call* questions in a calm, even tone, with a smile or a look of sincere interest.

Be cautious, then, of tying your *Cold Calls* to specific behaviors when you're not sure students are eager to be called on. If you say, "Hmm, I see you hiding over there, Caitlin," you not only risk making Caitlin self-conscious but also cause students to think about whether they look as though they are hiding and how they should look if they do (or don't) want to be *Cold Called*.

Of course there are times when the *Cold Call is* personal. Sometimes we do want to message to a student, *I chose you for a reason; I want to hear your opinion; your voice matters.* But that reason should almost always be a positive one. You are selected as an honor, or because of a unique perspective, or because I want you to know your voice matters. Brittney Moore's beautiful *Cold Calling* where she describes how she can't decide who to call on is a great example. Occasionally it will be clear to a student that they've been selected because they've made a common error that's worthy of study. If you intend to try that, make sure to read technique 12, *Culture of Error*, to make sure the context makes students feel secure and supported.

Na'Jee is also using *Cold Call* in a small group. In a way that's systematic, as it signals that *Cold Call* applies everywhere. Some teachers tend to think of small groups as more informal and not the place where systems and techniques apply. But it's also worth remembering why we are in small groups (for example, reading groups): We think what we're doing there is so important that we are willing to multiply the amount of resources we apply per student. If that's the case, we should use the systems that build productivity and focus too. Na'Jee is warm and welcoming with his reading group of four but he *Cold Calls* nonetheless. So do Brittney and Summer.

## Principle 4: *Cold Call* Intentionally

Perhaps this is the unspoken principle that supports the other four, but it is helpful to say directly: Although your *Cold Calls* may sometimes or often appear random to your students, they should usually be intentional and, often, planned before you execute. In Chapter Two, Lesson Structure, I discuss deciding in advance whom to call on—either specific students or categories. Your notes might say, *CC Abraham/Sasha* or *CC two quieter voices* or *circulate to CFU and CC an "almost right."* These require you to use data—either from assessments, such as *Exit Tickets*, or from real-time observations during the lesson. Brittney Moore *Cold Calls* one of her students three or four times in the lesson we taped. She wanted to give her extra practice because, in looking at the data the night before, Brittney had noticed that this student was struggling and wanted to make sure she got lots and lots of at-bats. Sometimes you will have to make the choice of whom to call on with a tighter turnaround, after *Active Observation*, for example. Then you'll want to use student responses to determine whom you will call on after the moment of *Everybody Writes* or *Turn and Talk*.

Most of the time when you *Cold Call* a student to contribute their thoughts to the conversation, you should have a decent guess of what they are going to say—or you should select them because of what you know about their patterns of academic participation, success, and struggle.

> **Pre-Call:** In Pre-Call, you reveal to the student you call on that your *Cold Call* is intentional by letting them know in advance that you will be asking them to speak. Christine Torres does this during her Keystone lesson when she tells Makaye during the *Turn and Talk*, "I'm coming to you to share." This tips a student off that you will *Cold Call* them. This can allow extra time to prepare or to imply that their idea is especially worthy, thus building positivity. You could also use pre-call before students have completed their work to incentivize effort. "I'm going to call on you for question #4. Make sure

you've taken time to double-check it." You can also occasionally use it to signal discussion dynamics from the outset. For example, after a few minutes of writing about how the protagonist is changing, you might kick off the conversation by saying, "Can't wait to hear your thoughts. Let's start the discussion with Jasmine, then Carlos, and then Imani. Make sure you build off each other and use your *Habits of Discussion* . . ."

Teachers are sometimes concerned that using *Cold Call* may be counterproductive by making students anxious. It's important to be aware of students' concerns and also to do our best to assuage their anxieties. I very rarely see a student who cannot adapt relatively quickly—almost never in classrooms where *Cold Call* has been rolled out positively and according to the principles I describe in this chapter. There is not much to be anxious about in being asked questions by a caring adult.

That said, no two human beings are the same and you may at some point have a student who struggles with *Cold Call*. I offer two bits of guidance in such a case: first, an extra bit of relationship building goes a long way. Speaking to a student privately and reassuring them of your appreciation of them and your belief in their ability to handle any of your classroom expectations is a good first step. Second, offer initial modifications; for example, let the student know in advance via a pre-call or perhaps a nod that a *Cold Call* is coming the first few times you use it. If that's the case I would also suggest engineering the student's first experiences so they are sure to be successful—and the student is able to answer and feel quietly successful (as opposed to heaping on a lot of praise, which might only make the student self-conscious). "Please read the directions for me, Chris," is a great starting point (the answer is right in front of them). It's worth noting that the most effective response to anxieties—even those far more pronounced and debilitating than a bit of nervousness—is "gradual systematic exposure" to anxiety-inducing phenomena, as Jonathan Haidt and Greg Lukianoff note.[10] The solution to a child who's afraid to jump into the pool is to encourage him to do so in an environment of psychological safety. The accomplishment of the task usually conquers the fear.

## Principle 5: Connect Your *Cold Calls*

From the teacher's perspective much of *Cold Calling* is about deciding strategically who will talk (though it may appear random from the student's seat). But in many ways *Cold Calling* is also about socializing *listening*, and the fifth principle is about maximizing that potential. Unbundling and using follow-on prompts are two ways to do that.

When you "unbundle," you break up larger questions into a series of smaller questions, ideally with contingent answers, and distribute them to multiple students. This can help build energy and momentum in your pacing; it also builds a culture of peer-to-peer accountability.

Answering one part of the question requires students to listen and react to the previous answer. Consider, first, Ms. Martin who has *Cold Called* D'Juan to ask him how to find the volume of a cylinder. The class listens while D'Juan ably describes the necessary calculations, but they become increasingly passive participants to the exchange. Actually, D'Juan really knows his stuff and he proudly stretches out his answer so it's as thorough and methodical as it can be. Ironically this has a counterproductive effect on the class. The longer the answer goes on, the easier it is to tune out. Students realize they won't be answering this question.

Now, compare that sequence to this one, in which Ms. Martin unbundles the question:

*Ms. Martin:*  How many variables and constants do we have to consider in finding the volume of a cylinder? D'Juan?

*D'Juan:*  Three of them.

*Ms. Martin:*  Good. Tell me one, Janella.

*Janella:*  Radius.

*Ms. Martin:*  OK, and D'Juan, is that a variable or a constant?

*D'Juan:*  Radius is a variable.

*Ms. Martin:*  OK, so what's the other variable, Carl?

*Carl:*  Height is the other variable.

*Ms. Martin:*  Good. So, what's the constant that we need, Kat?

*Kat:*  Pi.

*Ms. Martin:*  And how do we know it's a constant, Jameer?

*Jameer:*  Well, because it never changes.

*Ms. Martin:*  Good. So, Taylor, when I multiply my constant and my two variables, I get my volume, right?

*Taylor:*  Well, no, you need to square your radius.

*Ms. Martin:*  Ah, yes. Thank you, Taylor. Well done.

By breaking up a single question into pieces and *Cold Calling* multiple students, Ms. Martin keeps all students on their toes; in making questions contingent on one another, she causes students to attend even more closely to what the others say. Not only were six students engaged actively where only one had been before, but all students were likely thinking through the answers silently, given the plausibility of being called on. And because the students are all working together toward answering a question, unbundling tends to build a positive cohesive culture. It makes school a team sport.

Follow-on is the term for sequencing a series of more open-ended prompts that similarly cause students to listen to, reflect on, and expand one another's answers. Let's say Ms. Carrasco is teaching her students about plate tectonics.

| | |
|---|---|
| *Ms. Carrasco:* | Jennifer, what does this tell us causes earthquakes? |
| *Jennifer:* | The plates. |
| *Ms. Carrasco:* | Doing what? |
| *Jennifer:* | The plates colliding. |
| *Ms. Carrasco:* | Can you develop that a bit, please . . . Jalen? |
| *Jalen:* | Well the plates collide and sometimes one slides under the other but other times they scrape alongside each other. |
| *Ms. Carrasco:* | Good addition, Jalen. One thing we haven't talked about is the role of pressure. Teana, can you add to that? |
| *Teana:* | I think so. I think what happens is that as the plates collide in either of the ways Jalen talked about, the pressure builds up and builds up and then suddenly there's an earthquake. |

In this sequence Ms. Carrasco has used follow-on prompts—phrases that explicitly ask students to expand upon or react to the previous answer in order to build a culture of listening. Her phrases are *Can you develop that, Jalen?* and *Can you add to that, Teana?* I'm sure you can imagine others. Agree or disagree is a common one though I tend to prefer prompts that don't limit potential responses to just two. It's worth noting the difference in her follow-ons: the first, to Jalen is open ended—he can develop in whatever way he wants—but Teana's comes with guidance—please talk about the role of pressure. In either case, effective listening is reinforced and made critical to success.

## Four Purposes for *Cold Call*

In the previous section, I discussed principles for *how* to *Cold Call*, but it's also important to know *why* you are *Cold Calling* so you can make adaptations accordingly. I can think of at least four purposes for the technique.

### Purpose 1: Voice Equity

Let me begin by describing a *Cold Call* of my own, one you might not think of as a *Cold Call* at first but one that I hope will frame the conversation about it in a new light. I have three children and at dinner recently the discussion was dominated by my two older children. Their voices were confident. Of course, we would want to know what happened to Aijah and Jane in math class or Nilaan and Derrin at soccer practice. My littlest sat quietly at the end of the table, tracking the conversation with her eyes. Her brother and sister are five and seven years older, so perhaps she wondered: Were her stories from the day also relevant to the discussion? Would they meet with approval from her older siblings? When and how might she break in to try?

So I *Cold Called* her, turning to her at a tiny break in the discussion, and saying, "What about you, Goose? Are you still doing astronomy in science?"

She had not volunteered to join the conversation but I wanted her to know her voice mattered, and that her contributions were important. I wanted to show her the importance of her voice to the conversation. If she felt nervous, I wanted to break the ice for her.

There are few things more inclusive you can do than to ask for someone's opinion or input, especially when they do not yet know whether their voice is important in a room. To ask a student who has not volunteered, "What do you think?" is to tell them their voice matters. This idea is called "voice equity" and I first began to use it after a conversation with some colleagues who trained teachers for the Peace Corps in sub-Saharan Africa.

In many parts of the countries where they worked, "Girls are not called on," one of the team, Becky Banton, noted. There's an unspoken gender norm and girls often do not speak up readily. Sometimes the norm comes from their families and sometimes despite their families. The expectation is transmitted invisibly, socially, mysteriously—but inexorably.

"They sit quietly in the back of the room knowing the answers but not actively participating, not raising their hands, not going to the board," Becky noted.

"When our teachers *Cold Call*, especially when they know a girl has a good idea by having circulated first and they say, 'Come forward. Tell us your thinking,' the girls answer and they succeed and you see it in their faces," said Audrey Spencer. "It's so fast. In the space of a single class. It builds their confidence and then we see an increase in their achievement."

When there is a norm or an expectation that a student should not or cannot speak in class, be it societal (girls should be passive) or personal (there are three kids who volunteer; I am not one of them), the *Cold Call* breaks the norm *for* the student, absolving her of the responsibility for the violation of what is or appears to be a social code and perhaps even causing the student to see the code as a false construct.

*Cold Call* can remind a student that their voice matters and, often, that they are capable of participating credibly. In that sense it is a reminder that part of a teacher's responsibility is to reinforce everyone's right, legitimacy, and sometimes, just maybe, responsibility, to speak—for the sake of their own learning and to contribute to the classroom community.

In fact, a recent study suggests just how powerful *Cold Call* is in shaping students' beliefs and expectations about their own participation. The study, by Elisa Dallimore and colleagues, tested the effect of *Cold Call* on voluntary participation by assessing what happened over time to students in classes where *Cold Call* was frequently used by the teacher as compared to classes in which it was not used.[11] What they found was that "significantly more students answer questions voluntarily in classes with high cold-calling, and that the number of students voluntarily answering questions in high cold-calling classes increases over time." There is a double effect, in other words. Not only do more students participate in classes where the teacher *Cold Calls* because of the Cold Calls directly, but also because afterwards—perhaps because they experience success or perceive the norm of universal participation more strongly—*they begin to participate more by choice*. Further, the effect the authors describe "also increases over time." The more the *Cold Calling* becomes part of the fabric of class the more profoundly it causes students to choose to raise their hands. Finally, students' affective response to class discussion changed. The authors found that students' comfort in participating also increased. Being *Cold Called* didn't cause stress; it caused comfort and confidence.

Purpose 2: Creating a Culture of Engaged Attention and Loving Accountability

Later in this chapter—in technique 36, *Means of Participation*—you will see a soccer coach, James Beeston, explain to his players why he is going to *Cold Call* them during training: "Sometimes I might call on you guys even if your hand isn't raised, because the game requires you to be switched on at all times." What James knows is that if the game demands it, practice must prepare them for it. His job is to help them be the best athletes they can be. Prepare the child for the road, not the road for the child, as the expression goes. Somehow, we understand that a coach should prepare each athlete so they can hope to reach the highest level. This is the sign of a good coach and part of how a coach shows that he cares. Perhaps this is why the bonds between athletes and their coaches often run so deep.

Does it need to be said that teachers should prepare each learner as if they will go to the highest levels too? That this means a learning environment that also requires them to be, in James's words, "switched on at all times"? To care about young people is to build an environment that lovingly and supportively prepares them for success, and that requires most of all effort and attention. Where people direct and focus their attention and how successful they are at focusing that attention will play a large role in determining what they accomplish, in the classroom and more broadly. And attention is a habit, mostly shaped by both individual decisions and larger culture. The effect of smartphones on our capacity to concentrate should make that clear enough.

*Cold Call* is one of several tools that builds a lattice of loving accountability into your classroom culture. Certainly you can decide not to use it and leave your students' levels of effort and attention to chance. Many teachers do. But, in my opinion at least, it is a disservice to the young people we care about to not immerse them in a culture that socializes them to attend and focus and give their best every day. James *Cold Calls* because he cares. It is the same for a teacher.[12]

## Purpose 3: Checking for Understanding

As I discuss in Chapter Three, knowing the difference between "I taught it" and "They learned it" is the core challenge of teaching and requires effective, real-time data collection. This is one of *Cold Call*'s most important contributions. To fully assess what students in your class know you must be able to ask questions of any (and every) student at any time. Students who voluntarily participate are more likely to know the answer than the students who don't. If you are limited to assessing only these students when you ask a question, you will never be able to assess all members of the class, and you will always think the class has learned more than it has. When you set out to use questions to assess students' understanding, your default should be to use significant amounts of *Cold Call*. This will allow you to not only call on people "randomly" but to go one better and to call on what is likely to be a statistical sample of the room—or on students you are worried about. These things are critical to ensuring the accuracy of the data you gather.

A second, related application: One of the biggest challenges in checking for understanding is the gap between performance and learning. What our students appear to be able to do at the end of a lesson is almost always in part a false positive. They have not yet begun to forget. We assess what we think our students know at the end of a lesson and even if their answers are all correct, we are likely to overestimate their knowledge because forgetting has not yet occurred. What's critical to arresting the pervasive force of forgetting is *Retrieval Practice* (see technique 7) and *Cold Call* is the best way to build *Retrieval Practice* into your lessons. It allows you to make your *Retrieval Practice* speedy and energetic so you can do it frequently. Students like it and it allows you to maximize the number of students retrieving every answer. Denarius Frazier's video *Parts of a Circle* is an example of this: He has ensured long-term mastery of key geometric terms via *Retrieval Practice*, and the *Cold Calling* makes sure everyone is benefiting.

## Purpose 4: Pacing

Picture this scene from a classroom near you. Mr. K is reviewing a problem set from last night's homework. He says, "OK, who'd like to tell us how they answered number 2 on the homework?" Pause. Crickets. Finally, after five or six seconds, Natalie raises her hand. Unfortunately, Natalie also answered the previous question, so Mr. K tries another approach. "I'm seeing the same two or three hands," he says, scanning slowly and awkwardly. "Do I need to remind you that participation is graded in my class?" Teachers waste a great deal of time—ten or fifteen seconds per question, perhaps, but hours and hours over the long run, doing what Mr. K is doing: pleading for someone to answer their questions. What's worse, hearing your teacher plead for someone to participate slows the pacing—students' perception of passing time—to a crawl. It would have been a lot simpler, a lot faster, and a lot less painful for everyone for Mr. K to say, "OK, let's take a look at the second problem. How'd you answer that one, Mamadou?"

One of the best ways to engage students in learning is to make it feel dynamic and worthwhile, to give it flow. This makes it feel like something important and engaging. Pleading for hands is the anti-flow. It announces that the train has come to a halt and is stuck on the tracks. It causes students to lose faith in a teacher's competence ("See, nobody even participates in Mr. K's class; he's so boring") and in the value of the classroom. *Cold Call* is one of the best ways to control the pace of class, keeping things moving when you want (like Na'Jee Carter, who uses his *Cold Call* to keep things moving), or to slow things down a bit like Denarius Frazier, who uses it to disincentivize eager hand-raising that might put pressure on him and students to go faster.

## Two Common but Important Misconceptions

There are two common misconceptions about *Cold Call* that warrant discussion. In both cases they involve confusing *Cold Call* with a different technique.

The first misconception involves random generators—names of students written on popsicle sticks and drawn from a can or a computer app to select students at random to participate. Using such random generators is common and participants at workshops often suggest it as the best way to *Cold Call*. Random generators can be quite useful at times, but I want to explain why they are not to me an example of *Cold Calling*. Again, they're fine to use sometimes but the reasons they are not a form of *Cold Call* are important and I want to take a moment to explain them.

The first reason is that sticks aren't strategic. Intentionality—whom you call on and when—matters. You choose to call on Daniella or Domari because they have a great answer or because they've been quiet or because they are often confused in similar situations or because they are your "still waters run deep" students (the ones who never volunteer, yet jaws often drop after their unexpected, insightful comments). Earlier I discussed the importance of deciding whom you will *Cold Call* and why. *Cold Call is rarely actually random, though it may appear to be so from the students' perspective.*

In fact, it's often beneficial to *communicate this intentionality to students*. Using a random generator *makes it explicit that you are not making intentional decisions about who to call on*, but this is often the most important part. For example, to say: "David, what are you thinking?" tells David that you value his unique opinion and are thinking about his perspective at that moment. To use sticks is to say, "Anyone can go next. It's all about the same to me." There is no longer anything special about David being asked his opinion, then; a popsicle stick made the choice.[13] The message of inclusiveness—your voice matters—and voice equity is not communicated by randomness.

One other key difference is efficiency. Getting out the popsicle or lolly sticks takes time. Each time you pull one ("Oh, boy! Let's see who it is! Whoops, Jaden's not here . . .") takes time. And it interrupts the flow of normal conversation. It's hard for Amari to truly build off and elaborate on Janelle's point if there's a carnival event in between.

Again, I am not saying not to use popsicle sticks. One benefit is that they are psychologically easy and don't require as much bravery of teachers as *Cold Call,* so they can be a starting point for teachers who are anxious about not calling on students without their hands raised. And they can be a fun and easy way to remind your students that it's important for everyone to participate. They might work well with *Retrieval Practice*; the game-ishness of stick pulling is more of a match for content that is organized around specific questions than a discussion that relies on the continuity of comments. But please be clear: Popsicle sticks are not the same as *Cold Call.*

The second misconception has to do with a technique often called "hands down," in which the teacher tells students to put their hands down because she is *Cold Calling.* Do this too many times and students may not raise their hands. Again my argument is not that "hands down" is not a valid approach—it's an adaptation of *Cold Call*—but I think it is one with limitations, so it's important to understand the differences.

One of the primary purposes of *Cold Call* is to build student engagement and involvement. One of the most important results of being *Cold Called,* in fact, is the increased desire to *raise* one's hand and the increasing belief that one is capable of contributing. This was a big part of the story for my colleagues in the Peace Corps—not just that *Cold Calling* allowed girls to participate where otherwise they would have met with social sanction, but that *it caused them to gradually begin raising their hands on their own.* Therefore we want to balance *Cold Calling* with hand-raising to provide opportunities for students to *choose* to participate, even while we are choosing them via *Cold Call.* Further, hand-raising provides critical data. How many hands we see and how eagerly they have been raised tells us a lot about our class and their interests and confidence. Of course it's fine to occasionally tell students to put their hands down—it can be a nice change of pace and saying something like, "No hands for the next few minutes; I'm going to *Cold Call,*" can be especially helpful in making the Cold Call predictable. But since *Cold Calling* is something we can do just as easily when students are raising their hands, I think it's best to most often allow hand-raising during *Cold Call.*

So . . . can "hands down" or popsicle sticks be useful and an occasional fun change of pace? Yes. But teachers often assume they achieve the same ends and value as *Cold Call,* and I just want to be clear on why I think they are different.

### *Cold Call* in Synergy

The videos I've chosen of Denarius and Na'Jee's *Cold Calling* are unusual for a variety of reasons: first, because of the skill and proficiency they show. You're watching masters at work, at least in my opinion, and that's good to keep in mind if you're just beginning to use the technique. Your *Cold Calling* may not look like theirs right away. Another thing that's distinctive about these two videos is that they show Denarius and Na'Jee in the midst of sustained sequences of heavy reliance on *Cold Call*. This of course makes it easier to see and study how they do what they do. But it's also a distortion. Much of their and other masters' *Cold Calling* happens in combination with (and embedded within) other questioning and engagement techniques. In those instances the *Cold Call* itself occurs with less frequency but it is still essential because it works so well in synergy with other techniques. I write more about this synergy in technique 36, *Means of Participation*, and you can see this synergy in action in many of the Keystone videos.

In the video *Sadie McCleary: Keystone*, for example, Sadie begins reviewing answers as the *Do Now* ends. She *Cold Calls* Alissa, Alex, and N'Kaye, but then she sends students into a *Turn and Talk* to review the rules of particle motion. There's a *Cold Call* for Sterling. Then another *Turn and Talk*. J'Karah is *Cold Called* to review. Next, another *Turn and Talk* and a pre-call for Habib. For the follow-up—why isn't "average kinetic energy" incorrect?—she takes volunteers. Then another *Turn and Talk* followed by a bit of written practice. Back and forth she goes, changing the format or *Means of Participation* (technique 36). But the ways that *Cold Call* works particularly well in combination with other techniques deserve reflection. It is, for example, an ideal backstop to an activity like a *Turn and Talk*, which you might use to boost the ratio in your classroom, because *Cold Calling* afterwards increases accountability and therefore engagement in decentralized tasks where you can't monitor what everyone is doing. The *Turn and Talk*, on the other hand, provides a counterbalance to *Cold Call* as it takes the attentive focus developed via *Cold Call* and channels it into a peer-to-peer interaction that maximizes active engagement. So Sadie is especially likely to use *Cold Call* before or after a *Turn and Talk*.

*Cold Call* is similarly ideal for increasing student attentiveness and effort during an *Everybody Writes*. Giving students two minutes to write about how Jonas is changing in the chapter, for example, is a great activity, but it's even better if you *Cold Call* Ella coming out of it—"Ella, please share a bit of what you wrote about." And it's even better still if you *Circulate* slowly, reading students' thoughts as they write them and then *Cold Call* to validate and discuss one particular answer —"Ella, I was struck by your use of the phrase 'rising tension.' Can you tell us a bit about what you meant and where you see it?" A bit of loving accountability after independent work, accomplished through occasional *Cold Calling*, helps students get the most out of the independent task.

## Timing the Name

Deciding where in the *Cold Call* you will name the student who is to answer is important. The default approach is to ask the question, pause, and then name a student—for example, "What's three times nine [pause], James?" Using the sequence *question, pause, name* ensures that every student begins preparing an answer during the pause. For example, everyone does three times nine, with one student merely called on to give their answer aloud. Saying the name first, as in "Jairo, what's three times nine?" will result in fewer students preparing the answer because they know they won't be called on. Since the difference in ratio is significant (twenty-five students answering a question and one saying it aloud versus one student answering a question and twenty-five watching) is significant, so *question, pause, name* is the default.

In some cases, however, calling a student's name first—*name, pause, question*—can be beneficial. It can cue a student to listen attentively before the question has been asked and increase the likelihood of success. This can be especially effective with students who might be reluctant to be *Cold Called* or who might struggle the first few times, perhaps because of language processing difficulties, or because knowledge of English is still developing. Using the name first can also help establish clarity about your *Means of Participation* (see technique 36). After a chorus of *Call and Response* (technique 35), for example, saying, "And, Damari, why do we multiple there?" would signal to students that you're no longer asking students to call out answers. In some cases placing the name in the middle of the question—"And how does wind, Damani, play a role in the erosion process?"—can let your question pick up the conversational thread from the previous comment and create continuity, but confirm full attention from the student you're *Cold Calling* so they hear the question.

## TECHNIQUE 35: CALL AND RESPONSE

*Call and Response* has two parts: a teacher asking a question or sharing information and the whole class responding aloud in unison to answer the question or repeat the phrase—for emphasis or to help encode it in memory. If you are doing *Retrieval Practice*, for example, sprinkling in a few opportunities where everyone responds increases memory building.

*Teacher:* What do we call it when two very different characters are put side by side for emphasis?

*Class:* Juxtaposition!

Asking your class to answer or repeat in unison can also be a great change of pace that can expand participation and build energy and momentum. You can see Christine Torres using it at the beginning of the vocabulary section in her Keystone lesson. She introduces a new vocabulary word and asks her students to repeat it as a class.

*Christine:* The first word we're going to learn is the word *implore.* Implore on two— one, two . . .

*Class:* Implore!

*Christine:* And the word "implore" means what? Read it for me, please, loud and proud . . . [taking hands] . . . Jovon?

Why use *Call and Response* here? First it gives every student the opportunity for a bit of practice. The practice isn't exactly *Retrieval Practice* but rather pronunciation, which is important, especially with vocabulary. If students aren't confident saying a word, if they don't know how to pronounce it, they'll be much less likely to use it or attend to it as they are reading. Students tend to skip over words they can't pronounce.[14] So you'll notice then that every time Christine introduces a new word the whole class practices saying it, quickly and efficiently. Then, as they use the word, they're more confident and fluent in using it.

There are other reasons to use *Call and Response* here as well. Christine's class starts with a bang. The energy and enthusiasm are high. You might watch her and think, *Well, if my kids were that enthusiastic, I'd teach like that too,* but the converse is actually more true. Her students are enthusiastic because of her teaching moves. There is, for example, a connection between Christine's use of *Call and Response* and the fact that practically every hand in the room goes up when she asks for a volunteer to read the definition. For one thing, everyone has already participated. More broadly, people respond to norms and Christine has made the norm of participation visible and universal. The more consistent and visible norms are, the more they influence people. Everyone is involved and also sees everyone else around them positively engaged in the lesson. The natural thing to do, then, is to continue to match the norm of enthusiastic engagement that's been set. You're more likely now to raise your hand.

But there's even more going on in this moment of *Call and Response,* I'd argue. Humans have evolved to rely on what has led to our survival as a species. Those things have as much to do with our ability to coordinate and build mutual bonds as with anything we do as individuals. We survived by forming cohesive productive groups, and as a result we not only yearn to be a part of said groups, but also feel comfort and belonging when we are within one. "The brain is a social organ," Zaretta Hammond writes in *Culturally Responsive Teaching and the Brain.* "It has a 'contact' urge, a 'desire to be with other people.'" Every society on earth sings, for example, in part because singing is a way of becoming a part of the collective. We sing together and join our voices. The emotions of doing so are often surprisingly profound. This is why singing—and choral group singing specifically—is so often a part of worship all over the world.

Hammond also clarifies something fundamental about American—and Western— societies. We are ardent individualists. She cites Dutch psychologist Geert Hofstede's Cultural Dimensions Index, which includes a ranking of every country in the world according to its level of individualism in society. The United States is at the far end of the spectrum (with the UK not far behind). We are the most individualist—or the least collectivist—society on earth. This has its benefits—rugged can-do, get-it-done self-reliance is generally a good thing—but it also raises some questions. The first is what it is like to engage in the schools of an anomalously individualistic society if you come from a less individualistic one. Part of being responsive to students from other cultures is understanding that they have a more group-oriented view of the world. All that *me* and *you* can seem strange when you are accustomed to *we*.

A second question is what wisdom there is for our ardently individualistic schools in a more collective approach. Collective knowledge, group reliance, and identity derived through shared endeavor are in fact good things for learning. They make our schools more inclusive and increase the sense of belonging.

As I discuss in *Habits of Attention*, to feel a part of something is one of the most profound motivators in the world, as Daniel Coyle points out in *The Culture Code*. And we rarely change our minds about something we believe to be true unless we feel a strong sense of connection to the person sharing information that might cause us to change, Jonathan Haidt explains in *The Righteous Mind*. Our beliefs are a reflection of who we feel like we belong with. We take our identity from our community even if community is often fleeting in our society.

*Call and Response* is a tiny piece of the fabric of classroom culture, but done well it can create moments that build a sense of togetherness. Doing things in unison reminds us that we belong to a group. This is why *Call and Response* is motivating and why it is inclusive. It briefly but viscerally makes everyone in the room a part of something collective. Just maybe these moments feel a bit like the choral singing that is universal to societies and religions around the world.

It's worth observing that *Call and Response* can evoke this feeling only to the degree that the response reinforces togetherness, that is, students are truly in unison. That's why in-cues are so important. Christine's is the same each time she uses it. It's clear, crisp, and distinctive. If it's not clear what she is asking students to do and the cue is ambiguous, students might hesitate to follow through. Or not follow through at all. And then the momentary power of "all of us with one voice" is lost.

"The next word is caustic. Caustic on two—one, two . . ." Christine says, elevating her voice to make the cue distinctive in another way. The response is crisp and energetic again because the cue is consistent.

## More on the *Call and Response* In-Cue

### In-Cues

*Call and Response* is about universality. All students should respond or the message is perverse and the benefits lessened. But for students to participate enthusiastically, they must confidently know when to sing out without fear that they will be the only one singing. To ensure this is the case, use a specific signal—often verbal ("Class!" "Everybody!" "One, two . . .") to indicate that students should respond. Such a signal, called an *in-cue,* allows everyone to answer together and with confidence. Clarity of signal also lets you prevent called-out responses when you want to call on a student.

Because in-cues are critical, it's worth geeking out on them a little. There are several types of in-cues to consider.

### Count-Based In-Cue

Count-based in-cues are highly effective in that they are distinctive—you use them only for *Call and Response* and they make the timing of the response clear.[15] Because they have a short countdown (Christine says, "On two: one, two . . ."), they give students just a moment to prepare and ensure that everyone is likely to be on cue.

### Group Prompt

Using a collective term for the whole class can also work, especially since the prompts often remind students of group membership: Saying "Everybody" or "Class" reminds students to expect universal participation. Should you fail to get it, you can simply repeat the prompt with slightly greater emphasis: "*Every-body, please.*"

### Nonverbal Gesture

A third kind of in-cue is a nonverbal gesture: a point, a hand dropped, a looping motion with the finger. These have the advantage of speed and don't require you to interrupt the flow of the lesson. They can also be challenging, in that the tone has to be just right or they can seem schoolmarmish. Also there will be times when you might not have everyone's eyes (that is, finishing up notes or simply momentarily distracted), and then you run the risk of losing students in the response.

## Tone Shift

A fourth kind of in-cue employs a shift in tone and/or volume. The teacher increases inflection on and often the volume of the last few words of a sentence to imply a question; students recognize this as a prompt and respond crisply. This is often the most efficient form of *Call and Response*; in the long run, it's often the easiest to use—it's seamless, fast, and natural—but it's the hardest to use. It's easier for students to miss a cue and they will only recognize the in-cue if you use *Call and Response* consistently and frequently. If you don't feel immediately confident and comfortable with *Call and Response*, consider beginning, as many teachers do, by mastering a simpler cue.

Many teachers think of *Call and Response* as a technique that is applicable among younger students but less so among older students. They imagine both the ease and benefits of second graders, saying "Nice work, Cheyenne!" in unison as they do in the video *Akilah Bond: Keystone* or "Nailed it!" as a group to celebrate Akheem's work in *Sarah Wright: Tio Luis*.

But while it looks different with high school students, it is still valuable, as you can see in *Sadie McCleary: Means of Participation*. She calls on a student to explain what the Celsius temperature scale is based on, and when his response suggests that he is unclear about the boiling point of water, Sadie recognizes this as a key piece of information students will need in long-term memory. She uses *Call and Response* to cause them to practice recalling this piece of information, to better encode it.

Her cue is a *group prompt*—"Tell me"—and she uses it to allow her to clearly identify moments when she'd like students to call and respond throughout her lessons. Her *Call and Response* moments are fairly infrequent. This is perhaps part of why they work with older students; she doesn't overuse them. But it also means that the cue has to be clearer. Mixing in the odd *Call and Response* with high school students helps students focus attention and remain actively engaged. It's a bit of novelty and so draws attention. Evolutionarily, what's new and unexpected gets attended to more closely because in our ancient history as a species, it could contain survival information. This phenomenon is known as "novelty bias" and it tells us that even if *Call and Response* itself is not the most substantive way to interact with classroom content, judiciously done—as a variation rather than a theme—it can help build attention. But it also explains why Sadie quickly transitions away from *Call and Response* after one or two interactions. The benefits from novelty bias erode quickly.

Here's something seemingly obvious that both Christine and Sadie have in common. Their students are repeating something important. In Christine's class it's the vocabulary word she hopes to familiarize students with. In Sadie's class it's the freezing and boiling points of water.

This is important to note because *Call and Response* is one of those techniques that can have a bit of a catnip problem. It feels good to see your students engaged as a positive cohesive group. But this sense of momentary gratification also makes it easy to overuse the technique or to apply it in less optimal ways.

One interesting scene in Robert Pondiscio's outstanding *How the Other Half Learns*[16] involves Success Academy's CEO Eva Moskowitz observing a class with a group of school administrators.

Students are calculating the number of volleyballs in a group where the total number of balls is known, as well as the number of balls that are *not* volleyballs. The teacher calls on a child named Dmitri to discuss his work.

"The total is thirty-two," he concludes.

"The total number of what?" she pushes.

"Um . . . of . . . the . . ."

"The total number of . . .?" she loudly signals to the class to answer.

"Balls!" some, but not all, students call out.

"The total number of . . ."

"Balls!" This time the whole class answers in unison, each child seeming determined to yell louder than the next."

She goes back to the child who hesitated. "So, these thirty-two, Dmitri, are the total number of . . ."

The whole class again answers for Dmitri. "Balls!" they yell. It's deafening.

Moskowitz has seen enough and walks out. "You have an endemic problem with stupid shouting and call-and-response. Get them to a more intellectual place," she tells [the principal] back in the hallway . . . "They know what a ball is. They've known what a ball is since they were toddlers." Moskowitz is visibly irritated.

I agree with Moskowitz's assessment. With any "technique" there is the risk of overuse or misapplication. You get a hammer and suddenly everything looks like a nail. Multiply that risk times ten for *Call and Response* because of its appeal to teachers. It feels good to get a vibrant and upbeat response. The temptation can be to use it again and again. Suddenly it's a bit of a compulsion—overused with limited intentionality—that can easily devolve into poor execution. As with any technique you have to remain aware of the downside and answer the concerns that Moskowitz raises: For what purpose am I using it? What am I having students repeat and why? Am I overusing this technique?

### *Call and Response* with Reading

In a recent lesson, Eric Snider of Brooklyn was reading an article describing the characteristics of science fiction with his students. He began reading aloud with the expectation that his students would follow along, reading on their own at their seats. To help students feel motivated to follow along with him, he used a "*Call and Response* spot check."

"Some key facts to be mindful of," he began, reading, "Most science fiction writers create believable . . ." The next word was "worlds," but Eric didn't read it. Instead he signaled to his students, most of whom chimed in "worlds!" This appeared to demonstrate that they were successfully following along. Eric, however, was concerned. "That was about 80 percent [of us]," he noted, walking to the overhead projector on which he was displaying the text. "We are right here," he continued, pointing to the place in the text where he was reading. He then began again. "Most science fiction writers create believable worlds with familiar elements," he read, continuing past the point of the original spot check. "Science fiction often contains advanced . . ." Here he signaled again, whereupon all of his students chimed in: "*technologies!*" Having used *Call and Response* to gather data on who was reading along, and to reinforce their importance of reading along, he could now continue to read, knowing that students were more likely to be reading with him.

## TECHNIQUE 36: MEANS OF PARTICIPATION

The video *Sadie McCreary: Means of Participation* shows Sadie's AP Chemistry class at Eastern Guilford HS in Greensboro, North Carolina. Sadie is sailing along through the kind of lesson every teacher would wish for. Her students are willing and active participants. They're focused and productive. The lesson feels positive, rigorous, and dynamic. There's no downtime.

First, Sadie outlines a series of questions for students to answer "out loud with a partner." As she gives these directions the room crackles easily and naturally to life. Students chatter away, on task, without hesitation; everyone's participating. Coming out of the *Turn and Talk*, Sadie *Cold Calls* students warmly and inclusively to check their answers. These follow-up questions make sure the Think Ratio is high, too: "The Celsius temperature scale is based on what, Matthew?" she says.

Matthew is ready for her *Cold Call*, observing that the Celsius scale is based on the freezing point of water, and, with a gentle reminder, also its boiling point. Sadie switches to *Call and Response* to reinforce the importance of freezing point and boiling point and her students seem to read her mind, responding crisply and in unison. She switches back to *Cold Call* to assess how well students have understood the Kelvin scale and yet again things run almost perfectly to plan—she's easily able to sample the room and involve any student. An eager hand-raiser in the front corner really wants to say his piece. Some teachers might need to rely on him to drive the conversation—his is the only hand up at the moment —but not Sadie. The eager hand-raiser waits patiently—and does not call out—as she *Cold Calls* a few more students and then asks for volunteers, which she gets easily. There's no awkward pleading for more or different students to raise their hands. When Sadie asks them to take notes, students update their tidy and organized notes seamlessly.

The lesson seems to gallop along and yet it seems relatively effortless for Sadie, standing there at the front of the room, smiling graciously.

Sadie's lesson is so successful because of her clarity about what to do when. For students in her class, there are a series of familiar routines for how content will be engaged and there is no ambiguity about which routine to use when. We call these routines for engagement the *Means of Participation*. Investing time in planning them and ensuring that which you'll use when is clear to students makes you more likely to find yourself like Sadie: smiling in the midst of a class bursting with energy and productivity.

Routines are important. They "hack the attention economy in the classroom and help pupils learn hard things faster," writes Peps Mccrea, and allow working memory to focus on the academic task rather than the process for doing that task, which has become familiar and habitual. On the 100th *Turn and Talk* when you say, "With your partner, how does the structure of electron shells help us explain the behavior of the noble gases? Go," students have almost their entire working memory focused on the question and almost none on an array of potential extraneous distractions: *Who am I supposed to talk to? Does she want to talk to me? Is everyone else going to do it? Should I be writing this down?*

Cues are always the first step in any routine. "A routine," continues Mccrea, "is a sequence of actions triggered by a specific prompt or cue that is repeated so often it becomes an automatic [or nearly automatic] response." The cue starts the chain of actions for any habit. So *Means of Participation* involves framing clear routines for each of the formats by which students participate in your class and then signaling quickly, reliably (and often subtly) to students which format you'd like them to use. The cue sets students up to engage confidently, correctly, and with minimal load on working memory. If students participate in less than optimal ways—calling out answers when we don't want them to or not answering when we hope they will—it's often because we haven't clearly communicated the *Means of Participation* for a given question. Considering student responses through this lens can also help us to *assume the best* (see technique 59, *Positive Framing*). When students call out or engage in other behaviors we weren't expecting, considering whether our own framing of *Means of Participation* might have been unclear can be a helpful first step.

Watch again and you can see how intentional Sadie's cues are. Her "default"—the system of expectation for how to participate unless signaled otherwise—is that if she asks a question you raise your hand if you want to answer. There is always, also, the possibility of a *Cold Call*. This clarity about how to answer allows her to both take hand-raisers or *Cold Call* and to allow as much *Wait Time* as she likes. Students understand this because she has explained it to them. Occasionally, when she is especially eager for hands, she communicates that to her students by saying "Hands!" or raising her own. When she wants *Call and Response*, she says, "Tell me" and students understand that signal. When she says "With your partners," everyone knows a *Turn and Talk* is coming, and they know exactly how to engage their partner. Because Sadie has established these cues to make her *Means of Participation* clear, the room quickly comes to life whenever she asks a question.

In many classrooms, however, teachers ask students questions without signaling clearly in what format they should answer. When students have to wonder *Should I raise my hand? Can I call out? Was that question rhetorical? Should I write that down?* you get hesitation, confusion, and lack of follow-through instead of the crackling intellectual energy of Sadie's classroom. You get classrooms where teachers ask very good questions, but the same few students hesitantly call out answers again and again. Or classrooms where the teacher will ask a question and then after a few seconds of apparent impassivity from students, answer it herself. As I pointed out in the introduction to ratio, it doesn't matter how good the question is if only two or three students bother to answer it. *Means of Participation* is the signaling system by which you switch clearly and transparently among the formats in which students can answer, like *Cold Call*, taking volunteers, and *Turn and Talk* so everyone answers productively and confidently.

The word "default" here describes the basic rules of participation that are always in place in Sadie's classroom unless she signals otherwise. These are: raise your hand, don't call out, and know that I may ask you your opinion via *Cold Call*.

The first step in MOP, then, is the rollout where you explain the default (and perhaps some of the other systems you'll use for participation) and why. It should be brief but compelling. Better to just describe the default and add short descriptions of the other formats later rather than talk it to death on the first day!

Ironically one of the best models I have of a teacher doing this is not a classroom teacher but a soccer coach, James Beeston. The soccer field is not the classroom, but I submit that there's a lot for every educator to learn from how James rolls out his expectations in the video *James Beeston: Switched on at All Times*. I've transcribed what he says below:

> The main thing from tonight's session . . . It's going to require intensity from both a physical and a mental standpoint. I'm going to be asking you questions through-out, to check for understanding. Don't shout out the answer. That's a big, impor-tant thing because I want you to think about the answers that you're giving. If you know the answer and I go like that [raises hand], raise your hand. If you don't know the answer, that's OK. We'll work through it; we'll problem-solve together. Sometimes I might call on you guys even if your hand isn't raised, OK?, because the game requires you to be switched on at all times, so I am going to be calling on guys at times to make sure the focus is still there, all right, so we're locked in from the first minute to the last minute.

This "rollout" takes James about 45 seconds. He explains what he's going to do ("Some-times I might call on you guys even if your hand isn't raised") and why (". . . the game requires you to be switched on at all times"). He tells them what to do when he initiates a routine (". . . don't call out; I want you to think about the answers"). He sets his standards high but he also makes it safe to struggle ("We'll work through it; we'll problem-solve together"). And then he immediately begins practicing what he preaches so players understand that he means it because they start building the habit right away.

In fact a second video of James, *James Beeston: How Can We Use This?*, shows him ques-tioning his players a bit later (after they've practiced for 20 minutes or so). From a ratio perspective—how many participants think about his questions, how much of the time, and how deeply—it would be hard to do much better.

Sadie had a very similar rollout on her first day to set up her default. Then she layered in new routines and their cues using a chart like the following one, which captures some of the common routines students use to participate in class, the cues a teacher might use to signal them and some other factors to consider.

| MOP | Expectations | CUE | Notes |
| --- | --- | --- | --- |
| *Cold Call* (or Volunteers) | Raise your hand. I may call on hands or may *Cold Call*. | Default "I'll ask some of you to share" or "Be ready, I may *Cold Call*" to increase predictability. | Explain to students that if you don't signal anything else it means (1) raise your hand, (2) do not call out, (3) be ready for a *Cold Call*. |

| Volunteers (only) | I am looking to only call on volunteers, but I want lots of them. | "Hands!" "Your turn." Nonverbal: teacher raises hand as she asks. | Have a reminder ready if there are call outs (nonverbal or "Hands, please"). |
|---|---|---|---|
| Call and Response | You'll call out the answer in unison and on cue. | "Tell me." Inflection at end of question. | Sometimes use a signal that you're done with Call and Response too, e.g. "Now: hands" or "Now: Cold Call." |
| Turn and Talk | You'll Turn and Talk to a designated partner. | "With your partner . . ." "Turn and talk . . ." | Note that BreOnna Tindall has both shoulder and face partners. Cue is: "Face/shoulder partner." |
| Everybody Writes | You'll put pencil to paper . . . | "In your notes . . ." "Stop and jot . . ." "On your own . . ." "Silent solo . . ." | Have an "If you're stuck" starter ready. |
| Other "Means of Participation" might include Show Call, White Boards, and Hand Signals. | | | |

To establish this technique in your classroom, your might start by making a chart like the one above. Get specific as you plan about your expectations and cues. Finally, craft and practice your rollout. Read more about how to build a procedure into a routine in technique 50, *Routine Building*.

Once you've established the procedures, planning for your MOP can become part of your lesson preparation (see technique 3, *Delivery Moves*). To maximize engagement and flow, you'll want to be intentional about varying approaches. We see Sadie do this in her chemistry lesson. *Cold Call* into *Turn and Talk*, then some volunteers and a bit of *Call and Response*. After that a bit of *Everybody Writes*.

When I spoke with Sadie, she shared this guidance about how she plans for MOP: "On my best days I plan for it in advance. If it's a meatier question then I always have students write or *Turn and Talk* first to increase participation, then I circulate while they are talking and warm call a few students [I call this technique "pre-call"]. If it's a question that is easy enough to ask out loud and I want to gather data in the moment by calling on specific students, then I *Cold Call* students who are typically high or medium or low to get a sense of whether they understand the concept. For something really simple that I want all students to quickly remind themselves of—choral response and we all say it aloud."

# Frontloading

In a recent blog, London-based science teacher Adam Boxer shared an idea he called "frontloading" to get the most out of *Means of Participation*. His reflection started with the observation that even if you diligently communicate the desired *Means of Participation*, some students still may not hear it if it comes at the end of your directions. He gives this example:

> *"What is the word equation for photosynthesis? Please write your answer on your mini-whiteboard and hold it face down until I ask you to show me."*

"On the face of it, this is a good instruction. The question is clean and clear and the MOP is established in terms of how the students will write and present their answer," Boxer writes, but he adds that you may still end up with students raising their boards before you have asked them. "The second you ask them the question, they start writing down their answer (or at least thinking about it) and they are no longer listening to you. It's not that they are being defiant or messing around, they just didn't take in the instruction. And again, it's not because the instruction isn't clear . . . it's a property of its placement." He suggests frontloading—placing the *Means of Participation* at the beginning of the direction so that students hear it first and process it before they start thinking about the question.

> *"OK, in a second I'm going to ask a question. Please write your answer on your mini-whiteboard and hold it face down until I ask you to show me. What is the word equation for photosynthesis?"*

If routines aren't firmly established, he suggests using a script more like this to build reliable follow-through:

> *"OK, I'm going to ask a question and you are going to one [hold up a finger], write your answer on a mini-whiteboard; two [hold up two fingers], keep it face down; and three [hold up three fingers], show me only when I say."*

You might even ask students to repeat that back to you if you're still getting routines built, Boxer suggests.[17]

Here are some of his examples of other frontloaded *Means of Participation* phrases:

*"By putting your hand up in the air, I'd like you to tell me . . ."*

*"Without calling out, can anyone tell me . . ."*

*"In silence, you are going to . . ."*

"I'd wager ten quid that works better every time," he notes.

## Online Lessons: *Means of Participation* Icons

The shift to remote teaching posed a unique set of challenges to teachers' working memory—challenges my team and I felt ourselves when we led trainings online. Like so many teachers, we often found ourselves using a presentation to structure our session. As we presented one slide we were often thinking of what the next slide covered, and trying to assess how our participants were responding to the session—reading their expressions, toggling over to the chat to field their questions or respond to their comments, prepping a breakout room. The new setting and the addition of technology resulted in working memory overload and it was shockingly easy to forget how we wanted participants to engage in the content of each slide. Even if we'd planned our *Means of Participation* we sometimes forgot to use what we'd planned at the right time and in the right way. Or we remembered but struggled to listen and respond as well as we could have. Our solution was to use icons to make our *Means of Participation* easy to remember so our working memory could be focused on participants.

We developed a set of icons that we placed at the bottom of our slides to remind us of the *Means of Participation* we'd planned:

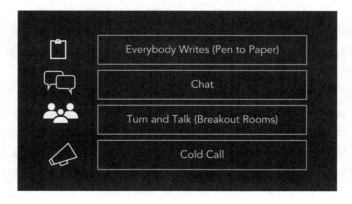

Suddenly we didn't have to strain to remember what participation moves we'd planned. With our working memory free we could listen far better to the discussion and think more deeply about the content. We shared this idea with several schools and watched them do remarkable things with it. Memphis Rise, a school in Memphis, Tennessee, for example, standardized the icons across the teaching staff and gave teachers a glossary of the terms and guidance on how to use them well. Here's a page from that document:

| Participation Method | Notes | Examples |
|---|---|---|
| 4. Chat to All – Wait Question<br><br>Wait | • **Definition:** Students type their responses into the chat to everyone and submit the responses on the teacher's cue.<br>• **Prior to Asking Question:** Make sure that chat setting is set to 'everyone publicly' and that students are clear on the whether the question is a speed question or wait question. When giving directions, you should make sure that students have selected "To: Everyone" in their chat menu.<br>• **Uses for Speed Questions:** Longer responses, responses that require more processing time, and data collection | • "For this question, I would like for you to prepare your response in the chat, but wait until I say 'go' to hit enter. We are going to give everyone a chance to get their thoughts together before we submit!"<br>• "Take two minutes to prepare your response in that chat. Wait to hit enter until I say go. Wow, nice work team. Take 1 minute to scroll back up and read the thoughts of your teammates. |
| 5. Cold Call | • **Best Practices Mirror 'In-Person' Instruction:** Cold call should be positively framed and used as a frequent participation method in the class. Language around 'cold call' should communicate an invitation to the discussion or to the class verbally.<br>• **Reminding Students of the Zoom Operations:** Especially early on in the school year, we should make sure that Cold Call questions include a prompt for students to 'unmute' themselves.<br>• **Uses for Cold Call:** Operational questions, low-level CFU questions, constructing discussion based off of chat responses | • "Why did Sean respond that way? Take 15 seconds to think about it. Mario, please unmute yourself and start us off with your thoughts."<br>• "Caleb, please pick up on 'When he...' unmute yourself, continue reading."<br>• "Rosa, you sent a beautiful response in that chat. Please unmute yourself and share it!"<br>• "Alex, please unmute yourself and build on that." |
| 6. Hand Raise<br><br>Raise Hand | • **Execution Notes:** Ask students to volunteer to respond to a question by raising their hand in the participants menu.<br>• **Narrated Wait Time:** Use narrated wait time prior to selecting a student so that all students have a chance to develop their response and navigate to the participants menu to raise their hand. | • "Number 3 was a little bit tricky for all of us. I am looking for someone to raise their hand and walk us through their thought process for it. If you're feeling confident, remember you can raise your hand by clicking participants and then 'raise hand'"<br>• "We have one minute to jot down our response. Raise your hand in the participants menu, if you want to start off our discussion. Ohhh, I got 2 hands already. Now 5 of us! Really nice work team!" |
| 7. Show Me | • **Definition:** Students share their responses visually on-screen.<br>• **Hand Signals:** Explain to students how to show their answer choices using their hands (1 for A, 2 for B, 3 for C, 4 for D)<br>   ◦ Ask a question, give students narrated wait time – to think or write – and then count down for the 'show me'<br>• **2.0 – White Board:** Have students write their answer to a problem or a question on a white board. On your cue, have students show their responses.<br>• **Uses for Show Me:** Note that 'Show Me' is very similar, in terms of outcomes, to a wait question or a private chat question. Use Show Me when you want to collect data from the entire class in a quick and efficient way. | • "When I say go, I would like for you to show me a 1 if you chose A, a 2 if your chose B, a 3 if you chose C, and a 4 if you chose D. Take 20 seconds to choose your answer go. Go!"<br>• "I would like for you to write your answer big to fit on your whiteboard. When I say go, show me your response." |

*Source:* Memphis Rise Academy, Memphis, Tennessee.

In the video *Madalyn McClelland: Maps*, you can see not only how Madalyn uses the icons to guide her own teaching but how to make participation transparent to students.

Interestingly, this is an idea that can also be productive in the classroom. One of my favorite schools in the UK, Torquay Academy in Torquay, has similarly developed a set of icons that they share with students. They also share the intent of the teaching techniques they represent so that when they see the "Wait Time" icon they know that the purpose is to think deeply and not rush, and so forth.[18]

# TECHNIQUE 37: BREAK IT DOWN

*Break It Down* is a powerful teaching tool, but it can be challenging to use because it is primarily a reactive strategy. It's useful immediately after an incorrect or insufficient answer.

How to respond effectively and efficiently in those situations is one of teaching's ongoing challenges. We know that repeating the question a little slower or louder isn't likely to help, but what do you do instead?

With *Break It Down,* the goal is to ask a question or present a piece of new information that will help the student answer correctly and will still cause the student to do as much of the thinking as possible. In the simplest terms, you want to provide the smallest viable hint, helping the student activate what he or she *does* know to get the correct answer.

In the video *Narlene Pacheco: Keystone,* you can see an example that shows both Narlene's skill and the challenges of the technique. Her kindergarteners are segmenting words—"bat" in this case—but one of her students has the letters out of order. She has b-t-a. "Segment bat for me," Narlene says, carefully managing her tell (see technique 12, *Culture of Error*). When her young scholar does this correctly, she points at her paper: "What did you write?" It's an ideal *Break It Down* since Narlene hasn't provided any new information. She's just asked her student to review her work with heightened attentiveness. If her scholar was able to get it right now it would be based entirely on a self-correction. But she does not yet see her mistake.

"Read what you have," Narlene now says, her second effort to *Break It Down,* but again it's not enough so Narlene goes a step further. "What's the first sound? Do you have that?" she asks. Her tone is impeccable: supportive, without a hint of frustration or judgment. "What's the second sound?" she continues. "Tuh" her student replies. She's narrowing her focus to a specific part of the work that's challenging. "What's the word?" Narlene now asks. "Buh-ah-tuh," her student says and in so doing catches her error and fixes it. Narlene has helped her student solve while doing as much of the work as she can, and her students is happy: She's figured it out rather than simply being told.

## Smallest Viable Hint

A teacher never really knows what knowledge a given student has, nor exactly how big the gap is between what the student knows and what he needs to know to succeed. Because the ideal is to cause a student to apply what he knows to the greatest degree possible, it's useful to try to provide the smallest (successful) hint possible.

Providing a minimal hint gets at the tension in *Break It Down.* Whereas one goal is to break things down to the least degree possible, another is to do it quickly, thus managing time and pace. Meticulously adding a thin slice of knowledge to each previous hint would be the perfect means of causing students to do the greatest amount of cognitive work, but would derail instruction in a series of exercises that destroyed your pacing and led to rapid frustration on your students' part.

Sometimes, in the face of a wrong answer, you'll have to move on to something else. So while your long-term goal is to maximize the cognitive work that students do, you'll also have to balance those long-term goals with practical short-term realities. The good news is that the more you use *Break it Down*, the better (and faster) your students will get at their half of the equation.

## How *Break It Down* Works

When you ask a questions and the answer is not sufficient to be considered correct, your first goal is to get the student to the correct answer. Your second goal is to keep your *Break It Down* rigorous by providing the smallest viable cue.

Take a look at the following figure. If you can provide a cue like A that makes the student fill in most of the gap, your student is likely to learn and remember more than if you use a cue like C. "Memory is the residue of thought," Daniel Willingham tells us. There's more thinking to remember in A.

Both are more challenging than D, which solves the problem without any *Break It Down* (by giving the answer or having another student give the answer). Again, you want the smallest cue that will work in consideration of pacing, timing, rigor, and so on. A is desirable if you can, but you won't always be able to. You'll have to use D sometimes, too.

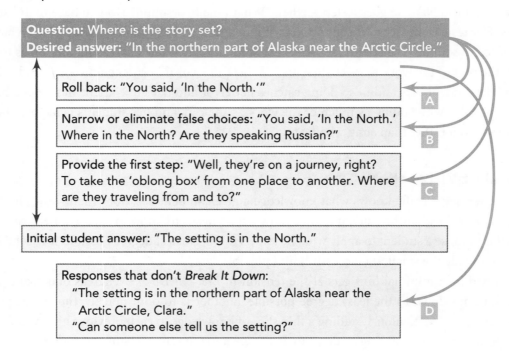

## Planning for *Break It Down*

One of the best ways to succeed with *Break It Down* is to prepare for it: with *Plan for Error* and *Exemplar Planning* (see Chapter Two), even if you don't predict the precise error students make, over time you'll get better at anticipating the kinds of things that students get wrong and the responses that help. You do an exercise like this, in other words, as part of a long-term investment in your own understanding.

As you plan to *Break It Down*—or even when you use the technique without planning—there are benefits to building your "range," the types of prompts you're comfortable using. We all tend to be creatures of habit; over time, our hints become predictable. Using a variety of ways to offer hints to students can help you connect with more kinds of thinkers, as well as provide a wider and more flexible array of help.

## Provide an Example

If you got a blank stare when you asked for the definition of a prime number, you might say, "Seven is one" or "Seven is one, and so is eleven." If you wanted to *Break It Down* further, you could cue: "Seven is one, but eight is not." You could then potentially take it a step further by observing, "Eight's factors include two and four." You can also provide additional examples if the question stumping the student was originally based on a category. For example, a student in Jaimie Brillante's fifth-grade writing class struggled to identify the part of speech of the word *owner*. Jaimie cued: "Well, *owner* would logically be the same part of speech as other words that end in *-er. Dancer, swimmer, singer*. What are those?" she asked. "They're people," the student replied. Jaimie prompted, "And people have to be . . . ," as the student chimed in, "Nouns!"

## Provide a Rule

In Christy Huelskamp's sixth-grade reading class at Williamsburg Collegiate in Brooklyn, a student guessed incorrectly that *indiscriminate* was a verb when used in the sentence, "James was an indiscriminate reader; he would pick up any book from the library and read it cover to cover." Christy replied with a rule: "A verb is an action or a state of being. Is 'indiscriminate' an action?" The student quickly recognized that it was modifying a noun. "It's an adjective," she said.

## Provide the Missing (or First) Step

When a student in her fifth-grade math class was unable to explain what was wrong with writing the number fifteen-sixths, Kelli Ragin cued: "Well, what do we always do when the numerator is larger than the denominator?" Instantly the student caught on. "Oh, we need to make a mixed number. So I divide six into fifteen."

## Roll-Back

Sometimes it's sufficient to repeat a student's answer back to him or her. Many of us instantly recognize our errors when they're played back for us, as if on tape. You can see a great example of this in the video *Jessica Bracey: What You Said Is*.

Jessica is reading a novel called *Circle of Gold* with her fifth graders. She calls on a student, Gavin, to analyze the character Toni's actions. His first answer is solid and he observes correctly that Toni is a sneaky character and that she is trying to trick Angel and Charlene into revealing their dishonesty, so Jessica follows up with another: "Why is that important?" Gavin does well here, too. It's important because if Toni tricks them, she'll reveal the truth about a stolen bracelet and defend her friend Mattie's honor. Now Jessica follows up again: "And what does that reveal about Toni as a friend?" This time however, Gavin gets stuck. He freezes and can't answer. To some degree this is inevitable . . . if we follow up good answers with further questions—be they *Stretch It* or *Right Is Right*—we are at some point going to get to the limits of what a student can answer at the moment. What then? How do we get the most out of them and foster success?

Jessica's response is simple and elegant. She uses a roll-back, simply repeating Gavin's words back to him: "So, Gavin, what you said is that Toni is sneaky and that she's a tricky person and that she's doing this because she is trying to get to the truth about who stole Angel's bracelet. Why is that important and what does that reveal about Toni as a friend?"

From there Gavin picks it up easily and closes out his analysis: this reveals that Toni is a helpful and good friend. She's trying to exonerate Mattie. He even uses the word "meticulous."

It's a great moment. Instead of being "stuck" and not only possibly feeling like he'd failed, Gavin persists and does another layer of analysis. He closes it out with success, doing the cognitive work himself.

## A Couple of Finer Points

Notice Jessica's affect, which is neutral and emotionally constant as she re-asks the question. She's not annoyed with Gavin. There's no negativity in the roll-back but there's also no sticky-sweet to it, either. She knows he can get it. So she is steady at the helm.

She also avoids "tipping" (see technique 32, *Phrasing Fundamentals*). That is, she's careful not to give too much away with her inflection. To understand how that might have happened, consider a roll-back in this situation:

You're studying the water cycle and you ask for an explanation of what happens to water vapor when it reaches the atmosphere. A student replies, "You get evaporation—water vapor forming droplets that become clouds." This is wrong, of course. He has confused evaporation with condensation.

Saying "You said, 'You get evaporation—water vapor forming droplets that become clouds,'" without discernible emphasis on any word makes your roll-back much more rigorous than if you said something like: "You said 'You get *evaporation*—water vapor forming droplets that become clouds.'" Emphasis on the word "evaporation" points the student to the fact that it is the error and he can much more easily make the correction. So managing inflection as Jessica does in the video builds rigor.

To be fair, if your student still couldn't answer your evaporation question, your next move might be to add some emphasis, but you'd want to start with the least hint possible because you want your student to do as much of the analysis as he can.

Jessica then wraps it up with another nice move. She reinforces Gavin's work positively—"That was really strong thinking" and then asks for positive reinforcement from the class.

## Eliminate Choices

When Jaimie Brillante's student struggled to recognize that *owner* was a noun, Jaimie could have eliminated some false choices as follows: "Well, let's go through some of the options. If it were a verb, it would be an action. Can you or I owner? Well, what about an adjective? Is it telling me what kind or how many of something?" Narlene also did this with her young scholar when she helped her to establish that her first sound had been segmented correctly.

## Fighting Rigor Collapse

Rigor collapse refers to what happens when you ask a hard question that students can't answer and progressively *Break It Down* until the big question is a question that now lacks the rigor of the original.

Scaling down the question gradually and cautiously so that students do as much of the cognitive work as possible is generally a good thing, but how do you achieve that without having a class consisting of simple, or even simplistic, questions?

In a lesson my team and I recently observed, a class was reading *The Outsiders,* and the teacher had asked students about the following exchange between Cherry, a "Soc" (that is, someone in a higher socioeconomic class) and Ponyboy, a "Greaser" (of a lower socioeconomic class):

> "You read a lot, don't you, Ponyboy?" Cherry asked.
>
> I was startled. "Yeah. Why?"
>
> She kind of shrugged. "I could just tell. I'll bet you watch sunsets, too. I used to watch sunsets, before I got so busy. I miss it."

The teacher asked what Cherry meant by "before I got so busy." Cherry was the sort of person who was likely "busy" doing things like schoolwork and activities, the sorts of things on her side of the class divide, whereas Ponyboy was not. They could have been kindred spirits—watchers of sunsets—but class and caste expectations (at least partly) put them in different places.

The kids didn't get this. When asked, students postulated that the sorts of things Cherry was doing included "going shopping and hanging out with friends." Because hanging out with friends was what Ponyboy would do, the teacher tried to break the complexity down a bit. "Can anyone connect this to the phrase 'the rat race'?" (They had discussed earlier Ponyboy's use of the term to disparage trying to succeed and cross the class divide.) Again students struggled to make the connection. So the teacher tried to break down the misunderstanding even further, hoping students would recognize the differences in how the two characters spent their time. Who was more likely to take music lessons? she asked. Cherry or Ponyboy? Why? Ponyboy didn't have parents to supervise him. If this was one sort of thing she might be doing when she was "busy," what were some others?

The good news is that the teacher uncovered and addressed the fundamental misunderstanding among her class, but the result was also that a rigorous, metaphorical conversation with implications about socioeconomic class had been replaced by a literal one. The sequence ended with a small and narrow inference about who was more likely to take music lessons and never got back to implications about character or class: rigor collapse.

After winnowing questions, then, it's often important to make broader sense of the answer students gave. Imagine, for example, if the teacher were to say something like, "Good; now connect that to one of the themes we've discussed from the book," or "Good; now connect that to our discussion of class divide."

If *Breaking It Down* takes a broad question and narrows it, a last move of connecting the narrow to a broader point is sometimes necessary.

## Notes

1. https://www.aft.org/sites/default/files/periodicals/willingham_0.pdf.
2. It's also worth noting that desirable difficulty assumes that students are successful in their thinking most of the time. We remember things better if we are able to answer, and less so, for the most part and for most of us it seems, if we cogitate on giant abstract questions of being and nothingness.
3. The term schema gets used vaguely and a bit recklessly—often in the classroom with very young students in a way-too-jargony way—so I tend to avoid it. I just refer to knowledge, which is really what it is: a lot of knowledge that is connected.
4. That is, if you know something you will begin to connect it to other things you are thinking and learning about and this will become a web of connections and facts.

Arguably this is the difference between knowledge and information and expresses why schools should be intentional about how they present knowledge—they can shape the organizational structure as much as the amount of knowledge that students learn (see technique 5, *Knowledge Organizers*). Ironically, though, those who claim that schools teach isolated facts not only don't appear to have been in many schools recently but appear to be lacking in knowledge about how human cognition works. As a side note, I am pretty sure the phrase "even isolated facts don't stay that way for long" comes from something Daisy Christodoulou has written but I have been unable to find a citation. Still, this is a good opportunity to recommend her book *Seven Myths About Education*.

5. An interview with Paul Simon on the Dick Cavett Show (https://www.youtube.com/watch?v=qFt0cP-klQI) provides a good example. Simon is discussing how he wrote the song *Bridge Over Troubled Water*. He describes being stuck and suddenly thinking of a Bach *Chorale*, which he transposed and inserted into the song. (But only because knowledge of chorales and what they sounded like was in his long-term memory.) At a second point, Simon recalls, a gospel album that had been "constantly on my mind" because he had been playing it over and over "must have subconsciously influenced me because I started to go to gospel changes. . . ." To do this he had to encode the knowledge of how gospel sounded generally and what gospel "changes" sounded like in his long-term memory by playing the record over and over. And understanding the idea of typical chord change patterns ("changes") itself relies of knowledge of musical theory; you have to know what "changes" are to listen for them. All of this caused insights to "come to him" suddenly while he was thinking about his own song. Inspiration and creativity relied on broad knowledge of Bach, gospel, and music theory. The insights were as much about the fusions of various schemes of knowledge as anything else.

6. Paul Simon, for example, would be extremely unlikely to think: I think I'll read up on Bach Chorales because just maybe they'd fit here in my song. He had to have the knowledge already to make the connection. The knowledge is what tells him what to "look up."

7. See Willingham, especially. "Memory is the residue of thought, meaning that the more *you think about* something, the more likely it is that you'll remember it later." Cognitive scientists like Willingham would argue that if you don't remember it, you haven't really learned it, which is why memory and learning are closely related. https://www.aft.org/sites/default/files/periodicals/willingham_0.pdf.

8. If there's one thing my work life under pandemic has taught me, it's that I need the possibility of having to answer in order to stay fully engaged. Having seen this in a thousand Zoom calls, I recognize its echoes in face-to-face interactions.

9. Another way that planning questions in advance can help: You're more likely to avoid asking a question for which, upon reflection, there is no clear answer.

10. Jonathan Haidt and Greg Lukianoff, *The Coddling of the American Mind* (Penguin Books, 2019), 29.

11. Elise J. Dallimore, Julie H. Hertenstein, and Marjorie B. Platt, "Impact of Cold-Calling on Student Voluntary Participation," *Journal of Education Management*, 2012. The authors compared 16 sections of a single course with 600-plus total students in which half of the teachers used *Cold Call* and half did not.

12. *Cold Call* is a great example of the Band-Aid Paradox from the Preface to this book. *Cold Calling* involves some anxiety for a teacher. Will it go well? Will it be stressful for students? It is harder to figure out how to remove Band-Aids slowly that to justify ripping them off quickly. Some people will choose the latter. But you don't have to.

13. I'm grateful to Ellie Ryall, a history teacher in England who shared this thought via Twitter. Since then, she has had the wisdom to ditch Twitter and therefore I can't give her the footnote she deserves.

14. You can read more about the impact of pronunciation and the importance of phonemic awareness in this seminal article on the Matthew effect in reading: https://www.psychologytoday.com/files/u81/Stanovich__1986_.pdf.

15. Also they can be cut short if students are not fully attentive in the lead-up to the *Call and Response*. A count of "One, two!" can occasionally be cut off by the teacher ("One . . .") to indicate that the class is not ready while still maintaining the anticipation of the fun that's to come.

16. The book is a profound and challenging reflection on schools, parents, and choice for dozens of reasons. I highly recommend it for far more substantive reasons than a reflection on *Call and Response*.

17. You can read the full blog post here: https://achemicalorthodoxy.wordpress.com/2020/10/14/front-loading/.

18. You can read more about Torquay Academy and Memphis Rise and their student-facing systems in the *Teach Like a Champion* "Field Notes." Memphis Rise: https://teachlikeachampion.com/blog/how-memphis-rise-helps-teachers-build-vibrant-online-culture/; Torquay Academy blog: https://teachlikeachampion.com/blog/learn-like-champion-torquay-academys-students-loop-tlac/.

# Chapter 8

# Building Ratio Through Writing

The amount and quality of writing students do in your classroom is one of the most important determinants of their academic success—possibly the single most important thing—so one of the simplest and most powerful shifts you can make is to increase the amount of writing—especially high-quality writing—your students do. Why ask, "Who can tell me what Jonas has just realized about what it means to be *released*?" and have one or two students answer, when you could say, "Please tell me what Jonas has just realized about what it means to be *released*. One minute to write some thoughts in your packet. Go!" This shift means every student answers and every student battles to frame the thought in precise syntax. Teachers often define a sentence as "a complete thought." By having students write more, we cause them to push their ideas from vague notions or developing ideas to complete thoughts; to practice developing complete thoughts is to practice perhaps the core task of thinking.

Increasing the amount of writing in your class raises important questions, however, from the practical (*How do I get them to actually write?*) to the philosophical (*Where in the sequence of learning is writing most valuable? How can I build a process-oriented culture of revision into my writing?*). For that reason, this chapter looks at techniques that can help you use writing for maximum effect on both Participation Ratio and Think Ratio.

# TECHNIQUE 38: EVERYBODY WRITES

When we think about writing that is part of the process of learning and mastering content, we see teachers use three primary types.

One of them, developmental writing, I'll define in technique 41, *Art of the Sentence*. For now I want to define a concept called *formative writing* and compare it to the more common *summative writing*. The technique *Everybody Writes* is about using formative writing prompts frequently throughout class.

Formative writing is writing in which students seek to decide rather than explain what they think. The purpose is to use writing as a tool to think: to develop and discover new insights rather than to justify an opinion they already have. In contrast, the purpose of summative writing is to explain or justify the writer's opinion and often to include evidence to create a supporting argument. Summative writing says: *Here is what I think and why*. To complete a summative writing task, students must already know what they think and be ready to marshal evidence and select an appropriate structure to make a cogent argument.

Summative writing is probably the most common form of analytical writing done in schools, in part because it looks like—and therefore (we often think) must prepare—students for the sorts of questions they are asked on assessments.

Again, in summative writing you have to know what you think before you start; in formative writing the purpose is to find out. Here's a gallery of summative and formative prompts from different subjects, placed side by side for comparison:

|  | Formative Prompts | Summative Prompts |
|---|---|---|
| ELA | What might the figs be symbolic of in this chapter? What are some reasons they keep appearing? | Explain the symbolism of the figs in the chapter and explain what Munoz-Ryan was attempting to accomplish with this symbol. Make reference to at least three occasions in which the figs appear. |
| Math | Why might solving this system of equations be more difficult than the last example? | Explain how you solved the system of equations above. |
| Science | Would you expect neurons to have a high or low surface area to volume ratio? Why? | Explain whether neurons have a high or low surface-area-to-volume ratio. Be sure to reference specific details about their cellular design. |
| History | What strikes you about Olmec civilization, especially any images or ideas that might appear in later Meso-American cultures? | Explain to what degree the Olmec civilization influenced subsequent civilizations in Mexico. Include two pieces of evidence to support your argument. |

| Early Elementary | How might Paddington be feeling in this moment? Why? | Based on this story, what are two character traits that describe Paddington? Support your answer with details from the text. |
|---|---|---|
| Arts | What ideas might the artist be attempting to convey with his choice of colors here? | Explain Picasso's theory of color during his Blue Period and the impact it had on the art world. |

One thing you've probably noticed is the openness of the formative prompts. They ask for "some reasons" rather than "the reason" or "the reasons"—all of them, presumably. The change encourages students to consider more than one possible answer and implies that it's hard to say how many reasons there might be. They ask questions for which it is hard to be wholly wrong as long as you are diligent and thoughtful, as in: "What strikes you about . . ." Perhaps the most important word in many formative prompts is the word "might." What *might* the figs be symbolic of? Rather than: What *are* the figs symbolic of? Or: What ideas *might* the artist be attempting to convey with his choice of colors? "Might" makes it clear that the goal is to explore, not to prove; the stakes are lowered.

The lowering of stakes can be powerful with writing. Putting words to the page is intimidating, so it is understandable that many students may have trouble beginning the process. "I don't know how to start," they tell us. Often, perhaps, that's because summative prompts set the bar so high. "Explain your opinion about X or Y." There are Xs and Ys in the world I have been thinking about for years and still have not fully arrived at an opinion about. I hereby propose that the ability to think without deciding too early is a very good thing intellectually. A formative prompt lets you start with maybe. *Maybe one reason is . . .*

A few years ago, we discussed the idea of formative writing with Ashley LaGrassa, then an eighth-grade English teacher at Rochester Prep in Rochester, New York, and she decided to give it a try. After all, eighth grade might be one of the toughest years for getting students to open up in writing.

"The idea that a simple change of format might make my classroom feel safer for students, leading them to take risks and engage more deeply, was too alluring to pass up," Ashley said, "and the result was one of the most joyful lessons of the year. My eighth graders jumped in to wrestle with challenging questions, pregnant with the possibility of multiple 'right' answers." Afterwards she reflected on what worked and why.

The lesson focused on Alice Walker's "Beauty: When the Other-Dancer Is the Self" and began with formative writing as part of the *Do Now*: "How might Alice Walker's experiences have influenced her writing?"

"My hope in including the word 'might' was to help students feel safe jumping in with thoughts rather than comprehensive answers," she said. Students jumped in and she was happily surprised to see "twice as many hands as usual" offering to share their answers. On a later question, *Reflect on the role of gender in Walker's experience*, she again found that "students went right to work. There was no flipping through the packet or rewriting of the question to pass time. Students began quickly jotting down their thoughts; seemingly, the sense of possibility within the question made students feel more comfortable with risk."

The subsequent discussion too crackled to life. "Within moments, students were deeply analyzing the impact a scar discussed in the text had on Walker in light of her gender, moving from her specific experience to a message about society at large. By asking students for their *reflections,* the question invited students to share all thoughts and suggested a validity in a variety of responses. This encouraged them and prepared them to take the risks."

Formative questions made writing a "low-risk adventure" in which students "didn't always have to have a final argument about the theme to discuss the story." You can see this play out in the video *Arielle Hoo: Keystone*. Arielle asks her students to write their "conjectures" to start their reflection on a problem. She is suggesting, "We're just thinking and experimenting with ideas at this point." She says *go* and the class springs into action.

Ironically, students are more likely to have a strong final argument about the theme if they'd had time to wrestle with the idea formatively first. In other words, the argument isn't that formative writing is "better" than summative writing, because it isn't. Both are important and students need to be able to do both. Rather, the argument is that formative writing is *also* necessary—if more likely to be overlooked—and that the two types of writing are synergistic in a dozen ways. For example, formative writing helps students engage in and care about the text so that they feel more vested in any argument they then decide to defend or explain in summative writing . . . which in turn helps them to understand what things they should seek to understand or figure out through formative writing.

One other key aspect of the writing prompts used in *Everybody Writes*: they occur and reoccur, midstream and throughout in the lesson, while ideas are fresh. Teachers often call their *Everybody Writes* prompts "Stop and Jots" for two reasons: (1) The word "jot" expresses the informality and conjectural nature of the exercise. And the responses are pretty short. These aren't essays. They're forty-five, sixty, and ninety-second reflections. (2) The "stop" implies that *students are in the midst* of doing something else. We want students to write formatively as they are experiencing an idea, a question, an uncertainty. We want them to "stop" and wrestle with it on the page while the question is fresh in their heads.

So the idea behind *Everybody Writes* is simple. Ask students to write frequently and formatively and do it midstream, in short bursts throughout your lesson. Suddenly you will awaken students to a whole new side of writing. You will help them learn to think in writing.

Some other benefits of *Everybody Writes*:

- Because you can review student ideas in advance by reading over their shoulders, you're able to select useful responses to begin discussion. Of course, there will be other times when rather than looking for exemplary responses, you will seek Stop and Jots that show ideas that are partially developed or show a common confusion. It all depends what you are looking for.

- If you use *Everybody Writes* before discussion, then every idea that gets shared aloud is in effect a second draft, a thought of higher quality than what would otherwise have been shared without the opportunity to think in writing first.

- *Everybody Writes* also allows you to *Cold Call* students with the confidence that they have been set up to succeed, because you know that everyone is prepared with thoughts. You can simply ask, "What did you write about, Avery?" to kick things off.

A final thought: the more you use writing, the better (and more efficient) your students get at using it. The first time you try it, it may take students a bit of time to get started; the quality may be only so-so. But by the time they are answering reflection prompt number 87, as students in *Jessica Bracey: Keystone* do, they are very good and very efficient at using the *Everybody Writes* moment as an opportunity to develop their thoughts. Practicing something important eighty-six times will have that effect. This was certainly evident in Jessica's class: not only was the post-writing discussion of high quality, but it began with almost every hand shooting into the air. Having had an opportunity to "write to determine what they think," they are now ready to discuss, expand, and refine their ideas in discussion.

## TECHNIQUE 39: SILENT SOLO

Successful teaching often consists of sublime moments achieved in part via mundane tools. That is certainly true of this chapter, which describes how changes in the ways we ask students to write can transform the ways they think and maximize the value and quality of other activities we engage in as well. If you can get everyone in the room to write for a sustained period of time, the benefits to student thinking and discussion will be many.

- Giving students the opportunity to write for a minute or so before a discussion will lead to better listening, more confident participation, and higher-quality ideas to share.

- Short, formative written reflections in the midst of learning can help students not just to document what they think but to discover and expand it.

- Glancing over students' shoulders at the ideas they are wrestling with in response to a question can allow you to "hunt" (select students or ideas that deserve the class's attention and focus) rather than "fish" (call on students blindly in hopes that what they share will be germane or apropos). A *Cold Call* that starts, "Tariq, you used a fascinating word in your reflection: spurned. Can you talk about that a bit?" changes not only the discussion but Tariq's sense of himself as a valued thinker in the classroom.

Those are powerful things. But the *if* in "If you can get everyone to write" is a big one, especially if you raise your sights even a little higher—as in: "If you can reliably get every student to write willingly, thoughtfully, and on cue, and to sustain the effort for a significant duration."

It's a case where the sublime rests upon mastery of the mundane. The technique *Silent Solo* involves an apparently mundane goal: teaching students to reliably write, on cue, as a matter of habit. Once established, the technique is nearly invisible, manifested in humble moments observers might overlook. You say, of the outcome of an experiment or a scene in the novel, "Well, that was unexpected. Take 90 seconds to reflect in writing on reasons why this might have happened. Go!" Even though suddenly every pencil is scratching, observers might yawn and glance out the windows. They might see it as downtime—a little break in class. They might think your students arrived in your classroom doing that naturally. They'd be wrong, of course.

*Silent Solo* lets you send students into a task where the Participation Ratio is high—everyone in the room answering the question at once—and the Think Ratio is as well—framing ideas carefully in words is an inherently rigorous task. But the ability to conjure a moment like that—reliably, over and over—requires consistency and attention to detail to establish.

I want to pause here and underscore the role of silence in *Silent Solo*. It's not just writing but *quiet writing* that's the necessary routine. For some, that's a tough sell. Your vision of an ideal class might be characterized by boisterous discussion or passionate debate. However, providing time for focused, thoughtful reflection (typically prior to that full-voiced discussion or debate) gives all students a moment to gather their ideas, to listen to their own inner voice, and capture elusive ideas that only yield when you stick with them. Silence is necessary to the deepest reflection.[1] Students deserve to experience it—doubly so in a screen-filled world where exactly that sustained, uninterrupted reflection is so rare. They may not get the opportunity anywhere else.

The time your students spend with their pencils transcribing the reflections of a quiet mind will build their ability to sustain focus and likely result in their best thinking. The resulting discussion will ironically be more likely to crackle with life if you allow it to be preceded by thoughtful silence.

You can see the power of the system at work in the video *Montage: Silent Solo*.

Within seconds of Hasan Clayton's prompt "eyes in," every student is at work, reflecting thoughtfully in writing on Hasan's question. They start on cue and sustain this for four solid minutes. Four minutes of sustained reflection in a world where attention is increasingly fractured and interrupted by technology is a profound thing.

At the drop of a hat, Tamesha McGuire's first graders are off and writing too, reflecting on the strategies they used to make sets of ten. Compare this to a typical classroom where a teacher might ask for verbal answers: "What strategies did you use to make ten?" In that case a few students might answer, describing gamely but perhaps imprecisely, what they did. In Tamesha's classroom everyone answers and describes their thinking with the precise word choice and syntax that writing demands. You can't flex the written word like the spoken one. To write is to think harder. Both ratios have been multiplied.

"Go ahead, take one minute," Jamila Hammet tells the students at her table; they grab their pencils and are off. The writing is of shorter duration than Hasan's. They're reading *Because of Winn-Dixie* and the question is about how they feel when looking at a picture of a dog. The lesson is about the nature of the bonds between animals and humans. She wants to insert a short period of personal reflection to help students understand the characters in the novel better. As they write, they are focused, intent, and quite happy to be putting their thoughts down on paper. Because the routine is so solid, Jamila can insert small bursts of writing like this at almost any point in her lesson to increase the quality of student reflection, the amount of participation, or to give students a moment to shift gears and respond thoughtfully.

You can see a version of this system, slightly modified for older students, in Sadie McCleary's Chemistry class. Her students answer three questions over six minutes. Efficient, focused, and effective, every student is on task and doing the core work of chemistry independently and in writing.

The goal of *Silent Solo*, as these teachers show, is a shared habit: one in which all students engage and some perhaps look forward to. There are clues in the montage as to how the habit was built and is maintained:

- Tamesha is warm, upbeat, and cheery. She first praises effort where she sees it, naming specific students so they feel seen and important, then quickly transitions to reading quietly over students' shoulders to show how much she values their ideas.

- Hasan, too, shows his appreciation for students who engage the writing straight away. He modulates his voice, lowering it to use a more reflective tone that matches the task. He reminds his students to write in complete sentences.

- Jamila's language—"go ahead"—and her hint of a smile imply that students must be eager to write and cherish the opportunity for reflection. Perhaps at first some did and some didn't, but I suspect her introduction made a least a few feel more excited.

- Sadie adapts her routine to a problem set. She's clear about the task and the time and graciously protects the transition to begin from disruption with a nonverbal "pause" signal and a promise to come check in with her students individually. To lose momentum would have been a catastrophe for the focus she'd created.

The downside of these videos is that they show you—mostly—what it looks likes *after* the routine is formed. Applying what we know about building strong and successful habits will be critical to understanding the initial steps required to establish *Silent Solo* in your classroom.

A habit is a chain of actions that happen in sequence. Since one action is dependent on the one prior we are required to be intentional about the design of the component parts and how students learn them. To sustain and maximize a habit we also have to think about motivation—how do we get students to embrace the habit willingly, as students appear to do in Hasan's, Tamesha's, Jamila's, and Sadie's classrooms, so that independent work becomes a joy rather than a chore? We have to ask: *What makes students likely to follow—eagerly even— the chain of actions in the habit?*

To turn an activity into a routine, make your directions *simple, clear cut,* and *stepped,* says Peps Mccrea.[2] You want first steps that are easily remembered and require few decisions. This makes the habit easy to activate, as a counter-example may show. Let's say you've planned for students to reflect on your question for three minutes in writing. You say, "Please take out a piece of paper and answer the question, Why do most animals live in the canopy of a typical rainforest?" Unfortunately, at this point, success is already in doubt. You have thirty students and some number of them will struggle to find paper. Someone will have to decide what kind of paper to use . . . and possibly discuss this with a peer . . . or ask you: *Is this paper OK? I don't have any notebook paper. Is this OK?* Someone else will ask for something to write on. Distraction will replace the quiet hum of thinking in writing—*Have we started yet, Ms. Collins?*—and the three minutes you've allocated for this written task will quickly evaporate.

If students already have journals handy or out on their desks, when you say, "Why do most animals live in the canopy of a typical rainforest? Go," initiating the chain of actions would be far easier and there would be fewer interruptions. Notice how this happens in the video *Jessica Bracey: Keystone.* She tells her students to start writing in their journals, which are on their desks. Within seconds they are all deeply engaged in the task. Every student. The speed of their response is important. It's not just that potentially wasted time is made productive;

it's that there is continuity of thinking. The ideas that were in their heads as they read are still in their heads as they write, undisturbed by a shuffle for paper or search for a pen. Routines like this harvest attention as much as they harvest time.

You could replace journals with notes or notebooks (as Sadie McCleary does) or with a packet. In fact, as I discuss in technique 4, *Double Plan*, one of the main benefits of having a packet—a single document where students can engage with all aspects of the lesson—is that it preserves continuity of student thought throughout the lesson. When the question is written down, students can check it so they don't lose sight of their focus as they write. Having the question prewritten also simplifies direction giving. One of the reasons directions are vague or unclear is that we are trying to frame the question as we assign it. Planning it in advance and writing it down protects against this.

Recall, for example, the packet from Reading Reconsidered Curriculum that I shared in technique 4, *Double Plan*. Since every student is working from the same page, and all have the same space in which to reflect before discussion, every brain maximizes its engagement with the academic task, rather than the logistics of how and where to complete it. When you give the cue, students dive into writing time with their thoughts intact. Simplicity has made the habit easy to activate, with benefits in focus and depth of thinking.

"Make the first action easy off the blocks," Mccrea continues, and students will be more vested in the rest of the routine. The videos in the montage show the power of this. The goal when you begin building the routine is the simplest possible activation step: to get pencils moving. All of them. Right away. Later, you can layer in further expectations; for now you want to make it as simple as possible to succeed. It helps if the cue to begin is consistent—same words every time—and if it's short and delivered in a crisp tone that "pops" so that students react quickly and decisively. Mccrea notes that a good cue should be "punchy"—short and delivered with a change of tone or pace. The cues in the video have this in common. We want students bursting out of the blocks. The synchrony of everyone taking action at once makes the norm more visible and reinforces it. "Go!" is a great punchy cue—as in *One minute to think in writing. Go!*—but there are alternatives: Hasan says "Eyes in" and Tamesha uses the slightly more playful "Go to work."

The second key aspect of the activation step is that it be *clear cut*. The less gray area, the better. "Where possible, actions should be things that can be considered done or not done, rather than partially done." It's clear, then, whether the routine is happening successfully and productively. That's why pencils moving is such an ideal first step. If students' pencils are moving, *Silent Solo* is happening. If they are not, it is not the habit you had envisioned and therefore not serving students to the best possible effect. Some teachers' in-cue when establishing the routine is "Pencils moving. Go!" Later they remove the "Pencils moving" part.

The importance of a crisp start raises an important question, however. Students, understandably, may ask for time to think before they write. As I discuss in technique 38, *Everybody Writes*, thinking *through* writing is, for most students, a new way of processing and students will initially want to process in the way they perceive themselves to have been most successful in the past, by first reflecting and then writing. This is where your rollout to students is key. You might say something like: "When I say go, please do your best to answer question 2 in your packet. This exercise is not for a grade—what you write is for you and you won't turn it in.[3] Challenge yourself to think in writing! I will expect to see your pencils moving the whole time. Go!" Or you might say, "It will be hard, but push yourself. You will learn to write your way through anxieties and concerns. If you get stuck, write about why you are stuck." Or say, "A better question might have been . . . But keep your pencil moving! Go!" The keys here are relieving the pressure students may be feeling to get the answer "right" and getting students started trying to think in writing. Later you can add expectations[4] and the technique will establish for your students an indispensable cognitive tool. For now you want a vibrant, positive norm.

You can also start small. The first time you assign *Silent Solo* writing, do it for forty-five seconds. Challenge students to see if they can write the whole way. Help them by making the initial question an interesting one and maybe by giving them a phrase to start off their answer if they get stuck. Ensuring success is ensuring buy-in. The next time your goal will be a minute. Later, ninety seconds. Within a month you'll be writing for five or ten minutes at a stretch. But if you try to start with ten minutes you likely won't get there because students will, effectively, practice struggling. You want them to practice succeeding.

Most likely, students will continue to seek assistance with this challenging task, even after the rollout and even after time has been extended. As you circulate, students will likely call you over and want to tell you what they are thinking instead of or before writing it down. Remember, allowing them to talk instead of writing to explore their thoughts won't help them learn to think in writing, and that is the cognitive habit we are aiming for. Try saying something like "I can't wait to read it once you've written it" or "Great, get it down before you forget it." This brief pep talk both refocuses students on the essential challenge of the task (the writing) and reassures them at a tough moment that whatever they get down will be valuable to themselves and to the class's discourse.

A few other implementation notes:

- Another key source of motivation is transparency of purpose. Understanding the "why" behind a task usually helps the reluctant or skeptical get started. You'd want to understand why this "silent writing" wasn't busy work, too. So you might preview—briefly!—what comes later in the lesson ("Take one minute *Silent Solo* to write down some ideas about what Esperanza's doll might represent. We're going to use these ideas to shape our discussion of symbolism when the timer goes off") or building investment up front ("Reading your faces, I think this chapter intrigued you. I can't wait to read some of your thoughts. Take one minute to jot your observations. Go!"). Linking moments of *Silent Solo* with the larger trajectory of the lesson can help students feel invested in their writing and more likely to make the most of the time provided.

- Student motivation is also impacted by what you do as they're working. If your affect and actions show students their ideas have value, it will provide an incentive to continue writing. As you circulate, remind students gently and warmly of expectations if needed— "keep those pencils moving"—but not exclusively or even primarily. Make sure to also take the time to read over shoulders, comment, and nod appreciatively. *Oh, that's interesting, Carol. Can't wait to talk about that, Grant. Nice, Israel. Great word . . .* or just raise your eyebrows and smile. Appreciating the content of what students have written makes them feel successful and scholarly and it will help make strong thinking a habit.

The clip *Emily Badillo: Three Minutes on Your Own* shows many of the elements of habit-building in action. Emily is a guest teacher in the classroom where this clip is filmed so it's her first time working with these students. (She's piloting the Reading Reconsidered Curriculum my team has developed.[5]) You can see that her question is already written in a packet that all students have on their desks. Students' task is to begin writing as soon as they read it. She explicitly calls the habit of independent writing *Silent Solo*, by the way. It's a catchy phrase but it also reminds her students of the rules. We took the name of this habit from hearing a teacher—we're not sure who!—use that phrase: *Silent Solo. Two minutes. What has Cassie just found out? Go.*

A few other things you'll see Emily do (and the time in the video where you see them):

0:18: Emily sets up a challenge task that students "get" to do if they're done early. It's framed positively (a challenge) but one big excuse for why they wouldn't be writing ("I'm done!") has already been eliminated.

0:26: Emily sets the timer. This makes the goal of writing for three minutes real and tangible. (For more, see technique 30, *Work the Clock*.)

0:29: Emily slows down her pace in circulating and looks carefully to see if students are following through—carefully enough for them to notice her in their peripheral vision. The message is: I am looking carefully to see if everyone is writing. If you show it matters to you, it will be far more likely to matter to students.

0:32: Emily narrates her expectation: She is "looking for a table where everybody's pencil is moving." There's that clear-cut unambiguous activation step.

0:35: Emily notes examples of good follow-through by Ezra, Logan, and others.

1:02: Emily tells one student who would prefer to talk than write: "Don't tell me, write it down." Her tone is appreciative, but she also reinforces expectations for writing.

1:19: Circulating, Emily focuses on engaging student ideas and asks questions to show she's reading carefully. At 1:50, Emily is careful to show appreciation for effort—"Nice job. Keep going." It's especially important that the last thing students hear is the phrase "Keep going." This ensures that her appreciation doesn't accidentally promote less follow-through.

You'll also notice that throughout there are long stretches of silence in which to think and work. Emily creates silence—she makes her expectations clear and enforces them—but also honors the silence herself. And of course after these three minutes of silent work, students will have a chance to share their ideas out loud with partners and with the rest of the room. By setting aside this time for silent writing, Emily ensures that students will have time to process and ideas to share.

## TECHNIQUE 40: FRONT THE WRITING

In many classes, writing serves as a capstone—to a discussion, a demonstration, a lab, a presentation, or some other part of the lesson. It's often right and good and logical that writing comes last. Writing is an ideal tool for synthesizing and processing ideas. But there's also immense value when the writing comes first. *Front the Writing* is about designing lessons so that the writing happens early on.

Consider, first, two common sequences—let's call them RDW and ADW (read-discuss-write and activity-discuss-write). You might do RDW if you were reading a short story with an ambiguous ending. You might finish the last paragraph and ask, "So tell me, what does the final line of the story mean? What happened and why?" A discussion might ensue, with students first making conjectures of varying types. Likely, they'd bring evidence as the details of the story's ending were discussed.

With ADW you might look at a chemical reaction or perhaps listen to a piece of music and then discuss it. What do we think is happening in the beaker and why? What do we think the composer was trying to communicate?

After those discussions you'd ask your students to write about the text they read or the activity they did. As they wrote, they'd be drawing on two sources of information: what they took from the story or the activity and what their classmates said in discussion. Ideally, a student would take his or her initial understanding from the reading or the activity and add some nuance and additional detail gleaned from discussion, but it doesn't always work that way. It especially doesn't work that way for your weakest students, with the weakest readers particularly at risk.

In many cases, students are able to use what they hear and learn in the discussion to write, convincing you that they understood the reading (or the lab experiment or a lecture) far better than they did. You might call this "piggybacking." So while it is valuable to use a final writing exercise to assess how much your students know or to allow them to synthesize ideas, the writing in this case conflates information gleaned from two sources, one often easier to understand than the other. You (and your students) could easily get a false positive—an erroneous indication of mastery—as a result of piggybacking.

This happened to some colleagues at a school I work with. They were doing a unit in which students read *Romeo and Juliet* and strove to have a college-level discussion about it. In this case, the discussion was held in part online and via chat—a fact that had the unanticipated result of allowing teachers to go back and analyze it later. As the discussion unfolded, they had cause to.

Originally my colleagues thought their unit had been a triumph. The discussions were rich and, thanks to the accountability of the chat structure, they could easily track who had participated how many times, ensuring that everyone contributed.

But as a capstone, students were asked to write a paper analyzing a passage from the play, and the papers were a stunning disappointment. You've been down this road once or twice probably. They couldn't wait to see what students wrote, but as they read each successive paper they moved from anticipation to disappointment to despondency and despair. Where had the trenchant insight and deep analysis gone? Then they realized they had a transcript of all of their discussions. They went back to look for clues. They found that the discussion was indeed full of outstanding ideas, but that, time and time again, those ideas were broached by just two students, with the rest of the class piggybacking on their breakthroughs. The class was able to reflect on a unique and powerful insight *once it was made*, but only two girls were consistently able to generate those underlying insights. They (and only they) were able to discern the germ of core conflicts and themes in Shakespeare's Elizabethan verbiage. Once they laid it out clearly, others were able to jump in. "Oh, it's about loyalty? I can speak to that!"

It's good in some ways that the ideas of these two scholars permeated the room. But it also convinced teachers that the students had greater and broader mastery of reading Shakespeare than they actually did. This was exacerbated by the fact that the teachers had had no tool to measure whether students were able to generate meaning directly from the text. Read—or analyze a data set or do another activity—then discuss, then assess, is problematic if you want to know if students can do the first task on their own. If you want to know that, you've got to get some form of assessment before the discussion.

As students advance in their educational careers, they will increasingly find themselves in situations where they must make sense of a text or an experiment or some other key learning activity on their own—without a group of thirty colleagues with whom to distill the information and discuss first. As they mature, they will add value in professional settings by being the ones who can themselves generate ideas directly from the initial experience.

One of the simplest ways to address this is to shift the cycle from RDW to RWD or ADW to AWD and put the writing before the discussion. You still get the benefit of an exchange of ideas at the end, but not before everyone practices thinking deeply and autonomously: *What did I just see? What did it mean? How can I make sense of it?* Beyond the other benefits of writing, this also allows you to assess what students know right away, before the discussion. You can even design the discussion to respond to the initial understanding you see on their papers.

But *Front the Writing* can go a step further. It can help students get much more out of the discussion itself. Think for a minute about what we want students to do, cognitively, during the part of discussion when they are listening to their peers. We want them to listen, of course, but what else? We often tacitly (or explicitly) ask them to decide whether they agree or disagree with the speaker, but this is a bit of an oversimplification of the sort of intellectual life our students might aspire to. In the conversations of life, those whose comments focus simply on "I agree" or "I disagree" are limited. Much more interesting are discussions with comments more like, "I agree that that evidence is important but I interpreted it differently," or "The first part of your comment is insightful but I think you may have exaggerated the significance."

Asking students to listen and focus on whether they agree or disagree can foment an unproductive situation: a discussion full of students with arms crossed saying, "Well, that's just what I think," perhaps a little more loudly the second time around. Learning and growth aren't maximized when students are focused on proving that their original opinion was right and "winning" the discussion, rather than, say, listening for information that might cause them to change their original thought, to develop a more nuanced and flexible opinion that moderates and modulates their initial reaction in light of others' perspectives. Surely we are exasperated when, in our lives outside of school, we come across people who want to win discussions instead of hear others out in the assumption that they might learn something. We should be careful about reinforcing that in our schools.

Next question, then: How can we socialize students to think of discussion as a tool to refine or revise their own thinking in light of the points made by others? One effective way is to ask them to write and then listen to the discussion *with the understanding that the next step will be to revise their original opinion*. That is, moving to RWDR or AWDR (read-write-discuss-revise or activity-write-discuss-revise) gives structure to the idea that during a discussion, what students should do is track ideas they will use to revise their opinion afterward. It makes a habit of it, in fact. The process ends with them changing their opinion. It expects them to.

This not only provides lots of practice revising—a skill I write about it in technique 42, *Regular Revision*, that is at least as important as writing an initial idea—but also causes students to engage in the discussion with a more flexible mindset: What can I learn here, and how will I apply it to my idea? This mindset is not just theoretical—someone tells me I ought to be doing that. In practice, as a student, I am prompted, ideally over and over again, to do it with the result being that I become very good at coming up with an initial opinion, writing it down to formulate it into words, engaging in an exchange with peers in which I harvest ideas that I can weave into my own thinking, and then revising my initial opinion in writing—locking down the changes in my thinking in specific, visible words and syntax. If students could do that every day, I suspect the difference for their learning, and also for a populace prone to righteous and reflexive confidence that their opinion is assuredly the only right one, would be significant.

Below you'll find a template we often use in our workshops to show how you might put this into practice in the classroom:

## *Front the Writing* Example in Student Work Packet

**Everybody Writes #1:** What might the figurative language in the first and second stanza tell us about the flowers?

_____

_____

_____

_____

_____

**Notes from Discussion Tracker**

**Rewrite Everybody Writes #1:** What might the figurative language in the first and second stanza tell us about the flowers?

_____

_____

_____

_____

_____

Notice the initial prompt is "formative" (see *Everybody Writes*, technique 38) and uses the word "might." Notice also the room provided for note-taking during the discussion and the fact that the postwrite *is the same question*. You *could* change it, of course, but I like the idea that the message is that I want you to answer the same question, just more insightfully. You could also add more lines beneath the prompt to suggest that you want more thinking after the discussion, but again I like the idea that it's exactly the same. The message is as much about changing what you wrote as it is adding to it. *I don't want more; I want better.* That said, subtle changes might be fine. One teacher at a workshop in London (I'm sorry I don't remember who!) noted that he would change the prompt slightly so that the first one asked *What does the figurative language in the first and second stanza tell* you *about the flowers?* and the second *What does the figurative language in the first and second stanza tell* us *about the flowers?* I like that idea—and the idea that there are lots of ways you could play with the concept of writing before and after a discussion in a disciplined way.

You can see several great examples of *Front the Writing* in two of the Keystone videos in this book. The explosion of hands two minutes into Jessica Bracey's clip is in part a result of the fact that students have all written first. So, too, the hands at the beginning of Arielle Hoo's class, when she asks them to write their conjectures. And of course at the end of Arielle's class there's a group revision in writing.

## TECHNIQUE 41: ART OF THE SENTENCE

In *Everybody Writes* I defined two types of writing: formative and summative. Now I want to introduce a third: developmental writing, which is writing designed to build *syntactic control* though *deliberate practice*. In a moment I will define those terms, but first I want to explain why developmental writing is so important.

Not long ago I visited a highly successful school. Instruction was strong and the kids had bought in to the culture. They loved being there, worked hard, and were happy; they were very successful—arguably the best school in the city it served. But the school had asked my team and me to help them think about their reading outcomes, which lagged behind the rest of their outstanding results.

I remember one English classroom in particular. Students were reading a challenging novel and paused to write about it during class. Their *Silent Solo* (technique 39) was perfect and they wrote with energy and commitment from the moment the teacher said "Go!" until she said, "OK, pencils down." But as they wrote I walked around the room and read over students' shoulders. What I saw was an immense amount of diligent but often inchoate writing—phrases and words strove to express ideas but were not quite coherent. There would often be a nicely chosen word, an insightful phrase in the midst of a ramshackle sentence, but the pieces did not add up. The whole was almost always lesser than the sum of the parts. Students tried hard but did not produce clear ideas or arguments.

What students lacked was syntactic control, which Bruce Saddler defines as "the ability to create a variety of sentences that clearly express an intended meaning."[6]

To master a sentence, to render unto it the power to capture a complex thought with nuance and precision, one must master a set of tools that are rarely named and even more rarely taught—in part, because we often scorn them.

The sentence in the previous paragraph, for example, required a pair of introductory prepositional phrases, the second echoing the first in vaguely appositive-like manner. It required an em dash. It required subordinating conjunctions. I had to construct a sentence in which the subject—"one," by the way—was the twentieth word.

Don't try to deny it. As soon as you read the words *introductory prepositional phrases*, the music stopped and the party ended. A few readers crossed themselves reflexively at the sound of those ancient pagan words. *Oh*, others thought, *he's going in for "grammar." I knew he was old school, but . . .*

Grammar, as all good people know, is cruel to children. Most modern teachers will tell you that it is of limited use, the passion of ancient scolds, only faintly visible, now, in the chalk dust of time.

"For me, grammar instruction is about sentence structure," writes Daisy Christodoulou. "It's about helping students to marshal their thoughts into coherent, logical sentences."[7] Its purpose is syntax, and mastery of syntax remains something that we can teach joyfully and successfully without memorizing a thousand terms, like *adverbial modifier*.[8] Syntactic forms are magical tools and, happily, carefully designed writing exercises can develop them.

Coordination and subordination are good examples. When used adroitly those *ands* and *buts* and *sos* and *despites* are tools of syntax. They wander the earth humbly seeking to explain to us the ways that ideas are connected. They quietly tell us: *There are two ideas here, but one is more important than the other.* Or *caused the other.* Or *the second idea is contingent upon the other happening first.* Or *contrasts with the first.*

It is a superpower, when a person can coordinate and subordinate deftly and smoothly. The connections between ideas often create the lion's share of the meaning. But they are also where it all comes apart for many students, in reading as well as writing. When reading complex text, the words and phrases within a sentence may be clear enough on their own, but piecing together the interrelationships among them can still pose a problem. Your student understands the idea in the first half of the sentence but misses the syntactic cue that explains its relationship to the second half. Suddenly she is lost. Readers who do not have mastery of the hidden vocabulary of syntax are always fighting a rising tide of meaninglessness. For writers who lack syntactic control, all but the simplest strands of thought resist their mastery. Precision matters because ideas are brought into being by the words that create them. Before that they are just the stuff of fog and instinct. "Language is the mother, not the handmaiden, of thought," is how W. H. Auden expressed this idea.

*Art of the Sentence* (AOS) is the name for tools designed to teach syntactic control, happily in quite enjoyable ways and without even a whiff of sentence diagramming.

Those tools rely in part on short exercises, each with a clear goal in which students use and master specific aspects of syntactic control. Deliberate practice, if you will. You probably think students already get a ton of practice with their writing but, as Judith Hochman notes in her outstanding book *The Writing Revolution*,[9] writing gets assigned a lot but not taught a lot.

There are two things a developmental writing exercise needs to work: depth of content and scarcity. The two work together. As Judith Hochman points out, developmental writing must always be embedded in the content you are teaching. Students have to have an idea of substance to wrestle with and they have to know things connected to that idea (recall Daniel

Willingham's observation that I discuss in Chapter One that higher-order thinking relies on background knowledge). When students have plenty to say about a concept and are driven to express it, you then introduce scarcity. Usually this means requiring them to write a single sentence. This causes outward pressure on the sentence—students who want to say a lot but are limited to a single sentence must suddenly begin using a new and expanded version of the sentence to get it all in. Necessity is the mother of syntactical invention.

You can see this in a moment from the video of Jamila Hammet's lesson that we watched in the discussion of *Silent Solo*. Her students are reading Kate DiCamillo's *Because of Winn-Dixie*, a novel about the deep relationship between a girl and her dog. Students are asked to look at a picture of an adorable and loving dog, who reminds them of Winn-Dixie perhaps, and describe how they feel when they look at the dog. Without scarcity a student could write: "I love this dog. He's cute and I'd want to play with him. I'd want to throw him a ball and let him fetch. I'd like to see if he wants to tuck in beside me and watch a movie."

What you might get, in other words, is what we do get so often. Relatively wooden, unimaginative writing using simple and receptive sentence construction.

But a student forced to put all their thoughts into a single sentence might write:

> *I love this dog because he's so cute and I imagine us playing, me throwing him a ball to fetch or else the two of us tucked in on the couch watching a movie.*

That's a sentence pushing outward on the student's limits. The student is expanding how much she can capture, and how well, in "a complete thought." Notice all the syntactic tools that have been brought to bear—I'm honestly not sure what to call them all. Scarcity caused that—scarcity combined with students having a lot to say and ideally knowing a fair amount about a topic.

You should also expect errors to show up as students try to write more complex sentences, by the way. Of course they will. It's a good thing—they're at the edge of their mastery. Make sure to combine AOS and other developmental writing exercises with technique 42, *Regular Revision*, to ensure a strong balance of exploration and accuracy.

But *Art of the Sentence* also often includes additional constraints and parameters that make the practice deliberate and cause students to focus on using specific syntactic tools. They also make the exercises even more interesting.

For example, Jamila might have asked her students to write a single sentence about the dog in the picture but begin with the phrase "Looking at the dog . . ." She would then cause students to practice using a sophisticated grammatical form—an introductory participial phrase. Or she could have asked them to start their sentence with: "When one looks at a dog like this . . ." Now she'd be causing them to use "one" as the subject. If students are going to read sentences like that, creating them intentionally can help a lot.

Or Jamila could have asked students to start "At first glance . . ." Now students would be using an introductory prepositional phrase, but she would also cause them to look at the picture twice. What did you not see at first that a second glance reveals?

Previously in her lesson Jamila had given students a nonfiction article to read about the history of animal-human bonds and the domestication of dogs. She could have asked students to "Write a single sentence describing how your reaction to the dog might explain some of the reasons why dogs became domesticated early on in human history. Use the word 'bond.' Or quote a word or phrase from the article in your sentence."

Rules like these allow you to deliberately choose words, phrases, or grammatical forms for students to practice using. Over time students develop facility with a wide range of them in their writing even if they don't know their names. As you're probably already thinking, this exposure strengthens students' ability to comprehend these sentences when they come across them while reading complex text.

## Sentence Starters and Sentence Parameters

Let's take a second to define three types of AOS sentences. The first use "sentence starters," specific verbiage that students must use at the outset of their writing such as:

> *Summarize the data from this graph in one complete well-written sentence that begins with the phrase "Over time . . ."*

At first glance, a prompt with a sentence starter may appear to be easier to respond to than a prompt without one because it contains scaffolding, but in many ways the opposite can be simultaneously true. The sentence is now pushed into new and often unfamiliar syntactical territory. Without being pushed and stretched in such ways, students aren't likely to expand their repertoire of syntactical forms very much. Now, imagine the different sorts of phrases with which you could ask students to begin a sentence:

> "Growing exponentially, . . ."
>
> "The line that expresses the function . . ."
>
> "The relationship between . . ."
>
> "In the long run, . . ."
>
> "When the line approaches vertical, . . ."

Each of these has a different effect on student writing and thinking, pushing them not only into new syntax but potentially into new thinking.

Another approach you can use to guide the sentences students write is *sentence parameters*. These range from asking students to use a specific word or phrase (for example, "Be sure to use the phrase 'stock character' in your answer" or "Use the word 'ambiguous'") to naming a specific grammatical form: "Write a sentence using a subordinate clause with the word 'despite'" or "Write a sentence beginning with a participial phrase." You could also give parameters for length. "In a sentence of no more than eight words . . ." Or perhaps, if you wanted to go beyond the 'rule' of a single sentence, you could teach sentence rhythm this way: "Describe the conflict in Goya's painting *The Third of May* in two sentences of at least twelve words and one of no more than five." I personally like word limits. An unintended consequence of using AOS tools can be the tacit reinforcement of *long* sentences—that's often an outcome of pushing one's syntactic limits. But of course while one needs to be able to construct a long and/or complex sentence, long and complex sentences are not always better. Short and sweet is often the definition of excellence. So one parameter you might occasionally use—implicit in one of the sentences in this example—is a word limit: "In a sentence of six or fewer words . . ."

The third kind of AOS prompts are nondenominational. They simply ask students to capture a big idea in a single sentence with no other rules, often with a phrase like "in one carefully crafted sentence" or "in one beautiful sentence" to encourage students to take pride in the implicit challenge.

I noted that the prompt with a parameter may surprisingly be more rigorous. This is often true, but of course not always. Sometimes an open-ended prompt, such as "Describe Christopher's reaction in one artfully crafted sentence" is ideal, especially for students who have developed increasing fluidity with sentence structures. The best results are likely to come, I suspect, from asking students to write a balance of sentences both with and without parameters.

Finally, one ideal place to use AOS is at the end of a lesson, given that part of its purpose is to help students synthesize and summarize. Imagine a school where every lesson in every subject ended with students writing (and revising!) a single, artfully crafted sentence capturing with nuance and sophistication the most important or challenging idea from that lesson. *Art of the Sentence*, in short, can do great service as an *Exit Ticket* or as the next day's *Do Now*. Imagine: You wrap up the lesson by having everyone distill a key idea in writing; the next day, students get their sentences back with individualized guidance, such as "Revise to use the phrase *in spite of*" or "Rewrite, clarifying what the pronoun 'it' refers to," or with a challenge like "Great! Now see if you can use the word *anabolic*."

### *Art of the Sentence* Meets the Little Ones

You might be wondering: is this idea feasible with my little ones? I think the answer is yes. A lovely video of Brittany Rumph with her K/1 students, *Brittany Rumph: Artful Sentence*, shows a bit of what's possible.

Notice that students draft their sentences on worksheets that frame the writing like art in a museum. Later Brittany will put many of the best up on the walls to celebrate and encourage them, but the implicit message is *By writing one beautiful sentence, every single one of you is creating art with your words.*

Even without that detail, you know Brittany makes a big deal of student writing. The tone of celebration is everywhere—in the way she reads great sentences aloud and does a *Call and Response* to put an exclamation point on one student's use of the word "magnificent." Her students' work, that of most students, is full as you might expect of invented spellings and the like. But it is also full of a capacity for complex syntax that's far ahead of what you might expect. Soon their spelling and handwriting will catch up and their syntactic control will serve them well. In Jeremiah's words, they'll be writing *juicy* sentences from the outset.

In the video *Sarah Fischler: Exhausting Six Months*, you can watch seventh-grade science teacher Sarah Fischler using AOS. My team and I love the range of prompts she uses—and the frequency, as well as the playful but practical specificity of her time limits (a great example of the effectiveness of precise time limits). Sarah's students process constantly in writing in a variety of ways and with pleasure.

---

# Required Reading: *The Writing Revolution*

No book is better at helping educators think about expanding students' ability to craft sentences and expand their syntactic control than Judith Hochman's *The Writing Revolution*.[10] Among the highlights are the developmental writing activities she suggests. These are similar to and work in synergy with *Art of the Sentence* work. We use them regularly in our Reading Reconsidered Curriculum. Some of the best extracts:

> *Because. But. So.* Take a "kernel sentence" (a short simple sentence) and expand it three times, once each time using each of the three conjunctions, *because, but,* and *so.* Not only does it teach a core piece of syntactic control but it causes students to think about an idea in three different ways.

> *Appositives.* Expand a kernel sentence with an appositive phrase. This teaches their use, the ability to insert ideas midsentence, and causes students to expand and apply more background knowledge.

*Sentence expansion.* Take a kernel sentence and expand it with some number of *who, when, what, where,* and *why.*

For examples of these and other Hochman gems, please see technique 42, *Regular Revision.*

---

One of the benefits of developmental writing is that it teaches grammar functionally, in the service of idea creation. To that end, schools might think about a scope and sequence of developmental writing activities to teach key elements of grammar in a systematic way. Here's a version of a very simple model I drafted while developing our Reading Reconsidered Curriculum:

| Developmental Writing Scope and Sequence | |
|---|---|
| **Progression** | **Core Developmental Writing Prompts** (examples use "Esperanza opened her eyes . . .") |
| **Grade 5** | • *Combine sentences:* Esperanza opened her eyes. She had been sleeping. She dreamed that her father was with her. |
| | • *Expand with because, but, so:* "Esperanza opened her eyes so she saw that it had not been a dream." |
| | • *Expand with after, during, before:* "Esperanza opened her eyes during a dream in which her father was still present." |
| | • *Expansion (E):* Add details explaining three to five of the Five Ws: "Esperanza opened her eyes when she woke up, feeling anxious, in her own bed." |
| | • *Expand with appositives:* "Esperanza, a young girl whose father had just been killed, opened her eyes." |
| **Grade 6** | **Previous prompts plus:** |
| | • *Because, But, So 2.0:* More sophisticated versions (for example, *although, consequently, as a result of*) <br> • Esperanza opened her eyes although she did so only reluctantly. |
| | **Develop with Prepositional Phrase:** |
| | • *Introductory:* "After a restless night's sleep, Esperanza opened her eyes . . ." |
| | • *Mid-sentence:* "Esperanza, in the middle of a bad dream, opened her eyes . . ." |
| | **Develop with Participial Phrase:** |
| | • *Introductory:* "Hoping it had all been a dream, Esperanza opened her eyes." |
| | • *Mid-sentence:* "Esperanza, dreaming of her father, opened her eyes." |

# TECHNIQUE 42: REGULAR REVISION

In the previous technique, *Art of the Sentence*, I described how short developmental writing exercises could harness the benefits of deliberate practice and help avoid a common trap for teachers—assigning a lot of writing but never managing to teach students the fundamental skills of expression or syntactic control.

Often, mastering syntactic tools comes as much from revision as it does from the initial act of writing. By revision, I mean the process of asking rigorous but straightforward questions about one's written idea formation: *Does that word capture exactly what I mean? Could I express my idea more precisely, perhaps with fewer words? If I change the order, how would that affect meaning? If my words are unclear, then what exactly did I mean?*[11]

Most of us submit our own writing to the revision process frequently and, for some of us, constantly. We revise even an informal email to a colleague perhaps, or scratch out and use a different word three times when texting an explanation to a friend about running late. Revision is an everyday thing in the real world but too often a special event in the classroom—a formal activity applied mostly with compositions and longer pieces. It's often encoded in what some teachers call *the writing process*, which can take a week to complete, with each step (drafting, revising, editing) getting its own day. Over the course of the year there are perhaps three or four "revision days."

I'd argue that to make students' writing powerful and also to allow writing to cause writers to think most deeply—to boost the Think Ratio, that is—revision should always be a part of writing. In some ways the less distinguishable as a "separate step," the better.

The technique *Regular Revision* pursues the simple idea that we can make student writing better by making revision an everyday act, often done in short simple doses, and by making it a habit to regularly revise all manner of writing, not only formal pieces.

I find this observation of Bruce Saddler's profound: "Sentences represent vehicles of communication that are literally *miniature compositions*," he writes. We could apply the drafting and revision process reserved for longer compositions more frequently, and probably more successfully, to smaller writing exercises just by thinking of them as compositions, too. Sentence-length developmental writing exercises, for example, are perfect vehicles for revising. Small and focused, they are perfect for successful, deliberate practice.[12]

Skills are mastered when practiced regularly, even if practiced in smaller chunks. You might call that the Yo-Yo Ma Effect. As a child, the great cellist's father taught him to play in short, frequent, and intense doses. He played better, and with more attention, because he played shorter. The frequency of practice and the level of focus and attention involved are often more important than the duration in shaping outcomes.[13] Five minutes of practice a day for ten days, done with focus and attention, will probably get you farther than an hour of practice on one occasion, even though the number of minutes applied is greater in the second instance. Doubly so if your level of attention starts to tail off at the end of the hour.

Revising smaller pieces of writing more frequently allows for focus and energy. It also allows us to have a single very specific goal for every round of practice—something the cognitive psychologist Anders Ericsson points out as being critical to accelerating learning in practice. If there's one thing to focus on and improve, it's easy to see—and then to support people as they apply that particular idea. *Let's add an active verb here. Let's figure out why this syntax doesn't work.* See the difference between those focused prompts and a more general "revise your paragraph?" There's a clear task to start with, so students know what to look for and to change; the task then ends with visible progress, giving students the sense of success that we discussed earlier. This will make them want to continue in the endeavor.

As it is now, teachers spend an immense amount of time giving students feedback on their writing. We mark up their essays with comment after comment we hope they'll read—when we return their papers in three or four weeks—and perhaps apply, at an undetermined time in the future. Often by the time they read our reams of feedback they barely remember writing the original. In addition to the time lag, there's also usually too much feedback to use. Most of it will get ignored and students will then practice ignoring feedback. I'm your student and among the fifteen suggestions you have on my three-page paper is to use more active verbs and to make my thesis statement clearer. Perhaps I'll find opportunities to use active verbs. Perhaps I won't. But usually there is no clear and immediate opportunity to even begin to try to respond and apply to this plethora of "opportunities for improvement." Even if I wanted to try to make all of your changes, it is likely to take another month to get an opportunity.

Of course you could guarantee me the chance to rewrite my thesis by asking me to revise the whole essay but the transaction cost is high. For both of us. I rewrite the essay—as do my twenty-nine classmates on their own essays—and you're back to three weeks of dreading the stack of thirty essays staring at you accusingly from the corner of your desk.

So what if we, as teachers, applied our feedback not to writing of the largest unit size but of the smallest? What if I wrote a sentence and you suggested I rewrite it with more active verbs and I did it right then and there? Three minutes later you'd say, "Yes, much better, Doug. See how different your sentence is?" And I'd agree, because I could see that I had made a difference by making an immediate and focused change. I could look at the before and after to see the change. And then perhaps you'd say, "Try another." Or next you might say, "Here's another one-sentence composition to write. Focus on active verbs." "*Yes,*" you'd say, reviewing my work only a matter of seconds after I had completed it. The feedback cycle is suddenly fast and focused and effective.

## Sentence-Level Revision Is High-Quality Practice

To maximize the benefits of practice, Ericsson suggests, the practice should first have well-defined, specific goals. "We're working on our writing" is insufficiently vague. "We're working on using active verbs in our writing" or "on incorporating indirect quotations into our writing" or "on starting sentences with prepositional phrases" are clear, specific goals.

We make more progress if we teach larger skills by linking a series of baby steps, aggregating smaller skills into a larger whole. For this we'll need sentence-level practice to happen frequently. Daisy Christodoulou makes a similar point in her outstanding book, *Making Good Progress*. We presume that the best way to prepare for a task we want to assess is to assign tasks just like it over and over. But this often overwhelms students' working memory, as cognitive load theory tells us. Students will show more mastery on the final, more complex task if they first build that mastery through practice on discrete, manageable chunks. To put it plainly, your students will write far better three-page compositions if, throughout their time with you, they have been regularly practicing writing and revising excellent sentences.

For maximum benefit, practice also requires a focused mindset and full attention, Ericsson advises. Obviously, this ability to focus is dictated in part by the vibrancy of classroom culture, but shorter activities are an ideal way to maximize the attentive capacity of students at any age. As the practice pays off and students experience success, their ability to expand the duration of their attentive focus will also grow. In other words, as I write about in technique 39, *Silent Solo*, start small.

Finally, according to Ericsson, effective practice requires the giving (and use) of quality feedback from a knowledgeable source. Again, with smaller units of writing, feedback can be given more quickly and students more easily socialized to use it. And of course as they do so and see positive changes, they're likely to become more motivated and to like writing.

## *Show Call*: Revision's Best Friend

To bring revision to life, teachers need a tool to make the process visible, and for that there is *Show Call* (technique 13). The technique is discussed extensively in Chapter Three but it also serves as a great tool for teaching revision. *Show Call* allows you to make the often private and individualized process of revision legible and meaningful to all the students in your classroom. That aspect is a game changer.

In many classrooms a typical "revision" exchange without *Show Call* might go something like this:

1. A student, Martina, reads her answer aloud.

2. The teacher says to the class, "Let's give Martina some feedback. What was effective about her answer?"

3. A classmate, working from her limited and fading memory of what Martina wrote, makes a vague observation: "She had really good details."

4. The teacher tries to elicit a specific example to discuss: "Good. What was good about her details?"

5. The commenting student, with memory rapidly fading, tries valiantly to respond but offers an even vaguer response. "Um, I don't remember exactly; I just remember they were really good."

This well-intentioned exchange is essentially a waste of time for both Martina and the class. If you are going to take class time to practice revision (and I certainly hope you do), then you need to make sure that both the original student author and the rest of the class (now in the role of "assistant-revisers") are able to derive meaning from the exercise. Therefore, we need to keep the writing we are talking about in students' working memory—it must remain visible to them. *Show Call* does that, enabling a teacher to ask for precise, actionable analysis. If I project Martina's writing, I can say, "I like Martina's thesis sentence, especially her use of a strong verb like 'devour,'" and then use the projected image to point it out for everyone. Or "I like Martina's thesis sentence, but it would be even better if she put it in the active voice. Who can show us how to do that?" This way, when we talk about what's good about a particular piece of writing, or how it can be improved, people are not just following along, but are able to actively think about the revision task. Since most of the information we take into our brains comes to us visually, students will now understand and remember the revision you are talking about far better.

Making a problem visible also allows you to ask perception-based questions. Asking a student, "Do you see any verbs we could improve on?" is far better than saying, "Amari has used a so-so verb here, let's see if we can improve it." The former question causes students not simply to exercise the skill of improving verbs but to recognize—and practice recognizing—places where it needs doing, where writing could benefit from improvement. Without the critical step of perceiving opportunities for revision on their own, they won't learn to write independently.

Finally, after leveraging the minds of all the students in the class and eliciting thoughts from several of them on the revision at hand, you can then create an opportunity for all students to apply the learning they've just done. "Great, now let's all go through our sentences, check the ones that are in the active voice, and revise any that are in the passive voice." Through the use of *Show Call*, the Think Ratio and Participation Ratio on the revision task has just increased exponentially.

Incidentally, a nice way I've seen teachers make sure that every student learns from each revision opportunity is by doing something called an "offline rewrite." After *Show Calling* student A's work, provide feedback, ask the class to revise, and then *Show Call* student Z's work to see if he or she applied the feedback as well. This ensures that everyone is accountable for applying the feedback, not just the person whose work was *Show Called*. It also gives students the time and space they need to make thoughtful revisions. This can be especially helpful for students who need additional processing time before they can effectively apply feedback.

## On Revising Writing

Here are some hints to help you make revisions as productive as possible.

Judith Hochman has observed that it is important to distinguish *editing*, which is fixing basic errors like capitalization, punctuation, and spelling, from *revising*, which is the task of improving writing—specifically by revising structure or word choice. As Hochman has pointed out, if you let students choose, they will generally edit, primarily because it is easier to add a missing capital letter than to revise a sentence so as to use a subordinating conjunction, for example. In fact, many teachers, too, will choose editing over revising for this reason. But of course the real work is in revision.

One high-value task Hochman suggests is to ask students to add an appositive phrase to a sentence that lacks substance. In a lesson at New Dorp High School in Staten Island, a teacher began revising the sentence "Gandhi had an impact." The teacher first asked her students to use a *Turn and Talk* to write four good appositives to describe Gandhi. Students then inserted the best appositives into the sentence so that it read, for example, "Gandhi, a pacifist and important leader, had an impact." After the teacher asked her students to add a few more clarifications, the students came up with sentences like these: "Gandhi, a pacifist and important leader in India, had a strong impact on society." And the best part was not so much that her students had made this sentence markedly better, it was that they were learning how to use a replicable device, the addition of an appositive phrase, to improve any sentence they might write. That's the power of a good revision task: it teaches a replicable skill.

With thanks to Hochman for the insights that inform some of these suggestions, here are a few more high-value revision tasks:

1. Take a look at Ivan's work here. I want you to find two places where more specific technical vocabulary could make his work even better.

2. Take a look at Ivan's work here. I want you to find at least one place where he could replace a direct quotation with a partial or full paraphrase. Be ready to show us how he could write into or out of the quotation.

3. Take a look at Ivan's work here. I want you to find his two best, most dynamic verbs and then find two verbs you could upgrade to make his writing stronger.

4. Take a look at Ivan's work here. I want you to use a subordinating conjunction to add crucial information.

5. Take a look at Ivan's work here. I want you to add a phrase beginning with "but," "because," or "so" to improve this sentence.

6. Take a look at Ivan's work here. I want you to take these two sentences and combine them to show how the ideas connect and make your writing more fluid.

## Notes

1. A recent study showed that background noise, especially background noise in the form of human voices, quickly reduced reading comprehension. The effect was strongest on the weakest readers. Is there any reason to think writing would be any different? See Giada Guerra et al., "Loudness and Intelligibility of Irrelevant Background Speech Differentially Hinder Children's Short Story Reading," *Mind, Brain, and Education* (October 2020).

2. In *Motivated Teaching*. Please read this book; truly, it is excellent.

3. Meaning you won't turn it in today. Once you've got everybody going you might collect occasionally or *Show Call* or any number of things, but first you just want students writing, so reduce questions, anxieties, and distractions wherever possible.

4. Some classes obviously will be ready for this right away and will need less encouragement and can offer more challenges, such as "Use your new vocabulary" or "Try to think of several reasons," from the outset.

5. For more on the curriculum check out the Teach Like a Champion website: https://teachlikeachampion.com/reading-reconsidered-curriculum/.

6. I like to use a slightly adapted version of Saddler's definition: "The ability to use a variety of syntactic structures to create a variety of sentences that clearly express an intended meaning."

7. https://www.ollielovell.com/tot/092/#Some_insightful_thoughts_on_teaching_Grammar_via_DaisyChristo.

8. I have no idea what the technical terms are to describe most of the elements of syntax I was using in that fancy sentence above (nor am I suggesting that fancy equals good).

"Vaguely appositive-like" is certainly not a technical term. But I can use most of those tools even if I don't know what they're called. I have at least fair-to-middling syntactic control.

9. Did you glance lovingly at your copy of her book, placed in a seat of honor on your bookshelf, as you read that? If not, it suggests you have not read it. You should.

10. To be fair, it's great about all aspects of writing. I'm just partial to her work on sentences.

11. A story from my childhood: In fifth grade I wrote a book report. My topic sentence said the book was interesting. "You cannot write a book report in which your topic sentence calls the book interesting," my mom said. "What kind of interesting? Why?" Back in my room I spent twenty minutes asking myself, "Well, what was so interesting about it? Why? What word could capture that?" I rewrote my sentence four or five times to understand and express more clearly what I felt. It's possible I still got a C.

12. Much of my discussion of deliberate practice draws on the insights of the late Anders Ericsson, perhaps the foremost researcher on the idea of "deliberate practice" and the coiner of that term. I highly recommend his book *Peak: Secrets from the New Science of Expertise.*

13. Admittedly, if you want to be Yo-Yo Ma, you'll need both.

# Chapter 9

# Building Ratio Through Discussion

Stephen Covey observed more than thirty years ago that "most people do not listen with the intent to understand. They listen with the intent to reply."[1] This observation has perhaps never been truer than today, when we risk running classrooms that echo the increasingly dominant and counterproductive forms of discussion evidenced on social media—one side blasting a point of view they are sure cannot be wrong or even nuanced at the opposite side, who are busy preparing an equally righteous return salvo. The goal of being proven right in a discussion is very different from the goal of learning from it. Without careful listening, a clear shared purpose, and a sense that discussion is supposed to add to our collective and individual understanding, we're not really getting what we should out of it. Perhaps without those things we're not even discussing at all.

It is at least worth asking whether our classrooms might unintentionally be contributing to the larger social trend of discourse characterized by an excess of righteous pronouncements and far less listening or seeking nuance. Do we teach our students to listen well? That a question can be more powerful than a pronouncement? To assume their first impression might be wrong, and just maybe to believe they have succeeded if and when they changed their thinking? Wisdom, mostly, is realizing how little you know. How much talking there is and how avidly it's offered is often the criteria by which we measure our discussions. Talking, after all, is easy to see and measure. But we might be better served by socializing students to listen and proceed with a mindset that says, "I probably have a lot to learn from others." It would be harder but perhaps more valuable to measure our discussions based on listening as much as talking.

*Effective* discussions in the classroom are rare. Many people might say this is because it's hard to get students to talk. In fact, what teachers *tell students* they want them to do during discussion is almost always to talk more. Students are graded on their participation and that usually means how often they talk, and perhaps with bonus points for strength of opinion. A *good* discussion, in this paradigm, is lots of students talking, and a *great* one is lots of students talking *and expressing opinions strongly and confidently*. Colby argues forcefully and repeatedly about the Kansas-Nebraska Act and we are happy. Look at him fighting for his ideas![2] He knows what he believes and won't be swayed!

To talk a lot is to succeed. To talk louder, to be more ardent in one's opinions and beliefs, is to succeed more.

But talking only improves student thinking if it is part of an exchange and if people are listening to one another—ideally with open minds inclined to consider and potentially change initial reactions and opinions. A true discussion requires students to listen well and respond after careful consideration. Perhaps the idea that Colby is sure of what he believes and won't be swayed is not an entirely good thing.

Further, for a discussion to be effective, the purpose must be more than to prove that you are right and others are wrong. The name for that is a debate. In the classroom, the goal should be to learn from rather than win the discussion—to inform rather than confirm what you thought you knew. All participants then are working to ultimately answer the question: what have I or we learned from this process?

In this chapter I am going to talk about talking but I am going to try to talk at least as much about listening. While we should encourage speaking, it's the listening—and maybe ideally the speaking in conjunction with careful listening—that's most valuable in our discussions.

A clear mental model is a good starting point. Something other than "talk more and talk louder" should shape our purpose. If we aren't clear on how discussion is different from students merely talking, students talking may be all we get.[3]

In this chapter I discuss tools for building more productive discussions. I'll begin with *Turn and Talk*, a procedure for pair discussions. One benefit of a classroom where pair conversations are excellent is that those conversations can support and improve many of the habits that support larger whole-group discussions. Second, I'll talk about *Habits of Discussion*, which describes how to build productive habits to foster collaboration and cohesiveness in discussions. I'll then discuss *Batch Processing*: letting students speak after and respond to one another often in short sequences. I'll close with *Disciplined Discussion*, which suggests that helping people stay on topic and follow a thread is an overlooked skill. We tend to valorize "outside the box" ideas but "inside the box" comments are often far more valuable.

## TECHNIQUE 43: TURN AND TALK

*Turn and Talk*—a short, contained pair discussion—is a common teaching tool used in thousands of classrooms and it offers a lot of benefits. Among others:

- It boosts Participation Ratio. You say "Why is Scout afraid? *Turn and Talk* to your partner for thirty seconds. Go!" and suddenly fifteen voices are going at once instead of just one. In a short time you've allowed almost everyone the chance to share an answer.

- It can increase reluctant students' willingness to speak in larger settings. A student rehearses an idea she might not offer in front of thirty people, and finds it comes out well or earns admiration from her partner. She becomes more willing to share her idea with the whole group.

- It's a great response when the class appears stuck. You ask a question, get only a smattering of hands or perhaps none at all, and respond: "Hmmm. No one seems quite sure. *Turn and Talk* with your partner for thirty seconds. See if you can come up with some ideas. Go!" Suddenly you have a workaround for explaining the answer.

- It can allow you to listen in on conversations and choose valuable comments to start discussion with, as in, "Maria, would you mind sharing what you and Justine talked about?"

But there are challenges to go with the benefits. Because it *can* result in fifteen people talking at once does not mean it *will*, and a disengaged *Turn and Talk* where there's little turning and even less talking is a culture killer. And there are a variety of accountability challenges:

- Conversations may wander off the assigned topic and may never even address the topic at all. (It is, after all, exciting to have the chance to chat with your friend in the middle of class.)

- There is the risk that students in a *Turn and Talk* listen poorly—that their partner is merely a target for their own words and not a source of insight.

- Even if everyone is on topic and listening their hardest, erroneous information could still spread. Billy Knowsforsure tells Tammy Tendstobelieve that to take the square root of something means to divide it by two; she nods, begins committing it to memory, and you never know it. Education researcher Graham Nuthall, carefully observing students during lessons,[4] found that students frequently persuaded their classmates that erroneous information was true. The most credulous were likely to be those with the weakest knowledge on a topic.

So *used frequently* does not always imply *used well*. The details of execution are critical. BreOnna Tindall's execution of her *Turn and Talk* in the video *BreOnna Tindall: Keystone* provides a road map. Students have read a short passage about the idea of "blind justice" and have been asked to discuss whether the idea of justice being blind is supposed to be a positive or a negative symbol. BreOnna gives a direction: "One minute to *Turn and Talk*. Share out your response with your face partner. Go!" Suddenly, the room crackles to life.

Her success starts with the directions. They are crisp and clear, without an extraneous word, *economy of language* exemplified. The speed and energy of the transition capped off by the cue to action "Go!" means that everyone starts at exactly the same time. No one has time or incentive to glance around and see if their peers are really doing it. In these ways her directions exemplify technique 28, *Brighten the Lines*.

Of course it's critical that *Turn and Talk* is a familiar procedure. BreOnna has taught her students how to do *Turn and Talk* well and they've practiced it. You can see their familiarity with it in the video. They know who their partner is without having to ask; they start their conversations comfortably and naturally; they speak at the appropriate volume. And perhaps most of all, the practice has taught them that since everyone is going to join in the *Turn and Talk* with energy and enthusiasm, they can safely do the same. This lack of hesitation is one of the main reasons why just seconds after the prompt, the room crackles to life.

Interestingly, it's not just one procedure. As the phrase "*Turn and Talk* with your face partner" implies, there are *face partners* and also *shoulder partners*. BreOnna can keep things fresh by shifting which partner students talk to. Her room layout is designed around *Turn and Talk*!

And don't overlook her phrase "share out your response" as it implies something important. Of course, they have plenty to say. Students have written first and are sharing what they wrote. As with whole group discussions, writing first means a more substantive and inclusive partner discussion (see technique 40, *Front the Writing*). As we will see, *Turn and Talk* works best when designed for synergy with what happens before and after.

Finally, BreOna tells her students they will have (just) one minute to talk. This helps them gauge the appropriate length of their comments. And, ironically, keeping the *Turn and Talk* short maximizes its value. It's a preliminary to the larger class discussion, so BreOnna wants students to have more to say, still, when it's over. She doesn't want them to say everything yet.

You can see many of the same themes in the video *Sarah Wright: Keystone*. First, Sarah asks a question: "Imagine you are Tio Luis [in Pam Muñoz-Ryan's novel *Esperanza Rising*], what would you say?" This is a reiteration of a question they have already responded to in writing, and now they get to share their brilliance. There are hands in the air. Lots. Students are eager to talk so this might seem like a surprising moment to choose a *Turn and Talk*. One of its best uses, I noted earlier, is to help build engagement when students are hesitant. But here it's useful for the opposite reason. When you have lots of eager hands, *Turn and Talk* can be a great way to let everyone get to talk and to minimize the *I had a great answer and didn't get to share it* frustration.

Like in BreOnna's classroom, Sarah's directions are crisp and clear with no extra words. They end in a consistent in-cue—the same as Breonna's, "Go!"—and again the room crackles to life. You can then see Sarah circulating, listening to answers, sharing her appreciation, and also perhaps deciding whom to call on.

But again, not every *Turn and Talk* looks like these. How does a teacher build this level of energy and productivity?

The first step is ensuring that students feel responsible for doing the task in front of them to the best of their ability. Once you've done that, you can begin to design the activity for maximum rigor. This "all in" attitude is achieved mostly through intentional habit-building. In the videos, neither BreOnna nor Sarah tells their students, "Be attentive; be active; do your best, and talk about the topic at hand." Those things are understood. Students do them automatically, which means they are carefully taught and reinforced until they become routine.

## Build the Routine

A *Turn and Talk* is a recurring classroom procedure; a common means for students to engage ideas. The more frequently something recurs in the classroom, the more important to make it a routine—to map the steps of the procedure, then rehearse and repeat it until it happens smoothly and with almost no drain on working memory. You can read more in Chapter Ten about installing routines but some specific aspects of the *Turn and Talk* routine deserve specific comment.

"My *Turn and Talks* actually used to be pretty ineffective," BreOnna shared. "[Students] would not talk—or they would talk about something else." Now, though, she builds in "an extensive rollout where I explain 'this is what I'm expecting [active on-topic conversations; asking questions of each other], this is the type of language I want to hear [academic vocabulary]. I want to see these actions [nodding; facing each other; showing your partner you're listening].' It could seem a little Type A but I honestly think kids just don't know how to have an academic conversation in a way that brings out the best in their partner. I try to make sure they have all the tools before they need them."

Who partners with whom should be set in advance so that conversations can begin without further action or discussion, as they do in BreOnna's and Sarah's classes. Generally, partners should be pairs who are sitting side by side and should commonly remain partners for the duration of a lesson—although, as I noted, BreOnna's students have two potential partner pairings: a shoulder partner and a face partner. In Sarah's class, there is just one partner but in both cases, that partner is clearly established before class begins.

The value is not just in the fact that when students are chatting with a partner within two seconds, they're using time efficiently. It's that a fast and familiar transition preserves continuity of thinking. Whatever was on their mind as they were writing remains in their working memory as they enter the *Turn and Talk*. Five or ten seconds spent looking for a partner or scanning the room to see if everybody is doing the *Turn and Talk* is more than enough to remove a key thought from working memory.

In other words, for the sake of the thinking, the transition needs to be smooth, precise, and almost invisibly efficient.

## The In-Cue

Watch the students during the *Turn and Talks* in the video *Christine Torres: Keystone*. The first one starts with Christine asking: "How does the image show *implore*? Fifteen seconds with your teammate. Go!"

A few minutes later she asks: "What *caustic* remark might the judge have made? Fifteen seconds to *Turn and Talk*. Go."

In each case the cue is short, crisp, and sharp and the response is decisive momentum-building energy—enthusiasm might be a better word—from the class.

Think high school students won't do that? Watch Denarius Frazier's students at the beginning of the video *Denarius Frazier: Keystone*: "Tell your neighbor what you want to remember every time we're doing synthetic division." Or Sadie McCleary's at the beginning of her Keystone: "With your partner: What happens as you increase temperature to the pressure of a gas and why, based on particle motion? Go!"

There's not an ounce of reluctance or cynicism in sight. Students in these videos are showing us that they perceive and react to classroom norms. If students look around the room and see hesitation, if they don't see others turning and talking right away, they won't perceive the activity to be the norm. Some students won't do it and those who do will be likely to feign as much participation as is required but to seek to do the bare minimum.

But if students perceive in the first fractions of a second that universal positive engagement is the norm, or if they assume—as they anticipate the *Turn and Talk* coming—that everyone will naturally participate with interest and enthusiasm, then you get the kind of crackling energy you see in Christine's, BreOnna's, Sarah's, Denarius's, and Sadie's classrooms.

It's critical that *Turn and Talk* become a familiar and well-rehearsed procedure, in other words, and it's critical that it be launched with an in-cue that is both a *direction*—here is what to do—and *signal* to start and so should be short, crisp, and clear. You need just enough words to clarify the question and the task; beyond that, keeping the in-cue short and punchy creates energy.

It's no coincidence then that the in-cues we see are so similar.

The recipe is **Frame. Name. [Time]. Go!** in almost every case. Teachers frame the question clearly, then identify that the task is a *Turn and Talk*, and then (sometimes) set a time context. Then they give a consistent signal to start. That the signal is so often "Go!" is no surprise, given the goal of building an immediately visible norm of positive engagement.

It's worth lingering for a moment on the first step, framing the question. Once a strong procedure has been installed (see techniques 49 and 50 in particular for guidance on this critical step), the framing is the trickiest part. It's very hard to jump into a discussion with energy and verve if you're not clear on the question or what it means. And this means, for teachers, the question for discussion should be carefully phrased and quite possibly drafted in advance. Sometimes you will use one reactively in the moment—"Hmm. We're a little divided on the answer. Turn and discuss with your partner. . ."—but for the most part teachers like the ones we've watched have likely drafted their *Turn and Talks* in their notes. You can see an example of how Christine prepares this part of her lesson in Chapter Two.

It's worth noting, too, that there might be cases in which you'd want to vary your cadence, tone, and inflection when framing a question. For example, if I thought the question was especially challenging and thoughtful and wanted students to think carefully as or before they began to *Turn and Talk*, I might give my directions with a slower cadence and a reflective tone. I watched Rue Ratray (then of Edward Brooke Charter School in Boston) do this masterfully in one of his lessons recently. Students were reading an interview with Lois Lowry about her novel *The Giver,* and came upon a sentence that required close reading. "I agree with Nijah," Rue said. "We do need to break down the phrase '*Rejecting the authority and wisdom of the governing body*.' What does *that* mean?" he asked. He spoke slowly and tilted his head slightly in apparent befuddlement. He paused for a few seconds to let the question sink in. Then: "*Turn and Talk* to your partner. Go!"

As he said this the class came to life. The phrase Rue used, "*Turn and Talk* to your partner. Go!" was central to this success. It was familiar because he'd been using it steadily for weeks as he dispatched them to *Turn and Talks*. But here he combined it with a bit of *Wait Time* beforehand . . . four or five seconds to begin reflecting before they spoke. Denarius Frazier, too, uses a long stretch of *Wait Time* before his crisp cue to *Turn and Talk* at the beginning of his Keystone to set a cerebral and reflective tone.

If the transition into *Turn and Talk* is crisp and the routine familiar, you can cue up a *Turn and Talk* on the spur of the moment. Notice how the *Turn and Talk* unfolds in the video *Alonte Johnson: Mother's Courage* during Alonte's lesson on on Edna St. Vincent Millay's poem "The Courage That My Mother Had." Alonte's *Turn and Talk* is unplanned—a reaction to the small number of hands he sees when he asks his question. He thinks—*Ah! They're reticent. I'll let them talk it out to build their ideas and their confidence.* He even shares that intention with them at the end: "Glad to see so many more hands.. . ." Only when the routine is seamless and clear can you drop it in impromptu like this. But if you *can* it's an ideal tool for responding to crickets.

## Managing Turns and Listening Behaviors

A quick, consistent *Turn and Talk* in-cue helps foster energetic discussion among all students. But to return to one of the themes of this chapter, the value of the discussion that comes after relies as much on the quality of the listening as it does on the quality of the talking, so it's worth taking a moment to consider some of the ways teachers can build and reinforce listening behaviors during *Turn and Talk*.

One of my favorites is the occasional use of managed turns—intentionally cuing one partner or the other to start first. This is valuable because we can make two important assumptions about most *Turn and Talks*. First, the talking within them won't be split evenly. Sometimes the first person to talk will talk through the whole *Turn and Talk*. This can be for legitimate reasons—the *Turn and Talk* is short, and it takes a while to make a point, or they're caught up in an idea. Second, we can assume that some students are more inclined to talk than others. They are likely to interpret the phrase "*Turn and Talk* to your partner, go!" as a cue to start talking themselves. Others are more reserved by nature. They are likely to interpret the phrase "*Turn and Talk* to your partner, go!" as a cue to glance at their partner and encourage them to start talking. Not always, of course, but there are tendencies, stronger or weaker, among specific students. If we pair them neutrally, those who tend to talk more will talk more—when perhaps it would be more beneficial for them to practice listening—and those who are quieter will be more inclined to listen—when perhaps it would be good for them to talk a little more.

Eric Snider of Achievement First Bushwick Middle School used the idea of managed turns to address that in a recent lesson. His class was reading Ray Bradbury. During a tense scene, Eric looked at his students. "What is David, the son, feeling worried about?" Pausing briefly, he added, "Long hair to short hair." That phrase was their prompt to *Turn and Talk*. It meant that the member of each pair with longer hair would start the conversation. Other times when Eric used the in-cue, he would say, "Short hair to long hair,"[5] to reverse whose turn came first and ensure balance in participation. Other times, of course, he would not specify who began and would leave it to students instead. The idea is to occasionally increase voice equity by balancing the talking and listening roles.

A related tool that can balance voice equity during *Turn and Talks* is to insert an intentional switch point. For instance, "We're halfway through your ninety seconds. Please be sure switch partners if you haven't already."

Another useful tool for socializing listening in *Turn and Talks* is to ask students to refer to their partner's idea when calling on them afterwards, as in: "Rodrigo, what did you and Kelsey talk about?" Or, after Rodrigo says, "I think the reaction is going to give off heat energy," asking, "Did Kelsey agree?" Or, on occasions when students spontaneously mention their partners' thinking—"We weren't sure but Kelsey thought it would be exothermic"—saying "Thank you for referencing your partner's ideas."

You could also be more meta: "I'd love to hear from some class members whose partner shared a particularly useful example during the *Turn and Talk*." Or "I'd like to start with someone whose partner said something surprising." Letting students know that we notice and care when they show they value their partner's contributions is one way to get them to do more of it.

"In questioning after a *Turn and Talk*, I ask about the conversations," Bill Wilkinson, deputy head of science at Beechen Cliff School, in Bath, England, noted. He suggests asking such questions as: (1) Which pairs disagreed on the answer at first? (2) Which pairs agreed by the end? (3) Which of you changed your mind? Tell us why. (4) Don't tell me what you thought, tell me what your partner thought.

## The Accountability Challenge

Here are some tools that can help to ensure that your *Turn and Talks* are accountable and focused—that is, that students feel gentle pressure to do their best work and stay on task.

Use *Cold Call* (technique 34) to set the expectation that everyone should be ready to talk about some insight he or she gleaned after the *Turn and Talk* is complete. Have a positive tone and make sure you sound genuinely interested: *Magalie, tell us a bit about what you and Donald spoke about. . .* If this is relatively predictable, students will know they have to be ready to summarize their conversation. You can often make this likelihood of a *Cold Call* more transparent by letting students know beforehand that it's likely to occur: "One minute to discuss the imagery you noticed with your partner. I may *Cold Call* a few of you to share, so be ready with what you and your partner discussed. Go!"

Circulating during the *Turn and Talk* and listening in on conversations gives you a double bonus—it allows you to show appreciation for and interest in good work and tacitly ensure students are focused and productive. You can see in the following pictures of Christine Torres, Sarah Wright, and BreOnna Tindall how they use body language and posture to show their interest in what they hear students say as they circulate. In some cases they are actually responding verbally. In others they are merely listening and showing how much they appreciate top effort.

*Turn and Task.* You can also turn your *Turn and Talk* into a *Turn and Task.* You can see a great example of this in the video *Gabby Woolf: Keystone.* After a round of *FASE Reading* (technique 24) with her class, Gabby assigns students to read the next section of text to one another in pairs. It's partner work but the work they do together is something other than discussion. That might mean saying: "With your partner, come up with a list of three words to describe the setting," or "With your partner, write a hypothesis describing the results you think you might see from the experiment." "With your partner, solve problem 4. I'll *Cold Call* some of you to hear your answers. Go!" Having a clear deliverable emphasizes accountability a bit more because the task is clearer. If it's a written task, it serves this purpose even better: you can observe the writing as you circulate. You can ask students to "share what you wrote." You can even collect the work to review it later.

One small lesson for teachers from the year 2020 and online instruction comes from doing *Turn and Talks* online via breakout rooms. The most common reason why pairs are off task in an online breakout room is that students can't remember or are not clear on the question!

So making sure that the question is absolutely clear—and possibly even written down some-where if the *Turn and Talk* is more than a minute in length—can help remind people of what they are supposed to be discussing.[6]

A final note on accountability and focus. Students engage fully in *Turn and Talks* in large part because it is their habit to do so. We want to avoid letting them get into the habit of sit-ting looking at each other during a *Turn and Talk* because they have little to say. In fact we want to avoid their even having that experience. We want them to assume the conversation will be active and useful. One reason why students might have experiences with disengaged and passive *Turn and Talks* is because otherwise productive *Turn and Talks* went on too long and resulted in awkward moments when they and their partners were all talked out. That's my first topic in the next section, but it's worth noting that keeping *Turn and Talks* short also plays a role in keeping students engaged.

## Design and Sequence for Rigor

Recently I watched a lesson from a middle school science class. The topic of the lesson was friction. The class had read an article on how friction might affect the movements of a bas-ketball during a game, and the teacher asked his students to *Turn and Talk* to discuss what they'd learned. The teacher's in-cue was crisp, and he had established a culture of positive accountability, so students buzzed into action, sharing their energy, their excitement, and, as it turned out afterwards, a great deal of misinformation.

When the teacher asked students to share the ideas they'd discussed in pairs, the first three out of four shared ideas that misapplied or misunderstood how friction worked. Almost everyone, the data was telling him, had shared and believed misreadings about the article. Suddenly, he had some mopping up to do.

There are times, this story reminds us, when even with efficient and accountable sys-tems, *Turn and Talks* can be dominated by the spread of low-quality ideas—or erroneous ones. In the class I watched, the teacher stumbled on this fact through the good fortune of hearing answers that revealed the problems, and the wise decision to process the *Turn and Talk* through a broader, teacher-led discussion afterwards. But let's pause here to consider all of the *Turn and Talks* where misinformation has blithely and earnestly been spread among participating students who did not know that what they were hearing (or saying and driv-ing into memory) was dead wrong, all without the teacher being aware of it. As Graham Nuthall points out in *The Hidden Lives of Learners*, peer-generated misinformation can be profoundly influential on student thinking.

A *Turn and Talk* by itself is a great tool for boosting Participation Ratio, then. It multiplies voices and gets everyone going by giving them a low-stakes way to share ideas, rehearse a larger thought, develop their first impression, or hear an alternative reaction, all in semi-private, where saying, "Whoops, actually that was a really bad idea!" is fine. But *Turn and Talk* can also involve students sharing ideas that need development and clarification. It can involve the spreading of misinformation and confirmation bias. It can generate thinking that requires more reflection and direction.

Perhaps the most useful way to think about *Turn and Talk* is as a rehearsal for some other activity: a whole-class discussion, a written synthesis, a charting and comparison of ideas generated. The *Turn and Talk*'s purpose is generative—let's get a lot of ideas going, figure out what makes sense, and why. After a *Turn and Talk,* the ideas that were generated get analyzed, studied, clarified, and confirmed—maybe even edited, revised, and prioritized—in a public way, so that students see what was good, what was better, and possibly what was wrong.

Here, then, are three key "after" activities to make sure that *Turn and Talk* brings rigor and high standards to your classroom.

## Whole-Class Analysis

Teach students that the first idea is not always the best idea, that developing a strong answer often requires going back through your initial thoughts and considering them in light of further criteria or analysis. This might sound like "Let's look at some of the ideas we came up with and see which ones make the most sense," or "Let's try to use what we know about friction to test a few of our ideas and see if they were accurate." Or you could try something like "Let's put a couple of these on the board and list the evidence that seems to support (or not support) some of our ideas."

## Whole-Class Discussion

Use *Turn and Talk* as the starting point for a deeper whole-class discussion that builds on and stretches students' initial thinking. This might sound like "Let's build on the thinking we've started," possibly with a coda, like "As we talk, feel free to add to what you already wrote down." Or you might try "Now let's try to put our ideas together to come up with a few 'best' examples." Or, finally, you could just acknowledge that the initial *Turn and Talk* was a warm-up: "Now that we've started to discuss some ideas, let's take a look at the sentence together and see if we can make sense of what it means."

## Whole-Class Note-Taking

Follow up the *Turn and Talk* by processing those initial thoughts—by having students share, improve, and prioritize the contents of their collective "pair" discussions. The expectation here is that they take what they talked about in their *Turn and Talk,* develop it by listening and comparing to what others took from the discussion, and track a wide array of thoughts on the topic, not just their own. This might sound like "Add two sentences to the bullets on page three" or "Now let's look at the passage and circle all the evidence we found as a group. Make sure to take notes on your sheet so you've got all of our class's ideas in your notes."

## What Comes First?

Another way to build more Think Ratio into your *Turn and Talk* is to add an activity before it occurs that boosts ratio.

Letting students write first is the most obvious. We can see the effects of this in BreOnna Tindall's classroom. What students are discussing in pairs is not their spur-of-the-moment reaction but something they've been wrestling into words for several minutes. The Think Ratio is higher. As I discuss in the chapter on writing for ratio, writing first helps any discussion—even a pair conversation. It adds rigor and allows people to listen better.

Think time prior to a *Turn and Talk* can also help. It's simple and fast and provides some of the benefit you get from allowing students to write first. That's what Rue Ratray was doing when he posed his question to his students about *The Giver*—"We do need to break down the phrase 'Rejecting the authority and wisdom of the governing body.' What does *that* mean?" As you'll recall he paused for four or five seconds before sending students to a *Turn and Talk.* Letting them reflect and generate initial ideas. You could easily stretch out this think time and make it more transparent

T: "We do need to break down the phrase 'Rejecting the authority and wisdom of the governing body.' What does *that* mean? Take ten seconds to think about what that phrase means before I let you talk to a partner about it. [Ten seconds elapses] OK. Share your thoughts with your partner. Go!"

Or

T: "We do need to break down the phrase 'Rejecting the authority and wisdom of the governing body.' What does *that* mean? Take fifteen seconds to jot down some ideas. What does that phrase mean? Then I'll let you talk to a partner about it. [Fifteen seconds elapses] OK. Share your thoughts with your partner. Go!"

In these two examples, you would make the *Turn and Talk* even better by making sure the question was jotted on the whiteboard or student packet, and thus helping students to remember the question once the conversation actually begins.

Inserting a *Turn and Talk* when you're stuck can also be a useful tool. Here you're not so much planning a preliminary activity as spotting a place where the Think Ratio is high and some more active thinking would help. That's what Alonte Johnson and Denarius Frazier are doing with their impromptu *Turn and Talks*. The moment when students are stuck is a great time to let them "think it out" in pairs.

## Priming

A final thought on building more rigor into *Turn and Talks*: In addition to a clear question, a time frame and a cue to begin, your *Turn and Talk* directions can also prompt students to use or discuss specific key ideas. For example: "Take forty-five seconds to discuss what's happening with your partner. Strive to use the words 'spindle fibers.' I'll put it up on the board to help you remember. If your partner doesn't use that phrase, ask them to restate using the key term, as we will be using it when we share out after your conversations."

## Crest of the Wave and Precise Time Limits

Two general rules of thumb can help you to manage time (and timing) during *Turn and Talks*. The first, *crest of the wave*, relates to the observation that a *Turn and Talk* is almost always a preliminary activity. It's rarely the capstone to work on a topic, but rather a midpoint where ideas are rehearsed and developed before they are harvested, refined, and developed. If you are transitioning from a *Turn and Talk* to an activity that allows for better synthesis, you want students to still be actively wrestling with ideas and eager to take them forward, rather than feeling "done" with an idea as the *Turn and Talk* ends. If it goes on too long and students have talked through all of their ideas, running out of things to say as the clock keeps ticking, this will sap energy and cause students to perceive *Turn and Talk* as an activity in which there's not much urgency to discuss things because there's likely to be dead time to fill. This perception will likely infect behavior in all *Turn and Talks*.

If you were to graph the level of energy during a *Turn and Talk*, it might look like a normal curve with a fat tail at the end. Ideally you would end it at its maximum point, when ideas were bursting and students eager to get to the next steps, before the long slope downward. That's the crest of the wave (see Figure 9.1).

## Precise, Clear Time Limits

Another general rule is to be precise with time. Imagine you're a student and are participating in a *Turn and Talk*, but you don't know how long it's going to last. Forty-five seconds? Two minutes? Fifteen minutes? Not knowing this basic information can make it hard for you to gauge how much to say. Do you need to get the basic idea out and stop so that the other person can broach an idea? Is your conversation about deep analysis? Should you ask your

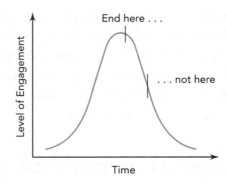

**Figure 9.1**    Crest of the Wave. Time your out-cue so that the *Turn and Talk* ends at the crest of interest and energy, not as it peters out.

partner a thoughtful question? Informing participants of the time parameters helps them manage their comments and their conversations to make the best use of time. Saying *"Turn and Talk* to your neighbor for the next thirty seconds" means just share some initial ideas. Be quick and then let the other person talk. Saying "Two-and-a-half minutes to discuss the role of setting. Go!" provides guidance; further, your use of specific and odd increments shows that your time allocation is careful, specific, and intentional. It tells students that time and its careful use matter to you, so they should matter to them. If you use a stopwatch to track those time allocations, it also helps you keep yourself accountable for moving the lesson forward and not losing track of time while checking in with a stuck or highly engaged pair, for example. And, over time, it will help you make smarter and more specific time allocations for *Turn and Talks*.

## Online Lessons: Remote *Turn and Talks*

*Turn and Talks* were critical to engagement during remote teaching. They allowed us to boost the ratio and let often isolated students talk to one another. But online *Turn and Talks*—breakout rooms in pairs—were also doubly challenging. The video *Ben Esser: Shorter Turn and Talk* shows how Ben solved many of these challenges. Students have written answers first, so this *Turn and Talk* is an opportunity to rehearse and explain ideas. Perhaps for that reason the time allocation is short, and Ben emphasizes this fact by telling students it will be short. He wants them to come out ready to talk to the whole group. Being clear about time helps students gauge how long to talk and making sure they have plenty to say helps overcome some potential awkwardness of being in a breakout room without much to say. You can also see that he's managing turns here—the person with the name that comes first in the alphabet goes first. He also addresses the possibility of students being off task by dropping into a few pairs conversations. In fact, Ben *Cold Calls* Suraya to speak because he dropped into her group and thought she had a strong idea. She most likely knows this and sees the *Cold Call* as an approval of her thinking.

## TECHNIQUE 44: HABITS OF DISCUSSION

Imagine for a moment that we're sitting with a group of people. You say, "I just finished *The Giver*. It's so good and psychologically jarring."

I say, "I'm almost done with *The Hunger Games*. It's so violent but still pretty good."

Then our friend Corinne joins in. "I just couldn't get into *The Hunger Games*," she says.

This series of comments does not quite qualify as a discussion—at least not in the fullest sense. Instead, it exemplifies what's often missing when we call disconnected verbal interactions a "discussion." Was my comment, "I'm almost done with *The Hunger Games*," a response to your comment about *The Giver*, for example? Did I say that because they are both dystopian novels and I see some connection? Did I hear your point about it being psychologically jarring? Am I comparing that to the violence of *Hunger Games*? Am I just using the opportunity to talk about a book that I like instead of one that you like? Am I trying to talk about *The Giver* or changing the subject? If I'd said something like, "I hear you about *The Giver*. Someone told me *The Hunger Games* would be similar but it's not as good to me. Maybe because it's so violent," I would be connecting my comment to yours and making it clear how they were related. And I would be making it clear that I had listened carefully to what you said.

Corinne's comment was similar. When she said, "I couldn't get into *The Hunger Games*," was she changing the subject due to her inability to finish books? Excusing herself from the conversation on the grounds that she hadn't read the book? Or was she saying she had stopped reading *The Hunger Games* because it was so violent? Was she following up on my comment? Did she hear it? A bit of framing—"Funny the violence didn't bother me but I couldn't get into *The Hunger Games*. It just wasn't as well written as *The Giver*"—could have helped us to see those connections and knit our comments together. She was in fact comparing the books we'd both mentioned and showing that she was thinking about the connection.

We all could have connected our ideas and demonstrated that we were listening, but we didn't. Our comments were related, but not really a discussion so much as a series of statements loosely grouped around an idea.

Conversations in the classroom are often similar. A discussion is supposed to be *a mutual endeavor by a group of people to develop, refine, or contextualize an idea or set of ideas,* and that's different from a series of loosely related comments. What characterizes discussion in the most successful classrooms is a commitment to connecting and relating ideas and opinions. A discussion that's valuable will feature comments that are consistently useful to others, not just interesting to those who made them, and which establish the speaker's understanding of and interest in what was previously said.

People who make a conversation effective *show* they are listening carefully by occasionally offering brief summaries of other participants' comments or by making a specific effort to connect the point they're making to what someone else said. A comment that refers back to earlier ideas and strives for that connection makes for a discussion—for example, saying "Funny, the violence didn't bother me" both clarifies the argument and shows appreciation for what other conversants have said. And it makes us feel like we belong and have things to contribute. It convinces us to share more, and perhaps to believe ourselves to be a little more capable.

Generally, of course, people don't consciously think, *I'll make it clear I'm building off someone else's point* or *I'll reinforce that I value the person I'm talking to right now even though I disagree.* Most positive discussion-building actions are habits triggered by a conversant's intuitive sense of how discussion should work—a mental model. So if a teacher can instill strong conversational habits and an effective mental model, she will help students quite naturally build discussions that are connected, in which participants show appreciation for one another.

Cultures that express appreciation during discussion and especially when there is disagreement are important for more reasons than cordiality. Jonathan Haidt explains in his book *The Righteous Mind* that people are much more likely to change their opinion when they like the person they are talking to and know he or she likes and cares about them. Ideas that change us come from people we perceive as allies. We like and trust them first; then we listen with openness. This is especially true when we already believe something. Someone who confronts us almost never changes an established belief; only someone we *want* to believe does that, Haidt finds. So when mutual respect and psychological safety pervade, and where the ethos is collaborative, and the message is *We are working together to understand this,* then, true open-mindedness and maximum learning are likely to occur.

In most cases, good discussion skills, those that allow certain people to bring out the best in their colleagues, are not "naturally occurring." Especially not today, when abrasive models of conversation are so commonly normalized on social media. To reliably have great discussions in your classroom, it's necessary to instill such behaviors deliberately. Doing so is a technique I call *Habits of Discussion*, and it's a powerful tool. The return on the investment in teaching students how to discuss is immense.

The first step in building strong *Habits of Discussion* is a series of nearly invisible behaviors displayed by participants in a conversation that signal the importance of the endeavor and remind other participants of their belonging in a community that values them. These include things like establishing and maintaining eye contact and engaging frequently in *prosocial nonverbal behaviors*, such as nodding to show understanding and others I described in the critical technique *Habits of Attention*. "A small signal can have a huge effect on people's sense of belonging and membership," social psychologist Gregory Walton tells Daniel Coyle in *The Culture Code*. "But the deeper thing to realize is that you can't just give the cue once." It has to occur frequently and steadily.

The fundamental actions participants take to build a strong discussion are listening carefully and showing speakers they care about what they're saying. No one makes a discussion-changing insight to a room full of people whose body language says *I don't care*. Maintaining eye contact not only helps communicate both ideas but helps students discipline themselves to "lock in" on the person they're listening to and helps them "hear more." By looking at the person talking, a listener picks up gestures and facial expressions that add meaning to the words themselves.

An additional fundamental comes from the technique *Format Matters*. Students have to speak loudly enough to be heard clearly. This works best when it is a habit. Nothing breaks the thread of a discussion like the teacher saying, "Carly, we can't hear you," or, worse, the situation going uncorrected. *It's fine if we can't hear you* makes a pretty clear statement about the importance afforded to Carly's thoughts. Not only can people not respond to what they can't hear, but when people are straining to hear, their facial expressions and body language change. You cannot make a what-you-are-saying-is-interesting face when you are making an I-can-barely-hear-you one.

To the importance of eye contact, listening behaviors, and reinforcing voice volume, we can add three specific additional fundamentals: names, reciprocal looking, and rephrasing.

Consider this moment from a discussion in an eighth-grade classroom about Lincoln's inaugural address.

"I think Lincoln looked weak and maybe conflicted in extending an 'olive branch' to the Southern states," Jabari says.

"No," Jamila counters, "He says he will enforce federal laws in states that secede. He's drawing a clear line in the sand but trying not to seem like he's provoking conflict." Jamila is looking at the teacher as she says this, implying that the teacher is the person whose opinion matters most. Jabari, and the fact that the argument she is responding to is his, is just not that relevant to Jamila.

Now imagine the scene slightly differently. Michelle turns to Jabari. "Jabari," she says, "I don't read Lincoln's words as 'conflicted.' He says he will enforce federal laws in states that secede. He's drawing a clear line in the sand but trying not to seem like he's provoking conflict."

In looking at Jabari, in using his name in the response and implicitly summarizing his point and using his exact words—"I don't read Lincoln's words as conflicted"—Michelle has emphasized the fact that she is responding to him directly. Her actions say, *I listened carefully to your argument; I understood and respect it.* Alex Pentland, who leads the program on Connection Studies at MIT, notes that studies on team performance have found that cultures where "members communicate directly with one another . . . not just the team leader"[7] tend to be the most successful and collaborative learning environments.

Reciprocally looking at Jabari—looking back at him to show she is responding to him—rephrasing his argument and using his name all build the fabric of support and connection. They reinforce a sense of community in the classroom throughout the discussion.

Perhaps this is why I often see positive outlier teachers reinforce this expectation in class, either verbally—"Great; turn to Janelle and tell her that"—or nonverbally, with a brief point of the finger or eyes reminding students to look at the person they're responding to. They're reminding their students of how important it is for people who intend to discuss an idea to talk to each other.

Now let's upgrade Michelle's response even a little more. If Michelle said, "I read that passage differently, Jabari. I don't read Lincoln's words as 'conflicted,'" her words "I read that passage a little differently" show that she is relating her argument to his. *I agree that these are important words; here's a different way to think about them.* Making the effort to frame the connection shows that she thinks Jabari's comment was important. Participants who, like Michelle, tacitly reference preceding comments via syntactical structures embedded within the grammar of their sentences, make them important. Some typical phrases that do that include:

"I understand why you'd say that, but . . ."

"I was just thinking of something similar, that . . ."

"And then there was another example of that . . ."

"The thing that doesn't take into account is . . ."

"I want to build on what you said . . ."

In each of these examples—whether the new speaker is agreeing with the first speaker, disagreeing with her, or somewhere in between—the comment begins by framing the relationship between the present comment and the previous one, ideally in some respectful way. Teaching students to use frames like this to weave their comments together with those around them results in more cohesive discussions. It is usually accomplished through the use of *sentence starters*—short phrases that teachers socialize students to use and adapt, that facilitate building off someone else's idea.

Many teachers start by posting sentence starters like these on their wall and spending a few days asking students to practice using basic ones, saying things like, "Great; can you use a sentence starter to frame that response and talk directly to Aleisha?" or "Today I'm just going to listen for how well you use our sentence starters to build off one another during our discussion." Or, as BreOnna Tindall described, praising effective use of them, "Oh, you built on that idea so well. That was so good!" Over time, the list itself would become less critical as using the sentence starters and adaptations of them become a habit.

The simplest sentence starters are "I agree because . . ." or "I disagree because . . ." These are useful, especially, for getting students started in responding to one another and situating their comments within the larger conversation, but as many of the teachers I know have developed their use of sentence starters over time, they've pushed to get beyond "agree" or "disagree" pretty quickly. But sentence starters don't just reflect how students think during discussions; they shape it, too—in this case tending to socialize students to take sides, to focus on "winning" the discussion, to dig in their heels and try to prove their original comment was right. The best discussions are less about proving oneself right than they are about finding nuanced common ground. Agree/disagree is an acceptable starting point but students can and should think in more complex ways. So it's important to introduce students to sentence starters that push them to find other ways of connecting their arguments' to others:

"There's another piece of evidence to think about . . ."

"There's some evidence that makes me not sure what to think . . ."

"I'd like to build on _____'s idea . . ."

"I think there are two ways of reading that . . ."

"There's another example of what _____ is talking about . . ."

"Another way you might interpret that is . . ."

"I think it's more complex than what we've been saying because . . ."

Nonverbals, too, can be critical to building up the habit of using sentence starters. Maggie Johnson, a reading teacher at Troy Prep Middle School, developed different hand signals that her students used when they wanted to develop someone else's idea as opposed to making a new comment. When they want to make a new point during a discussion, they raise their hand in the usual fashion. When they want to "add on," develop, or respond to the previous point, they raise two fingers. This allows Maggie to shape the direction of the discussion even without participating in it. She can decide whether it's more valuable to stick with the present point or move on to a new one, and she can move in that direction merely by choosing whom she calls on to go next. In fact, keeping a discussion focused on a point of importance or value is one of the most important things for a teacher to attend to during discussion, a topic I will discuss in technique 46, *Disciplined Discussion*.

A last element of *Habits of Discussion* is the addition of teaching moves that cause students to build the habit—and ideally a mental model—of one speaker building off the previous. Follow-on questioning—an adaptation of the "follow-on" from the *Cold Call* (technique 34)—and follow-on prompting can help. In a follow-on, the teacher consistently asks one student to respond to something another student has said, whether or not the second student has volunteered to do so. Something as simple as, "Skylar, do you agree with Markus?" (asked in good faith and not as a "gotcha"; see *Cold Call* for more details) establishes the expectation that Skylar must always be listening well enough to be able to offer a reasonable response, even if only to say that he's not sure about a particular point. Expecting Skylar to be able to respond reinforces peer-to-peer listening and, importantly, reinforces that listening is an expectation no matter who is speaking—it is a courtesy not merely reserved for the teacher. Of course to build the habit of follow-on in discussion you could use it without the *Cold Call*. Skylar might have raised his hand and instead of simply calling on him by saying his name you might remind him of the expectation that he develop the previous comment by saying, "Skylar, what do you think of what Markus just said?"

Instead of asking a directive question like, "Skylar, do you agree with Markus?" follow-on prompting is nondirective, with the result that it disrupts the thread of the conversation less and avoids steering the second student's response, which in some cases is part of the purpose of discussion. A teacher who's using follow-on prompting might keep his students on their toes and listening to one another by using fast follow-on prompts five or six times per class— enough to be predictably unpredictable without breaking the flow of students responding directly to one another via *Cold Call*.

You can see Christine Torres doing this in the second half of her Keystone video. She asks students to opine on whether Kirsty is brave when she talks back to Nazi soldiers in a key scene of *Number the Stars*.

Mark says yes: She's young and vulnerable and brave in speaking up to those in power.

"Build on, Jasmine . . ." Christine says. This prompt reminds Jasmine to refer back to Mark's answer and contextualize her remarks accordingly. Like saying *develop* or *weigh in* or *say more*, *build on* reminds a student to both refer back to the previous comment and stay on the topic at hand, but unlike the more commonly used *agree or disagree* (or *do you agree?*) it also allows for a wider array of possible responses. Encouraging students to agree/disagree focuses them on who's right rather than more nuanced forms of thinking. It narrows the range of potential responses.

In this case Jasmine chooses a relatively straightforward connection between her comment and Mark's: "I agree with you, Mark," she says, "and I'd like to build on to it . . ." She's connected directly to Mark to show it's a discussion and indicated how her comment is related. She will be describing further evidence of Kirsty's bravery.

Next to be called on is Nate. "What do you think, Nate?" Christine says. It's a subtle reminder to situate his remark relative to Mark and Jasmine's comments.

"I respectfully disagree with you, Mark and Jasmine," Nate begins.

Through this approach, prompts like "develop" allow Christine to remind her students to practice responding to one another with little intervention from her.

There's a certain amount of sophistication and maturity evident in a class that uses *Habits of Discussion*, but the technique is effective even with younger students. For example, Anthony in Akilah Bond's Keystone video responds to Cheyenne about halfway through by saying, "I kind of agree with you, Cheyenne," and Michael begins to add, "What we're missing from Sonoa's response is . . ."

## TECHNIQUE 45: BATCH PROCESS

You can see some of the elements of strong *Habits of Discussion* and other elements from this book in the video *Jason Brewer: Batch Process*. Discussing changes in labor brought about by the early stages of industrialization in the United States, student are attentive and supportive of one another. Their prosocial listening behaviors and tracking (see *Habits of Attention*, technique 48) are strong. It feels like the kind of classroom where you can have a substantive conversation in a supportive environment. You'll probably also notice Jason's outstanding *Wait Time* (technique 33) before he calls on his first student, Mahaira. Her answer is wrong, but her classmates remain supportive and respectful and Jason manages his tell (see technique 12, *Culture of Error*) beautifully. He merely says, "Agree or disagree? . . . Nyesha . . ." It's a textbook follow-on prompt, reminding Nyesha to ground her comment in Mahaira's.

"I respectfully disagree with you, Mahaira," Nyesha begins, proceeding to point out how the rise of replaceable parts required less skill from laborers, allowing factory owners to replace them as they wished. She speaks directly to Mahaira and refers back to her classmate's answer gracefully.

Jason then calls on a third student, "Marty, what do you think?" reminding him to sustain focus on the present topic with a follow-on prompt that gives wide latitude and opens the opportunity for him to incorporate his classmate's comments into his own reflections.

It's a short discussion but a productive one. Jason says almost nothing about the content of the conversation in the spaces between his three students' comments except to call on the next speaker and gently remind them of discussion norms. He doesn't say, "That's right, would anyone like to build off of Nyesha's idea?" or "Marty has made an important point!" or "Almost, Mahaira, but I think you've left something out." Only at the end after three comments from students does he step in, asking the class questions about a hypothetical example in which Drayvon works in a factory and asks for more pay.

In addition to socializing strong *Habits of Discussion*, Jason is *Batch Processing*, establishing very short sequences in which students have mini peer-to-peer discussions even within other lesson activities, such as direct instruction or questioning (see Chapter 6). Jason doesn't have to stop class and announce: "OK, we'll have a discussion now." Merely by letting three students have turns directly in a row and not taking a turn himself until the end, he allows a mini-discussion to emerge naturally. He speaks only after three students have offered their commentary rather than responding to each individually. Rather than playing tennis (comments going student-teacher-student-teacher-student-teacher) in Jason's class, they play volleyball: the comments go student-student-student-teacher.

You can see another example in the video *Josh Sullivan: Say More About That*. As they respond to his question, Josh chooses to let three students speak in a row without comment from him. Or at least without verbal comment. His expression and gestures and the notes he silently writes on the board show that he is listening and that ideas of merit are emerging as students speak. In an environment where strong norms like *Habits of Attention, Habits of Discussion*, and of course volunteering through hand-raising are in place, this can facilitate short bursts of student-to-student discourse in the midst of other activities.

Obviously the key is to resist mediating every comment and allow short strings of three or four students to speak in a row. (Then you can step in to comment and steer.) But it's also important to model thoughtful, attentive listening. Not only does this reinforce the importance of student comments, but it helps you resist talking since much of what we say between comments is designed to show the sort of interest and approval we can often express without words. I personally prefer saying students' names rather than just pointing at speakers and it's also sometimes useful to add low-transaction-cost reminders of established discussion norms, such as, "Build on that, Henry." It's still *Batch Processing* if you speak between student comments as long as what you say is merely to manage the process (i.e. choose who's next) as opposed to commenting on ideas. And of course it can still be beneficial for the teacher to comment on ideas offered during *Batch Processing*—you just have to wait a bit so students get to talk to each other first.

Another benefit of *Batch Processing* is that it meshes perfectly with our understanding of deliberate practice. Short iterations of spaced practice will build a skill more completely than larger but less frequent doses. Do something a little bit every day—for two minutes, say—and you'll get better at it than if you do it twice a month in a larger block—forty minutes, say. In one school we worked closely with, where students were especially adept at discussion, the key to transformation was the principal's request that all teachers take one minute during every lesson to practice the fundamentals of peer-to-peer discussion. That small amount of daily practice turned out to be more productive and easier to orchestrate than the more elaborate forms of discussions that required fifteen hypothetical minutes everyone was hoping would still be there at the end of a lesson.

History teacher Ryan Miller used this approach for student-to-student discussion at Williamsburg Collegiate Charter School in Brooklyn. In every lesson, Ryan asked what he thought would be a challenging and interesting question, set a clock for two minutes, and then stepped back and let students talk and respond directly to one another with little mediation or intervention from him except to identify the next speaker. He found two minutes to be plenty of time, and transparently using a timer brought out the best ideas—students had to make valuable contributions, not fill time—without letting things go on for too long. Suddenly he could drop into a two-minute discussion at any point: *Let's pause as Kennedy and his cabinet are planning their response to the missiles and put two minutes on the clock. What were some alternative actions they could have considered?*

Some other points Ryan made about his daily *Batch Process*: he's always disciplined about making the conversation connect to the central idea of the lesson. And he trained his students carefully on *Habits of Discussion* so they were effective at responding to building off each other's ideas. Ryan would step in to guide students in staying on task and avoiding off-task comments, straying from the topic, or not developing the previous idea. Those actions are part of the final technique in this chapter, *Disciplined Discussion*.

My colleague Hannah Solomon, who has made a habit of running schools characterized by rigor and joy, offered some suggestions to consider if you choose to try this idea:

- Student preparation is critical for this to succeed—kids need to be clear on the question, have ample processing time (preferably in writing, so teachers can use *Cold Call* to stir the pot if the conversation slows), and have received support in how to respond to each other (i.e. *Habits of Discussion*) before the teacher sets the timer and sits back.

- Teachers need to choose intentionally whether or not to summarize key takeaways at the end of the two minutes—either by clarifying misconceptions or by stating something like, "Let's keep wrestling with this challenge as we move forward."

- Teachers should be transparent about the *Means of Participation*—is it all volunteers or some *Cold Calls* or some other model?

- One challenge with techniques similar to this in younger grades is that so much misinformation can get shared that teachers then need to tidy up after—so the role of knowledge feeding is important to consider. This is an activity that works much better when everyone has learned a lot and has strong background knowledge.

## Charting Aids Discussion by Aiding Memory

One way to help students stay on topic and validate their classmates' ideas is to help them to remember them. This may seem trivial but we know that people can only keep one or two ideas in working memory at a time and that recall fades quickly. Thirty seconds after hearing Kimani's great idea it will be hard for his classmates to remember exactly what he said. You can write a brief reminder on the board. "Jonas alarmed by feelings bc he doesn't know what they are" or perhaps simply "'Jonas doesn't know what feelings are'—Kimani."

Now students can think about Kimani's comment. Remember it. Refer back to it. Even with several comments made in between, they can use *Habits of Discussion* not just to build off of the most recent comment but those that happened several minutes ago. It provides the assist when a student says, "I'd like to build off of what Kimani said earlier about Jonas not knowing what feelings are . . ."

You can do this on the whiteboard, the overhead projector, or chart paper. It's important to note that it is different from technique 22, *Board = Paper*, because students may well *not* be writing what you write. You are the memory scribe. Their job is to listen. Here's Jessica Bracey doing that as Omar comments in her Keystone video.

She is helping to keep his idea alive for students to use throughout discussion and you can see the results.

Of course, as with anything else, there's some explicit instruction to be done. Students won't know what you're doing and how to make use of it when you chart unless you tell them: *I'm writing down key ideas up here so you can refer back to them and tie your ideas together. It will help us have a real discussion where we connect and remember one another's ideas.*

## TECHNIQUE 46: DISCIPLINED DISCUSSION

An effective discussion needs a shared purpose—on two levels. It needs a specific topic participants tacitly agree to discuss, and it needs a shared mental model of what it means to discuss something. If people are just trying to prove they are right, it's a debate. Discussion should involve some reflection along the lines of, what have I, or we, learned here? And a discussion is often better if it's cohesive. "If you chase five rabbits you catch none," a friend of mine says, meaning that if you try to talk about everything, you resolve nothing.

With that in mind, here's a key moment from a discussion in Rue Ratray's English class, taped when he taught at Edward Brooke Charter School in Boston. The discussion was about Lois Lowry's novel *The Giver*, specifically the relationship of individuals to authority. The community was very accepting of government dictates, students observed. Then a student named Sofia commented that Jonas was an exception. He was "not willing to accept or agree with the ideas of the government." Rue called on another student, Khalid, but Khalid suddenly shifted the subject.

"Carol and I talked about how we liked this phrase that . . ."

"Wait a minute, Khalid," Rue enjoined. "What do you think about what Sofia said?"

When Rue redirected Khalid before he could share his idea, he risked disrupting his train of thought. He might forget what he had been about to say. Why do that? The reason is that Rue's eye was on the long game—he was reminding Khalid that a comment too disconnected from the previous comment or topic detracted from discussion even if it was interesting to him. Rue was teaching students a critical aspect of having a successful discussion by reminding them of the self-discipline necessary to discussion. Effective contributors to a discussion recognize when changing the subject detracts from the overall conversation. Giving students the opportunity to practice the skills of discussion means supporting them as they develop this meta-awareness.

Unfortunately, in many classrooms, the moment when someone finishes a thought means it's open season; there's no expectation that the next comment will stick with the same topic and the result is conversations that have a fractured and scattered feel. In fact, students will often say, "What I was going to talk about was . . ." which implies that they are changing the topic (and that the previous comment was relatively unremarkable). Do this enough and you prevent the substance and depth that come from wrestling with the nuances of a specific issue. And it suggests to previous speakers that their comments weren't worth making. Why keep contributing if you say something you've been thinking about and it's ignored by the next speaker as if it never happened? It's easily overlooked, in other words, that one of the most important characteristics of a good discussion is topicality.

Ryan Miller used a similar move in a recent lesson. Students were examining primary source documents about President Teddy Roosevelt's intervention in Panama. One student commented that Roosevelt's claims that the United States was not involved were an effort to hide the government's intentions. The subsequent student made a sudden change of topic, almost as if the previous point had never been made, so Ryan stepped in: "That's interesting, but I'd like to hear someone respond to Sara's comment before we move on to another one."

Ryan's and Rue's goal in these interventions was to have students internalize a mental model of discussion that includes self-discipline and a recognition of the need to read one's audience among participants. In a good discussion people don't just talk about anything they want at any time.

This is an example of what I call *managing the meta*, the first part of the technique *Disciplined Discussion*, which encourages focus and self-awareness in discussion. That sometimes requires keeping a discussion "inside the box," and reminding students "Let's stay on our original topic right now" or asking, "How is this connected to the topic at hand?"

The second part of *Disciplined Discussions* is *intentional reflection,* an adaptation of *stamping,* a term Paul Bambrick-Santoyo uses to describe writing after a discussion in which participants summarize key ideas or, in this case, reflect deliberately on questions like: "What did I (or we) learn from our discussion?" or "How did your opinions change?" Writing about these topics gives them importance and permanence and ensures that time spent in discussion isn't wasted. As Paul Kirscher and colleagues remind us, learning is a change in long-term memory. The discussion may be rich but unless students remember it, they won't have learned much. Writing helps bridge that gap.

The more time you spend in discussion, the more important it is to make sure that clear takeaways are framed and the process of encoding them in long-term memory is begun. *Intentional reflection* means a discussion doesn't just end with the teacher saying it's over. It ends with the teacher saying something like:

"Take a minute to jot down your takeaways from the discussion."

Or (to emphasize listening a bit more): "Take a minute to jot down a summary of some of the more useful comments from your peers."

Or (to emphasize openness to new ideas): "Take a minute to jot down the ways your perspective changed in the course of the discussion."

This would also be a great occasional application of *Art of the Sentence* (technique 41):

"Great discussion. Two minutes now to capture your most important takeaway in one carefully crafted sentence."

Or, "Great discussion. Two minutes to capture the two differing points of view we heard in one complete sentence."

Of course you don't have to be a purist about using *Art of the Sentence. Silent Solo* could suffice. "Two minutes to capture the three key historical events we discussed and how they were connected. Go!"

I prefer writing over *Turn and Talk,* though. Writing encodes ideas more deeply in memory—we remember what we think about, Daniel Willingham tells us, and writing is usually a harder form of thinking than talking. Plus it leaves students with a written record they can refer back to.

Interestingly, in her Keystone, Arielle Hoo concludes her class discussion of parallel overlapping lines with a written summary, but she makes it a shared class activity. She provides a sentence starter and various students contribute ideas. She refines and selects from among them, creating a summary that is superior in content to what any single student could have created. Students then copy this down as their record of the proceedings. My team and I call this sort of written summary—one that's both a shared creation and curated by the teacher, one that results in an exemplar of higher quality than any individual might produce—a *Collectively Worked Example*. It's a great way to end a class.

## Managing the Meta—The Case for Inside the Box

We tend to valorize "thinking outside the box." The phrase evokes creativity, cognitive leaps, and the raw stuff of insight. In classroom discussion, however, keeping it *inside* the box—staying focused on a specific topic, maintaining steady, deep reflection on all sides of an idea—is often more valuable. Of course, the two aren't mutually exclusive, but there is a certain tension between them. Students sometimes reach for comments that are far afield rather than focused and topical because they believe that's how "outside the box" happens. We sometimes even encourage their doing so. Still, if we don't teach students how to keep insights on topic, we are guaranteed great leaps sideways, occasionally at the expense of forward progress. Let me give you an example.

I spent some time observing classes in a school near me, and one of the things that struck me was the way the discussions differed among classrooms. In some, students made relevant and insightful contributions. In others, comments were interesting to the student who made them, but not as useful or thought-provoking to others. They were arcane and solipsistic—smart, perhaps, but so self-absorbed that it was hard to say. The curious thing is that I was observing the same group of students in different rooms. I started to wonder, "Why were they so alert to their peers' perspective in one class and the opposite in another?"

In one classroom, the teacher asked, "What is fairness?" One student answered with an obscure quotation from a comic book that no one else had heard of. Another replied that it was like pizza. They veered from one obscure analogy to another. They were certainly outside the box. The teacher too made obscure connections. The text they were reading was like "that commercial on TV." Then it was "like that song," and he quoted some lyrics. He called these text-to-text connections, but they weren't. Their effect was not to cast the text in a new and revealing light but to distract the class from any sustained reflection on it. Student comments mirrored his choices. They referred to something arcane or comprehensible only to them and he never helped them think about how useful their comments were to others. Perhaps his mental model was vague and he didn't envision discussions as being characterized by comments that were topical and timely. I once had a professor who would occasionally respond to comments, "How does that relate to what we were just talking about?" His doing so helped us see very quickly that discussion was not just about us and our desire to talk about what thoughts were on our minds, but about the mutual goal of developing shared insight on a topic.

The power of framing expectations about discussion was evident in the math class many of the same students had been in earlier in the day. It was their first day studying rate of change, and their teacher had just observed that time was almost always an independent variable when it appeared in a rate-of-change problem. "It's going to be your independent variable 99 percent of the time," he said. He asked students if they had any questions. Several ensued in which students reflected on how certain rate-of-change problems would be represented on a line graph. Then a student asked for an example of a situation in which time could be the dependent variable, and the teacher said, "To think of an example, I'd have to come up with something pretty obscure. Maybe we'll do that later, but for now let's just assume it's going to be the independent variable."

Despite his hint, another student raised her hand and began brainstorming "what ifs," wondering aloud how time might become a dependent variable. It was great that she was asking herself this question, and although many teachers might have encouraged it, her comment was less useful to others in the room. The teacher was trying to help the class come to a collective understanding of rate of change at a conceptual level, not to digress into an area he'd just indicated was not worth the time. His response was brilliant: "You're thinking outside the box. But I want us to focus on thinking inside the box right now, on really understanding rate of change, what it is and how it works. So let's stay there right now." Then he smiled genuinely and sincerely and they went back to talking about rate of change.

Although some teachers might be reluctant to circumscribe discussion in this way, his doing so was immensely productive. Essentially he said, "Here's what we're doing as a group right now. That's something you should pay attention to when you speak up—what the group is trying to do and why." Part of a teacher's responsibility is to teach students when and how to participate productively in a discussion.

In short, you *manage the meta* when, through feedback and modeling, you guide students in the dynamics of building conversation, specifically how to make the kinds of comments that are most productive in a given setting. Rather than assuming they know how to make a discussion valuable, you invest in teaching them as they struggle forward. Perhaps there are times when you want *more* outside the box. If that's the case, you might use meta comments like, "I want to hear some people who are willing to make some broader connections." Either way, managing the meta relies on two key tools: modeling the kind of participation you want in a discussion and providing constant supportive feedback on how to engage your peers in a meaningful, connected, and mutually productive way.

## Notes

1. Most people, you may have noticed, are confident that this applies to people other than themselves.
2. We should realize another risk: students often recognize that expressing ardent opinions—even ones they may not truly hold—shows interest and is a route to a higher grade. Colby may well know that punching up his passion about the Kansas Nebraska Act is a great way to enhance his grade.
3. To be clear, there are times when we encourage talking to allow students to process or to increase Participation Ratio. This is great, but is different from discussion, when we must support students in remembering and building their skills for the listening portion of the process.
4. There are several vignettes about this in *The Hidden Lives of Learners*.
5. There are lots of different ways to designate the two halves of each pair—"window" and "door" or "wall" (designating which part of the classroom they are closer to) often works.
6. Another realization about *Turn and Talks* that comes from online teaching is that a lot of time gets wasted in the awkward social dance of starting the conversation. Who will go first? What do you say to begin? Shaping the routine early in the year—for example, by saying "When you get to your breakout room, simply greet your partner and say 'What did you think?'"—helped a lot of teachers with this. Perhaps there's a classroom equivalent.
7. Quoted in Daniel Coyle, *The Culture Code*.

# Chapter 10

# Procedures and Routines

I wish everyone could have seen Sam DeLuke and Meghan Hurley's second-grade classroom at Troy Prep Elementary School on the day I visited recently. When I first walked in, I found Sam sitting in one corner, listening in on five students discussing a chapter book. As I inched closer, I overheard students making sophisticated statements like "I think you missed one piece of evidence, Zariah" and "I agree with David's point and want to develop it" (see technique 44, *Habits of Discussion*). In another corner, Meghan read a book about ants aloud to ten students who hung on every word. In the center of the room, six students sat engrossed in the pages of their independent reading, while another group had hunkered down to draft paragraphs explaining the theme of a story they had read.

A few minutes later, on Sam's cue, one of the groups from the center put their things away, stood, and walked quietly to Meghan's corner. Others, who did not transition, kept working away. Later, with a subtle gesture and without ever interrupting her instruction, she prompted a student to distribute books to peers who didn't have them.

Students in Sam and Meghan's class worked in an atmosphere of independence and self-management. Executive function is usually described as including the following sorts of skills:

- Paying attention
- Organizing, planning, and prioritizing

- Starting tasks and staying focused on them to completion
- Understanding different points of view
- Regulating emotions
- Self-monitoring (keeping track of what you're doing)

Students paced themselves and managed their own time. They listened carefully and drew out the best from their classmates when they worked together. The room seemed to run itself.

Paradoxically, the autonomy and self-management that were so much a part of the student experience were the products of structure and planning; students had made habits of a series of procedures Sam and Meghan had designed—how to work at your desk; how to manage materials; how to move from place to place in the room; how to ask for help if you were confused and the teacher was busy teaching others—and it was this very structure and planning, ironically, that allowed for greater autonomy. The moments when a brief reminder from Sam initiated a perfectly orchestrated transition were not in contrast to the moments when students worked at their desks with independence; they allowed them, fostered them, and made them productive.

Sam and Meghan had invested heavily in their *procedures,* which provide students with explicit guidance on how to execute recurring tasks such as working independently, transitioning between small groups, and answering questions in class. During the first few weeks of the year, they relied on constant practice to reinforce expectations. If you'd seen them then, you might not have understood where it was all leading—*Why all the structure? Why all the "just so" with every little piece? Why so much focus on the process for moving from place to place or participating in discussion?* But each of those "just so" pieces took its place within a system, a network of procedures that allowed Sam and Meghan to teach students habits that ultimately led to more independence. Over time, these procedures became automatic, or *routine*—students could, for the most part, execute them on their own. From that point, Sam and Meghan could afford to give their students autonomy because students knew how to manage it productively and because teachers could initiate it, adjust it, or correct it with a single word or gesture.

This is an idea that is not unique to the classroom. Classroom procedures and routines like Sam and Meghan's represent essentially the intentional internalization of shared classroom habits. And habits, it is worth noting, have a profound influence on our lives. They become keystones. You develop a healthy positive habit in your life like reading or working out and it's more likely to result in your developing others. "Typically, people who exercise start eating better and becoming more productive at work. They smoke less and show more patience with colleagues and family. They use their credit cards less frequently and say they feel less stressed. Exercise is a keystone habit that triggers widespread change," Charles Duhigg writes in *The Power of Habit*. This sort of behavior looks like self-discipline—well, it *is* self-discipline, but self-discipline made easy. Productive habits make it easy to be productive. And this is important for students because studies find that self-discipline predicts academic performance "more robustly than . . . IQ," Duhigg writes, and has a "bigger effect on academic performance than does intellectual talent."

This chapter is the study of the way we develop shared positive habits in the classroom. That discussion can benefit from definitions of some key terms:

- **Procedure:** the design a teacher establishes for the way she and her students will efficiently and productively execute a recurring task or action in the classroom.

- **System:** a network of related procedures that help teachers accomplish end goals: help students maintain an organized binder, manage behavior, move materials, participate successfully in a discussion, and so on.

- **Routine:** a procedure or system that has become automatic, which students do either without much oversight, without intentional cognition (in other words, as a habit), and/or of their own volition and without teacher prompting (for example, note-taking while reading).

In the video *Nikki Bowen: Stand Up*, originally published in the book *Great Habits, Great Readers* by Paul Bambrick-Santoyo, Aja Settles, and Juliana Worrell, you can see Nikki's impressive system for students switching literacy groups. Not only does it maximize time for learning by making transitions fast, but it ensures that students arrive at each station with minds focused and ready to learn. Within seconds they're off and running. Among other things, this is a great example of how the terms *system*, *procedure*, and *routine* intersect. Nikki's system for transitions is actually made up of a series of separate component procedures. Once students learned the procedures, practiced them, and linked them together smoothly as habit, they became a *routine*. Separating the *system* into a series of *procedures* allowed Nikki to break the learning process into chunks (in consideration of students' working memory) and to apply the chunks in other classroom systems as well. All of her classroom transitions start with "Learner's Position"—that is, students showing they are attentive and ready—and the process of walking pathways is similar no matter where a student is walking within the room.

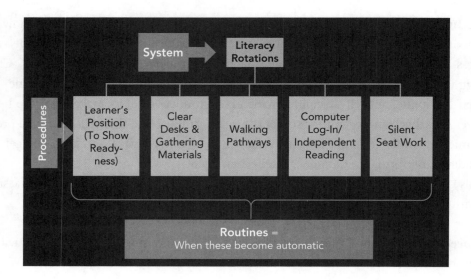

My goal in this chapter is to pull back the curtain a bit and reveal the ways in which teachers like Nikki, Sam, and Meghan use procedures and routines to create rigorous, joyful, and orderly classrooms that grant students real independence. At the beginning of the chapter we'll look specifically at two familiar and important routines that are linked to form a system for the beginning of class: *Threshold and Strong Start*. After that, we'll study *Habits of Attention*, which is a routine for basic social interactions by and among students during learning. But of course a great classroom has far more procedures and routines than that, so afterwards, we'll explore the "how" behind designing and installing procedures and routines so that you can set up students for success in your classroom and beyond.

That said, it's also important to note how many examples of procedures and routines are described *elsewhere* in this book. Doing so can also help us glimpse the range in types of systems you can include in your classroom.

There are three broad categories of Procedures and Routines:

1. **Academic Routines:** Help students complete tasks they engage in as part of the learning process. Elsewhere in the book you will find myriad examples of such routines. *Turn and Talk* is essentially a routine for peer-to-peer conversations. *Habits of Discussion* are a set of procedures for use and adaptation during larger discussions. *Silent Solo* is a routine for making independent writing happen smoothly and universally among students. *FASE Reading* is a tool for making a productive routine out of student oral reading. *Show Me* is a routine—or a group of routines—that allow you to check student work simply and easily. All of these live and die by the effectiveness of implementation. So, in the end, all your *Means of Participation—Cold Call, Show Call*, and *Call and Response*—work if

they are predictable routines in which when you call on students, they expect you might do it, understand the spirit in which it's done, and know how to respond.

2. **Procedural Routines:** Help students manage materials and get from one place to another while maximizing efficiency. There are a dozen routines you could install to make the mundane logistics of the classroom work more smoothly: lining up at the doorway, passing out and collecting papers, moving to the carpet for little ones, getting out materials. In this chapter I'll discuss two such routines: *Threshold* and *Strong Start* for beginning class. They may seem mundane, but after reading about them I hope you will see their profound importance. But there are more elsewhere—*All Hands*, in Chapter Six, for example.

3. **Cultural Routines:** Help students express shared values, norms, and aspirations. Perhaps you noticed in Jessica Bracey's or Denarius Frazier's classroom how students praise each other for effort or quality thinking, either when the teacher suggests it or of their own volition (see also the video *John Bogard: Go to IP*). Perhaps you are aware of how some teachers socialize their students to "send magic" to a peer who is temporarily stuck while trying to answer a question. In place of calling out, they make a gesture that says: *I support you; I know you'll get it.* The first among these by far is *Habits of Attention* and its importance is captured in this photograph:

This is Jessica's student, Omar, answering her question about the protagonist's motivation in the novel they're reading. He's a tiny bit nervous at first. Does he have it right? Has he said it well? Is it safe to share? But he answers at length—he keeps going, giving more detail and opinion and gathering confidence. In part he does this because of the social routine you can see here: his peers looking at him and affirming that they are listening and that his words matter.

It's worth noting also that teachers' own routines are a critical part of a successful classroom. Chapter Two is really a study of preparation procedures that hopefully become routine. How you circulate and observe for data are other examples of critical teacher-facing routines.

A word about the collective power of routines before we push on: Let's say everyone in your class had their own routine for getting their materials out and could complete the process in a few seconds. Would it be just as good as a shared routine where everyone does it the same way? Better even? Everyone accomplishing the same task in the same handful of seconds, each by doing it their own way sounds a lot more compelling. Why, this is to say, do routines have to be collective?

The first reason is that it makes them easy to support and manage. It's a long shot that everyone could find their own way to do that same thing—you'd be unlikely to get the outcome you wanted—but even if they did you'd be hard-pressed to help a student who struggled without steps to guide him through, even with the understanding that there was a right way to do it. *You'll need to make sure your notebook is in your desk every morning when you unpack* as opposed to asking, *Well where do you usually like to keep your notebook, in your backpack or in your desk*? As the epically disorganized child who was the one least likely to figure out the right way in middle school, I can also tell you that I was among the least likely to take anyone's guidance on how to be more productive. I didn't get it and so I didn't see the wisdom of, and was resistant to, what people were trying to tell me.

And of course group productivity requires coordination. You can move from chair to desk any way you want when you're the only one in the room. When thirty people are doing it at the same time, the only way to avoid unnecessary collisions or negotiated settlements over who will transition first down this row or that column is to organize it.

A second reason for coordination is that clear procedures and routines are extremely effective at norm setting: "When we are uncertain of how to behave," Tom Bennett writes, "we look to other people as a safe guide of what to do. This is called social proof, a term coined by Cialdini in 1984. By seeing what others do, we have 'proof' that it's the right thing." A clear norm not only encourages people to follow, but often gives them comfort. It reduces the anxiety many students feel that they might do the wrong thing and look foolish. As the video *Nicole Warren: Keystone* reveals, Nicole's class is full of routines her students know well. This helps her create a sense of flow and momentum that enhances motivation. There's an unbroken flow of energy. But notice also how happy her students are to know exactly what to do, to see others around them doing the same, and to join with them. To return to a point I made in Chapter Seven, Zaretta Hammond calls the brain "a social organ," and notes that it "has a 'contact' urge, a 'desire to be with other people.'" This is often reflected in the universality and power of singing—in every culture in the world, singing together is a way of becoming a part of a unified group collective, literally and symbolically. We join our voices—in worship or otherwise—and the emotions of doing so are surprisingly profound. Part of it is the music and part of it is the certainty of belonging created by the coordination. It can be overdone and misused, of course, but it's also profound and elemental. Tom Bennett writes of the psychological benefits of the "collective sensation of being part of a large group sharing goals and activities."[1] It reminds students that they belong. Far from being militaristic and soulless, managed properly, executed with a pinch of happiness or even joy, and invested with meaning by a teacher, shared routines are often comforting.

A third reason collective routines are powerful is that, ironically, they help us focus our cognition where it is more useful. Having a habit for how to write a midstream response to a novel—what I call Stop and Jot in the *Everybody Writes* section—sets students free to write more and better since their minds are on the book and not where to write and whether to use pencil or pen. Similarly, making a habit of doing something productive makes it easy to do and lets you save willpower and self-discipline for other things. This is in part a hidden story of schooling. Success relies on a lot of things but one of them is getting all your tasks and assignments completed, on time and whether or not you particularly feel like it that day. When scientists analyze people who appear to have the greatest amounts of self-discipline, James Clear writes, it turns out they are actually better at "structuring their lives in a way that does not require heroic willpower and self-control."[2] They have better habits and make productive behaviors automatic. They don't need to draw on self-discipline to take care of daily habits because their routines and habits do that. Advising individuals in how to change their lives for the better, Clear essentially describes a high-performing classroom with strong procedures and routines. "One of the most effective things you can do to build better habits is to join a culture where your desired behavior is the normal behavior. . . . Your culture sets your expectations for what is 'normal.' Surround yourself with people who have the habits you want. . . . You'll rise together."[3]

Classroom procedures and routines, in other words, which are really shared habits, carefully designed by a loving adult, are critical to almost every goal we seek in schools.

## TECHNIQUE 47: THRESHOLD AND STRONG START

People constantly read environments and take social cues from them, and this process starts within seconds of entering a space. Less than that, actually. We form many of our impressions and opinions almost instantaneously, Jonathan Haidt explains in *The Righteous Mind*, often creating logical explanations for our responses only later. Like so much of our behavior, this process is hidden from us—we are not aware that we do it, but we do it just the same. The "we" in this statement includes your students.

Their first impressions matter, not just on the first day of school, but every day, and so how class begins—and in fact how culture and expectations are communicated in the ambiguous and liminal time *before* class has begun—is critical in setting norms, communicating culture. How you choose to greet students when they cross the threshold of your doorway communicates to students what is likely to happen when they enter your classroom, and what people expect to happen is much more likely to come about. With culture, getting it right and keeping it right are much easier than fixing it once it goes wrong. *Threshold* ensures that you make a habit of getting it right at the start of each day.

Students' arrival in the classroom should result in their receiving the message that they belong; that their teacher is prepared and capable; and that as learners their time will be well spent. It's also important to offer a subtle reminder that expectations in your classroom are elevated over what they are in the hallway or any other space. What happens in your classroom is more important, and a subtle shift should happen when students enter, not unlike what the great majority of people do upon entering a church, mosque, or synagogue—they will drop their voices and change the tenor of their interactions to reflect the dignity of the space. Their actions say, *What happens here is important.* No one tells them to make this change. They read it in the cues offered by the environment and the way others around them act. A classroom is not a house of worship—we don't want a shift to the same culture you'd see there—what we want is a shift, a recognition that the students are entering a place of shared value and heightened importance.

With that in mind, watch the first moments in the classrooms of Sadie McCleary, Darren Hollingsworth, Trona Cenac, Steve Chiger, and Tamesha McGuire, all of which are different and yet in a way similar. Each communicates different cultures, but they communicate and reinforce culture clearly. They use different routines but signal that this place you are entering will be a productive learning space. We are watching teachers who are all *culture shapers* rather than *culture takers*.

Start with *Darren Hollingsworth: Smart. Smart!* How could you not start with Darren? We can't see him at the outset, but we can hear him greeting students in the hallway: "Look at this! Smart.[4] Smart!" Describing his students generally and a few individuals, he says, "Super smart." He's upbeat and irrepressible but also confident and absolutely clear in his mind on what is supposed to happen when students enter his room. He greets students by name, communicating that they are known and important, but as they enter there's a clear task to follow through on ("My group, go straight in. Equipment out, ladies and gents!") and students follow along with clear expectations, setting the norm for a happy and productive start to class. This soon becomes routine. It's how class starts with Mr. Hollingsworth. Students will feel known and included and also expect to have their time well spent.

Note something that will become a theme. Darren is positioned at the point of entry where he can clearly see his room and also greet every student. There's no other way in, and this allows him to slow the flow into the room and if need be to remind students of elevated expectations. He does this, in fact, pausing the line briefly because it isn't tidy enough. He playfully calls it a rabble—it clearly isn't—but students fix their already productive behavior to make it even better. Joy, inclusion, and high expectations are successfully messaged.

In *Sadie McCleary: Grab One of Each*, Sadie is perhaps slightly less ebullient but no less warm, genuine, and gracious as she greets her students. There are little moments of dialogue— "Hi, N'Kaye. Nice to see you," "Hi, Alexa," and "I like your glasses"—and reminders about materials so everyone has what they need from the outset. "Grab one of each [there are two handouts by the door] and a calculator if you need one." There are also minor reminders of elevated expectation: "Cell phones away, please," she tells one student. Students take the *Do Now* from the basket, proceed to their desks, and start working. It's a topsy-turvy morning for Sadie because there are cameras recording the class and not everyone has signed a permission to be filmed, so during the *Threshold* she's also shuffling students around to put them in unfamiliar seats (with some out of view of the camera) but all of this goes remarkably smoothly because everyone knows what to do and because she appears at the door signaling organization and preparedness and expectation. Students feel seen and cared about but also get down to work quickly. The *Threshold* might seem like downtime, in other words, but it's not. One student lingers a little too long talking about something that's best dealt with later ("Let me come help you with that in a second," Sadie says). This time is actually crucial in setting expectations. It's not downtime for Sadie.

Notice some of the similarities in Darren and Sadie's technique. They both stand in the doorway where they can control the flow of students into the room, even though Sadie's students arrive episodically and don't line up outside the door. She takes the opportunity to both set a warm, gracious tone and remind students in simple ways that when they enter the classroom the expectations are different, elevated—what we do here matters deeply. Great teachers often combine these minor resets and reminders with warm and gracious, "I see you" moments—"Love the new glasses," "Good to see you," "How'd the debate go?"—seizing on many opportunities to use students' names. All of this builds relationships by making students feel "known" (part of the *safe, successful, and known* recipe my colleague Dan Cotton framed).

Trona (*Trona Cenac: It's Gonna Be Fine*) is greeting her students at the beginning of the year. They've had various adventures and have much to tell her. There's excitement and good feeling, but she also channels this into the first tasks. The message is: *It's great to see you; I care about you and also, we have a lot to do and here's how to get started.* She's a little more explicit about the daily expectations because it's early in the year. Like Darren and Sadie, she's at the narrow point in the threshold so she can control the flow into the classroom. And Trona makes sure she can maintain her vision of the classroom as well as the hallway as students enter. You'll notice how much of the work she does outside the room. If you can do this, it's smart, because habits are powerful. It means that the classroom is your space and students never see it in any way other than as you wish it. Therefore the process of entering and shifting slightly in demeanor becomes a matter of habit.

Steve Chiger applies similar ideas (*Steve Chiger: Knowing What to Do*). He greets students warmly but simply by name and seems upbeat about the class, and even though students are very attentive, also pauses the process of entry ever so briefly because he "thought he heard something." Afterwards you can see students productively engage in their entry routine. He's signaled expectations and elevated the importance of the space, and students react accordingly.

Tamesha McGuire shows a slightly different setting (*Tamesha McGuire: Tuck Your Chair*). She's already in the room chatting amiably and lovingly with her boys and getting ready for her lesson when the girls, who've been elsewhere, enter. She claps twice and shifts her tone to show that class has started now, and her girls know instantly that they've entered a space of elevated importance. She's actually not at the door, but it's a *Threshold*, nonetheless.

The themes thus far include greeting your students by standing in the physical threshold of the classroom when possible—astride the door, taking the opportunity to remind students where they are (they are with you now, and no matter what the expectations elsewhere, you will always expect their best), how you feel toward them (caring, warm, but also with a hint that strictness can emerge as needed), and what you will expect of them (excellence, scholarship, and effort). During this routine, each student who enters greets you, shakes your hand, looks you in the eye, and offers a civil and cordial greeting, and vice versa. It's a ritual of courtesy and caring.

You can use the greeting to engage students briefly and build rapport: "Loved your homework, David"; "Nice game last night, Shayna"; "Looking for great things from you today, Mr. Williams!"; "Your hair looks great, Shanice!" You won't have time to say something like this to every student, but you can pick a few each day, over time connecting with each student and reminding them all that you know them as individuals. You can also build rapport while reinforcing expectations for *Threshold* by warmly acknowledging students with strong greetings: "Nice strong shake, Jamal"; "I love the enthusiasm, Terry."

You can also welcome students with a description of what's to come and a reminder of what's expected: "We have a quiz today. Better use that *Do Now* to get ready." You should also use *Threshold* to set expectations by correcting weak handshakes, untidy attire, apathetic greetings, or poor eye contact. Fortunately, this is easy to do because *Threshold* has a built-in consequence. Get it wrong, and if necessary you go back and try it again.

When you stand at the doorway, position yourself to *see both sides* so that you can maintain visibility of students who have already entered your classroom as well as those you're greeting. Once they enter, narrate a bit of positive behavior: "Thanks for getting *right* to work"; "Good work, Jamila. Appreciate you getting that homework right out." If you notice that several students in class are not meeting expectations, you can warmly remind them of what they should be doing: "Make sure those chairs are tucked in so that everyone can get by," or "Remember, we enter with 'voices off.'"

If it's not possible for you to greet students at the door (either for school policy reasons or because you float to classrooms), invent another ritual to signify the start of something formal, as Tamesha does. What matters is that you use the power of ritual to help students see, from the moment they enter your classroom, that it is different from the other places they go.

For busy teachers, the time just after students have entered class—while they're walking in, getting seated, and hopefully working on a *Do Now*—can sometimes be a bit of an afterthought. Some use it to complete clerical tasks—stapling packets, organizing instructional materials, writing lesson objectives on the board, or briefly collecting their thoughts. In their eyes, the opening minutes of class are ideal for preparing for a lesson that won't begin until they start delivering new content.

Of course there are times when you have to grab a minute to attend to some task, but it's important to recognize that every lesson begins *as soon as students walk through the door*. Two minutes at this point counts just as much in terms of potential learning as two minutes during the heart of your lesson and, of course, you and your classroom norms are still communicating to students *Here's what to do here; here's what to expect*.

So it's worth being intentional about the start of class, planning a most efficient *right* way for students to enter the classroom, complete the *Do Now,* get their learning materials ready, and transition to the heart of the lesson—and then making a consistent habit of it for every student. When that happens, once it's a routine, it's a win-win situation. Students are productive, you're productive, and with everything moving with tidy efficiency you're actually more likely to get time to review your lesson, tidy the room, catch up with individual students, and just maybe have a sip of coffee.

## Strong Start

*Strong Start* is about designing the sequence of events in the classroom from the moment students enter the room, presumably after your Threshold, until the heart of the lesson begins. It's critical for three reasons:

1. It sets the tone for everything that comes after. Classroom culture is not static from day to day. It is shaped by the opening minutes of a lesson—whether you intentionally engineer them or not.

2. From a *pacing* perspective, a strong, energetic start to your lesson builds momentum. It socializes students to work with discipline, urgency, and efficiency as soon as they walk through the door. Get off to a slow start, and you could find yourself spending the rest of your lesson fighting to rebuild momentum you lost and may never win back.

3. *Strong Start* usually includes a Do Now, which sets the table for mastery by efficiently previewing or reviewing high-quality content students need to master. It builds the academic habits students will need to succeed.

If you stepped inside a highly successful classroom shortly after the bell rang, you would probably find that you could divide the routine students use to start the lesson into three parts: (1) from door to *Do Now,* (2) *Do Now,* and (3) review of the *Do Now.*

The first component of *Strong Start* comprises how students get from the door to their *Do Now.* Unlike *Threshold,* which immediately precedes students' entry into the room and focuses on setting behavioral norms and expectations, from the door to *Do Now* is about making a habit out of what's efficient, productive, and scholarly as students take their seats.

A typical arrangement might look something like this: as soon as students cross the threshold of the classroom door, they pick up a packet of materials from a table or counter just inside as Sadie McCleary does. In some cases, especially at the elementary grades, packets might already be at students' desks. You can see that Christine Torres has done this at the outset of her lesson in the video *Christine Torres: Silently to Your Seats.*

A bit of warm and appreciative affirmation like Christine's lets students know you value their efforts. "Thanks for getting *right* to work, James," "Lindsay is already answering question number one on the *Do Now,*" and the like). Discipline your narration so that it's pithy and precise, and quietly reinforces industrious behavior. Once the opening procedures become routine, use narration with diminished frequency. The goal is to get to a point where you need to say very little—if anything—to set your door to *Do Now* routine in motion. When

Christine offers her appreciation, comments are carefully spaced and there's lots of quiet think time. She wants to avoid making her affirmations feel mechanical—this can happen if there are too many and they sound repetitive—and wants to be sure to create a working environment where students can be productive and not have their thinking interrupted.

A couple of key points maximize the effectiveness of the door to *Do Now*:

- It's more efficient to have students pick up their packets from a table than it is for you to try to hand the packets to them at the door. The latter approach slows you down and forces you to multitask when your mind should be on setting expectations and building relationships.

- Students should know where to sit. Time spent milling around, looking for a seat, deciding where to sit, or talking about deciding where to sit ("Can I sit next to him? Will he think I'm flirting?") is a waste of learning time and energy. Assign seats or allow students to sign up for regular seats.

- Whatever students need to do with homework (put it in a basket, place it on the front left corner their desk, pass it to a proctor), they should do the same way every day without prompting. This lets you collect it seamlessly, and collecting it at the start of every class tacitly underscores its importance.

- Put your *Do Now* (the second part of this routine) in the same place every day: on the board, on an interactive handout, or in the packet. The objectives for the lesson, the agenda, and the homework for the coming evening should be on the board already, also in the same predictable place every day.

As part of *Strong Start,* establishing the routine of the *Do Now* is critical. A *Do Now* enables you to maximize instructional time, build industrious habits, and make use of a discrete block of time when your students can practice and thus sustain and build their proficiency with skills they've already mastered. This issue—making sure students don't lose through disuse what they'd once mastered—is one of the hidden challenges of teaching.

I discuss the details of an effective *Do Now* in technique 20.

## TECHNIQUE 48: HABITS OF ATTENTION

"What few people ever appreciate is how central attention is for every function we perform," writes reading researcher Maryanne Wolf. "What we attend to is ultimately what we learn," concurs Peps Mccrea. It is the unheralded "gatekeeper" of learning. The ability to sustain focus and concentration is the unacknowledged source of many students' success, and the inability to attend is the undoing of others.

"Neuroscience reminds us that before we can be motivated to learn what is in front of us, we must pay attention to it," says Zaretta Hammond. "The hallmark of an independent learner is his ability to direct his attention toward his own leaning."[5] To build strong attentional habits is to give students stewardship of their own thinking.

*Selective attention* is the term for the ability to select what you pay attention to—to lock out distractions and lock in on the task at hand. It has "reverberating effects" on success in language, literacy, and mathematics, note cognitive scientists Courtney Stevens and Daphne Bavelier. They add that there are potentially "large benefits to incorporating attention-training activities into the school context."[6]

If young people can build habits of sustained selective attention, their likelihood of success is higher. This has always been true but is magnified today when much of our universe—the online portion of it—is designed to fragment our attention and draw it to where it can be marketed and sold.

The technique *Habits of Attention* seeks to establish routines that cause students to focus their attention during class and build stronger attentional habits. In addition, it seeks to use the signals people send when they attend to someone else to build a stronger, more inclusive learning community.

I used to call the technique STAR/SLANT after the acronyms that schools often used to describe its component expectations in the classroom. I still suggest the use of an acronym to describe core attentional habits, but I've changed the name and the description to focus more on *why*. Understand the purpose of the technique and you are far more likely to use it effectively.

The "habits" in the technique focus in particular on eye-tracking and pro-social body language—language that communicates support for, and the belonging of, speakers. It may be helpful, before reading more, to watch these things in action in a classroom. I suggest you do so in two parts, first watching Christine Torres's Keystone video, which shows two broad segments of her lesson, as she first teaches new vocabulary words and then leads a discussion of Lois Lowry's novel *Number the Stars*. Christine's students, I think you will agree, are unusually engaged and attentive: They enthusiastically wrestle with new words and are cerebral, respectful, and attentive in discussing a difficult question. Next watch the video *Christine Torres: Habits of Attention Outtakes* to see a montage of moments extracted from this lesson. Note how important it is that students look at one another, how their body language shows classmates that they belong and their ideas are welcome. Note how attentive, confident, and productive they are as a result.

"Visual cues," writes James Clear in *Atomic Habits*, "are the greatest catalyst of our behavior. Where we look shapes our attention more than any single factor."[7] We are often not fully intentional or even conscious of where we look and why, however, so shaping students' habits of looking can lead to a profound change, not only in their actions and cognition, but in those around them. For example, engaging in behaviors that show a speaker that you are listening carefully—nodding, for example, and looking interested—are often self-actualizing. They cause you to pay better attention and cause the speaker to feel a strong sense of affirmation and belonging as well. Note therefore how often—and how deftly—Christine reinforces these things.

There is a strong connection between such behaviors and our ability to build community in the classroom. Belonging[8] is arguably the most powerful motivator there is. Our unconscious brains are "obsessed with it" writes Daniel Coyle in his book, *The Culture Code,* but he adds that the brain "needs to be continually fed by signals of safe connection." Surveying the research, he notes that "Posture and expression are incredibly important. It's the way we prove we are in synch with someone." However, "a mere hint of belonging is not enough . . . we are built to require lots of signaling, over and over."

You can see this happening in Christine's classroom. Her students are constantly signaling to one another that they belong. They turn and face each other. They nod, react, and encourage. And this signal is strongest when their classmates are sharing important ideas. There is a risk that every student takes in raising their hand. To raise your hand and say something truthful in front of a group of peers is to risk failure or, worse, judgment by them. Yes, your answer could be disastrously wrong, but even worse, your classmates' nonverbal response could say: *None of us could care less about what you just said* or *Oh, wait, did you say something? I barely even noticed* or *please tell me you didn't just make a comment about the book.* If that is the case, only a rare student will raise her hand.[9] The learning journey is forestalled when students must risk social transgression to embark upon it. "Regardless of how strong the logic of your pep talk," Peps Mccrea writes, "few pupils will ask more questions in class if they sense it will result in being mocked by their mates."

But in Christine's classroom, to raise your hand and to begin to formulate a thought is to bask in the warm glow of acceptance and encouragement. The culture in her classroom does not just *allow* students to take this necessary risk, it lovingly draws them into the light. It is profound and beautiful—a gift to young people, and most of all to the hesitant and reluctant. But what you see in her classroom is not something that will happen naturally, among any group of people, unless the teacher intentionally builds it.

There are people who will tell you that building such culture is coercive and repressive, and sometimes that this is "controlling Black and Brown bodies." I hope this discussion will make it clear that this is a not the case.[10] To ask students to be attentive to their bodies is to *create* opportunities for their minds and spirits; to help them build habits that help them focus is to help them harness the power of their thinking. When classmates intentionally signal belonging and encouragement to one another, they release them from invisible barriers that constrain them, barriers that for some students will exist in the majority of classrooms they will enter in their lives. To shape these signals is to give students power and community in place of dependence and isolation.

Eye contact and body language are the means we use to show someone that they matter and belong. Understanding our evolution as a species can help us to understand why.

Let's start with our eyes, which have a white outer portion called the sclera. In all of the other primates, the area surrounding the pupil is dark and as a result you cannot clearly track eye movements. Scientists explain this singular aspect of human evolution via the Cooperative Eye Hypothesis. Humans act with a level of cooperation unseen in the mammal kingdom. As a species we survived because of this unequaled ability (and desire) to coordinate and collaborate. For most of evolutionary history to be cast out of the group was certain death. Our eyes have adapted to look the way they do because the information contained in the gaze of our peers—*Am I accepted and respected? What is my status? Do I belong?*—is central to survival. "For hundreds of thousands of years, we needed ways to develop cohesion because we depended so much on each other. We used signals long before we used language," says Alex Pentland of the MIT Human Dynamics Lab.[11] Our physiology is designed to communicate these signals and we are profoundly sensitive to what is told in our peers' eyes—even if we are often unconscious of it.

"Belonging feels like it happens from the inside out," summarizes Coyle, "but in fact it happens from the outside in." Students in Christine's classroom feel like they belong because their peers are signaling to them that they belong—and that they *still* belong—just possibly they *especially* belong—when and if they participate in learning.

The original version of this technique—and its name—referred to acronyms such as SLANT, which several outstanding schools used to articulate the signals of belonging and attentiveness that people use when in groups:

**S**it up

**L**isten

**A**sk and answer questions

**N**od your head

**T**rack the speaker

Especially crucial elements from that list were tracking the speaker—that is, following the person talking with your eyes—and sitting up—you don't learn well if you are slouched, or at all if you have your head down on your desk, and allowing yourself to check out physically causes you to check out mentally. If we care about young people, if we believe their learning and their futures are important, we can't allow them to simply opt out of attending to learning.

Handy acronyms such as SLANT allow teachers to explain and reinforce the component behaviors: "Don't forget to SLANT" or "Check your S" (that is, make sure you're sitting up); "Please track Guadeloupe while she shares her answer." Or simply calling on Guadeloupe by saying "Track Guadeloupe, please." But there can be challenges with these acronyms. First, they focus on the action without always fully describing its purpose and a good thing can easily become distorted when the purpose isn't clear. The component parts of SLANT, for example, are easy to manage and so teachers—perhaps a struggling teacher for whom an orderly classroom has been elusive—can lock in on the behavior without pursuing its purpose.

An additional challenge can be that managing attention behaviors can prove successful enough that it can lead to a spread in managing behaviors less clearly tied to attention: hands folded on the desk; back flat against the chair, and so forth. To be clear, these behaviors are not something I've discussed in *Teach Like a Champion*, but I have certainly seen classrooms where they are reinforced in a counterproductive way and sometimes in the belief that this book endorses them. Reminding students who are at risk of becoming distracted—or who are sending unsupportive messages to peers—to Track or SLANT can be useful; telling students to keep their feet flat on the floor or interrupting them when they are productively engaged in a discussion to tell them to fold their hands on the desk is not.[12] What if they want to take notes?

*Habits of Attention* also implies asking students to track us as teachers at times. There are people who will tell you this, too, is a form of tyranny, but telling children they needn't pay attention to adults is a cheap version of freedom to trade an education for. "When parents asked me why their students should have to track me when I spoke, I explained, 'If I can't see your son's eyes I don't know if he heard. I don't know if he will be able to complete the learning task,'" my colleague Darryl Williams says of his school leadership days. "I explained it from an equity perspective. One of the reasons we get students' attention is to give them the opportunity to be successful at a task." That's an educator who is clear on his purpose and who understands what supports autonomy for young people.

To address these challenges, I'm going to propose what I think is a better acronym—with the caveat that I think each school or classroom should reflect individually on any acronym they choose. Are these the tools we think will build positive attention habits in our students?

If students work hard and meet these expectations, will it improve their ability to learn in a positive way? The answer must be yes, or the expectations are not worth including. But if the answer is yes, you should not shrink from including them.

With all of that in mind, it's clear that there's information we can add to descriptions of attention habits to provide more consistent reminders to teachers and students about their purpose. Consider the "N" in SLANT, that is, nodding your head. This not only shows interest in another person's ideas, it also causes you to engage actively in listening. Here is an updated list for *Habits of Attention*, with the acronym STAR, revised to emphasize purpose more clearly:

- **Sit up** to look interested and stay engaged.
- **Track the speaker** to show other people their ideas matter.
- **Appreciate your classmates' ideas** by nodding, smiling, and so on when they speak.
- **Rephrase the words of the person who spoke** before you so they know you were listening.

In this acronym you can see I've added details about purpose. Nodding is included in the "appreciate" step to emphasize the importance of appreciating your classmates. That said, you might replace the "Appreciate" A with an A called "Active listening" (to help you focus and show that you value your classmates). "Sit up" includes a purpose as well, *so you look interested and engaged.* You'll also notice that I've brought in an idea from the *Habits of Discussion* technique, "rephrasing," but you could drop it if you wanted, perhaps replacing it with something else. Again, I am describing options here because the behaviors described in any acronym (and the expectations) should be carefully thought through at the school or classroom level. My version of STAR may be helpful, but the adaptations you make to it will make it even better.

There's one other piece that's needed, though. *Habits of Attention* only work if they become *habits*. You can see how important this is to Christine Torres. Her classroom culture is strong—exceptional, you might argue. It's warm and encouraging and inclusive of all. It's fun and funny and scholarly. And yet, she is still shaping and reinforcing and lovingly correcting for *Habits of Attention* all the way through. She strikes a careful balance. If you have to explain and remind every time you want eye contact to validate a speaker, then it will become a constant disruption to the conversation you are trying to honor. But just because things are going well does not mean she forgets about maintaining the environment. She reinforces it lovingly, early, and often with a hint of humor so her reminders are gentle. Having an acronym helps her because it allows for easy abbreviated reminders.

Some details to notice from Christine's class:

- Frequently she reminds students to track in advance via the language she uses to call on a student, as in segment 1: "What did the girl do in the situation? Track, Etani . . ."

- Occasionally she narrates the positive to make the norm more visible, as in segment 2: "Track, Azariah. Jada's tracking; Juju's tracking." Once she reminds a student to reciprocate the signal—to turn and face his classmates as they are tracking him. Other times she reminds students indirectly and playfully as in segment 4: "Ooh, Jasmine, girl, wait until you have all eyes."

- You can also see habits in formation. Notice how, without her asking students to, students turn and engage face-to-face and expressively in their *Turn and Talk*. Many a teacher can tell you tales of flat affect and disinterest expressed in pair conversations, but not in Christine's class.

- The culture carries over, too, in the moment when she calls on Nate without asking for tracking . . . still his classmates turn to face him. The signal of belonging is loud and clear.

- The montage ends with Christine asking for students to track her. She's giving them a key piece of information. It's critical that they hear and attend. By asking for tracking she signals the extra importance of the moment. Students lock in and, without her asking them to, adjust their own posture.

That said, even a well-established routine is a default—understood as the base condition but a condition that can be changed or turned off. I witnessed an example of this in Torian Black's history class at Freedom Prep in Memphis one morning not too long ago.

During his lesson he gave students a variety of reading and writing tasks to complete in groups. The tasks were complex and afforded students a significant amount of autonomy, so it was important that they listen carefully and get the directions right. His gentle reminders to "make sure you're listening" were accompanied by a warm and gracious smile. This not only communicated trust and caring but confidence. As a result, things were pretty crisp and class time was spent on the activities as planned.

But here was my favorite part. As he reviewed a portion of the directions, Torian said, "No need to track me; you can just read along on the page in front of you."

Later he summarized the directions and used that phrase again in a warm and quiet voice, "No need to track me." So students read along.

I love that phrase . . . "No need to track me." It does several things at once.

First, it reminds students that there is an intact expectation in the classroom that listeners track speakers. But it also shows intentionality on Torian's part. A really useful rule of thumb for managing a classroom is *Because you can does not mean you must.* Could Torian enforce the expectation that students track him while he gave direction? Yes. Must he? No. And in fact he wanted them reading the directions, not looking at him in this case. Or perhaps he wanted to give them an inch of extra flexibility because they were so on-point. He gave them permission not to follow the default while reminding them that it was still the default—a perfect and elegant way to prevent ambiguity. But he also reminded them that the lack of tracking was intentional and not an accident. The system and the exception coexisted happily and his phrase allowed Torian to turn off the tracking default temporarily while reinforcing it as an expectation.

Let's close then with two examples of what classrooms with strong *Habits of Attention* look like. First, check out the Keystone video of BreOnna Tindall's classroom. Her students look at each other as they share their thoughts about *The Narrative of the Life of Frederick Douglass*. You can feel their confidence as their ideas are validated by the group. The importance of their contributions is reinforced at every turn and so the scholarly side of students is drawn out, even for the students who are at first hesitant to speak. The environment, the culture, changes them.

But notice in particular how, after the initial *Turn and Talk*, one student, Adriel, is called on to share his response. It's a *Cold Call*, by the way. Adriel hadn't raised his hand. But voice equity is important. In a good classroom, everyone's voice matters and BreOnna expresses that with her *Cold Call*. Is Adriel nervous? Perhaps. But in addition to BreOnna's sincere interest and gracious smile, his classmates track him to show his ideas matter to them. This draws him out. They snap occasionally as he speaks to encourage and appreciate his thinking. In the glow of their respect, he speaks earnestly and with depth. He would not do that if their eye contact and body language did not encourage him to; if they slouched and looked away out the window. No one would. Left on his own, he might have sat silently but here he is drawn out into the sunlight of his peers. Changing the social cues he sees changes his behavior. He is discovering that his ideas are worthy of appreciation from his peers. A classroom with strong *Habits of Attention* I noted earlier, is like a bright mirror. It reflects its students' talents, but it is changing them at the same time.

Adriel's relationship with BreOnna certainly influences his work in school, but not as much as the interactions with his peers do. Thus BreOnna has sought to shape and guide them so they are as beneficial as possible.

Notice also that BreOnna calls next on Renee. She's got plenty to say as well and we can see that she knows the culture of the classroom will embrace her cerebral reflections. But notice also how she builds off of Adriel. This happens in part because of the classroom's habits but it's important to recognize that *Habits of Discussion* rely on *Habits of Attention*. She is attentive and focused during both the *Turn and Talk*—when she tracked and nodded and encouraged and so locked into her conversations—and while Adriel was speaking. Her answer reflects strong attention habits.

Finally, check out Denarius Frazier's tenth-grade math classroom at Uncommon Collegiate High School in Brooklyn (*Denarius Frazier: Solutions*). Using *Habits of Attention* with high schoolers might seem daunting but the results are surprisingly similar. As you watch, I hope you note the high "ratio" in the classroom—it's the students who do the work. They actively engage in tasks both challenging and worthy. The level of the discussion is high. You might also note the open-mindedness of Vanessa, who begins to defend her answer, recognizes her mistake, and changes her thinking without defensiveness. Look at the still image of the moment when this happens. The eye contact—tracking—is important and so are the facial expressions. The moment happens because she is receiving strong signals of psychological safety and belonging throughout: her classmates' eyes and faces and body language say *We are with you*.

What we're seeing is in part unnatural. At least it starts that way. At first, no group of people will of their own accord behave in a manner educationally optimal for the group as a whole. So it may be true that students begin tracking mostly because a teacher has asked them to. They are nudged, to use Richard Thaler and Cass Sunstein's term for an environment that encourages optimal decision making from participants, but once the nudge has happened, the action often becomes their own, a vehicle by which they express a culture of belonging and supporting one another of their own volition. They feel the difference and having felt it, embrace it. The classroom is more humanized than "dehumanized" by the tracking.

## TECHNIQUE 49: ENGINEER EFFICIENCY

Whether they use the term or not, nearly all educators develop *procedures*—set ways to complete recurring tasks—and teach them to students. One reason why procedures are so ubiquitous in classrooms is that, when designed well, they help teachers conserve time for learning. A second reason is that procedures "hack attention"; they save working memory for more important things. A third slightly more hidden benefit is that when students know what to do without being told, teachers have to make fewer corrections and can talk to them about more important or more positive things. Still, as every teacher knows, not all procedures are created equal. Sometimes, a procedure that's poorly designed can make doing a task more difficult. To avoid this pitfall, I recommend designing procedures that satisfy five criteria: Simplicity, Plan the Words, Quick Is King, Little Narration Required, and Double Planned.

**Simplicity.** Plan the simplest way to complete each key task correctly. Although this point might seem obvious, teachers are sometimes tempted to design elaborate procedures because executing them can be fun. Adding that extra sequence of *Call and Response* or holding students in a crisp line for an additional fifteen seconds can also make things feel orderly. But in the end, these are perverse incentives. You want procedures so that you can get to learning. Period. The simplest version is the best.

If you're not sure whether or not you should add something to your procedure, ask yourself: Does it help my students accomplish the task? Will I want to require them to do this step every time they do this task for the rest of the year? Will the productivity I gain be greater than the cost in time? The answer will often be yes, but strive to make certain of that for each step, and trim the procedure down to a handful of actions.

**Plan the Words.** "First, there is a cue, a trigger that tells your brain . . . which habit to use," writes Charles Duhigg in *The Power of Habit*, "Then there is the routine." The words that cue a procedure to begin and the ones that guide its steps *are part of the routine*. They should be planned as carefully and used as consistently as any other part. Notice how carefully Nikki Bowen says the word "transition" to her first graders in the video *Nikki Bowen: Stand Up* and how "shoulder partners" or "table partners" is the cue for different version of *Turn and Talk* in the video *BreOnna Tindall: Keystone*.

**Quick Is King.** Make the most of class time by showing students the fastest right way to do something. Even tightening your procedures by mere seconds can lead to big savings over the course of a school year. To get a sense of just how much time is at stake, let's say that your students completed ten transitions per day. Next, imagine that you pruned these transitions down by a minute apiece and sustained that pace for two hundred school days. Practically speaking, this would enable you to add back an entire *week's* worth of instructional time. That's one more week you could spend analyzing the themes in *Animal Farm,* teaching students how to dissect a frog, or helping students master the skill of adding fractions with unlike denominators. Looking at it the opposite way can give you a sense of just how much time inefficient procedures can steal from you and your students.

To challenge your students to get it right as quickly as possible and to discipline yourself to focus on speed, practice procedures against the clock. Use a stopwatch to measure and celebrate progress while continuously challenging kids to execute the procedures a little faster. "We did this in sixteen seconds yesterday; let's shoot for twelve today!"

That said, keep in mind that you are shooting for the fastest possible "right version"; if your students go so fast that they get it wrong, it's better to have them go back, do it slower but just right, and then keep practicing. Once it's done correctly you can speed it up.

**Little Narration Required.** When it comes to establishing a procedure, using fewer words to manage the execution is preferable. The goal is autonomy, and too many directions from the teacher keeps students from internalizing how to do it on their own. Autonomy is also lost if students need you there to explain each detail.

Further, providing too much verbal support (in the form of hints or reminders) cheapens the sense of satisfaction students get from successfully completing a procedure without your help. Saying less helps them feel more independent and take more ownership of it.

Plan the phrases you want to use at each step to ensure their clarity and efficiency. Use them consistently and with as little other verbiage as possible. Over time, remove verbal reminders and use only nonverbals, which students can refer to only if they need them. In time, remove those reminders as well; only step in to reinforce the procedure if students show you they need it.

**Double Planned.** Plan for what both you *and* your students will do at every step in a procedure. Then walk through the procedure yourself or with peers to make sure it works and there are no unexpected blind spots.

# TECHNIQUE 50: ROUTINE BUILDING

A beautifully designed procedure is not yet a tool for success in your classroom until it has become habit, and there are six keys to "installing" a routine. *Routine Building* lays the groundwork for success, paving the way via clear explanation and consistent reinforcement that disappears as excellence becomes habitual—but never goes away entirely.

The process of installation starts with a "rollout," a short speech in which you explain not only the *what* but the *why*. Students will be more invested if they understand your purpose and the value they put on such an understanding increases with every grade level. A rollout doesn't have to be a long description; you'll want to install a lot of routines so, for many, a sentence or a phrase will do. "We want to make sure to spend our time on more important things so we want to do it quickly." Other, more significant routines might warrant a bit more explanation—a rollout speech of a few sentences. See, for example, soccer coach James Beeston explaining his means of participation to his athletes in practice. He'll *Cold Call*, he tells them, because the game will demand a lot from them so training should, too. It wouldn't be hard to make a classroom version of that. Just be careful to not overdo it. Don't apologize for wanting what's best for students, just help them understand why it's best. Be crisp and clear and honest. And smile, as Jo Facer says in *Simplicity Rules*. You're helping students do things that will cause them to thrive and be successful. That's a good thing.

Next you'll want to outline the procedure, probably walk students through it if it's complex—pack up your things, stand up, push in your chair, and get ready to line up at the door—and if students are younger, maybe even number the steps at first so you can practice more intentionally, saying "Let's make sure we've got step number 2 down" or using nonverbal cues, as Lauren Moyle does in the video *Lauren Moyle: This Is Your Challenge*. Numbering has the effect of chunking the procedure into discrete steps that students can master and commit more easily to long-term memory. If you're teaching students how to transition from one location to another, it can also help to use a method called *point-to-point movement*. The idea is to identify a location or an action and then prompt students to move to that point and stop (for example, "Please stop at the corner of the hallway"). Parsing the transition into steps provides you with clear starting and stopping points, allowing you to control the pace with more precision. If you don't establish clear end points, releasing students to practice a new transition can lead to a mass of confusion, shoving, and squabbling that's difficult to stop, let alone manage.

Then model and describe. That is, explain and show students how to do the procedure. Doing both gives students a visual road map that they can follow and establishes a common language around the procedure. This is especially useful for "pain points," parts of the procedure that often prove tricky for students and that you therefore want to see and understand especially well in advance, or common mistakes that students will make when raising their hands ("I'm not waving it in the air. I'm not holding it over my head"). This makes the difference between correct and incorrect more visible to students. And a demonstration contains more detail than you can ever get in words, and research suggests that working memory for auditory and visual information may be additive. That is, students can absorb twice as much before working memory becomes overloaded.

After you've modeled and described, you'll want to let students practice. Lots. To truly master procedures, students need repeated practice with timely feedback on their execution. Far too often, teachers don't ask students to practice enough before releasing them to execute procedures on their own. This sets up students for failure. With younger students you may wish to practice in isolation—that is, to separate the practice from the context in which it will be executed and be very deliberate: "Let's practice pushing in our chairs and getting ready to line up now." We often see teachers with the most effective procedures using Pretend Practice—that is, distorting practice deliberately in ways that make it less realistic but more focused and effective at building skills. For a transition in an art room where there are lots of materials, you might start by having students practice without materials first to get the routine down and then add back in the crayons and the glue and the paint to make sure they can do it at full complexity—and full potential for spillage—when they already know their way through it.

Here are some ways you might see Pretend Practice:

1. *Isolated step*. Sometimes teachers will choose just one small aspect of a procedure and practice it over and over or at half speed to make sure their students get it. Only then will they speed it up to real time or link it to the steps before and after it.

2. *Strategically simplified*. Sometimes a teacher will remove a distraction to make practice more effective—for example, by practicing a transition without books the first few times ("Imagine you're carrying your books") or by practicing the process for putting materials away in art class without the actual supplies the first few times. That way students can lock in on the steps with simplicity and without pencils and crayons rolling around on the floor.

3. *Faux errors*. Other times, a teacher will ask students to deliberately make a common error to role-play how to respond. "What do you do if you go to the left if everyone is going to the right? Let's try it and work it out."

With older students, the practice is much more compelling if it's embedded in real content, even relatively simple orientation content. The video *Mallory Grossman: Quick Poll* is a great example. Mallory contrives a way for students to practice their new routines three times over the course of the first lesson. My colleagues on the *TLAC* team and I have also come to believe in something else Mallory is doing here—embedding practice of procedures in content for students above the primary level. This allows the students to feel the benefits of the routines and makes practice more natural.

A common mistake is to stop practicing once a routine appears stable. Routines require periodic maintenance to make sure they stay in ideal running order. Occasional feedback or a *Do It Again*—"Whoops, we were a little slow getting started with our Stop and Jot or our *Turn and Talk* there. Let's practice that again"—is important. And remember the Forgetting Curve: to learn something students have to begin to forget and then come back to something—usually multiple times. And a strong rotuine in October does not guarantee a strong routine in December. A little refresher, even before it is becomes necessary, is always smart, doubly so because you can practice without implying anything is wrong: "Let's be super attentive to our *Habits of Discussion* or *Habits of Attention* today."

Once students are able to complete a procedure in the right way, strive to transfer ownership, passing some of the responsibility to students. Doing so gives students a greater sense of accomplishment, independence, and ownership over classroom structures.

Recently, we taped a lesson to watch Maggie Johnson's eighth-grade English class at Troy Preparatory Middle School and uncovered a hidden gem in the first few seconds of the video.

"Pencils down when you hear the beep," she said, referring to the timer that's about to go off and signifies the end of independent work. "No countdown today." In fact, there would be no countdown as part of Maggie's routine for the rest of the year, she later told them. Maggie was transitioning her kids from one highly effective system to another—replacing a teacher-narrated countdown with a simpler, faster, and more mature system wherein her students come to attention on their own at the beep. Maggie's countdown system was very effective, and sometimes it's the things that go well in our classes that we hold on to hardest— sometimes for a fraction too long, or that's the risk at least. In Maggie's case, despite the effective system already in place, she realized either that as eighth graders, her students were ready for a bit more autonomy and self-management, or that eliminating the countdown would be faster and less disruptive to the work they were doing, or both.

In short, what we were observing in Maggie's class was a transfer of ownership. In effect, Maggie was saying, "You've proven you can master this part of being scholars on your own, so now I give you more autonomy. You 'own' the rate at which you earn more freedom to self-manage." This can be a powerful trade, especially when students understand that the autonomy is earned via mastery and follow-though.

**Other Notes on Transferring Ownership**

- **Say "You're Ready":** Remind students that you are giving them more autonomy in appreciation of their maturity and responsibility . . . that they've earned it. It's often great to make this a gradual process since it's better to give than to take away.

- **"You Know":** As you remove scaffolding, add language to make your actions transparent. Remind students that (1) they know what to do, and (2) you are aware of and appreciate this. "You don't need reminders from me anymore. . . . "

- **A Little Less in Sync:** You can transfer responsibility to students by simplifying a routine or eliminating steps, or by simply allowing them to complete the procedure without requiring that it be done in exact coordination with classmates.

- **Shared Leadership:** Let students assume leadership roles—cuing their classmates to begin stages of a routine, monitoring or evaluating its success, modeling for others, having specific jobs or responsibilities.

A caveat is important here: some teachers assume that because earned autonomy is an effective form of transferred ownership, they would do well to transfer ownership at the outset with a tacit bargain: "I'm going to give you a lot of autonomy, but I want you to show me that you understand how to use it, or I'll take it away." This is usually less effective. Unless you've started with discipline—teaching and establishing what routines should look like—students won't know what you mean by "how to use it" and will likely struggle. Your choice will then be to remove the autonomy you initially offered—potentially messaging that the systems you now establish are a punishment rather than "how we do things," and undertaking a more difficult installation (taking away freedom is harder than giving it)—or to fail to rein in the freedoms when students struggle, which means poor systems and routines for the year. Earning autonomy will help students value and understand it.

## Better Late Than Never: Tips for Rebooting Procedures and Routines

Procedures are best installed and routinized at the beginning of the year, but there are always times when a new procedure or system (that is, a set of related procedures) needs to be installed midyear. Culture has begun to slip, or morale to wane. You realize several months into the year that there's something you wish you'd routinized from the outset. Perhaps you've even arrived new, midyear, and in the wake of a teacher without systems and have been asked to rebuild the culture. A classroom "reset," which often involves rolling out brand-new systems and reintroducing or modifying old ones, can be a necessity. Before you reset, consider these tips to ensure that it goes as smoothly as possible:

- **Set a goal:** Connect the reboot to an inspiring, headline-grabbing goal or important date—right now or in the future (for example, "We only have 60 days left until we take our comprehensive exams. We need to be ready so we're going to sharpen up the little things").

- **Reboot after a break.** Take advantage of these periods away from class; they provide you with a natural excuse to reintroduce old procedures or to make a clean break from the past. ("We're just back from the long weekend and it's a good time to get all our procedures sharpened up so we're really focused and engaged for our next novel.")

- **Be transparent.** Briefly explain *why* you're rebooting. If you don't, you risk confusing students and losing their buy-in. "Sometimes when we do things over and over, we get a little sloppy with our execution. It's normal for everyone, but it's causing us to lose important learning time that you need to get ready for college. We're going to think back to when I taught you X at the beginning of the year—we'll review what we need to do and practice doing it not just well, but perfectly."

- **Coordinating with your team.** Coordinating your reboot with other teachers at your grade level, in your hall or across the school, provides more consistent reinforcement for students and thus easier and quicker change.

- **Follow up with precise praise.** Acknowledge progress, and praise students who exceed your expectations. If students pick up the procedures with less practice than they did at the beginning of the year, recognize their growth. This shows students that your reset isn't a punishment or indictment, but rather an expression of your belief in their ability to meet your high expectations.

## Props

Props are a form of public praise for students who demonstrate excellence or exemplify virtues. If you can consistently enable classmates to deliver resounding praise to one another in two seconds flat, you can build a culture that valorizes achievement and effort without sacrificing order or time on task. As students come to relish the culture of Props, you might even teach them a wide variety of them (see the end of the chapter for a list of suggestions) and let a student nominate Props for a classmate who did a great job.

The key is to invest the time at the outset to teach students to give Props the right way: crisply, quickly, and enthusiastically, just as you would with any routine. Ensuring that you teach your students to deliver Props that meet the following criteria will go a long way to ensuring your success:

- **Quick.** You should be able to cue a Prop in one second. Similarly, the Prop itself should be fast because you don't have time to waste and because there's nothing less energizing than an exhortation that starts strong but peters out. If it's not sharp, reinforce with *Do It Again* (technique 51, later in this chapter) and make sure to get it right.

- **Visceral.** Props are often powerful when they rely on movement and sound, especially percussive sound. Props that don't use much in the way of words are less likely to get tiresome; their half-life is longer because there's no phrase to wear out. A quick "Oh, yeah," is fine, but something like "On the way to college!" is likely to get old (and show its age) quickly. Furthermore, there's something fun and muscular about the thunder of group percussion.

- **Universal.** When you give Props, everybody joins in. It's up to you to set and enforce this expectation.

- **Enthusiastic.** The tone is energetic and lively. It should be a break—brief and fun—from hard work. Resist the temptation to make it too grown-up; it doesn't have to narrate values and express a mission-aligned personal credo. If it's a little bit of silly, it will reinforce moments when students have already demonstrated those things. Props are the exclamation point, not the sentence.

- **Evolving.** Let your students suggest and develop ideas for Props. They will constantly renew the systems with fresh and funky ideas and will participate more vigorously because they have helped invent them. And if students are forever thinking of new ones, Props will never get tired, boring, or obligatory.

## TECHNIQUE 51: DO IT AGAIN

Routines give students a clear model of how to execute common tasks successfully and clear working memory for higher-order tasks. If the transition is quick and automatic, students' minds can be free to roam or to reflect on content, like yours on your drive to work, perhaps. The more familiar the routine, the more it benefits your classroom and your students, in other words. What that implies is lots of practice. Practice with feedback and correction is the only way to build a habit. That's where *Do It Again* comes in. It is a very simple idea: when we are learning something and need to refine the routine or when we have not done something as well as we might, the most productive response is simply to do it over, a little better, a little sharper. This response—"That wasn't quite right; let's try it again," or "That was good, but let's try it again and see if we can be great"—is far superior to the alternatives: either ignoring the issue and letting quality of follow-through degrade, or chastening students for poor execution, or loading up their working memory with feedback they don't really get to use. By having students strive to do it over and better, you leverage the power of repetition and practice to painlessly build strong culture and self-discipline.

*Do It Again*, in other words, is the perfect tool to help maintain proficiency at something your students know how to do. It can as easily be applied to math procedures—"Try that again and make sure your decimals are lined up"—and classroom habits—"Just a minute, guys. Carlton, please start your answer over again and we'll all make sure we're giving you strong eye contact while you're speaking."

In a range of situations it's effective because:

- *It shortens the feedback loop.* Behavioral science has shown that the shorter the time lag between an action and a response, the more effective the response will be in changing the behavior. Let's say you have a clear expectation for entering the classroom, and a group of students comes in from recess in a disorderly way. Having the group stay in for recess three hours later is less likely to change their behavior than is a lesser response that occurs right away. If the reaction comes immediately after, while the original action is fresh in the students' minds, the two will be more clearly associated in their memory. In the three-hours-later scenario, they will be more likely to think, "She kept me in for recess." In the moment, they are more likely to recall and reflect on how they entered the classroom. *Doing It Again* shortens the feedback loop in comparison to almost any other consequence.

- *It sets a standard of excellence, not just minimal follow-through.* Do It Again is appropriate not just for times when students do something poorly; it's ideal for times when students do something "just fine" when the goal is excellence. Saying, "That was good, but I want great" or "In this class, we're going to strive to do everything world class; let's see if we can use a bit more expression when we read" enables a teacher to set a standard of excellence, where good can always be better and better can always shoot for best. This can drive your classroom culture by replacing acceptable with excellent, first in the small things and then in all things.

- *It promotes group culture and accountability.* Although individuals can easily be asked to *Do It Again,* the technique is especially effective as a response to group endeavors. If three or four students don't bother to engage in the *Turn and Talk* the best solution may be to pause the whole class and say, "Just a second. A couple of us might have been distracted at the beginning of that *Turn and Talk*. It's important that we all engage the question and our partner. I'll cue you again and I look forward to seeing your best conversational skills. Go!" As an aside, there are times when it feels wrong to hold groups too accountable for individuals who try to co-opt their purposes. Suffice it to say that because you *can* leverage group accountability does not mean you *should* in every situation.

- *It ends with success.* The last thing you remember of an event often shapes your perception of it more broadly. *Do It Again* ends a situation where a process was done with insufficient quality with success. The last thing students do in a sequence is to do an activity the right way. This helps engrain the perception and memory of what right looks like. It also helps build muscle memory. Students build the habit of doing it right, over and over. In fact one of the most interesting times to *Do It Again* is to encode success. As in: "That was perfect. Do it again just like that so you remember just what it feels like." The "it" could be a math problem or playing a perfect eighth note. In fact, watch the video *John Burmeister: Trill*. In it, John, who is one of my favorite music teachers, is teaching cello to an individual student. Notice how many times she plays a trill in the course of learning it—eleven times, actually. Sometimes because it's not quite there; sometimes to add a layer of detail; sometimes to encode success—three more just like that.

- *It is reusable.* As John's cello video shows, *Do It Again* can be reused frequently so you always have a way to respond that's productive. You don't need to keep inventing new responses. You can be positive in administering the third iteration: "I still think we can do this even better. Let's give it one more shot!" Add a stopwatch to some routines, and the challenge of *Do It Again* (and do it better) only becomes more powerful.

However, it's important to execute the technique well. *Do It Again* should be positive whenever possible, with a keen focus on getting better and, in a great classroom, informed by a constant narrative of "good, better, best." That is, "just doing it" gets replaced by doing it well. In fact, one colleague suggested that a better name for this technique is *Do It Better,* as *better* captures the idea that doing things over again to be as good as you can be is what school is about. The goal is not merely compliance but excellence, even in the little things.

*Do It Again* can be an effective tool for managing affect. Sometimes people's attitudes change from the outside in. Asking a low-energy class to repeat something with enthusiasm (especially, and critically, while modeling those attributes yourself) can start to be a self-fulfilling prophecy. *Do It Again* is a great opportunity to challenge students positively to show you their best. Saying, "Oooh, let's line up again and prove why we're the best reading group in the school" is often better than saying, "Class, that was very sloppy. We're going to do it again until we get it exactly right," even if the purpose in both cases is to *Do It Again* until you get it exactly right. You can see Kirby Jarrell do a lovely job of that in *Kirby Jarrell: Go Brown*. The class is timing themselves at how long it takes to get materials from the previous class put away and to have their novels out and ready. Michaela is running the clock and she reports that it took 48 seconds, an excellent time, so Kirby playfully decides to celebrate by having her kids say, "48 seconds? Go Brown!" [They're nicknamed after the university]. Students do it and the energy is a bit mixed. With a warm smile and a bit of bravery—everyone wants to cut bait when an idea appears not to work—Kirby playfully asks students to do it again with more enthusiasm. And they do it! And the energy level rises in the class and students appear energized a bit. It's a tiny throwaway moment but imagine—maybe Kirby keeps the chant for next class, maybe she doesn't—but imagine the message if she'd just let the mediocre follow-through remain the end point. The message might have been *Oh, that was awkward. If Ms. Jarrell asks you to do something silly just wait it out and we'll give up on it*. Here it ends pleasant and off-handed but at no loss to her enthusiastic and playful classroom culture.

Lastly, teachers sometimes think they need to wait until an entire routine or activity is done before asking the class to try it again. In fact, you should have students go back and try it again as soon as you know that the level of execution will not meet the standard you set for it. Don't wait for the routine to end. Again, this will better connect the stimulus to the response. Let's say students are lining up for lunch, and the drill is to stand up quietly, push in their chairs, turn to face the door, and then follow the table leader to the door. If students forget to push in their chairs, have them sit back down and try it again right then. This saves time and reinforces instant accountability.

## Putting It All Together

In the video *Montage: Do It Again*, you can see a few intriguing video examples of *Do It Again* in the classroom. You'll have to watch carefully because they come and go fast, which is part of the point. The less fuss, less disruption, and less censuring of students, the better. Simple and clear, nonjudgmental, and even positive when possible. You can see that in Erica Lim's class. She's starting for the day and wants to make sure to set expectations for follow-through on the greeting. It's not a big thing, yet you don't have to do it if you don't want to make follow-through questionable on all tasks. So she offers a simple and quick and emotionally constant reminder of what she knows her high schoolers know how to do. Denarius Frazier, too, is emotionally constant. If we're going to try to use tools that build positive culture and show appreciation for success, they'll be positive only if they are universal. When the response is spotty, Denarius asks quickly for a redo—the quicker the better—and is almost deadpan, showing a hint of a surprise. Much better, he says, when students follow through. He's reinforced this routine and the norm of follow-through on all such routines. It's a tiny but important movement and it's the simplicity of the responses and Denarius's lack of fuss that makes it successful. Sarah Ott's approach is similar and different. When students are slow in wrapping up and responding to her, she's playful and upbeat and energetic rather than steady, but she still gets her *Do It Again* done fast. It's a technique that usually gets more out of less.

## Notes

1. Tom Bennett, *Running the Room*, p. 104.
2. James Clear, *Atomic Habits*, p. 93.
3. Ibid, p. 117.
4. For U.S. readers: in England calling students "smart" means they look sharp and ready to go.
5. Hammond discusses attention in *Culturally Responsive Teaching and the Brain*. Learning, she goes on to say, "requires focused attention. active engagement and conscious processing by the learner" (p. 48).
6. www.researchgate.net/publication/225304965_The_role_of_selective_attention_on_academic_foundations_A_cognitive_neuroscience_perspective.
7. It's not a coincidence that tech engineers use the phrase "eyeballs" to describe the level of attention commanded by their software. Eyeballs are the currency of the gig economy, though of course the purpose of software is the opposite of a teacher's—it seeks to win attention through distraction. Teachers seek to build the ability to sustain and focus concentration. Is it necessary to point out that the winner of this battle—whether young people flick reactively from one push notification to the next or can sustain focus on what's most important—is of profound importance for the cognitive habits of a generation?
8. Also referred to as psychological safety.
9. You can see the story of one such example in Ron Suskind's outstanding book *A Hope in the Unseen* about Cedric Jennings, who manages to get from his high school in Anacostia to Brown University. The price of his success is massive. Everywhere he goes he is an outsider and more— a constant target of mockery. Humans are deeply social

and precious few people will embark on a journey that will result in their being made a pariah.

10. Why do people traffic in this distortion? Perhaps some genuinely believe it because they have not seen classrooms like Christine's. Some perhaps mistake the benign and beneficial authority of a teacher with authoritarianism—the abuse of authority. But for others it is a selfish act. They use words like "carceral" to describe it, to exonerate themselves from responsibility. No one doubts that ours is an education system that systematically constrains the opportunities of poor and minority children. For some, making their own protest is the priority; their goal is to make it clear that they are not responsible. Unfortunately, shouting slogans doesn't solve problems. I prefer to solve the problem and make classrooms better even if it opens me up to simplistic and self-serving calumny.

11. Pentland is quoted in Coyle's *The Culture Code*.

# Chapter 11

# High Behavioral Expectations

A classroom must be orderly for learning to take place.

Some educators will take exception with that statement.

"Not at all," they might say. "Learning is messy, chaotic, loud, and unpredictable. Disorder is part of education."

But what they'd mean by disorder would be a classroom in which, after forty minutes of the frenetic building of suspension bridges with toothpicks and gumdrops, everyone cleaned up nicely and the teacher had a few moments to ask with a puckish grin: "Well, class, what have we learned?"

They'd mean a class where young people enthusiastically engaged in a ramshackle discussion with lively disagreement—about a book that everyone had read and had a copy of at the ready.

They wouldn't mean a classroom where it would take them ten minutes to get students to hear and follow directions for the bridge building or a classroom where students who raised their hand during the discussion risked violating powerful, unspoken social norms. Or where a student muttered and smirked every time the two girls in front of him spoke out loud. Or where they had to wonder what that student was saying under his breath to the girls.

What they would mean by disorderly would be just the right amount of untidiness and unpredictability when they'd chosen it, designed it, and delegated it. Order, in other words.

One of the core challenges of teaching is that it is very, very hard to create classrooms reliably characterized by psychological safety and where students encourage the best from one another; where, when necessary, students can think deeply amidst quiet and develop their capacity to pay attention; where some students' desire to pursue learning assiduously is honored and supported, even when others don't really feel like it.

It's far easier to say that order doesn't matter, or is counterproductive. It's easier to claim that a teacher's responsibility to be able to judiciously enforce quiet is the same as a craven desire to suppress student voices. It's easier to argue that the exercise of benevolent and necessary authority is a form of authoritarianism and to conflate those similar sounding but very different words. Establishing orderly classrooms is an ideal place for the Band-Aid Paradox.[1]

Democracy, in a classroom, is problematic when twenty-eight people want to learn chemistry and two want to persist in making hilarious burping noises. The twenty-eight do not require a mere majority to proceed. They need unanimity. One or two students' freedom to make those clever noises or to say no to the idea of listening and following directions is often a *de facto* decision for everyone else in the room. The lesson will not proceed as planned.

This is an age-old challenge but also one that is increasingly difficult to bridge. Our society is the most individualistic on the planet (adapting to its individualism is one of the biggest challenges for students who come here from other cultures) and it is growing more so by the moment. There are precious few times and places where people will accept that they must be willing to constrain their own behaviors and desires for the common good. This used to be taken for granted; people were proud to do their part and raised their children to expect to as well, but no more. The refusal of some individuals to wear masks to help mitigate an epidemic, for example, underscores how hard it is to socialize such actions in our society. And yet schools are among the last institutions that ask for and depend on this increasingly unfamiliar behavior—where a greater common good (learning and knowledge for all) is achieved through small personal sacrifice (show, or perhaps even feign interest in what your classmates are saying even on days when you don't really feel like it).

At any given moment, the students in your classroom will be a mix of the stoic and the impulsive; the selfless and the selfish; the virtuous and the thoughtless; the wise and the silly.[2] Hopefully more virtuous and wise than thoughtless and silly, but surely some of both. And in that mixture, the rights of those who dream of atoms and cell structure or insight into Grant's mindset as dawn broke over Vicksburg are fragile. They require protection. The more virtue and wisdom among the majority of your young people, the more imperative that you protect their right to learn in an optimal setting. And let me say a word here for the silly—of which I can say I was often one. Part of teaching is graciously and humanely preventing the puckishness of the child inclined to occasional silliness from becoming a bar to their own and others' learning. Short-sighted decisions by young people are to be expected. Everyone chooses hilarity over chemistry at some point. That such inclinations are natural and common does not mean that we should indiscriminately allow them, or that constraining them need be cruel or harsh—the opposite, in fact, and with skill such actions can feel like (and be) a form of caring. There is plenty of room for laughter at the right time.

The video *Emily Bisso: Write What I Write* tells a version of that story. Emily's class is taking notes. Except Joshua. He's distracted and wants Emily's attention and is going to miss out on the learning. I'll unpack the details of her lovely interaction to get him back to learning later in the chapter, but it's not just her tone that expresses love and caring. It's the action itself. It will matter that Joshua learn the content of this lesson and learn to be a scholar if he is to thrive. To care about him is to get him back on track.

"It is not possible for everyone's desires to be met at the same time as everyone else's," Tom Bennett reminds us in *Running the Room*. "At times individual wants will be balanced with the greater good of the community. . . . It is impossible for everyone to behave as they please." This is to say that you cannot be a teacher and not be prepared to ask or require some students to sometimes do what they are not inclined to do. Doing so is the exercise of the responsibility we are entrusted with, not the abuse of authority.

And—here comes a summary of what this chapter is about—most of the tasks required of us to ensure the right kind and amount of order can be done warmly and graciously, in a caring manner and often with a smile. With skill they can be made less visible (in fact one of the main skills I try to point out in technique 55, *Least Invasive Intervention*, is making them as invisible as you can) and can be stripped of caustic emotions (technique 56, *Firm, Calm Finesse*). Or, even better, moments of conflict can be headed off and prevented before they even happen. Or many of them can. We cannot all achieve Emily Bisso's state of grace in the Joshua interaction; not every interaction can be solved quite so simply and happily. But the goal is to remember what Emily is telling us as much as what she is telling Joshua: *I do this because I care and in being attentive to my technique I am most able to do it in ways that help students thrive.* In fact, Emily's success is as much a result of her mastery of "quiet presence," "economy of language," and "live in the now" (elements of *Strong Voice* I discuss later in the chapter, and of *Positive Framing*, which I discuss in the next chapter) as it is of her intention to be caring. Nobody takes this job because they want to shout at young people and have caustic interactions with them. But teachers by the thousand do so every day. They do so because the situations we are placed in as teachers are immensely challenging. They require more than good intentions to resolve optimally. They require technique. The grace that a teacher like Emily shows, we should all understand, is at least in part technique in disguise.

But before we go to technique it is necessary to establish that to excuse (or worse, justify) disorderly classrooms is to allow precious opportunity to be stolen from young people—usually the most vulnerable. Teachers are invested with authority to ensure that certain rights are protected precisely because those rights are preciously important and require everyone's cooperation to sustain. And teachers for the most part are insufficiently trained and prepared for this small but critical part of the job.

This is no small failing. A recent national survey of teachers[3] found that *more than three quarters* (77 percent) believed that "most students suffered" because a few students were persistently disruptive. But of course, school problems, like everything else, are not evenly distributed in society. In schools with more than 75 percent of students eligible for free or reduced-price lunches, more than half of teachers[4] went further and said that "student behavior problems contributed to a disorderly or unsafe environment that made it difficult for many students to learn." For those who might be wondering, the authors also disaggregated the results by race of teacher and found few differences. On the question of whether student behavior "contributed to a disorderly or unsafe environment that made it difficult for many students to learn," for example, Black teachers said yes at roughly the same rate as White teachers: 60 percent for Black teachers to 57 percent for White teachers. The issue, in other words, does not appear to be White teachers seeing harmless behavior among kids of color and reading danger and defiance where none exists, although, of course, we should always be aware that this is a risk. The data suggest that the issue is that almost every student assigned to a school not characterized by economic privilege is consigned to spend a significant portion of their learning years in classrooms where a lack of order makes it difficult for them to learn.

That is the norm.

Additionally, students themselves feel unsafe much of the time in school. A 2018 study by the United Negro College Fund reported that fewer than half of African American students (43 percent) feel safe at school.[5] Think for a moment about the enormity of that finding—feeling unsafe is *normal*—it is how the average Black student feels in school, according to the survey. And those data are not disaggregated to show the disparate impact on Black students in high poverty schools, specifically.

Parents, not surprisingly, worry too. Another report by UNCF found that parents prioritized a safe, secure, and violence-free environment as the most important single factor when choosing a school for their child.[6]

Given that effective schools are the single most important vehicle in society for ensuring equality of and access to opportunity, these data represent a massive and regressive tax on families of poverty. But it is not just egregious behavior that is a problem. Low-level disruptions are chronic in many classrooms and result in not only lost learning time but disruption of student focus. A report by the UK Government in 2013–2014 found such behaviors as calling out without permission, talking unnecessarily while the teacher was teaching, being slow to start work or follow directions, showing lack of respect for peers or teacher, not arriving to class with necessary materials, and using mobile devices to be chronic problems in many classrooms. "The findings in this report are deeply worrying," Her Majesty's Chief Inspectorate wrote, "not because pupils' safety is at risk . . . but because this type of behavior has a detrimental impact on the life chances of too many pupils. It can also drive away hard-working teachers from the profession."[7]

And yet, there is still more to the story. Unnecessary suspensions are a chronic problem in schools and they, too, can have cascading consequences for students who are suspended—they miss class and fall further behind; they are then more likely to drop out of school or become further disengaged. That said, permitting the behaviors that lead to suspension should not be an option, for reasons reflected in the data mentioned earlier. At least two steps are central—and often overlooked—in addressing this challenge. The first is that schools must become more inclined to use teaching as a response when students are disruptive. To that end, my colleague Hilary Lewis has developed a Dean of Students' curriculum, for example. It offers robust and productive lessons that provide replacement behaviors and opportunities for developing knowledge and sustaining reflection in place of mere punishment when students behave in a disruptive or counterproductive manner.[8] The other step is for teachers to develop the capacity to prevent issues from escalating to the point where students require such disciplinary measures. Calmly and efficiently resolving the natural tensions that arise in the classroom is a core skill of a master teacher. Prevention and deescalation are almost always preferable to a post-event response, no matter how good.

There is a tendency among some educators to equate orderly classrooms with higher rates of suspension and other harsh disciplinary consequences, but in fact the opposite is the case. Norms are the most pervasive influence on the behaviors of individuals. Students are more likely to engage in more extreme behaviors in environments in which those behaviors appear plausible or even common, where things spiral quickly out of control, where there is little learning going on, where there is peer pressure to test limits, and where the culture does little to check this impulse. Sadly, when this is the case, students often feel tacit pressure to engage in behaviors they don't especially want to do and know are wrong. Every principal will tell you that some portion of suspensions are of young people who lack a positive and productive relationship to school, and some portion are of kids who like school and want to succeed there and nonetheless do something dangerous, stupid, or mean-spirited in a way that seems utterly out of character. A teacher who can use the tools in this chapter to establish a warm, caring, and humane learning environment that offers consistent limits is engaged in the work of preventing suspensions.

There is a final element to an orderly classroom that is also easily overlooked. "Self-discipline, self-regulation, hard work, [and] patience," Tom Bennett writes in *Running the Room*, are all "enormously important characteristics of successful people in a variety of contexts. . . . Everything of value you can conceive of was acquired through sustained effort, practice, and delayed gratification." An orderly classroom builds these habits—you want to speak but you discipline yourself to listen first; you are tired some days but complete your tasks regardless.

Productive and positive behavior, in other words, is part of an invisible curriculum in schools that reinforces executive functioning skills and allows students to thrive. Students learn to understand how to work within the parameters of a group or organization. Young people who are rude to teachers and classmates and who talk back and struggle to embrace common goals "are not going to magically transform themselves into prime candidates for the best jobs" or into collaborative members of the project team, observes Jo Facer in *Simplicity Rules*. To learn those things is to be ready to start your own business, raise children, or be the sort of valued colleague who brings greatness to a team or project.

And just because we teach students to understand how to work within the parameters of a group or organization "does not mean they cannot push back intellectually," Facer continues. Learning to be a productive member of a group does not prevent you from taking political or social action in the face of unjust broader societal norms. Students who have been in well-run classrooms have not been "socialized to be compliant." I do not buy the argument that if you call out in class and don't follow your teacher's direction you are learning independent thought and a commitment to justice. Or that co-opting productive meetings and being inattentive to the needs of the group is preparing for leadership. Conflating schools without rules as crucibles of liberation proposes a fairly unrealistic vision of what civil disobedience and organized dissent entail. There are actually a fairly large number of meetings required to organize groups and clarify goals. Better to have learned to clearly express your ideas, to learn how to work within group norms. Such students remain empowered to stand up to injustice when doing so is warranted and in fact have more tools to do so when required—a good education teaches students many things, including the history and tools of resistance to injustice.

This causes me to return to the phrase "productive and positive" behavior, which I used previously. That phrase reminds us that the purpose of these techniques is not so much to forestall negative behavior as it is to socialize positive and productive behaviors that help young people thrive in all the settings of their lives. Our goal is to create something good, and one outcome will be the prevention of the negative behaviors along the way.

## TECHNIQUE 52: WHAT TO DO

Giving directions is one of the most overlooked aspects of teaching both because of its mundanity and its familiarity. We are forever doing it but it feels about as profound as ordering a sandwich.

But poor directions—those that are unclear or meandering (which is to say unclear and compounded by length and repetition)—have consequences that are far-reaching. For example:

- My directions aren't clear, so some students don't follow through on them and we waste time.

- My directions aren't clear, so some students do the task incorrectly and are confused.

- My directions aren't clear, so some students are confused, and I get mad at them for not doing what I wanted. They feel my sense of frustration and are frustrated in return.

- My directions aren't clear, so students assume I'm flustered or not prepared or am not really all that clear on what I want.

- My directions aren't clear, so some enterprising student takes advantage of the gray area and pretends to misunderstand by doing something else entirely. Wouldn't that be funny!

Turns out giving effective directions is one of teaching's core competencies and *What to Do* is the art of giving directions effectively. It is a case study in little things with big consequences.

The most basic version of poor directions occurs when teachers tell students what *not* to do. Let me offer a few examples:

"Kevin, you shouldn't be looking out the window."

"Cheryl, don't get distracted."

"Class, don't hand me messy disorganized work."

Now let me rewrite them to show how they might be different (acknowledging that a master teacher would probably make them far better):

"Kevin, make sure you're getting everything on the board into your notes."

"Cheryl, please turn to Carly and share your thoughts about the beginning of Chapter Two."

"Class, make sure your decimals are lined up, you write neatly, and circle your final answer."

In each of these cases, the revision is likely to help students be successful because it describes specific, concrete, and observable actions. When there are multiple steps, they are in a clear sequence.

**Specific Directions.** Effective directions break down larger tasks into manageable steps that students can take. I could have corrected "don't hand me messy or disorganized work" with "make sure your work is neat and organized," for example. That might be fine. But it's a bit of an assumption that students know what it means to do neat and organized work. And even if they do, a reminder always helps. So breaking the task apart into more specific steps is, in a sense, teaching students the component steps of organization.

You can get a sense for how clear and specific directions help students succeed and engage productively in the work of class in the video *Denarius Frazier: Check in with Your Neighbor*. The incipient sense of flow, the way Denarius is building a sense of uninterrupted focus and momentum, derives from his simple clear directions coming out of the *Do Now*—"Pencils down and track me"—and to start the *Turn and Talk*: "Go ahead and check in with your neighbor. You have thirty seconds. Go." Crisp and clear and all but impossible to misinterpret. Or watch the moment at the beginning of the video *Gabby Woolf: Keystone*. "We're going to be reading the beginning of Chapter Four," Gabby notes and students look placidly back at her. Then she adds a clear and specific direction: "Have your text in front of you, please." Notice how many students suddenly swing into action and get their books. Notice how many students didn't think to have their books ready and how much unproductive learning time has been avoided by the simple clarity of that small phrase inserted at the outset of the activity.

**Concrete Directions.** Effective directions involve, when possible, clear, actionable tasks that students know how to execute. It's not just that the direction about neat and organized work breaks it into clear and manageable steps but that the steps are concrete enough to be hard to misinterpret. They refer to things like lining up decimals rather than "carefully presented work." The former is much more concrete and ideally, I'd have taught students to line up decimals, so they knew exactly what I meant and were likely to be successful. Same for my direction to Cheryl, who, let's assume, is missing out on a *Turn and Talk* and is distracted or perhaps turned around and trying to get the attention of someone else in class. *Cheryl, please start the Turn and Talk* would tell her what to do, but it's vague. In other words, what do I mean by that? Cheryl might misunderstand. Though many readers will probably come up with even better examples, I've tried to "shrink the change" as Chip and Dan Heath describe it in *Switch*. I've made the first step easier to follow by making it clearer and smaller.

You can see how Sadie McCleary's specific and concrete directions to her chemistry class help every student to get ready simply and easily in the video *Sadie McCleary: Notes for Today*.

Sadie has taught students how to head a paper to take notes on so when she says, "Today is lesson 14," they understand that this is what they should write at the top of their notes under the phrase "Unit 2: Matter," which they've already written at the top. Notice how specific she is even about what exactly they should write. In addition to ensuring they are ready to take notes, this signals her own careful preparation to students.

**Sequential Directions.** I mentioned earlier that effective directions should describe a sequence of concrete, specific actions. This allows you to pace them: If there are a series of steps and a student is inclined to distraction, you might parse them out more slowly or even one by one, checking for completion or at least progress on one before naming the next. I learned this as a parent when my children were small. There might be days when I could say: *OK, towel off, get your jammies on, and brush those teeth* successfully. There were also days when that many directions at once would end in disaster. If one of my kids was getting out of the tub and feeling giddy or distracted, I would pace the directions. I'd start: *OK. Get your towel and dry off*. When that was done, I'd say: *Great. Now get into your jammies*. When that was done, I'd say, *Good, now over to the sink to brush your teeth*. So you might pace your directions to Cheryl if you weren't sure of her mindset and the likelihood of her follow-through. *Cheryl, turn and face Carly. Good, please give her a bit of eye contact so she knows you're listening. OK, now share your thought or ask her what she thought.*

Jason Brewer does a really nice job of pacing his sequential *What to Do* directions for a different reason in the video *Jason Brewer: Pencils Are Down*. He wants to give students time to finish each task in his directions well, without rushing, so he parses them one by one with lots of space in between and with a calm and easy voice.

**Observable Directions.** The more observable you make a direction the more you can assess follow-through and, if necessary, reinforce accountability for a student who's confused, distracted, or not especially inclined to follow through at the moment. Telling a student to "pay attention" is the classic counterexample. It's non-observable. So if I tell Caleb to pay attention and in my estimation he does not improve and I say, "Caleb, I asked you to pay attention," he would likely reply, "But I *was* paying attention," either because he believed he was or because he was seeking to avoid responsibility. But if my directions were observable: "Caleb, pick up your pencil and take notes in the space at the top of your paper," and Caleb continued to struggle, I could first say, "Caleb, pick up your pencil please," and watch for his follow-through, pacing my further directions from there based on his response. It's much harder to sustain an "I did pick up my pencil" argument when your pencil is not in your hand than it is to sustain an "I was paying attention" argument. Now Caleb's lack of follow-through is clear and unambiguous so if I must respond with a consequence of some sort, it will be clear—to me and to him—that it is justified.

In the video *Arielle Hoo: Eyes Up Here*, Arielle's *What to Do* directions—impeccable, clear, warm, and gracious—always start with an observable direction: "Eyes up here" or "Track up here." This allows her to scan for follow-through and attention and make sure students hear all the math. She combines her WTD directions with several exceptional examples of technique 53, *Radar and Be Seen Looking*.

## Keys to Effective Delivery with *What to Do*

**Economy of Language**: Maybe the most useful piece of advice for making *What to Do* directions effective is to use as few words as possible. More words often make the necessary task less clear or more ambiguous. You might think economy of language would make you sound stern, but of course crispness can be done with grace and warmth, as the clip *Tamesha McGuire: Baseline* beautifully demonstrates. Tamesha's directions are: "Tuck your chairs," "Pencils up," and "Write your name." The longest has three words, which helps her kindergartners to get happily to work and gives her lots of time to circulate and share the warmth instead of offering repeated reminders. This is especially important with your first direction. You can see that play out in *Denarius Frazier: Try That Grid*, in which Denarius's directions sound much like Tamesha's: "In pairs." "Two minutes." "You do one." "Try that grid, fill in all the blanks that you can." The crispness and clarity of the first two directions earns students' attention and focus.

A second key to success is to use *Emotional Constancy*, that is to deliver directions and corrections in an even tone, even if you are feeling a little frazzled or frustrated, so students focus on and respond to your words, not your emotions. That's pretty evident in all the examples we've seen so far. There's no tension to distract students from the task at hand.

**Consistent *What to Do*:** Use consistent language as often as you can so the directions themselves are a sort of routine in and of themselves. For example, always saying "Pencils in the tray" often works better than an unpredictable combination of "Pencils in your trays," "Pencils in their homes," "Pencils down," "Put your pencils down," "Let's put those pencils away," and so on. You don't have to be obsessive about it but increasing the consistency of the language in your directions allows you to make the direction more like a habit. This frees you up to focus on your lesson and makes it easier for students to do what you've asked. Part of the reason Denarius's class starts so smoothly is that he is consistent about the phrase he uses to close the *Do Now* nearly every day. It's almost always "Pencils down and eyes up here" or something very similar. If there are moments when you most want follow-through, use the most familiar version of the direction.

Giving a ***What to Do* Out Front**, that is, in advance of a cue to begin, is a great way to make sure students hear all of your directions and aren't distracted as you give them. For example, saying, "When I say 'go,' please turn to your partner and discuss your observations about the beginning of the chapter," gives you the opportunity to make sure everyone has heard the direction and is attentive and to add further detail—"I'll ask a few of you to share your partner's observation"—before students rush off to *Turn and Talk*. If your class is especially enthusiastic and it's a task they're excited to do, you might even say, "When I say 'go,' but not before I say 'go,' please turn to your partner and discuss your observations . . ." This also, by the way, makes a crisper and more visible start to the *Turn and Talk*, and norms that are more visible are more likely to become universal quickly.

On the other hand, you may notice the directions in *Arielle Hoo: Eyes Up Here*, where she says, "Eyes up here in four . . . three . . . two . . ." She's given her *What to Do* but also given a countdown to students before the cue so they have a bit of time and space and can finish what they are writing.

## Simplified *What to Do*

If a student does not respond to your *What to Do* direction, simplify it, either by removing words, requesting an even more concrete action, or reducing the number of steps you've asked the student to follow through on. For example, if you say to a student, "Pick up your pencil and take notes at the top of the page," and she doesn't do it, you might say, "Pick up your pencil, please." If you still don't get follow-through, you might point to the pencil. "Pencil in your hand, please, Roberta." Breaking down directions makes it easier to teach and reinforce your expectations for how students should complete a task.

What about when your direction is explicitly in response to a student who needs redirection? Adapting *What to Do* to the type of situation—and your assessment of its possible causes—can help ensure success in terms of both the task getting done and relationships being preserved.

**Standard**: The cause of poor follow-through is unclear and could plausibly be benign, such as distraction or confusion:

*Assume the Best*: "Hmm, I must not have been clear. When we are in 'Learner's Position,' that means our voices are off."

*Act As If*: After delivering a *What to Do* correction, glance away as if you're sure that they'll follow through. Then use a confirmation glance as needed to monitor.

**Ambiguous:** The cause of poor follow-through is unclear, but it has been persistent or seems like it could include some taking advantage of gray area.

*Simplify:* Remove words, choose just one step.

*Emotional Constancy:* Double-check that you are calm and steady; remove emotional variables.

**Challenging:** The cause of poor follow-through appears to be deliberate or limit-testing. Behavior is repeated or the situation is especially challenging.

*Shrink the Change:* Break the next step down into the smallest possible task. For example, you say to a student, "Stand up at your desk and walk to the door, please," but she doesn't do it. You say, "Stand up at your desk, please." She still doesn't do it. You say, "Push your chair back. Good. Now stand up. Thank you."

*Insert Careful Acknowledgments:* When a student is in a negative cycle, help them perceive each productive step back toward the path to success by acknowledging it in a muted tone. For example, a dean of students dealing with an upset student might say: "Please sit in this chair" very calmly and then add "thank you" (with very little affect) when the student has done it. Then perhaps: "Please turn and face me so I know you're ready to discuss this." As soon as it happens, the dean might acknowledge that the student is making an effort: "That's much better. Thank you." Then he or she might try, "Now when you're ready to talk, please give me a nod." Again you might acknowledge with, "Thank you," perhaps adding "I appreciate you showing me you're ready to talk about this. I appreciate that."

---

## Online Lessons: Remote *What to Do*

The importance of directions is critical—and critically overlooked—in most settings. Teaching remotely caused many of us to confront the challenges of clarity in this new setting. With glitchy Internet and an increased potential for distractions, with the difficulty of pairing nonverbal cues with directions and the fact that teachers' directions suddenly were given in a tiny voice emanating from a window in the corner of a screen, it was many times easier for students to miss a direction online. And of course the safety net that has existed for students for time immemorial—if you don't know what to do, look at what the people next to you are doing—also disappears when you are sitting alone at your kitchen table.

Under such conditions teachers learned a thing or two about giving directions. One of our favorite videos was this one of Alonzo Hall's "orientation screen" at the beginning of his lesson. His verbal directions are also given visually, with absolute clarity and absolute simplicity so they are much harder to miss or misunderstand. *Here's what to do*, they say, with the most important parts highlighted in yellow.

**Let's Get Organized!**

- **Welcome back to math class!**
- For this lesson, you need:
    1. A few pieces of paper (notebook or blank paper is fine)
    2. A pencil
- Please pause the video and gather your materials. Press play when you have everything ready to go!

And here's Eric Snider making the directions for independent work both visual and oral and *leaving a version of them up for students to reference throughout the activity* so they can always reorient.

| Independent Work until <u>1:30</u> |
| --- |
| ☐ 1.   Read pages 195-199. It's finally the girls' time to perform! Find out what happens and be ready for. . . a plot twist. |
| ☐ 2.   Answer questions 4-6 in classwork. |
| ☐ 3.   Take Socrative Quiz. |
| ☐ 4.   Make sure <u>ALL</u> questions are answered then → "Turn In" Classwork. |
| ☐ 5.   Begin IR for your reading log. We will come back together at <u>1:30</u> |

**What Alonzo and Eric are doing ties in to cognitive science.** "Spoken words disappear," Oliver Caviglioli points out in his book on the science of visuals, *Dual Coding*. This is called the *Transient Information Effect* and it reminds us that anything that is exclusively verbal is harder to study and remember and often exerts a heavy load on working memory. This has instructional implications but also cultural ones: we should put reminders everywhere if we want people to remember.

**But our reminders should be simple!** Limiting extraneous information is another piece of advice Caviglioli provides about visuals. Graphics are most useful when spare and focused: simple and without extraneous info; for example, fewer colors are better and line drawings are often better than photos if we want people to focus on the content and process the key ideas.

## TECHNIQUE 53: RADAR AND BE SEEN LOOKING

In technique 52, *What to Do*, I shared a video of Arielle Hoo giving directions to her math class (*Arielle Hoo: Eyes Up Here*). She's a model of clarity and her students respond beautifully, working attentively, thoughtfully, and contentedly.

You can get an even clearer sense of the culture of Arielle's room in the video *Arielle Hoo: Keystone*, taken from the same lesson. Notice two very simple but very important things she does after giving her directions: "Eyes up here in four . . . three . . ."

I've cut and pasted a series of still shots taken from the video here and numbered them one through four to show what she does a little more clearly:

The first thing Arielle does is to look. She gives her directions and, instead of looking down at her notes or at the board, she takes a second to scan the room, right to left. This lets her confirm that students are following her directions. If they're not, she'd want to adjust. Perhaps she wasn't clear enough and she'd want to regive her directions with a bit of assuming the best: "Whoops, let me be a little clearer. . . ." Perhaps they're a little giddy and she'll want to slow her voice slightly to set a calmer tone. For sure, she won't want to push on too fast if students are showing signs of distraction. Either way, the lesson is that a teacher can manage only what she sees so actions that allow you to see more clearly and comprehensively are critical. Actions that allow teachers to see well constitute a critical set of skills and one that is too rarely talked about. I call such actions *Building Radar*.

To return to Arielle's classroom, and her glance up at her class to see whether they've followed through, what her action tells students in that moment is at least as important as what she learns from looking. Her message is: *I care whether you do what I asked. I will notice whether you do so or not.* When we show that it matters to us, it matters more to students. Just by looking, and having students know that we look, we make it more likely that they will follow through; perhaps in part because we've eliminated some gray area, but more likely because we've simply shown that it matters. If you have a strong relationship with students, this will be profoundly influential. If you are still building it, the clarity and competence you show will help earn their trust and respect.

A brief digression here before I return to the second thing Arielle does. Watch the very short video of fourth-grade teacher Katie Kroell (*Katie Kroell: Sacrifice*). She's an excellent teacher but I've chosen this clip mostly because it is a study of human nature. Notice the young man in the left foreground. He's getting something out of his backpack. It could be anything, honestly: an extra pencil or something he wants to show a classmate. About ten seconds into the video, Katie glances in his direction:

She doesn't do anything else. She doesn't nod her head or wag her finger or frown. It's actually not even clear how she feels about what the student is doing. She merely looks and he decides of his own volition not to get whatever it was out of his backpack. It's his choice, but his choice changes because he knows his teacher is aware of it. *I don't need that right now.* When people know others are aware of what they are doing, they become more aware of their own choices and they choose differently. This is true almost everywhere in our lives. There's a street near my house where a device on the roadside shows your speed as you drive past. It doesn't take a picture. There are no consequences. It simply tells you how fast you are going. And yet every driver I have ever driven behind slows down.[9]

That's part of what's happening in Arielle's classroom. When students know that their teacher sees and cares whether they follow a direction, they are suddenly much more likely to follow it.

And this brings me to the second thing Arielle does. She exaggerates her looking ever so slightly so students will be more aware of it. You can see this best in the photos. She lifts her chin in a tiny bit of pantomime. *See me looking?* This enhances the effect of the preventive benefits of looking, especially for students who are least likely to notice without the extra emphasis. I call this idea *Be Seen Looking.* Looking is most effective when students are aware of it, so we can help them become more aware of it via subtle nonverbal actions and thus prevent behaviors that would require correction. It's a gift to everybody.

To go back to the photo from Katie's classroom, it's worth asking whether her student would have seen her questioning glance if she hadn't, like Arielle, lifted her chin slightly to make her looking more legible to her student.

Let's call that move *Chin Up* to make it easy to remember and replicate. And while we're at it, let's call a deliberate scan from one side of the room—to build a habit of looking well—a *Swivel.* Radar's foundation is the *Swivel*—the deliberate scan of the classroom that causes you to be sure to see as much as you can. It takes only a second or two. Ideally it would become a habit—you'd give directions and scan without even really thinking to do it.[10] It looks like it's a habit for Arielle—her mind is on other things as she scans. But it helps her keep everyone positively engaged and defends against blind spots. And if she sees something small she can redirect it simply and quickly while it's still small. The idea of catching things early while they're tiny so the fix can also be tiny is called "catch it early." It'll come up later in this chapter. But to catch it early you have to see it early. So you have to look systematically.

You can observe Arielle responding to what her Swivel reveals when she says, "Waiting on two." As we'll discuss in a few pages this is called an anonymous individual correction. It lets students know she's aware they're a bit behind while preserving their anonymity. In this case they quickly catch up. A potential problem is averted.

You also might notice that Arielle takes a half step back when she scans. It's the equivalent of stepping back when you are taking a photograph to get everyone in the frame. It allows her to see more of the class with less of a Swivel, and it reminds us that where you stand is a major factor in what and how well you see.

Julia Addeo's Swivel is especially good. It's a critical part of her transition about two minutes into her keystone. "Just one piece of feedback. Track up here," she says to make sure students who were working on their problem set now attend to the discussion. She's at the overhead projector and can't afford to move to a new spot. Perhaps because of this she scans left to right and then back to the left, making it clear without any words that their focus is critical and matters to her. Her students recognize this and seconds later she's teaching to a locked-in room of thirty.

The video *Denarius Frazier: Keystone* shows Denarius using a Swivel to scan the room several times. The clearest and best example occurs at about 10:20 because his range of motion is relatively narrow. That's because he's taken an even more intentional approach to the question of where to stand. When you stand in the corner of the room you dramatically reduce the field of vision you have to scan and otherwise manage. This makes it simpler to see everything. I call this position Pastore's Perch, after the first teacher I observed using it consistently and intentionally, Patrick Pastore.

You can see math teacher Rodolfo Loureiro standing consistently in Pastore's Perch to see better in *Rodolfo Loureiro: Fix Your Mistakes*. Each time he gives a direction he walks to the corner of his room and observes from there. This makes it easy for him to see whether students follow through. The movement to the corner also probably makes it clearer to students that he's looking and that it's time for task completion. The combination of these two effects allows Rodolfo to relax and smile warmly. Bonus points to Rodolfo for using different corners so he sees different students with more clarity each time and is in tune with how everyone is doing.

Here's a quick graphic that demonstrates the importance of Pastore's Perch. To see the classroom from the front center you have to scan a field of about 150 degrees. That's a lot to see, but scan carefully and pay special attention to the blind spots in the corners of the visual field. However, if you walk to the corner of your room, you can see the whole room by scanning a visual field of just 80 degrees. It's now simpler to scan.

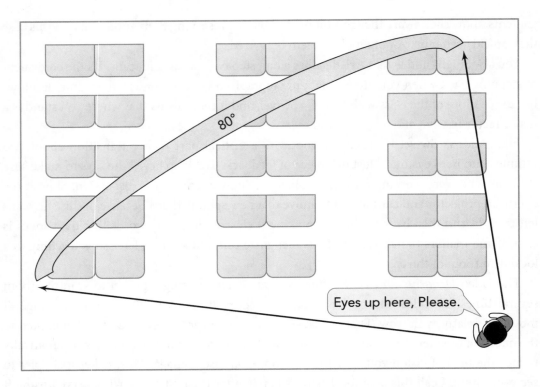

*Be Seen Looking* is the yin to *Radar*'s yang. One is seeing well, and the other is contriving ways to subtly remind students that you see them.

In *Marisa Ancona: Pens to Paper*, you can see Marisa doing this even before class has started. Notice how industriously her students get settled and ready for class. In large part this is because she puts such value on it. She is visibly watching, steadily and calmly with a bit of *Chin Up*, and making her way from one corner of the room to the other the whole time. What the teacher shows she values, students are more likely to value, and Marisa demonstrates how much she values student focus without saying a word.

Watching the various unspoken pantomimes teachers use to ensure that their students notice them looking, my colleagues on the TLAC team began to give humorous and lighthearted names for the most common among them. They include the *Swivel* and the *Chin Up* described earlier in addition to the *Sprinkler*, an adaptation of the *Swivel* wherein a teacher starts to Swivel then momentarily doubles back midstream in the direction she'd just scanned as if to say, momentarily, "Oh, I think I just saw something. No. Everything is OK." It makes the deliberateness of the scan more visible. We called it the *Sprinkler* because someone in the room noticed that it looked like the 1980s dance move of the same name, and the gag was on. We started to give dance names to all the *Be Seen Looking* moves. Here are a few more of our favorites:

**The Invisible Column:** A teacher moves his head slightly to the side after giving a direction as if he's trying to look around something (an invisible column). You can see Rodolfo Loureiro model his version of this timeless move in the video *Montage: Be Seen Looking*.

**The Tiptoes:** A teacher stands for a moment on her tiptoes while looking out at the room, as if she's just making doubly sure everything is OK in some hard-to-see spot in the room. Kirby Jarrell models an especially impressive version of this in the video *Montage: Be Seen Looking*.

**The Disco Finger:** A teacher traces the track of her gaze in a *Swivel* with her finger outstretched, pointer style, like one of the killer disco moves you haven't dusted off in a decade or two. It intimates, *Let me just check all of these places* and makes the Swivel obvious to those who are least likely to notice it. Tamesha McGuire takes this to the next level with her kindergartners in the video *Montage: Be Seen Looking*. Obviously, her goal here is to make her action especially visible to her little ones. Just a hint of disco finger, low, subtle, perhaps with your finger about at your midriff is probably the trick for your eighth graders.

**The Politician:** A teacher acts like an aspiring office holder who walks onstage before a big speech and points in recognition to all of her apparent friends and supporters in the audience—one over here, one over there. As a teacher, you send a similar upbeat message of "I see you all out there" when you gesture briefly to the folks in the audience who are similarly demonstrating that they are with you. The irrepressible Darren Hollingsworth models a useful version of this move in the video *Montage: Be Seen Looking* and you can see Patrick Pastore doing his version there as well—while standing in Pastore's Perch, no less.

**The QB:** A teacher moves like an NFL quarterback (QB) who, crouching behind the center, gazes quickly at the defense. Just because he's low doesn't mean he's not going to scan. Similarly, as champion teachers crouch to confer with a scholar, they flash their eyes briefly across the room, to make sure they see the field. Kathryn Orfuss isn't conferencing with a student in her clip in the video *Montage: Be Seen Looking*—she's at the overhead projector—but it gives you a good sense for how to look up and glance proactively when you're doing something else.

To summarize, not looking for follow-through after we give a direction can suggest that we don't notice or don't care whether students follow through on our directions, but doing the reverse—showing that we care that they do what we asked—is actually a very strong positive incentive for most students.

# TECHNIQUE 54: MAKE EXPECTATIONS VISIBLE

As a rule of thumb, the more visible the action you ask students to execute, the easier it is for you to see whether students follow through, and the more that students implicitly recognize that you can clearly see what they do. This makes them more likely to do what you've asked and makes it easier for you to hold them accountable. Some of the most effective teachers have a way of making "observable directions" fun and tactile, increasing both the incentive to follow through and their ability to manage.

A colleague of mine, David McBride, used this idea to help a teacher who was struggling at the time to keep students focused. Drawing on *Radar* and *Be Seen Looking*, David asked the teacher to script three points into his lesson when he would give a clear task and ensure that he got 100 percent of students doing it, even if at first this was only temporary. He wanted to start by showing the teacher that students would and could follow his directions; that a room where everyone was productively engaged was within his reach.

David asked him to:

- Give an observable direction.
- Use *Radar* to scan intentionally and strategically to see whether it's being done.
- Stand in Pastore's Perch while scanning.
- Narrate the follow-through of at least two students who've done right away what the teacher has asked.
- Warmly correct at least one student if students were not meeting expectations.

David called this a "reset" and it worked in some cases, but in others it was less helpful because the teacher didn't always see off-task behaviors. So David changed his guidance to emphasize making expectations visible.

"I want you to choose an especially visible direction. Something you know students will know you can see them do. Substitute '*Pencils down* and eyes on me' for 'Eyes on me,' for example, and then look for that as you scan."

The results were dramatic. Students putting their pencils down were ten times more visible to the teacher than was fleeting and hard-to-gauge eye contact. It was easier to see who was following through as asked. Not only that, but students sensed the increased clarity implicit in the new directions.

It was evident to them that it would be obvious to the teacher whether they followed through. There were a few challenging kids in the group but there was a far larger number of students who had begun to sense that not doing as the teacher asked was a bit of a game in this classroom—a challenge to see if they could not do as the teacher asked without him noticing. Soon, playing that game had become a norm. There were games the kids played at recess and to play them was to be in the club. A version of that had started to emerge in the classroom, too.

But suddenly, with the gray era eliminated, a larger number of students who had not been following through consistently began to change their behavior. The norm suddenly shifted. The challenging kids were still there but suddenly they were few and far between. There had been one or two bold rebels who induced those around them to follow them in testing the teacher but suddenly the rebels had no followers. It was a case study in the Heath Brothers' observation that the size of the problem does necessarily correlate with the size of the solution.

This story of a classroom reinvigorated, and a teacher saved—he was at the point of giving up—began with making a simple direction more visible and thereby eliminating ambiguity. Follow-through is easier to manage and monitor when directions ask students to do something visible. If you can see it, you can manage it.

Here are a few more examples of how you might make expectations more visible:

- Say "Pencils in the tray" instead of "Pencils down."
- Say "Books open in front of you" instead of "Books out."
- Say "Let me see those pencils moving" instead of "You should be writing."

I hope my story here won't make it seem as though making expectations visible is primarily a reactive strategy or a fix-it strategy for a struggling teacher. You may have noticed that Denarius Frazier, who appears throughout this book and who is surely one of the most exceptional teachers I have met, begins his class in the video *Denarius Frazier: Check in with Your Neighbor* with almost the exact direction David asked his struggling teacher to use: "Pencils down and track me in three . . . two . . . one."

## TECHNIQUE 55: LEAST INVASIVE INTERVENTION

The goal of behavioral interventions is to get 100 percent of students on task, attentive, and positively engaged in the best possible lesson. Ironically, constant, time-consuming interventions intended to ensure that everyone is with you can sometimes make it all but impossible to teach. When instruction comes to a halt, whether it is because of a disruption or because of the response to the disruption by the teacher, the result is that *no one* is on task because when the teacher is not teaching there usually is no task. And during the hiatus that can result from an interruption many students will find something else to pay attention to—their minds will wander; they will turn to look out the window, they will turn to a friend and raise an eyebrow. When instruction finally restarts, they are more distracted and less attentive, so the trick is to fix any problems or disruptions using the least invasive intervention and ensure that everyone can keep working.

Let's say I am teaching but Roberta has flopped her head down on her desk and, eyes closed, is either asleep or feigning sleep. I am keenly aware of the importance of fixing the situation. Not only will Roberta miss out on the lesson if I allow her to sleep—thus compounding whatever has caused her to be tired with a gap in her learning—but her action is a statement to other students that they, too, might put their heads down and sleep if they're tired or are just not "feeling it" that day. I should make sure after class that Roberta is all right if I have doubts—it's possible there are issues that require support, but let's also not rush to assume that; there's also a chance that Roberta is simply tired, as teenagers often are, and that this is a moment for loving accountability. If I allow Roberta to take a nap it won't be the last time this happens: I will soon have a classroom where, when it suits them, some number of my students will flop their heads down—some in silent judgment of school or society or adults or my teaching and some just because they can. Or because it's become the norm.

Let's say that, knowing all this, I stop my lesson on the Great Depression and speak to Roberta: "Roberta, what we're studying today is really important for you to know about. We're going to be writing essays about it, but you'll also talk about this era constantly in college; please pick your head up and stay with us." Even in the best-case scenario—Roberta raising her head and getting back to work right away—my interaction took several seconds, and, during that time, there was no further discussion of the Great Depression. It's not just that learning stopped; engagement stopped, and sharp minds are now looking for a substitute.

It could even be that now I'll have other fires to fight. "Jane, there are no cell phones allowed in this class," I say to my student who took one out during the hiatus. "Carlos, I need you paying attention." Each time I stop to correct one student, I risk losing another. I may never catch up.

It's going to be a struggle from here to get the momentum back. Attention residue, which I discuss in Chapter One, means that part of what students thought about while the task was interrupted will remain on their minds when the interruption is over. And if the stops are frequent, we'll never reach the kind of uninterrupted flow state that characterizes instruction at its best.

And of course there are all the questions about how Roberta will feel to have everyone looking at her. Yes, she needs to be awake and engaged in class. But having everyone staring at her hardly helps her concentrate. And it may make her resent me or even refuse to sit up.

So how would an expert teacher handle this? Would they intervene with Roberta? Almost assuredly. She may not feel that way at the moment but ten years from now she will wish she had not slept through classes. And if asked, her parents would be unlikely to say, "Please let my child sleep through classes."

The goal might be the same, then, but the *how* would be very different. The teacher would seek to make the correction as invisible as possible and, perhaps more important, they would make the correction *while still teaching*. They would put a premium on privacy. They might walk by while still teaching and put a gentle hand on Roberta's elbow but direct their gaze out toward the class (rather than down at Roberta) while they did this, to give Roberta as much privacy as possible to recover her attention. If Roberta was still slow to react, they might whisper to her in a tiny pause, "Make sure you're sitting up please, Roberta." If that didn't work, they might find a plausible moment to ask the class to engage in some other task such as a *Turn and Talk*—"Please take 30 seconds to review the definition of the Civilian Conservation Corps with your partner. Go!"—and then make a brief, low-key intervention: "Roberta, I can tell you're tired, but class is too important for me to allow you to sleep. Open to a clean sheet of paper. Your heading should say 'Great Depression.' I'll be back to check on you in thirty seconds."

They would be calm and steady. But most of all, they would be as fast as possible in order to keep the thread of instruction alive for the other twenty-nine students in the classroom. And therein lies the secret: if you can manage to correct noninvasively, you are likely to be able to set and reinforce expectations successfully and consistently.

## Six Interventions

In watching great classroom managers, my team and I have made a list of six useful interventions, ranked in order of invasiveness from least to most. The goal, generally speaking, is to be as near to the top of this list as possible as often as possible.

### Intervention 1: Nonverbal Intervention

First on the list is a *nonverbal intervention*. I observed this during a recent lesson taught by Ashley Hinton. As Ashley taught her students to write descriptive paragraphs, she constantly made micro corrections with either a hand gesture or intentional modeling of the action she expected students to take. As she did this, she never broke the thread of her engaging teaching; distracted students were corrected in privacy and at no cost to the lesson.

You can watch Ashley do this in the video *Ashley Hinton: Nonverbal Montage*. Notice how Ashley addresses minor issues with subtle and well-timed nonverbal interventions while they're still small and can be fixed with a tiny adjustment—small problem equals small solution and, in this case, no disruption. This also makes it easy for Ashley to stay positive in her tone as she makes her corrections. In addition, Ashley *Circulates* (technique 25) constantly while she makes her corrections. Always on the move, she's able to approach a student to give a bit more clarity to her corrections without other students noticing. Her gestures are consistent—she focuses on just two or three expectations that she wants to see—and, of course, she keeps teaching.

It's important to remember that a nonverbal intervention is not inherently noninvasive, even if it looks that way when Ashley does it. To be noninvasive, you have to keep teaching and keep moving, embedding corrections in the larger flow of class. I was recently watching a teacher struggling to use nonverbals to address behavior in her classroom. The reason? She failed to continue teaching while making nonverbal corrections. She broke off her discussion and walked two rows to her left as the class watched her intently. She stopped and made a dramatic gesture to a student to sit up and stared at him waiting for him to follow her directions. At this point, with no instruction going on, everyone was staring at her and the student in question. Despite the nonverbal nature of the interaction, her intervention failed the "noninvasive" test.

Last, nonverbals work best when they are consistent and limited in scope. To begin using nonverbals, I might choose the one or two most common low-level distractions in my classrooms and develop a consistent nonverbal for each. If there are only a few signals, you can use them, and your students can process them without distracting any of you from the content of the lesson. For her part, Ashley Hinton chose to use gestures to remind her students to track the speaker with their eyes (see technique 48, *Habits of Attention*) to put their hands down when a classmate was talking, and to sit attentively.

### Intervention 2: Positive Group Correction

Slightly more invasive but still with a very small footprint is *positive group correction*—a quick, verbal reminder offered to the entire group, advising them to take a specific action. Like a nonverbal intervention, a positive group correction is ideal for catching off-task behavior early. The word "positive" comes from the concept that this intervention always describes the solution (a positive) rather than the problem (a negative). "Group" refers to the fact that it's directed to the entire class as opposed to specific students. Because the goal is to be noninvasive, this form of correction tends to be very short and preserves economy of language. "Check that you're sitting up straight" (or "Check your SLANT," if you use the acronym) is a classic. About a second, and you're back to teaching. If you need to boost the level of accountability with specific students, you might do that nonverbally at the same time; that is, you might say, "I need to see everyone writing," while you briefly focus on an individual student who needs a bit more support with some eye contact and perhaps a slight nod of your head. The idea is that, in speaking to the group, it also corrects those students whom you might not see.

Of course, while you can establish nonverbal accountability for individuals, you keep non-compliers off the public stage. Saying a student's name usually causes people to look at him, and this can cause resentment or sometimes reward (i.e. being looked at is what the student wants). If you make the effort to show that you are trying to solve something without "calling a student out" and while preserving their privacy, the result is usually positive.

### Intervention 3: Anonymous Individual Correction

The next intervention, an *anonymous individual correction*, is similar to a *positive group correction* in that it describes the solution; however, it makes it explicit that there are people (as yet anonymous) who have not yet met expectations. You might combine it with a positive group correction to make it sound like this: "Eyes up here, please [*positive group correction*]. I need two more sets of eyes [*anonymous individual correction*]."

As with the positive group correction, you can supplement an anonymous individual correction with nonverbals, especially eye contact and a quick nod, to establish directly and privately whom you are expecting to fix the situation fast. The combination of verbal group accountability and nonverbal individual accountability can be especially effective.

Laura Baxter does a nice job of this in *Laura Baxter: Orange Row*. Twice she pauses briefly to remind students that their focus needs improving or they need to face forward, but she's always calm and keeps the individuals she's referring to anonymous, although in one case you can see there's some subtle eye contact—subtle enough that you don't see classmates turning around to see who is causing the problem. Her economy of language is also great.

### Intervention 4: Private Individual Correction (PIC)

The next level of intervention is a *private individual correction*. When you have to name names, you can still make use of privacy. And when you need to take more time with a student, you can make it less invasive by asking the class to work independently, or by making your intervention at a time when it's easy to be offstage.

That was one of the strategies I suggested a master teacher might try, especially if Roberta had not responded to earlier less invasive efforts to get her on task—"Please take thirty seconds to review the definition of the Civilian Conservation Corps with your partner. Go!"[11]— And then make a brief intervention that was as private as possible. "Roberta, I can tell you're tired, but class is too important for me to allow you to sleep. Open up your notebook to a clean sheet of paper. Your heading should say 'Great Depression.' I'll be back to check on you in thirty seconds."

Here, with your voice dropped to show you are not trying to make something public out of it, the intervention is likely to be more effective, especially if you are careful to describe the solution, not the problem (see technique 52, *What to Do*) and to emphasize purpose ("This is important for you to learn") over power (which is why something like "When I ask someone to sit up, I expect to see them do it" is generally ineffective).

You can see Josh Goodrich, then of Oasis South Bank in London, make a private individual correction in the video *Josh Goodrich: Let's Get to It*. Most of his students are working industriously but one student has just not been able to get himself going. Josh spots him and walks over, dropping his voice to a whisper. "I need to see you writing within ten seconds. Let's get to it, mate." His tone is calm and steady. His directions are clear. He whispers to preserve privacy and he's quick. You could be sitting two seats away and miss the whole thing.

### Balance with Private Individual Precise Praise (PIPP)

We call a *private individual correction* a PIC for short, and its partner is the PIPP, or *private individual precise praise*. When you use PIPP, you walk over to a student, just as you would when you make a PIC, but whisper positive feedback instead of criticism. If students come to expect that a private intervention could be either positive or corrective, they will be more open to you as you approach them. You also earn trust for your criticism by balancing it with praise. Most of all, you build a defense against the sort of eavesdropping that students do when they are curious about or take delight in the misfortune of others. In other words, if the content is unpredictable—sometimes positive, sometimes corrective or constructive— the urgent need to listen for the juicy bits of discipline disappears. Frankly, the idea that you might approach Roberta and say, "I thought that answer was outstanding. Keep up the good work" is not terribly intriguing to eavesdroppers. Such positive comments can help to protect the privacy of the student when you need to tell Roberta to sit up.

### Intervention 5: Lightning-Quick Public Correction

It would be great if you could make every correction quick and private, but we all know that in a complex place like a classroom it just doesn't work like that. You will be forced, at times, to make corrections or give reminders to individual students during public moments. In those cases, your goals should be to limit the amount of time a student is "onstage" for something negative, to focus on telling the student what to do right rather what he or she did wrong, and then to call everyone's attention to something else, ideally something more positive, and doubly so if it helps build reinforce positive norms. This is called a *lightning-quick public correction,* and it might sound something like, "Quentin, I need your pencil moving . . . just like those sharp-looking scholars in my back row!" or "Quentin, I need your pencil moving" and then "Josefina, I can't wait to hear what you're writing about."

Perhaps the most effective single action for "hiding" a public correction or reminder is whispering it. Even if you're in public. Even if everyone can still hear you. You can see this done effectively in the video *Jason Armstrong: Don't Miss It.* Jason, in fact, makes two corrections of students who are off task, and both are essentially public and audible. He's standing in front of the class when he makes them, but they *feel* like private individual corrections because he whispers them. By dropping his voice he is reminding the students he is correcting that he is doing everything he can to keep it as private as he can, that he's sensitive to and respectful of their feelings and does not want to embarrass them. A whisper, even if everyone else can hear it, says, "I am trying to do this without calling too much attention to you." It creates trust and the illusion of privacy. For this reason a *whisper correction* is one of the most powerful tools a teacher can use.

### Intervention 6: Consequence

The last form of intervention is a consequence. Giving consequences is technical and challenging—enough so that it is the subject of its own technique later in this chapter; however, it's worth noting that many of the elements of noninvasiveness I have discussed (whispering, making the conversation private, etc.) can also be applied to a consequence.

## Common Misperceptions

One common misperception about the levels of intervention is that they represent a process or a formula—that you should always progress methodically through each level, trying all six types of correction in sequence before giving a consequence. Although the goal is to be as close to the top of the list as possible, great classroom managers maintain fidelity to what works. Sometimes they go straight to a consequence, sometimes back and forth among the levels; and occasionally they use several interventions with an off-task student. In fact, using levels 1 to 5 implies that students are making (or appear likely to be making) a good-faith effort to comply with expectations when reminded. Behavior that is deliberate and is disruptive most often is behavior that should earn a consequence.

Another common misperception is that ignoring misbehavior—or addressing it by praising students who are behaving—is the least invasive form of intervention. In fact, ignoring misbehavior is the *most* invasive form of intervention, because the behavior becomes more likely to persist and expand. The goal is to address behavior quickly, while its manifestation is still minimal and the required response still small.

## TECHNIQUE 56: FIRM, CALM FINESSE

Great classroom managers are steady at the helm. They may show passion when discussing history or science, but when they ask a student to get to work or not to call out answers, they are calm and composed. They act as if they couldn't imagine a universe in which students wouldn't follow through, and this, in turn, causes students to follow through. These teachers do their work with finesse, and generally take steps to engage students without conflict. Here are six general rules for teaching with *Firm, Calm Finesse*.

### Rule 1: Catch It Early

Sometimes we want to believe that a problem, left alone, will cure itself. Most often, it persists or gets worse because we've sent the message that we'll tolerate it for a while. Eventually, we have to step in with a bigger fix, in part because the behavior has gotten more bold or disruptive, and in part because we are starting to get frustrated. Here's a phrase my team uses that teachers have often found helpful for self-reflection: If you're mad, you've waited too long. It's usually better to fix something with a tiny adjustment very early than to make a bigger intervention later. You're far more likely to correct positively and with a smile when your corrections feel like tiny adjustments to you as well as to your students.

### Rule 2: Value Purpose over Power

The reason you correct behaviors in the classroom is that doing so leads to a vibrant, positive learning environment, student achievement, and even habits of self-discipline. Strive to make your language constantly stress that the goal is helping students learn and succeed, not reinforcing your own power. Statements like "When I ask you to sit up, I want to see you sitting up" are best avoided. "Please get this down so you're prepared for the test" or "You'll need to be on time to class so we have a full 60 minutes together" are much better. Keep corrections tight and crisp, but try to remind students (and yourself) that your high expectations are, in the end, about the students, not you.

### Rule 3: Remember That "Thank You" Is the Strongest Phrase

Saying "Thank you" after a student follows a direction is one of the most subtly powerful things you can do, for two reasons. First, it is a sign that a strong community characterized by civility and mutual appreciation is in existence when "please" and "thank you" are frequently used. So it's good to model "please" and "thank you" in your classroom, especially at moments when students might question whether they still apply; for example, are they still full members of the community when they receive a redirection? Of course, but when you say, "Hands folded in front of you, please, Maya," it subtly reminds her of that. Then, when Maya folds her hands, you can say, in a low and slightly muted tone: "Thank you."

Saying "thank you" also reinforces expectations and normalizes follow-through. You would only say "thank you" because Maya had followed your direction. It shows your appreciation to her and it subtly reminds everyone else in the class that the norm is to do what the teacher has asked you.

## Rule 4: Use Universal Language

Look for chances to remind students that expectations are universal and not personal. Although "I need you with me" is fine, "We need you with us" is better. It suggests that learning is a team sport, and subtly says that the rest of the class is also meeting the expectations you are asking an individual to adhere to. "Let's make sure we're all tracking the speaker," as an alternate to "Please make sure you're tracking the speaker," reminds everyone that the expectation is universal.

## Rule 5: Bright Face

Your bright face is your teaching smile—or at least your age-appropriate, default expression of "I like this work, I like the people here, and I'm pretty confident that I'm in charge." You can see Patrick Pastore's bright face when he looks up to scan his class most days. He starts with a smile, not a scowl. His bright, pleasant face is confident. His plan, it says, is to trust but verify. This is very different from a teacher whose scowl says *I'm not happy here, I'm worried about students following my directions*, or even *I'm waiting for them not to do what I ask, because I'm sure it's going to happen.* That can be a self-fulfilling prophecy.

To underscore, your bright face does not have to be a huge, beaming smile especially if it's not sincere. It's just a pleasant expression that exudes a degree of positivity and confidence that matches your style and the age group of your students. With kindergartners, it might really be an irrepressible smile. With high schoolers, it might be a bit more subdued.

It's important to use such a face whenever possible but it's especially good to show it immediately after or even during a redirection or correction—first, to remind students generally that all is well, and second, to remind particularly the student who you may have had to redirect that they are still in your good stead.

## Rule 6: Use Your Confirmation Glance

Trust, and demonstrating trust, are among the most important things you can communicate in building a relationship with others. Showing trust is self-fulfilling—if you signal that you trust, students will follow through when you make a request.

There are times when it's critical to ask and then look or walk away and show that you trust students to follow through. A confirmation glance is the ideal tool to use to verify follow-through. To use it, you walk away and then glance strategically back. Sometimes a student needs just a bit of space to pull it together and decide he or she wants to do the right thing, and a confirmation glance can provide it. It's best to begin by being brief with the delay before a confirmation glance, and then extend it a bit longer over your time with the class. Sometimes teachers use it explicitly with students, as in, "I'm going to walk away, and when I look back, I am going to see you with your pencil in your hand, writing your response." Of course, you will need to follow up decisively if your confirmation glance reveals lack of follow-through, but using it can intimate a potent, calm, self-assuredness to your class.

## TECHNIQUE 57: ART OF THE CONSEQUENCE

Unfortunately, despite your best efforts to redirect nonproductive behavior with subtlety and grace, to prevent small things from becoming bigger things and to encourage students to choose to do the most positive things, you will have to give consequences in your classroom. This is all but inevitable and it is not a statement about what you believe or don't believe about students. You should love your students and want the best for them. You will still occasionally be in a situation that calls for consequences. In many cases you will give consequences *because* you care about your students. The key is to give consequences judiciously, justly, and humanely with the purpose of changing nonproductive behaviors into positive behaviors rather than punishing.

And in the end if your consequences are appropriate—that is, in most cases they let students learn lessons at small cost—given with humanity and supported by teaching, they are a useful thing. "Treating students as having responsibility over their actions is vital if we are to teach them how to accept responsibility for themselves, to manage their own lives, to grow in maturity," writes Tom Bennett. "Students must learn to self-regulate, to restrain their own immediate desires and whims, to persevere even when they don't want to before they can learn . . . independent behavior."

Bennett's observations lead us to recognize something we often lose sight of: a just, fair, and manageable consequence is an act of caring to a student who must learn to respect and set limits and self-regulate. Of course we don't wish to make them unhappy now; but a small unhappiness now is preferable to larger disappointments later—and of course to allowing the rights and dignity of others to be trammeled. To a student who is too impulsive, life may bring an array of potential challenges we would never wish them to have to struggle with. If consequences in school can help them to replace their impulsiveness with more disciplined responses, we have done students a favor. Try to express to students if and when you must give consequences that they are an act of caring.

But all this talk of consequences as an act of caring only goes so far when they backfire. And consequences are notoriously tricky. As I'm sure nearly every teacher can attest, they do not always have the intended effect. Who hasn't given a consequence that, instead of reducing a negative behavior, actually made it worse? As my team and I set out to learn from great teachers, we observed classrooms where consequences had the intended effect, not just some of the time but nearly all of the time, and these observations inform what I have dubbed *Art of the Consequence*.

## Principles of the Effective Consequence

Consequences, used properly, are not merely punishments with a sanitized name. Their purpose is to efficiently reinforce sound decision making—to respond to situations in which mistakes are made so that students learn from them. Their goal should be to develop and teach, and this goal can and should be evident in how you employ consequences. The following sections describe a few principles of effective consequences.

### Incremental

It isn't the size of a consequence that changes student behavior but the consistency of it. Designing consequences so that they can be allocated in smaller increments lets students learn from mistakes at manageable cost. "Small mistake, small consequence" works really well for students, and it's better for you as well. If your consequences are heartbreaking for the students you love, you will hesitate and probably not use them. Plan out a system of consequences that starts small and scales up gradually in severity. The first response should be a disincentive, not a life-altering event.

We've all seen an elementary school student become bereft over a color change. This is one reason why in many classrooms I have seen a color change chart that shows everyone on green while the teacher is near tears with frustration. The system isn't incremental, so it doesn't get used. One simple change is to subdivide a color change (green to yellow or yellow to red) into a series of three checks. If a student is calling out and you've asked him to stop but the action persists, he is telling you he needs a clearer reminder, but a check is far more useful than an color change. "That's a check for you, Donald," you might whisper, "Please work harder not to call out when it's someone else's turn."

Another benefit of small, scaled consequences is that they enable you to respond consistently, but still offer students a clear and feasible path to success. A student who loses all of his or her privileges has no incentive to stay in the game.

### Quick

An immediate consequence is more closely associated with the action that caused it than a delayed consequence. If the goal is to shape behavior rather than to punish it, try to give a consequence right away. A smaller consequence in the moment (for example, "Scholars, go back to the door and come into this classroom quietly please") will often be more effective than a larger consequence that occurs later ("Gentlemen, I will see you here after school"). Quick consequences also reduce the amount of time a student's behavior remains onstage. This latter benefit removes students' incentive to engage in attention-seeking behavior and minimizes the odds of escalating behavior.

### Consistent

Responses should be predictable in students' minds: "If I do X, Y will happen." If they aren't sure what will happen, then they have an incentive to "test" and see. Thus consistency and incrementalism go together. We are trying to teach, not punish, so the message should not be *It's OK sometimes, but not other times.*

Consistently using the same language reduces the transaction costs involved with giving consequences, and also makes them more legible to students (for example, "Michael, please don't call out, two scholar dollars" or "Michael, calling out, two scholar dollars"[12]). Students won't have to worry about trying to decipher your consequences and you won't have to spend time and explaining. And of course you'll want to explain what calling out is and why it's a problem in advance. What is expected of students should be defined for them.

If you and your students shift activities or move to different areas of the room, your management system should follow. Whether you're teaching from desks or the carpet, stick with the system and approach that students know and understand. Otherwise, students will quickly learn when and where they can test the limits.

### As Private as Possible

In technique 55, *Least Invasive Intervention*, I discuss the benefits of privacy. When you seek to employ it, you remind a student that you are not trying to embarrass them, and you avoid situations where responses are public and a relationship-corrosive back and forth may ensue. These things are doubly important when giving consequences. We want students to know we give consequences when we must, and we should be prepared for them not to be happy about it. In both cases privacy helps. Using a whisper correction, a nonverbal gesture, or a private individual correction can help.

### Depersonalized

Avoid personalizing consequences by keeping them as private as possible (with a whisper, during a one-on-one interaction, for example) and by judging actions instead of people (for example, "That was inconsiderate of your classmates, Daniel," versus "You are very inconsiderate, Daniel."). Maintaining privacy shows consideration to the student, which can go a long way toward preserving your relationship with him or her. It also keeps behavior offstage, which reduces the likelihood of attention-seeking behavior or a public standoff that benefits no one.

Finally, strive to remember that strong teacher emotions distract students from reflecting on the behavior(s) that resulted in a consequence. Maintain a neutral facial expression and steady tone of voice when you deliver the consequence, and then continue teaching with warmth and enthusiasm.

## Notes on Delivery

In addition to exuding *Emotional Constancy,* protecting privacy, and making sure consequences are focused on purpose, not power, teachers who give consequences that reliably change behavior for the better follow the principles described in the next sections.

### Use a Bounce-Back Statement

It's probably safe to say that every teacher has encountered a student who shuts down once he or she receives a consequence. In that instant, some students feel as though the whole world is against them, including you, so they convince themselves that they should cut their losses and stop trying. Your goal is to suggest otherwise and nudge them forward into a productive direction. One way is by delivering a "bounce-back" statement that shows students that success is still within their grasp. For example, you might say something like "Michael, please don't call out. That's two scholar dollars. I know you can do this" or "That's two scholar dollars. I can't wait to see your hand up so I can call on you." When you use bounce-back statements, you socialize students to persist in the face of emotional duress, which is a life skill that will benefit them long after they leave your classroom.

### Maintain the Pace

Responding to behavior by lecturing or giving a speech disengages the rest of the class and increases the likelihood of other fires sprouting up. Here are a couple of tips for maintaining the pace when emotions run high and you have to give a consequence:

Describe what students *should be doing* as opposed to what they *are not doing* ("Michael, I need your eyes" is better than "Michael, for the last time, stop getting distracted!").

Use the least amount of verbiage you can ("That's two bucks. I need you tracking," rather than "You just earned a two-scholar-dollar deduction because you chose to draw cartoons when you were supposed to be listening to my lecture. You should know better . . . ," and so forth). Doing so maximizes instructional time and minimizes the amount of time students are left onstage.

### Get Back on Track

When it comes to consequences, the goal is to get in, get out, and *move on* with the business of teaching. Teachers who are able to get *all* students back on track after a consequence remember to show that it's over.

What you focus on after you give a consequence speaks volumes to students about what you value. If you want students to carry on with learning, resume instruction with warmth and energy. Find an opportunity to talk to students in a calm, relaxed manner to show that the interaction is over. You can even go a step further by getting the student who received a consequence positively back into the flow of class by asking a question or acknowledging his or her work. Doing so models forgiveness and shows students that you still value them and want them to be successful.

## The Million-Dollar Question: Consequence or Correction?

One of the trickiest aspects of managing a classroom is deciding when to give a consequence rather than a correction. The question is tough, in part because teachers must decide on a case-by-case basis. That being said, here are some helpful rules of thumb:

**Persistence and repetition.** When students *persistently* engage in off-task behavior that they know they shouldn't, this should push you more toward a consequence. This is especially true when students continue in spite of your correction(s). If, instead, the behavior appears to be a one time error caused by distraction or misunderstanding, then err on the side of correction.

**Degree of disruption.** If a student's behavior doesn't disrupt others' learning, then it's more likely that a correction is warranted. In contrast, if the student's behavior distracts or disrupts others, a consequence is more likely to be warranted. You have a responsibility to maintain the group environment.

**Motivation.** If a student is clearly testing your expectations, give a consequence. Tolerating willful defiance corrodes your authority in the eyes of the student as well as the rest of the class. Just be sure that's the case before you rush to judge.

## What Comes After

Many of the actions we take when we give a consequence are shaped by the necessary fact that we are teaching or are in charge of a group of people while we give them in most cases. That said there is an immense opportunity and often a responsibility for a follow-up conversation designed to explain and even better to teach. Here are some notes.

### Explained, With Love

The first thing is to remind students that you have to give them consequences because you care about them. You want them to understand something that they are struggling to learn or hear something that they are struggling to hear because you care about them and want the best for them. Distinguish between the behavior and the person. "I believe in you and think you're a great kid; but of course I can't allow you to push someone else in the classroom, just like it wouldn't be OK with me if someone else pushed you." Do this with calmness and *Emotional Constancy*. If you're upset don't attempt an explanation until you're confident you can sustain *Emotional Constancy*.

### Teaching a Replacement Behavior

It's not enough in the long run to tell someone *not* to do something. Our job as educators is to teach people *what to do*, instead. What a student can do, instead, at the moment when they are inclined to do something counterproductive, is known as a **replacement behavior**. *Instead of reacting quickly in anger at a classmate, here are three questions to ask myself. Instead of calling out I can jot down what I wanted to say or send magic to a classmate, so they suspect I know the answer, too.*

It won't be enough for a student to know a replacement behavior, of course. If they're likely to be able to use it, they'll need to practice it a bit. As in: *I'm going to ask you some questions that you know the answer to, and you're going to practice writing down a word or two, to remind you of what you want to say rather than calling out, OK?* and that can be a great way to make "talking it over" a productive and active task.

Background knowledge is profoundly important to learning. That starts with vocabulary. To name something is to conjure it into being. *When you keep from doing something you have an urge to do, it's called self-regulation.* That makes it easier to talk about.

But background knowledge can go further. You could give an impulsive student a short article about the role of the amygdala in mindfulness—summarizing the idea that if you can delay your response by even a second you can better regulate it. If students understand the science behind what is happening to them, they can often be more successful in making changes.

A good, brief article on the role of the amygdala can be hard to find the moment you need it, obviously, so it might be worth keeping a few articles about predictable challenges at the ready. That's the idea behind the Dean of Students' Curriculum[13] my team developed under Hilary Lewis's leadership. It's a set of dozens of reflective knowledge-based lessons to help students reflect on common nonproductive behaviors.

## Self-Checking

Giving consequences to students is hard. It rarely makes them happy. It rarely make teachers happy. There's the risk that despite your best efforts to always be fair and accurate and judicious you will be wrong in giving a consequence, in the single case or perhaps you will have misunderstood a particular student even more broadly. There will be a student in whom you somehow see the wrong more than she deserves or one whom you never quite notice when she gives her best. And yet it's necessary to set limits for students. Tom Bennett's guidance that "Treating students as having responsibility over their actions is vital if we are to teach them to accept responsibility for themselves, to manage their own lives and grow in maturity" is helpful to keep in mind. So are these four sets of questions to ask yourself, to help you make sure you're on the right path.

- **About Design:** Is your consequence system scaled and gradual? Are there small consequences students can use to learn lessons at low cost? Are the consequences incremental and scaled? Do they always specify the behavior that caused them so students know and can learn from what they did wrong? Is the system aligned across the school? Are there positive consequences as well, so students' positive behavior is also reinforced? Is positive reinforcement intermittent, occasional, and framed in appreciation of extra effort (rather than an expectation)?

- **About the Decision:** Am I more inclined to give consequences for persistent and repetitive behaviors and less inclined to give corrections for single low-level incidents? Am I more inclined to give consequences for behaviors that disrupt the learning opportunities for other students or endanger their safety? Am I more inclined to give corrections for behavior that only affects the student involved? Do I take motivation into account when I can? Do we as a school or a grade-team make these decisions similarly and consistently?

- **About Delivery:** Am I as private as I can be? Do I attempt to drop my voice or whisper if in public? Am I emotionally constant in asking the student to focus on his or her own actions? Do I tag the behavior, so my students know what I think they've done wrong? Am I quick and do I get back to teaching promptly, ideally including the student in question in the lesson?

- **Discipline:** Have I explained and taught my expectations? Have I explained and maybe even practiced with my students what to do when a consequence is given, generally and specifically, and what to do when and if a consequence is given and the student(s) do not agree? Is there a process for students who get consequences they don't agree with to follow?

## TECHNIQUE 58: STRONG VOICE

The communication we are consciously aware of amounts to only a portion—sometimes a small one—of the communication we actually do.[14] We may *think* our listeners are attending to the content of our words but that's only partly true. When people listen, they react to an array of signals (tone, expression, and body language) that begin influencing them right away. "Affective reactions are so tightly integrated with perception that we find ourselves liking or disliking something the instant we notice it, sometimes even before we know what it is," writes the social psychologist Jonathan Haidt.[15] In his book *The Righteous Mind* he describes the process of belief and opinion formation in cognitive terms and finds that humans typically have instant reactions based on factors they perceive subconsciously, and then later create explanations and justifications for those responses. Those justifications and responses are often "based on socially strategic purposes." We react in a fraction of a second and afterwards try to convince ourselves that our responses were justified and look to use our responses to build the social bonds that are so important to us.

*Ha! That was funny. I laughed too!*

*Ha! What a fool he is. You and I, we are smarter than that.*

The chain of reactions that begins with how people read our tone, expression, and body language is long and complex. *Strong Voice* helps you attend to signals communicated by such factors in your communication as a teacher and use them to increase the likelihood that students will react productively and positively to the things you ask of them. This is especially important because attending to such signals can be especially valuable in avoiding or resolving situations where emotions run hot and where the follow-through required from students is far better achieved without raised voices or recrimination.

Aligning your tone, expression, and body language signals to the rest of your communication helps you to build stronger relationships, ensure productivity and, especially, avoid the sorts of showdowns that can spiral into negativity. A shouting match is a disaster for teacher and student, in the moment it happens and over the long run of a relationship that often struggles to recover. Needless to say there is a lot more to building relationships than the topics discussed here. They are merely one contributing aspect—a critical one for a person charged with responsibility for ensuring that thirty students get from point A to point B in a timely manner so learning can happen and regardless of whatever is on their personal agendas at the moment.

While *Strong Voice* is a critical technique for teachers to master, it is also one that is easily misunderstood, so I begin with some important notes on the purpose and even the name of the technique, which, to be honest, I almost changed for this version of the book, in part because "strong voice" has always been a bit of a misnomer. It is a technique as much about body language as about voice, for example. More importantly, the strength implied is in most cases about steadiness and self-control, about maintaining poise and composure, especially under duress.

Social science research tells us that emotions broadcast to others are contagious. When we're conversing, we're not merely exchanging ideas, we're often shaping the listener's mindset and emotions. Researchers have found that emotions can spread between individuals even when their contact with each other is *entirely nonverbal*. In one study, three strangers were observed facing one another in silence. Researchers found that an emotionally expressive person transmitted his or her mood to the other two without uttering a word.[16] What we do with our voice, words, and body language can cause others to shift into modes of communication more like our own and this phenomenon has a name, "mirroring," which refers to the way in which we unconsciously synchronize our emotional state to match that of another person's during an interaction. One implication for teachers is that if we can keep our composure, or even noticeably recompose ourselves as things get tense, others are likely to follow. And of course if we lose our composure others are more likely to as well.

Young people's emotions are real and often intense; our job as teachers is not to tell them not to feel them. However, part of our job *is* to help them manage emotions, keep control, and match their response to the setting. I am sure there are people who will see this as "controlling," but I think most teachers are clear on the benefits to young people when we help them learn to self-regulate as they enter society.

To return briefly to the word "strong," however, at trainings my team and I run, our coaching often involves helping teachers not to come on so "strong" with their *Strong Voice*—to be calmer and quieter, to appear self-assured, not loud. One potential reason people might try to be more forceful in tone and body language than necessary is the name itself: something called *Strong Voice* must be about being overpowering, right?

Wrong. A composed teacher makes it more likely that students will maintain their composure, will focus on the message, and not be distracted by how it was delivered. Being more aware of your body language and tone of voice and keeping them purposeful, poised, and confident helps you *and* your students.

So while I toyed with the idea of renaming *Strong Voice*, I have kept it for continuity's sake—and chosen instead to add framing to help make sure the purpose is clear.

## The Six Principles of Strong Voice

Over the years, my team and I have had the privilege of watching hundreds of teachers who lead vibrant, rigorous, and joyful classrooms that are also productive and orderly. These two things are related. When students follow directions, teachers can make engaging and rigorous activities happen with a minimum of fuss. And teachers who provide quality lessons are more likely to get students to do as they ask. Neither of these causes the other, but attending to both helps.

The more we studied such teachers, the more we noticed patterns in what they did to ensure follow-through when they asked students to do things.

We have distilled these observations into six replicable principles that teachers can name a practice.

### Principle 1: Shift Your Register

Watch the body language of Arielle Hoo and Denarius Frazier in the short video *Hoo and Frazier: Register Shift*. In the moment when each asks for students' attention, their body language shifts slightly. Arielle steps back from the projector, holds herself upright and symmetrical, and scans the room. She does this for perhaps a second. Beforehand, she's more fluid in her motions and posture and by the time she has said, "Great, let's take a look at Tyler's work," she has shifted back to this more informal body language once again, but in that short moment of formality she signals to her class the importance of what they are about to do and they respond. She's asked for their eye contact with her words but, also, with the signals of body language and tone.

So, too, does Denarius. Preparing students to analyze an example of student work, he steps forward slightly, so students can see him better. He stands upright, chin slightly raised, and symmetrical. His cadence slows slightly. Again there's an air of formality. And then, like Arielle, the formality dissolves into a more casual tone, "On a few of our papers . . ." he says, his voice now sounding more relaxed. But that short shift has signaled to students that what we are doing is important, worthy of increased attention, and they have intuitively responded.

Neither teacher is tense, mind you, just slightly formal and this moment of heightened formality is like a punctuation mark: short but legible and shaping the meaning of what gets said before and after.

This is what I call a **register shift** and to understand it further it will be helpful to first define the term *register*, which I use to refer to the overall tone communicated by a teacher's affect—her voice, her body language, her facial expressions, and so on. In our study of classrooms, we typically observe teachers shifting between three registers: casual, formal, and urgent.

The table titled "Three Registers" further differentiates typical features.

## Three Registers

| Register | Voice/Words | Body Language |
|----------|-------------|---------------|
| Casual | • Words may run together (e.g. with a pitter-patter rhythm) <br> • Frequent vocal inflections and a wide range of pitch <br> • Use of colloquial language | • Asymmetrical distribution of weight on each foot (e.g. leaning more on one foot) <br> • Relaxed posture <br> • Inconsistent eye contact |
| Formal | • Clearly articulated words and syllables <br> • Carefully chosen words that describe the solution or next step forward <br> • Intentionally slows or pauses speech for emphasis <br> • Drops intonation at the end of sentences to signal certainty and finality | • Symmetrical distribution of weight on feet, which are placed shoulder-width apart <br> • Upright posture <br> • Steady eye contact <br> • Hands relaxed at one's sides or clasped in front or behind back |
| Urgent | • Loud volume, intensity of tone and emotion <br> • Words run together <br> • Exaggerated emphasis on a specific word or words | • Widened eyes <br> • Leaning in versus standing straight up <br> • Rushed and abrupt gestures |

When teachers want students to hear and follow through on their requests, they often shift into a version of the *formal register*, using their body language and tone to emphasize the importance of what they're saying. This might mean doing some of the things Arielle and Denarius were doing: standing symmetrically, and with an upright posture, slowing the cadence of speech, minimizing inflection, and articulating each word with intentional clarity. Or modulating movements slightly. When Arielle and Denarius move during a register shift, they do so with poise and purpose. They reduce the amount and scope of hand gestures. They are often deliberately still. These things send a clear message that what they're saying is important and deserves attention and follow-through.

This formal register contrasts with the *casual register*, which signals relaxed openness and but also optionality—to be casual is to say *Take it or leave it* or *We're just chatting here*. When teachers assume a casual register, we often observe them standing with a relaxed posture. If they're *very* casual, they might be leaning against a wall or piece of classroom furniture. They often allow their words to run together, the words coming fast like raindrops, each hard to differentiate from the previous with absolute clarity, and their range of infection varies widely.

Teachers often use some version of a more casual register when delivering content. For example, to become animated in an art class when you talk about shading and cross-hatching is to express enthusiasm and energy for these methods, and students commonly respond to enthusiasm and energy. To state the obvious, a range of casual registers exists. Each person's register is different, qualitatively but also quantitatively: versions of casual speech can communicate everything from "Oh, man, I looove this passage," to "Let us relax a bit and take pleasure in reading the novel aloud for a moment." Some teachers rarely use the casual register at all and maintain, quite successfully, an air of seriousness and formality throughout. Each teacher has his or her own style of teaching, and this is as it should be. Variety is beneficial; the core work of teaching can be done in a wide range of casual and formal registers. You be you.

But every teacher also needs to be able to shift, for example, into the formal from the casual or into a higher degree of formality from their everyday self in moments when, like Arielle and Denarius, they want to signal that paying attention and following through are now especially important. There are two parts to that observation: the work is done by *both* the tone *and* the shift. The discernable change in affect draws students' attention; the formal affect expresses importance once you have their attention.

You can see an especially clear and effective example of this in the video *Trona Cenac: Register Shifts*. As the video opens, Trona is chatting casually with students before the beginning of class on the first day of school at Troy Prep High School. Her body language is casual: loose and asymmetrical. You can tell from the student's use of language ("I did that packet and I was like . . .") that she reads the casualness of the situation. Suddenly it's time to start class. Trona signals this in part through her voice and more upright body language. Her shoulders are back and her chin is raised. Students are quickly attentive, though, and everything is going well so she moves to the front of the group and greets students in the casual register. She's asymmetrical with a relaxed smile. Soon after there are important directions to hear.

Trona emphasizes this by assuming a more formal bearing. Here's a series of still shots from the video that show the clear differences in Trona's body language from when she is casual to when she is formal.

casual          formal          casual          formal

The following graphic may help you to conceptualize the idea of shifting registers. Your range of normal teaching may be somewhere within a range of casual to formal, depending on your personal style. Likely your range varies slightly from day to day and moment to moment depending on factors such as the content you're teaching.

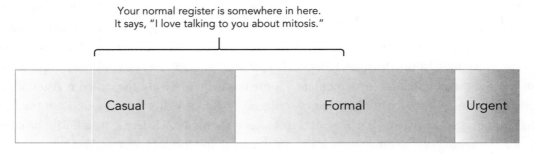

But when you need students' fullest attention you shift briefly to the right . . .

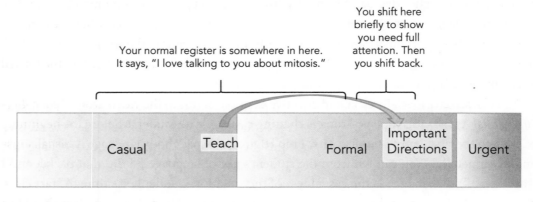

and then return quickly to your usual range.

I should note that I have discussed only two of the three available registers. The urgent register is, for the most part, counterproductive in classrooms, except in the case of absolute emergencies. Using this register increases tension and anxiety. It may be useful if someone is in danger of imminent physical harm, for example, but use it in other situations and you'll likely come off as nervous and panicky or you'll ratchet up the level of tension at exactly the moment when you want things to remain calm. It will just as likely become a self-fulfilling prophecy. If it becomes familiar, students may experience "urgency fatigue" and grow immune to it. Then you won't have it if you ever really need it.

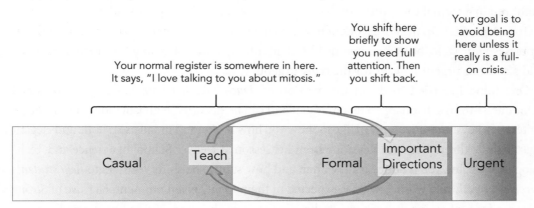

More relevant to most teachers, however, is that creeping hint of urgency that can sneak into our communication when things aren't going as we'd like. Students aren't following directions and seem to be, perhaps deliberately, not doing what is expected. We speak as if through gritted teeth. Our posture becomes stilted and tense and that tension creeps into our voices, too. We can begin slipping into it without realizing it. My team and I find it useful to practice listening for this, to take a phrase we might say in the classroom and practice saying it casually and formally so we can hear the difference and find the tone that feels right, and then practice saying it in an urgent register so we become attuned to what we sound like when we start to slip. If we are aware, if we hear it when it happens, we can correct it more quickly.

As this implies there are several skills implicit in managing your register. The first is awareness: What register am I in right now? What is it communicating? Does my register align to my words? Are my words saying "I need your attention" but my body language that "We're just hanging out here"? Am I saying, "I'm not frustrated" when the edge in my voice confirms the contrary?

The second is making changes in register evident with the right degree of emphasis and speed. The changes are subtle in Arielle's and Denarius's classrooms. They might be less so in other cases.

Register shifts can also be useful when students have not responded as they should the first time. If a student fails to follow a direction, a good first response is to shift noticeably (that is, visibly and, if possible, audibly) into a more formal register, perhaps putting your hands behind your back and changing to a more symmetrical stance—a lot of teachers add a raised eyebrow here as if to show surprise—and then giving the directions again, modulating your voice and leaving a clear gap between each word, which suggests that you have chosen each . . . word . . . very . . . carefully. "Please give me your eyes." Once this is done you would likely shift back toward something more casual to show the moment is over, though you might retain a formal tone until you begin to see a response from your student.

To summarize: Do the core work of teaching in whatever balance of casual and formal that expresses your style, but when you need full attention, shift noticeably into formal register. And save your urgent register for the truly urgent.

One thing I've tried to do in this version of *Teach Like a Champion* is to show small techniques—things that happen in a moment and can be distorted with isolation—in the larger context of a keystone video, and I'd like to show you how BreOnna Tindall uses subtle and elegant register shifts throughout the Keystone from her lesson at Denver School of Science and Technology. One thing you'll notice is how often and how subtly she shifts registers to *help students perceive correctly and warmly* what is expected of them in any given moment. Her use of *Strong Voice* is a form of caring that she uses to help her students be successful in knowing what to do and study an inspiring book (*Narrative of the Life of Frederick Douglass*) without interruption or distraction. Her moves are subtle so I will describe them with time codes and still photos.

As the timer goes off at the beginning of the clip, you can see BreOnna walk to the corner of the room (Pastore's Perch; see technique 53). "That's time," she says and, wanting to ensure she gets all eyes and ears for her upcoming directions, she "goes formal," very briefly raising her chin, standing symmetrically, leaving a distinct space between each word as she speaks.

Here she is asking for eyes:

Even as she does this—you might argue *because* she does this, at least in part—she gets an eager and positive response from her students and you can hear her relax her tone slightly afterwards and include a tiny gesture that feels more casual as she says "with your face partner."

Then students are off on their *Turn and Talk* (technique 43) where they are industrious and engaged. Her casual body language as she chats with students reaffirms this:

At 1:14 in the video, BreOnna calls an end to the *Turn and Talk*. Her first words are, "Check your SLANT" and her tone is casual here because she is reinforcing a habit almost everyone has been attentive to rather than issuing a reminder about an expectation some have neglected. Using a more casual register suggests this and implies that she assumes the best (see technique 59, *Positive Framing*). If she were less happy with the level of follow-through, we might expect her request, "Check your SLANT," to be accompanied by a clearer shift to greater formality.

In her next sentence, however, BreOnna edges toward slightly more formality. There's a brief pause where she uses *Radar and Be Seen Looking* (technique 53) to scan the room and ensure everyone listening for the coming direction. Again her upright and symmetrical body language suggests the importance of attention, so her words don't have to. She doesn't have to give a verbal reminder because she is reinforcing the point nonverbally. Then she drops her voice and begins her next sentence, "We're gonna go ahead and track Adriel . . ."

Her register shifts in the middle of the sentence, I'd argue. In the first half (above picture) it is formal—I need you with me; class is starting—but in the second half of her sentence—as she *Cold Calls* Adriel—you probably notice a distinct shift to the casual. This is because—as I interpret it—her body language is now signaling information about the *Cold Call* rather than the preceding direction. She wants to make sure it feels inclusive and positive to Adriel. In his book *Culturally Responsive Teaching in the Classroom*, Adeyemi Stembridge reminds us that how students perceive our actions is as important as how we intend them, and as you can see in the picture below, BreOnna's bright smile and relaxed posture as she asks Adriel's classmates to "snap it up" for him ensures her actions will be received as they are intended. She wants to diffuse any tension and ensure that Adriel feels support and sunshine from his classmates.

Adriel does well, and Breonna then *Cold Calls* Renee to "share her response." Notice her casual body language just after she reminds the class in the most lilting of voices that they should be "Tracking Renee." In *Running the Room*, Tom Bennett makes the point that behavioral reinforcements are most important to give when things are going well, as they certainly are here, because it allows us to build culture positively and preventatively. Again, the pairing of the reminder and a more casual register makes it easy for BreOnna to do that. Her mastery of register allows her to consistently reinforce expectations with just the right level of gentleness or emphasis.

Now here's BreOnna as Renee answers:

She's relaxed, standing small instead of standing tall, asymmetrical instead of symmetrical, because she is deflecting attention from herself. She wants students to be tracking their classmate. Notice also how doubly casual BreOnna is when she interrupts Renee to praise her use of the word "exonerated." As she breaks in, she wants to reassure Renee and communicate immediately that the interruption is a good thing.

It's a master class, frankly, in building not just loving positive culture but rigorous academic culture at the same time, and though you might not expect this to be a classroom where *Strong Voice* is key, among the sources of BreOnna's success is her remarkable ability to shift registers to communicate nonverbally both her affection for students and the importance of their attention in critical moments.

Principle 2: Show Both Shoulders/Stand Still

Many times when we give a direction, we communicate to listeners that the direction is an afterthought, because we appear to be doing something else while we give it. The message is *Something else is foremost in my mind relative to this direction.* If you are passing out papers while you direct students, you suggest that your directions aren't that important. If you stop moving, you show that there is nothing more important than the direction you are giving. When you want directions to be followed, don't engage in other tasks at the same time. It may even help to strike a formal pose.

You can see an example of this in the video of BreOnna Tindall. At about 3:25, BreOnna has wrapped up the discussion and is transitioning to the next task, introducing the passage the class will read during the day's lesson.

"I'd like for us to be thinking about 'blind justice,'" she says. But here she's getting her materials ready and placing them on the projector. You'll notice she starts to slow down her pace of diction, almost as if she's stalling. She doesn't want to engage the topic fully until she's done with that task and can face students fully to show its importance.

Here's what that moment looks like.

A few seconds later, however, she turns to face the class to frame the topic for the day. Suddenly it feels as if we are no longer in transition. Below is a still shot of BreOnna having turned to face the class fully to show that they, and the coming task, are her singular priority. Notice that students are now looking at her, whereas in the first image they were not. She's shown them that what she's saying to them is her priority and they've responded accordingly.

Another observation: when you learn to shoot a basketball, the first bit of advice you get is to square up[17] to the basket. It's hard to get the right result if you're not facing your objective fully. With human communication it's similar. You show what is important to you by facing it. Glance over your shoulder and say to David, *please put that away*, and you are saying that what you are facing with your shoulders is still more important to you. That may be fine for an off-hand reminder. Or it could help you surreptitiously give a student a reminder you want to keep as private as possible. But if you are not getting the follow-through you need from students, try facing them more intentionally as you give directions or if you must repeat them. In this way the orientation of your body reinforces the importance of your words.

Notice, too, Matthew Gray's body language in his lesson at the beginning of his class at Oasis South Bank. His class of Year Sixes has just arrived and are a bit fidgety. Matthew is careful to hold very still and face them as he gives directions. There's an air of formality; he is still and stands with both shoulders squared to the class throughout, no matter where he stands. Soon his class is focused and hard at work.

### Principle 3: Use Economy of Language

When you're communicating what you want students to do, strive to use the fewest words possible. Demonstrating Economy of Language shows students that you are prepared, composed, know your purpose in speaking, and that what you are saying is worth hearing. Conversely, when people are nervous, they tend to use more filler words as they decide what to say. Flip the script and start using filler words and one outcome can be that you appear nervous.

Another benefit of Economy of Language is that it focuses listeners on the most important points of what you said, eliminating the distraction of unnecessary language.

When emotions are running high, and your students' thinking brains may be clouded with negative emotion, brevity can be a powerful ally. By keeping your directions simple and concise, you can cut through the brain fog wrought by an active limbic system and help students stay focused on the path forward. This simplicity and repetition is crucial, as researchers have found that when you're under duress, your emotions "swamp the thinking brain's capacity to focus" on even the simplest of tasks.[18] Striving for Economy of Language can also discipline you to resist the temptation to engage in the kind of unnecessary argument and debate that can make a tense situation worse.

To be clear, I am not suggesting that you need to use Economy of Language when you are discussing anaerobic respiration or the last chapter of *Lord of the Flies*—just when you're discussing behavior and when there are potential distractions. If anything, maintaining

Economy of Language when you're correcting unproductive behavior or giving directions helps you conserve your time, words, and energy for such academic instruction.

Most of the Keystone clips contain examples of strong Economy of Language in critical moments, particularly the start of class or a transition where the teacher wants to maintain energy and momentum. Nicole Warren is a good example; her bright joyful energy is emphasized by her choice of few words when students are getting started with the lesson: "Eyes up here . . . waiting on one . . . tell your partner . . ." Or Jessica Bracey, who transitions from Omar to Danielle amidst a remarkable discussion by saying, "Habits of Discussion . . . Paraphrase . . . push it even further. Please track . . . Danielle." She can't build *Habits of Discussion* (technique 44) without reminding students to use them and in particular to remember to restate Omar's point. She wants to call on Danielle. She wants to remind students to direct their eyes to the speaker. All of these things are important but she does not want to disrupt the momentum or distract from Omar's excellent comment, so she uses tiny reminder phrases. Ten words and perhaps three seconds and she's done it all.

### Principle 4: Quiet Presence

There's a tendency to think that louder is stronger, but this is usually not the case. For the most part, raised voices rarely correlate with better listening. You give a direction but there's a background noise of talking and shuffling of papers, for example. You increase your voice level to be heard above the bustle, but students get a little louder, too, and suddenly you sound like you are speaking through a bullhorn.

Going louder emphasizes the clamor and suggests to students that things are unraveling. Often raising your voice will increase the sense of tension, especially if you are speaking at a faster pace, too. If there is an opportunist in the group, this may signal that that you're getting flustered, and he or she may take the opportunity to goad you a bit—to see how flustered you'll get. Better to set out to modulate your voice as much as possible from the beginning or to progressively modulate it as you speak. If students are already noisy, starting to speak and then self-interrupting (see further on) can help you do that—to gain students' attention while demonstrating that you won't talk over noise. But often it's we who start the process. We speak in voices that suggest they expect to be broadcast over a bed of noise. As if we are anticipating it. And in that case the anticipated noise is usually not far behind.

The best tool of prevention, however, is to help students to build a habit of listening to and listening for information that comes quietly from the outset. We want students to consistently associate quiet voices with attentiveness.

Notice, for example, how Arielle Hoo does this in the register shift clip at the beginning of the chapter. "Great, and track up here in five, four . . ." she begins. Her voice is a bit louder than her normal speaking voice here. Not a shout, certainly, but projected enough to make sure everyone knows she's speaking and looks up. But notice also the way her voice drops, even over the brief length of the countdown. By the time she's at "one" she's speaking at a conversational volume. She uses the shortest possible spike in volume; it's momentary and by the time her phrase ends she has already returned to speaking volume. From there she gets even quieter. Her final direction, *Make sure books are closed*, is at a very low volume but by this time students are listening attentively. If a tiny bit of raised volume helps you draw eyes, it helps best when it is a tiny burst, a fraction of a second. Once that's happened its work is done and Arielle, for one, is always trying to move toward quiet. Her voice drop to a near-whisper is also an investment in the future. *She wants students to make a habit of listening to and for information delivered quietly.*

When you want students to listen and follow through on an important request, especially when emotions are running high, strive to exude Quiet Presence. If you have to raise your voice slightly at first to show you are speaking, modulate quickly to a lower volume. Drop your pitch and speak more quietly even as you progress through a single sentence. Speak slowly and calmly; again, slowing yourself even over the course of the sentence if necessary. This helps you bring a calming effect to students in an escalating situation. And to yourself. Teachers often find that making a habit of using Quiet Presence, of always working toward quiet like Arielle does, helps them tamp down their emotions. You feel calmer because you speak more calmly and this help ensure that the interaction ends successfully.

You can see an excellent example of how speaking quietly and slowly signals caring and focus to students in Emily Bisso's lovely interaction with a student, Joshua, in *Emily Bisso: Write What I Write*. As the clip opens, Joshua is eagerly seeking Emily's attention to the detriment of his note-taking. It's counterproductive but also signals a student with whom she has a positive and caring relationship. She'd like to preserve that, not to mention Joshua's feelings. As Joshua waves his paper at her, Emily lowers her voice and uses impeccable economy of language. She "lives in the now" (see technique 59, *Positive Framing*) as well in describing what the solution looks like in the very next moment. "Write what I write, Joshua. Thank you, sweetie." Receiving the signal that Emily is seeking to communicate her corrective guidance privately and quietly, and hearing the opposite of tension in the calm steadiness of her voice, Joshua returns happily to his work.

### Principle 5: Self-Interrupt (Formerly *Do Not Talk Over*)

If what you're saying is worth students' attention—you are explaining the task they need to complete for the next six minutes or explaining the symbolism of the conch in *Lord of the Flies*—every student has the right to hear and the responsibility to allow others to do so. If students cannot hear you say these things, they cannot complete learning tasks or understand what they need to understand to succeed. Not every utterance you make in the classroom has this level of importance, but it remains true that being able to hear the teacher—and not talking while the teacher is talking—is an equity issue. The costs of even low-level disruptions (as discussed in the introduction to this chapter) are both massive and most likely to be paid by students already in suboptimal settings or most prone to distraction. "One of the reasons we get students' attention is to give them the opportunity to be successful at a task," my colleague Darryl Williams reminded me. There are times, in other words, when your words are the most important in the room, and you must be able to ensure that they do not compete for attention with other voices.

In many cases, the solution is to start in order to stop—that is, start a sentence and break it off, even in the middle of a word, to show that you do not yet have full attention. This is called a self-interrupt. The noticeable break makes the explanation—*I have stopped talking because not everyone is listening and right now you must listen*—unnecessary. A brief pause and an effort to proceed again is often all that's required. Sometimes a second start-then-stop is required. Sometimes breaking mid-word to make the pause more evident is surprisingly effective. Adding a shift in register helps, too. But used consistently and used early—before it is attempting to compete with the auditory equivalent of Times Square—this technique is one of the most useful and simple tricks in a teacher's arsenal.

Laura Fern models this beautifully in the video *Self-Interrupt Montage*. She's cheery and bright, walking across the front of the classroom as she responds to a student, "That's excellent, Cameron. That's one way that while bo—" A student in the front row is mesmerized by the camera and is no longer listening. He's lost the lesson. But hearing the sudden and unexpected break in Laura's voice causes him to turn face forward, to return to the math. Notice that there's no lecture here for him. The break itself brings him back. Notice how much the unexpectedness of it calls his attention. Putting the break in the middle of a word—as opposed to just after one—maximizes this effect. Notice also how Laura's body freezes. Her face goes very briefly expressionless and formal as she pauses, but a warmer expression replaces that "teacher look" when her student refocuses, and a second or so later she's back to teaching with the problem solved. (Notice, though, how she uses a **confirmation glance** afterwards to double-check that he remains focused.) Also in the montage you can see Eric Snider self-interrupting with his middler school students (and thus sparing them the lecture) as well as Sadie McCleary using the technique with high school students.

Principle 6: Time and Place (Formerly *Do Not Engage*)

There are times when we initiate a topic of discussion with students that requires timely resolution on their part. There are times when those students may wish to avoid the timely resolution. Changing the subject is often one way to do that. This action may be deliberate or accidental, the result of distraction, intense emotion, or perhaps a bit of strategy.

Here's one example:

*Teacher:* James, we don't laugh when a classmate struggles. Please move your card to yellow.

*James:* It wasn't me!

*Teacher:* Please move your card to yellow.

*James:* Shannon was laughing! Not me!

*Teacher:* If you think I am mistaken you may discuss with me after class. Please get up and move your card to yellow.

It may be reasonable for the teacher to discuss who was talking with James, but the expectation needs to be that the latter conversation doesn't happen until James has first done what his teacher asked. That's why the name for this principle is *Time and Place*. Sometimes the things students would rather discuss are frivolous. Sometimes they are legitimate. But the time and place for them is rarely when you have just asked them to do something else or when you are trying to attend to the needs of thirty classmates.

Either way, *Time and Place* is the skill of not engaging a new topic until you have achieved resolution on the one you've suggested.

One of my favorite examples of *Time and Place* is this example from Christy Lundy's classroom. Note the light circle. There's some drama afoot (sorry for the pun) and Christy can't see it! She calls on Patience, whose goal in answering, it soon turns out, has more to do with the kicking battle than anything having to do with *The Mouse and the Motorcycle*. "He's kicking me!" she states. An argument ensues.

We've all been there and we all know where this sort of situation can go. It's not bringing us back to the Beverly Cleary novel any time soon. Yes, Christy's students feel the situation keenly. The emotions are real. And also, yes, it is a distraction—the kind of thing that waylays a lesson and the kind of thing students who would rather not read can learn: *If I can create some drama right now, I will not have to do the work.* You will meet this student at least once in your career. She deserves a teacher who will ensure that she does the work. It's not the time and place, in other words.

"Three . . . two . . . one," says Christy, the brief short countdown giving Patience a bit of time to compose herself. Just a bit of space. She's has done two things here: She's reminded

Patience that there *is* an appropriate time to discuss the issue. She doesn't dismiss Patience's complaint; she just needs her to understand that it will have to wait till later. Then she returns Patience to the task: "You need to answer my question." Patience, it turns out, is capable of putting the kicking behind her. It wasn't perhaps the crisis it appeared to be, and Christy rewards her with a bright, warm smile. Notice also the impeccable Economy of Language Christy uses. "Three . . . two . . . one. Inappropriate time. You need to answer my question." It takes only ten words to resolve the crisis. Twenty words would probably do the opposite.

## Notes

1. This term is discussed in the Preface to this edition. Roughly it describes a caregiver's tendency to give lower-quality treatment to a patient rather than one harder to administer but preferential on the grounds that it is in the patient's interests.

2. I don't mean the young people themselves; I mean the behaviors they may manifest. I don't believe in the fixity of traits and propose instead that the overwhelming majority of students will show grace, curiosity, and virtue if we build classrooms that socialize those things intentionally enough.

3. https://fordhaminstitute.org/national/research/discipline-reform-through-the-eyes-of-teachers. David Griffith and Adam Tyner surveyed over 1,200 teachers from every type of public school, asking about the behavioral environment as they experienced it. Crucially, they separated the data according to school and teacher characteristics.

4. Fifty-eight percent. More than half also reported that they dealt with verbal disrespect from students daily or weekly.

5. https://www.uncf.org/wp-content/uploads/reports/Advocacy_ASATTBro_4-18F_Digital.pdf

6. https://uncf.org/pages/perceptions-done-to-us-not-with-us-african-american-parent-perceptions-of-k

7. https://assets.publishing.service.gov.uk/government/uploads/system/uploads/attachment_data/file/379249/Below_20the_20radar_20-_20low-level_20disruption_20in_20the_20country_E2_80_99s_20classrooms.pdf.

8. You can find out more here: https://teachlikeachampion.com/dean-of-students-curriculum/.

9. Except possibly the students who are so distracted by their phones they don't even notice. Please don't allow phones in your classroom.

10. You could probably build this habit by spacing out five minutes of practice four or five times over a few weeks. See technique 7, *Retrieval Practice*.

11. Yet another reason why having such means of participation well-oiled routines is so critical.

12. Scholar dollars are an example of a consequence system that is designed to be incremental and therefore allow teachers to negatively reinforce behaviors at low cost. Typically students start the week with 50 scholar dollars. Calling out might result in a two-dollar deduction. A student might earn back a few scholar dollars for a special act of consideration. At the end of the week students might purchase special items (lunch with a teacher for them and three friends, for example) with their scholar dollars if they had a significant number remaining.

13. https://teachlikeachampion.com/dean-of-students-curriculum/.

14. A. Mehrabian and M. Wiener, "Decoding of Inconsistent Communications," *Journal of Personality and Social Psychology* 6, no. 1 (1967): 109–114.

15. Jonathan Haidt, *The Righteous Mind*, p. 65. I can't recommend this book strongly enough!

16. H. Friedman and R. Riggio. "Effect of Individual Differences in Nonverbal Expressiveness on Transmission of Emotions," *Journal of Nonverbal Behavior* 6 (1981): 32–58.

17. The phrase "squaring up" also means to initiate confrontation with someone, so while I originally wrote this section on *Strong Voice* while thinking about squaring up in basketball, the potential for people to see it as confrontational is significant, so I suggest using the phrase "show both shoulders" instead.

18. Daniel Goleman, Richard Boyatzis, and Annie McKee, *Primal Leadership: Unleashing the Power of Emotional Intelligence* (p. 45).

# Chapter 12

# Building Student Motivation and Trust

This is a book about the tools teachers can use to build dynamic and inclusive classrooms that foster the greatest amount of learning and achievement possible and ensure that students thrive. But even seemingly successful methods, Adeyemi Stembridge reminds us, "can fall utterly flat" if they don't find receptiveness among students.

This receptiveness is fostered via cultural and relational means. We must seek to make all students feel known and understood by their teacher, experience connection to the content, and trust in the endeavor of school. But there are psychological aspects, mindsets held internally by students that are critical factors in whether we (and they) succeed. Motivation is first among these. Learning requires effort, self-discipline, struggle, and perseverance; students will have to give and sustain effort and attention to succeed. They will have to decide, in short, that learning is worth working for.

It is hard to help a student achieve something they are not motivated to learn. For some students, motivation is a bright flame that merely has to be protected and fed with opportunity; for others it has scarcely (yet) been sparked. With some students we have to do everything we can to keep them in the game until they come to see the value of playing: They need, but do not yet want, what schools offer.

The range of students we encounter is wide, but in almost every case, engendering and fostering the internal desire to learn is a part of the work of teaching, one in which we are always engaged, whether we realize that or not.

That's a key realization: we are always influencing motivation. The moment when we have a good long talk with students about effort and motivation may help, but less probably than the daily habits students fall into, the pervasive influence of what those around them do, and the compounded effect of a thousand small interactions we have with them when our minds are on something else.

One of the requirements of motivation—particularly for those students who begin with a skeptical attitude—is trust. Students have to come to believe in the endeavor of school and, as a result, be willing to try. I say that trust is a requirement but not a prerequisite of motivation because building trust can take time. It has to happen eventually for teaching to take hold. That does not mean it has to be there for you to start. Trust can take a long time—longer than you have before you start teaching. Happily, teaching well is one of the primary ways trust is built.

My colleague Dan Cotton framed for our team a model for how trust is built that continues to be meaningful for us. To feel trust, students have to feel safe, successful, and known.

Feeling *safe* means being physically safe—students can't feel at risk of being bullied or threatened—but also psychologically safe—it has to be OK to try, to be wrong, to take risks. There can never be snickers for trying and failing or, worse, for trying at all. As Zaretta Hammond writes, "Neuroscience tells us the brain feels safest and most relaxed when we are connected to others we trust to treat us well." If we truly want our students to be prepared for the transformative experience of learning, then we must establish for them that the classroom is a place in which they belong and will be respected.

Feeling *known* refers to having a sense of belonging and importance. Students have to feel like their teacher—and the institution—knows them and sees them as both a part of a community and as an individual—not just one of a group of students in third period or eighth grade. Of course that means they have to know that their identities and cultures are welcomed and valued, but in a much more everyday sense students have to feel seen, literally and figuratively—with the literal often causing the figurative. This is often expressed in small moments. Using student names, and inventing opportunities to greet students by name, is hugely important, for example. Saying someone's name is a small reminder of something larger: that we know them for themselves; that we see them in the crowd. One of the reasons I love it when teachers greet students as they enter the room is so they can say, "We missed you yesterday," "I love your hair," "Are those new glasses?" and, yes, "Make sure to get me your essay; it was due yesterday." That, too, tells a student they matter. But Denarius Frazier (see *Denarius Frazier:*

*Remainder*) is also making students feel known when he circulates in his math class and sees their work and the products of their minds. "Much better," he tells one student. The message is: "I saw what you did today and how it was different from what you did yesterday."

*Successful* is perhaps the easiest of the three elements to overlook, though its role in motivation is larger than most people realize. Motivation, Peps Mccrea explains,[1] is "as much a product of learning as it is the driver of it. . . . If we care about building motivation for the long run, we must prioritize proficiency. It is the ultimate self-fulfilling engine of education."

Accomplishing a task successfully and learning that they can succeed leads students to want more. That's why effective teaching that leads to student mastery is one of the greatest long-term sources of student motivation and trust. Part of why Christine Torres's students love and trust her and work so hard throughout each lesson is her skill as a teacher. Every day they enter a place that's orderly and productive and see themselves learning and accomplishing things. They feel capable and accomplished and, naturally, like that feeling. Peps Mccrea calls this "scholarly identity" and it often comes from the outside in. They see themselves doing well at English and conclude they must like and value English.

But motivation is shaped most of all by norms. That's the hidden secret. It's the most important factor and it's mostly invisible to us. People are evolved to be supremely social—think here of the "cooperative eye" hypothesis—and will be inclined to do what the group is doing even without realizing it. "Norms are so powerful they override more formal school policies or rules. However, their largely invisible and unconscious nature makes them easy to underestimate if not totally ignore," writes Mccrea. Norms will emerge, in any setting where there are people, and they will shape behavior. It is merely a question of whether they are deliberate or accidental norms. In many schools it is the latter.

The strength of a norm's influence over us, however, also depends on how much we feel a part of and identify with those exhibiting the norms. Motivation is mediated by belonging.

What I focus on in this chapter is how to make students feel belonging, trust, and motivation, so that teachers find a receptive audience for learning. Put another way, this chapter describes rules of thumb for the daily interactions with students in which motivation and trust are built.

## TECHNIQUE 59: POSITIVE FRAMING

People are motivated by the positive far more than by the negative. Seeking success and happiness will spur stronger action than seeking to avoid punishment. "When we are happy—when our mindset and mood are positive—we are smarter, more motivated, and thus more successful. Happiness is the center, and success revolves around it," concludes Shawn Achor, summarizing years of studying happiness. Positivity inspires and motivates and that should influence the way we teach. But positivity, particularly in learning settings, is often misunderstood.

One flaw is the assumption that praise is the same thing as positivity. *Praise* is telling someone they have done something well. *Positivity* (in this case) is the delivery of information students need in a manner that motivates, inspires, and communicates our belief in their capacity. This is important because teachers are often told to use a "praise sandwich" or to praise five times as often as they criticize. But telling someone they're doing great several times so that you can then say *And you have to line up your decimals consistently* is problematic.

Believing that you must wrap criticism with praise assumes that students are fragile and can't take constructive feedback—that criticism is something a teacher has to trick them into hearing. Most students want to understand how to get better and come to trust adults who tell them the truth when they also know that those adults believe in them.

Inaccurate or unwarranted praise "is unlikely to stand for long in the face of contrary experience," writes Peps Mccrea. "Promises of success that don't eventually materialize will only serve to undermine motivation and erode trust."

We all know the teacher who's inclined to describe every idea, every answer, every action as "awesome." Soon enough that word and his praise more generally become less meaningful. When everything is awesome, nothing is.

Which isn't to say praise isn't profoundly important and motivating. It is. But that's all the more reason to preserve its value.

So the key is often not to praise more. Rather, aspire to give a range of useful and honest feedback and guidance that includes both praise and critical or corrective feedback, but do so positively, *in a manner that motivates, inspires, and communicates our belief in our students' capacity.*

Using *Positive Framing* allows you to give all kinds of feedback, as required by the situation, while keeping culture strong and students motivated. Doubly so for redirections—moments when we say to a student, "Do that differently." If those moments remind the person you're talking to that you want them to be successful and that you believe in and trust their intentions, students will trust you more and be motivated to follow your guidance.

*Positive Framing*, then, is the technique of framing interactions—particularly academic or behavioral redirections—so that they reinforce a larger picture of faith and trust, even while you remind students of a better course of action.

Next are six rules of thumb to follow. As you read about them, be sure to check out the classroom examples in the video *Montage: Positive Framing.*

## Assume the Best

One of the most pervasive tendencies in human psychology is the Fundamental Attribution Error—the idea that, when in doubt, we tend to attribute another person's actions to their character or personality rather than to the situation. We often assume intentionality behind a mistake.

You can hear this in classrooms where a teacher's words imply that a student did something wrong deliberately when in fact there is little ground to assume that.

"Stop trying to disrupt class!" "Why won't you use the feedback I gave you on your first draft?" or "Just a minute, class; some people seem to think they don't have to push in their chairs when we line up." Such statements attribute ill intention to what could be the result of distraction, lack of practice, or genuine misunderstanding. What if the student had tried to incorporate your feedback, or just plain forgot about the chair? How might hearing statements like these make a confused or flustered student feel? Unless you have clear evidence that a behavior was intentional, it's better to assume that your students have tried (and will try) to do as you've asked.

This mindset also helps us as teachers maintain our emotional constancy and equilibrium. Rather than feeling flustered or defensive—*Why won't he follow my directions? Is she trying to get under my skin? How many times have I said this?*—assuming the best helps us model calm assurance. This in turn builds trust—students know we will give them the benefit of the doubt and support them through confusion or struggles without jumping to conclusions or taking their actions too personally.

One of the most useful words for assuming the best is *forgot,* as in, "Just a minute; a couple of us seem to have forgotten to push in their chairs. Let's try that again." Given the benefit of the doubt, your scholars can focus their energy on doing the task right instead of feeling defensive.

Further, this approach shows your students that you assume they want to do well and believe they can—it's just a matter of nailing down some details.

*Confused* is another good assume-the-best word, as in, "Just a minute; some people appear to be confused about the directions, so let me give them again." Another approach is to assume that the error is your own: "Just a minute, class; I must not have been clear: I want you to find every verb in the paragraph working silently on your own. Do that now." This last one is especially useful. It draws students' attention more directly to your belief that only your own lack of clarity would mean lack of instant follow-through by your focused and diligent charges. And, of course, it also forces you to contemplate that, in fact, you may not have been all that clear.

It is important to note that these phrases will not likely work—nor will this approach—if you do not actually believe the best about the students in front of you. As Adeyemi Stembridge writes, "Authenticity is a must for our students. One of their assets is that they can spot frauds at great distances." If you are doubtful about student confusion, or worse, if you deliver this observation in a sarcastic tone, then you may actually damage the very relationships that you intend to build up.

Another nice way to assume the best is to see minor struggles as the result of misdirected enthusiasm. When you think this way, you suggest that there was a positive intention for a behavior that merely went awry. In a behavioral situation, this might sound like, "Gentlemen, I appreciate your enthusiasm to get to math class, but we need to walk to the door. Let me see you go back and do it the right way." In an academic setting, it might sound like, "I appreciate that you are trying to build complex and expressive sentences, but this one might have a little too much in it for clarity."

Assuming the best is especially effective for errors on challenging academic work. Learning is full of mistakes done for good reasons. There are those that spring from an overabundance of diligence—"You told me to use transition words so I used far too many"—and those rooted in too much enthusiasm—"I've just learned to reduce fractions and now I want to reduce and reduce and reduce everything . . . even when I can't."

Assuming the best might give credit for a good idea and then offer the correction: "I like that you're looking to reduce. But we can't do that here." Or "I love to see you trying to use those transition words but there are so many they've gotten a bit confusing." Looking for the good intention behind the mistake, looking to assume the best, has the additional benefit of causing *you* to think about all the good reasons why students might have done something that at first looks egregious. Assuming well-intentioned errors can help you to see more of the positivity that already exists.

It's important to remember that you, too, participate in setting the norms of your classroom by describing what you expect. Assuming the best reinforces positive norms (and expresses a quiet confidence). It suggests that you struggle to imagine a universe in which students would not be productive, considerate, and scholarly because of your faith both in them and in the culture of your own classroom. You implicitly describe the norm you believe to be there—everyone making a good faith effort. If by contrast you were to assume the worst, you would be suggesting that sloppiness, inconsiderateness, and whatever else were what you yourself expected in your classroom.

Of course, you'll want to be careful not to overuse the assume-the-best approach. If a student is clearly struggling—refusing to follow a clearly delivered instruction and is signaling to you that they are in an agitated, emotional state—don't pretend. In such cases, addressing the behavior directly with something more substantive, such as a private individual correction, also helps to get the student back into a productive mode without the attention of the rest of the class.

Even in the most challenging cases, however—say a student has done something really negative like stealing or belittling a classmate—be careful to let your words judge a specific behavior ("That was dishonest") rather than a person ("You are dishonest"). Perhaps even say, "That was dishonest, but I know that's not who you are." A person is always more and better than the moments in which he or she errs, and our language choices give us the opportunity to show in those moments that we still see the best in the people around us.

## Live in the Now

In most cases—during class and while your lesson is underway, for example—avoid talking about what went wrong and what students can no longer fix. Talk about what should happen next. Describing what's no longer within your control is negative and demotivating. There's a time and place for processing what went wrong, but the right time is not when your lesson hangs in the balance or when action is required.

When you have to give constructive feedback, start by giving instructions that describe as specifically as possible the next move on the path to success (see technique 52, *What to Do*).

If David is whispering to his neighbor instead of taking notes, say, "I need to see you taking notes, David," or, better, because it is more specific, "I should see your pencil moving," rather than, "Stop talking, David," or "I've told you before to take notes, David."

In the previous chapter we saw Emily Bisso use this to great effect: "Write what I write, Joshua."

Again, the clearer you can be about the next step, the better. As Chip and Dan Heath point out in *Switch*, "what looks like resistance is often a lack of clarity." So provide clarity without judgment. If you deliver the directions in a neutral tone, with no frustration evident in your voice, you may be surprised by how helpful it is. Most students want to succeed; by providing them with a clear next step you are helping both of you to get closer to your shared goal.

One challenge here is that we often are too vague in our instructions. When in doubt, shrink the change—a phrase that also comes from the Heath brothers. "One way to motivate action, then, is to make people feel as though they're already closer to the finish line than they might have thought." Name a small first step that feels doable. So, "Please start taking notes, David," becomes "Pencil in hand, please." It's much easier for a potentially reluctant or confused student to engage in a task that is bite-size than one that might feel more overwhelming.

For what it's worth, this is part of the coaching philosophy of the famously positive and successful football coach Pete Carroll, one of the game's best motivators. "We're really disciplined as coaches to always talk about what we want to see," he says of his entire coaching staff's approach. They always strive to focus on "the desired outcome, not about what went wrong or what the mistake was. We have to be disciplined and always use our language to talk about the next thing you can do right. It's always about what we want to happen, not about the other stuff."[2]

## Allow Plausible Anonymity

You can often allow students the opportunity to strive to reach your expectations in plausible anonymity as long as they are making a good-faith effort. This would mean, as I discuss in Chapter Eleven, beginning by correcting them without using their names when possible. If a few students are not yet completely ready to move on with the activities of the class, consider making your first correction something like "Check yourself to make sure you've followed the directions." In most cases, this will yield results faster than calling out individual students by name. It doesn't feel good to hear your teacher say, "Evan, put down the pencil," if you knew you were about to do just that. Saying to your class, "Wait a minute, Morehouse (or "Tigers" or "fifth grade" or just "guys"), I hear a few voices still talking. I need to see you quiet and ready to go!" is better than lecturing the talkers in front of the class. This plausible anonymity is another way of communicating to students that you believe the best about their intentions and are certain they are just seconds away from being fully ready to move forward with the tasks necessary to learn.

## Narrate the Positive and Build Momentum

Compare the statements two teachers recently made in their respective classrooms:

*Teacher 1: (pausing after giving a direction)* Monique and Emily are there. I see rows three and four are fully prepared. Just need three people. Thank you for fixing that, David. Ah, now we're there, so let's get started.

*Teacher 2: (same setting)* I need two people paying attention at this table. Some people don't appear to be listening. *This* table also has some students who are not paying attention to my directions. I'll wait, gentlemen, and if I have to give consequences, I will.

In the first teacher's classroom, things appear to be moving in the right direction because the teacher narrates the evidence of student follow-through, of students doing as they're asked, of things getting done. He calls his students' attention to this fact, thereby normalizing it. He doesn't praise when students do what he asks, but merely acknowledges or describes. He wants them to know he sees it, but he also doesn't want to confuse doing what's expected with doing "great." If I am sitting in this classroom and seek, as most students do, to be normal, I now sense the normality of positive, on-task behavior and will likely choose to do the same.

The second teacher is telling a different story. Things are going poorly and getting worse. He's doing his best to call our attention to the normality of his being ignored and the fact that this generally occurs without consequence. The second teacher is helping students to see negative norms as they develop and, in broadcasting his anxieties, making them even more visible and prominent as well. In a sense he's creating a self-fulfilling prophecy: he narrates negative behavior into being.

"To modify motivation," writes Peps Mccrea, "change what . . . pupils see." If teachers make "desirable norms"(people doing positive things) more visible to students they will be more likely to join with them. Mccrea calls this "elevating visibility." To elevate visibility of a norm you want more people to follow, increase their "profusion"—the proportion of students who appear to follow them—and their "prominence"—how much you notice when people do it.

The first teacher is helping students to see more readily how profuse positive and constructive behavior is, and he is making it more prominent to students by letting them know that he sees and that it matters.

Narrating the positive, though useful, is also extremely vulnerable to misapplication, so here are a couple of key rules:

- Use *Narrate the Positive* as a tool to motivate group behavior as students are deciding whether to work to meet expectations, not as a way to correct individual students after they clearly have not met expectations.

- If you narrate positive on-task behavior *during* a countdown you are describing behavior that has exceeded expectations. You gave students ten seconds to get their binders out and be ready to take notes, but Jabari is ready at five seconds. It's fine to call that out. It's very different to call out Jabari for having his binder out after your countdown has ended. At that point it might seem as though you are using Jabari's readiness to plead with others who have not followed through in the time you allotted.

Another common misapplication would be this: You're ready to discuss *Tuck Everlasting*, but Susan is off task, giggling and trying to get Martina's attention. You would not be using positive framing or narrating the positive effectively if you circum-narrated a "praise circle" around Susan: "I see Danni is ready to go. And Elisa. Alexis has her book out." In this case, I recommend that you address Susan directly but positively: "Susan, show me your best, with your notebook out. We've got lots to do." If you use the praise circle, students will be pretty aware of what you're doing and are likely to see your positive reinforcement as contrived and disingenuous. And they're likely to think you're afraid to just address Susan. In fact, Susan may think that as well. By directly reminding Susan what is expected—and why—you have helped her get ready to engage with the learning and maintained the norm of readiness that is shared by the class.

## Challenge!

Students love to be challenged, to prove they can do things, to compete, to win. So challenge them: exhort them to prove what they can do by building competition into the day. Students can be challenged as individuals or, usually better, as groups, and those groups can compete in various ways:

Against other groups within the class (e.g. rows, tables)

Against other groups outside the class (another homeroom)

Against an impersonal foe (the clock; the test, to prove they're better than it is; their age— "That was acceptable work for seventh graders, but I want to see if we can kick it up to eighth-grade quality.")

Against an abstract standard ("I want to see whether you guys have what it takes!")

Here are some examples to get you started. I'm sure you'll find it fun to think of more:

"You guys have been doing a great job this week. Let's see if you can take it up a notch."

"I love the work I'm seeing. I wonder what happens when we add in another factor."

"Let's see if we can write for ten minutes straight without stopping. Ready?!"

"Ms. Austin said she didn't think you guys could knock out your math tables faster than her class. Let's show 'em what we've got."

## Talk Expectations and Aspirations

When you ask students to do something differently or better, you are helping them become the people they wish to be or to achieve enough to have their choice of dreams. You can use the moments where you ask for better work to remind them of this. When you ask your students to revise their thesis paragraphs, tell them you want them to write as though "you're in college already" or that "with one more draft, you'll be on your way to college." If your students are fourth graders, ask them to try to look as sharp as the fifth graders. Or tell them you want to do one more draft of their work and have them "really use the words of a scientist [or historian, and so on] this time around." Tell them you want them to listen to each other like Supreme Court Justices. Although it's nice that you're proud of them (and it's certainly wonderful to tell them that), the goal in the end is not for them to please you but for them to leave you behind on a long journey toward a more distant and more important goal. It's useful if your framing connects them to that goal.

# TECHNIQUE 60: PRECISE PRAISE

Whereas *Positive Framing* focuses on how you make constructive or critical feedback feel motivating, caring, and purposeful to the recipient, *Precise Praise* is about managing positive feedback to maximize its focus, benefit, and credibility. Although it might seem like the simplest thing in the world, positive reinforcement helps students more if it's intentional, and you must constantly defend against the potential for it to become empty or disingenuous, especially through overuse. When we over-rely on "excellent" and "awesome" to stamp every interaction we have with a child—what I sometimes call the state of "awesome awesomeness"—we eliminate our ability to truly and genuinely celebrate the accomplishments that are indeed *excellent* and *awesome* when they really do occur.

## Reinforce Actions, Not Traits

Positive reinforcement is a response to an action that has just occurred: a student does something well, and you tell her she's done a nice job. At its best, positive reinforcement is also about the future. You don't just want a student to feel good about having done something correctly, you want to help her understand how to succeed again the next time. Even more deeply, you want to reinforce a way of thinking about learning that embraces struggle and adversity—relishes it even. Carol Dweck's seminal research on this topic, discussed in her book *Mindset,* has shown that in the long run, people who have a growth mindset far outpace those with a fixed mindset. Her research suggests that the difference is one of the strongest predictors of success. People with a fixed mindset see intelligence and skill as something static. You're smart, or you're not. You're good at something, or you're not. People with a growth mindset see intelligence and skill as something you develop. You work hard, and you get better. Smart isn't what you are; it's what you do. Individuals with a fixed mindset see a challenge and think, "Oh, no. This is going to be difficult." Individuals with a growth mindset see a challenge and think, "Oh, boy. This is going to be difficult."

Dweck finds that praise is central to the development of growth mindset. If students are praised for traits ("You're smart"), they become risk averse: they worry that if they fail, they won't be smart anymore. If students are praised for actions ("You worked hard, and look!"), they become risk tolerant because they understand that the things within their control— their actions—determine results. It's critical then to praise actions, not traits, and further to carefully identify actions that students can replicate. You are praising them in part to help them see the inside of the success machine: the more actionable the thing you reinforce, the more students can replicate their success. "Go back and look at your draft, Maria. See those cross-outs and rewrites? That's why your final draft is so strong."

You can see this in the video *Steve Chiger: Kudos*, of North Star Academy English teacher Steve Chiger. At first Steve walks up to a student and tells her she's done well. We pause the video here to let you reflect: What's her takeaway? What does she conclude about her success? She knows Mr. Chiger thinks she did something great, but not what and why. Not how to do it again. Perhaps his praise made her feel good, but with so many questions maybe it doesn't quite feel genuine.

But then it's as if Steve recognizes this. He doubles back and answers all of those questions. The student realizes *I was sharp in class because I prepped well and read carefully and made notes. I can do that again.*

Suddenly the praise has taken on a whole new role. She can see the road map that was hidden before. He has helped her to see what has caused her success and what to keep doing.

## Offer Objective-Aligned Praise

I have a secret life working with coaches of sports franchises. (If you want to know more about it, you can check out my book *The Coach's Guide to Teaching*.) In that world, one of my favorite videos to show is of all-world basketball player Steph Curry getting feedback from all-world basketball coach Steve Kerr.

The interaction (you can watch it here: https://www.coachsguidetoteaching.com/; scroll down through about 12 videos) takes place on the bench as Kerr shows Curry a set of data about his performance in the game so far. Uncharacteristically, Curry is having a rough night—or at least a less-brilliant-than-usual night.

But Kerr wants Curry to be aware of the things he is doing right, so he will persist in doing them. In the long run, they will cause Curry and the team to succeed. One of the most important things a coach can do is to help players attend to the signal (what's important to success) and not the noise (all the other things that distract us from what's important). *What are the actions that will cause me to be successful over the long run, regardless of the outcome of this single moment?*

That's what Kerr does in the video. He's helping Curry—yes, even Steph Curry—see the signal: when he is on the floor and plays up-tempo, great things that he is not fully aware of are happening and will continue to happen. The goal of the praise is not to make Curry feel better and build his confidence—Curry has plenty of that. The goal is to help him know what to replicate. That is in many ways the greatest power of praise.

One of the keys to helping students succeed is giving them **accurate attributions**, to "regularly point out the causes of pupil success and failure [and] help them see how effort and approach make a difference," in Mccrea's words. Kerr is helping Curry make an accurate attribution. Play up-tempo—replicate what you are doing in that aspect of your game—and you will succeed. As indeed Curry did, being crowned NBA champion later that year.

Of course, praising (or positively reinforcing) actions means calling out things like hard work and diligence, but some of the best teachers I've observed align their praise to learning objectives. Suppose students are working on including strong transitions in their writing. As you *Circulate* (technique 25) and observe, you specifically reinforce those who have used transitions or, better, those who have gone back and added to or revised their transitions to make them better. Perhaps you even use a *Show Call* (technique 13) to show off their work. "Scholars, look up here. This is Melanie's paper. Look at this paragraph. She included a solid transition, but then she went back and revised it to make it capture the contrast between the paragraphs more clearly. Now her paper really holds together. That's how you do it." Now, not only does Melanie know what was behind her success, not only does she understand that success is determined directly by her own actions, but the rest of the class sees it, too.

Another benefit of *Precise Praise* connects back to what Shawn Achor calls the Tetris Effect. Essentially, by training our brains to look for and appreciate the positive, we learn to see things more positively overall. Achor writes, "Just as it takes days of concentrated practice to master a video game, training your brain to notice more opportunities takes practice focusing on the positive." By using *Precise Praise* to help students notice all that they are doing that is right or exceptional, we are also training them to see the learning community as a positive place. We are also, of course, training ourselves to see the same. Imagine the effect that this habit has on the struggling first-year teacher, in the classroom where everything may not be exactly as she or he had hoped. By training herself to precisely name that which is going well, she not only makes that behavior more replicable for students, but lets herself celebrate that which is worthy—and hopefully avoids the doom loop of narration that can overwhelm so many well-intended, early-career teachers.

## Differentiate Acknowledgment from Praise

Acknowledgment is what you often use when a student meets your expectations. Praise is what you use when a student exceeds expectations. An acknowledgment merely describes a productive behavior or perhaps thanks a student for doing it, without adding a value judgment and with a modulated tone. Praise adds judgment words like "great" or "fantastic" or the kind of enthusiastic tone that implies that such words might apply. "Thanks for that comment, Marcus" is an acknowledgment; "Fantastic insight, Marcus" is praise. "Marcus is ready" is acknowledgment; "Great job, Marcus" is praise. Distinguishing the two is important, as reversing some of the examples will demonstrate. If I tell Marcus it's fantastic that he's ready for class, I suggest that this is more than I expect from my students. Ironically, in praising this behavior I tell my students that my standards are pretty low and that perhaps I am a bit surprised that Marcus met my expectations. Perhaps they aren't expectations after all. Either way, praising students for merely meeting expectations may reduce the degree to which they do so over the long run. It also makes your praise seem "cheap." If that happens, it also means that when Marcus writes a powerful response to a piece of literature and you call it "fantastic," you will be describing it in a manner on par with how you described coming to class on time, and this may perversely diminish the accomplishment in his eyes. In the long run, a teacher who continually praises what's expected risks trivializing both the praise and the things she really wishes to label "great," eroding the ability to give meaningful verbal rewards and to identify behavior that is truly worthy of notice. In short, save your praise for when it is truly earned and use acknowledgment freely to reinforce expectations.

It's important to add that, as with any technique, it is essential here that you deeply know your students. There may be students for whom completing a homework assignment is, in fact, extraordinary. When that is the case, a more private moment in which you praise and appreciate the effort it may have taken for that student to set themselves up for success and to establish a new and better habit is more than warranted, it is desirable. What you want to avoid is public praise for a behavior that, for most students, is not out of the ordinary at all.

## Modulate and Vary Your Delivery

Because teachers most often give reinforcement, positive and negative, in a public setting (that is, in a room with twenty-five other people in it), it's critical to be attentive to the degree to which a statement engages others in the room: Is it loud or quiet, public or private? Do others overhear it?

Generally, privacy is beneficial with critical feedback. As I discuss in Chapter Eleven, whispered or nonverbal reminders assume the best about students: they allow them to self-correct without being called out in public. The private individual correction discussed in technique 55, *Least Invasive Intervention,* is a classic example of this. But what about the reverse? Should praise therefore be loud? Turns out it's not quite that simple. Positive reinforcement works best when it is genuine and memorable. To make it memorable, you'll want it to stand out a bit, keeping its format a bit unpredictable.

A bit of public praise can be powerful—you stop the class to read Shanice's sentence aloud and say to the class, "Now that is how a strong, active verb can give muscle to a sentence!" People can't replicate it if they don't know about it, so that's one clear benefit to public praise. In addition, the fact that you thought Shanice's work was so good that everybody should hear will make your words memorable to her—but they will stand out more if *all* praise isn't public. Part of what's powerful about the public delivery is that it's a bit unexpected, so it can also be powerful to walk up to Shanice and whisper, "Now that is a strong, active verb. It sounds like you wrote this for a college paper." In fact, you capture the greatest benefit by delivering positive reinforcement using an unpredictable variety of settings and volumes.

Among the benefits of private praise is that it often sounds especially genuine to the listener because, implicitly, it *is* private and therefore only about her, as opposed to public praise, which is also about those who hear it and your desire for them to observe and possibly replicate what the student you're praising has done. The power of pulling Shanice aside as she enters the classroom and saying, "I just wanted to tell you that I graded the exams last night, and yours was really outstanding," may be equal to or even greater than your public recognition of her work. When a teacher takes a moment to speak to a student privately, she intimates that what she is going to say to that student is very, very important, and this raises a question: What could be so important? To find that it is a response to your excellent work is both powerful and unexpected for a student.

One further benefit of private praise is that it creates uncertainty and additional privacy around all private interactions, and this is immensely productive. If all of my private and quiet conversations with students were critical (that is, they were all private individual corrections), students might become defensive upon my approach. Further, other students might be motivated to eavesdrop, knowing that listening in might provide them with the juicy details of a classmate's misfortune. Most people can't help but be curious about such things. If, however, my approaching or leaning down to speak quietly with a student is just as likely to be an example of private individual precise praise (PIPP, also discussed in Chapter Eleven), then students will consider the approach with balanced equanimity, and their classmates will have no incentive to eavesdrop. Either message is thus heard more openly by the intended recipient and ignored by those for whom it's not intended.

That said, there are also benefits to loud praise and praise that's semiprivate—that is, deliberately intended to be overheard by others. Praise always walks the line between the benefit of allowing others to overhear what's praiseworthy and thus encouraging them to seek to emulate it, and the benefit of the genuine sincerity of its just being about the recipient. In terms of how to balance these benefits, my sense is that both are more powerful if they aren't entirely predictable and that although socializing and influencing others through praise are beneficial, they're less critical than the long-term benefit of maintaining the credibility and genuineness of praise. I would skew toward privacy a bit more for the most substantive feedback to a student.

## TECHNIQUE 61: WARM/STRICT

In *Culturally Responsive Teaching and the Brain*, Zaretta Hammond describes the critical importance of teachers who are what she calls "warm demanders": those who combine personal warmth with high expectations and "active demandingness," which, she writes, "isn't defined as just a no-nonsense firmness with regard to behavior but an insistence on excellence and academic effort."

But warm demanders can be rare because so many people perceive high expectations, firmness, and relentlessness about academic content and firm discipline to be something you do, not because you love young people, but because, somehow, you don't. You are one or the other: caring or demanding. They are opposites. But of course this is an illusion. The magic lies in the correlation, in fact, in being the person who can be both at the same time, who can say *I believe in you and I care about you and therefore I will not accept anything but your best. You must rewrite the paragraph, complete the homework, apologize to a peer you have wronged—because you are worthy of as much.*

To do that is to push a student to be their very best.

You can get a glimpse of how those two apparently contradictory ideas live in harmony in watching a video we also saw in Chapter 11: *Trona Cenac: Register Shifts.* The video is shot on one of the first days of school and Trona is in the hallway, setting norms and expectations before students come into class. You can sense right away how glad she is to see her students and how glad they are to see her. She's warm, gracious, and caring—full of smiles and reassurance. But she's also really clear about what's expected of them and what they need to do to be successful. They need to come in, take a seat, and get started on their work with urgency. There's work to be done. It's not optional. Within this single interaction she tells students she cares about them and expects a lot from them—essentially at the same time.

A teacher like Trona includes the *come in, take a seat, get started right away* part *because* she cares deeply about her students. Being willing to do so is part of what adults who care for and about young people do. Certainly it would be easier for her not to shift into the *we have work to do, please sharpen up* mode, but to merely be adoring and adored. Her students might like her even more, at least for a while, if she did. It would be easier to let them saunter in and get settled on their own time, start class only when they seemed ready, teach for 45 instead of 52 minutes per day, and show movies sometimes just because a movie is a nice break. It would be easier to give almost everyone an A on every paper or better yet not grade papers at all, the better to never have anyone resent you or argue a grade.

Hammond has a name for this type of teacher: the sentimentalist. The sentimentalist is willing to reduce standards for students—either to be more liked by them or, as Hammond writes, "out of pity or because of poverty or oppression." The sentimentalist "allows students to engage in behavior that is not in their best interest." The sentimentalist, in other words, means well but loves to be loved; needs to be needed too much, or chooses the short-term benefits to herself of satisfying personal relationships over students' long-term success and the ways in which strong relationships can be used to foster that. Sentimentalism is an occupational hazard. It's better to name it so that we can all check ourselves as we move through the journey of teaching. Am I too often doing what is easy because I want students to like me? Or am I pushing them—and myself—in a loving way that expects the best of all of us?

For me the technique of learning to be able to be both warm and strict *at exactly the same time* and finding the optimal balance of those things based on how it affects student learning is called *Warm/Strict*. It's learning to be caring, funny, warm, concerned, and nurturing—but also strict, by the book, relentless, and sometimes uncompromising with students. It means establishing the importance of deadlines and expectations and procedures and, yes, rules. But *Warm/Strict* does *not* mean being unreasonable or inhumane. It does *not* mean never making an exception; rather, it means making such decisions not based on popularity, but based on long-term commitment to your students' growth.

"In society we don't get very far if we are rude, if we talk back, if we talk over others, if we don't listen," writes UK Headteacher and author Jo Facer. "In schools we need to escape the idea that teaching children how to behave is teaching them 'obedience,' a word that for many has connotations of oppression and fear." Children who treat others poorly are not going to "magically transform themselves," Facer goes on to point out. They rely on adults, ideally in partnership in and outside the classroom, to steer them towards behaviors that not only allow schools to function well but, more importantly, prepare them to be successful and valued members of society and community down the road.

I want to say a bit about the word "strict" specifically. It's a fraught word for some but I think it is worth using because it reminds us of something important: A teacher sets limits and expectations for and on behalf of a group, a culture. Young people with whom we are strict may not always be happy with those limits in the moment, but they also usually recognize in the long run that being held accountable by someone who cares about you is an important part of learning to make your way in the world. They are especially likely to arrive at this realization when the adult who is strict shows them that they care—deeply. The world will penalize a person who cannot meet deadlines. The caring teacher is not the one who allows a young person to make a habit of missing them again and again. The caring teacher says you have an immense capacity for excellence but deadlines matter and I want you to get this in on time. The caring teacher may even work with the student for whom this is a struggle, setting benchmarks, texting a reminder the night before. But in the end the teacher may also have to set limits. If the work is late, there should be a penalty. You prepare the child for the road, not the road for the child.

There are caveats, of course. Sustaining strictness in the long run requires caring and warmth; students have to trust your intentions to do what is best for them even if they don't always like each decision. And ideally they should feel the caring most *in the moments you set limits*. A reset on expectations is a good time to smile. If there's one thing I've learned from studying teachers as a parent it is that if you said you'd give a consequence, you give the consequence, but you are also quick to tell the person you care about them and can't wait for things to be back to normal; for example, *You'll have to serve your detention, Michael, but I look forward to seeing you back in class tomorrow*. As Jo Facer puts it, "Having strict rules means you love children and want the best for them. Make sure you communicate that with your face and body language."

Consider this interaction between Hasan Clayton and one of his students, a fifth grader whom I'll call Kevin, after Hasan noticed Kevin sleeping during a remote lesson (in 2020, that is). After class Hasan asked Kevin to stay on the call after his classmates left.

| | |
|---|---|
| *Hasan:* | I noticed you were sleeping in class, Kevin. |
| *Kevin:* | *(Long pause. No answer.)* |
| *Hasan:* | Am I correct? Or am I wrong? |
| *Kevin:* | You're correct. |
| *Hasan:* | Why were you sleeping in class? |
| *Kevin:* | I don't know. I thought I got a good sleep yesterday, but I still got tired. |
| *Hasan:* | That's not good. Do you know how much material you're missing when you're sleeping? |
| *Kevin:* | Yes. |
| *Hasan:* | Do you know how it makes me feel when you're sleeping? |
| *Kevin:* | It makes you feel sad. |
| *Hasan:* | It makes me feel like you don't think what we're doing in class is important. |
| *Kevin:* | So during independent practice today, what if I redo the lesson. |
| *Hasan:* | Yes, I would appreciate you doing that, going back and answering all the questions and then turning it in. We have to think about how our actions are affecting ourselves and our community. |
| *Kevin:* | OK. |
| *Hasan:* | All right, Kevin, I hope to see you later. If not, I'll see you tomorrow. |

Some notes:

- Throughout the conversation Hasan never raised his voice or sounded angry. He also never sounded sweet or apologetic. I would describe him as composed. This is important. His goal was to cause Kevin to reflect on the cost of sleeping in class, not distract him with thoughts about whether Mr. Clayton was angry at him or induce defensiveness because he was being shouted at. *Emotional Constancy* was the order of the day.

- Hasan required that Kevin acknowledge the fact that he was sleeping. When Kevin didn't respond to his initial statement *I noticed you were sleeping in class,* Hasan didn't say anything for a full six or seven seconds! He refused to bail Kevin out by chattering through the awkward silence with "It's OK. Everyone gets tired sometimes." After the silence, Hasan persisted: "Am I correct or am I wrong?" He tacitly required Kevin to take ownership of his actions by acknowledging them.

- Once Kevin acknowledged his actions, Hasan's tone lightened ever so slightly and he asked: Why were you sleeping? He was still reserved. There's no baby talk—you could imagine a teacher using a *Why were you so-o-o sleepy?* approach here—but his tone reacts subtly to the degree to which Kevin owns the issue.

- When Kevin describes what's wrong with sleeping in class, Hasan does not excuse the action. He explains the problem and pauses again. His economy of language is noticeable. Adding extraneous verbiage makes the interaction more casual (see technique 58, *Strong Voice*), but Hasan wants formality here.

- Hasan focuses on depersonalizing the interaction and stressing *Purpose Over Power* (technique 56, *Firm, Calm Finesse*) rephrasing Kevin's assertion that he might have made Hasan "sad" to focus on learning—*It makes me feel like you don't think what we're doing in class is important.*

- Kevin suggests a consequence and Hasan agrees to it. A lot of teachers might say, "That's OK," but Hasan accepts Kevin's proposed consequence because the consequence will help Kevin remember and allow Kevin to make a gesture of resolution—this is an important step in resolution and closure. Hasan tells Kevin he appreciates his solution and then, a bit warmer, reminds him that he looks forward to seeing him back in class.

Some useful tools for achieving *Warm/Strict*:

*Explain to students why you're doing what you're doing* and how it is designed to help them:[3] "Priya, we don't do that in this classroom because it keeps us from making the most of our learning time." This emphasizes purpose rather than power.

*Use please and thank you.* "Please" and "thank you" cement the bonds of civility and community. We use them to show cordiality, appreciation, and respect. You want students to treat you and others with decency, civility, and caring, even if you must ask them to do things they may not be inclined to do, and therefore you should model that same decency, civility, and caring. "Please" and "thank you" do this. They help you express your caring and respect for students. This is especially important in moments that are most fraught.

Can "please" sound wrong? Of course, so some clarification is in order: It should not be a pleading please but a firm, respectful please. Usually that means very little pause after the "please" and a minimal degree of emphasis on the word. "Please take out your notebooks" in a steady rhythm with "please" no more emphasized than the rest of the words. "*Please* . . . take out your notebooks" is a sign of trouble—a subtle difference, but important.

*Distinguish between behavior and people.* When we give critical feedback or set limits, we want to say, "I believe in you" and "That can be better" at the same time. The first step is to frame critical comments as a judgment on an action, not a person.

Think for a moment about the phrase "You don't," as in: "**You don't** put effort into your lab write-ups."

Compare it to the same statement but with *didn't* substituted for *don't*: "**You didn't** put much effort into this lab write-up."

The word *don't* judges. *This thing that you did is something you always do.* It globalizes a mistake and implies it is an enduring flaw. Maybe even hints at deliberateness. The word *didn't* judges a one-time event. It leaves open the possibility that the person you are talking to usually does the right thing but failed to in this instance. It's one moment; we can fix it quickly.

But as some readers may have already noticed, even *didn't* focuses on the problem rather than the solution. Compare: "You ***didn't*** put effort into your lab write-up" to "You ***must always*** put your best effort into your lab write-ups." Or "You ***are capable of much more carefully written write-ups***."

*Demonstrate that consequences are temporary.* Move on quickly and show students that when they have responded to a mistake via consequence or restitution, it is then in the past. Smile and greet them naturally as soon as possible afterwards to show that they are starting with a clean slate. You might tell a student, regarding her consequence, "After you're done, I can't wait to have you come back and show us your best."

# TECHNIQUE 62: EMOTIONAL CONSTANCY

School is a sort of social laboratory for students; it is often the place where the greatest number of their interactions with broader society occur, and where, inevitably and fittingly, they experiment with decisions about the nature of their relationships with the people and institutions around them.

Even an experiment that ends perfectly contains some trial and error. A theory is developed ("Perhaps I don't need to do my homework every day"), tested, and evaluated ("OK, I think it is better when I do my homework"). Theory testing is one of the primary activities of youth, as I suspect your recollections of your own can attest—mine certainly do. In many ways we are evolved to use our adolescent years to test limits and theories.

What that means is that the environment should provide the necessary feedback on experiments—the goal is not to tell young people that skipping homework is OK—in an atmosphere that treats experimentation as an expected event. We want to help those experiments yield useful and productive lessons, but also to remember that the behaviors we see often are experiments and that students themselves may not consciously realize that they are experimenting.

If this is the case, then maintaining *Emotional Constancy*—lessening the intensity of strong emotion, especially frustration and disappointment—is a key part of our job.

Generally speaking, strong negative emotions by teachers only intensify emotions among students. A student behaves poorly and takes a bit of an attitude; the teacher bristles back; the student reacts to the rising emotion by talking back more strongly, and a small mistake becomes larger. Or a student makes a mistake and a teacher snaps angrily at him while giving a consequence; part of him thinks, *Why is she yelling at me? Does she yell at me more than she yells at others?* He has these thoughts instead of reflecting on the connection between his actions and the consequence. The teacher's emotions insert another variable into the equation and distract him from his own behavior.

Compare that to Hasan Clayton's interaction with Kevin. With studious calm Hasan asked Kevin to take responsibility, and explained why the experiment led to poor outcome. And then Kevin proposed a consequence. This is to say, *Kevin heard everything Hasan said, in part because Hasan was not shouting it or reacting with shock.* Kevin shouldn't have slept through class but it was not thoroughly unexpected that he tried.

One of the most important tools you can use to maintain emotional constancy is to **Walk Slow,** which I mean literally and figuratively. Teaching young people to slow down their decisions is a good way to help them make better decisions—with the cortex and not the amygdala. Even a fraction of a second can make a difference. It's the same for teachers.

As you approach a situation that you yourself are emotional about, walk slowly—I mean this metaphorically—don't rush to react—but also quite literally, move slowly when you feel yourself getting upset. I once observed Bridget McElduff in a lesson where a student laughed at another student for struggling to read a series of challenging words correctly aloud. Bridget was angry. She loved her students and felt a strong desire in particular to defend a student from mockery, especially in her own classroom, especially when it was a result of her taking exactly the sort of risk that was necessary to learning. Bridget began walking briskly over to address the laughing student, who was on the other side of the room.

But Bridget was able to tell herself to take a route around the back of the room and as she did that, she slowed her pace. This gave her a few precious seconds to compose herself and choose her words carefully. By the time Bridget got to the young man she was able to calmly explain why his behavior was unacceptable and remind him that she knew he was better than that. The walk was key. She needed a moment to get over her momma-bear anger. All it took was three or four seconds, but it really made a difference. Suddenly she realized that he was conducting an experiment. She had to help him reject the hypothesis: *laughing at a classmate was acceptable*. But she also had to understand that testing is what young people do.

Fools rush in. Anytime you feel yourself having a negative emotional response, strive to "walk slow"—literally or figuratively. A fraction of a second is often enough.

Here are some additional tips for maintaining your *Emotional Constancy*:

**Criticize behaviors rather than people.** "That behavior is inconsiderate" is a statement about a temporary situation. It's also a statement that, with a bit of tweaking, would allow you to show that you don't think that it's typical of a given student: "It's unlike you to behave this way. Please fix it immediately." This is better than making a permanent statement about a student: "You are inconsiderate." If your goal is trust, it can be a long way back from too many statements of that kind.

**Avoid globalizing.** Saying "You always" do X or asking "Why are you always doing" Y makes the conversation about events that are no longer within a student's control—and that he or she may not even remember. This makes the issue seem bigger and less focused on a specific action, and can make your correction feel like a "gotcha."

**Take your relationship out of it.** Telling a student you feel disappointed or betrayed by his or her actions, or personalizing your response—for example, "I thought I could trust you"—makes the interaction about you rather than about a student learning productive and socially responsible behavior. Framing things impersonally diffuses emotion and keeps your role in the conversation to that of coach and mediator, helping the student to learn those behaviors that will benefit her most in the long run.

# TECHNIQUE 63: JOY FACTOR

The finest teachers offer up the work of learning to students with generous servings of joy expressed through passion, enthusiasm, humor, and the like—not necessarily as the antidote to work but because those are some of the primary ways that work gets done—and just possibly because work, done right, can evoke joy. The classroom can and should be a joyful place and a few points of emphasis and understanding can help bring that to the fore in a sustainable and productive way. This is beneficial to achievement as well. A place where students (and teachers) feel satisfaction, gratification, and happiness is also likely to be a place where they work hard and persist, learn more, and are just possibly more creative. A bit of *Joy Factor* can help make yours not just a happy classroom but a high-achieving one.

Joy is complex, though—it can take a surprisingly wide array of forms. It can (but need not) involve singing or dancing, but it can just as easily be quiet: the pleasure of doing a challenging problem well, or as a team, or of seeing your work praised by your classmates. It is experienced by individuals and in small or large groups—for the most part, it is enhanced by sharing in some ways with others, which makes it ideal for classrooms. In *The Happiness Advantage*, Shawn Achor discusses research on three component elements of happiness: pleasure, engagement, and meaning. We are happy when we find pleasure, but happiness goes well beyond that. We are happy when we are connected and when we perceive ourselves to be doing something important. "People who pursue only pleasure experience only part of the benefits happiness can bring while those who pursue all three routes lead the fullest lives," Achor continues. Pleasure, engagement, and meaning: all three should be the foci of our efforts to make our classrooms joyful places.

Let me start by drawing a small distinction between joy and fun.[4] I don't draw this distinction to rule out fun in the classroom. Fun is part of joy. But joy is broader than fun. And seeking fun as a purpose rather than joy in learning can lead us astray and so deserves caution. Let me explain both of those ideas.

In distinguishing joy from fun, one teacher wrote me to emphasize the feeling of joy brought about by "the feeling of success after hard work" and the "celebration of success, both individual and collective," not to mention "a bit of awe and wonder—experiencing something new and amazing."[5]

Two powerful sources of joy that I have discussed elsewhere in this book are belonging and flow. Belonging is an intense feeling of membership in group. Inclusion in groups wa maybe the single most important factor in our evolutionary success as a species. Those were able to join with, collaborate in, and maintain membership with groups survived that weren't, didn't. We evolved to be intensely sensitive to the status of our own mer

"Belonging feels like it happens from the inside out, but in fact it happens from the outside in," writes Daniel Coyle in *The Culture Code*. But, he adds, people don't just need to hear once that they are included; they need to receive signals over and over, to be happy. Belonging, according to Coyle, is "a flame that needs to be continually fed by signals of safe connection."

We often feel the greatest joy when we feel belonging. This perhaps is why singing, in particular choral singing, is part of practically every culture on earth and specifically a feature of worship in those cultures. When we sing together we affirm that we all know the words, literally and metaphorically, and show our ability to coordinate. We subsume our own yearnings in the group. Done even briefly this can have a profound effect on us, which is especially worth remembering in the midst of the most individualistic society in the world. The wholeness and joy of belonging that our evolutionary self requires is something [or *the thing*, or *the one thing*] that our rational self is most likely to overlook or even scorn.

This is something we can unlock in the classroom. Singing is an obvious example. Watch the joy in the faces of Nicole Warren's students as they start their class signing a math song they know by heart (see *Nicole Warren: Keystone*). It's everything a part of us is socialized to scorn: rote, ritual, memorized, familiar to the point of repetitive. And yet the students are clearly happy. (Note also the joy in their faces at the end of the video when Nicole circulates and helps them to see their accomplishments.) Note that the gestures emphasize the chorality of the experience—people love to "know the moves," and here knowing the moves is visible and so therefore is the belonging. Our own math song is even better than one lots of people know; we all know the words and can voice in unison something other people don't know about. *Knowing things others don't know or aren't aware of* is a key to belonging.

Music can be a source of joy even when it is not choral. It is unclear why, but every culture on earth sings and creates music. They use those things to define themselves. Some evolutionary biologists suggest that singing predated language as we know it—that before we had words we had music, which allowed us to express emotion and urgent information over distance. We sang ourselves into battle or into comfort afterwards, and this is wired into us. We have evolved with a proclivity for music, so we can assume it had evolutionary benefit in some way and that we evolved to take pleasure in it.

You can hear snippets of song throughout some of the videos in this book, such as Summer Payne in *Cold Call* singing, "individual tur-urns listen for your na-ame," or Christine ___s in *Format Matters* singing, "don't turn to the wall 'cuz the wall don't care." And every ___ use *Call and Response* (technique 35) you are in fact using a sort of simple chanting: *one voice*, you are saying, we all belong.

___, especially shared songs, can be a source of joy. But it can also remind us of ___ coordinated activity is to building a sense of belonging. Even sharing the

*Like a Champion* 3.0

experience together of hearing a text read aloud or reading a text aloud together as a group (see technique 24, *FASE Reading*), taking turns and bringing a whole to life through our efforts as individuals can awaken this feeling—the construction of a whole in which we subsume our individuality briefly and emerge gratified and infused with a sense of belonging and meaning.

Knowing "what to do" makes us feel as if we belong. Perhaps this explains the unexpected happiness students sometimes exude in learning the routines of the classroom. We think we're teaching a tool for efficiency but students are receiving a signal that they belong. Done well, known routines and choral behaviors can be the seeds of membership.

Several pages back, now, I also mentioned "flow" and this too is critical to understanding the difference between joy and fun: We like to lose ourselves in a challenging activity that sweeps us up in its momentum. We are often happiest when this happens. Any coach will tell you that one of the biggest teaching challenges in a sports setting is breaking the flow. You blow the whistle to talk about how the defense should be positioned and after a few seconds you start to see a gradual lurking frustration: *We want to play, Coach; please stop talking so we can play*. This reminds us that the core activity and its design are critical and that when they are well designed, joy is powerful because it is sprinkled in small moments—playful, silly, absurd, expressing belonging—that come and go quickly enough to augment and work in synergy with the sense of flow.

Consider how Christine Torres drops quick humorous comments into her lesson. The vocabulary word is "caustic" and the *Turn and Talk* asks students to engage an inside joke: "Imagine Ms. Torres is a contestant on *American Idol*; what's a 'caustic' remark a judge might make about her singing?" Don't be silly, she adds, he would never make a caustic remark about Ms. Torres's singing. Maybe you see the belonging cues there: Ms. Torres's talent as a singer is an ongoing discussion, a sort of inside joke you would only get if you were in her class. But also note the speed of it. It's a quick laugh that preserves the sense of flow. The joy students feel comes as much from their engaged study of the vocabulary as it does from the joke. Christine's humor sits off stage and comments amusingly on the main action, but the lesson is still the star. Nicole Warren's math song works because it is fast. It would be half as joyful if it were twice as long.

This, I think, is another reason why it's important to differentiate joy from fun. We can play *Jeopardy!* to review during class today and that will be fun, but interestingly it may not also be joyful unless we engineer it well so that it is designed for flow. We can all recall the "fun" activity we designed that sparked no joy because the flow wasn't there or because the group dynamics didn't work well. And while we're at it, please recognize that the word "fun" can distract us. Most young people have fun when they play video games—though interestingly I am not sure they are joyful, perhaps because the degree of connection and belonging is missing. You can refer to "having fun" by itself but you don't "have joy" by itself. You *take joy or feel joy in doing something.* "Joy" is clearer on purpose than "fun." It has meaning and engagement.

In a recent social media post I asked teachers for insights on how they thought about joy in the classroom. How did they create "productive joy"? I asked. I used the phrase to stress the idea that what we sought was joy that served learning. That seemed obvious to me. "Sounds controlling," one skeptic responded. She wanted to know why I felt the need to make it "productive" and to dictate the terms of someone else's happiness. But I hope it is obvious to the great majority of teachers that the goal is to achieve joy *in the tasks of learning.* If we don't seek to make joy a cause of as much learning as possible and the maximum amount of learning joyful, we have lost our way. But of course there is the risk that the fun runs away from us and we forget that it is there to serve the learning. Happily it is not only possible to do both, but the goals are just possibly synergistic. People generally like learning things. Don't play *Jeopardy!* unless it is rigorous enough to support learning, but also know that if it is challenging and engaging, joy will be more likely to arise from it.

Let me apply the conversation about flow and belonging to an additional source of classroom joy: humor is immensely beneficial to creating joy—we almost always smile when we laugh, and we often remember the joke forever (see note 7 in this chapter for an example). But *small recurring inside jokes* are especially powerful because of the way they maximize belonging and flow: Christine Torres joking about her excellent singing; a nickname for a character in history (one teacher called Orsino in *Twelfth Night* "wet wipe" because he was so spineless compared to the female leads in the play[6]); or consider my high school history teacher, Mr. Gilhool, who was the master of the inside joke: he (and soon we) always referred to the city of "Amsterdarn" to civilize its "vulgar" name; he dramatized Count von Schlieffen on his deathbed advising Bismarck "to keep the West strong" and afterwards anytime anyone mentioned World War I military tactics, Gilhool would remind us of von Schlieffen's words with a brief dramatization (except in cases where we remembered to do it first).

These jokes all happened in less than a second. That was part of the fun. Mr. Gilhool was also teaching with substance and pace while the inside jokes were coming at you fast, so you had to be paying attention or you'd miss the moment when he made a brief motion like he was weighing something on scales when he mentioned any philosopher's name,[7] which was why everyone around you was laughing. (See note 7 for an explanation.) Part of what made Mr. Gilhool great was that we were learning a ton and part of it was getting the joke. These things were synergistic; so were the memory aspects. For what it's worth I still sometimes say "Amsterdarn" to this day and more importantly I still remember the Schlieffen Plan. Humor is powerful, especially when it is *used in the service of learning* via *small recurring inside jokes*.[8]

I'd like to make mention of the importance with *Joy Factor* of "being you." I could probably come up with a few inside jokes—my children might weigh in on the small likelihood of their being funny—but I cannot and could not sing. Which is important to recognize and respect. No singing for some of us. Steer carefully with humor if you can't pull it off.

I mention this also because I'm about to discuss a video of a teacher who is brilliant at what he does and when I watch him I know I could not do those things. Joyful things are hard to force. The message of the video *Darren Hollingsworth: Rabble* is that enthusiasm matters. Enthusiasm can look a lot of ways. It doesn't have to be as extroverted as Darren's but his is certainly magic to listen to. He's greeting students passing in the hallway and at the *Threshold* (see technique 47) before class at Great Yarmouth Academy in Great Yarmouth, England. His banter is priceless. Consider the student to whom he says, "Are you Mr. Pellow's brother?" He's new to the school and suddenly feels known, picked out of the mass of students in the hallway, called a "top man." (But also, à la *Warm/Strict*, reminded that "Yes, sir" is the proper response to an adult.[9]) The students are greeted joyfully, playfully, warmly, individually, and by name as they enter. Stopped and called—tongue in cheek—"a rabble" because the line is not tidy, but they're also expected to fix the line and come in properly. There's joy and there's high expectation and regularly the twain shall meet.

Most people can't be Darren but everyone can find a version of themselves that evokes a unique form of joy. And it's worth remarking on the power of the happiness whatever form it takes. "Students primed to feel happy before taking math tests far outperformed their neutral peers," Shawn Achor writes in the *Happiness Advantage*. "Our brains are wired to work best when we are happy." So simply smiling, and saying, "I think you'll enjoy this lesson today," can be almost as good a starting point.

## Notes

1. In his short, elegant, and immensely useful book *Motivated Teaching*. I recommend it unreservedly.
2. Carroll says this in a video the Seahawks produced called *Practice Is Everything* (https://www.youtube.com/watch?v=NMLa6fM10KA).
3. A technique called *Explain Everything* is highlighted in the first edition of this book. The technique helps students understand how what you and they are doing in the classroom will advance them academically. For more information, visit www.teachlikea-champion.com/yourlibrary.

4. I am indebted to Mark Chatley of Maidstone, England, who pointed out this distinction in a tweet when I asked for guidance from educators recently.

5. These are Mark's words. I am grateful for them.

6. "Leane Elizabeth" from Leicester, England, shared this in a tweet. The best part was that she had to explain the reference to me in a subsequent note *because it was an inside joke.*

7. This requires a note but the note requires a warning: I am going to tell you a story about long ago. It involves an approach to teaching that *I am not advocating and not advising you consider using.* Mr. Gilhool memorably opined, while making a movement as if balancing two sides of a scale: "Goethe, Herder, Hegel: I'd trade 'em all for a six-pack and a tank of gas," by which he meant to argue the point of view that philosophers were of small practical value to most of society. If he mentioned some great thinker who might be high-minded and out of touch with society he would make the weighing motion and we would think about his hilarious words trading philosophers for something practical and be reminded of the pragmatist's argument in a way we found hilarious. Again, I hope it is clear that you should *not* say this to students now. When Mr. G said this in the 1980s, people said and thought different things. We were seniors in high school and the drinking age was 18. Nonetheless, before you scorn Mr. Gilhool, let it be known that I would never have heard of Herder were it not for Mr. Gilhool and I read Goethe for the first time in part because I wanted to see what Gilhool was talking about, just as I remember the Schlieffen Plan today in large part because of his humorous portrayal of it.

8. Thank you to Ian White, a teacher in Hackney, London, who used the phrase "little inside jokes" in responding to a post I'd written on Twitter, which gave rise to this meditation and my phrase "small recurring inside jokes." His phrase is probably better.

9. I am not arguing for students calling adults "Sir" and "Ma'am." It's not part of any technique or guidance. They do it in a lot of English schools. It can be lovely. I'd be happy if Darren were my teacher and warmly set expectations for me like that, but you might feel differently. Do this if it inspires you; don't do it if you don't like it.

# How to Access the Videos

Access the videos in the text at www.wiley.com/go/teachlikeachampion3. The password is the first word of Chapter 4, in all lowercase letters. Enter it where prompted.

## CUSTOMER CARE

If you have trouble accessing this content, please contact Wiley Product Technical Support at http://support.wiley.com. Or, you can also call the Wiley Product Technical Support phone number at 800-762-2974. Outside the United States, call 317-572-3994.

# Ready to Learn More?

## ENGAGE WITH THE *TEACH LIKE A CHAMPION* TEAM

Doug and his team offer further support for teachers, leaders, and schools at teachlikeachampion.com.

There, you can read and subscribe to Doug's "Field Notes" blog, sign up for workshops, request training for your schools, and learn about TLAC Online modules and other training materials. You can also learn more about the Reading Reconsidered ELA Curriculum and TLAC's Dean of Students Curriculum.

# Index